GNU C Library 2.22 Reference Manual 1/2

A catalogue record for this book is available from the Hong Kong Public Libraries.

Published in Hong Kong by Samurai Media Limited.

Email: info@samuraimedia.org

ISBN 978-988-8381-07-4

Short Contents

Table of Contents

17 Low-Level Terminal Interface 477

18 Syslog................................... 504

25   The Basic Program/System Interface..... 705

1 Introduction

The C language provides no built-in facilities for performing such common operations as input/output, memory management, string manipulation, and the like. Instead, these facilities are defined in a standard *library*, which you compile and link with your programs.

The GNU C Library, described in this document, defines all of the library functions that are specified by the ISO C standard, as well as additional features specific to POSIX and other derivatives of the Unix operating system, and extensions specific to GNU systems.

The purpose of this manual is to tell you how to use the facilities of the GNU C Library. We have mentioned which features belong to which standards to help you identify things that are potentially non-portable to other systems. But the emphasis in this manual is not on strict portability.

1.1 Getting Started

This manual is written with the assumption that you are at least somewhat familiar with the C programming language and basic programming concepts. Specifically, familiarity with ISO standard C (see Section 1.2.1 [ISO C], page 2), rather than "traditional" pre-ISO C dialects, is assumed.

The GNU C Library includes several *header files*, each of which provides definitions and declarations for a group of related facilities; this information is used by the C compiler when processing your program. For example, the header file `stdio.h` declares facilities for performing input and output, and the header file `string.h` declares string processing utilities. The organization of this manual generally follows the same division as the header files.

If you are reading this manual for the first time, you should read all of the introductory material and skim the remaining chapters. There are a *lot* of functions in the GNU C Library and it's not realistic to expect that you will be able to remember exactly *how* to use each and every one of them. It's more important to become generally familiar with the kinds of facilities that the library provides, so that when you are writing your programs you can recognize *when* to make use of library functions, and *where* in this manual you can find more specific information about them.

1.2 Standards and Portability

This section discusses the various standards and other sources that the GNU C Library is based upon. These sources include the ISO C and POSIX standards, and the System V and Berkeley Unix implementations.

The primary focus of this manual is to tell you how to make effective use of the GNU C Library facilities. But if you are concerned about making your programs compatible with these standards, or portable to operating systems other than GNU, this can affect how you use the library. This section gives you an overview of these standards, so that you will know what they are when they are mentioned in other parts of the manual.

See Appendix B [Summary of Library Facilities], page 892, for an alphabetical list of the functions and other symbols provided by the library. This list also states which standards each function or symbol comes from.

1.2.1 ISO C

The GNU C Library is compatible with the C standard adopted by the American National Standards Institute (ANSI): *American National Standard X3.159-1989—"ANSI C"* and later by the International Standardization Organization (ISO): *ISO/IEC 9899:1990, "Programming languages—C"*. We here refer to the standard as ISO C since this is the more general standard in respect of ratification. The header files and library facilities that make up the GNU C Library are a superset of those specified by the ISO C standard.

If you are concerned about strict adherence to the ISO C standard, you should use the '-ansi' option when you compile your programs with the GNU C compiler. This tells the compiler to define *only* ISO standard features from the library header files, unless you explicitly ask for additional features. See Section 1.3.4 [Feature Test Macros], page 15, for information on how to do this.

Being able to restrict the library to include only ISO C features is important because ISO C puts limitations on what names can be defined by the library implementation, and the GNU extensions don't fit these limitations. See Section 1.3.3 [Reserved Names], page 14, for more information about these restrictions.

This manual does not attempt to give you complete details on the differences between ISO C and older dialects. It gives advice on how to write programs to work portably under multiple C dialects, but does not aim for completeness.

1.2.2 POSIX (The Portable Operating System Interface)

The GNU C Library is also compatible with the ISO *POSIX* family of standards, known more formally as the *Portable Operating System Interface for Computer Environments* (ISO/IEC 9945). They were also published as ANSI/IEEE Std 1003. POSIX is derived mostly from various versions of the Unix operating system.

The library facilities specified by the POSIX standards are a superset of those required by ISO C; POSIX specifies additional features for ISO C functions, as well as specifying new additional functions. In general, the additional requirements and functionality defined by the POSIX standards are aimed at providing lower-level support for a particular kind of operating system environment, rather than general programming language support which can run in many diverse operating system environments.

The GNU C Library implements all of the functions specified in *ISO/IEC 9945-1:1996, the POSIX System Application Program Interface*, commonly referred to as POSIX.1. The primary extensions to the ISO C facilities specified by this standard include file system interface primitives (see Chapter 14 [File System Interface], page 377), device-specific terminal control functions (see Chapter 17 [Low-Level Terminal Interface], page 477), and process control functions (see Chapter 26 [Processes], page 749).

Some facilities from *ISO/IEC 9945-2:1993, the POSIX Shell and Utilities standard* (POSIX.2) are also implemented in the GNU C Library. These include utilities for dealing with regular expressions and other pattern matching facilities (see Chapter 10 [Pattern Matching], page 222).

1.2.2.1 POSIX Safety Concepts

This manual documents various safety properties of GNU C Library functions, in lines that follow their prototypes and look like:

Preliminary: | MT-Safe | AS-Safe | AC-Safe |

The properties are assessed according to the criteria set forth in the POSIX standard for such safety contexts as Thread-, Async-Signal- and Async-Cancel- -Safety. Intuitive definitions of these properties, attempting to capture the meaning of the standard definitions, follow.

- `MT-Safe` or Thread-Safe functions are safe to call in the presence of other threads. MT, in MT-Safe, stands for Multi Thread.

  Being MT-Safe does not imply a function is atomic, nor that it uses any of the memory synchronization mechanisms POSIX exposes to users. It is even possible that calling MT-Safe functions in sequence does not yield an MT-Safe combination. For example, having a thread call two MT-Safe functions one right after the other does not guarantee behavior equivalent to atomic execution of a combination of both functions, since concurrent calls in other threads may interfere in a destructive way.

  Whole-program optimizations that could inline functions across library interfaces may expose unsafe reordering, and so performing inlining across the GNU C Library interface is not recommended. The documented MT-Safety status is not guaranteed under whole-program optimization. However, functions defined in user-visible headers are designed to be safe for inlining.

- `AS-Safe` or Async-Signal-Safe functions are safe to call from asynchronous signal handlers. AS, in AS-Safe, stands for Asynchronous Signal.

  Many functions that are AS-Safe may set `errno`, or modify the floating-point environment, because their doing so does not make them unsuitable for use in signal handlers. However, programs could misbehave should asynchronous signal handlers modify this thread-local state, and the signal handling machinery cannot be counted on to preserve it. Therefore, signal handlers that call functions that may set `errno` or modify the floating-point environment *must* save their original values, and restore them before returning.

- `AC-Safe` or Async-Cancel-Safe functions are safe to call when asynchronous cancellation is enabled. AC in AC-Safe stands for Asynchronous Cancellation.

  The POSIX standard defines only three functions to be AC-Safe, namely `pthread_cancel`, `pthread_setcancelstate`, and `pthread_setcanceltype`. At present the GNU C Library provides no guarantees beyond these three functions, but does document which functions are presently AC-Safe. This documentation is provided for use by the GNU C Library developers.

  Just like signal handlers, cancellation cleanup routines must configure the floating point environment they require. The routines cannot assume a floating point environment, particularly when asynchronous cancellation is enabled. If the configuration of the floating point environment cannot be performed atomically then it is also possible that the environment encountered is internally inconsistent.

- `MT-Unsafe`, `AS-Unsafe`, `AC-Unsafe` functions are not safe to call within the safety contexts described above. Calling them within such contexts invokes undefined behavior.

  Functions not explicitly documented as safe in a safety context should be regarded as Unsafe.

- `Preliminary` safety properties are documented, indicating these properties may *not* be counted on in future releases of the GNU C Library.

Such preliminary properties are the result of an assessment of the properties of our current implementation, rather than of what is mandated and permitted by current and future standards.

Although we strive to abide by the standards, in some cases our implementation is safe even when the standard does not demand safety, and in other cases our implementation does not meet the standard safety requirements. The latter are most likely bugs; the former, when marked as `Preliminary`, should not be counted on: future standards may require changes that are not compatible with the additional safety properties afforded by the current implementation.

Furthermore, the POSIX standard does not offer a detailed definition of safety. We assume that, by "safe to call", POSIX means that, as long as the program does not invoke undefined behavior, the "safe to call" function behaves as specified, and does not cause other functions to deviate from their specified behavior. We have chosen to use its loose definitions of safety, not because they are the best definitions to use, but because choosing them harmonizes this manual with POSIX.

Please keep in mind that these are preliminary definitions and annotations, and certain aspects of the definitions are still under discussion and might be subject to clarification or change.

Over time, we envision evolving the preliminary safety notes into stable commitments, as stable as those of our interfaces. As we do, we will remove the `Preliminary` keyword from safety notes. As long as the keyword remains, however, they are not to be regarded as a promise of future behavior.

Other keywords that appear in safety notes are defined in subsequent sections.

1.2.2.2 Unsafe Features

Functions that are unsafe to call in certain contexts are annotated with keywords that document their features that make them unsafe to call. AS-Unsafe features in this section indicate the functions are never safe to call when asynchronous signals are enabled. AC-Unsafe features indicate they are never safe to call when asynchronous cancellation is enabled. There are no MT-Unsafe marks in this section.

- `lock`

  Functions marked with `lock` as an AS-Unsafe feature may be interrupted by a signal while holding a non-recursive lock. If the signal handler calls another such function that takes the same lock, the result is a deadlock.

  Functions annotated with `lock` as an AC-Unsafe feature may, if cancelled asynchronously, fail to release a lock that would have been released if their execution had not been interrupted by asynchronous thread cancellation. Once a lock is left taken, attempts to take that lock will block indefinitely.

- `corrupt`

  Functions marked with `corrupt` as an AS-Unsafe feature may corrupt data structures and misbehave when they interrupt, or are interrupted by, another such function. Unlike functions marked with `lock`, these take recursive locks to avoid MT-Safety problems, but this is not enough to stop a signal handler from observing a partially-updated data structure. Further corruption may arise from the interrupted function's failure to notice updates made by signal handlers.

Functions marked with `corrupt` as an AC-Unsafe feature may leave data structures in a corrupt, partially updated state. Subsequent uses of the data structure may misbehave.

- `heap`

  Functions marked with `heap` may call heap memory management functions from the `malloc/free` family of functions and are only as safe as those functions. This note is thus equivalent to:

  | AS-Unsafe lock | AC-Unsafe lock fd mem |

- `dlopen`

  Functions marked with `dlopen` use the dynamic loader to load shared libraries into the current execution image. This involves opening files, mapping them into memory, allocating additional memory, resolving symbols, applying relocations and more, all of this while holding internal dynamic loader locks.

  The locks are enough for these functions to be AS- and AC-Unsafe, but other issues may arise. At present this is a placeholder for all potential safety issues raised by `dlopen`.

- `plugin`

  Functions annotated with `plugin` may run code from plugins that may be external to the GNU C Library. Such plugin functions are assumed to be MT-Safe, AS-Unsafe and AC-Unsafe. Examples of such plugins are stack unwinding libraries, name service switch (NSS) and character set conversion (iconv) back-ends.

  Although the plugins mentioned as examples are all brought in by means of dlopen, the `plugin` keyword does not imply any direct involvement of the dynamic loader or the `libdl` interfaces, those are covered by `dlopen`. For example, if one function loads a module and finds the addresses of some of its functions, while another just calls those already-resolved functions, the former will be marked with `dlopen`, whereas the latter will get the `plugin`. When a single function takes all of these actions, then it gets both marks.

- `i18n`

  Functions marked with `i18n` may call internationalization functions of the `gettext` family and will be only as safe as those functions. This note is thus equivalent to:

  | MT-Safe env | AS-Unsafe corrupt heap dlopen | AC-Unsafe corrupt |

- `timer`

  Functions marked with `timer` use the `alarm` function or similar to set a time-out for a system call or a long-running operation. In a multi-threaded program, there is a risk that the time-out signal will be delivered to a different thread, thus failing to interrupt the intended thread. Besides being MT-Unsafe, such functions are always AS-Unsafe, because calling them in signal handlers may interfere with timers set in the interrupted code, and AC-Unsafe, because there is no safe way to guarantee an earlier timer will be reset in case of asynchronous cancellation.

1.2.2.3 Conditionally Safe Features

For some features that make functions unsafe to call in certain contexts, there are known ways to avoid the safety problem other than refraining from calling the function altogether. The keywords that follow refer to such features, and each of their definitions indicate how the whole program needs to be constrained in order to remove the safety problem indicated by the keyword. Only when all the reasons that make a function unsafe are observed and addressed, by applying the documented constraints, does the function become safe to call in a context.

- `init`

  Functions marked with `init` as an MT-Unsafe feature perform MT-Unsafe initialization when they are first called.

  Calling such a function at least once in single-threaded mode removes this specific cause for the function to be regarded as MT-Unsafe. If no other cause for that remains, the function can then be safely called after other threads are started.

  Functions marked with `init` as an AS- or AC-Unsafe feature use the internal `libc_once` machinery or similar to initialize internal data structures.

  If a signal handler interrupts such an initializer, and calls any function that also performs `libc_once` initialization, it will deadlock if the thread library has been loaded.

  Furthermore, if an initializer is partially complete before it is canceled or interrupted by a signal whose handler requires the same initialization, some or all of the initialization may be performed more than once, leaking resources or even resulting in corrupt internal data.

  Applications that need to call functions marked with `init` as an AS- or AC-Unsafe feature should ensure the initialization is performed before configuring signal handlers or enabling cancellation, so that the AS- and AC-Safety issues related with `libc_once` do not arise.

- `race`

  Functions annotated with `race` as an MT-Safety issue operate on objects in ways that may cause data races or similar forms of destructive interference out of concurrent execution. In some cases, the objects are passed to the functions by users; in others, they are used by the functions to return values to users; in others, they are not even exposed to users.

  We consider access to objects passed as (indirect) arguments to functions to be data race free. The assurance of data race free objects is the caller's responsibility. We will not mark a function as MT-Unsafe or AS-Unsafe if it misbehaves when users fail to take the measures required by POSIX to avoid data races when dealing with such objects. As a general rule, if a function is documented as reading from an object passed (by reference) to it, or modifying it, users ought to use memory synchronization primitives to avoid data races just as they would should they perform the accesses themselves rather than by calling the library function. `FILE` streams are the exception to the general rule, in that POSIX mandates the library to guard against data races in many functions that manipulate objects of this specific opaque type. We regard this as a convenience provided to users, rather than as a general requirement whose expectations should extend to other types.

  In order to remind users that guarding certain arguments is their responsibility, we will annotate functions that take objects of certain types as arguments. We draw the line for objects passed by users as follows: objects whose types are exposed to users, and that users are expected to access directly, such as memory buffers, strings, and various user-visible `struct` types, do *not* give reason for functions to be annotated with `race`. It would be noisy and redundant with the general requirement, and not many would be surprised by the library's lack of internal guards when accessing objects that can be accessed directly by users.

As for objects that are opaque or opaque-like, in that they are to be manipulated only by passing them to library functions (e.g., `FILE`, `DIR`, `obstack`, `iconv_t`), there might be additional expectations as to internal coordination of access by the library. We will annotate, with `race` followed by a colon and the argument name, functions that take such objects but that do not take care of synchronizing access to them by default. For example, `FILE` stream `unlocked` functions will be annotated, but those that perform implicit locking on `FILE` streams by default will not, even though the implicit locking may be disabled on a per-stream basis.

In either case, we will not regard as MT-Unsafe functions that may access user-supplied objects in unsafe ways should users fail to ensure the accesses are well defined. The notion prevails that users are expected to safeguard against data races any user-supplied objects that the library accesses on their behalf.

This user responsibility does not apply, however, to objects controlled by the library itself, such as internal objects and static buffers used to return values from certain calls. When the library doesn't guard them against concurrent uses, these cases are regarded as MT-Unsafe and AS-Unsafe (although the `race` mark under AS-Unsafe will be omitted as redundant with the one under MT-Unsafe). As in the case of user-exposed objects, the mark may be followed by a colon and an identifier. The identifier groups all functions that operate on a certain unguarded object; users may avoid the MT-Safety issues related with unguarded concurrent access to such internal objects by creating a non-recursive mutex related with the identifier, and always holding the mutex when calling any function marked as racy on that identifier, as they would have to should the identifier be an object under user control. The non-recursive mutex avoids the MT-Safety issue, but it trades one AS-Safety issue for another, so use in asynchronous signals remains undefined.

When the identifier relates to a static buffer used to hold return values, the mutex must be held for as long as the buffer remains in use by the caller. Many functions that return pointers to static buffers offer reentrant variants that store return values in caller-supplied buffers instead. In some cases, such as `tmpname`, the variant is chosen not by calling an alternate entry point, but by passing a non-`NULL` pointer to the buffer in which the returned values are to be stored. These variants are generally preferable in multi-threaded programs, although some of them are not MT-Safe because of other internal buffers, also documented with `race` notes.

- `const`

  Functions marked with `const` as an MT-Safety issue non-atomically modify internal objects that are better regarded as constant, because a substantial portion of the GNU C Library accesses them without synchronization. Unlike `race`, that causes both readers and writers of internal objects to be regarded as MT-Unsafe and AS-Unsafe, this mark is applied to writers only. Writers remain equally MT- and AS-Unsafe to call, but the then-mandatory constness of objects they modify enables readers to be regarded as MT-Safe and AS-Safe (as long as no other reasons for them to be unsafe remain), since the lack of synchronization is not a problem when the objects are effectively constant.

The identifier that follows the `const` mark will appear by itself as a safety note in readers. Programs that wish to work around this safety issue, so as to call writers, may use a non-recursve `rwlock` associated with the identifier, and guard *all* calls to functions marked with `const` followed by the identifier with a write lock, and *all* calls to functions marked with the identifier by itself with a read lock. The non-recursive locking removes the MT-Safety problem, but it trades one AS-Safety problem for another, so use in asynchronous signals remains undefined.

- `sig`

Functions marked with `sig` as a MT-Safety issue (that implies an identical AS-Safety issue, omitted for brevity) may temporarily install a signal handler for internal purposes, which may interfere with other uses of the signal, identified after a colon.

This safety problem can be worked around by ensuring that no other uses of the signal will take place for the duration of the call. Holding a non-recursive mutex while calling all functions that use the same temporary signal; blocking that signal before the call and resetting its handler afterwards is recommended.

There is no safe way to guarantee the original signal handler is restored in case of asynchronous cancellation, therefore so-marked functions are also AC-Unsafe.

Besides the measures recommended to work around the MT- and AS-Safety problem, in order to avert the cancellation problem, disabling asynchronous cancellation *and* installing a cleanup handler to restore the signal to the desired state and to release the mutex are recommended.

- `term`

Functions marked with `term` as an MT-Safety issue may change the terminal settings in the recommended way, namely: call `tcgetattr`, modify some flags, and then call `tcsetattr`; this creates a window in which changes made by other threads are lost. Thus, functions marked with `term` are MT-Unsafe. The same window enables changes made by asynchronous signals to be lost. These functions are also AS-Unsafe, but the corresponding mark is omitted as redundant.

It is thus advisable for applications using the terminal to avoid concurrent and reentrant interactions with it, by not using it in signal handlers or blocking signals that might use it, and holding a lock while calling these functions and interacting with the terminal. This lock should also be used for mutual exclusion with functions marked with `race:tcattr(fd)`, where *fd* is a file descriptor for the controlling terminal. The caller may use a single mutex for simplicity, or use one mutex per terminal, even if referenced by different file descriptors.

Functions marked with `term` as an AC-Safety issue are supposed to restore terminal settings to their original state, after temporarily changing them, but they may fail to do so if cancelled.

Besides the measures recommended to work around the MT- and AS-Safety problem, in order to avert the cancellation problem, disabling asynchronous cancellation *and* installing a cleanup handler to restore the terminal settings to the original state and to release the mutex are recommended.

1.2.2.4 Other Safety Remarks

Additional keywords may be attached to functions, indicating features that do not make a function unsafe to call, but that may need to be taken into account in certain classes of programs:

- `locale`

  Functions annotated with `locale` as an MT-Safety issue read from the locale object without any form of synchronization. Functions annotated with `locale` called concurrently with locale changes may behave in ways that do not correspond to any of the locales active during their execution, but an unpredictable mix thereof.

  We do not mark these functions as MT- or AS-Unsafe, however, because functions that modify the locale object are marked with `const:locale` and regarded as unsafe. Being unsafe, the latter are not to be called when multiple threads are running or asynchronous signals are enabled, and so the locale can be considered effectively constant in these contexts, which makes the former safe.

- `env`

  Functions marked with `env` as an MT-Safety issue access the environment with `getenv` or similar, without any guards to ensure safety in the presence of concurrent modifications.

  We do not mark these functions as MT- or AS-Unsafe, however, because functions that modify the environment are all marked with `const:env` and regarded as unsafe. Being unsafe, the latter are not to be called when multiple threads are running or asynchronous signals are enabled, and so the environment can be considered effectively constant in these contexts, which makes the former safe.

- `hostid`

  The function marked with `hostid` as an MT-Safety issue reads from the system-wide data structures that hold the "host ID" of the machine. These data structures cannot generally be modified atomically. Since it is expected that the "host ID" will not normally change, the function that reads from it (`gethostid`) is regarded as safe, whereas the function that modifies it (`sethostid`) is marked with `const:hostid`, indicating it may require special care if it is to be called. In this specific case, the special care amounts to system-wide (not merely intra-process) coordination.

- `sigintr`

  Functions marked with `sigintr` as an MT-Safety issue access the `_sigintr` internal data structure without any guards to ensure safety in the presence of concurrent modifications.

  We do not mark these functions as MT- or AS-Unsafe, however, because functions that modify the this data structure are all marked with `const:sigintr` and regarded as unsafe. Being unsafe, the latter are not to be called when multiple threads are running or asynchronous signals are enabled, and so the data structure can be considered effectively constant in these contexts, which makes the former safe.

- `fd`

  Functions annotated with `fd` as an AC-Safety issue may leak file descriptors if asynchronous thread cancellation interrupts their execution.

Functions that allocate or deallocate file descriptors will generally be marked as such. Even if they attempted to protect the file descriptor allocation and deallocation with cleanup regions, allocating a new descriptor and storing its number where the cleanup region could release it cannot be performed as a single atomic operation. Similarly, releasing the descriptor and taking it out of the data structure normally responsible for releasing it cannot be performed atomically. There will always be a window in which the descriptor cannot be released because it was not stored in the cleanup handler argument yet, or it was already taken out before releasing it. It cannot be taken out after release: an open descriptor could mean either that the descriptor still has to be closed, or that it already did so but the descriptor was reallocated by another thread or signal handler.

Such leaks could be internally avoided, with some performance penalty, by temporarily disabling asynchronous thread cancellation. However, since callers of allocation or deallocation functions would have to do this themselves, to avoid the same sort of leak in their own layer, it makes more sense for the library to assume they are taking care of it than to impose a performance penalty that is redundant when the problem is solved in upper layers, and insufficient when it is not.

This remark by itself does not cause a function to be regarded as AC-Unsafe. However, cumulative effects of such leaks may pose a problem for some programs. If this is the case, suspending asynchronous cancellation for the duration of calls to such functions is recommended.

- `mem`

    Functions annotated with `mem` as an AC-Safety issue may leak memory if asynchronous thread cancellation interrupts their execution.

    The problem is similar to that of file descriptors: there is no atomic interface to allocate memory and store its address in the argument to a cleanup handler, or to release it and remove its address from that argument, without at least temporarily disabling asynchronous cancellation, which these functions do not do.

    This remark does not by itself cause a function to be regarded as generally AC-Unsafe. However, cumulative effects of such leaks may be severe enough for some programs that disabling asynchronous cancellation for the duration of calls to such functions may be required.

- `cwd`

    Functions marked with `cwd` as an MT-Safety issue may temporarily change the current working directory during their execution, which may cause relative pathnames to be resolved in unexpected ways in other threads or within asynchronous signal or cancellation handlers.

    This is not enough of a reason to mark so-marked functions as MT- or AS-Unsafe, but when this behavior is optional (e.g., `nftw` with `FTW_CHDIR`), avoiding the option may be a good alternative to using full pathnames or file descriptor-relative (e.g. `openat`) system calls.

- `!posix`

    This remark, as an MT-, AS- or AC-Safety note to a function, indicates the safety status of the function is known to differ from the specified status in the POSIX standard. For example, POSIX does not require a function to be Safe, but our implementation is, or vice-versa.

For the time being, the absence of this remark does not imply the safety properties we documented are identical to those mandated by POSIX for the corresponding functions.

- `:identifier`

  Annotations may sometimes be followed by identifiers, intended to group several functions that e.g. access the data structures in an unsafe way, as in `race` and `const`, or to provide more specific information, such as naming a signal in a function marked with `sig`. It is envisioned that it may be applied to `lock` and `corrupt` as well in the future.

  In most cases, the identifier will name a set of functions, but it may name global objects or function arguments, or identifiable properties or logical components associated with them, with a notation such as e.g. `:buf(arg)` to denote a buffer associated with the argument *arg*, or `:tcattr(fd)` to denote the terminal attributes of a file descriptor *fd*.

  The most common use for identifiers is to provide logical groups of functions and arguments that need to be protected by the same synchronization primitive in order to ensure safe operation in a given context.

- `/condition`

  Some safety annotations may be conditional, in that they only apply if a boolean expression involving arguments, global variables or even the underlying kernel evaluates evaluates to true. Such conditions as `/hurd` or `/!linux!bsd` indicate the preceding marker only applies when the underlying kernel is the HURD, or when it is neither Linux nor a BSD kernel, respectively. `/!ps` and `/one_per_line` indicate the preceding marker only applies when argument *ps* is NULL, or global variable *one_per_line* is nonzero.

  When all marks that render a function unsafe are adorned with such conditions, and none of the named conditions hold, then the function can be regarded as safe.

1.2.3 Berkeley Unix

The GNU C Library defines facilities from some versions of Unix which are not formally standardized, specifically from the 4.2 BSD, 4.3 BSD, and 4.4 BSD Unix systems (also known as *Berkeley Unix*) and from *SunOS* (a popular 4.2 BSD derivative that includes some Unix System V functionality). These systems support most of the ISO C and POSIX facilities, and 4.4 BSD and newer releases of SunOS in fact support them all.

The BSD facilities include symbolic links (see Section 14.5 [Symbolic Links], page 393), the `select` function (see Section 13.8 [Waiting for Input or Output], page 342), the BSD signal functions (see Section 24.10 [BSD Signal Handling], page 703), and sockets (see Chapter 16 [Sockets], page 429).

1.2.4 SVID (The System V Interface Description)

The *System V Interface Description* (SVID) is a document describing the AT&T Unix System V operating system. It is to some extent a superset of the POSIX standard (see Section 1.2.2 [POSIX (The Portable Operating System Interface)], page 2).

The GNU C Library defines most of the facilities required by the SVID that are not also required by the ISO C or POSIX standards, for compatibility with System V Unix and other Unix systems (such as SunOS) which include these facilities. However, many of the more obscure and less generally useful facilities required by the SVID are not included. (In fact, Unix System V itself does not provide them all.)

The supported facilities from System V include the methods for inter-process communication and shared memory, the `hsearch` and `drand48` families of functions, `fmtmsg` and several of the mathematical functions.

1.2.5 XPG (The X/Open Portability Guide)

The X/Open Portability Guide, published by the X/Open Company, Ltd., is a more general standard than POSIX. X/Open owns the Unix copyright and the XPG specifies the requirements for systems which are intended to be a Unix system.

The GNU C Library complies to the X/Open Portability Guide, Issue 4.2, with all extensions common to XSI (X/Open System Interface) compliant systems and also all X/Open UNIX extensions.

The additions on top of POSIX are mainly derived from functionality available in System V and BSD systems. Some of the really bad mistakes in System V systems were corrected, though. Since fulfilling the XPG standard with the Unix extensions is a precondition for getting the Unix brand chances are good that the functionality is available on commercial systems.

1.3 Using the Library

This section describes some of the practical issues involved in using the GNU C Library.

1.3.1 Header Files

Libraries for use by C programs really consist of two parts: *header files* that define types and macros and declare variables and functions; and the actual library or *archive* that contains the definitions of the variables and functions.

(Recall that in C, a *declaration* merely provides information that a function or variable exists and gives its type. For a function declaration, information about the types of its arguments might be provided as well. The purpose of declarations is to allow the compiler to correctly process references to the declared variables and functions. A *definition*, on the other hand, actually allocates storage for a variable or says what a function does.)

In order to use the facilities in the GNU C Library, you should be sure that your program source files include the appropriate header files. This is so that the compiler has declarations of these facilities available and can correctly process references to them. Once your program has been compiled, the linker resolves these references to the actual definitions provided in the archive file.

Header files are included into a program source file by the '`#include`' preprocessor directive. The C language supports two forms of this directive; the first,

```
#include "header"
```

is typically used to include a header file *header* that you write yourself; this would contain definitions and declarations describing the interfaces between the different parts of your particular application. By contrast,

```
#include <file.h>
```

is typically used to include a header file `file.h` that contains definitions and declarations for a standard library. This file would normally be installed in a standard place by your system administrator. You should use this second form for the C library header files.

Typically, '`#include`' directives are placed at the top of the C source file, before any other code. If you begin your source files with some comments explaining what the code in the file does (a good idea), put the '`#include`' directives immediately afterwards, following the feature test macro definition (see Section 1.3.4 [Feature Test Macros], page 15).

For more information about the use of header files and '`#include`' directives, see Section "Header Files" in *The GNU C Preprocessor Manual*.

The GNU C Library provides several header files, each of which contains the type and macro definitions and variable and function declarations for a group of related facilities. This means that your programs may need to include several header files, depending on exactly which facilities you are using.

Some library header files include other library header files automatically. However, as a matter of programming style, you should not rely on this; it is better to explicitly include all the header files required for the library facilities you are using. The GNU C Library header files have been written in such a way that it doesn't matter if a header file is accidentally included more than once; including a header file a second time has no effect. Likewise, if your program needs to include multiple header files, the order in which they are included doesn't matter.

Compatibility Note: Inclusion of standard header files in any order and any number of times works in any ISO C implementation. However, this has traditionally not been the case in many older C implementations.

Strictly speaking, you don't *have to* include a header file to use a function it declares; you could declare the function explicitly yourself, according to the specifications in this manual. But it is usually better to include the header file because it may define types and macros that are not otherwise available and because it may define more efficient macro replacements for some functions. It is also a sure way to have the correct declaration.

1.3.2 Macro Definitions of Functions

If we describe something as a function in this manual, it may have a macro definition as well. This normally has no effect on how your program runs—the macro definition does the same thing as the function would. In particular, macro equivalents for library functions evaluate arguments exactly once, in the same way that a function call would. The main reason for these macro definitions is that sometimes they can produce an inline expansion that is considerably faster than an actual function call.

Taking the address of a library function works even if it is also defined as a macro. This is because, in this context, the name of the function isn't followed by the left parenthesis that is syntactically necessary to recognize a macro call.

You might occasionally want to avoid using the macro definition of a function—perhaps to make your program easier to debug. There are two ways you can do this:

- You can avoid a macro definition in a specific use by enclosing the name of the function in parentheses. This works because the name of the function doesn't appear in a syntactic context where it is recognizable as a macro call.

- You can suppress any macro definition for a whole source file by using the '#undef' preprocessor directive, unless otherwise stated explicitly in the description of that facility.

For example, suppose the header file stdlib.h declares a function named abs with

```
extern int abs (int);
```

and also provides a macro definition for abs. Then, in:

```
#include <stdlib.h>
int f (int *i) { return abs (++*i); }
```

the reference to abs might refer to either a macro or a function. On the other hand, in each of the following examples the reference is to a function and not a macro.

```
#include <stdlib.h>
int g (int *i) { return (abs) (++*i); }
```

```
#undef abs
int h (int *i) { return abs (++*i); }
```

Since macro definitions that double for a function behave in exactly the same way as the actual function version, there is usually no need for any of these methods. In fact, removing macro definitions usually just makes your program slower.

1.3.3 Reserved Names

The names of all library types, macros, variables and functions that come from the ISO C standard are reserved unconditionally; your program **may not** redefine these names. All other library names are reserved if your program explicitly includes the header file that defines or declares them. There are several reasons for these restrictions:

- Other people reading your code could get very confused if you were using a function named exit to do something completely different from what the standard exit function does, for example. Preventing this situation helps to make your programs easier to understand and contributes to modularity and maintainability.

- It avoids the possibility of a user accidentally redefining a library function that is called by other library functions. If redefinition were allowed, those other functions would not work properly.

- It allows the compiler to do whatever special optimizations it pleases on calls to these functions, without the possibility that they may have been redefined by the user. Some library facilities, such as those for dealing with variadic arguments (see Section A.2 [Variadic Functions], page 878) and non-local exits (see Chapter 23 [Non-Local Exits], page 652), actually require a considerable amount of cooperation on the part of the C compiler, and with respect to the implementation, it might be easier for the compiler to treat these as built-in parts of the language.

In addition to the names documented in this manual, reserved names include all external identifiers (global functions and variables) that begin with an underscore ('_') and all identifiers regardless of use that begin with either two underscores or an underscore followed by a capital letter are reserved names. This is so that the library and header files can define functions, variables, and macros for internal purposes without risk of conflict with names in user programs.

Some additional classes of identifier names are reserved for future extensions to the C language or the POSIX.1 environment. While using these names for your own purposes right now might not cause a problem, they do raise the possibility of conflict with future versions of the C or POSIX standards, so you should avoid these names.

- Names beginning with a capital 'E' followed a digit or uppercase letter may be used for additional error code names. See Chapter 2 [Error Reporting], page 22.

- Names that begin with either 'is' or 'to' followed by a lowercase letter may be used for additional character testing and conversion functions. See Chapter 4 [Character Handling], page 77.

- Names that begin with 'LC_' followed by an uppercase letter may be used for additional macros specifying locale attributes. See Chapter 7 [Locales and Internationalization], page 169.

- Names of all existing mathematics functions (see Chapter 19 [Mathematics], page 511) suffixed with 'f' or 'l' are reserved for corresponding functions that operate on `float` and `long double` arguments, respectively.

- Names that begin with 'SIG' followed by an uppercase letter are reserved for additional signal names. See Section 24.2 [Standard Signals], page 663.

- Names that begin with 'SIG_' followed by an uppercase letter are reserved for additional signal actions. See Section 24.3.1 [Basic Signal Handling], page 672.

- Names beginning with 'str', 'mem', or 'wcs' followed by a lowercase letter are reserved for additional string and array functions. See Chapter 5 [String and Array Utilities], page 87.

- Names that end with '_t' are reserved for additional type names.

In addition, some individual header files reserve names beyond those that they actually define. You only need to worry about these restrictions if your program includes that particular header file.

- The header file `dirent.h` reserves names prefixed with 'd_'.
- The header file `fcntl.h` reserves names prefixed with 'l_', 'F_', 'O_', and 'S_'.
- The header file `grp.h` reserves names prefixed with 'gr_'.
- The header file `limits.h` reserves names suffixed with '_MAX'.
- The header file `pwd.h` reserves names prefixed with 'pw_'.
- The header file `signal.h` reserves names prefixed with 'sa_' and 'SA_'.
- The header file `sys/stat.h` reserves names prefixed with 'st_' and 'S_'.
- The header file `sys/times.h` reserves names prefixed with 'tms_'.
- The header file `termios.h` reserves names prefixed with 'c_', 'V', 'I', 'O', and 'TC'; and names prefixed with 'B' followed by a digit.

1.3.4 Feature Test Macros

The exact set of features available when you compile a source file is controlled by which *feature test macros* you define.

If you compile your programs using 'gcc -ansi', you get only the ISO C library features, unless you explicitly request additional features by defining one or more of the feature macros. See Section "GNU CC Command Options" in *The GNU CC Manual*, for more information about GCC options.

You should define these macros by using '#define' preprocessor directives at the top of your source code files. These directives *must* come before any #include of a system header file. It is best to make them the very first thing in the file, preceded only by comments. You could also use the '-D' option to GCC, but it's better if you make the source files indicate their own meaning in a self-contained way.

This system exists to allow the library to conform to multiple standards. Although the different standards are often described as supersets of each other, they are usually incompatible because larger standards require functions with names that smaller ones reserve to the user program. This is not mere pedantry — it has been a problem in practice. For instance, some non-GNU programs define functions named getline that have nothing to do with this library's getline. They would not be compilable if all features were enabled indiscriminately.

This should not be used to verify that a program conforms to a limited standard. It is insufficient for this purpose, as it will not protect you from including header files outside the standard, or relying on semantics undefined within the standard.

_POSIX_SOURCE   [Macro]
> If you define this macro, then the functionality from the POSIX.1 standard (IEEE Standard 1003.1) is available, as well as all of the ISO C facilities.
>
> The state of _POSIX_SOURCE is irrelevant if you define the macro _POSIX_C_SOURCE to a positive integer.

_POSIX_C_SOURCE   [Macro]
> Define this macro to a positive integer to control which POSIX functionality is made available. The greater the value of this macro, the more functionality is made available.
>
> If you define this macro to a value greater than or equal to 1, then the functionality from the 1990 edition of the POSIX.1 standard (IEEE Standard 1003.1-1990) is made available.
>
> If you define this macro to a value greater than or equal to 2, then the functionality from the 1992 edition of the POSIX.2 standard (IEEE Standard 1003.2-1992) is made available.
>
> If you define this macro to a value greater than or equal to 199309L, then the functionality from the 1993 edition of the POSIX.1b standard (IEEE Standard 1003.1b-1993) is made available.
>
> Greater values for _POSIX_C_SOURCE will enable future extensions. The POSIX standards process will define these values as necessary, and the GNU C Library should support them some time after they become standardized. The 1996 edition of POSIX.1 (ISO/IEC 9945-1: 1996) states that if you define _POSIX_C_SOURCE to a value greater than or equal to 199506L, then the functionality from the 1996 edition is made available.

_XOPEN_SOURCE   [Macro]
_XOPEN_SOURCE_EXTENDED   [Macro]
> If you define this macro, functionality described in the X/Open Portability Guide is included. This is a superset of the POSIX.1 and POSIX.2 functionality and in fact _POSIX_SOURCE and _POSIX_C_SOURCE are automatically defined.

As the unification of all Unices, functionality only available in BSD and SVID is also included.

If the macro `_XOPEN_SOURCE_EXTENDED` is also defined, even more functionality is available. The extra functions will make all functions available which are necessary for the X/Open Unix brand.

If the macro `_XOPEN_SOURCE` has the value 500 this includes all functionality described so far plus some new definitions from the Single Unix Specification, version 2.

`_LARGEFILE_SOURCE`   [Macro]

If this macro is defined some extra functions are available which rectify a few short-comings in all previous standards. Specifically, the functions `fseeko` and `ftello` are available. Without these functions the difference between the ISO C interface (`fseek`, `ftell`) and the low-level POSIX interface (`lseek`) would lead to problems.

This macro was introduced as part of the Large File Support extension (LFS).

`_LARGEFILE64_SOURCE`   [Macro]

If you define this macro an additional set of functions is made available which enables 32 bit systems to use files of sizes beyond the usual limit of 2GB. This interface is not available if the system does not support files that large. On systems where the natural file size limit is greater than 2GB (i.e., on 64 bit systems) the new functions are identical to the replaced functions.

The new functionality is made available by a new set of types and functions which replace the existing ones. The names of these new objects contain `64` to indicate the intention, e.g., `off_t` vs. `off64_t` and `fseeko` vs. `fseeko64`.

This macro was introduced as part of the Large File Support extension (LFS). It is a transition interface for the period when 64 bit offsets are not generally used (see `_FILE_OFFSET_BITS`).

`_FILE_OFFSET_BITS`   [Macro]

This macro determines which file system interface shall be used, one replacing the other. Whereas `_LARGEFILE64_SOURCE` makes the 64 bit interface available as an additional interface, `_FILE_OFFSET_BITS` allows the 64 bit interface to replace the old interface.

If `_FILE_OFFSET_BITS` is undefined, or if it is defined to the value 32, nothing changes. The 32 bit interface is used and types like `off_t` have a size of 32 bits on 32 bit systems.

If the macro is defined to the value 64, the large file interface replaces the old interface. I.e., the functions are not made available under different names (as they are with `_LARGEFILE64_SOURCE`). Instead the old function names now reference the new functions, e.g., a call to `fseeko` now indeed calls `fseeko64`.

This macro should only be selected if the system provides mechanisms for handling large files. On 64 bit systems this macro has no effect since the `*64` functions are identical to the normal functions.

This macro was introduced as part of the Large File Support extension (LFS).

`_ISOC99_SOURCE`   [Macro]

> Until the revised ISO C standard is widely adopted the new features are not automatically enabled. The GNU C Library nevertheless has a complete implementation of the new standard and to enable the new features the macro `_ISOC99_SOURCE` should be defined.

`_GNU_SOURCE`   [Macro]

> If you define this macro, everything is included: ISO C89, ISO C99, POSIX.1, POSIX.2, BSD, SVID, X/Open, LFS, and GNU extensions. In the cases where POSIX.1 conflicts with BSD, the POSIX definitions take precedence.

`_DEFAULT_SOURCE`   [Macro]

> If you define this macro, most features are included apart from X/Open, LFS and GNU extensions: the effect is to enable features from the 2008 edition of POSIX, as well as certain BSD and SVID features without a separate feature test macro to control them. Defining this macro, on its own and without using compiler options such as `-ansi` or `-std=c99`, has the same effect as not defining any feature test macros; defining it together with other feature test macros, or when options such as `-ansi` are used, enables those features even when the other options would otherwise cause them to be disabled.

`_REENTRANT`   [Macro]
`_THREAD_SAFE`   [Macro]

> If you define one of these macros, reentrant versions of several functions get declared. Some of the functions are specified in POSIX.1c but many others are only available on a few other systems or are unique to the GNU C Library. The problem is the delay in the standardization of the thread safe C library interface.
>
> Unlike on some other systems, no special version of the C library must be used for linking. There is only one version but while compiling this it must have been specified to compile as thread safe.

We recommend you use `_GNU_SOURCE` in new programs. If you don't specify the '`-ansi`' option to GCC, or other conformance options such as `-std=c99`, and don't define any of these macros explicitly, the effect is the same as defining `_DEFAULT_SOURCE` to 1.

When you define a feature test macro to request a larger class of features, it is harmless to define in addition a feature test macro for a subset of those features. For example, if you define `_POSIX_C_SOURCE`, then defining `_POSIX_SOURCE` as well has no effect. Likewise, if you define `_GNU_SOURCE`, then defining either `_POSIX_SOURCE` or `_POSIX_C_SOURCE` as well has no effect.

1.4 Roadmap to the Manual

Here is an overview of the contents of the remaining chapters of this manual.

- Chapter 2 [Error Reporting], page 22, describes how errors detected by the library are reported.

- Chapter 3 [Virtual Memory Allocation And Paging], page 39, describes the GNU C Library's facilities for managing and using virtual and real memory, including dynamic allocation of virtual memory. If you do not know in advance how much memory your program needs, you can allocate it dynamically instead, and manipulate it via pointers.

- Chapter 4 [Character Handling], page 77, contains information about character classification functions (such as `isspace`) and functions for performing case conversion.

- Chapter 5 [String and Array Utilities], page 87, has descriptions of functions for manipulating strings (null-terminated character arrays) and general byte arrays, including operations such as copying and comparison.

- Chapter 6 [Character Set Handling], page 127, contains information about manipulating characters and strings using character sets larger than will fit in the usual `char` data type.

- Chapter 7 [Locales and Internationalization], page 169, describes how selecting a particular country or language affects the behavior of the library. For example, the locale affects collation sequences for strings and how monetary values are formatted.

- Chapter 9 [Searching and Sorting], page 212, contains information about functions for searching and sorting arrays. You can use these functions on any kind of array by providing an appropriate comparison function.

- Chapter 10 [Pattern Matching], page 222, presents functions for matching regular expressions and shell file name patterns, and for expanding words as the shell does.

- Chapter 11 [Input/Output Overview], page 243, gives an overall look at the input and output facilities in the library, and contains information about basic concepts such as file names.

- Chapter 12 [Input/Output on Streams], page 248, describes I/O operations involving streams (or `FILE *` objects). These are the normal C library functions from `stdio.h`.

- Chapter 13 [Low-Level Input/Output], page 323, contains information about I/O operations on file descriptors. File descriptors are a lower-level mechanism specific to the Unix family of operating systems.

- Chapter 14 [File System Interface], page 377, has descriptions of operations on entire files, such as functions for deleting and renaming them and for creating new directories. This chapter also contains information about how you can access the attributes of a file, such as its owner and file protection modes.

- Chapter 15 [Pipes and FIFOs], page 424, contains information about simple interprocess communication mechanisms. Pipes allow communication between two related processes (such as between a parent and child), while FIFOs allow communication between processes sharing a common file system on the same machine.

- Chapter 16 [Sockets], page 429, describes a more complicated interprocess communication mechanism that allows processes running on different machines to communicate over a network. This chapter also contains information about Internet host addressing and how to use the system network databases.

- Chapter 17 [Low-Level Terminal Interface], page 477, describes how you can change the attributes of a terminal device. If you want to disable echo of characters typed by the user, for example, read this chapter.

- Chapter 19 [Mathematics], page 511, contains information about the math library functions. These include things like random-number generators and remainder functions on integers as well as the usual trigonometric and exponential functions on floating-point numbers.

- Chapter 20 [Low-Level Arithmetic Functions], page 559, describes functions for simple arithmetic, analysis of floating-point values, and reading numbers from strings.

- Chapter 21 [Date and Time], page 595, describes functions for measuring both calendar time and CPU time, as well as functions for setting alarms and timers.

- Chapter 23 [Non-Local Exits], page 652, contains descriptions of the `setjmp` and `longjmp` functions. These functions provide a facility for `goto`-like jumps which can jump from one function to another.

- Chapter 24 [Signal Handling], page 661, tells you all about signals—what they are, how to establish a handler that is called when a particular kind of signal is delivered, and how to prevent signals from arriving during critical sections of your program.

- Chapter 25 [The Basic Program/System Interface], page 705, tells how your programs can access their command-line arguments and environment variables.

- Chapter 26 [Processes], page 749, contains information about how to start new processes and run programs.

- Chapter 28 [Job Control], page 763, describes functions for manipulating process groups and the controlling terminal. This material is probably only of interest if you are writing a shell or other program which handles job control specially.

- Chapter 29 [System Databases and Name Service Switch], page 782, describes the services which are available for looking up names in the system databases, how to determine which service is used for which database, and how these services are implemented so that contributors can design their own services.

- Section 30.13 [User Database], page 810, and Section 30.14 [Group Database], page 814, tell you how to access the system user and group databases.

- Chapter 31 [System Management], page 821, describes functions for controlling and getting information about the hardware and software configuration your program is executing under.

- Chapter 32 [System Configuration Parameters], page 838, tells you how you can get information about various operating system limits. Most of these parameters are provided for compatibility with POSIX.

- Appendix A [C Language Facilities in the Library], page 877, contains information about library support for standard parts of the C language, including things like the `sizeof` operator and the symbolic constant `NULL`, how to write functions accepting variable numbers of arguments, and constants describing the ranges and other properties of the numerical types. There is also a simple debugging mechanism which allows you to put assertions in your code, and have diagnostic messages printed if the tests fail.

- Appendix B [Summary of Library Facilities], page 892, gives a summary of all the functions, variables, and macros in the library, with complete data types and function prototypes, and says what standard or system each is derived from.

- Appendix C [Installing the GNU C Library], page 995, explains how to build and install the GNU C Library on your system, and how to report any bugs you might find.

- Appendix D [Library Maintenance], page 1003, explains how to add new functions or port the library to a new system.

If you already know the name of the facility you are interested in, you can look it up in Appendix B [Summary of Library Facilities], page 892. This gives you a summary of its syntax and a pointer to where you can find a more detailed description. This appendix is particularly useful if you just want to verify the order and type of arguments to a function, for example. It also tells you what standard or system each function, variable, or macro is derived from.

2 Error Reporting

Many functions in the GNU C Library detect and report error conditions, and sometimes your programs need to check for these error conditions. For example, when you open an input file, you should verify that the file was actually opened correctly, and print an error message or take other appropriate action if the call to the library function failed.

This chapter describes how the error reporting facility works. Your program should include the header file `errno.h` to use this facility.

2.1 Checking for Errors

Most library functions return a special value to indicate that they have failed. The special value is typically `-1`, a null pointer, or a constant such as `EOF` that is defined for that purpose. But this return value tells you only that an error has occurred. To find out what kind of error it was, you need to look at the error code stored in the variable `errno`. This variable is declared in the header file `errno.h`.

`volatile int errno`   [Variable]

> The variable `errno` contains the system error number. You can change the value of `errno`.
>
> Since `errno` is declared `volatile`, it might be changed asynchronously by a signal handler; see Section 24.4 [Defining Signal Handlers], page 678. However, a properly written signal handler saves and restores the value of `errno`, so you generally do not need to worry about this possibility except when writing signal handlers.
>
> The initial value of `errno` at program startup is zero. Many library functions are guaranteed to set it to certain nonzero values when they encounter certain kinds of errors. These error conditions are listed for each function. These functions do not change `errno` when they succeed; thus, the value of `errno` after a successful call is not necessarily zero, and you should not use `errno` to determine *whether* a call failed. The proper way to do that is documented for each function. *If* the call failed, you can examine `errno`.
>
> Many library functions can set `errno` to a nonzero value as a result of calling other library functions which might fail. You should assume that any library function might alter `errno` when the function returns an error.
>
> **Portability Note:** ISO C specifies `errno` as a "modifiable lvalue" rather than as a variable, permitting it to be implemented as a macro. For example, its expansion might involve a function call, like `*__errno_location ()`. In fact, that is what it is on GNU/Linux and GNU/Hurd systems. The GNU C Library, on each system, does whatever is right for the particular system.
>
> There are a few library functions, like `sqrt` and `atan`, that return a perfectly legitimate value in case of an error, but also set `errno`. For these functions, if you want to check to see whether an error occurred, the recommended method is to set `errno` to zero before calling the function, and then check its value afterward.

All the error codes have symbolic names; they are macros defined in `errno.h`. The names start with 'E' and an upper-case letter or digit; you should consider names of this form to be reserved names. See Section 1.3.3 [Reserved Names], page 14.

The error code values are all positive integers and are all distinct, with one exception: EWOULDBLOCK and EAGAIN are the same. Since the values are distinct, you can use them as labels in a switch statement; just don't use both EWOULDBLOCK and EAGAIN. Your program should not make any other assumptions about the specific values of these symbolic constants.

The value of errno doesn't necessarily have to correspond to any of these macros, since some library functions might return other error codes of their own for other situations. The only values that are guaranteed to be meaningful for a particular library function are the ones that this manual lists for that function.

Except on GNU/Hurd systems, almost any system call can return EFAULT if it is given an invalid pointer as an argument. Since this could only happen as a result of a bug in your program, and since it will not happen on GNU/Hurd systems, we have saved space by not mentioning EFAULT in the descriptions of individual functions.

In some Unix systems, many system calls can also return EFAULT if given as an argument a pointer into the stack, and the kernel for some obscure reason fails in its attempt to extend the stack. If this ever happens, you should probably try using statically or dynamically allocated memory instead of stack memory on that system.

2.2 Error Codes

The error code macros are defined in the header file errno.h. All of them expand into integer constant values. Some of these error codes can't occur on GNU systems, but they can occur using the GNU C Library on other systems.

int EPERM   [Macro]
> Operation not permitted; only the owner of the file (or other resource) or processes with special privileges can perform the operation.

int ENOENT   [Macro]
> No such file or directory. This is a "file doesn't exist" error for ordinary files that are referenced in contexts where they are expected to already exist.

int ESRCH   [Macro]
> No process matches the specified process ID.

int EINTR   [Macro]
> Interrupted function call; an asynchronous signal occurred and prevented completion of the call. When this happens, you should try the call again.
>
> You can choose to have functions resume after a signal that is handled, rather than failing with EINTR; see Section 24.5 [Primitives Interrupted by Signals], page 687.

int EIO   [Macro]
> Input/output error; usually used for physical read or write errors.

int ENXIO   [Macro]
> No such device or address. The system tried to use the device represented by a file you specified, and it couldn't find the device. This can mean that the device file was installed incorrectly, or that the physical device is missing or not correctly attached to the computer.

int **E2BIG**   [Macro]

> Argument list too long; used when the arguments passed to a new program being executed with one of the **exec** functions (see Section 26.5 [Executing a File], page 752) occupy too much memory space. This condition never arises on GNU/Hurd systems.

int **ENOEXEC**   [Macro]

> Invalid executable file format. This condition is detected by the **exec** functions; see Section 26.5 [Executing a File], page 752.

int **EBADF**   [Macro]

> Bad file descriptor; for example, I/O on a descriptor that has been closed or reading from a descriptor open only for writing (or vice versa).

int **ECHILD**   [Macro]

> There are no child processes. This error happens on operations that are supposed to manipulate child processes, when there aren't any processes to manipulate.

int **EDEADLK**   [Macro]

> Deadlock avoided; allocating a system resource would have resulted in a deadlock situation. The system does not guarantee that it will notice all such situations. This error means you got lucky and the system noticed; it might just hang. See Section 13.15 [File Locks], page 368, for an example.

int **ENOMEM**   [Macro]

> No memory available. The system cannot allocate more virtual memory because its capacity is full.

int **EACCES**   [Macro]

> Permission denied; the file permissions do not allow the attempted operation.

int **EFAULT**   [Macro]

> Bad address; an invalid pointer was detected. On GNU/Hurd systems, this error never happens; you get a signal instead.

int **ENOTBLK**   [Macro]

> A file that isn't a block special file was given in a situation that requires one. For example, trying to mount an ordinary file as a file system in Unix gives this error.

int **EBUSY**   [Macro]

> Resource busy; a system resource that can't be shared is already in use. For example, if you try to delete a file that is the root of a currently mounted filesystem, you get this error.

int **EEXIST**   [Macro]

> File exists; an existing file was specified in a context where it only makes sense to specify a new file.

int **EXDEV**   [Macro]

> An attempt to make an improper link across file systems was detected. This happens not only when you use **link** (see Section 14.4 [Hard Links], page 392) but also when you rename a file with **rename** (see Section 14.7 [Renaming Files], page 397).

`int` `ENODEV`   [Macro]

> The wrong type of device was given to a function that expects a particular sort of device.

`int` `ENOTDIR`   [Macro]

> A file that isn't a directory was specified when a directory is required.

`int` `EISDIR`   [Macro]

> File is a directory; you cannot open a directory for writing, or create or remove hard links to it.

`int` `EINVAL`   [Macro]

> Invalid argument. This is used to indicate various kinds of problems with passing the wrong argument to a library function.

`int` `EMFILE`   [Macro]

> The current process has too many files open and can't open any more. Duplicate descriptors do count toward this limit.
>
> In BSD and GNU, the number of open files is controlled by a resource limit that can usually be increased. If you get this error, you might want to increase the `RLIMIT_NOFILE` limit or make it unlimited; see Section 22.2 [Limiting Resource Usage], page 632.

`int` `ENFILE`   [Macro]

> There are too many distinct file openings in the entire system. Note that any number of linked channels count as just one file opening; see Section 13.5.1 [Linked Channels], page 334. This error never occurs on GNU/Hurd systems.

`int` `ENOTTY`   [Macro]

> Inappropriate I/O control operation, such as trying to set terminal modes on an ordinary file.

`int` `ETXTBSY`   [Macro]

> An attempt to execute a file that is currently open for writing, or write to a file that is currently being executed. Often using a debugger to run a program is considered having it open for writing and will cause this error. (The name stands for "text file busy".) This is not an error on GNU/Hurd systems; the text is copied as necessary.

`int` `EFBIG`   [Macro]

> File too big; the size of a file would be larger than allowed by the system.

`int` `ENOSPC`   [Macro]

> No space left on device; write operation on a file failed because the disk is full.

`int` `ESPIPE`   [Macro]

> Invalid seek operation (such as on a pipe).

`int` `EROFS`   [Macro]

> An attempt was made to modify something on a read-only file system.

`int` `EMLINK`   [Macro]

Too many links; the link count of a single file would become too large. `rename` can cause this error if the file being renamed already has as many links as it can take (see Section 14.7 [Renaming Files], page 397).

`int` `EPIPE`   [Macro]

Broken pipe; there is no process reading from the other end of a pipe. Every library function that returns this error code also generates a `SIGPIPE` signal; this signal terminates the program if not handled or blocked. Thus, your program will never actually see `EPIPE` unless it has handled or blocked `SIGPIPE`.

`int` `EDOM`   [Macro]

Domain error; used by mathematical functions when an argument value does not fall into the domain over which the function is defined.

`int` `ERANGE`   [Macro]

Range error; used by mathematical functions when the result value is not representable because of overflow or underflow.

`int` `EAGAIN`   [Macro]

Resource temporarily unavailable; the call might work if you try again later. The macro `EWOULDBLOCK` is another name for `EAGAIN`; they are always the same in the GNU C Library.

This error can happen in a few different situations:

- An operation that would block was attempted on an object that has non-blocking mode selected. Trying the same operation again will block until some external condition makes it possible to read, write, or connect (whatever the operation). You can use `select` to find out when the operation will be possible; see Section 13.8 [Waiting for Input or Output], page 342.

  Portability Note: In many older Unix systems, this condition was indicated by `EWOULDBLOCK`, which was a distinct error code different from `EAGAIN`. To make your program portable, you should check for both codes and treat them the same.

- A temporary resource shortage made an operation impossible. `fork` can return this error. It indicates that the shortage is expected to pass, so your program can try the call again later and it may succeed. It is probably a good idea to delay for a few seconds before trying it again, to allow time for other processes to release scarce resources. Such shortages are usually fairly serious and affect the whole system, so usually an interactive program should report the error to the user and return to its command loop.

`int` `EWOULDBLOCK`   [Macro]

In the GNU C Library, this is another name for `EAGAIN` (above). The values are always the same, on every operating system.

C libraries in many older Unix systems have `EWOULDBLOCK` as a separate error code.

`int` `EINPROGRESS`   [Macro]

An operation that cannot complete immediately was initiated on an object that has non-blocking mode selected. Some functions that must always block (such as `connect`;

see Section 16.9.1 [Making a Connection], page 456) never return `EAGAIN`. Instead, they return `EINPROGRESS` to indicate that the operation has begun and will take some time. Attempts to manipulate the object before the call completes return `EALREADY`. You can use the `select` function to find out when the pending operation has completed; see Section 13.8 [Waiting for Input or Output], page 342.

`int EALREADY`   [Macro]
    An operation is already in progress on an object that has non-blocking mode selected.

`int ENOTSOCK`   [Macro]
    A file that isn't a socket was specified when a socket is required.

`int EMSGSIZE`   [Macro]
    The size of a message sent on a socket was larger than the supported maximum size.

`int EPROTOTYPE`   [Macro]
    The socket type does not support the requested communications protocol.

`int ENOPROTOOPT`   [Macro]
    You specified a socket option that doesn't make sense for the particular protocol being used by the socket. See Section 16.12 [Socket Options], page 472.

`int EPROTONOSUPPORT`   [Macro]
    The socket domain does not support the requested communications protocol (perhaps because the requested protocol is completely invalid). See Section 16.8.1 [Creating a Socket], page 453.

`int ESOCKTNOSUPPORT`   [Macro]
    The socket type is not supported.

`int EOPNOTSUPP`   [Macro]
    The operation you requested is not supported. Some socket functions don't make sense for all types of sockets, and others may not be implemented for all communications protocols. On GNU/Hurd systems, this error can happen for many calls when the object does not support the particular operation; it is a generic indication that the server knows nothing to do for that call.

`int EPFNOSUPPORT`   [Macro]
    The socket communications protocol family you requested is not supported.

`int EAFNOSUPPORT`   [Macro]
    The address family specified for a socket is not supported; it is inconsistent with the protocol being used on the socket. See Chapter 16 [Sockets], page 429.

`int EADDRINUSE`   [Macro]
    The requested socket address is already in use. See Section 16.3 [Socket Addresses], page 431.

`int EADDRNOTAVAIL`   [Macro]
    The requested socket address is not available; for example, you tried to give a socket a name that doesn't match the local host name. See Section 16.3 [Socket Addresses], page 431.

`int` `ENETDOWN`   [Macro]
>   A socket operation failed because the network was down.

`int` `ENETUNREACH`   [Macro]
>   A socket operation failed because the subnet containing the remote host was unreachable.

`int` `ENETRESET`   [Macro]
>   A network connection was reset because the remote host crashed.

`int` `ECONNABORTED`   [Macro]
>   A network connection was aborted locally.

`int` `ECONNRESET`   [Macro]
>   A network connection was closed for reasons outside the control of the local host, such as by the remote machine rebooting or an unrecoverable protocol violation.

`int` `ENOBUFS`   [Macro]
>   The kernel's buffers for I/O operations are all in use. In GNU, this error is always synonymous with `ENOMEM`; you may get one or the other from network operations.

`int` `EISCONN`   [Macro]
>   You tried to connect a socket that is already connected. See Section 16.9.1 [Making a Connection], page 456.

`int` `ENOTCONN`   [Macro]
>   The socket is not connected to anything. You get this error when you try to transmit data over a socket, without first specifying a destination for the data. For a connectionless socket (for datagram protocols, such as UDP), you get `EDESTADDRREQ` instead.

`int` `EDESTADDRREQ`   [Macro]
>   No default destination address was set for the socket. You get this error when you try to transmit data over a connectionless socket, without first specifying a destination for the data with `connect`.

`int` `ESHUTDOWN`   [Macro]
>   The socket has already been shut down.

`int` `ETOOMANYREFS`   [Macro]
>   ???

`int` `ETIMEDOUT`   [Macro]
>   A socket operation with a specified timeout received no response during the timeout period.

`int` `ECONNREFUSED`   [Macro]
>   A remote host refused to allow the network connection (typically because it is not running the requested service).

int ELOOP   [Macro]
> Too many levels of symbolic links were encountered in looking up a file name. This
> often indicates a cycle of symbolic links.

int ENAMETOOLONG   [Macro]
> Filename too long (longer than PATH_MAX; see Section 32.6 [Limits on File System
> Capacity], page 850) or host name too long (in gethostname or sethostname; see
> Section 31.1 [Host Identification], page 821).

int EHOSTDOWN   [Macro]
> The remote host for a requested network connection is down.

int EHOSTUNREACH   [Macro]
> The remote host for a requested network connection is not reachable.

int ENOTEMPTY   [Macro]
> Directory not empty, where an empty directory was expected. Typically, this error
> occurs when you are trying to delete a directory.

int EPROCLIM   [Macro]
> This means that the per-user limit on new process would be exceeded by an attempted
> fork. See Section 22.2 [Limiting Resource Usage], page 632, for details on the RLIMIT_
> NPROC limit.

int EUSERS   [Macro]
> The file quota system is confused because there are too many users.

int EDQUOT   [Macro]
> The user's disk quota was exceeded.

int ESTALE   [Macro]
> Stale file handle. This indicates an internal confusion in the file system which is due
> to file system rearrangements on the server host for NFS file systems or corruption
> in other file systems. Repairing this condition usually requires unmounting, possibly
> repairing and remounting the file system.

int EREMOTE   [Macro]
> An attempt was made to NFS-mount a remote file system with a file name that
> already specifies an NFS-mounted file. (This is an error on some operating systems,
> but we expect it to work properly on GNU/Hurd systems, making this error code
> impossible.)

int EBADRPC   [Macro]
> ???

int ERPCMISMATCH   [Macro]
> ???

int EPROGUNAVAIL   [Macro]
> ???

`int` **EPROGMISMATCH**   [Macro]

???

`int` **EPROCUNAVAIL**   [Macro]

???

`int` **ENOLCK**   [Macro]

No locks available. This is used by the file locking facilities; see Section 13.15 [File
Locks], page 368. This error is never generated by GNU/Hurd systems, but it can
result from an operation to an NFS server running another operating system.

`int` **EFTYPE**   [Macro]

Inappropriate file type or format. The file was the wrong type for the operation, or
a data file had the wrong format.

On some systems `chmod` returns this error if you try to set the sticky bit on a non-
directory file; see Section 14.9.7 [Assigning File Permissions], page 410.

`int` **EAUTH**   [Macro]

???

`int` **ENEEDAUTH**   [Macro]

???

`int` **ENOSYS**   [Macro]

Function not implemented. This indicates that the function called is not implemented
at all, either in the C library itself or in the operating system. When you get this
error, you can be sure that this particular function will always fail with `ENOSYS` unless
you install a new version of the C library or the operating system.

`int` **ENOTSUP**   [Macro]

Not supported. A function returns this error when certain parameter values are valid,
but the functionality they request is not available. This can mean that the function
does not implement a particular command or option value or flag bit at all. For
functions that operate on some object given in a parameter, such as a file descriptor
or a port, it might instead mean that only *that specific object* (file descriptor, port,
etc.) is unable to support the other parameters given; different file descriptors might
support different ranges of parameter values.

If the entire function is not available at all in the implementation, it returns `ENOSYS`
instead.

`int` **EILSEQ**   [Macro]

While decoding a multibyte character the function came along an invalid or an incomplete sequence of bytes or the given wide character is invalid.

`int` **EBACKGROUND**   [Macro]

On GNU/Hurd systems, servers supporting the `term` protocol return this error for
certain operations when the caller is not in the foreground process group of the terminal. Users do not usually see this error because functions such as `read` and `write`
translate it into a `SIGTTIN` or `SIGTTOU` signal. See Chapter 28 [Job Control], page 763,
for information on process groups and these signals.

`int EDIED`   [Macro]

> On GNU/Hurd systems, opening a file returns this error when the file is translated by a program and the translator program dies while starting up, before it has connected to the file.

`int ED`   [Macro]

> The experienced user will know what is wrong.

`int EGREGIOUS`   [Macro]

> You did **what**?

`int EIEIO`   [Macro]

> Go home and have a glass of warm, dairy-fresh milk.

`int EGRATUITOUS`   [Macro]

> This error code has no purpose.

`int EBADMSG`   [Macro]

`int EIDRM`   [Macro]

`int EMULTIHOP`   [Macro]

`int ENODATA`   [Macro]

`int ENOLINK`   [Macro]

`int ENOMSG`   [Macro]

`int ENOSR`   [Macro]

`int ENOSTR`   [Macro]

`int EOVERFLOW`   [Macro]

`int EPROTO`   [Macro]

`int ETIME`   [Macro]

`int ECANCELED`   [Macro]

> Operation canceled; an asynchronous operation was canceled before it completed. See Section 13.10 [Perform I/O Operations in Parallel], page 346. When you call `aio_cancel`, the normal result is for the operations affected to complete with this error; see Section 13.10.4 [Cancellation of AIO Operations], page 356.

The following error codes are defined by the Linux/i386 kernel. They are not yet documented.

`int ERESTART`   [Macro]

`int ECHRNG`   [Macro]

`int EL2NSYNC`   [Macro]

`int EL3HLT`   [Macro]

`int EL3RST`   [Macro]

`int ELNRNG`   [Macro]

`int EUNATCH`	[Macro]
`int ENOCSI`	[Macro]
`int EL2HLT`	[Macro]
`int EBADE`	[Macro]
`int EBADR`	[Macro]
`int EXFULL`	[Macro]
`int ENOANO`	[Macro]
`int EBADRQC`	[Macro]
`int EBADSLT`	[Macro]
`int EDEADLOCK`	[Macro]
`int EBFONT`	[Macro]
`int ENONET`	[Macro]
`int ENOPKG`	[Macro]
`int EADV`	[Macro]
`int ESRMNT`	[Macro]
`int ECOMM`	[Macro]
`int EDOTDOT`	[Macro]
`int ENOTUNIQ`	[Macro]
`int EBADFD`	[Macro]
`int EREMCHG`	[Macro]
`int ELIBACC`	[Macro]
`int ELIBBAD`	[Macro]
`int ELIBSCN`	[Macro]
`int ELIBMAX`	[Macro]
`int ELIBEXEC`	[Macro]
`int ESTRPIPE`	[Macro]
`int EUCLEAN`	[Macro]
`int ENOTNAM`	[Macro]
`int ENAVAIL`	[Macro]
`int EISNAM`	[Macro]
`int EREMOTEIO`	[Macro]
`int ENOMEDIUM`	[Macro]
`int EMEDIUMTYPE`	[Macro]

int ENOKEY   [Macro]

int EKEYEXPIRED   [Macro]

int EKEYREVOKED   [Macro]

int EKEYREJECTED   [Macro]

int EOWNERDEAD   [Macro]

int ENOTRECOVERABLE   [Macro]

int ERFKILL   [Macro]

int EHWPOISON   [Macro]

2.3 Error Messages

The library has functions and variables designed to make it easy for your program to report informative error messages in the customary format about the failure of a library call. The functions `strerror` and `perror` give you the standard error message for a given error code; the variable `program_invocation_short_name` gives you convenient access to the name of the program that encountered the error.

char * strerror (*int errnum*)   [Function]
> Preliminary: | MT-Unsafe race:strerror | AS-Unsafe heap i18n | AC-Unsafe mem | See Section 1.2.2.1 [POSIX Safety Concepts], page 2.

> The `strerror` function maps the error code (see Section 2.1 [Checking for Errors], page 22) specified by the *errnum* argument to a descriptive error message string. The return value is a pointer to this string.

> The value *errnum* normally comes from the variable `errno`.

> You should not modify the string returned by `strerror`. Also, if you make subsequent calls to `strerror`, the string might be overwritten. (But it's guaranteed that no library function ever calls `strerror` behind your back.)

> The function `strerror` is declared in `string.h`.

char * strerror_r (*int errnum, char *buf, size_t n*)   [Function]
> Preliminary: | MT-Safe | AS-Unsafe i18n | AC-Unsafe | See Section 1.2.2.1 [POSIX Safety Concepts], page 2.

> The `strerror_r` function works like `strerror` but instead of returning the error message in a statically allocated buffer shared by all threads in the process, it returns a private copy for the thread. This might be either some permanent global data or a message string in the user supplied buffer starting at *buf* with the length of *n* bytes.

> At most *n* characters are written (including the NUL byte) so it is up to the user to select the buffer large enough.

> This function should always be used in multi-threaded programs since there is no way to guarantee the string returned by `strerror` really belongs to the last call of the current thread.

> This function `strerror_r` is a GNU extension and it is declared in `string.h`.

void perror (*const char *message*)   [Function]

   Preliminary: | MT-Safe race:stderr | AS-Unsafe corrupt i18n heap lock | AC-Unsafe corrupt lock mem fd | See Section 1.2.2.1 [POSIX Safety Concepts], page 2.

   This function prints an error message to the stream **stderr**; see Section 12.2 [Standard Streams], page 248. The orientation of **stderr** is not changed.

   If you call **perror** with a *message* that is either a null pointer or an empty string, **perror** just prints the error message corresponding to **errno**, adding a trailing newline.

   If you supply a non-null *message* argument, then **perror** prefixes its output with this string. It adds a colon and a space character to separate the *message* from the error string corresponding to **errno**.

   The function **perror** is declared in **stdio.h**.

strerror and **perror** produce the exact same message for any given error code; the precise text varies from system to system. With the GNU C Library, the messages are fairly short; there are no multi-line messages or embedded newlines. Each error message begins with a capital letter and does not include any terminating punctuation.

Many programs that don't read input from the terminal are designed to exit if any system call fails. By convention, the error message from such a program should start with the program's name, sans directories. You can find that name in the variable **program_invocation_short_name**; the full file name is stored the variable **program_invocation_name**.

char * program_invocation_name   [Variable]

   This variable's value is the name that was used to invoke the program running in the current process. It is the same as **argv[0]**. Note that this is not necessarily a useful file name; often it contains no directory names. See Section 25.1 [Program Arguments], page 705.

   This variable is a GNU extension and is declared in **errno.h**.

char * program_invocation_short_name   [Variable]

   This variable's value is the name that was used to invoke the program running in the current process, with directory names removed. (That is to say, it is the same as **program_invocation_name** minus everything up to the last slash, if any.)

   This variable is a GNU extension and is declared in **errno.h**.

The library initialization code sets up both of these variables before calling **main**.

Portability Note: If you want your program to work with non-GNU libraries, you must save the value of **argv[0]** in **main**, and then strip off the directory names yourself. We added these extensions to make it possible to write self-contained error-reporting subroutines that require no explicit cooperation from **main**.

Here is an example showing how to handle failure to open a file correctly. The function **open_sesame** tries to open the named file for reading and returns a stream if successful. The **fopen** library function returns a null pointer if it couldn't open the file for some reason. In that situation, **open_sesame** constructs an appropriate error message using the **strerror** function, and terminates the program. If we were going to make some other library calls before passing the error code to `strerror`, we'd have to save it in a local variable instead, because those other library functions might overwrite `errno` in the meantime.

```
#define _GNU_SOURCE

#include <errno.h>
#include <stdio.h>
#include <stdlib.h>
#include <string.h>

FILE *
open_sesame (char *name)
{
  FILE *stream;

  errno = 0;
  stream = fopen (name, "r");
  if (stream == NULL)
    {
      fprintf (stderr, "%s: Couldn't open file %s; %s\n",
               program_invocation_short_name, name, strerror (errno));
      exit (EXIT_FAILURE);
    }
  else
    return stream;
}
```

Using `perror` has the advantage that the function is portable and available on all systems implementing ISO C. But often the text `perror` generates is not what is wanted and there is no way to extend or change what `perror` does. The GNU coding standard, for instance, requires error messages to be preceded by the program name and programs which read some input files should provide information about the input file name and the line number in case an error is encountered while reading the file. For these occasions there are two functions available which are widely used throughout the GNU project. These functions are declared in `error.h`.

void **error** (*int* **status**, *int* **errnum**, *const char* *****format**, *. . .*)   [Function]
    Preliminary: | MT-Safe locale | AS-Unsafe corrupt heap i18n | AC-Safe | See Section 1.2.2.1 [POSIX Safety Concepts], page 2.

    The **error** function can be used to report general problems during program execution. The *format* argument is a format string just like those given to the `printf` family of functions. The arguments required for the format can follow the *format* parameter. Just like `perror`, **error** also can report an error code in textual form. But unlike `perror` the error value is explicitly passed to the function in the *errnum* parameter. This eliminates the problem mentioned above that the error reporting function must be called immediately after the function causing the error since otherwise `errno` might have a different value.

    The **error** prints first the program name. If the application defined a global variable **error_print_progname** and points it to a function this function will be called to print the program name. Otherwise the string from the global variable **program_name** is used. The program name is followed by a colon and a space which in turn is followed by the output produced by the format string. If the *errnum* parameter is non-zero the format string output is followed by a colon and a space, followed by the error message for the error code *errnum*. In any case is the output terminated with a newline.

The output is directed to the **stderr** stream. If the **stderr** wasn't oriented before the call it will be narrow-oriented afterwards.

The function will return unless the *status* parameter has a non-zero value. In this case the function will call **exit** with the *status* value for its parameter and therefore never return. If **error** returns the global variable **error_message_count** is incremented by one to keep track of the number of errors reported.

void error_at_line (*int* **status**, *int* **errnum**, *const char* ***fname**,   [Function]
          unsigned int **lineno**, *const char* ***format**, . . .)
Preliminary: | MT-Unsafe race:error_at_line/error_one_per_line locale | AS-Unsafe corrupt heap i18n | AC-Unsafe corrupt/error_one_per_line | See Section 1.2.2.1 [POSIX Safety Concepts], page 2.

The **error_at_line** function is very similar to the **error** function. The only difference are the additional parameters *fname* and *lineno*. The handling of the other parameters is identical to that of **error** except that between the program name and the string generated by the format string additional text is inserted.

Directly following the program name a colon, followed by the file name pointer to by *fname*, another colon, and a value of *lineno* is printed.

This additional output of course is meant to be used to locate an error in an input file (like a programming language source code file etc).

If the global variable **error_one_per_line** is set to a non-zero value **error_at_line** will avoid printing consecutive messages for the same file and line. Repetition which are not directly following each other are not caught.

Just like **error** this function only returned if *status* is zero. Otherwise **exit** is called with the non-zero value. If **error** returns the global variable **error_message_count** is incremented by one to keep track of the number of errors reported.

As mentioned above the **error** and **error_at_line** functions can be customized by defining a variable named **error_print_progname**.

void (*error_print_progname) (void)   [Variable]
If the **error_print_progname** variable is defined to a non-zero value the function pointed to is called by **error** or **error_at_line**. It is expected to print the program name or do something similarly useful.

The function is expected to be print to the **stderr** stream and must be able to handle whatever orientation the stream has.

The variable is global and shared by all threads.

unsigned int error_message_count   [Variable]
The **error_message_count** variable is incremented whenever one of the functions **error** or **error_at_line** returns. The variable is global and shared by all threads.

int error_one_per_line   [Variable]
The **error_one_per_line** variable influences only **error_at_line**. Normally the **error_at_line** function creates output for every invocation. If **error_one_per_line** is set to a non-zero value **error_at_line** keeps track of the last file name and

line number for which an error was reported and avoid directly following messages for the same file and line. This variable is global and shared by all threads.

A program which read some input file and reports errors in it could look like this:

```
{
  char *line = NULL;
  size_t len = 0;
  unsigned int lineno = 0;

  error_message_count = 0;
  while (! feof_unlocked (fp))
    {
      ssize_t n = getline (&line, &len, fp);
      if (n <= 0)
        /* End of file or error.  */
        break;
      ++lineno;

      /* Process the line.  */
      ...

      if (Detect error in line)
        error_at_line (0, errval, filename, lineno,
                       "some error text %s", some_variable);
    }

  if (error_message_count != 0)
    error (EXIT_FAILURE, 0, "%u errors found", error_message_count);
}
```

error and error_at_line are clearly the functions of choice and enable the programmer to write applications which follow the GNU coding standard. The GNU C Library additionally contains functions which are used in BSD for the same purpose. These functions are declared in err.h. It is generally advised to not use these functions. They are included only for compatibility.

void warn (*const char *format*, ...)   [Function]

> Preliminary: | MT-Safe locale | AS-Unsafe corrupt heap i18n | AC-Unsafe corrupt lock mem | See Section 1.2.2.1 [POSIX Safety Concepts], page 2.

> The warn function is roughly equivalent to a call like

>> error (0, errno, format, the parameters)

> except that the global variables error respects and modifies are not used.

void vwarn (*const char *format*, va_list *ap*)   [Function]

> Preliminary: | MT-Safe locale | AS-Unsafe corrupt heap i18n | AC-Unsafe corrupt lock mem | See Section 1.2.2.1 [POSIX Safety Concepts], page 2.

> The vwarn function is just like warn except that the parameters for the handling of the format string *format* are passed in as a value of type va_list.

void warnx (*const char *format*, ...)   [Function]

> Preliminary: | MT-Safe locale | AS-Unsafe corrupt heap | AC-Unsafe corrupt lock mem | See Section 1.2.2.1 [POSIX Safety Concepts], page 2.

> The warnx function is roughly equivalent to a call like

```
error (0, 0, format, the parameters)
```
except that the global variables **error** respects and modifies are not used. The difference to **warn** is that no error number string is printed.

void vwarnx (*const char *format*, *va_list* **ap**)   [Function]
Preliminary: | MT-Safe locale | AS-Unsafe corrupt heap | AC-Unsafe corrupt lock mem | See Section 1.2.2.1 [POSIX Safety Concepts], page 2.

The **vwarnx** function is just like **warnx** except that the parameters for the handling of the format string *format* are passed in as a value of type **va_list**.

void err (*int* **status**, *const char *format*, ...)   [Function]
Preliminary: | MT-Safe locale | AS-Unsafe corrupt heap i18n | AC-Unsafe corrupt lock mem | See Section 1.2.2.1 [POSIX Safety Concepts], page 2.

The **err** function is roughly equivalent to a call like
```
error (status, errno, format, the parameters)
```
except that the global variables **error** respects and modifies are not used and that the program is exited even if *status* is zero.

void verr (*int* **status**, *const char *format*, *va_list* **ap**)   [Function]
Preliminary: | MT-Safe locale | AS-Unsafe corrupt heap i18n | AC-Unsafe corrupt lock mem | See Section 1.2.2.1 [POSIX Safety Concepts], page 2.

The **verr** function is just like **err** except that the parameters for the handling of the format string *format* are passed in as a value of type **va_list**.

void errx (*int* **status**, *const char *format*, ...)   [Function]
Preliminary: | MT-Safe locale | AS-Unsafe corrupt heap | AC-Unsafe corrupt lock mem | See Section 1.2.2.1 [POSIX Safety Concepts], page 2.

The **errx** function is roughly equivalent to a call like
```
error (status, 0, format, the parameters)
```
except that the global variables **error** respects and modifies are not used and that the program is exited even if *status* is zero. The difference to **err** is that no error number string is printed.

void verrx (*int* **status**, *const char *format*, *va_list* **ap**)   [Function]
Preliminary: | MT-Safe locale | AS-Unsafe corrupt heap | AC-Unsafe corrupt lock mem | See Section 1.2.2.1 [POSIX Safety Concepts], page 2.

The **verrx** function is just like **errx** except that the parameters for the handling of the format string *format* are passed in as a value of type **va_list**.

3 Virtual Memory Allocation And Paging

This chapter describes how processes manage and use memory in a system that uses the GNU C Library.

The GNU C Library has several functions for dynamically allocating virtual memory in various ways. They vary in generality and in efficiency. The library also provides functions for controlling paging and allocation of real memory.

Memory mapped I/O is not discussed in this chapter. See Section 13.7 [Memory-mapped I/O], page 337.

3.1 Process Memory Concepts

One of the most basic resources a process has available to it is memory. There are a lot of different ways systems organize memory, but in a typical one, each process has one linear virtual address space, with addresses running from zero to some huge maximum. It need not be contiguous; i.e., not all of these addresses actually can be used to store data.

The virtual memory is divided into pages (4 kilobytes is typical). Backing each page of virtual memory is a page of real memory (called a *frame*) or some secondary storage, usually disk space. The disk space might be swap space or just some ordinary disk file. Actually, a page of all zeroes sometimes has nothing at all backing it – there's just a flag saying it is all zeroes.

The same frame of real memory or backing store can back multiple virtual pages belonging to multiple processes. This is normally the case, for example, with virtual memory occupied by GNU C Library code. The same real memory frame containing the `printf` function backs a virtual memory page in each of the existing processes that has a `printf` call in its program.

In order for a program to access any part of a virtual page, the page must at that moment be backed by ("connected to") a real frame. But because there is usually a lot more virtual memory than real memory, the pages must move back and forth between real memory and backing store regularly, coming into real memory when a process needs to access them and then retreating to backing store when not needed anymore. This movement is called *paging*.

When a program attempts to access a page which is not at that moment backed by real memory, this is known as a *page fault*. When a page fault occurs, the kernel suspends the process, places the page into a real page frame (this is called "paging in" or "faulting in"), then resumes the process so that from the process' point of view, the page was in real memory all along. In fact, to the process, all pages always seem to be in real memory. Except for one thing: the elapsed execution time of an instruction that would normally be a few nanoseconds is suddenly much, much, longer (because the kernel normally has to do I/O to complete the page-in). For programs sensitive to that, the functions described in Section 3.4 [Locking Pages], page 72 can control it.

Within each virtual address space, a process has to keep track of what is at which addresses, and that process is called memory allocation. Allocation usually brings to mind meting out scarce resources, but in the case of virtual memory, that's not a major goal, because there is generally much more of it than anyone needs. Memory allocation within a process is mainly just a matter of making sure that the same byte of memory isn't used to store two different things.

Processes allocate memory in two major ways: by exec and programmatically. Actually, forking is a third way, but it's not very interesting. See Section 26.4 [Creating a Process], page 751.

Exec is the operation of creating a virtual address space for a process, loading its basic program into it, and executing the program. It is done by the "exec" family of functions (e.g. `execl`). The operation takes a program file (an executable), it allocates space to load all the data in the executable, loads it, and transfers control to it. That data is most notably the instructions of the program (the *text*), but also literals and constants in the program and even some variables: C variables with the static storage class (see Section 3.2.1 [Memory Allocation in C Programs], page 41).

Once that program begins to execute, it uses programmatic allocation to gain additional memory. In a C program with the GNU C Library, there are two kinds of programmatic allocation: automatic and dynamic. See Section 3.2.1 [Memory Allocation in C Programs], page 41.

Memory-mapped I/O is another form of dynamic virtual memory allocation. Mapping memory to a file means declaring that the contents of certain range of a process' addresses shall be identical to the contents of a specified regular file. The system makes the virtual memory initially contain the contents of the file, and if you modify the memory, the system writes the same modification to the file. Note that due to the magic of virtual memory and page faults, there is no reason for the system to do I/O to read the file, or allocate real memory for its contents, until the program accesses the virtual memory. See Section 13.7 [Memory-mapped I/O], page 337.

Just as it programmatically allocates memory, the program can programmatically deallocate (*free*) it. You can't free the memory that was allocated by exec. When the program exits or execs, you might say that all its memory gets freed, but since in both cases the address space ceases to exist, the point is really moot. See Section 25.7 [Program Termination], page 744.

A process' virtual address space is divided into segments. A segment is a contiguous range of virtual addresses. Three important segments are:

*
    The *text segment* contains a program's instructions and literals and static constants. It is allocated by exec and stays the same size for the life of the virtual address space.

* The *data segment* is working storage for the program. It can be preallocated and preloaded by exec and the process can extend or shrink it by calling functions as described in See Section 3.3 [Resizing the Data Segment], page 72. Its lower end is fixed.

* The *stack segment* contains a program stack. It grows as the stack grows, but doesn't shrink when the stack shrinks.

3.2 Allocating Storage For Program Data

This section covers how ordinary programs manage storage for their data, including the famous `malloc` function and some fancier facilities special the GNU C Library and GNU Compiler.

3.2.1 Memory Allocation in C Programs

The C language supports two kinds of memory allocation through the variables in C programs:

- *Static allocation* is what happens when you declare a static or global variable. Each static or global variable defines one block of space, of a fixed size. The space is allocated once, when your program is started (part of the exec operation), and is never freed.

- *Automatic allocation* happens when you declare an automatic variable, such as a function argument or a local variable. The space for an automatic variable is allocated when the compound statement containing the declaration is entered, and is freed when that compound statement is exited.

  In GNU C, the size of the automatic storage can be an expression that varies. In other C implementations, it must be a constant.

A third important kind of memory allocation, *dynamic allocation*, is not supported by C variables but is available via GNU C Library functions.

3.2.1.1 Dynamic Memory Allocation

Dynamic memory allocation is a technique in which programs determine as they are running where to store some information. You need dynamic allocation when the amount of memory you need, or how long you continue to need it, depends on factors that are not known before the program runs.

For example, you may need a block to store a line read from an input file; since there is no limit to how long a line can be, you must allocate the memory dynamically and make it dynamically larger as you read more of the line.

Or, you may need a block for each record or each definition in the input data; since you can't know in advance how many there will be, you must allocate a new block for each record or definition as you read it.

When you use dynamic allocation, the allocation of a block of memory is an action that the program requests explicitly. You call a function or macro when you want to allocate space, and specify the size with an argument. If you want to free the space, you do so by calling another function or macro. You can do these things whenever you want, as often as you want.

Dynamic allocation is not supported by C variables; there is no storage class "dynamic", and there can never be a C variable whose value is stored in dynamically allocated space. The only way to get dynamically allocated memory is via a system call (which is generally via a GNU C Library function call), and the only way to refer to dynamically allocated space is through a pointer. Because it is less convenient, and because the actual process of dynamic allocation requires more computation time, programmers generally use dynamic allocation only when neither static nor automatic allocation will serve.

For example, if you want to allocate dynamically some space to hold a `struct foobar`, you cannot declare a variable of type `struct foobar` whose contents are the dynamically allocated space. But you can declare a variable of pointer type `struct foobar *` and assign it the address of the space. Then you can use the operators '`*`' and '`->`' on this pointer variable to refer to the contents of the space:

```
{
```

```
    struct foobar *ptr
        = (struct foobar *) malloc (sizeof (struct foobar));
    ptr->name = x;
    ptr->next = current_foobar;
    current_foobar = ptr;
}
```

3.2.2 Unconstrained Allocation

The most general dynamic allocation facility is `malloc`. It allows you to allocate blocks of memory of any size at any time, make them bigger or smaller at any time, and free the blocks individually at any time (or never).

3.2.2.1 Basic Memory Allocation

To allocate a block of memory, call `malloc`. The prototype for this function is in `stdlib.h`.

void * malloc (*size_t size*)   [Function]
> Preliminary: | MT-Safe | AS-Unsafe lock | AC-Unsafe lock fd mem | See Section 1.2.2.1 [POSIX Safety Concepts], page 2.
>
> This function returns a pointer to a newly allocated block *size* bytes long, or a null pointer if the block could not be allocated.

The contents of the block are undefined; you must initialize it yourself (or use `calloc` instead; see Section 3.2.2.5 [Allocating Cleared Space], page 45). Normally you would cast the value as a pointer to the kind of object that you want to store in the block. Here we show an example of doing so, and of initializing the space with zeros using the library function `memset` (see Section 5.4 [Copying and Concatenation], page 91):

```
    struct foo *ptr;
    ...
    ptr = (struct foo *) malloc (sizeof (struct foo));
    if (ptr == 0) abort ();
    memset (ptr, 0, sizeof (struct foo));
```

You can store the result of `malloc` into any pointer variable without a cast, because ISO C automatically converts the type `void *` to another type of pointer when necessary. But the cast is necessary in contexts other than assignment operators or if you might want your code to run in traditional C.

Remember that when allocating space for a string, the argument to `malloc` must be one plus the length of the string. This is because a string is terminated with a null character that doesn't count in the "length" of the string but does need space. For example:

```
    char *ptr;
    ...
    ptr = (char *) malloc (length + 1);
```

See Section 5.1 [Representation of Strings], page 87, for more information about this.

3.2.2.2 Examples of `malloc`

If no more space is available, `malloc` returns a null pointer. You should check the value of *every* call to `malloc`. It is useful to write a subroutine that calls `malloc` and reports an error if the value is a null pointer, returning only if the value is nonzero. This function is conventionally called `xmalloc`. Here it is:

```
void *
xmalloc (size_t size)
{
  void *value = malloc (size);
  if (value == 0)
    fatal ("virtual memory exhausted");
  return value;
}
```

Here is a real example of using `malloc` (by way of `xmalloc`). The function `savestring` will copy a sequence of characters into a newly allocated null-terminated string:

```
char *
savestring (const char *ptr, size_t len)
{
  char *value = (char *) xmalloc (len + 1);
  value[len] = '\0';
  return (char *) memcpy (value, ptr, len);
}
```

The block that `malloc` gives you is guaranteed to be aligned so that it can hold any type of data. On GNU systems, the address is always a multiple of eight on 32-bit systems, and a multiple of 16 on 64-bit systems. Only rarely is any higher boundary (such as a page boundary) necessary; for those cases, use `aligned_alloc` or `posix_memalign` (see Section 3.2.2.7 [Allocating Aligned Memory Blocks], page 46).

Note that the memory located after the end of the block is likely to be in use for something else; perhaps a block already allocated by another call to `malloc`. If you attempt to treat the block as longer than you asked for it to be, you are liable to destroy the data that `malloc` uses to keep track of its blocks, or you may destroy the contents of another block. If you have already allocated a block and discover you want it to be bigger, use `realloc` (see Section 3.2.2.4 [Changing the Size of a Block], page 44).

3.2.2.3 Freeing Memory Allocated with `malloc`

When you no longer need a block that you got with `malloc`, use the function `free` to make the block available to be allocated again. The prototype for this function is in `stdlib.h`.

void **free** (*void *ptr*)   [Function]
> Preliminary: | MT-Safe | AS-Unsafe lock | AC-Unsafe lock fd mem | See Section 1.2.2.1 [POSIX Safety Concepts], page 2.

> The `free` function deallocates the block of memory pointed at by *ptr*.

void **cfree** (*void *ptr*)   [Function]
> Preliminary: | MT-Safe | AS-Unsafe lock | AC-Unsafe lock fd mem | See Section 1.2.2.1 [POSIX Safety Concepts], page 2.

> This function does the same thing as `free`. It's provided for backward compatibility with SunOS; you should use `free` instead.

Freeing a block alters the contents of the block. **Do not expect to find any data (such as a pointer to the next block in a chain of blocks) in the block after freeing it.** Copy whatever you need out of the block before freeing it! Here is an example of the proper way to free all the blocks in a chain, and the strings that they point to:

```
struct chain
  {
    struct chain *next;
    char *name;
  }

void
free_chain (struct chain *chain)
{
  while (chain != 0)
    {
      struct chain *next = chain->next;
      free (chain->name);
      free (chain);
      chain = next;
    }
}
```

Occasionally, **free** can actually return memory to the operating system and make the process smaller. Usually, all it can do is allow a later call to **malloc** to reuse the space. In the meantime, the space remains in your program as part of a free-list used internally by **malloc**.

There is no point in freeing blocks at the end of a program, because all of the program's space is given back to the system when the process terminates.

3.2.2.4 Changing the Size of a Block

Often you do not know for certain how big a block you will ultimately need at the time you must begin to use the block. For example, the block might be a buffer that you use to hold a line being read from a file; no matter how long you make the buffer initially, you may encounter a line that is longer.

You can make the block longer by calling **realloc**. This function is declared in **stdlib.h**.

void * realloc (*void *ptr*, *size_t newsize*)   [Function]
> Preliminary: | MT-Safe | AS-Unsafe lock | AC-Unsafe lock fd mem | See Section 1.2.2.1 [POSIX Safety Concepts], page 2.
>
> The **realloc** function changes the size of the block whose address is *ptr* to be *newsize*.
>
> Since the space after the end of the block may be in use, **realloc** may find it necessary to copy the block to a new address where more free space is available. The value of **realloc** is the new address of the block. If the block needs to be moved, **realloc** copies the old contents.
>
> If you pass a null pointer for *ptr*, **realloc** behaves just like '**malloc (*newsize*)**'. This can be convenient, but beware that older implementations (before ISO C) may not support this behavior, and will probably crash when **realloc** is passed a null pointer.

Like **malloc**, **realloc** may return a null pointer if no memory space is available to make the block bigger. When this happens, the original block is untouched; it has not been modified or relocated.

In most cases it makes no difference what happens to the original block when **realloc** fails, because the application program cannot continue when it is out of memory, and the only thing to do is to give a fatal error message. Often it is convenient to write and use a subroutine, conventionally called `xrealloc`, that takes care of the error message as `xmalloc` does for `malloc`:

```
void *
xrealloc (void *ptr, size_t size)
{
  void *value = realloc (ptr, size);
  if (value == 0)
    fatal ("Virtual memory exhausted");
  return value;
}
```

You can also use `realloc` to make a block smaller. The reason you would do this is to avoid tying up a lot of memory space when only a little is needed. In several allocation implementations, making a block smaller sometimes necessitates copying it, so it can fail if no other space is available.

If the new size you specify is the same as the old size, `realloc` is guaranteed to change nothing and return the same address that you gave.

3.2.2.5 Allocating Cleared Space

The function `calloc` allocates memory and clears it to zero. It is declared in `stdlib.h`.

`void * calloc` (*size_t count*, *size_t eltsize*)   [Function]
  Preliminary: | MT-Safe | AS-Unsafe lock | AC-Unsafe lock fd mem | See
  Section 1.2.2.1 [POSIX Safety Concepts], page 2.

  This function allocates a block long enough to contain a vector of *count* elements,
  each of size *eltsize*. Its contents are cleared to zero before `calloc` returns.

  You could define `calloc` as follows:

```
void *
calloc (size_t count, size_t eltsize)
{
  size_t size = count * eltsize;
  void *value = malloc (size);
  if (value != 0)
    memset (value, 0, size);
  return value;
}
```

But in general, it is not guaranteed that `calloc` calls `malloc` internally. Therefore, if an application provides its own `malloc`/`realloc`/`free` outside the C library, it should always define `calloc`, too.

3.2.2.6 Efficiency Considerations for `malloc`

As opposed to other versions, the `malloc` in the GNU C Library does not round up block sizes to powers of two, neither for large nor for small sizes. Neighboring chunks can be coalesced on a `free` no matter what their size is. This makes the implementation suitable for all kinds of allocation patterns without generally incurring high memory waste through fragmentation.

Very large blocks (much larger than a page) are allocated with `mmap` (anonymous or via `/dev/zero`) by this implementation. This has the great advantage that these chunks are returned to the system immediately when they are freed. Therefore, it cannot happen that a large chunk becomes "locked" in between smaller ones and even after calling `free` wastes memory. The size threshold for `mmap` to be used can be adjusted with `mallopt`. The use of `mmap` can also be disabled completely.

3.2.2.7 Allocating Aligned Memory Blocks

The address of a block returned by `malloc` or `realloc` in GNU systems is always a multiple of eight (or sixteen on 64-bit systems). If you need a block whose address is a multiple of a higher power of two than that, use `aligned_alloc` or `posix_memalign`. `aligned_alloc` and `posix_memalign` are declared in `stdlib.h`.

void * aligned_alloc (*size_t* `alignment`, *size_t* `size`)   [Function]
> Preliminary: | MT-Safe | AS-Unsafe lock | AC-Unsafe lock fd mem | See Section 1.2.2.1 [POSIX Safety Concepts], page 2.
>
> The `aligned_alloc` function allocates a block of *size* bytes whose address is a multiple of *alignment*. The *alignment* must be a power of two and *size* must be a multiple of *alignment*.
>
> The `aligned_alloc` function returns a null pointer on error and sets `errno` to one of the following values:
>
> ENOMEM   There was insufficient memory available to satisfy the request.
>
> EINVAL   *alignment* is not a power of two.
>
> > This function was introduced in ISO C11 and hence may have better portability to modern non-POSIX systems than `posix_memalign`.

void * memalign (*size_t* `boundary`, *size_t* `size`)   [Function]
> Preliminary: | MT-Safe | AS-Unsafe lock | AC-Unsafe lock fd mem | See Section 1.2.2.1 [POSIX Safety Concepts], page 2.
>
> The `memalign` function allocates a block of *size* bytes whose address is a multiple of *boundary*. The *boundary* must be a power of two! The function `memalign` works by allocating a somewhat larger block, and then returning an address within the block that is on the specified boundary.
>
> The `memalign` function returns a null pointer on error and sets `errno` to one of the following values:
>
> ENOMEM   There was insufficient memory available to satisfy the request.
>
> EINVAL   *alignment* is not a power of two.
>
> The `memalign` function is obsolete and `aligned_alloc` or `posix_memalign` should be used instead.

int posix_memalign (*void **memptr*, *size_t* `alignment`, *size_t* `size`)   [Function]
> Preliminary: | MT-Safe | AS-Unsafe lock | AC-Unsafe lock fd mem | See Section 1.2.2.1 [POSIX Safety Concepts], page 2.
>
> The `posix_memalign` function is similar to the `memalign` function in that it returns a buffer of *size* bytes aligned to a multiple of *alignment*. But it adds one requirement

to the parameter *alignment*: the value must be a power of two multiple of `sizeof` (`void *`).

If the function succeeds in allocation memory a pointer to the allocated memory is returned in **memptr* and the return value is zero. Otherwise the function returns an error value indicating the problem. The possible error values returned are:

ENOMEM   There was insufficient memory available to satisfy the request.

EINVAL   *alignment* is not a power of two multiple of `sizeof` (`void *`).

This function was introduced in POSIX 1003.1d. Although this function is superseded by `aligned_alloc`, it is more portable to older POSIX systems that do not support ISO C11.

`void * valloc (`*size_t* `size)`   [Function]
> Preliminary: | MT-Unsafe init | AS-Unsafe init lock | AC-Unsafe init lock fd mem | See Section 1.2.2.1 [POSIX Safety Concepts], page 2.
>
> Using `valloc` is like using `memalign` and passing the page size as the value of the second argument. It is implemented like this:
> ```
> void *
> valloc (size_t size)
> {
>   return memalign (getpagesize (), size);
> }
> ```
> Section 22.4.2 [How to get information about the memory subsystem?], page 648 for more information about the memory subsystem.
>
> The `valloc` function is obsolete and `aligned_alloc` or `posix_memalign` should be used instead.

3.2.2.8 Malloc Tunable Parameters

You can adjust some parameters for dynamic memory allocation with the `mallopt` function. This function is the general SVID/XPG interface, defined in `malloc.h`.

`int mallopt (`*int* `param`, *int* `value)`   [Function]
> Preliminary: | MT-Unsafe init const:mallopt | AS-Unsafe init lock | AC-Unsafe init lock | See Section 1.2.2.1 [POSIX Safety Concepts], page 2.
>
> When calling `mallopt`, the *param* argument specifies the parameter to be set, and *value* the new value to be set. Possible choices for *param*, as defined in `malloc.h`, are:
>
> M_MMAP_MAX
> > The maximum number of chunks to allocate with `mmap`. Setting this to zero disables all use of `mmap`.
>
> M_MMAP_THRESHOLD
> > All chunks larger than this value are allocated outside the normal heap, using the `mmap` system call. This way it is guaranteed that the memory for these chunks can be returned to the system on `free`. Note that requests smaller than this threshold might still be allocated via `mmap`.

M_PERTURB

> If non-zero, memory blocks are filled with values depending on some low order bits of this parameter when they are allocated (except when allocated by `calloc`) and freed. This can be used to debug the use of uninitialized or freed heap memory. Note that this option does not guarantee that the freed block will have any specific values. It only guarantees that the content the block had before it was freed will be overwritten.

M_TOP_PAD

> This parameter determines the amount of extra memory to obtain from the system when a call to `sbrk` is required. It also specifies the number of bytes to retain when shrinking the heap by calling `sbrk` with a negative argument. This provides the necessary hysteresis in heap size such that excessive amounts of system calls can be avoided.

M_TRIM_THRESHOLD

> This is the minimum size (in bytes) of the top-most, releasable chunk that will cause `sbrk` to be called with a negative argument in order to return memory to the system.

3.2.2.9 Heap Consistency Checking

You can ask `malloc` to check the consistency of dynamic memory by using the `mcheck` function. This function is a GNU extension, declared in `mcheck.h`.

int mcheck (*void (*abortfn) (enum mcheck_status status*))   [Function]
> Preliminary: | MT-Unsafe race:mcheck const:malloc_hooks | AS-Unsafe corrupt | AC-Unsafe corrupt | See Section 1.2.2.1 [POSIX Safety Concepts], page 2.

> Calling `mcheck` tells `malloc` to perform occasional consistency checks. These will catch things such as writing past the end of a block that was allocated with `malloc`.

> The *abortfn* argument is the function to call when an inconsistency is found. If you supply a null pointer, then `mcheck` uses a default function which prints a message and calls `abort` (see Section 25.7.4 [Aborting a Program], page 747). The function you supply is called with one argument, which says what sort of inconsistency was detected; its type is described below.

> It is too late to begin allocation checking once you have allocated anything with `malloc`. So `mcheck` does nothing in that case. The function returns `-1` if you call it too late, and `0` otherwise (when it is successful).

> The easiest way to arrange to call `mcheck` early enough is to use the option '`-lmcheck`' when you link your program; then you don't need to modify your program source at all. Alternatively you might use a debugger to insert a call to `mcheck` whenever the program is started, for example these gdb commands will automatically call `mcheck` whenever the program starts:

```
(gdb) break main
Breakpoint 1, main (argc=2, argv=0xbffff964) at whatever.c:10
(gdb) command 1
Type commands for when breakpoint 1 is hit, one per line.
End with a line saying just "end".
>call mcheck(0)
```

```
>continue
>end
(gdb) ...
```

This will however only work if no initialization function of any object involved calls any of the `malloc` functions since `mcheck` must be called before the first such function.

enum mcheck_status mprobe (*void *pointer*)   [Function]
> Preliminary: | MT-Unsafe race:mcheck const:malloc_hooks | AS-Unsafe corrupt | AC-Unsafe corrupt | See Section 1.2.2.1 [POSIX Safety Concepts], page 2.
>
> The `mprobe` function lets you explicitly check for inconsistencies in a particular allocated block. You must have already called `mcheck` at the beginning of the program, to do its occasional checks; calling `mprobe` requests an additional consistency check to be done at the time of the call.
>
> The argument *pointer* must be a pointer returned by `malloc` or `realloc`. `mprobe` returns a value that says what inconsistency, if any, was found. The values are described below.

enum mcheck_status   [Data Type]
> This enumerated type describes what kind of inconsistency was detected in an allocated block, if any. Here are the possible values:
>
> MCHECK_DISABLED
> > `mcheck` was not called before the first allocation. No consistency checking can be done.
>
> MCHECK_OK
> > No inconsistency detected.
>
> MCHECK_HEAD
> > The data immediately before the block was modified. This commonly happens when an array index or pointer is decremented too far.
>
> MCHECK_TAIL
> > The data immediately after the block was modified. This commonly happens when an array index or pointer is incremented too far.
>
> MCHECK_FREE
> > The block was already freed.

Another possibility to check for and guard against bugs in the use of `malloc`, `realloc` and `free` is to set the environment variable `MALLOC_CHECK_`. When `MALLOC_CHECK_` is set, a special (less efficient) implementation is used which is designed to be tolerant against simple errors, such as double calls of `free` with the same argument, or overruns of a single byte (off-by-one bugs). Not all such errors can be protected against, however, and memory leaks can result. If `MALLOC_CHECK_` is set to 0, any detected heap corruption is silently ignored; if set to 1, a diagnostic is printed on `stderr`; if set to 2, `abort` is called immediately. This can be useful because otherwise a crash may happen much later, and the true cause for the problem is then very hard to track down.

There is one problem with `MALLOC_CHECK_`: in SUID or SGID binaries it could possibly be exploited since diverging from the normal programs behavior it now writes something to the standard error descriptor. Therefore the use of `MALLOC_CHECK_` is disabled by default for SUID and SGID binaries. It can be enabled again by the system administrator by adding a file `/etc/suid-debug` (the content is not important it could be empty).

So, what's the difference between using `MALLOC_CHECK_` and linking with '-lmcheck'? `MALLOC_CHECK_` is orthogonal with respect to '-lmcheck'. '-lmcheck' has been added for backward compatibility. Both `MALLOC_CHECK_` and '-lmcheck' should uncover the same bugs - but using `MALLOC_CHECK_` you don't need to recompile your application.

3.2.2.10 Memory Allocation Hooks

The GNU C Library lets you modify the behavior of `malloc`, `realloc`, and `free` by specifying appropriate hook functions. You can use these hooks to help you debug programs that use dynamic memory allocation, for example.

The hook variables are declared in `malloc.h`.

`__malloc_hook`   [Variable]
> The value of this variable is a pointer to the function that `malloc` uses whenever it is called. You should define this function to look like `malloc`; that is, like:
>
>   void *function (size_t size, const void *caller)
>
> The value of *caller* is the return address found on the stack when the `malloc` function was called. This value allows you to trace the memory consumption of the program.

`__realloc_hook`   [Variable]
> The value of this variable is a pointer to function that `realloc` uses whenever it is called. You should define this function to look like `realloc`; that is, like:
>
>   void *function (void *ptr, size_t size, const void *caller)
>
> The value of *caller* is the return address found on the stack when the `realloc` function was called. This value allows you to trace the memory consumption of the program.

`__free_hook`   [Variable]
> The value of this variable is a pointer to function that `free` uses whenever it is called. You should define this function to look like `free`; that is, like:
>
>   void function (void *ptr, const void *caller)
>
> The value of *caller* is the return address found on the stack when the `free` function was called. This value allows you to trace the memory consumption of the program.

`__memalign_hook`   [Variable]
> The value of this variable is a pointer to function that `aligned_alloc`, `memalign`, `posix_memalign` and `valloc` use whenever they are called. You should define this function to look like `aligned_alloc`; that is, like:
>
>   void *function (size_t alignment, size_t size, const void *caller)
>
> The value of *caller* is the return address found on the stack when the `aligned_alloc`, `memalign`, `posix_memalign` or `valloc` functions are called. This value allows you to trace the memory consumption of the program.

You must make sure that the function you install as a hook for one of these functions does not call that function recursively without restoring the old value of the hook first! Otherwise, your program will get stuck in an infinite recursion. Before calling the function recursively, one should make sure to restore all the hooks to their previous value. When coming back from the recursive call, all the hooks should be resaved since a hook might modify itself.

__malloc_initialize_hook   [Variable]

The value of this variable is a pointer to a function that is called once when the malloc implementation is initialized. This is a weak variable, so it can be overridden in the application with a definition like the following:

```
void (*__malloc_initialize_hook) (void) = my_init_hook;
```

An issue to look out for is the time at which the malloc hook functions can be safely installed. If the hook functions call the malloc-related functions recursively, it is necessary that malloc has already properly initialized itself at the time when **__malloc_hook** etc. is assigned to. On the other hand, if the hook functions provide a complete malloc implementation of their own, it is vital that the hooks are assigned to *before* the very first **malloc** call has completed, because otherwise a chunk obtained from the ordinary, un-hooked malloc may later be handed to **__free_hook**, for example.

In both cases, the problem can be solved by setting up the hooks from within a user-defined function pointed to by **__malloc_initialize_hook**—then the hooks will be set up safely at the right time.

Here is an example showing how to use **__malloc_hook** and **__free_hook** properly. It installs a function that prints out information every time **malloc** or **free** is called. We just assume here that **realloc** and **memalign** are not used in our program.

```
/* Prototypes for __malloc_hook, __free_hook */
#include <malloc.h>

/* Prototypes for our hooks.  */
static void my_init_hook (void);
static void *my_malloc_hook (size_t, const void *);
static void my_free_hook (void*, const void *);

/* Override initializing hook from the C library. */
void (*__malloc_initialize_hook) (void) = my_init_hook;

static void
my_init_hook (void)
{
  old_malloc_hook = __malloc_hook;
  old_free_hook = __free_hook;
  __malloc_hook = my_malloc_hook;
  __free_hook = my_free_hook;
}

static void *
my_malloc_hook (size_t size, const void *caller)
{
  void *result;
  /* Restore all old hooks */
  __malloc_hook = old_malloc_hook;
  __free_hook = old_free_hook;
  /* Call recursively */
  result = malloc (size);
  /* Save underlying hooks */
```

```
        old_malloc_hook = __malloc_hook;
        old_free_hook = __free_hook;
        /* printf might call malloc, so protect it too. */
        printf ("malloc (%u) returns %p\n", (unsigned int) size, result);
        /* Restore our own hooks */
        __malloc_hook = my_malloc_hook;
        __free_hook = my_free_hook;
        return result;
     }

     static void
     my_free_hook (void *ptr, const void *caller)
     {
        /* Restore all old hooks */
        __malloc_hook = old_malloc_hook;
        __free_hook = old_free_hook;
        /* Call recursively */
        free (ptr);
        /* Save underlying hooks */
        old_malloc_hook = __malloc_hook;
        old_free_hook = __free_hook;
        /* printf might call free, so protect it too. */
        printf ("freed pointer %p\n", ptr);
        /* Restore our own hooks */
        __malloc_hook = my_malloc_hook;
        __free_hook = my_free_hook;
     }

     main ()
     {
        ...
     }
```

The `mcheck` function (see Section 3.2.2.9 [Heap Consistency Checking], page 48) works by installing such hooks.

3.2.2.11 Statistics for Memory Allocation with `malloc`

You can get information about dynamic memory allocation by calling the `mallinfo` function. This function and its associated data type are declared in `malloc.h`; they are an extension of the standard SVID/XPG version.

struct mallinfo   [Data Type]

This structure type is used to return information about the dynamic memory allocator. It contains the following members:

int arena   This is the total size of memory allocated with `sbrk` by `malloc`, in bytes.

int ordblks

> This is the number of chunks not in use. (The memory allocator internally gets chunks of memory from the operating system, and then carves them up to satisfy individual `malloc` requests; see Section 3.2.2.6 [Efficiency Considerations for `malloc`], page 45.)

int smblks

> This field is unused.

int hblks   This is the total number of chunks allocated with `mmap`.

int hblkhd
:   This is the total size of memory allocated with mmap, in bytes.

int usmblks
:   This field is unused.

int fsmblks
:   This field is unused.

int uordblks
:   This is the total size of memory occupied by chunks handed out by malloc.

int fordblks
:   This is the total size of memory occupied by free (not in use) chunks.

int keepcost
:   This is the size of the top-most releasable chunk that normally borders the end of the heap (i.e., the high end of the virtual address space's data segment).

struct mallinfo mallinfo (*void*)   [Function]
Preliminary: | MT-Unsafe init const:mallopt | AS-Unsafe init lock | AC-Unsafe init lock | See Section 1.2.2.1 [POSIX Safety Concepts], page 2.

This function returns information about the current dynamic memory usage in a structure of type struct mallinfo.

3.2.2.12 Summary of malloc-Related Functions

Here is a summary of the functions that work with malloc:

void *malloc (size_t *size*)
:   Allocate a block of *size* bytes. See Section 3.2.2.1 [Basic Memory Allocation], page 42.

void free (void **addr*)
:   Free a block previously allocated by malloc. See Section 3.2.2.3 [Freeing Memory Allocated with malloc], page 43.

void *realloc (void **addr*, size_t *size*)
:   Make a block previously allocated by malloc larger or smaller, possibly by copying it to a new location. See Section 3.2.2.4 [Changing the Size of a Block], page 44.

void *calloc (size_t *count*, size_t *eltsize*)
:   Allocate a block of *count* * *eltsize* bytes using malloc, and set its contents to zero. See Section 3.2.2.5 [Allocating Cleared Space], page 45.

void *valloc (size_t *size*)
:   Allocate a block of *size* bytes, starting on a page boundary. See Section 3.2.2.7 [Allocating Aligned Memory Blocks], page 46.

void *aligned_alloc (size_t *size*, size_t *alignment*)
:   Allocate a block of *size* bytes, starting on an address that is a multiple of *alignment*. See Section 3.2.2.7 [Allocating Aligned Memory Blocks], page 46.

`int posix_memalign (void **memptr, size_t alignment, size_t size)`

Allocate a block of *size* bytes, starting on an address that is a multiple of *alignment*. See Section 3.2.2.7 [Allocating Aligned Memory Blocks], page 46.

`void *memalign (size_t size, size_t boundary)`

Allocate a block of *size* bytes, starting on an address that is a multiple of *boundary*. See Section 3.2.2.7 [Allocating Aligned Memory Blocks], page 46.

`int mallopt (int param, int value)`

Adjust a tunable parameter. See Section 3.2.2.8 [Malloc Tunable Parameters], page 47.

`int mcheck (void (*abortfn) (void))`

Tell `malloc` to perform occasional consistency checks on dynamically allocated memory, and to call *abortfn* when an inconsistency is found. See Section 3.2.2.9 [Heap Consistency Checking], page 48.

`void *(*__malloc_hook) (size_t size, const void *caller)`

A pointer to a function that `malloc` uses whenever it is called.

`void *(*__realloc_hook) (void *ptr, size_t size, const void *caller)`

A pointer to a function that `realloc` uses whenever it is called.

`void (*__free_hook) (void *ptr, const void *caller)`

A pointer to a function that `free` uses whenever it is called.

`void (*__memalign_hook) (size_t size, size_t alignment, const void *caller)`

A pointer to a function that `aligned_alloc`, `memalign`, `posix_memalign` and `valloc` use whenever they are called.

`struct mallinfo mallinfo (void)`

Return information about the current dynamic memory usage. See Section 3.2.2.11 [Statistics for Memory Allocation with `malloc`], page 52.

3.2.3 Allocation Debugging

A complicated task when programming with languages which do not use garbage collected dynamic memory allocation is to find memory leaks. Long running programs must assure that dynamically allocated objects are freed at the end of their lifetime. If this does not happen the system runs out of memory, sooner or later.

The `malloc` implementation in the GNU C Library provides some simple means to detect such leaks and obtain some information to find the location. To do this the application must be started in a special mode which is enabled by an environment variable. There are no speed penalties for the program if the debugging mode is not enabled.

3.2.3.1 How to install the tracing functionality

`void mtrace (void)`   [Function]

Preliminary: | MT-Unsafe env race:mtrace const:malloc_hooks init | AS-Unsafe init heap corrupt lock | AC-Unsafe init corrupt lock fd mem | See Section 1.2.2.1 [POSIX Safety Concepts], page 2.

When the `mtrace` function is called it looks for an environment variable named `MALLOC_TRACE`. This variable is supposed to contain a valid file name. The user must have write access. If the file already exists it is truncated. If the environment variable is not set or it does not name a valid file which can be opened for writing nothing is done. The behavior of `malloc` etc. is not changed. For obvious reasons this also happens if the application is installed with the SUID or SGID bit set.

If the named file is successfully opened, `mtrace` installs special handlers for the functions `malloc`, `realloc`, and `free` (see Section 3.2.2.10 [Memory Allocation Hooks], page 50). From then on, all uses of these functions are traced and protocolled into the file. There is now of course a speed penalty for all calls to the traced functions so tracing should not be enabled during normal use.

This function is a GNU extension and generally not available on other systems. The prototype can be found in `mcheck.h`.

void muntrace (*void*)   [Function]
Preliminary: | MT-Unsafe race:mtrace const:malloc_hooks locale | AS-Unsafe corrupt heap | AC-Unsafe corrupt mem lock fd | See Section 1.2.2.1 [POSIX Safety Concepts], page 2.

The `muntrace` function can be called after `mtrace` was used to enable tracing the `malloc` calls. If no (successful) call of `mtrace` was made `muntrace` does nothing.

Otherwise it deinstalls the handlers for `malloc`, `realloc`, and `free` and then closes the protocol file. No calls are protocolled anymore and the program runs again at full speed.

This function is a GNU extension and generally not available on other systems. The prototype can be found in `mcheck.h`.

3.2.3.2 Example program excerpts

Even though the tracing functionality does not influence the runtime behavior of the program it is not a good idea to call `mtrace` in all programs. Just imagine that you debug a program using `mtrace` and all other programs used in the debugging session also trace their `malloc` calls. The output file would be the same for all programs and thus is unusable. Therefore one should call `mtrace` only if compiled for debugging. A program could therefore start like this:

```
#include <mcheck.h>

int
main (int argc, char *argv[])
{
#ifdef DEBUGGING
  mtrace ();
#endif
  ...
}
```

This is all what is needed if you want to trace the calls during the whole runtime of the program. Alternatively you can stop the tracing at any time with a call to `muntrace`. It is even possible to restart the tracing again with a new call to `mtrace`. But this can cause unreliable results since there may be calls of the functions which are not called. Please note that not only the application uses the traced functions, also libraries (including the C library itself) use these functions.

This last point is also why it is no good idea to call `muntrace` before the program terminated. The libraries are informed about the termination of the program only after the program returns from `main` or calls `exit` and so cannot free the memory they use before this time.

So the best thing one can do is to call `mtrace` as the very first function in the program and never call `muntrace`. So the program traces almost all uses of the `malloc` functions (except those calls which are executed by constructors of the program or used libraries).

3.2.3.3 Some more or less clever ideas

You know the situation. The program is prepared for debugging and in all debugging sessions it runs well. But once it is started without debugging the error shows up. A typical example is a memory leak that becomes visible only when we turn off the debugging. If you foresee such situations you can still win. Simply use something equivalent to the following little program:

```
#include <mcheck.h>
#include <signal.h>

static void
enable (int sig)
{
  mtrace ();
  signal (SIGUSR1, enable);
}

static void
disable (int sig)
{
  muntrace ();
  signal (SIGUSR2, disable);
}

int
main (int argc, char *argv[])
{
  ...

  signal (SIGUSR1, enable);
  signal (SIGUSR2, disable);

  ...
}
```

I.e., the user can start the memory debugger any time s/he wants if the program was started with `MALLOC_TRACE` set in the environment. The output will of course not show the allocations which happened before the first signal but if there is a memory leak this will show up nevertheless.

3.2.3.4 Interpreting the traces

If you take a look at the output it will look similar to this:

```
= Start
[0x8048209] - 0x8064cc8
[0x8048209] - 0x8064ce0
[0x8048209] - 0x8064cf8
[0x80481eb] + 0x8064c48 0x14
[0x80481eb] + 0x8064c60 0x14
[0x80481eb] + 0x8064c78 0x14
[0x80481eb] + 0x8064c90 0x14
= End
```

What this all means is not really important since the trace file is not meant to be read by a human. Therefore no attention is given to readability. Instead there is a program which comes with the GNU C Library which interprets the traces and outputs a summary in an user-friendly way. The program is called **mtrace** (it is in fact a Perl script) and it takes one or two arguments. In any case the name of the file with the trace output must be specified. If an optional argument precedes the name of the trace file this must be the name of the program which generated the trace.

```
drepper$ mtrace tst-mtrace log
No memory leaks.
```

In this case the program **tst-mtrace** was run and it produced a trace file **log**. The message printed by **mtrace** shows there are no problems with the code, all allocated memory was freed afterwards.

If we call **mtrace** on the example trace given above we would get a different outout:

```
drepper$ mtrace errlog
- 0x08064cc8 Free 2 was never alloc'd 0x8048209
- 0x08064ce0 Free 3 was never alloc'd 0x8048209
- 0x08064cf8 Free 4 was never alloc'd 0x8048209

Memory not freed:
-----------------
   Address     Size    Caller
0x08064c48     0x14  at 0x80481eb
0x08064c60     0x14  at 0x80481eb
0x08064c78     0x14  at 0x80481eb
0x08064c90     0x14  at 0x80481eb
```

We have called **mtrace** with only one argument and so the script has no chance to find out what is meant with the addresses given in the trace. We can do better:

```
drepper$ mtrace tst errlog
- 0x08064cc8 Free 2 was never alloc'd /home/drepper/tst.c:39
- 0x08064ce0 Free 3 was never alloc'd /home/drepper/tst.c:39
- 0x08064cf8 Free 4 was never alloc'd /home/drepper/tst.c:39
```

```
Memory not freed:
-----------------
     Address    Size     Caller
  0x08064c48    0x14   at /home/drepper/tst.c:33
  0x08064c60    0x14   at /home/drepper/tst.c:33
  0x08064c78    0x14   at /home/drepper/tst.c:33
  0x08064c90    0x14   at /home/drepper/tst.c:33
```

Suddenly the output makes much more sense and the user can see immediately where the function calls causing the trouble can be found.

Interpreting this output is not complicated. There are at most two different situations being detected. First, **free** was called for pointers which were never returned by one of the allocation functions. This is usually a very bad problem and what this looks like is shown in the first three lines of the output. Situations like this are quite rare and if they appear they show up very drastically: the program normally crashes.

The other situation which is much harder to detect are memory leaks. As you can see in the output the **mtrace** function collects all this information and so can say that the program calls an allocation function from line 33 in the source file **/home/drepper/tst-mtrace.c** four times without freeing this memory before the program terminates. Whether this is a real problem remains to be investigated.

3.2.4 Obstacks

An *obstack* is a pool of memory containing a stack of objects. You can create any number of separate obstacks, and then allocate objects in specified obstacks. Within each obstack, the last object allocated must always be the first one freed, but distinct obstacks are independent of each other.

Aside from this one constraint of order of freeing, obstacks are totally general: an obstack can contain any number of objects of any size. They are implemented with macros, so allocation is usually very fast as long as the objects are usually small. And the only space overhead per object is the padding needed to start each object on a suitable boundary.

3.2.4.1 Creating Obstacks

The utilities for manipulating obstacks are declared in the header file **obstack.h**.

struct obstack   [Data Type]

An obstack is represented by a data structure of type **struct obstack**. This structure has a small fixed size; it records the status of the obstack and how to find the space in which objects are allocated. It does not contain any of the objects themselves. You should not try to access the contents of the structure directly; use only the functions described in this chapter.

You can declare variables of type **struct obstack** and use them as obstacks, or you can allocate obstacks dynamically like any other kind of object. Dynamic allocation of obstacks allows your program to have a variable number of different stacks. (You can even allocate an obstack structure in another obstack, but this is rarely useful.)

All the functions that work with obstacks require you to specify which obstack to use. You do this with a pointer of type `struct obstack *`. In the following, we often say "an obstack" when strictly speaking the object at hand is such a pointer.

The objects in the obstack are packed into large blocks called *chunks*. The `struct obstack` structure points to a chain of the chunks currently in use.

The obstack library obtains a new chunk whenever you allocate an object that won't fit in the previous chunk. Since the obstack library manages chunks automatically, you don't need to pay much attention to them, but you do need to supply a function which the obstack library should use to get a chunk. Usually you supply a function which uses `malloc` directly or indirectly. You must also supply a function to free a chunk. These matters are described in the following section.

3.2.4.2 Preparing for Using Obstacks

Each source file in which you plan to use the obstack functions must include the header file `obstack.h`, like this:

```
#include <obstack.h>
```

Also, if the source file uses the macro `obstack_init`, it must declare or define two functions or macros that will be called by the obstack library. One, `obstack_chunk_alloc`, is used to allocate the chunks of memory into which objects are packed. The other, `obstack_chunk_free`, is used to return chunks when the objects in them are freed. These macros should appear before any use of obstacks in the source file.

Usually these are defined to use `malloc` via the intermediary `xmalloc` (see Section 3.2.2 [Unconstrained Allocation], page 42). This is done with the following pair of macro definitions:

```
#define obstack_chunk_alloc xmalloc
#define obstack_chunk_free free
```

Though the memory you get using obstacks really comes from `malloc`, using obstacks is faster because `malloc` is called less often, for larger blocks of memory. See Section 3.2.4.10 [Obstack Chunks], page 67, for full details.

At run time, before the program can use a `struct obstack` object as an obstack, it must initialize the obstack by calling `obstack_init`.

`int obstack_init (`*`struct obstack *obstack-ptr`*`)`   [Function]

Preliminary: | MT-Safe race:obstack-ptr | AS-Safe | AC-Safe mem | See Section 1.2.2.1 [POSIX Safety Concepts], page 2.

Initialize obstack *obstack-ptr* for allocation of objects. This function calls the obstack's `obstack_chunk_alloc` function. If allocation of memory fails, the function pointed to by `obstack_alloc_failed_handler` is called. The `obstack_init` function always returns 1 (Compatibility notice: Former versions of obstack returned 0 if allocation failed).

Here are two examples of how to allocate the space for an obstack and initialize it. First, an obstack that is a static variable:

```
static struct obstack myobstack;
...
obstack_init (&myobstack);
```

Second, an obstack that is itself dynamically allocated:

```
struct obstack *myobstack_ptr
  = (struct obstack *) xmalloc (sizeof (struct obstack));

obstack_init (myobstack_ptr);
```

`obstack_alloc_failed_handler`   [Variable]

> The value of this variable is a pointer to a function that `obstack` uses when `obstack_chunk_alloc` fails to allocate memory. The default action is to print a message and abort. You should supply a function that either calls `exit` (see Section 25.7 [Program Termination], page 744) or `longjmp` (see Chapter 23 [Non-Local Exits], page 652) and doesn't return.
>
> ```
> void my_obstack_alloc_failed (void)
> ...
> obstack_alloc_failed_handler = &my_obstack_alloc_failed;
> ```

3.2.4.3 Allocation in an Obstack

The most direct way to allocate an object in an obstack is with `obstack_alloc`, which is invoked almost like `malloc`.

`void * obstack_alloc (struct obstack *obstack-ptr, int size)`   [Function]

> Preliminary: | MT-Safe race:obstack-ptr | AS-Safe | AC-Unsafe corrupt mem | See Section 1.2.2.1 [POSIX Safety Concepts], page 2.
>
> This allocates an uninitialized block of *size* bytes in an obstack and returns its address. Here *obstack-ptr* specifies which obstack to allocate the block in; it is the address of the **struct obstack** object which represents the obstack. Each obstack function or macro requires you to specify an *obstack-ptr* as the first argument.
>
> This function calls the obstack's `obstack_chunk_alloc` function if it needs to allocate a new chunk of memory; it calls `obstack_alloc_failed_handler` if allocation of memory by `obstack_chunk_alloc` failed.

For example, here is a function that allocates a copy of a string *str* in a specific obstack, which is in the variable **string_obstack**:

```
struct obstack string_obstack;

char *
copystring (char *string)
{
  size_t len = strlen (string) + 1;
  char *s = (char *) obstack_alloc (&string_obstack, len);
  memcpy (s, string, len);
  return s;
}
```

To allocate a block with specified contents, use the function `obstack_copy`, declared like this:

`void * obstack_copy (struct obstack *obstack-ptr, void *address,`   [Function]
`        int size)`

> Preliminary: | MT-Safe race:obstack-ptr | AS-Safe | AC-Unsafe corrupt mem | See Section 1.2.2.1 [POSIX Safety Concepts], page 2.

This allocates a block and initializes it by copying *size* bytes of data starting at *address*. It calls `obstack_alloc_failed_handler` if allocation of memory by `obstack_chunk_alloc` failed.

void * obstack_copy0 (*struct obstack *obstack-ptr*, *void *address*,   [Function]
     int size)

Preliminary: | MT-Safe race:obstack-ptr | AS-Safe | AC-Unsafe corrupt mem | See Section 1.2.2.1 [POSIX Safety Concepts], page 2.

Like `obstack_copy`, but appends an extra byte containing a null character. This extra byte is not counted in the argument *size*.

The `obstack_copy0` function is convenient for copying a sequence of characters into an obstack as a null-terminated string. Here is an example of its use:

```
char *
obstack_savestring (char *addr, int size)
{
  return obstack_copy0 (&myobstack, addr, size);
}
```

Contrast this with the previous example of `savestring` using `malloc` (see Section 3.2.2.1 [Basic Memory Allocation], page 42).

3.2.4.4 Freeing Objects in an Obstack

To free an object allocated in an obstack, use the function `obstack_free`. Since the obstack is a stack of objects, freeing one object automatically frees all other objects allocated more recently in the same obstack.

void obstack_free (*struct obstack *obstack-ptr*, *void *object*)   [Function]

Preliminary: | MT-Safe race:obstack-ptr | AS-Safe | AC-Unsafe corrupt | See Section 1.2.2.1 [POSIX Safety Concepts], page 2.

If *object* is a null pointer, everything allocated in the obstack is freed. Otherwise, *object* must be the address of an object allocated in the obstack. Then *object* is freed, along with everything allocated in *obstack* since *object*.

Note that if *object* is a null pointer, the result is an uninitialized obstack. To free all memory in an obstack but leave it valid for further allocation, call `obstack_free` with the address of the first object allocated on the obstack:

```
obstack_free (obstack_ptr, first_object_allocated_ptr);
```

Recall that the objects in an obstack are grouped into chunks. When all the objects in a chunk become free, the obstack library automatically frees the chunk (see Section 3.2.4.2 [Preparing for Using Obstacks], page 59). Then other obstacks, or non-obstack allocation, can reuse the space of the chunk.

3.2.4.5 Obstack Functions and Macros

The interfaces for using obstacks may be defined either as functions or as macros, depending on the compiler. The obstack facility works with all C compilers, including both ISO C and traditional C, but there are precautions you must take if you plan to use compilers other than GNU C.

If you are using an old-fashioned non-ISO C compiler, all the obstack "functions" are actually defined only as macros. You can call these macros like functions, but you cannot use them in any other way (for example, you cannot take their address).

Calling the macros requires a special precaution: namely, the first operand (the obstack pointer) may not contain any side effects, because it may be computed more than once. For example, if you write this:

```
obstack_alloc (get_obstack (), 4);
```

you will find that **get_obstack** may be called several times. If you use *obstack_list_ ptr++ as the obstack pointer argument, you will get very strange results since the incrementation may occur several times.

In ISO C, each function has both a macro definition and a function definition. The function definition is used if you take the address of the function without calling it. An ordinary call uses the macro definition by default, but you can request the function definition instead by writing the function name in parentheses, as shown here:

```
char *x;
void *(*funcp) ();
/* Use the macro.  */
x = (char *) obstack_alloc (obptr, size);
/* Call the function.  */
x = (char *) (obstack_alloc) (obptr, size);
/* Take the address of the function.  */
funcp = obstack_alloc;
```

This is the same situation that exists in ISO C for the standard library functions. See Section 1.3.2 [Macro Definitions of Functions], page 13.

Warning: When you do use the macros, you must observe the precaution of avoiding side effects in the first operand, even in ISO C.

If you use the GNU C compiler, this precaution is not necessary, because various language extensions in GNU C permit defining the macros so as to compute each argument only once.

3.2.4.6 Growing Objects

Because memory in obstack chunks is used sequentially, it is possible to build up an object step by step, adding one or more bytes at a time to the end of the object. With this technique, you do not need to know how much data you will put in the object until you come to the end of it. We call this the technique of *growing objects*. The special functions for adding data to the growing object are described in this section.

You don't need to do anything special when you start to grow an object. Using one of the functions to add data to the object automatically starts it. However, it is necessary to say explicitly when the object is finished. This is done with the function **obstack_finish**.

The actual address of the object thus built up is not known until the object is finished. Until then, it always remains possible that you will add so much data that the object must be copied into a new chunk.

While the obstack is in use for a growing object, you cannot use it for ordinary allocation of another object. If you try to do so, the space already added to the growing object will become part of the other object.

void obstack_blank (*struct obstack *obstack-ptr*, *int* size)   [Function]
> Preliminary: | MT-Safe race:obstack-ptr | AS-Safe | AC-Unsafe corrupt mem | See Section 1.2.2.1 [POSIX Safety Concepts], page 2.

> The most basic function for adding to a growing object is obstack_blank, which adds space without initializing it.

void obstack_grow (*struct obstack *obstack-ptr*, *void *data*, *int*   [Function]
> size)
> Preliminary: | MT-Safe race:obstack-ptr | AS-Safe | AC-Unsafe corrupt mem | See Section 1.2.2.1 [POSIX Safety Concepts], page 2.

> To add a block of initialized space, use obstack_grow, which is the growing-object analogue of obstack_copy. It adds *size* bytes of data to the growing object, copying the contents from *data*.

void obstack_grow0 (*struct obstack *obstack-ptr*, *void *data*, *int*   [Function]
> size)
> Preliminary: | MT-Safe race:obstack-ptr | AS-Safe | AC-Unsafe corrupt mem | See Section 1.2.2.1 [POSIX Safety Concepts], page 2.

> This is the growing-object analogue of obstack_copy0. It adds *size* bytes copied from *data*, followed by an additional null character.

void obstack_1grow (*struct obstack *obstack-ptr*, *char c*)   [Function]
> Preliminary: | MT-Safe race:obstack-ptr | AS-Safe | AC-Unsafe corrupt mem | See Section 1.2.2.1 [POSIX Safety Concepts], page 2.

> To add one character at a time, use the function obstack_1grow. It adds a single byte containing *c* to the growing object.

void obstack_ptr_grow (*struct obstack *obstack-ptr*, *void *data*)   [Function]
> Preliminary: | MT-Safe race:obstack-ptr | AS-Safe | AC-Unsafe corrupt mem | See Section 1.2.2.1 [POSIX Safety Concepts], page 2.

> Adding the value of a pointer one can use the function obstack_ptr_grow. It adds sizeof (void *) bytes containing the value of *data*.

void obstack_int_grow (*struct obstack *obstack-ptr*, *int data*)   [Function]
> Preliminary: | MT-Safe race:obstack-ptr | AS-Safe | AC-Unsafe corrupt mem | See Section 1.2.2.1 [POSIX Safety Concepts], page 2.

> A single value of type int can be added by using the obstack_int_grow function. It adds sizeof (int) bytes to the growing object and initializes them with the value of *data*.

void * obstack_finish (*struct obstack *obstack-ptr*)   [Function]
> Preliminary: | MT-Safe race:obstack-ptr | AS-Safe | AC-Unsafe corrupt | See Section 1.2.2.1 [POSIX Safety Concepts], page 2.

> When you are finished growing the object, use the function obstack_finish to close it off and return its final address.

> Once you have finished the object, the obstack is available for ordinary allocation or for growing another object.

This function can return a null pointer under the same conditions as `obstack_alloc` (see Section 3.2.4.3 [Allocation in an Obstack], page 60).

When you build an object by growing it, you will probably need to know afterward how long it became. You need not keep track of this as you grow the object, because you can find out the length from the obstack just before finishing the object with the function `obstack_object_size`, declared as follows:

int obstack_object_size (*struct obstack *obstack-ptr*)   [Function]
  Preliminary: | MT-Safe race:obstack-ptr | AS-Safe | AC-Safe | See Section 1.2.2.1 [POSIX Safety Concepts], page 2.

  This function returns the current size of the growing object, in bytes. Remember to call this function *before* finishing the object. After it is finished, `obstack_object_size` will return zero.

If you have started growing an object and wish to cancel it, you should finish it and then free it, like this:

```
obstack_free (obstack_ptr, obstack_finish (obstack_ptr));
```

This has no effect if no object was growing.

You can use `obstack_blank` with a negative size argument to make the current object smaller. Just don't try to shrink it beyond zero length—there's no telling what will happen if you do that.

3.2.4.7 Extra Fast Growing Objects

The usual functions for growing objects incur overhead for checking whether there is room for the new growth in the current chunk. If you are frequently constructing objects in small steps of growth, this overhead can be significant.

You can reduce the overhead by using special "fast growth" functions that grow the object without checking. In order to have a robust program, you must do the checking yourself. If you do this checking in the simplest way each time you are about to add data to the object, you have not saved anything, because that is what the ordinary growth functions do. But if you can arrange to check less often, or check more efficiently, then you make the program faster.

The function `obstack_room` returns the amount of room available in the current chunk. It is declared as follows:

int obstack_room (*struct obstack *obstack-ptr*)   [Function]
  Preliminary: | MT-Safe race:obstack-ptr | AS-Safe | AC-Safe | See Section 1.2.2.1 [POSIX Safety Concepts], page 2.

  This returns the number of bytes that can be added safely to the current growing object (or to an object about to be started) in obstack *obstack* using the fast growth functions.

While you know there is room, you can use these fast growth functions for adding data to a growing object:

void **obstack_1grow_fast** (*struct obstack *obstack-ptr*, *char c*)   [Function]
> Preliminary: | MT-Safe race:obstack-ptr | AS-Safe | AC-Unsafe corrupt mem | See Section 1.2.2.1 [POSIX Safety Concepts], page 2.

> The function `obstack_1grow_fast` adds one byte containing the character *c* to the growing object in obstack *obstack-ptr*.

void **obstack_ptr_grow_fast** (*struct obstack *obstack-ptr*, *void*   [Function]
>   **data*)
> Preliminary: | MT-Safe race:obstack-ptr | AS-Safe | AC-Safe | See Section 1.2.2.1 [POSIX Safety Concepts], page 2.

> The function `obstack_ptr_grow_fast` adds `sizeof (void *)` bytes containing the value of *data* to the growing object in obstack *obstack-ptr*.

void **obstack_int_grow_fast** (*struct obstack *obstack-ptr*, *int*   [Function]
>   *data*)
> Preliminary: | MT-Safe race:obstack-ptr | AS-Safe | AC-Safe | See Section 1.2.2.1 [POSIX Safety Concepts], page 2.

> The function `obstack_int_grow_fast` adds `sizeof (int)` bytes containing the value of *data* to the growing object in obstack *obstack-ptr*.

void **obstack_blank_fast** (*struct obstack *obstack-ptr*, *int size*)   [Function]
> Preliminary: | MT-Safe race:obstack-ptr | AS-Safe | AC-Safe | See Section 1.2.2.1 [POSIX Safety Concepts], page 2.

> The function `obstack_blank_fast` adds *size* bytes to the growing object in obstack *obstack-ptr* without initializing them.

When you check for space using `obstack_room` and there is not enough room for what you want to add, the fast growth functions are not safe. In this case, simply use the corresponding ordinary growth function instead. Very soon this will copy the object to a new chunk; then there will be lots of room available again.

So, each time you use an ordinary growth function, check afterward for sufficient space using `obstack_room`. Once the object is copied to a new chunk, there will be plenty of space again, so the program will start using the fast growth functions again.

Here is an example:

```
    void
    add_string (struct obstack *obstack, const char *ptr, int len)
    {
      while (len > 0)
        {
          int room = obstack_room (obstack);
          if (room == 0)
            {
              /* Not enough room.  Add one character slowly,
                 which may copy to a new chunk and make room.   */
              obstack_1grow (obstack, *ptr++);
              len--;
            }
          else
            {
              if (room > len)
                room = len;
              /* Add fast as much as we have room for. */
              len -= room;
              while (room-- > 0)
                obstack_1grow_fast (obstack, *ptr++);
            }
        }
    }
```

3.2.4.8 Status of an Obstack

Here are functions that provide information on the current status of allocation in an obstack. You can use them to learn about an object while still growing it.

void * obstack_base (*struct obstack *obstack-ptr*) [Function]

Preliminary: | MT-Safe | AS-Unsafe corrupt | AC-Safe | See Section 1.2.2.1 [POSIX Safety Concepts], page 2.

This function returns the tentative address of the beginning of the currently growing object in *obstack-ptr*. If you finish the object immediately, it will have that address. If you make it larger first, it may outgrow the current chunk—then its address will change!

If no object is growing, this value says where the next object you allocate will start (once again assuming it fits in the current chunk).

void * obstack_next_free (*struct obstack *obstack-ptr*) [Function]

Preliminary: | MT-Safe | AS-Unsafe corrupt | AC-Safe | See Section 1.2.2.1 [POSIX Safety Concepts], page 2.

This function returns the address of the first free byte in the current chunk of obstack *obstack-ptr*. This is the end of the currently growing object. If no object is growing, obstack_next_free returns the same value as obstack_base.

int obstack_object_size (*struct obstack *obstack-ptr*) [Function]

Preliminary: | MT-Safe race:obstack-ptr | AS-Safe | AC-Safe | See Section 1.2.2.1 [POSIX Safety Concepts], page 2.

This function returns the size in bytes of the currently growing object. This is equivalent to

```
    obstack_next_free (obstack-ptr) - obstack_base (obstack-ptr)
```

3.2.4.9 Alignment of Data in Obstacks

Each obstack has an *alignment boundary*; each object allocated in the obstack automatically starts on an address that is a multiple of the specified boundary. By default, this boundary is aligned so that the object can hold any type of data.

To access an obstack's alignment boundary, use the macro `obstack_alignment_mask`, whose function prototype looks like this:

int `obstack_alignment_mask` (*struct obstack *obstack-ptr*)   [Macro]
> Preliminary: | MT-Safe | AS-Safe | AC-Safe | See Section 1.2.2.1 [POSIX Safety Concepts], page 2.
>
> The value is a bit mask; a bit that is 1 indicates that the corresponding bit in the address of an object should be 0. The mask value should be one less than a power of 2; the effect is that all object addresses are multiples of that power of 2. The default value of the mask is a value that allows aligned objects to hold any type of data: for example, if its value is 3, any type of data can be stored at locations whose addresses are multiples of 4. A mask value of 0 means an object can start on any multiple of 1 (that is, no alignment is required).
>
> The expansion of the macro `obstack_alignment_mask` is an lvalue, so you can alter the mask by assignment. For example, this statement:
>
> ```
> obstack_alignment_mask (obstack_ptr) = 0;
> ```
>
> has the effect of turning off alignment processing in the specified obstack.

Note that a change in alignment mask does not take effect until *after* the next time an object is allocated or finished in the obstack. If you are not growing an object, you can make the new alignment mask take effect immediately by calling `obstack_finish`. This will finish a zero-length object and then do proper alignment for the next object.

3.2.4.10 Obstack Chunks

Obstacks work by allocating space for themselves in large chunks, and then parceling out space in the chunks to satisfy your requests. Chunks are normally 4096 bytes long unless you specify a different chunk size. The chunk size includes 8 bytes of overhead that are not actually used for storing objects. Regardless of the specified size, longer chunks will be allocated when necessary for long objects.

The obstack library allocates chunks by calling the function `obstack_chunk_alloc`, which you must define. When a chunk is no longer needed because you have freed all the objects in it, the obstack library frees the chunk by calling `obstack_chunk_free`, which you must also define.

These two must be defined (as macros) or declared (as functions) in each source file that uses `obstack_init` (see Section 3.2.4.1 [Creating Obstacks], page 58). Most often they are defined as macros like this:

```
#define obstack_chunk_alloc malloc
#define obstack_chunk_free free
```

Note that these are simple macros (no arguments). Macro definitions with arguments will not work! It is necessary that `obstack_chunk_alloc` or `obstack_chunk_free`, alone, expand into a function name if it is not itself a function name.

If you allocate chunks with `malloc`, the chunk size should be a power of 2. The default chunk size, 4096, was chosen because it is long enough to satisfy many typical requests on the obstack yet short enough not to waste too much memory in the portion of the last chunk not yet used.

int obstack_chunk_size (*struct obstack *obstack-ptr*)   [Macro]
> Preliminary: | MT-Safe | AS-Safe | AC-Safe | See Section 1.2.2.1 [POSIX Safety Concepts], page 2.

> This returns the chunk size of the given obstack.

Since this macro expands to an lvalue, you can specify a new chunk size by assigning it a new value. Doing so does not affect the chunks already allocated, but will change the size of chunks allocated for that particular obstack in the future. It is unlikely to be useful to make the chunk size smaller, but making it larger might improve efficiency if you are allocating many objects whose size is comparable to the chunk size. Here is how to do so cleanly:

```
if (obstack_chunk_size (obstack_ptr) < new-chunk-size)
  obstack_chunk_size (obstack_ptr) = new-chunk-size;
```

3.2.4.11 Summary of Obstack Functions

Here is a summary of all the functions associated with obstacks. Each takes the address of an obstack (`struct obstack *`) as its first argument.

void obstack_init (*struct obstack *obstack-ptr*)
> Initialize use of an obstack. See Section 3.2.4.1 [Creating Obstacks], page 58.

void *obstack_alloc (*struct obstack *obstack-ptr*, int *size*)
> Allocate an object of *size* uninitialized bytes. See Section 3.2.4.3 [Allocation in an Obstack], page 60.

void *obstack_copy (*struct obstack *obstack-ptr*, void **address*, int *size*)
> Allocate an object of *size* bytes, with contents copied from *address*. See Section 3.2.4.3 [Allocation in an Obstack], page 60.

void *obstack_copy0 (*struct obstack *obstack-ptr*, void **address*, int *size*)
> Allocate an object of *size*+1 bytes, with *size* of them copied from *address*, followed by a null character at the end. See Section 3.2.4.3 [Allocation in an Obstack], page 60.

void obstack_free (*struct obstack *obstack-ptr*, void **object*)
> Free *object* (and everything allocated in the specified obstack more recently than *object*). See Section 3.2.4.4 [Freeing Objects in an Obstack], page 61.

void obstack_blank (*struct obstack *obstack-ptr*, int *size*)
> Add *size* uninitialized bytes to a growing object. See Section 3.2.4.6 [Growing Objects], page 62.

void obstack_grow (*struct obstack *obstack-ptr*, void **address*, int *size*)
> Add *size* bytes, copied from *address*, to a growing object. See Section 3.2.4.6 [Growing Objects], page 62.

void obstack_grow0 (struct obstack *obstack-ptr, void *address, int size)
> Add size bytes, copied from address, to a growing object, and then add another
> byte containing a null character. See Section 3.2.4.6 [Growing Objects], page 62.

void obstack_1grow (struct obstack *obstack-ptr, char data-char)
> Add one byte containing data-char to a growing object. See Section 3.2.4.6
> [Growing Objects], page 62.

void *obstack_finish (struct obstack *obstack-ptr)
> Finalize the object that is growing and return its permanent address. See
> Section 3.2.4.6 [Growing Objects], page 62.

int obstack_object_size (struct obstack *obstack-ptr)
> Get the current size of the currently growing object. See Section 3.2.4.6 [Growing Objects], page 62.

void obstack_blank_fast (struct obstack *obstack-ptr, int size)
> Add size uninitialized bytes to a growing object without checking that there is
> enough room. See Section 3.2.4.7 [Extra Fast Growing Objects], page 64.

void obstack_1grow_fast (struct obstack *obstack-ptr, char data-char)
> Add one byte containing data-char to a growing object without checking
> that there is enough room. See Section 3.2.4.7 [Extra Fast Growing Objects],
> page 64.

int obstack_room (struct obstack *obstack-ptr)
> Get the amount of room now available for growing the current object. See
> Section 3.2.4.7 [Extra Fast Growing Objects], page 64.

int obstack_alignment_mask (struct obstack *obstack-ptr)
> The mask used for aligning the beginning of an object. This is an lvalue. See
> Section 3.2.4.9 [Alignment of Data in Obstacks], page 67.

int obstack_chunk_size (struct obstack *obstack-ptr)
> The size for allocating chunks. This is an lvalue. See Section 3.2.4.10 [Obstack
> Chunks], page 67.

void *obstack_base (struct obstack *obstack-ptr)
> Tentative starting address of the currently growing object. See Section 3.2.4.8
> [Status of an Obstack], page 66.

void *obstack_next_free (struct obstack *obstack-ptr)
> Address just after the end of the currently growing object. See Section 3.2.4.8
> [Status of an Obstack], page 66.

3.2.5 Automatic Storage with Variable Size

The function alloca supports a kind of half-dynamic allocation in which blocks are allocated
dynamically but freed automatically.

Allocating a block with alloca is an explicit action; you can allocate as many blocks as
you wish, and compute the size at run time. But all the blocks are freed when you exit the
function that alloca was called from, just as if they were automatic variables declared in
that function. There is no way to free the space explicitly.

The prototype for alloca is in stdlib.h. This function is a BSD extension.

void * alloca (*size_t size*)   [Function]
>   Preliminary: | MT-Safe | AS-Safe | AC-Safe | See Section 1.2.2.1 [POSIX Safety
>   Concepts], page 2.
>
>   The return value of alloca is the address of a block of *size* bytes of memory, allocated
>   in the stack frame of the calling function.

Do not use alloca inside the arguments of a function call—you will get unpredictable results, because the stack space for the alloca would appear on the stack in the middle of the space for the function arguments. An example of what to avoid is foo (x, alloca (4), y).

3.2.5.1 alloca Example

As an example of the use of alloca, here is a function that opens a file name made from concatenating two argument strings, and returns a file descriptor or minus one signifying failure:

```
int
open2 (char *str1, char *str2, int flags, int mode)
{
  char *name = (char *) alloca (strlen (str1) + strlen (str2) + 1);
  stpcpy (stpcpy (name, str1), str2);
  return open (name, flags, mode);
}
```

Here is how you would get the same results with malloc and free:

```
int
open2 (char *str1, char *str2, int flags, int mode)
{
  char *name = (char *) malloc (strlen (str1) + strlen (str2) + 1);
  int desc;
  if (name == 0)
    fatal ("virtual memory exceeded");
  stpcpy (stpcpy (name, str1), str2);
  desc = open (name, flags, mode);
  free (name);
  return desc;
}
```

As you can see, it is simpler with alloca. But alloca has other, more important advantages, and some disadvantages.

3.2.5.2 Advantages of alloca

Here are the reasons why alloca may be preferable to malloc:

- Using alloca wastes very little space and is very fast. (It is open-coded by the GNU C compiler.)

- Since alloca does not have separate pools for different sizes of block, space used for any size block can be reused for any other size. alloca does not cause memory fragmentation.

- Nonlocal exits done with longjmp (see Chapter 23 [Non-Local Exits], page 652) automatically free the space allocated with alloca when they exit through the function that called alloca. This is the most important reason to use alloca.

To illustrate this, suppose you have a function `open_or_report_error` which returns a descriptor, like `open`, if it succeeds, but does not return to its caller if it fails. If the file cannot be opened, it prints an error message and jumps out to the command level of your program using `longjmp`. Let's change `open2` (see Section 3.2.5.1 [alloca Example], page 70) to use this subroutine:

```
int
open2 (char *str1, char *str2, int flags, int mode)
{
  char *name = (char *) alloca (strlen (str1) + strlen (str2) + 1);
  stpcpy (stpcpy (name, str1), str2);
  return open_or_report_error (name, flags, mode);
}
```

Because of the way `alloca` works, the memory it allocates is freed even when an error occurs, with no special effort required.

By contrast, the previous definition of `open2` (which uses `malloc` and `free`) would develop a memory leak if it were changed in this way. Even if you are willing to make more changes to fix it, there is no easy way to do so.

3.2.5.3 Disadvantages of `alloca`

These are the disadvantages of `alloca` in comparison with `malloc`:

- If you try to allocate more memory than the machine can provide, you don't get a clean error message. Instead you get a fatal signal like the one you would get from an infinite recursion; probably a segmentation violation (see Section 24.2.1 [Program Error Signals], page 663).

- Some non-GNU systems fail to support `alloca`, so it is less portable. However, a slower emulation of `alloca` written in C is available for use on systems with this deficiency.

3.2.5.4 GNU C Variable-Size Arrays

In GNU C, you can replace most uses of `alloca` with an array of variable size. Here is how `open2` would look then:

```
int open2 (char *str1, char *str2, int flags, int mode)
{
  char name[strlen (str1) + strlen (str2) + 1];
  stpcpy (stpcpy (name, str1), str2);
  return open (name, flags, mode);
}
```

But `alloca` is not always equivalent to a variable-sized array, for several reasons:

- A variable size array's space is freed at the end of the scope of the name of the array. The space allocated with `alloca` remains until the end of the function.

- It is possible to use `alloca` within a loop, allocating an additional block on each iteration. This is impossible with variable-sized arrays.

NB: If you mix use of `alloca` and variable-sized arrays within one function, exiting a scope in which a variable-sized array was declared frees all blocks allocated with `alloca` during the execution of that scope.

3.3 Resizing the Data Segment

The symbols in this section are declared in `unistd.h`.

You will not normally use the functions in this section, because the functions described in Section 3.2 [Allocating Storage For Program Data], page 40 are easier to use. Those are interfaces to a GNU C Library memory allocator that uses the functions below itself. The functions below are simple interfaces to system calls.

int `brk` (*void *addr*) [Function]

> Preliminary: | MT-Safe | AS-Safe | AC-Safe | See Section 1.2.2.1 [POSIX Safety Concepts], page 2.
>
> `brk` sets the high end of the calling process' data segment to *addr*.
>
> The address of the end of a segment is defined to be the address of the last byte in the segment plus 1.
>
> The function has no effect if *addr* is lower than the low end of the data segment. (This is considered success, by the way).
>
> The function fails if it would cause the data segment to overlap another segment or exceed the process' data storage limit (see Section 22.2 [Limiting Resource Usage], page 632).
>
> The function is named for a common historical case where data storage and the stack are in the same segment. Data storage allocation grows upward from the bottom of the segment while the stack grows downward toward it from the top of the segment and the curtain between them is called the *break*.
>
> The return value is zero on success. On failure, the return value is `-1` and `errno` is set accordingly. The following `errno` values are specific to this function:
>
> ENOMEM   The request would cause the data segment to overlap another segment or exceed the process' data storage limit.

void `*sbrk` (*ptrdiff_t delta*) [Function]

> Preliminary: | MT-Safe | AS-Safe | AC-Safe | See Section 1.2.2.1 [POSIX Safety Concepts], page 2.
>
> This function is the same as `brk` except that you specify the new end of the data segment as an offset *delta* from the current end and on success the return value is the address of the resulting end of the data segment instead of zero.
>
> This means you can use 'sbrk(0)' to find out what the current end of the data segment is.

3.4 Locking Pages

You can tell the system to associate a particular virtual memory page with a real page frame and keep it that way — i.e., cause the page to be paged in if it isn't already and mark it so it will never be paged out and consequently will never cause a page fault. This is called *locking* a page.

The functions in this chapter lock and unlock the calling process' pages.

3.4.1 Why Lock Pages

Because page faults cause paged out pages to be paged in transparently, a process rarely needs to be concerned about locking pages. However, there are two reasons people sometimes are:

- Speed. A page fault is transparent only insofar as the process is not sensitive to how long it takes to do a simple memory access. Time-critical processes, especially realtime processes, may not be able to wait or may not be able to tolerate variance in execution speed.

    A process that needs to lock pages for this reason probably also needs priority among other processes for use of the CPU. See Section 22.3 [Process CPU Priority And Scheduling], page 636.

    In some cases, the programmer knows better than the system's demand paging allocator which pages should remain in real memory to optimize system performance. In this case, locking pages can help.

- Privacy. If you keep secrets in virtual memory and that virtual memory gets paged out, that increases the chance that the secrets will get out. If a password gets written out to disk swap space, for example, it might still be there long after virtual and real memory have been wiped clean.

Be aware that when you lock a page, that's one fewer page frame that can be used to back other virtual memory (by the same or other processes), which can mean more page faults, which means the system runs more slowly. In fact, if you lock enough memory, some programs may not be able to run at all for lack of real memory.

3.4.2 Locked Memory Details

A memory lock is associated with a virtual page, not a real frame. The paging rule is: If a frame backs at least one locked page, don't page it out.

Memory locks do not stack. I.e., you can't lock a particular page twice so that it has to be unlocked twice before it is truly unlocked. It is either locked or it isn't.

A memory lock persists until the process that owns the memory explicitly unlocks it. (But process termination and exec cause the virtual memory to cease to exist, which you might say means it isn't locked any more).

Memory locks are not inherited by child processes. (But note that on a modern Unix system, immediately after a fork, the parent's and the child's virtual address space are backed by the same real page frames, so the child enjoys the parent's locks). See Section 26.4 [Creating a Process], page 751.

Because of its ability to impact other processes, only the superuser can lock a page. Any process can unlock its own page.

The system sets limits on the amount of memory a process can have locked and the amount of real memory it can have dedicated to it. See Section 22.2 [Limiting Resource Usage], page 632.

In Linux, locked pages aren't as locked as you might think. Two virtual pages that are not shared memory can nonetheless be backed by the same real frame. The kernel does this in the name of efficiency when it knows both virtual pages contain identical data, and does it even if one or both of the virtual pages are locked.

But when a process modifies one of those pages, the kernel must get it a separate frame and fill it with the page's data. This is known as a *copy-on-write page fault*. It takes a small amount of time and in a pathological case, getting that frame may require I/O.

To make sure this doesn't happen to your program, don't just lock the pages. Write to them as well, unless you know you won't write to them ever. And to make sure you have pre-allocated frames for your stack, enter a scope that declares a C automatic variable larger than the maximum stack size you will need, set it to something, then return from its scope.

3.4.3 Functions To Lock And Unlock Pages

The symbols in this section are declared in **sys/mman.h**. These functions are defined by POSIX.1b, but their availability depends on your kernel. If your kernel doesn't allow these functions, they exist but always fail. They *are* available with a Linux kernel.

Portability Note: POSIX.1b requires that when the **mlock** and **munlock** functions are available, the file **unistd.h** define the macro **_POSIX_MEMLOCK_RANGE** and the file **limits.h** define the macro **PAGESIZE** to be the size of a memory page in bytes. It requires that when the **mlockall** and **munlockall** functions are available, the **unistd.h** file define the macro **_POSIX_MEMLOCK**. The GNU C Library conforms to this requirement.

int mlock (*const void *addr, size_t* len)   [Function]

> Preliminary: | MT-Safe | AS-Safe | AC-Safe | See Section 1.2.2.1 [POSIX Safety Concepts], page 2.
>
> mlock locks a range of the calling process' virtual pages.
>
> The range of memory starts at address *addr* and is *len* bytes long. Actually, since you must lock whole pages, it is the range of pages that include any part of the specified range.
>
> When the function returns successfully, each of those pages is backed by (connected to) a real frame (is resident) and is marked to stay that way. This means the function may cause page-ins and have to wait for them.
>
> When the function fails, it does not affect the lock status of any pages.
>
> The return value is zero if the function succeeds. Otherwise, it is **-1** and **errno** is set accordingly. **errno** values specific to this function are:
>
> ENOMEM
>
> > • At least some of the specified address range does not exist in the calling process' virtual address space.
> >
> > • The locking would cause the process to exceed its locked page limit.
>
> EPERM   The calling process is not superuser.
>
> EINVAL   *len* is not positive.
>
> ENOSYS   The kernel does not provide **mlock** capability.
>
> You can lock *all* a process' memory with **mlockall**. You unlock memory with **munlock** or **munlockall**.
>
> To avoid all page faults in a C program, you have to use **mlockall**, because some of the memory a program uses is hidden from the C code, e.g. the stack and automatic variables, and you wouldn't know what address to tell **mlock**.

int munlock (*const void *addr, size_t* `len`)   [Function]
> Preliminary: | MT-Safe | AS-Safe | AC-Safe | See Section 1.2.2.1 [POSIX Safety Concepts], page 2.
>
> `munlock` unlocks a range of the calling process' virtual pages.
>
> `munlock` is the inverse of `mlock` and functions completely analogously to `mlock`, except that there is no `EPERM` failure.

int mlockall (*int* `flags`)   [Function]
> Preliminary: | MT-Safe | AS-Safe | AC-Safe | See Section 1.2.2.1 [POSIX Safety Concepts], page 2.
>
> `mlockall` locks all the pages in a process' virtual memory address space, and/or any that are added to it in the future. This includes the pages of the code, data and stack segment, as well as shared libraries, user space kernel data, shared memory, and memory mapped files.
>
> *flags* is a string of single bit flags represented by the following macros. They tell `mlockall` which of its functions you want. All other bits must be zero.
>
> `MCL_CURRENT`
>> Lock all pages which currently exist in the calling process' virtual address space.
>
> `MCL_FUTURE`
>> Set a mode such that any pages added to the process' virtual address space in the future will be locked from birth. This mode does not affect future address spaces owned by the same process so exec, which replaces a process' address space, wipes out `MCL_FUTURE`. See Section 26.5 [Executing a File], page 752.
>
> When the function returns successfully, and you specified `MCL_CURRENT`, all of the process' pages are backed by (connected to) real frames (they are resident) and are marked to stay that way. This means the function may cause page-ins and have to wait for them.
>
> When the process is in `MCL_FUTURE` mode because it successfully executed this function and specified `MCL_CURRENT`, any system call by the process that requires space be added to its virtual address space fails with `errno` = `ENOMEM` if locking the additional space would cause the process to exceed its locked page limit. In the case that the address space addition that can't be accommodated is stack expansion, the stack expansion fails and the kernel sends a `SIGSEGV` signal to the process.
>
> When the function fails, it does not affect the lock status of any pages or the future locking mode.
>
> The return value is zero if the function succeeds. Otherwise, it is `-1` and `errno` is set accordingly. `errno` values specific to this function are:
>
> `ENOMEM`
>> • At least some of the specified address range does not exist in the calling process' virtual address space.
>> • The locking would cause the process to exceed its locked page limit.

EPERM   The calling process is not superuser.

EINVAL   Undefined bits in *flags* are not zero.

ENOSYS   The kernel does not provide `mlockall` capability.

You can lock just specific pages with `mlock`. You unlock pages with `munlockall` and `munlock`.

`int munlockall (void)`   [Function]
    Preliminary: | MT-Safe | AS-Safe | AC-Safe | See Section 1.2.2.1 [POSIX Safety Concepts], page 2.

    `munlockall` unlocks every page in the calling process' virtual address space and turn off `MCL_FUTURE` future locking mode.

    The return value is zero if the function succeeds. Otherwise, it is −1 and `errno` is set accordingly. The only way this function can fail is for generic reasons that all functions and system calls can fail, so there are no specific `errno` values.

4 Character Handling

Programs that work with characters and strings often need to classify a character—is it alphabetic, is it a digit, is it whitespace, and so on—and perform case conversion operations on characters. The functions in the header file `ctype.h` are provided for this purpose.

Since the choice of locale and character set can alter the classifications of particular character codes, all of these functions are affected by the current locale. (More precisely, they are affected by the locale currently selected for character classification—the `LC_CTYPE` category; see Section 7.3 [Locale Categories], page 170.)

The ISO C standard specifies two different sets of functions. The one set works on `char` type characters, the other one on `wchar_t` wide characters (see Section 6.1 [Introduction to Extended Characters], page 127).

4.1 Classification of Characters

This section explains the library functions for classifying characters. For example, `isalpha` is the function to test for an alphabetic character. It takes one argument, the character to test, and returns a nonzero integer if the character is alphabetic, and zero otherwise. You would use it like this:

```
if (isalpha (c))
    printf ("The character '%c' is alphabetic.\n", c);
```

Each of the functions in this section tests for membership in a particular class of characters; each has a name starting with 'is'. Each of them takes one argument, which is a character to test, and returns an `int` which is treated as a boolean value. The character argument is passed as an `int`, and it may be the constant value `EOF` instead of a real character.

The attributes of any given character can vary between locales. See Chapter 7 [Locales and Internationalization], page 169, for more information on locales.

These functions are declared in the header file `ctype.h`.

int **islower** (*int c*)   [Function]
    Preliminary: | MT-Safe | AS-Safe | AC-Safe | See Section 1.2.2.1 [POSIX Safety Concepts], page 2.

    Returns true if *c* is a lower-case letter. The letter need not be from the Latin alphabet, any alphabet representable is valid.

int **isupper** (*int c*)   [Function]
    Preliminary: | MT-Safe | AS-Safe | AC-Safe | See Section 1.2.2.1 [POSIX Safety Concepts], page 2.

    Returns true if *c* is an upper-case letter. The letter need not be from the Latin alphabet, any alphabet representable is valid.

int **isalpha** (*int c*)   [Function]
    Preliminary: | MT-Safe | AS-Safe | AC-Safe | See Section 1.2.2.1 [POSIX Safety Concepts], page 2.

    Returns true if *c* is an alphabetic character (a letter). If `islower` or `isupper` is true of a character, then `isalpha` is also true.

In some locales, there may be additional characters for which `isalpha` is true—letters which are neither upper case nor lower case. But in the standard `"C"` locale, there are no such additional characters.

`int isdigit (`*int c*`)` [Function]
> Preliminary: | MT-Safe | AS-Safe | AC-Safe | See Section 1.2.2.1 [POSIX Safety Concepts], page 2.
>
> Returns true if *c* is a decimal digit ('0' through '9').

`int isalnum (`*int c*`)` [Function]
> Preliminary: | MT-Safe | AS-Safe | AC-Safe | See Section 1.2.2.1 [POSIX Safety Concepts], page 2.
>
> Returns true if *c* is an alphanumeric character (a letter or number); in other words, if either `isalpha` or `isdigit` is true of a character, then `isalnum` is also true.

`int isxdigit (`*int c*`)` [Function]
> Preliminary: | MT-Safe | AS-Safe | AC-Safe | See Section 1.2.2.1 [POSIX Safety Concepts], page 2.
>
> Returns true if *c* is a hexadecimal digit. Hexadecimal digits include the normal decimal digits '0' through '9' and the letters 'A' through 'F' and 'a' through 'f'.

`int ispunct (`*int c*`)` [Function]
> Preliminary: | MT-Safe | AS-Safe | AC-Safe | See Section 1.2.2.1 [POSIX Safety Concepts], page 2.
>
> Returns true if *c* is a punctuation character. This means any printing character that is not alphanumeric or a space character.

`int isspace (`*int c*`)` [Function]
> Preliminary: | MT-Safe | AS-Safe | AC-Safe | See Section 1.2.2.1 [POSIX Safety Concepts], page 2.
>
> Returns true if *c* is a *whitespace* character. In the standard `"C"` locale, `isspace` returns true for only the standard whitespace characters:
>
> | | |
> |---|---|
> | `' '` | space |
> | `'\f'` | formfeed |
> | `'\n'` | newline |
> | `'\r'` | carriage return |
> | `'\t'` | horizontal tab |
> | `'\v'` | vertical tab |

`int isblank (`*int c*`)` [Function]
> Preliminary: | MT-Safe | AS-Safe | AC-Safe | See Section 1.2.2.1 [POSIX Safety Concepts], page 2.
>
> Returns true if *c* is a blank character; that is, a space or a tab. This function was originally a GNU extension, but was added in ISO C99.

`int` **isgraph** (*int c*) [Function]

Preliminary: | MT-Safe | AS-Safe | AC-Safe | See Section 1.2.2.1 [POSIX Safety Concepts], page 2.

Returns true if *c* is a graphic character; that is, a character that has a glyph associated with it. The whitespace characters are not considered graphic.

`int` **isprint** (*int c*) [Function]

Preliminary: | MT-Safe | AS-Safe | AC-Safe | See Section 1.2.2.1 [POSIX Safety Concepts], page 2.

Returns true if *c* is a printing character. Printing characters include all the graphic characters, plus the space (' ') character.

`int` **iscntrl** (*int c*) [Function]

Preliminary: | MT-Safe | AS-Safe | AC-Safe | See Section 1.2.2.1 [POSIX Safety Concepts], page 2.

Returns true if *c* is a control character (that is, a character that is not a printing character).

`int` **isascii** (*int c*) [Function]

Preliminary: | MT-Safe | AS-Safe | AC-Safe | See Section 1.2.2.1 [POSIX Safety Concepts], page 2.

Returns true if *c* is a 7-bit `unsigned char` value that fits into the US/UK ASCII character set. This function is a BSD extension and is also an SVID extension.

4.2 Case Conversion

This section explains the library functions for performing conversions such as case mappings on characters. For example, `toupper` converts any character to upper case if possible. If the character can't be converted, `toupper` returns it unchanged.

These functions take one argument of type `int`, which is the character to convert, and return the converted character as an `int`. If the conversion is not applicable to the argument given, the argument is returned unchanged.

Compatibility Note: In pre-ISO C dialects, instead of returning the argument unchanged, these functions may fail when the argument is not suitable for the conversion. Thus for portability, you may need to write `islower(c) ? toupper(c) : c` rather than just `toupper(c)`.

These functions are declared in the header file `ctype.h`.

`int` **tolower** (*int c*) [Function]

Preliminary: | MT-Safe | AS-Safe | AC-Safe | See Section 1.2.2.1 [POSIX Safety Concepts], page 2.

If *c* is an upper-case letter, `tolower` returns the corresponding lower-case letter. If *c* is not an upper-case letter, *c* is returned unchanged.

`int` **toupper** (*int c*) [Function]

Preliminary: | MT-Safe | AS-Safe | AC-Safe | See Section 1.2.2.1 [POSIX Safety Concepts], page 2.

If *c* is a lower-case letter, `toupper` returns the corresponding upper-case letter. Otherwise *c* is returned unchanged.

int toascii (*int c*)   [Function]
      Preliminary: | MT-Safe | AS-Safe | AC-Safe | See Section 1.2.2.1 [POSIX Safety Concepts], page 2.

      This function converts *c* to a 7-bit `unsigned char` value that fits into the US/UK ASCII character set, by clearing the high-order bits. This function is a BSD extension and is also an SVID extension.

int _tolower (*int c*)   [Function]
      Preliminary: | MT-Safe | AS-Safe | AC-Safe | See Section 1.2.2.1 [POSIX Safety Concepts], page 2.

      This is identical to `tolower`, and is provided for compatibility with the SVID. See Section 1.2.4 [SVID (The System V Interface Description)], page 11.

int _toupper (*int c*)   [Function]
      Preliminary: | MT-Safe | AS-Safe | AC-Safe | See Section 1.2.2.1 [POSIX Safety Concepts], page 2.

      This is identical to `toupper`, and is provided for compatibility with the SVID.

4.3 Character class determination for wide characters

Amendment 1 to ISO C90 defines functions to classify wide characters. Although the original ISO C90 standard already defined the type `wchar_t`, no functions operating on them were defined.

The general design of the classification functions for wide characters is more general. It allows extensions to the set of available classifications, beyond those which are always available. The POSIX standard specifies how extensions can be made, and this is already implemented in the GNU C Library implementation of the `localedef` program.

The character class functions are normally implemented with bitsets, with a bitset per character. For a given character, the appropriate bitset is read from a table and a test is performed as to whether a certain bit is set. Which bit is tested for is determined by the class.

For the wide character classification functions this is made visible. There is a type classification type defined, a function to retrieve this value for a given class, and a function to test whether a given character is in this class, using the classification value. On top of this the normal character classification functions as used for `char` objects can be defined.

wctype_t   [Data type]
      The `wctype_t` can hold a value which represents a character class. The only defined way to generate such a value is by using the `wctype` function.

      This type is defined in `wctype.h`.

wctype_t wctype (*const char *property*)   [Function]
      Preliminary: | MT-Safe locale | AS-Safe | AC-Safe | See Section 1.2.2.1 [POSIX Safety Concepts], page 2.

The `wctype` returns a value representing a class of wide characters which is identified by the string *property*. Beside some standard properties each locale can define its own ones. In case no property with the given name is known for the current locale selected for the `LC_CTYPE` category, the function returns zero.

The properties known in every locale are:

```
"alnum"          "alpha"          "cntrl"          "digit"
"graph"          "lower"          "print"          "punct"
"space"          "upper"          "xdigit"
```

This function is declared in `wctype.h`.

To test the membership of a character to one of the non-standard classes the ISO C standard defines a completely new function.

`int iswctype (wint_t wc, wctype_t desc)`   [Function]

> Preliminary: | MT-Safe | AS-Safe | AC-Safe | See Section 1.2.2.1 [POSIX Safety Concepts], page 2.
>
> This function returns a nonzero value if *wc* is in the character class specified by *desc*. *desc* must previously be returned by a successful call to `wctype`.
>
> This function is declared in `wctype.h`.

To make it easier to use the commonly-used classification functions, they are defined in the C library. There is no need to use `wctype` if the property string is one of the known character classes. In some situations it is desirable to construct the property strings, and then it is important that `wctype` can also handle the standard classes.

`int iswalnum (wint_t wc)`   [Function]

> Preliminary: | MT-Safe locale | AS-Safe | AC-Safe | See Section 1.2.2.1 [POSIX Safety Concepts], page 2.
>
> This function returns a nonzero value if *wc* is an alphanumeric character (a letter or number); in other words, if either `iswalpha` or `iswdigit` is true of a character, then `iswalnum` is also true.
>
> This function can be implemented using
>
> ```
> iswctype (wc, wctype ("alnum"))
> ```
>
> It is declared in `wctype.h`.

`int iswalpha (wint_t wc)`   [Function]

> Preliminary: | MT-Safe locale | AS-Safe | AC-Safe | See Section 1.2.2.1 [POSIX Safety Concepts], page 2.
>
> Returns true if *wc* is an alphabetic character (a letter). If `iswlower` or `iswupper` is true of a character, then `iswalpha` is also true.
>
> In some locales, there may be additional characters for which `iswalpha` is true—letters which are neither upper case nor lower case. But in the standard "C" locale, there are no such additional characters.
>
> This function can be implemented using
>
> ```
> iswctype (wc, wctype ("alpha"))
> ```
>
> It is declared in `wctype.h`.

int **iswcntrl** (*wint_t wc*)   [Function]

> Preliminary: | MT-Safe locale | AS-Safe | AC-Safe | See Section 1.2.2.1 [POSIX Safety Concepts], page 2.
>
> Returns true if *wc* is a control character (that is, a character that is not a printing character).
>
> This function can be implemented using
>
>   iswctype (wc, wctype ("cntrl"))
>
> It is declared in `wctype.h`.

int **iswdigit** (*wint_t wc*)   [Function]

> Preliminary: | MT-Safe locale | AS-Safe | AC-Safe | See Section 1.2.2.1 [POSIX Safety Concepts], page 2.
>
> Returns true if *wc* is a digit (e.g., '0' through '9'). Please note that this function does not only return a nonzero value for *decimal* digits, but for all kinds of digits. A consequence is that code like the following will **not** work unconditionally for wide characters:
>
> ```
> n = 0;
> while (iswdigit (*wc))
>   {
>     n *= 10;
>     n += *wc++ - L'0';
>   }
> ```
>
> This function can be implemented using
>
>   iswctype (wc, wctype ("digit"))
>
> It is declared in `wctype.h`.

int **iswgraph** (*wint_t wc*)   [Function]

> Preliminary: | MT-Safe locale | AS-Safe | AC-Safe | See Section 1.2.2.1 [POSIX Safety Concepts], page 2.
>
> Returns true if *wc* is a graphic character; that is, a character that has a glyph associated with it. The whitespace characters are not considered graphic.
>
> This function can be implemented using
>
>   iswctype (wc, wctype ("graph"))
>
> It is declared in `wctype.h`.

int **iswlower** (*wint_t wc*)   [Function]

> Preliminary: | MT-Safe locale | AS-Safe | AC-Safe | See Section 1.2.2.1 [POSIX Safety Concepts], page 2.
>
> Returns true if *wc* is a lower-case letter. The letter need not be from the Latin alphabet, any alphabet representable is valid.
>
> This function can be implemented using
>
>   iswctype (wc, wctype ("lower"))
>
> It is declared in `wctype.h`.

int iswprint (*wint_t wc*)   [Function]

Preliminary: | MT-Safe locale | AS-Safe | AC-Safe | See Section 1.2.2.1 [POSIX Safety Concepts], page 2.

Returns true if *wc* is a printing character. Printing characters include all the graphic characters, plus the space (' ') character.

This function can be implemented using

```
iswctype (wc, wctype ("print"))
```

It is declared in `wctype.h`.

int iswpunct (*wint_t wc*)   [Function]

Preliminary: | MT-Safe locale | AS-Safe | AC-Safe | See Section 1.2.2.1 [POSIX Safety Concepts], page 2.

Returns true if *wc* is a punctuation character. This means any printing character that is not alphanumeric or a space character.

This function can be implemented using

```
iswctype (wc, wctype ("punct"))
```

It is declared in `wctype.h`.

int iswspace (*wint_t wc*)   [Function]

Preliminary: | MT-Safe locale | AS-Safe | AC-Safe | See Section 1.2.2.1 [POSIX Safety Concepts], page 2.

Returns true if *wc* is a *whitespace* character. In the standard `"C"` locale, `iswspace` returns true for only the standard whitespace characters:

`L' '`   space

`L'\f'`   formfeed

`L'\n'`   newline

`L'\r'`   carriage return

`L'\t'`   horizontal tab

`L'\v'`   vertical tab

This function can be implemented using

```
iswctype (wc, wctype ("space"))
```

It is declared in `wctype.h`.

int iswupper (*wint_t wc*)   [Function]

Preliminary: | MT-Safe locale | AS-Safe | AC-Safe | See Section 1.2.2.1 [POSIX Safety Concepts], page 2.

Returns true if *wc* is an upper-case letter. The letter need not be from the Latin alphabet, any alphabet representable is valid.

This function can be implemented using

```
iswctype (wc, wctype ("upper"))
```

It is declared in `wctype.h`.

`int` `iswxdigit` (*wint_t wc*)   [Function]
>   Preliminary: | MT-Safe locale | AS-Safe | AC-Safe | See Section 1.2.2.1 [POSIX Safety Concepts], page 2.
>
>   Returns true if *wc* is a hexadecimal digit. Hexadecimal digits include the normal decimal digits '0' through '9' and the letters 'A' through 'F' and 'a' through 'f'.
>
>   This function can be implemented using
>
>   `iswctype (wc, wctype ("xdigit"))`
>
>   It is declared in `wctype.h`.

The GNU C Library also provides a function which is not defined in the ISO C standard but which is available as a version for single byte characters as well.

`int` `iswblank` (*wint_t wc*)   [Function]
>   Preliminary: | MT-Safe locale | AS-Safe | AC-Safe | See Section 1.2.2.1 [POSIX Safety Concepts], page 2.
>
>   Returns true if *wc* is a blank character; that is, a space or a tab. This function was originally a GNU extension, but was added in ISO C99. It is declared in `wchar.h`.

4.4 Notes on using the wide character classes

The first note is probably not astonishing but still occasionally a cause of problems. The `iswXXX` functions can be implemented using macros and in fact, the GNU C Library does this. They are still available as real functions but when the `wctype.h` header is included the macros will be used. This is the same as the `char` type versions of these functions.

The second note covers something new. It can be best illustrated by a (real-world) example. The first piece of code is an excerpt from the original code. It is truncated a bit but the intention should be clear.

```
int
is_in_class (int c, const char *class)
{
  if (strcmp (class, "alnum") == 0)
    return isalnum (c);
  if (strcmp (class, "alpha") == 0)
    return isalpha (c);
  if (strcmp (class, "cntrl") == 0)
    return iscntrl (c);
  ...
  return 0;
}
```

Now, with the `wctype` and `iswctype` you can avoid the `if` cascades, but rewriting the code as follows is wrong:

```
int
is_in_class (int c, const char *class)
{
  wctype_t desc = wctype (class);
  return desc ? iswctype ((wint_t) c, desc) : 0;
}
```

The problem is that it is not guaranteed that the wide character representation of a single-byte character can be found using casting. In fact, usually this fails miserably. The correct solution to this problem is to write the code as follows:

```
    int
    is_in_class (int c, const char *class)
    {
      wctype_t desc = wctype (class);
      return desc ? iswctype (btowc (c), desc) : 0;
    }
```

See Section 6.3.3 [Converting Single Characters], page 133, for more information on `btowc`. Note that this change probably does not improve the performance of the program a lot since the `wctype` function still has to make the string comparisons. It gets really interesting if the `is_in_class` function is called more than once for the same class name. In this case the variable *desc* could be computed once and reused for all the calls. Therefore the above form of the function is probably not the final one.

4.5 Mapping of wide characters.

The classification functions are also generalized by the ISO C standard. Instead of just allowing the two standard mappings, a locale can contain others. Again, the `localedef` program already supports generating such locale data files.

`wctrans_t`   [Data Type]
> This data type is defined as a scalar type which can hold a value representing the locale-dependent character mapping. There is no way to construct such a value apart from using the return value of the `wctrans` function.
>
> This type is defined in `wctype.h`.

`wctrans_t wctrans` (*const char *property*)   [Function]
> Preliminary: | MT-Safe locale | AS-Safe | AC-Safe | See Section 1.2.2.1 [POSIX Safety Concepts], page 2.
>
> The `wctrans` function has to be used to find out whether a named mapping is defined in the current locale selected for the `LC_CTYPE` category. If the returned value is non-zero, you can use it afterwards in calls to `towctrans`. If the return value is zero no such mapping is known in the current locale.
>
> Beside locale-specific mappings there are two mappings which are guaranteed to be available in every locale:
>
> `"tolower"`   `"toupper"`
>
> These functions are declared in `wctype.h`.

`wint_t towctrans` (*wint_t wc*, *wctrans_t desc*)   [Function]
> Preliminary: | MT-Safe | AS-Safe | AC-Safe | See Section 1.2.2.1 [POSIX Safety Concepts], page 2.
>
> `towctrans` maps the input character *wc* according to the rules of the mapping for which *desc* is a descriptor, and returns the value it finds. *desc* must be obtained by a successful call to `wctrans`.
>
> This function is declared in `wctype.h`.

For the generally available mappings, the ISO C standard defines convenient shortcuts so that it is not necessary to call `wctrans` for them.

wint_t towlower (*wint_t wc*)   [Function]
> Preliminary: | MT-Safe locale | AS-Safe | AC-Safe | See Section 1.2.2.1 [POSIX Safety Concepts], page 2.
>
> If *wc* is an upper-case letter, **towlower** returns the corresponding lower-case letter. If *wc* is not an upper-case letter, *wc* is returned unchanged.
>
> **towlower** can be implemented using
>
> ```
> towctrans (wc, wctrans ("tolower"))
> ```
>
> This function is declared in **wctype.h**.

wint_t towupper (*wint_t wc*)   [Function]
> Preliminary: | MT-Safe locale | AS-Safe | AC-Safe | See Section 1.2.2.1 [POSIX Safety Concepts], page 2.
>
> If *wc* is a lower-case letter, **towupper** returns the corresponding upper-case letter. Otherwise *wc* is returned unchanged.
>
> **towupper** can be implemented using
>
> ```
> towctrans (wc, wctrans ("toupper"))
> ```
>
> This function is declared in **wctype.h**.

The same warnings given in the last section for the use of the wide character classification functions apply here. It is not possible to simply cast a **char** type value to a **wint_t** and use it as an argument to **towctrans** calls.

5 String and Array Utilities

Operations on strings (or arrays of characters) are an important part of many programs. The GNU C Library provides an extensive set of string utility functions, including functions for copying, concatenating, comparing, and searching strings. Many of these functions can also operate on arbitrary regions of storage; for example, the `memcpy` function can be used to copy the contents of any kind of array.

It's fairly common for beginning C programmers to "reinvent the wheel" by duplicating this functionality in their own code, but it pays to become familiar with the library functions and to make use of them, since this offers benefits in maintenance, efficiency, and portability.

For instance, you could easily compare one string to another in two lines of C code, but if you use the built-in `strcmp` function, you're less likely to make a mistake. And, since these library functions are typically highly optimized, your program may run faster too.

5.1 Representation of Strings

This section is a quick summary of string concepts for beginning C programmers. It describes how character strings are represented in C and some common pitfalls. If you are already familiar with this material, you can skip this section.

A *string* is an array of `char` objects. But string-valued variables are usually declared to be pointers of type `char *`. Such variables do not include space for the text of a string; that has to be stored somewhere else—in an array variable, a string constant, or dynamically allocated memory (see Section 3.2 [Allocating Storage For Program Data], page 40). It's up to you to store the address of the chosen memory space into the pointer variable. Alternatively you can store a *null pointer* in the pointer variable. The null pointer does not point anywhere, so attempting to reference the string it points to gets an error.

"string" normally refers to multibyte character strings as opposed to wide character strings. Wide character strings are arrays of type `wchar_t` and as for multibyte character strings usually pointers of type `wchar_t *` are used.

By convention, a *null character*, `'\0'`, marks the end of a multibyte character string and the *null wide character*, `L'\0'`, marks the end of a wide character string. For example, in testing to see whether the `char *` variable *p* points to a null character marking the end of a string, you can write `!*p` or `*p == '\0'`.

A null character is quite different conceptually from a null pointer, although both are represented by the integer `0`.

String literals appear in C program source as strings of characters between double-quote characters (`'"'`) where the initial double-quote character is immediately preceded by a capital 'L' (ell) character (as in `L"foo"`). In ISO C, string literals can also be formed by *string concatenation*: `"a" "b"` is the same as `"ab"`. For wide character strings one can either use `L"a" L"b"` or `L"a" "b"`. Modification of string literals is not allowed by the GNU C compiler, because literals are placed in read-only storage.

Character arrays that are declared `const` cannot be modified either. It's generally good style to declare non-modifiable string pointers to be of type `const char *`, since this often allows the C compiler to detect accidental modifications as well as providing some amount of documentation about what your program intends to do with the string.

The amount of memory allocated for the character array may extend past the null character that normally marks the end of the string. In this document, the term *allocated size* is always used to refer to the total amount of memory allocated for the string, while the term *length* refers to the number of characters up to (but not including) the terminating null character.

A notorious source of program bugs is trying to put more characters in a string than fit in its allocated size. When writing code that extends strings or moves characters into a pre-allocated array, you should be very careful to keep track of the length of the text and make explicit checks for overflowing the array. Many of the library functions *do not* do this for you! Remember also that you need to allocate an extra byte to hold the null character that marks the end of the string.

Originally strings were sequences of bytes where each byte represents a single character. This is still true today if the strings are encoded using a single-byte character encoding. Things are different if the strings are encoded using a multibyte encoding (for more information on encodings see Section 6.1 [Introduction to Extended Characters], page 127). There is no difference in the programming interface for these two kind of strings; the programmer has to be aware of this and interpret the byte sequences accordingly.

But since there is no separate interface taking care of these differences the byte-based string functions are sometimes hard to use. Since the count parameters of these functions specify bytes a call to `strncpy` could cut a multibyte character in the middle and put an incomplete (and therefore unusable) byte sequence in the target buffer.

To avoid these problems later versions of the ISO C standard introduce a second set of functions which are operating on *wide characters* (see Section 6.1 [Introduction to Extended Characters], page 127). These functions don't have the problems the single-byte versions have since every wide character is a legal, interpretable value. This does not mean that cutting wide character strings at arbitrary points is without problems. It normally is for alphabet-based languages (except for non-normalized text) but languages based on syllables still have the problem that more than one wide character is necessary to complete a logical unit. This is a higher level problem which the C library functions are not designed to solve. But it is at least good that no invalid byte sequences can be created. Also, the higher level functions can also much easier operate on wide character than on multibyte characters so that a general advise is to use wide characters internally whenever text is more than simply copied.

The remaining of this chapter will discuss the functions for handling wide character strings in parallel with the discussion of the multibyte character strings since there is almost always an exact equivalent available.

5.2 String and Array Conventions

This chapter describes both functions that work on arbitrary arrays or blocks of memory, and functions that are specific to null-terminated arrays of characters and wide characters.

Functions that operate on arbitrary blocks of memory have names beginning with 'mem' and 'wmem' (such as `memcpy` and `wmemcpy`) and invariably take an argument which specifies the size (in bytes and wide characters respectively) of the block of memory to operate on. The array arguments and return values for these functions have type `void *` or `wchar_t`. As a matter of style, the elements of the arrays used with the 'mem' functions are referred to as "bytes". You can pass any kind of pointer to these functions, and the `sizeof` operator is useful in computing the value for the size argument. Parameters to the 'wmem' functions must be of type `wchar_t *`. These functions are not really usable with anything but arrays of this type.

In contrast, functions that operate specifically on strings and wide character strings have names beginning with 'str' and 'wcs' respectively (such as `strcpy` and `wcscpy`) and look for a null character to terminate the string instead of requiring an explicit size argument to be passed. (Some of these functions accept a specified maximum length, but they also check for premature termination with a null character.) The array arguments and return values for these functions have type `char *` and `wchar_t *` respectively, and the array elements are referred to as "characters" and "wide characters".

In many cases, there are both 'mem' and 'str'/'wcs' versions of a function. The one that is more appropriate to use depends on the exact situation. When your program is manipulating arbitrary arrays or blocks of storage, then you should always use the 'mem' functions. On the other hand, when you are manipulating null-terminated strings it is usually more convenient to use the 'str'/'wcs' functions, unless you already know the length of the string in advance. The 'wmem' functions should be used for wide character arrays with known size.

Some of the memory and string functions take single characters as arguments. Since a value of type `char` is automatically promoted into a value of type `int` when used as a parameter, the functions are declared with `int` as the type of the parameter in question. In case of the wide character function the situation is similarly: the parameter type for a single wide character is `wint_t` and not `wchar_t`. This would for many implementations not be necessary since the `wchar_t` is large enough to not be automatically promoted, but since the ISO C standard does not require such a choice of types the `wint_t` type is used.

5.3 String Length

You can get the length of a string using the `strlen` function. This function is declared in the header file `string.h`.

`size_t strlen (const char *s)` [Function]

> Preliminary: | MT-Safe | AS-Safe | AC-Safe | See Section 1.2.2.1 [POSIX Safety Concepts], page 2.
>
> The `strlen` function returns the length of the null-terminated string s in bytes. (In other words, it returns the offset of the terminating null character within the array.)
>
> For example,
>
> ```
> strlen ("hello, world")
>     ⇒ 12
> ```
>
> When applied to a character array, the `strlen` function returns the length of the string stored there, not its allocated size. You can get the allocated size of the character array that holds a string using the `sizeof` operator:
>
> ```
> char string[32] = "hello, world";
> sizeof (string)
>     ⇒ 32
> strlen (string)
>     ⇒ 12
> ```

But beware, this will not work unless *string* is the character array itself, not a pointer to it. For example:

```
char string[32] = "hello, world";
char *ptr = string;
sizeof (string)
    ⇒ 32
sizeof (ptr)
    ⇒ 4   /* (on a machine with 4 byte pointers) */
```

This is an easy mistake to make when you are working with functions that take string arguments; those arguments are always pointers, not arrays.

It must also be noted that for multibyte encoded strings the return value does not have to correspond to the number of characters in the string. To get this value the string can be converted to wide characters and `wcslen` can be used or something like the following code can be used:

```
/* The input is in string.
   The length is expected in n.  */
{
  mbstate_t t;
  char *scopy = string;
  /* In initial state. */
  memset (&t, '\0', sizeof (t));
  /* Determine number of characters. */
  n = mbsrtowcs (NULL, &scopy, strlen (scopy), &t);
}
```

This is cumbersome to do so if the number of characters (as opposed to bytes) is needed often it is better to work with wide characters.

The wide character equivalent is declared in `wchar.h`.

size_t wcslen (*const wchar_t *ws*)   [Function]
 Preliminary: | MT-Safe | AS-Safe | AC-Safe | See Section 1.2.2.1 [POSIX Safety Concepts], page 2.

 The `wcslen` function is the wide character equivalent to `strlen`. The return value is the number of wide characters in the wide character string pointed to by *ws* (this is also the offset of the terminating null wide character of *ws*).

 Since there are no multi wide character sequences making up one character the return value is not only the offset in the array, it is also the number of wide characters.

 This function was introduced in Amendment 1 to ISO C90.

size_t strnlen (*const char *s*, *size_t maxlen*)   [Function]
 Preliminary: | MT-Safe | AS-Safe | AC-Safe | See Section 1.2.2.1 [POSIX Safety Concepts], page 2.

 The `strnlen` function returns the length of the string *s* in bytes if this length is smaller than *maxlen* bytes. Otherwise it returns *maxlen*. Therefore this function is equivalent to (`strlen (s)` < *maxlen* ? `strlen (s)` : *maxlen*) but it is more efficient and works even if the string *s* is not null-terminated.

```
char string[32] = "hello, world";
strnlen (string, 32)
    ⇒ 12
strnlen (string, 5)
```

⇒ 5

This function is a GNU extension and is declared in `string.h`.

`size_t wcsnlen` (*const wchar_t *ws*, *size_t* `maxlen`)   [Function]
> Preliminary: | MT-Safe | AS-Safe | AC-Safe | See Section 1.2.2.1 [POSIX Safety Concepts], page 2.
>
> `wcsnlen` is the wide character equivalent to `strnlen`. The *maxlen* parameter specifies the maximum number of wide characters.
>
> This function is a GNU extension and is declared in `wchar.h`.

5.4 Copying and Concatenation

You can use the functions described in this section to copy the contents of strings and arrays, or to append the contents of one string to another. The 'str' and 'mem' functions are declared in the header file `string.h` while the 'wstr' and 'wmem' functions are declared in the file `wchar.h`.

A helpful way to remember the ordering of the arguments to the functions in this section is that it corresponds to an assignment expression, with the destination array specified to the left of the source array. All of these functions return the address of the destination array.

Most of these functions do not work properly if the source and destination arrays overlap. For example, if the beginning of the destination array overlaps the end of the source array, the original contents of that part of the source array may get overwritten before it is copied. Even worse, in the case of the string functions, the null character marking the end of the string may be lost, and the copy function might get stuck in a loop trashing all the memory allocated to your program.

All functions that have problems copying between overlapping arrays are explicitly identified in this manual. In addition to functions in this section, there are a few others like `sprintf` (see Section 12.12.7 [Formatted Output Functions], page 278) and `scanf` (see Section 12.14.8 [Formatted Input Functions], page 300).

`void * memcpy` (*void *restrict* `to`, *const void *restrict* `from`, *size_t* `size`)   [Function]
> Preliminary: | MT-Safe | AS-Safe | AC-Safe | See Section 1.2.2.1 [POSIX Safety Concepts], page 2.
>
> The `memcpy` function copies *size* bytes from the object beginning at *from* into the object beginning at *to*. The behavior of this function is undefined if the two arrays *to* and *from* overlap; use `memmove` instead if overlapping is possible.
>
> The value returned by `memcpy` is the value of *to*.
>
> Here is an example of how you might use `memcpy` to copy the contents of an array:
> ```
> struct foo *oldarray, *newarray;
> int arraysize;
> ...
> memcpy (new, old, arraysize * sizeof (struct foo));
> ```

`wchar_t * wmemcpy` (*wchar_t *restrict* `wto`, *const wchar_t *restrict*   [Function]
> `wfrom`, *size_t* `size`)
> Preliminary: | MT-Safe | AS-Safe | AC-Safe | See Section 1.2.2.1 [POSIX Safety Concepts], page 2.

The `wmemcpy` function copies *size* wide characters from the object beginning at *wfrom* into the object beginning at *wto*. The behavior of this function is undefined if the two arrays *wto* and *wfrom* overlap; use `wmemmove` instead if overlapping is possible.

The following is a possible implementation of `wmemcpy` but there are more optimizations possible.

```
wchar_t *
wmemcpy (wchar_t *restrict wto, const wchar_t *restrict wfrom,
         size_t size)
{
  return (wchar_t *) memcpy (wto, wfrom, size * sizeof (wchar_t));
}
```

The value returned by `wmemcpy` is the value of *wto*.

This function was introduced in Amendment 1 to ISO C90.

void * mempcpy (*void *restrict* **to**, *const void *restrict* **from**, *size_t*   [Function]
        size)

Preliminary: | MT-Safe | AS-Safe | AC-Safe | See Section 1.2.2.1 [POSIX Safety Concepts], page 2.

The `mempcpy` function is nearly identical to the `memcpy` function. It copies *size* bytes from the object beginning at `from` into the object pointed to by *to*. But instead of returning the value of *to* it returns a pointer to the byte following the last written byte in the object beginning at *to*. I.e., the value is `((void *) ((char *) to + size))`.

This function is useful in situations where a number of objects shall be copied to consecutive memory positions.

```
void *
combine (void *o1, size_t s1, void *o2, size_t s2)
{
  void *result = malloc (s1 + s2);
  if (result != NULL)
    mempcpy (mempcpy (result, o1, s1), o2, s2);
  return result;
}
```

This function is a GNU extension.

wchar_t * wmempcpy (*wchar_t *restrict* **wto**, *const wchar_t *restrict*   [Function]
        wfrom, *size_t* **size**)

Preliminary: | MT-Safe | AS-Safe | AC-Safe | See Section 1.2.2.1 [POSIX Safety Concepts], page 2.

The `wmempcpy` function is nearly identical to the `wmemcpy` function. It copies *size* wide characters from the object beginning at `wfrom` into the object pointed to by *wto*. But instead of returning the value of *wto* it returns a pointer to the wide character following the last written wide character in the object beginning at *wto*. I.e., the value is `wto + size`.

This function is useful in situations where a number of objects shall be copied to consecutive memory positions.

The following is a possible implementation of `wmemcpy` but there are more optimizations possible.

```
wchar_t *
wmempcpy (wchar_t *restrict wto, const wchar_t *restrict wfrom,
          size_t size)
{
  return (wchar_t *) mempcpy (wto, wfrom, size * sizeof (wchar_t));
}
```

This function is a GNU extension.

void * memmove (*void *to, const void *from, size_t size*)   [Function]
Preliminary: | MT-Safe | AS-Safe | AC-Safe | See Section 1.2.2.1 [POSIX Safety Concepts], page 2.

memmove copies the *size* bytes at *from* into the *size* bytes at *to*, even if those two blocks of space overlap. In the case of overlap, memmove is careful to copy the original values of the bytes in the block at *from*, including those bytes which also belong to the block at *to*.

The value returned by memmove is the value of *to*.

wchar_t * wmemmove (*wchar_t *wto, const wchar_t *wfrom, size_t size*)   [Function]
Preliminary: | MT-Safe | AS-Safe | AC-Safe | See Section 1.2.2.1 [POSIX Safety Concepts], page 2.

wmemmove copies the *size* wide characters at *wfrom* into the *size* wide characters at *wto*, even if those two blocks of space overlap. In the case of overlap, memmove is careful to copy the original values of the wide characters in the block at *wfrom*, including those wide characters which also belong to the block at *wto*.

The following is a possible implementation of wmemcpy but there are more optimizations possible.

```
wchar_t *
wmempcpy (wchar_t *restrict wto, const wchar_t *restrict wfrom,
          size_t size)
{
  return (wchar_t *) mempcpy (wto, wfrom, size * sizeof (wchar_t));
}
```

The value returned by wmemmove is the value of *wto*.

This function is a GNU extension.

void * memccpy (*void *restrict to, const void *restrict from, int c, size_t*   [Function]
   size)
Preliminary: | MT-Safe | AS-Safe | AC-Safe | See Section 1.2.2.1 [POSIX Safety Concepts], page 2.

This function copies no more than *size* bytes from *from* to *to*, stopping if a byte matching *c* is found. The return value is a pointer into *to* one byte past where *c* was copied, or a null pointer if no byte matching *c* appeared in the first *size* bytes of *from*.

void * memset (*void *block, int c, size_t size*)   [Function]
Preliminary: | MT-Safe | AS-Safe | AC-Safe | See Section 1.2.2.1 [POSIX Safety Concepts], page 2.

This function copies the value of *c* (converted to an **unsigned char**) into each of the first *size* bytes of the object beginning at *block*. It returns the value of *block*.

`wchar_t * wmemset` (*wchar_t *block*, *wchar_t wc*, *size_t* `size`)   [Function]
>   Preliminary: | MT-Safe | AS-Safe | AC-Safe | See Section 1.2.2.1 [POSIX Safety
>   Concepts], page 2.
>
>   This function copies the value of *wc* into each of the first *size* wide characters of the
>   object beginning at *block*. It returns the value of *block*.

`char * strcpy` (*char *restrict* `to`, *const char *restrict* `from`)   [Function]
>   Preliminary: | MT-Safe | AS-Safe | AC-Safe | See Section 1.2.2.1 [POSIX Safety
>   Concepts], page 2.
>
>   This copies characters from the string *from* (up to and including the terminating null
>   character) into the string *to*. Like `memcpy`, this function has undefined results if the
>   strings overlap. The return value is the value of *to*.

`wchar_t * wcscpy` (*wchar_t *restrict* `wto`, *const wchar_t *restrict* `wfrom`)   [Function]
>   Preliminary: | MT-Safe | AS-Safe | AC-Safe | See Section 1.2.2.1 [POSIX Safety
>   Concepts], page 2.
>
>   This copies wide characters from the string *wfrom* (up to and including the terminat-
>   ing null wide character) into the string *wto*. Like `wmemcpy`, this function has undefined
>   results if the strings overlap. The return value is the value of *wto*.

`char * strncpy` (*char *restrict* `to`, *const char *restrict* `from`, *size_t*   [Function]
>   `size`)
>   Preliminary: | MT-Safe | AS-Safe | AC-Safe | See Section 1.2.2.1 [POSIX Safety
>   Concepts], page 2.
>
>   This function is similar to `strcpy` but always copies exactly *size* characters into *to*.
>
>   If the length of *from* is more than *size*, then `strncpy` copies just the first *size* charac-
>   ters. Note that in this case there is no null terminator written into *to*.
>
>   If the length of *from* is less than *size*, then `strncpy` copies all of *from*, followed by
>   enough null characters to add up to *size* characters in all. This behavior is rarely
>   useful, but it is specified by the ISO C standard.
>
>   The behavior of `strncpy` is undefined if the strings overlap.
>
>   Using `strncpy` as opposed to `strcpy` is a way to avoid bugs relating to writing past
>   the end of the allocated space for *to*. However, it can also make your program much
>   slower in one common case: copying a string which is probably small into a potentially
>   large buffer. In this case, *size* may be large, and when it is, `strncpy` will waste a
>   considerable amount of time copying null characters.

`wchar_t * wcsncpy` (*wchar_t *restrict* `wto`, *const wchar_t *restrict*   [Function]
>   `wfrom`, *size_t* `size`)
>   Preliminary: | MT-Safe | AS-Safe | AC-Safe | See Section 1.2.2.1 [POSIX Safety
>   Concepts], page 2.
>
>   This function is similar to `wcscpy` but always copies exactly *size* wide characters into
>   *wto*.
>
>   If the length of *wfrom* is more than *size*, then `wcsncpy` copies just the first *size* wide
>   characters. Note that in this case there is no null terminator written into *wto*.

If the length of *wfrom* is less than *size*, then `wcsncpy` copies all of *wfrom*, followed by enough null wide characters to add up to *size* wide characters in all. This behavior is rarely useful, but it is specified by the ISO C standard.

The behavior of `wcsncpy` is undefined if the strings overlap.

Using `wcsncpy` as opposed to `wcscpy` is a way to avoid bugs relating to writing past the end of the allocated space for *wto*. However, it can also make your program much slower in one common case: copying a string which is probably small into a potentially large buffer. In this case, *size* may be large, and when it is, `wcsncpy` will waste a considerable amount of time copying null wide characters.

char * strdup (*const char *s*)   [Function]
Preliminary: | MT-Safe | AS-Unsafe heap | AC-Unsafe mem | See Section 1.2.2.1 [POSIX Safety Concepts], page 2.

This function copies the null-terminated string *s* into a newly allocated string. The string is allocated using `malloc`; see Section 3.2.2 [Unconstrained Allocation], page 42. If `malloc` cannot allocate space for the new string, `strdup` returns a null pointer. Otherwise it returns a pointer to the new string.

wchar_t * wcsdup (*const wchar_t *ws*)   [Function]
Preliminary: | MT-Safe | AS-Unsafe heap | AC-Unsafe mem | See Section 1.2.2.1 [POSIX Safety Concepts], page 2.

This function copies the null-terminated wide character string *ws* into a newly allocated string. The string is allocated using `malloc`; see Section 3.2.2 [Unconstrained Allocation], page 42. If `malloc` cannot allocate space for the new string, `wcsdup` returns a null pointer. Otherwise it returns a pointer to the new wide character string.

This function is a GNU extension.

char * strndup (*const char *s, size_t size*)   [Function]
Preliminary: | MT-Safe | AS-Unsafe heap | AC-Unsafe mem | See Section 1.2.2.1 [POSIX Safety Concepts], page 2.

This function is similar to `strdup` but always copies at most *size* characters into the newly allocated string.

If the length of *s* is more than *size*, then `strndup` copies just the first *size* characters and adds a closing null terminator. Otherwise all characters are copied and the string is terminated.

This function is different to `strncpy` in that it always terminates the destination string.

`strndup` is a GNU extension.

char * stpcpy (*char *restrict to, const char *restrict from*)   [Function]
Preliminary: | MT-Safe | AS-Safe | AC-Safe | See Section 1.2.2.1 [POSIX Safety Concepts], page 2.

This function is like `strcpy`, except that it returns a pointer to the end of the string *to* (that is, the address of the terminating null character `to + strlen (from)`) rather than the beginning.

For example, this program uses `stpcpy` to concatenate 'foo' and 'bar' to produce 'foobar', which it then prints.

```
#include <string.h>
#include <stdio.h>

int
main (void)
{
  char buffer[10];
  char *to = buffer;
  to = stpcpy (to, "foo");
  to = stpcpy (to, "bar");
  puts (buffer);
  return 0;
}
```

This function is not part of the ISO or POSIX standards, and is not customary on Unix systems, but we did not invent it either. Perhaps it comes from MS-DOG.

Its behavior is undefined if the strings overlap. The function is declared in `string.h`.

wchar_t * wcpcpy (*wchar_t *restrict **wto**, const wchar_t *restrict **wfrom***)   [Function]
Preliminary: | MT-Safe | AS-Safe | AC-Safe | See Section 1.2.2.1 [POSIX Safety Concepts], page 2.

This function is like `wcscpy`, except that it returns a pointer to the end of the string *wto* (that is, the address of the terminating null character `wto + strlen (wfrom)`) rather than the beginning.

This function is not part of ISO or POSIX but was found useful while developing the GNU C Library itself.

The behavior of `wcpcpy` is undefined if the strings overlap.

`wcpcpy` is a GNU extension and is declared in `wchar.h`.

char * stpncpy (*char *restrict **to**, const char *restrict **from**, size_t*   [Function]
     size)
Preliminary: | MT-Safe | AS-Safe | AC-Safe | See Section 1.2.2.1 [POSIX Safety Concepts], page 2.

This function is similar to `stpcpy` but copies always exactly *size* characters into *to*.

If the length of *from* is more than *size*, then `stpncpy` copies just the first *size* characters and returns a pointer to the character directly following the one which was copied last. Note that in this case there is no null terminator written into *to*.

If the length of *from* is less than *size*, then `stpncpy` copies all of *from*, followed by enough null characters to add up to *size* characters in all. This behavior is rarely useful, but it is implemented to be useful in contexts where this behavior of the `strncpy` is used. `stpncpy` returns a pointer to the *first* written null character.

This function is not part of ISO or POSIX but was found useful while developing the GNU C Library itself.

Its behavior is undefined if the strings overlap. The function is declared in `string.h`.

wchar_t * wcpncpy (*wchar_t *restrict **wto**, const wchar_t *restrict*   [Function]
    *wfrom, size_t **size**)*

> Preliminary: | MT-Safe | AS-Safe | AC-Safe | See Section 1.2.2.1 [POSIX Safety Concepts], page 2.
>
> This function is similar to `wcpcpy` but copies always exactly *wsize* characters into *wto*.
>
> If the length of *wfrom* is more than *size*, then `wcpncpy` copies just the first *size* wide characters and returns a pointer to the wide character directly following the last non-null wide character which was copied last. Note that in this case there is no null terminator written into *wto*.
>
> If the length of *wfrom* is less than *size*, then `wcpncpy` copies all of *wfrom*, followed by enough null characters to add up to *size* characters in all. This behavior is rarely useful, but it is implemented to be useful in contexts where this behavior of the `wcsncpy` is used. `wcpncpy` returns a pointer to the *first* written null character.
>
> This function is not part of ISO or POSIX but was found useful while developing the GNU C Library itself.
>
> Its behavior is undefined if the strings overlap.
>
> `wcpncpy` is a GNU extension and is declared in `wchar.h`.

char * strdupa (*const char *s*)   [Macro]

> Preliminary: | MT-Safe | AS-Safe | AC-Safe | See Section 1.2.2.1 [POSIX Safety Concepts], page 2.
>
> This macro is similar to `strdup` but allocates the new string using `alloca` instead of `malloc` (see Section 3.2.5 [Automatic Storage with Variable Size], page 69). This means of course the returned string has the same limitations as any block of memory allocated using `alloca`.
>
> For obvious reasons `strdupa` is implemented only as a macro; you cannot get the address of this function. Despite this limitation it is a useful function. The following code shows a situation where using `malloc` would be a lot more expensive.

```
#include <paths.h>
#include <string.h>
#include <stdio.h>

const char path[] = _PATH_STDPATH;

int
main (void)
{
  char *wr_path = strdupa (path);
  char *cp = strtok (wr_path, ":");

  while (cp != NULL)
    {
      puts (cp);
      cp = strtok (NULL, ":");
    }
  return 0;
}
```

Please note that calling `strtok` using *path* directly is invalid. It is also not allowed to call `strdupa` in the argument list of `strtok` since `strdupa` uses `alloca` (see Section 3.2.5 [Automatic Storage with Variable Size], page 69) can interfere with the parameter passing.

This function is only available if GNU CC is used.

char * **strndupa** (*const char* ***s**, *size_t* **size**)   [Macro]
Preliminary: | MT-Safe | AS-Safe | AC-Safe | See Section 1.2.2.1 [POSIX Safety Concepts], page 2.

This function is similar to `strndup` but like `strdupa` it allocates the new string using `alloca` see Section 3.2.5 [Automatic Storage with Variable Size], page 69. The same advantages and limitations of `strdupa` are valid for `strndupa`, too.

This function is implemented only as a macro, just like `strdupa`. Just as `strdupa` this macro also must not be used inside the parameter list in a function call.

`strndupa` is only available if GNU CC is used.

char * **strcat** (*char* *restrict **to**, *const char* *restrict **from**)   [Function]
Preliminary: | MT-Safe | AS-Safe | AC-Safe | See Section 1.2.2.1 [POSIX Safety Concepts], page 2.

The `strcat` function is similar to `strcpy`, except that the characters from *from* are concatenated or appended to the end of *to*, instead of overwriting it. That is, the first character from *from* overwrites the null character marking the end of *to*.

An equivalent definition for `strcat` would be:

```
char *
strcat (char *restrict to, const char *restrict from)
{
  strcpy (to + strlen (to), from);
  return to;
}
```

This function has undefined results if the strings overlap.

wchar_t * **wcscat** (*wchar_t* *restrict **wto**, *const wchar_t* *restrict **wfrom**)   [Function]
Preliminary: | MT-Safe | AS-Safe | AC-Safe | See Section 1.2.2.1 [POSIX Safety Concepts], page 2.

The `wcscat` function is similar to `wcscpy`, except that the characters from *wfrom* are concatenated or appended to the end of *wto*, instead of overwriting it. That is, the first character from *wfrom* overwrites the null character marking the end of *wto*.

An equivalent definition for `wcscat` would be:

```
wchar_t *
wcscat (wchar_t *wto, const wchar_t *wfrom)
{
  wcscpy (wto + wcslen (wto), wfrom);
  return wto;
}
```

This function has undefined results if the strings overlap.

Programmers using the `strcat` or `wcscat` function (or the following `strncat` or `wcsncar` functions for that matter) can easily be recognized as lazy and reckless. In almost all situations the lengths of the participating strings are known (it better should be since how can one otherwise ensure the allocated size of the buffer is sufficient?) Or at least, one could know them if one keeps track of the results of the various function calls. But then it is very inefficient to use `strcat`/`wcscat`. A lot of time is wasted finding the end of the destination string so that the actual copying can start. This is a common example:

```
/* This function concatenates arbitrarily many strings.  The last
   parameter must be NULL.  */
char *
concat (const char *str, ...)
{
  va_list ap, ap2;
  size_t total = 1;
  const char *s;
  char *result;

  va_start (ap, str);
  va_copy (ap2, ap);

  /* Determine how much space we need.  */
  for (s = str; s != NULL; s = va_arg (ap, const char *))
    total += strlen (s);

  va_end (ap);

  result = (char *) malloc (total);
  if (result != NULL)
    {
      result[0] = '\0';

      /* Copy the strings.  */
      for (s = str; s != NULL; s = va_arg (ap2, const char *))
        strcat (result, s);
    }

  va_end (ap2);

  return result;
}
```

This looks quite simple, especially the second loop where the strings are actually copied. But these innocent lines hide a major performance penalty. Just imagine that ten strings of 100 bytes each have to be concatenated. For the second string we search the already stored 100 bytes for the end of the string so that we can append the next string. For all strings in total the comparisons necessary to find the end of the intermediate results sums up to 5500! If we combine the copying with the search for the allocation we can write this function more efficient:

```
char *
concat (const char *str, ...)
{
  va_list ap;
  size_t allocated = 100;
  char *result = (char *) malloc (allocated);
```

```
      if (result != NULL)
        {
          char *newp;
          char *wp;
          const char *s;

          va_start (ap, str);

          wp = result;
          for (s = str; s != NULL; s = va_arg (ap, const char *))
            {
              size_t len = strlen (s);

              /* Resize the allocated memory if necessary.  */
              if (wp + len + 1 > result + allocated)
                {
                  allocated = (allocated + len) * 2;
                  newp = (char *) realloc (result, allocated);
                  if (newp == NULL)
                    {
                      free (result);
                      return NULL;
                    }
                  wp = newp + (wp - result);
                  result = newp;
                }

              wp = mempcpy (wp, s, len);
            }

          /* Terminate the result string.  */
          *wp++ = '\0';

          /* Resize memory to the optimal size.  */
          newp = realloc (result, wp - result);
          if (newp != NULL)
            result = newp;

          va_end (ap);
        }

      return result;
    }
```

With a bit more knowledge about the input strings one could fine-tune the memory allocation. The difference we are pointing to here is that we don't use `strcat` anymore. We always keep track of the length of the current intermediate result so we can safe us the search for the end of the string and use `mempcpy`. Please note that we also don't use `stpcpy` which might seem more natural since we handle with strings. But this is not necessary since we already know the length of the string and therefore can use the faster memory copying function. The example would work for wide characters the same way.

Whenever a programmer feels the need to use `strcat` she or he should think twice and look through the program whether the code cannot be rewritten to take advantage of already calculated results. Again: it is almost always unnecessary to use `strcat`.

char * strncat (char *restrict *to*, const char *restrict *from*, size_t   [Function]
      size)

Preliminary: | MT-Safe | AS-Safe | AC-Safe | See Section 1.2.2.1 [POSIX Safety
Concepts], page 2.

This function is like `strcat` except that not more than *size* characters from *from* are
appended to the end of *to*. A single null character is also always appended to *to*, so
the total allocated size of *to* must be at least *size* + 1 bytes longer than its initial
length.

The `strncat` function could be implemented like this:

```
char *
strncat (char *to, const char *from, size_t size)
{
  memcpy (to + strlen (to), from, strnlen (from, size));
  to[strlen (to) + strnlen (from, size)] = '\0';
  return to;
}
```

The behavior of `strncat` is undefined if the strings overlap.

wchar_t * wcsncat (wchar_t *restrict *wto*, const wchar_t *restrict   [Function]
      wfrom, size_t *size*)

Preliminary: | MT-Safe | AS-Safe | AC-Safe | See Section 1.2.2.1 [POSIX Safety
Concepts], page 2.

This function is like `wcscat` except that not more than *size* characters from *from* are
appended to the end of *to*. A single null character is also always appended to *to*, so
the total allocated size of *to* must be at least *size* + 1 bytes longer than its initial
length.

The `wcsncat` function could be implemented like this:

```
wchar_t *
wcsncat (wchar_t *restrict wto, const wchar_t *restrict wfrom,
         size_t size)
{
  memcpy (wto + wcslen (wto), wfrom, wcsnlen (wfrom, size) * sizeof (wchar_t));
  wto[wcslen (to) + wcsnlen (wfrom, size)] = '\0';
  return wto;
}
```

The behavior of `wcsncat` is undefined if the strings overlap.

Here is an example showing the use of `strncpy` and `strncat` (the wide character version
is equivalent). Notice how, in the call to `strncat`, the *size* parameter is computed to avoid
overflowing the character array `buffer`.

```
#include <string.h>
#include <stdio.h>

#define SIZE 10

static char buffer[SIZE];

int
main (void)
{
```

```
        strncpy (buffer, "hello", SIZE);
        puts (buffer);
        strncat (buffer, ", world", SIZE - strlen (buffer) - 1);
        puts (buffer);
    }
```

The output produced by this program looks like:

```
hello
hello, wo
```

void **bcopy** (*const void *from, void *to, size_t size*)   [Function]
> Preliminary: | MT-Safe | AS-Safe | AC-Safe | See Section 1.2.2.1 [POSIX Safety Concepts], page 2.

> This is a partially obsolete alternative for **memmove**, derived from BSD. Note that it is not quite equivalent to **memmove**, because the arguments are not in the same order and there is no return value.

void **bzero** (*void *block, size_t size*)   [Function]
> Preliminary: | MT-Safe | AS-Safe | AC-Safe | See Section 1.2.2.1 [POSIX Safety Concepts], page 2.

> This is a partially obsolete alternative for **memset**, derived from BSD. Note that it is not as general as **memset**, because the only value it can store is zero.

5.5 String/Array Comparison

You can use the functions in this section to perform comparisons on the contents of strings and arrays. As well as checking for equality, these functions can also be used as the ordering functions for sorting operations. See Chapter 9 [Searching and Sorting], page 212, for an example of this.

Unlike most comparison operations in C, the string comparison functions return a nonzero value if the strings are *not* equivalent rather than if they are. The sign of the value indicates the relative ordering of the first characters in the strings that are not equivalent: a negative value indicates that the first string is "less" than the second, while a positive value indicates that the first string is "greater".

The most common use of these functions is to check only for equality. This is canonically done with an expression like '! strcmp (s1, s2)'.

All of these functions are declared in the header file **string.h**.

int **memcmp** (*const void *a1, const void *a2, size_t size*)   [Function]
> Preliminary: | MT-Safe | AS-Safe | AC-Safe | See Section 1.2.2.1 [POSIX Safety Concepts], page 2.

> The function **memcmp** compares the *size* bytes of memory beginning at *a1* against the *size* bytes of memory beginning at *a2*. The value returned has the same sign as the difference between the first differing pair of bytes (interpreted as **unsigned char** objects, then promoted to **int**).

> If the contents of the two blocks are equal, **memcmp** returns 0.

int wmemcmp (const wchar_t *a1, const wchar_t *a2, size_t size)   [Function]
    Preliminary: | MT-Safe | AS-Safe | AC-Safe | See Section 1.2.2.1 [POSIX Safety
    Concepts], page 2.

    The function wmemcmp compares the size wide characters beginning at a1 against the
    size wide characters beginning at a2. The value returned is smaller than or larger
    than zero depending on whether the first differing wide character is a1 is smaller or
    larger than the corresponding character in a2.

    If the contents of the two blocks are equal, wmemcmp returns 0.

On arbitrary arrays, the memcmp function is mostly useful for testing equality. It usually
isn't meaningful to do byte-wise ordering comparisons on arrays of things other than bytes.
For example, a byte-wise comparison on the bytes that make up floating-point numbers isn't
likely to tell you anything about the relationship between the values of the floating-point
numbers.

wmemcmp is really only useful to compare arrays of type wchar_t since the function looks
at sizeof (wchar_t) bytes at a time and this number of bytes is system dependent.

You should also be careful about using memcmp to compare objects that can contain
"holes", such as the padding inserted into structure objects to enforce alignment requirements, extra space at the end of unions, and extra characters at the ends of strings whose
length is less than their allocated size. The contents of these "holes" are indeterminate and
may cause strange behavior when performing byte-wise comparisons. For more predictable
results, perform an explicit component-wise comparison.

For example, given a structure type definition like:

```
struct foo
  {
    unsigned char tag;
    union
      {
        double f;
        long i;
        char *p;
      } value;
  };
```

you are better off writing a specialized comparison function to compare struct foo objects
instead of comparing them with memcmp.

int strcmp (const char *s1, const char *s2)   [Function]
    Preliminary: | MT-Safe | AS-Safe | AC-Safe | See Section 1.2.2.1 [POSIX Safety
    Concepts], page 2.

    The strcmp function compares the string s1 against s2, returning a value that has the
    same sign as the difference between the first differing pair of characters (interpreted
    as unsigned char objects, then promoted to int).

    If the two strings are equal, strcmp returns 0.

    A consequence of the ordering used by strcmp is that if s1 is an initial substring of
    s2, then s1 is considered to be "less than" s2.

    strcmp does not take sorting conventions of the language the strings are written in
    into account. To get that one has to use strcoll.

int **wcscmp** (*const wchar_t *ws1, const wchar_t *ws2*)   [Function]
: Preliminary: | MT-Safe | AS-Safe | AC-Safe | See Section 1.2.2.1 [POSIX Safety Concepts], page 2.

    The **wcscmp** function compares the wide character string *ws1* against *ws2*. The value returned is smaller than or larger than zero depending on whether the first differing wide character is *ws1* is smaller or larger than the corresponding character in *ws2*.

    If the two strings are equal, **wcscmp** returns 0.

    A consequence of the ordering used by **wcscmp** is that if *ws1* is an initial substring of *ws2*, then *ws1* is considered to be "less than" *ws2*.

    wcscmp does not take sorting conventions of the language the strings are written in into account. To get that one has to use **wcscoll**.

int **strcasecmp** (*const char *s1, const char *s2*)   [Function]
: Preliminary: | MT-Safe locale | AS-Safe | AC-Safe | See Section 1.2.2.1 [POSIX Safety Concepts], page 2.

    This function is like **strcmp**, except that differences in case are ignored. How uppercase and lowercase characters are related is determined by the currently selected locale. In the standard "C" locale the characters Ä and ä do not match but in a locale which regards these characters as parts of the alphabet they do match.

    strcasecmp is derived from BSD.

int **wcscasecmp** (*const wchar_t *ws1, const wchar_t *ws2*)   [Function]
: Preliminary: | MT-Safe locale | AS-Safe | AC-Safe | See Section 1.2.2.1 [POSIX Safety Concepts], page 2.

    This function is like **wcscmp**, except that differences in case are ignored. How uppercase and lowercase characters are related is determined by the currently selected locale. In the standard "C" locale the characters Ä and ä do not match but in a locale which regards these characters as parts of the alphabet they do match.

    wcscasecmp is a GNU extension.

int **strncmp** (*const char *s1, const char *s2, size_t size*)   [Function]
: Preliminary: | MT-Safe | AS-Safe | AC-Safe | See Section 1.2.2.1 [POSIX Safety Concepts], page 2.

    This function is the similar to **strcmp**, except that no more than *size* characters are compared. In other words, if the two strings are the same in their first *size* characters, the return value is zero.

int **wcsncmp** (*const wchar_t *ws1, const wchar_t *ws2, size_t size*)   [Function]
: Preliminary: | MT-Safe | AS-Safe | AC-Safe | See Section 1.2.2.1 [POSIX Safety Concepts], page 2.

    This function is the similar to **wcscmp**, except that no more than *size* wide characters are compared. In other words, if the two strings are the same in their first *size* wide characters, the return value is zero.

int **strncasecmp** (*const char *s1, const char *s2, size_t n*)   [Function]
: Preliminary: | MT-Safe locale | AS-Safe | AC-Safe | See Section 1.2.2.1 [POSIX Safety Concepts], page 2.

This function is like `strncmp`, except that differences in case are ignored. Like `strcasecmp`, it is locale dependent how uppercase and lowercase characters are related.

`strncasecmp` is a GNU extension.

int **wcsncasecmp** (*const wchar_t *ws1, const wchar_t *s2, size_t n*)   [Function]
Preliminary: | MT-Safe locale | AS-Safe | AC-Safe | See Section 1.2.2.1 [POSIX Safety Concepts], page 2.

This function is like `wcsncmp`, except that differences in case are ignored. Like `wcscasecmp`, it is locale dependent how uppercase and lowercase characters are related.

`wcsncasecmp` is a GNU extension.

Here are some examples showing the use of `strcmp` and `strncmp` (equivalent examples can be constructed for the wide character functions). These examples assume the use of the ASCII character set. (If some other character set—say, EBCDIC—is used instead, then the glyphs are associated with different numeric codes, and the return values and ordering may differ.)

```
strcmp ("hello", "hello")
    ⇒ 0    /* These two strings are the same. */
strcmp ("hello", "Hello")
    ⇒ 32    /* Comparisons are case-sensitive. */
strcmp ("hello", "world")
    ⇒ -15   /* The character 'h' comes before 'w'. */
strcmp ("hello", "hello, world")
    ⇒ -44   /* Comparing a null character against a comma. */
strncmp ("hello", "hello, world", 5)
    ⇒ 0    /* The initial 5 characters are the same. */
strncmp ("hello, world", "hello, stupid world!!!", 5)
    ⇒ 0    /* The initial 5 characters are the same. */
```

int **strverscmp** (*const char *s1, const char *s2*)   [Function]
Preliminary: | MT-Safe locale | AS-Safe | AC-Safe | See Section 1.2.2.1 [POSIX Safety Concepts], page 2.

The `strverscmp` function compares the string *s1* against *s2*, considering them as holding indices/version numbers. The return value follows the same conventions as found in the `strcmp` function. In fact, if *s1* and *s2* contain no digits, `strverscmp` behaves like `strcmp`.

Basically, we compare strings normally (character by character), until we find a digit in each string - then we enter a special comparison mode, where each sequence of digits is taken as a whole. If we reach the end of these two parts without noticing a difference, we return to the standard comparison mode. There are two types of numeric parts: "integral" and "fractional" (those begin with a '0'). The types of the numeric parts affect the way we sort them:

- integral/integral: we compare values as you would expect.

- fractional/integral: the fractional part is less than the integral one. Again, no surprise.

- fractional/fractional: the things become a bit more complex. If the common prefix contains only leading zeroes, the longest part is less than the other one; else the comparison behaves normally.

```
strverscmp ("no digit", "no digit")
    ⇒ 0     /* same behavior as strcmp. */
strverscmp ("item#99", "item#100")
    ⇒ <0    /* same prefix, but 99 < 100. */
strverscmp ("alpha1", "alpha001")
    ⇒ >0    /* fractional part inferior to integral one. */
strverscmp ("part1_f012", "part1_f01")
    ⇒ >0    /* two fractional parts. */
strverscmp ("foo.009", "foo.0")
    ⇒ <0    /* idem, but with leading zeroes only. */
```

This function is especially useful when dealing with filename sorting, because filenames frequently hold indices/version numbers.

`strverscmp` is a GNU extension.

int bcmp (*const void *a1, const void *a2, size_t size*)   [Function]
   Preliminary: | MT-Safe | AS-Safe | AC-Safe | See Section 1.2.2.1 [POSIX Safety Concepts], page 2.

   This is an obsolete alias for `memcmp`, derived from BSD.

5.6 Collation Functions

In some locales, the conventions for lexicographic ordering differ from the strict numeric ordering of character codes. For example, in Spanish most glyphs with diacritical marks such as accents are not considered distinct letters for the purposes of collation. On the other hand, the two-character sequence 'll' is treated as a single letter that is collated immediately after 'l'.

You can use the functions `strcoll` and `strxfrm` (declared in the headers file `string.h`) and `wcscoll` and `wcsxfrm` (declared in the headers file `wchar`) to compare strings using a collation ordering appropriate for the current locale. The locale used by these functions in particular can be specified by setting the locale for the `LC_COLLATE` category; see Chapter 7 [Locales and Internationalization], page 169.

In the standard C locale, the collation sequence for `strcoll` is the same as that for `strcmp`. Similarly, `wcscoll` and `wcscmp` are the same in this situation.

Effectively, the way these functions work is by applying a mapping to transform the characters in a string to a byte sequence that represents the string's position in the collating sequence of the current locale. Comparing two such byte sequences in a simple fashion is equivalent to comparing the strings with the locale's collating sequence.

The functions `strcoll` and `wcscoll` perform this translation implicitly, in order to do one comparison. By contrast, `strxfrm` and `wcsxfrm` perform the mapping explicitly. If you are making multiple comparisons using the same string or set of strings, it is likely to be more efficient to use `strxfrm` or `wcsxfrm` to transform all the strings just once, and subsequently compare the transformed strings with `strcmp` or `wcscmp`.

int strcoll (*const char *s1, const char *s2*)   [Function]
   Preliminary: | MT-Safe locale | AS-Unsafe heap | AC-Unsafe mem | See Section 1.2.2.1 [POSIX Safety Concepts], page 2.

The `strcoll` function is similar to `strcmp` but uses the collating sequence of the current locale for collation (the `LC_COLLATE` locale).

`int wcscoll` (*const wchar_t *ws1, const wchar_t *ws2*)   [Function]
   Preliminary: | MT-Safe locale | AS-Unsafe heap | AC-Unsafe mem | See
   Section 1.2.2.1 [POSIX Safety Concepts], page 2.

   The `wcscoll` function is similar to `wcscmp` but uses the collating sequence of the current locale for collation (the `LC_COLLATE` locale).

Here is an example of sorting an array of strings, using `strcoll` to compare them. The actual sort algorithm is not written here; it comes from `qsort` (see Section 9.3 [Array Sort Function], page 213). The job of the code shown here is to say how to compare the strings while sorting them. (Later on in this section, we will show a way to do this more efficiently using `strxfrm`.)

```
/* This is the comparison function used with qsort. */

int
compare_elements (const void *v1, const void *v2)
{
  char * const *p1 = v1;
  char * const *p2 = v2;

  return strcoll (*p1, *p2);
}

/* This is the entry point—the function to sort
   strings using the locale's collating sequence. */

void
sort_strings (char **array, int nstrings)
{
  /* Sort temp_array by comparing the strings. */
  qsort (array, nstrings,
         sizeof (char *), compare_elements);
}
```

`size_t strxfrm` (*char *restrict to, const char *restrict from, size_t*   [Function]
     size)
   Preliminary: | MT-Safe locale | AS-Unsafe heap | AC-Unsafe mem | See
   Section 1.2.2.1 [POSIX Safety Concepts], page 2.

   The function `strxfrm` transforms the string *from* using the collation transformation determined by the locale currently selected for collation, and stores the transformed string in the array *to*. Up to *size* characters (including a terminating null character) are stored.

   The behavior is undefined if the strings *to* and *from* overlap; see Section 5.4 [Copying and Concatenation], page 91.

   The return value is the length of the entire transformed string. This value is not affected by the value of *size*, but if it is greater or equal than *size*, it means that the transformed string did not entirely fit in the array *to*. In this case, only as much of the string as actually fits was stored. To get the whole transformed string, call `strxfrm` again with a bigger output array.

The transformed string may be longer than the original string, and it may also be shorter.

If *size* is zero, no characters are stored in *to*. In this case, `strxfrm` simply returns the number of characters that would be the length of the transformed string. This is useful for determining what size the allocated array should be. It does not matter what *to* is if *size* is zero; *to* may even be a null pointer.

`size_t` **wcsxfrm** (*wchar_t* *restrict **wto**, *const wchar_t* ***wfrom**, *size_t*   [Function]
    size)

Preliminary: | MT-Safe locale | AS-Unsafe heap | AC-Unsafe mem | See Section 1.2.2.1 [POSIX Safety Concepts], page 2.

The function `wcsxfrm` transforms wide character string *wfrom* using the collation transformation determined by the locale currently selected for collation, and stores the transformed string in the array *wto*. Up to *size* wide characters (including a terminating null character) are stored.

The behavior is undefined if the strings *wto* and *wfrom* overlap; see Section 5.4 [Copying and Concatenation], page 91.

The return value is the length of the entire transformed wide character string. This value is not affected by the value of *size*, but if it is greater or equal than *size*, it means that the transformed wide character string did not entirely fit in the array *wto*. In this case, only as much of the wide character string as actually fits was stored. To get the whole transformed wide character string, call `wcsxfrm` again with a bigger output array.

The transformed wide character string may be longer than the original wide character string, and it may also be shorter.

If *size* is zero, no characters are stored in *to*. In this case, `wcsxfrm` simply returns the number of wide characters that would be the length of the transformed wide character string. This is useful for determining what size the allocated array should be (remember to multiply with `sizeof (wchar_t)`). It does not matter what *wto* is if *size* is zero; *wto* may even be a null pointer.

Here is an example of how you can use `strxfrm` when you plan to do many comparisons. It does the same thing as the previous example, but much faster, because it has to transform each string only once, no matter how many times it is compared with other strings. Even the time needed to allocate and free storage is much less than the time we save, when there are many strings.

```
struct sorter { char *input; char *transformed; };

/* This is the comparison function used with qsort
   to sort an array of struct sorter. */

int
compare_elements (const void *v1, const void *v2)
{
  const struct sorter *p1 = v1;
  const struct sorter *p2 = v2;

  return strcmp (p1->transformed, p2->transformed);
}
```

```
/* This is the entry point—the function to sort
   strings using the locale's collating sequence. */

void
sort_strings_fast (char **array, int nstrings)
{
  struct sorter temp_array[nstrings];
  int i;

  /* Set up temp_array.  Each element contains
     one input string and its transformed string. */
  for (i = 0; i < nstrings; i++)
    {
      size_t length = strlen (array[i]) * 2;
      char *transformed;
      size_t transformed_length;

      temp_array[i].input = array[i];

      /* First try a buffer perhaps big enough.  */
      transformed = (char *) xmalloc (length);

      /* Transform array[i].  */
      transformed_length = strxfrm (transformed, array[i], length);

      /* If the buffer was not large enough, resize it
         and try again.  */
      if (transformed_length >= length)
        {
          /* Allocate the needed space. +1 for terminating
             NUL character.  */
          transformed = (char *) xrealloc (transformed,
                                           transformed_length + 1);

          /* The return value is not interesting because we know
             how long the transformed string is.  */
          (void) strxfrm (transformed, array[i],
                          transformed_length + 1);
        }

      temp_array[i].transformed = transformed;
    }

  /* Sort temp_array by comparing transformed strings. */
  qsort (temp_array, nstrings,
         sizeof (struct sorter), compare_elements);

  /* Put the elements back in the permanent array
     in their sorted order. */
  for (i = 0; i < nstrings; i++)
    array[i] = temp_array[i].input;

  /* Free the strings we allocated. */
  for (i = 0; i < nstrings; i++)
    free (temp_array[i].transformed);
}
```

The interesting part of this code for the wide character version would look like this:

```
      void
      sort_strings_fast (wchar_t **array, int nstrings)
      {
        ...
            /* Transform array[i]. */
            transformed_length = wcsxfrm (transformed, array[i], length);

            /* If the buffer was not large enough, resize it
               and try again.  */
            if (transformed_length >= length)
              {
                /* Allocate the needed space. +1 for terminating
                   NUL character.  */
                transformed = (wchar_t *) xrealloc (transformed,
                                                    (transformed_length + 1)
                                                    * sizeof (wchar_t));

                /* The return value is not interesting because we know
                   how long the transformed string is.  */
                (void) wcsxfrm (transformed, array[i],
                                transformed_length + 1);
              }
        ...
```

Note the additional multiplication with `sizeof (wchar_t)` in the `realloc` call.

Compatibility Note: The string collation functions are a new feature of ISO C90. Older C dialects have no equivalent feature. The wide character versions were introduced in Amendment 1 to ISO C90.

5.7 Search Functions

This section describes library functions which perform various kinds of searching operations on strings and arrays. These functions are declared in the header file `string.h`.

void * memchr (*const void *block, int c, size_t size*)   [Function]
> Preliminary: | MT-Safe | AS-Safe | AC-Safe | See Section 1.2.2.1 [POSIX Safety Concepts], page 2.
>
> This function finds the first occurrence of the byte *c* (converted to an `unsigned char`) in the initial *size* bytes of the object beginning at *block*. The return value is a pointer to the located byte, or a null pointer if no match was found.

wchar_t * wmemchr (*const wchar_t *block, wchar_t wc, size_t size*)   [Function]
> Preliminary: | MT-Safe | AS-Safe | AC-Safe | See Section 1.2.2.1 [POSIX Safety Concepts], page 2.
>
> This function finds the first occurrence of the wide character *wc* in the initial *size* wide characters of the object beginning at *block*. The return value is a pointer to the located wide character, or a null pointer if no match was found.

void * rawmemchr (*const void *block, int c*)   [Function]
> Preliminary: | MT-Safe | AS-Safe | AC-Safe | See Section 1.2.2.1 [POSIX Safety Concepts], page 2.
>
> Often the `memchr` function is used with the knowledge that the byte *c* is available in the memory block specified by the parameters. But this means that the *size* parameter

is not really needed and that the tests performed with it at runtime (to check whether the end of the block is reached) are not needed.

The `rawmemchr` function exists for just this situation which is surprisingly frequent. The interface is similar to `memchr` except that the *size* parameter is missing. The function will look beyond the end of the block pointed to by *block* in case the programmer made an error in assuming that the byte *c* is present in the block. In this case the result is unspecified. Otherwise the return value is a pointer to the located byte.

This function is of special interest when looking for the end of a string. Since all strings are terminated by a null byte a call like

```
rawmemchr (str, '\0')
```

will never go beyond the end of the string.

This function is a GNU extension.

---

void * memrchr (*const void *block, int c, size_t size*)   [Function]
Preliminary: | MT-Safe | AS-Safe | AC-Safe | See Section 1.2.2.1 [POSIX Safety Concepts], page 2.

The function `memrchr` is like `memchr`, except that it searches backwards from the end of the block defined by *block* and *size* (instead of forwards from the front).

This function is a GNU extension.

---

char * strchr (*const char *string, int c*)   [Function]
Preliminary: | MT-Safe | AS-Safe | AC-Safe | See Section 1.2.2.1 [POSIX Safety Concepts], page 2.

The `strchr` function finds the first occurrence of the character *c* (converted to a `char`) in the null-terminated string beginning at *string*. The return value is a pointer to the located character, or a null pointer if no match was found.

For example,

```
strchr ("hello, world", 'l')
    ⇒ "llo, world"
strchr ("hello, world", '?')
    ⇒ NULL
```

The terminating null character is considered to be part of the string, so you can use this function get a pointer to the end of a string by specifying a null character as the value of the *c* argument.

When `strchr` returns a null pointer, it does not let you know the position of the terminating null character it has found. If you need that information, it is better (but less portable) to use `strchrnul` than to search for it a second time.

---

wchar_t * wcschr (*const wchar_t *wstring, int wc*)   [Function]
Preliminary: | MT-Safe | AS-Safe | AC-Safe | See Section 1.2.2.1 [POSIX Safety Concepts], page 2.

The `wcschr` function finds the first occurrence of the wide character *wc* in the null-terminated wide character string beginning at *wstring*. The return value is a pointer to the located wide character, or a null pointer if no match was found.

The terminating null character is considered to be part of the wide character string, so you can use this function get a pointer to the end of a wide character string by specifying a null wude character as the value of the *wc* argument. It would be better (but less portable) to use `wcschrnul` in this case, though.

char * strchrnul (*const char *string*, *int c*)   [Function]
> Preliminary: | MT-Safe | AS-Safe | AC-Safe | See Section 1.2.2.1 [POSIX Safety Concepts], page 2.
>
> `strchrnul` is the same as `strchr` except that if it does not find the character, it returns a pointer to string's terminating null character rather than a null pointer.
>
> This function is a GNU extension.

wchar_t * wcschrnul (*const wchar_t *wstring*, *wchar_t wc*)   [Function]
> Preliminary: | MT-Safe | AS-Safe | AC-Safe | See Section 1.2.2.1 [POSIX Safety Concepts], page 2.
>
> `wcschrnul` is the same as `wcschr` except that if it does not find the wide character, it returns a pointer to wide character string's terminating null wide character rather than a null pointer.
>
> This function is a GNU extension.

One useful, but unusual, use of the `strchr` function is when one wants to have a pointer pointing to the NUL byte terminating a string. This is often written in this way:

```
s += strlen (s);
```

This is almost optimal but the addition operation duplicated a bit of the work already done in the `strlen` function. A better solution is this:

```
s = strchr (s, '\0');
```

There is no restriction on the second parameter of `strchr` so it could very well also be the NUL character. Those readers thinking very hard about this might now point out that the `strchr` function is more expensive than the `strlen` function since we have two abort criteria. This is right. But in the GNU C Library the implementation of `strchr` is optimized in a special way so that `strchr` actually is faster.

char * strrchr (*const char *string*, *int c*)   [Function]
> Preliminary: | MT-Safe | AS-Safe | AC-Safe | See Section 1.2.2.1 [POSIX Safety Concepts], page 2.
>
> The function `strrchr` is like `strchr`, except that it searches backwards from the end of the string *string* (instead of forwards from the front).
>
> For example,
> ```
> strrchr ("hello, world", 'l')
>     ⇒ "ld"
> ```

wchar_t * wcsrchr (*const wchar_t *wstring*, *wchar_t c*)   [Function]
> Preliminary: | MT-Safe | AS-Safe | AC-Safe | See Section 1.2.2.1 [POSIX Safety Concepts], page 2.
>
> The function `wcsrchr` is like `wcschr`, except that it searches backwards from the end of the string *wstring* (instead of forwards from the front).

char * **strstr** (*const char* ***haystack**, *const char* ***needle**)   [Function]
  Preliminary: | MT-Safe | AS-Safe | AC-Safe | See Section 1.2.2.1 [POSIX Safety Concepts], page 2.

  This is like **strchr**, except that it searches *haystack* for a substring *needle* rather than just a single character. It returns a pointer into the string *haystack* that is the first character of the substring, or a null pointer if no match was found. If *needle* is an empty string, the function returns *haystack*.

  For example,
```
strstr ("hello, world", "l")
    ⇒ "llo, world"
strstr ("hello, world", "wo")
    ⇒ "world"
```

wchar_t * **wcsstr** (*const wchar_t* ***haystack**, *const wchar_t* ***needle**)   [Function]
  Preliminary: | MT-Safe | AS-Safe | AC-Safe | See Section 1.2.2.1 [POSIX Safety Concepts], page 2.

  This is like **wcschr**, except that it searches *haystack* for a substring *needle* rather than just a single wide character. It returns a pointer into the string *haystack* that is the first wide character of the substring, or a null pointer if no match was found. If *needle* is an empty string, the function returns *haystack*.

wchar_t * **wcswcs** (*const wchar_t* ***haystack**, *const wchar_t* ***needle**)   [Function]
  Preliminary: | MT-Safe | AS-Safe | AC-Safe | See Section 1.2.2.1 [POSIX Safety Concepts], page 2.

  wcswcs is a deprecated alias for **wcsstr**. This is the name originally used in the X/Open Portability Guide before the Amendment 1 to ISO C90 was published.

char * **strcasestr** (*const char* ***haystack**, *const char* ***needle**)   [Function]
  Preliminary: | MT-Safe locale | AS-Safe | AC-Safe | See Section 1.2.2.1 [POSIX Safety Concepts], page 2.

  This is like **strstr**, except that it ignores case in searching for the substring. Like **strcasecmp**, it is locale dependent how uppercase and lowercase characters are related.

  For example,
```
strcasestr ("hello, world", "L")
    ⇒ "llo, world"
strcasestr ("hello, World", "wo")
    ⇒ "World"
```

void * **memmem** (*const void* ***haystack**, *size_t* **haystack-len**,   [Function]
      const void ***needle**, *size_t* **needle-len**)
  Preliminary: | MT-Safe | AS-Safe | AC-Safe | See Section 1.2.2.1 [POSIX Safety Concepts], page 2.

  This is like **strstr**, but *needle* and *haystack* are byte arrays rather than null-terminated strings. *needle-len* is the length of *needle* and *haystack-len* is the length of *haystack*.

  This function is a GNU extension.

size_t strspn (*const char ***string**, *const char ***skipset**)   [Function]
Preliminary: | MT-Safe | AS-Safe | AC-Safe | See Section 1.2.2.1 [POSIX Safety Concepts], page 2.

The **strspn** ("string span") function returns the length of the initial substring of *string* that consists entirely of characters that are members of the set specified by the string *skipset*. The order of the characters in *skipset* is not important.

For example,

```
strspn ("hello, world", "abcdefghijklmnopqrstuvwxyz")
    ⇒ 5
```

Note that "character" is here used in the sense of byte. In a string using a multibyte character encoding (abstract) character consisting of more than one byte are not treated as an entity. Each byte is treated separately. The function is not locale-dependent.

size_t wcsspn (*const wchar_t ***wstring**, *const wchar_t ***skipset**)   [Function]
Preliminary: | MT-Safe | AS-Safe | AC-Safe | See Section 1.2.2.1 [POSIX Safety Concepts], page 2.

The **wcsspn** ("wide character string span") function returns the length of the initial substring of *wstring* that consists entirely of wide characters that are members of the set specified by the string *skipset*. The order of the wide characters in *skipset* is not important.

size_t strcspn (*const char ***string**, *const char ***stopset**)   [Function]
Preliminary: | MT-Safe | AS-Safe | AC-Safe | See Section 1.2.2.1 [POSIX Safety Concepts], page 2.

The **strcspn** ("string complement span") function returns the length of the initial substring of *string* that consists entirely of characters that are *not* members of the set specified by the string *stopset*. (In other words, it returns the offset of the first character in *string* that is a member of the set *stopset*.)

For example,

```
strcspn ("hello, world", " \t\n,.;!?")
    ⇒ 5
```

Note that "character" is here used in the sense of byte. In a string using a multibyte character encoding (abstract) character consisting of more than one byte are not treated as an entity. Each byte is treated separately. The function is not locale-dependent.

size_t wcscspn (*const wchar_t ***wstring**, *const wchar_t ***stopset**)   [Function]
Preliminary: | MT-Safe | AS-Safe | AC-Safe | See Section 1.2.2.1 [POSIX Safety Concepts], page 2.

The **wcscspn** ("wide character string complement span") function returns the length of the initial substring of *wstring* that consists entirely of wide characters that are *not* members of the set specified by the string *stopset*. (In other words, it returns the offset of the first character in *string* that is a member of the set *stopset*.)

char * strpbrk (*const char *string, const char *stopset*)   [Function]
> Preliminary: | MT-Safe | AS-Safe | AC-Safe | See Section 1.2.2.1 [POSIX Safety Concepts], page 2.
>
> The strpbrk ("string pointer break") function is related to strcspn, except that it returns a pointer to the first character in *string* that is a member of the set *stopset* instead of the length of the initial substring. It returns a null pointer if no such character from *stopset* is found.
>
> For example,
>
>   strpbrk ("hello, world", " \t\n,.;!?")
>   ⇒ ", world"
>
> Note that "character" is here used in the sense of byte. In a string using a multibyte character encoding (abstract) character consisting of more than one byte are not treated as an entity. Each byte is treated separately. The function is not locale-dependent.

wchar_t * wcspbrk (*const wchar_t *wstring, const wchar_t *stopset*)   [Function]
> Preliminary: | MT-Safe | AS-Safe | AC-Safe | See Section 1.2.2.1 [POSIX Safety Concepts], page 2.
>
> The wcspbrk ("wide character string pointer break") function is related to wcscspn, except that it returns a pointer to the first wide character in *wstring* that is a member of the set *stopset* instead of the length of the initial substring. It returns a null pointer if no such character from *stopset* is found.

5.7.1 Compatibility String Search Functions

char * index (*const char *string, int c*)   [Function]
> Preliminary: | MT-Safe | AS-Safe | AC-Safe | See Section 1.2.2.1 [POSIX Safety Concepts], page 2.
>
> index is another name for strchr; they are exactly the same. New code should always use strchr since this name is defined in ISO C while index is a BSD invention which never was available on System V derived systems.

char * rindex (*const char *string, int c*)   [Function]
> Preliminary: | MT-Safe | AS-Safe | AC-Safe | See Section 1.2.2.1 [POSIX Safety Concepts], page 2.
>
> rindex is another name for strrchr; they are exactly the same. New code should always use strrchr since this name is defined in ISO C while rindex is a BSD invention which never was available on System V derived systems.

5.8 Finding Tokens in a String

It's fairly common for programs to have a need to do some simple kinds of lexical analysis and parsing, such as splitting a command string up into tokens. You can do this with the strtok function, declared in the header file string.h.

char * strtok (*char *restrict newstring, const char *restrict*   [Function]
> *delimiters*)
>
> Preliminary: | MT-Unsafe race:strtok | AS-Unsafe | AC-Safe | See Section 1.2.2.1 [POSIX Safety Concepts], page 2.

A string can be split into tokens by making a series of calls to the function `strtok`.

The string to be split up is passed as the *newstring* argument on the first call only. The `strtok` function uses this to set up some internal state information. Subsequent calls to get additional tokens from the same string are indicated by passing a null pointer as the *newstring* argument. Calling `strtok` with another non-null *newstring* argument reinitializes the state information. It is guaranteed that no other library function ever calls `strtok` behind your back (which would mess up this internal state information).

The *delimiters* argument is a string that specifies a set of delimiters that may surround the token being extracted. All the initial characters that are members of this set are discarded. The first character that is *not* a member of this set of delimiters marks the beginning of the next token. The end of the token is found by looking for the next character that is a member of the delimiter set. This character in the original string *newstring* is overwritten by a null character, and the pointer to the beginning of the token in *newstring* is returned.

On the next call to `strtok`, the searching begins at the next character beyond the one that marked the end of the previous token. Note that the set of delimiters *delimiters* do not have to be the same on every call in a series of calls to `strtok`.

If the end of the string *newstring* is reached, or if the remainder of string consists only of delimiter characters, `strtok` returns a null pointer.

Note that "character" is here used in the sense of byte. In a string using a multibyte character encoding (abstract) character consisting of more than one byte are not treated as an entity. Each byte is treated separately. The function is not locale-dependent.

wchar_t * wcstok (*wchar_t *newstring*, *const wchar_t *delimiters*,   [Function]
    wchar_t **save_ptr)
Preliminary: | MT-Safe | AS-Safe | AC-Safe | See Section 1.2.2.1 [POSIX Safety Concepts], page 2.

A string can be split into tokens by making a series of calls to the function `wcstok`.

The string to be split up is passed as the *newstring* argument on the first call only. The `wcstok` function uses this to set up some internal state information. Subsequent calls to get additional tokens from the same wide character string are indicated by passing a null pointer as the *newstring* argument, which causes the pointer previously stored in *save_ptr* to be used instead.

The *delimiters* argument is a wide character string that specifies a set of delimiters that may surround the token being extracted. All the initial wide characters that are members of this set are discarded. The first wide character that is *not* a member of this set of delimiters marks the beginning of the next token. The end of the token is found by looking for the next wide character that is a member of the delimiter set. This wide character in the original wide character string *newstring* is overwritten by a null wide character, the pointer past the overwritten wide character is saved in *save_ptr*, and the pointer to the beginning of the token in *newstring* is returned.

On the next call to `wcstok`, the searching begins at the next wide character beyond the one that marked the end of the previous token. Note that the set of delimiters *delimiters* do not have to be the same on every call in a series of calls to `wcstok`.

If the end of the wide character string *newstring* is reached, or if the remainder of string consists only of delimiter wide characters, wcstok returns a null pointer.

Warning: Since strtok and wcstok alter the string they is parsing, you should always copy the string to a temporary buffer before parsing it with strtok/wcstok (see Section 5.4 [Copying and Concatenation], page 91). If you allow strtok or wcstok to modify a string that came from another part of your program, you are asking for trouble; that string might be used for other purposes after strtok or wcstok has modified it, and it would not have the expected value.

The string that you are operating on might even be a constant. Then when strtok or wcstok tries to modify it, your program will get a fatal signal for writing in read-only memory. See Section 24.2.1 [Program Error Signals], page 663. Even if the operation of strtok or wcstok would not require a modification of the string (e.g., if there is exactly one token) the string can (and in the GNU C Library case will) be modified.

This is a special case of a general principle: if a part of a program does not have as its purpose the modification of a certain data structure, then it is error-prone to modify the data structure temporarily.

The function strtok is not reentrant, whereas wcstok is. See Section 24.4.6 [Signal Handling and Nonreentrant Functions], page 684, for a discussion of where and why reentrancy is important.

Here is a simple example showing the use of strtok.

```
#include <string.h>
#include <stddef.h>

...

const char string[] = "words separated by spaces -- and, punctuation!";
const char delimiters[] = " .,;:!-";
char *token, *cp;

...

cp = strdupa (string);          /* Make writable copy.  */
token = strtok (cp, delimiters);     /* token => "words" */
token = strtok (NULL, delimiters);   /* token => "separated" */
token = strtok (NULL, delimiters);   /* token => "by" */
token = strtok (NULL, delimiters);   /* token => "spaces" */
token = strtok (NULL, delimiters);   /* token => "and" */
token = strtok (NULL, delimiters);   /* token => "punctuation" */
token = strtok (NULL, delimiters);   /* token => NULL */
```

The GNU C Library contains two more functions for tokenizing a string which overcome the limitation of non-reentrancy. They are only available for multibyte character strings.

char * strtok_r (*char *newstring*, *const char *delimiters*, *char*   [Function]
    ***save_ptr*)
Preliminary: | MT-Safe | AS-Safe | AC-Safe | See Section 1.2.2.1 [POSIX Safety Concepts], page 2.

Just like strtok, this function splits the string into several tokens which can be accessed by successive calls to strtok_r. The difference is that, as in wcstok, the information about the next token is stored in the space pointed to by the third argument, *save_ptr*, which is a pointer to a string pointer. Calling `strtok_r` with a null pointer for *newstring* and leaving *save_ptr* between the calls unchanged does the job without hindering reentrancy.

This function is defined in POSIX.1 and can be found on many systems which support multi-threading.

char * strsep (*char **string_ptr, const char *delimiter*)   [Function]
Preliminary: | MT-Safe | AS-Safe | AC-Safe | See Section 1.2.2.1 [POSIX Safety Concepts], page 2.

This function has a similar functionality as `strtok_r` with the *newstring* argument replaced by the *save_ptr* argument. The initialization of the moving pointer has to be done by the user. Successive calls to `strsep` move the pointer along the tokens separated by *delimiter*, returning the address of the next token and updating *string_ptr* to point to the beginning of the next token.

One difference between `strsep` and `strtok_r` is that if the input string contains more than one character from *delimiter* in a row `strsep` returns an empty string for each pair of characters from *delimiter*. This means that a program normally should test for `strsep` returning an empty string before processing it.

This function was introduced in 4.3BSD and therefore is widely available.

Here is how the above example looks like when `strsep` is used.

```
#include <string.h>
#include <stddef.h>

...

const char string[] = "words separated by spaces -- and, punctuation!";
const char delimiters[] = " .,;:!-";
char *running;
char *token;

...

running = strdupa (string);
token = strsep (&running, delimiters);    /* token => "words" */
token = strsep (&running, delimiters);    /* token => "separated" */
token = strsep (&running, delimiters);    /* token => "by" */
token = strsep (&running, delimiters);    /* token => "spaces" */
token = strsep (&running, delimiters);    /* token => "" */
token = strsep (&running, delimiters);    /* token => "" */
token = strsep (&running, delimiters);    /* token => "" */
token = strsep (&running, delimiters);    /* token => "and" */
token = strsep (&running, delimiters);    /* token => "" */
token = strsep (&running, delimiters);    /* token => "punctuation" */
token = strsep (&running, delimiters);    /* token => "" */
token = strsep (&running, delimiters);    /* token => NULL */
```

char * basename (*const char *filename*)   [Function]
Preliminary: | MT-Safe | AS-Safe | AC-Safe | See Section 1.2.2.1 [POSIX Safety Concepts], page 2.

The GNU version of the `basename` function returns the last component of the path in *filename*. This function is the preferred usage, since it does not modify the argument, *filename*, and respects trailing slashes. The prototype for `basename` can be found in `string.h`. Note, this function is overriden by the XPG version, if `libgen.h` is included.

Example of using GNU `basename`:

```
#include <string.h>

int
main (int argc, char *argv[])
{
  char *prog = basename (argv[0]);

  if (argc < 2)
    {
      fprintf (stderr, "Usage %s <arg>\n", prog);
      exit (1);
    }

  ...
}
```

Portability Note: This function may produce different results on different systems.

`char * basename (char *path)`   [Function]
    Preliminary: | MT-Safe | AS-Safe | AC-Safe | See Section 1.2.2.1 [POSIX Safety Concepts], page 2.

    This is the standard XPG defined `basename`. It is similar in spirit to the GNU version, but may modify the *path* by removing trailing '/' characters. If the *path* is made up entirely of '/' characters, then "/" will be returned. Also, if *path* is `NULL` or an empty string, then "." is returned. The prototype for the XPG version can be found in `libgen.h`.

    Example of using XPG `basename`:

```
#include <libgen.h>

int
main (int argc, char *argv[])
{
  char *prog;
  char *path = strdupa (argv[0]);

  prog = basename (path);

  if (argc < 2)
    {
      fprintf (stderr, "Usage %s <arg>\n", prog);
      exit (1);
    }

  ...

}
```

`char * dirname (char *path)`   [Function]
    Preliminary: | MT-Safe | AS-Safe | AC-Safe | See Section 1.2.2.1 [POSIX Safety Concepts], page 2.

The `dirname` function is the compliment to the XPG version of `basename`. It returns the parent directory of the file specified by *path*. If *path* is NULL, an empty string, or contains no '/' characters, then "." is returned. The prototype for this function can be found in `libgen.h`.

5.9 strfry

The function below addresses the perennial programming quandary: "How do I take good data in string form and painlessly turn it into garbage?" This is actually a fairly simple task for C programmers who do not use the GNU C Library string functions, but for programs based on the GNU C Library, the `strfry` function is the preferred method for destroying string data.

The prototype for this function is in `string.h`.

`char * strfry (`*char *string*`)`   [Function]

> Preliminary: | MT-Safe | AS-Safe | AC-Safe | See Section 1.2.2.1 [POSIX Safety Concepts], page 2.
>
> `strfry` creates a pseudorandom anagram of a string, replacing the input with the anagram in place. For each position in the string, `strfry` swaps it with a position in the string selected at random (from a uniform distribution). The two positions may be the same.
>
> The return value of `strfry` is always *string*.
>
> **Portability Note:** This function is unique to the GNU C Library.

5.10 Trivial Encryption

The `memfrob` function converts an array of data to something unrecognizable and back again. It is not encryption in its usual sense since it is easy for someone to convert the encrypted data back to clear text. The transformation is analogous to Usenet's "Rot13" encryption method for obscuring offensive jokes from sensitive eyes and such. Unlike Rot13, `memfrob` works on arbitrary binary data, not just text.

For true encryption, See Chapter 33 [DES Encryption and Password Handling], page 859.

This function is declared in `string.h`.

`void * memfrob (`*void *mem, size_t length*`)`   [Function]

> Preliminary: | MT-Safe | AS-Safe | AC-Safe | See Section 1.2.2.1 [POSIX Safety Concepts], page 2.
>
> `memfrob` transforms (frobnicates) each byte of the data structure at *mem*, which is *length* bytes long, by bitwise exclusive oring it with binary 00101010. It does the transformation in place and its return value is always *mem*.
>
> Note that `memfrob` a second time on the same data structure returns it to its original state.
>
> This is a good function for hiding information from someone who doesn't want to see it or doesn't want to see it very much. To really prevent people from retrieving the information, use stronger encryption such as that described in See Chapter 33 [DES Encryption and Password Handling], page 859.
>
> **Portability Note:** This function is unique to the GNU C Library.

5.11 Encode Binary Data

To store or transfer binary data in environments which only support text one has to encode the binary data by mapping the input bytes to characters in the range allowed for storing or transferring. SVID systems (and nowadays XPG compliant systems) provide minimal support for this task.

char * l64a (*long int n*)   [Function]
> Preliminary: | MT-Unsafe race:l64a | AS-Unsafe | AC-Safe | See Section 1.2.2.1 [POSIX Safety Concepts], page 2.
>
> This function encodes a 32-bit input value using characters from the basic character set. It returns a pointer to a 7 character buffer which contains an encoded version of *n*. To encode a series of bytes the user must copy the returned string to a destination buffer. It returns the empty string if *n* is zero, which is somewhat bizarre but mandated by the standard.
>
> **Warning:** Since a static buffer is used this function should not be used in multithreaded programs. There is no thread-safe alternative to this function in the C library.
>
> **Compatibility Note:** The XPG standard states that the return value of l64a is undefined if *n* is negative. In the GNU implementation, l64a treats its argument as unsigned, so it will return a sensible encoding for any nonzero *n*; however, portable programs should not rely on this.
>
> To encode a large buffer l64a must be called in a loop, once for each 32-bit word of the buffer. For example, one could do something like this:

```
char *
encode (const void *buf, size_t len)
{
  /* We know in advance how long the buffer has to be. */
  unsigned char *in = (unsigned char *) buf;
  char *out = malloc (6 + ((len + 3) / 4) * 6 + 1);
  char *cp = out, *p;

  /* Encode the length. */
  /* Using 'htonl' is necessary so that the data can be
     decoded even on machines with different byte order.
     'l64a' can return a string shorter than 6 bytes, so
     we pad it with encoding of 0 ('.') at the end by
     hand. */

  p = stpcpy (cp, l64a (htonl (len)));
  cp = mempcpy (p, "......", 6 - (p - cp));

  while (len > 3)
    {
      unsigned long int n = *in++;
      n = (n << 8) | *in++;
      n = (n << 8) | *in++;
      n = (n << 8) | *in++;
      len -= 4;
      p = stpcpy (cp, l64a (htonl (n)));
      cp = mempcpy (p, "......", 6 - (p - cp));
    }
  if (len > 0)
```

```
        {
          unsigned long int n = *in++;
          if (--len > 0)
            {
              n = (n << 8) | *in++;
              if (--len > 0)
                n = (n << 8) | *in;
            }
          cp = stpcpy (cp, l64a (htonl (n)));
        }
      *cp = '\0';
      return out;
    }
```

It is strange that the library does not provide the complete functionality needed but so be it.

To decode data produced with **l64a** the following function should be used.

long int a64l (*const char *string*)   [Function]

Preliminary: | MT-Safe | AS-Safe | AC-Safe | See Section 1.2.2.1 [POSIX Safety Concepts], page 2.

The parameter *string* should contain a string which was produced by a call to **l64a**. The function processes at least 6 characters of this string, and decodes the characters it finds according to the table below. It stops decoding when it finds a character not in the table, rather like **atoi**; if you have a buffer which has been broken into lines, you must be careful to skip over the end-of-line characters.

The decoded number is returned as a **long int** value.

The **l64a** and **a64l** functions use a base 64 encoding, in which each character of an encoded string represents six bits of an input word. These symbols are used for the base 64 digits:

	0	1	2	3	4	5	6	7
0	.	/	0	1	2	3	4	5
8	6	7	8	9	A	B	C	D
16	E	F	G	H	I	J	K	L
24	M	N	O	P	Q	R	S	T
32	U	V	W	X	Y	Z	a	b
40	c	d	e	f	g	h	i	j
48	k	l	m	n	o	p	q	r
56	s	t	u	v	w	x	y	z

This encoding scheme is not standard. There are some other encoding methods which are much more widely used (UU encoding, MIME encoding). Generally, it is better to use one of these encodings.

5.12 Argz and Envz Vectors

argz vectors are vectors of strings in a contiguous block of memory, each element separated from its neighbors by null-characters ('\0').

Envz vectors are an extension of argz vectors where each element is a name-value pair, separated by a '=' character (as in a Unix environment).

5.12.1 Argz Functions

Each argz vector is represented by a pointer to the first element, of type `char *`, and a size, of type `size_t`, both of which can be initialized to 0 to represent an empty argz vector. All argz functions accept either a pointer and a size argument, or pointers to them, if they will be modified.

The argz functions use `malloc`/`realloc` to allocate/grow argz vectors, and so any argz vector creating using these functions may be freed by using `free`; conversely, any argz function that may grow a string expects that string to have been allocated using `malloc` (those argz functions that only examine their arguments or modify them in place will work on any sort of memory). See Section 3.2.2 [Unconstrained Allocation], page 42.

All argz functions that do memory allocation have a return type of `error_t`, and return 0 for success, and `ENOMEM` if an allocation error occurs.

These functions are declared in the standard include file `argz.h`.

`error_t argz_create` (*char *const* `argv[]`, *char* **`argz`, *size_t*   [Function]
    *`argz_len`)
> Preliminary: | MT-Safe | AS-Unsafe heap | AC-Unsafe mem | See Section 1.2.2.1 [POSIX Safety Concepts], page 2.
>
> The `argz_create` function converts the Unix-style argument vector *argv* (a vector of pointers to normal C strings, terminated by `(char *)0`; see Section 25.1 [Program Arguments], page 705) into an argz vector with the same elements, which is returned in *argz* and *argz_len*.

`error_t argz_create_sep` (*const char* *`string`, *int* `sep`, *char* **`argz`,   [Function]
    size_t *`argz_len`)
> Preliminary: | MT-Safe | AS-Unsafe heap | AC-Unsafe mem | See Section 1.2.2.1 [POSIX Safety Concepts], page 2.
>
> The `argz_create_sep` function converts the null-terminated string *string* into an argz vector (returned in *argz* and *argz_len*) by splitting it into elements at every occurrence of the character *sep*.

`size_t argz_count` (*const char* *`argz`, *size_t* `arg_len`)   [Function]
> Preliminary: | MT-Safe | AS-Safe | AC-Safe | See Section 1.2.2.1 [POSIX Safety Concepts], page 2.
>
> Returns the number of elements in the argz vector *argz* and *argz_len*.

`void argz_extract` (*const char* *`argz`, *size_t* `argz_len`, *char* **`argv`)   [Function]
> Preliminary: | MT-Safe | AS-Safe | AC-Safe | See Section 1.2.2.1 [POSIX Safety Concepts], page 2.
>
> The `argz_extract` function converts the argz vector *argz* and *argz_len* into a Unix-style argument vector stored in *argv*, by putting pointers to every element in *argz* into successive positions in *argv*, followed by a terminator of 0. *Argv* must be pre-allocated with enough space to hold all the elements in *argz* plus the terminating `(char *)0` (`(argz_count (argz, argz_len) + 1) * sizeof (char *)` bytes should be enough). Note that the string pointers stored into *argv* point into *argz*—they are not copies— and so *argz* must be copied if it will be changed while *argv* is still active. This

function is useful for passing the elements in *argz* to an exec function (see Section 26.5 [Executing a File], page 752).

void argz_stringify (*char *argz*, *size_t* **len**, *int* **sep**)   [Function]
Preliminary: | MT-Safe | AS-Safe | AC-Safe | See Section 1.2.2.1 [POSIX Safety Concepts], page 2.

The **argz_stringify** converts *argz* into a normal string with the elements separated by the character *sep*, by replacing each '\0' inside *argz* (except the last one, which terminates the string) with *sep*. This is handy for printing *argz* in a readable manner.

error_t argz_add (*char **argz*, *size_t *argz_len*, *const char *str*)   [Function]
Preliminary: | MT-Safe | AS-Unsafe heap | AC-Unsafe mem | See Section 1.2.2.1 [POSIX Safety Concepts], page 2.

The **argz_add** function adds the string *str* to the end of the argz vector ***argz**, and updates ***argz** and ***argz_len** accordingly.

error_t argz_add_sep (*char **argz*, *size_t *argz_len*, *const char*   [Function]
     *str, *int* **delim**)
Preliminary: | MT-Safe | AS-Unsafe heap | AC-Unsafe mem | See Section 1.2.2.1 [POSIX Safety Concepts], page 2.

The **argz_add_sep** function is similar to **argz_add**, but *str* is split into separate elements in the result at occurrences of the character *delim*. This is useful, for instance, for adding the components of a Unix search path to an argz vector, by using a value of ':' for *delim*.

error_t argz_append (*char **argz*, *size_t *argz_len*, *const char*   [Function]
     *buf, *size_t* **buf_len**)
Preliminary: | MT-Safe | AS-Unsafe heap | AC-Unsafe mem | See Section 1.2.2.1 [POSIX Safety Concepts], page 2.

The **argz_append** function appends *buf_len* bytes starting at *buf* to the argz vector ***argz**, reallocating ***argz** to accommodate it, and adding *buf_len* to ***argz_len**.

void argz_delete (*char **argz*, *size_t *argz_len*, *char *entry*)   [Function]
Preliminary: | MT-Safe | AS-Unsafe heap | AC-Unsafe mem | See Section 1.2.2.1 [POSIX Safety Concepts], page 2.

If *entry* points to the beginning of one of the elements in the argz vector ***argz**, the **argz_delete** function will remove this entry and reallocate ***argz**, modifying ***argz** and ***argz_len** accordingly. Note that as destructive argz functions usually reallocate their argz argument, pointers into argz vectors such as *entry* will then become invalid.

error_t argz_insert (*char **argz*, *size_t *argz_len*, *char *before*,   [Function]
     const char *entry)
Preliminary: | MT-Safe | AS-Unsafe heap | AC-Unsafe mem | See Section 1.2.2.1 [POSIX Safety Concepts], page 2.

The **argz_insert** function inserts the string *entry* into the argz vector ***argz** at a point just before the existing element pointed to by *before*, reallocating ***argz** and updating ***argz** and ***argz_len**. If *before* is 0, *entry* is added to the end instead (as if by **argz_add**). Since the first element is in fact the same as ***argz**, passing in ***argz** as the value of *before* will result in *entry* being inserted at the beginning.

char * argz_next (*const char* **argz**, *size_t* **argz_len**, *const char*   [Function]
    entry)

> Preliminary: | MT-Safe | AS-Safe | AC-Safe | See Section 1.2.2.1 [POSIX Safety Concepts], page 2.
>
> The `argz_next` function provides a convenient way of iterating over the elements in the argz vector *argz*. It returns a pointer to the next element in *argz* after the element *entry*, or 0 if there are no elements following *entry*. If *entry* is 0, the first element of *argz* is returned.
>
> This behavior suggests two styles of iteration:
>
> ```
> char *entry = 0;
> while ((entry = argz_next (argz, argz_len, entry)))
>   action;
> ```
>
> (the double parentheses are necessary to make some C compilers shut up about what they consider a questionable `while`-test) and:
>
> ```
> char *entry;
> for (entry = argz;
>      entry;
>      entry = argz_next (argz, argz_len, entry))
>   action;
> ```
>
> Note that the latter depends on *argz* having a value of 0 if it is empty (rather than a pointer to an empty block of memory); this invariant is maintained for argz vectors created by the functions here.

error_t argz_replace (*char* ****argz**, *size_t* ***argz_len**,   [Function]
    const char ***str**, *const char* ***with**, *unsigned* ***replace_count**)

> Preliminary: | MT-Safe | AS-Unsafe heap | AC-Unsafe mem | See Section 1.2.2.1 [POSIX Safety Concepts], page 2.
>
> Replace any occurrences of the string *str* in *argz* with *with*, reallocating *argz* as necessary. If *replace_count* is non-zero, `*replace_count` will be incremented by number of replacements performed.

5.12.2 Envz Functions

Envz vectors are just argz vectors with additional constraints on the form of each element; as such, argz functions can also be used on them, where it makes sense.

Each element in an envz vector is a name-value pair, separated by a '=' character; if multiple '=' characters are present in an element, those after the first are considered part of the value, and treated like all other non-'\0' characters.

If *no* '=' characters are present in an element, that element is considered the name of a "null" entry, as distinct from an entry with an empty value: `envz_get` will return 0 if given the name of null entry, whereas an entry with an empty value would result in a value of `""`; `envz_entry` will still find such entries, however. Null entries can be removed with `envz_strip` function.

As with argz functions, envz functions that may allocate memory (and thus fail) have a return type of `error_t`, and return either 0 or `ENOMEM`.

These functions are declared in the standard include file `envz.h`.

char * envz_entry (*const char* **envz**, *size_t* **envz_len**, *const char*   [Function]
          name)
>   Preliminary: | MT-Safe | AS-Safe | AC-Safe | See Section 1.2.2.1 [POSIX Safety
>   Concepts], page 2.
>
>   The **envz_entry** function finds the entry in *envz* with the name *name*, and returns a
>   pointer to the whole entry—that is, the argz element which begins with *name* followed
>   by a '=' character. If there is no entry with that name, 0 is returned.

char * envz_get (*const char* **envz**, *size_t* **envz_len**, *const char* **name**)   [Function]
>   Preliminary: | MT-Safe | AS-Safe | AC-Safe | See Section 1.2.2.1 [POSIX Safety
>   Concepts], page 2.
>
>   The **envz_get** function finds the entry in *envz* with the name *name* (like **envz_entry**),
>   and returns a pointer to the value portion of that entry (following the '='). If there
>   is no entry with that name (or only a null entry), 0 is returned.

error_t envz_add (*char* **envz**, *size_t* **envz_len**, *const char* **name**,   [Function]
          const char **value**)
>   Preliminary: | MT-Safe | AS-Unsafe heap | AC-Unsafe mem | See Section 1.2.2.1
>   [POSIX Safety Concepts], page 2.
>
>   The **envz_add** function adds an entry to **envz** (updating **envz** and **envz_len**)
>   with the name *name*, and value *value*. If an entry with the same name already exists
>   in *envz*, it is removed first. If *value* is 0, then the new entry will the special null type
>   of entry (mentioned above).

error_t envz_merge (*char* **envz**, *size_t* **envz_len**, *const char*   [Function]
          envz2, *size_t* **envz2_len**, *int* **override**)
>   Preliminary: | MT-Safe | AS-Unsafe heap | AC-Unsafe mem | See Section 1.2.2.1
>   [POSIX Safety Concepts], page 2.
>
>   The **envz_merge** function adds each entry in *envz2* to *envz*, as if with **envz_add**,
>   updating **envz** and **envz_len**. If *override* is true, then values in *envz2* will supersede
>   those with the same name in *envz*, otherwise not.
>
>   Null entries are treated just like other entries in this respect, so a null entry in *envz*
>   can prevent an entry of the same name in *envz2* from being added to *envz*, if *override*
>   is false.

void envz_strip (*char* **envz**, *size_t* **envz_len**)   [Function]
>   Preliminary: | MT-Safe | AS-Safe | AC-Safe | See Section 1.2.2.1 [POSIX Safety
>   Concepts], page 2.
>
>   The **envz_strip** function removes any null entries from *envz*, updating **envz** and
>   **envz_len**.

void envz_remove (*char* **envz**, *size_t* **envz_len**, *const char* **name**)   [Function]
>   Preliminary: | MT-Safe | AS-Unsafe heap | AC-Unsafe mem | See Section 1.2.2.1
>   [POSIX Safety Concepts], page 2.
>
>   The **envz_remove** function removes an entry named *name* from *envz*, updating **envz**
>   and **envz_len**.

6 Character Set Handling

Character sets used in the early days of computing had only six, seven, or eight bits for each character: there was never a case where more than eight bits (one byte) were used to represent a single character. The limitations of this approach became more apparent as more people grappled with non-Roman character sets, where not all the characters that make up a language's character set can be represented by 2^8 choices. This chapter shows the functionality that was added to the C library to support multiple character sets.

6.1 Introduction to Extended Characters

A variety of solutions is available to overcome the differences between character sets with a 1:1 relation between bytes and characters and character sets with ratios of 2:1 or 4:1. The remainder of this section gives a few examples to help understand the design decisions made while developing the functionality of the C library.

A distinction we have to make right away is between internal and external representation. *Internal representation* means the representation used by a program while keeping the text in memory. External representations are used when text is stored or transmitted through some communication channel. Examples of external representations include files waiting in a directory to be read and parsed.

Traditionally there has been no difference between the two representations. It was equally comfortable and useful to use the same single-byte representation internally and externally. This comfort level decreases with more and larger character sets.

One of the problems to overcome with the internal representation is handling text that is externally encoded using different character sets. Assume a program that reads two texts and compares them using some metric. The comparison can be usefully done only if the texts are internally kept in a common format.

For such a common format (= character set) eight bits are certainly no longer enough. So the smallest entity will have to grow: *wide characters* will now be used. Instead of one byte per character, two or four will be used instead. (Three are not good to address in memory and more than four bytes seem not to be necessary).

As shown in some other part of this manual, a completely new family has been created of functions that can handle wide character texts in memory. The most commonly used character sets for such internal wide character representations are Unicode and ISO 10646 (also known as UCS for Universal Character Set). Unicode was originally planned as a 16-bit character set; whereas, ISO 10646 was designed to be a 31-bit large code space. The two standards are practically identical. They have the same character repertoire and code table, but Unicode specifies added semantics. At the moment, only characters in the first `0x10000` code positions (the so-called Basic Multilingual Plane, BMP) have been assigned, but the assignment of more specialized characters outside this 16-bit space is already in progress. A number of encodings have been defined for Unicode and ISO 10646 characters: UCS-2 is a 16-bit word that can only represent characters from the BMP, UCS-4 is a 32-bit word than can represent any Unicode and ISO 10646 character, UTF-8 is an ASCII compatible encoding where ASCII characters are represented by ASCII bytes and non-ASCII characters by sequences of 2-6 non-ASCII bytes, and finally UTF-16 is an extension of UCS-2 in which pairs of certain UCS-2 words can be used to encode non-BMP characters up to `0x10ffff`.

To represent wide characters the `char` type is not suitable. For this reason the ISO C standard introduces a new type that is designed to keep one character of a wide character string. To maintain the similarity there is also a type corresponding to `int` for those functions that take a single wide character.

`wchar_t`   [Data type]

> This data type is used as the base type for wide character strings. In other words, arrays of objects of this type are the equivalent of `char[]` for multibyte character strings. The type is defined in `stddef.h`.
>
> The ISO C90 standard, where `wchar_t` was introduced, does not say anything specific about the representation. It only requires that this type is capable of storing all elements of the basic character set. Therefore it would be legitimate to define `wchar_t` as `char`, which might make sense for embedded systems.
>
> But in the GNU C Library `wchar_t` is always 32 bits wide and, therefore, capable of representing all UCS-4 values and, therefore, covering all of ISO 10646. Some Unix systems define `wchar_t` as a 16-bit type and thereby follow Unicode very strictly. This definition is perfectly fine with the standard, but it also means that to represent all characters from Unicode and ISO 10646 one has to use UTF-16 surrogate characters, which is in fact a multi-wide-character encoding. But resorting to multi-wide-character encoding contradicts the purpose of the `wchar_t` type.

`wint_t`   [Data type]

> `wint_t` is a data type used for parameters and variables that contain a single wide character. As the name suggests this type is the equivalent of `int` when using the normal `char` strings. The types `wchar_t` and `wint_t` often have the same representation if their size is 32 bits wide but if `wchar_t` is defined as `char` the type `wint_t` must be defined as `int` due to the parameter promotion.
>
> This type is defined in `wchar.h` and was introduced in Amendment 1 to ISO C90.

As there are for the `char` data type macros are available for specifying the minimum and maximum value representable in an object of type `wchar_t`.

`wint_t WCHAR_MIN`   [Macro]

> The macro `WCHAR_MIN` evaluates to the minimum value representable by an object of type `wint_t`.
>
> This macro was introduced in Amendment 1 to ISO C90.

`wint_t WCHAR_MAX`   [Macro]

> The macro `WCHAR_MAX` evaluates to the maximum value representable by an object of type `wint_t`.
>
> This macro was introduced in Amendment 1 to ISO C90.

Another special wide character value is the equivalent to `EOF`.

`wint_t WEOF`   [Macro]

> The macro `WEOF` evaluates to a constant expression of type `wint_t` whose value is different from any member of the extended character set.
>
> `WEOF` need not be the same value as `EOF` and unlike `EOF` it also need *not* be negative. In other words, sloppy code like

```
{
  int c;
  ...
  while ((c = getc (fp)) < 0)
    ...
}
```

has to be rewritten to use WEOF explicitly when wide characters are used:

```
{
  wint_t c;
  ...
  while ((c = wgetc (fp)) != WEOF)
    ...
}
```

This macro was introduced in Amendment 1 to ISO C90 and is defined in wchar.h.

These internal representations present problems when it comes to storing and transmittal. Because each single wide character consists of more than one byte, they are affected by byte-ordering. Thus, machines with different endianesses would see different values when accessing the same data. This byte ordering concern also applies for communication protocols that are all byte-based and therefore require that the sender has to decide about splitting the wide character in bytes. A last (but not least important) point is that wide characters often require more storage space than a customized byte-oriented character set.

For all the above reasons, an external encoding that is different from the internal encoding is often used if the latter is UCS-2 or UCS-4. The external encoding is byte-based and can be chosen appropriately for the environment and for the texts to be handled. A variety of different character sets can be used for this external encoding (information that will not be exhaustively presented here–instead, a description of the major groups will suffice). All of the ASCII-based character sets fulfill one requirement: they are "filesystem safe." This means that the character '/' is used in the encoding *only* to represent itself. Things are a bit different for character sets like EBCDIC (Extended Binary Coded Decimal Interchange Code, a character set family used by IBM), but if the operating system does not understand EBCDIC directly the parameters-to-system calls have to be converted first anyhow.

- The simplest character sets are single-byte character sets. There can be only up to 256 characters (for 8 bit character sets), which is not sufficient to cover all languages but might be sufficient to handle a specific text. Handling of a 8 bit character sets is simple. This is not true for other kinds presented later, and therefore, the application one uses might require the use of 8 bit character sets.

- The ISO 2022 standard defines a mechanism for extended character sets where one character *can* be represented by more than one byte. This is achieved by associating a state with the text. Characters that can be used to change the state can be embedded in the text. Each byte in the text might have a different interpretation in each state. The state might even influence whether a given byte stands for a character on its own or whether it has to be combined with some more bytes.

  In most uses of ISO 2022 the defined character sets do not allow state changes that cover more than the next character. This has the big advantage that whenever one can identify the beginning of the byte sequence of a character one can interpret a text correctly. Examples of character sets using this policy are the various EUC character sets (used by Sun's operating systems, EUC-JP, EUC-KR, EUC-TW, and EUC-CN) or Shift_JIS (SJIS, a Japanese encoding).

But there are also character sets using a state that is valid for more than one character and has to be changed by another byte sequence. Examples for this are ISO-2022-JP, ISO-2022-KR, and ISO-2022-CN.

- Early attempts to fix 8 bit character sets for other languages using the Roman alphabet lead to character sets like ISO 6937. Here bytes representing characters like the acute accent do not produce output themselves: one has to combine them with other characters to get the desired result. For example, the byte sequence `0xc2 0x61` (non-spacing acute accent, followed by lower-case 'a') to get the "small a with acute" character. To get the acute accent character on its own, one has to write `0xc2 0x20` (the non-spacing acute followed by a space).

  Character sets like ISO 6937 are used in some embedded systems such as teletex.

- Instead of converting the Unicode or ISO 10646 text used internally, it is often also sufficient to simply use an encoding different than UCS-2/UCS-4. The Unicode and ISO 10646 standards even specify such an encoding: UTF-8. This encoding is able to represent all of ISO 10646 31 bits in a byte string of length one to six.

  There were a few other attempts to encode ISO 10646 such as UTF-7, but UTF-8 is today the only encoding that should be used. In fact, with any luck UTF-8 will soon be the only external encoding that has to be supported. It proves to be universally usable and its only disadvantage is that it favors Roman languages by making the byte string representation of other scripts (Cyrillic, Greek, Asian scripts) longer than necessary if using a specific character set for these scripts. Methods like the Unicode compression scheme can alleviate these problems.

The question remaining is: how to select the character set or encoding to use. The answer: you cannot decide about it yourself, it is decided by the developers of the system or the majority of the users. Since the goal is interoperability one has to use whatever the other people one works with use. If there are no constraints, the selection is based on the requirements the expected circle of users will have. In other words, if a project is expected to be used in only, say, Russia it is fine to use KOI8-R or a similar character set. But if at the same time people from, say, Greece are participating one should use a character set that allows all people to collaborate.

The most widely useful solution seems to be: go with the most general character set, namely ISO 10646. Use UTF-8 as the external encoding and problems about users not being able to use their own language adequately are a thing of the past.

One final comment about the choice of the wide character representation is necessary at this point. We have said above that the natural choice is using Unicode or ISO 10646. This is not required, but at least encouraged, by the ISO C standard. The standard defines at least a macro `__STDC_ISO_10646__` that is only defined on systems where the `wchar_t` type encodes ISO 10646 characters. If this symbol is not defined one should avoid making assumptions about the wide character representation. If the programmer uses only the functions provided by the C library to handle wide character strings there should be no compatibility problems with other systems.

6.2 Overview about Character Handling Functions

A Unix C library contains three different sets of functions in two families to handle character set conversion. One of the function families (the most commonly used) is specified in the ISO C90 standard and, therefore, is portable even beyond the Unix world. Unfortunately this family is the least useful one. These functions should be avoided whenever possible, especially when developing libraries (as opposed to applications).

The second family of functions got introduced in the early Unix standards (XPG2) and is still part of the latest and greatest Unix standard: Unix 98. It is also the most powerful and useful set of functions. But we will start with the functions defined in Amendment 1 to ISO C90.

6.3 Restartable Multibyte Conversion Functions

The ISO C standard defines functions to convert strings from a multibyte representation to wide character strings. There are a number of peculiarities:

- The character set assumed for the multibyte encoding is not specified as an argument to the functions. Instead the character set specified by the `LC_CTYPE` category of the current locale is used; see Section 7.3 [Locale Categories], page 170.

- The functions handling more than one character at a time require NUL terminated strings as the argument (i.e., converting blocks of text does not work unless one can add a NUL byte at an appropriate place). The GNU C Library contains some extensions to the standard that allow specifying a size, but basically they also expect terminated strings.

Despite these limitations the ISO C functions can be used in many contexts. In graphical user interfaces, for instance, it is not uncommon to have functions that require text to be displayed in a wide character string if the text is not simple ASCII. The text itself might come from a file with translations and the user should decide about the current locale, which determines the translation and therefore also the external encoding used. In such a situation (and many others) the functions described here are perfect. If more freedom while performing the conversion is necessary take a look at the `iconv` functions (see Section 6.5 [Generic Charset Conversion], page 148).

6.3.1 Selecting the conversion and its properties

We already said above that the currently selected locale for the `LC_CTYPE` category decides about the conversion that is performed by the functions we are about to describe. Each locale uses its own character set (given as an argument to `localedef`) and this is the one assumed as the external multibyte encoding. The wide character set is always UCS-4 in the GNU C Library.

A characteristic of each multibyte character set is the maximum number of bytes that can be necessary to represent one character. This information is quite important when writing code that uses the conversion functions (as shown in the examples below). The ISO C standard defines two macros that provide this information.

int MB_LEN_MAX   [Macro]

> MB_LEN_MAX specifies the maximum number of bytes in the multibyte sequence for a
> single character in any of the supported locales. It is a compile-time constant and is
> defined in limits.h.

int MB_CUR_MAX   [Macro]

> MB_CUR_MAX expands into a positive integer expression that is the maximum number
> of bytes in a multibyte character in the current locale. The value is never greater than
> MB_LEN_MAX. Unlike MB_LEN_MAX this macro need not be a compile-time constant, and
> in the GNU C Library it is not.
>
> MB_CUR_MAX is defined in stdlib.h.

Two different macros are necessary since strictly ISO C90 compilers do not allow variable
length array definitions, but still it is desirable to avoid dynamic allocation. This incomplete
piece of code shows the problem:

```
{
  char buf[MB_LEN_MAX];
  ssize_t len = 0;

  while (! feof (fp))
    {
      fread (&buf[len], 1, MB_CUR_MAX - len, fp);
      /* ... process buf */
      len -= used;
    }
}
```

The code in the inner loop is expected to have always enough bytes in the array *buf*
to convert one multibyte character. The array *buf* has to be sized statically since many
compilers do not allow a variable size. The **fread** call makes sure that MB_CUR_MAX bytes
are always available in *buf*. Note that it isn't a problem if MB_CUR_MAX is not a compile-time
constant.

6.3.2 Representing the state of the conversion

In the introduction of this chapter it was said that certain character sets use a *stateful*
encoding. That is, the encoded values depend in some way on the previous bytes in the
text.

Since the conversion functions allow converting a text in more than one step we must
have a way to pass this information from one call of the functions to another.

mbstate_t   [Data type]

> A variable of type mbstate_t can contain all the information about the *shift state*
> needed from one call to a conversion function to another.
>
> mbstate_t is defined in wchar.h. It was introduced in Amendment 1 to ISO C90.

To use objects of type mbstate_t the programmer has to define such objects (normally
as local variables on the stack) and pass a pointer to the object to the conversion functions.
This way the conversion function can update the object if the current multibyte character
set is stateful.

There is no specific function or initializer to put the state object in any specific state. The rules are that the object should always represent the initial state before the first use, and this is achieved by clearing the whole variable with code such as follows:

```
{
  mbstate_t state;
  memset (&state, '\0', sizeof (state));
  /* from now on state can be used.  */
  ...
}
```

When using the conversion functions to generate output it is often necessary to test whether the current state corresponds to the initial state. This is necessary, for example, to decide whether to emit escape sequences to set the state to the initial state at certain sequence points. Communication protocols often require this.

int mbsinit (*const mbstate_t *ps*)   [Function]

> Preliminary: | MT-Safe | AS-Safe | AC-Safe | See Section 1.2.2.1 [POSIX Safety Concepts], page 2.
>
> The `mbsinit` function determines whether the state object pointed to by *ps* is in the initial state. If *ps* is a null pointer or the object is in the initial state the return value is nonzero. Otherwise it is zero.
>
> `mbsinit` was introduced in Amendment 1 to ISO C90 and is declared in `wchar.h`.

Code using `mbsinit` often looks similar to this:

```
{
  mbstate_t state;
  memset (&state, '\0', sizeof (state));
  /* Use state.  */
  ...
  if (! mbsinit (&state))
    {
      /* Emit code to return to initial state.  */
      const wchar_t empty[] = L"";
      const wchar_t *srcp = empty;
      wcsrtombs (outbuf, &srcp, outbuflen, &state);
    }
  ...
}
```

The code to emit the escape sequence to get back to the initial state is interesting. The `wcsrtombs` function can be used to determine the necessary output code (see Section 6.3.4 [Converting Multibyte and Wide Character Strings], page 139). Please note that with the GNU C Library it is not necessary to perform this extra action for the conversion from multibyte text to wide character text since the wide character encoding is not stateful. But there is nothing mentioned in any standard that prohibits making `wchar_t` using a stateful encoding.

6.3.3 Converting Single Characters

The most fundamental of the conversion functions are those dealing with single characters. Please note that this does not always mean single bytes. But since there is very often a subset of the multibyte character set that consists of single byte sequences, there are functions to help with converting bytes. Frequently, ASCII is a subpart of the multibyte character set. In such a scenario, each ASCII character stands for itself, and all other characters have at least a first byte that is beyond the range 0 to 127.

wint_t btowc (*int c***)**   [Function]

>   Preliminary: | MT-Safe | AS-Unsafe corrupt heap lock dlopen | AC-Unsafe corrupt lock mem fd | See Section 1.2.2.1 [POSIX Safety Concepts], page 2.
>
>   The `btowc` function ("byte to wide character") converts a valid single byte character *c* in the initial shift state into the wide character equivalent using the conversion rules from the currently selected locale of the `LC_CTYPE` category.
>
>   If (`unsigned char`) *c* is no valid single byte multibyte character or if *c* is `EOF`, the function returns `WEOF`.
>
>   Please note the restriction of *c* being tested for validity only in the initial shift state. No `mbstate_t` object is used from which the state information is taken, and the function also does not use any static state.
>
>   The `btowc` function was introduced in Amendment 1 to ISO C90 and is declared in `wchar.h`.

Despite the limitation that the single byte value is always interpreted in the initial state, this function is actually useful most of the time. Most characters are either entirely single-byte character sets or they are extension to ASCII. But then it is possible to write code like this (not that this specific example is very useful):

```
wchar_t *
itow (unsigned long int val)
{
  static wchar_t buf[30];
  wchar_t *wcp = &buf[29];
  *wcp = L'\0';
  while (val != 0)
    {
      *--wcp = btowc ('0' + val % 10);
      val /= 10;
    }
  if (wcp == &buf[29])
    *--wcp = L'0';
  return wcp;
}
```

Why is it necessary to use such a complicated implementation and not simply cast `'0'` + `val % 10` to a wide character? The answer is that there is no guarantee that one can perform this kind of arithmetic on the character of the character set used for `wchar_t` representation. In other situations the bytes are not constant at compile time and so the compiler cannot do the work. In situations like this, using `btowc` is required.

There is also a function for the conversion in the other direction.

int wctob (*wint_t c***)**   [Function]

>   Preliminary: | MT-Safe | AS-Unsafe corrupt heap lock dlopen | AC-Unsafe corrupt lock mem fd | See Section 1.2.2.1 [POSIX Safety Concepts], page 2.
>
>   The `wctob` function ("wide character to byte") takes as the parameter a valid wide character. If the multibyte representation for this character in the initial state is

exactly one byte long, the return value of this function is this character. Otherwise the return value is EOF.

wctob was introduced in Amendment 1 to ISO C90 and is declared in wchar.h.

There are more general functions to convert single character from multibyte representation to wide characters and vice versa. These functions pose no limit on the length of the multibyte representation and they also do not require it to be in the initial state.

size_t mbrtowc (wchar_t *restrict **pwc**, const char *restrict **s**, size_t **n**,   [Function]
          mbstate_t *restrict **ps**)

Preliminary: | MT-Unsafe race:mbrtowc/!ps | AS-Unsafe corrupt heap lock dlopen | AC-Unsafe corrupt lock mem fd | See Section 1.2.2.1 [POSIX Safety Concepts], page 2.

The mbrtowc function ("multibyte restartable to wide character") converts the next multibyte character in the string pointed to by s into a wide character and stores it in the wide character string pointed to by pwc. The conversion is performed according to the locale currently selected for the LC_CTYPE category. If the conversion for the character set used in the locale requires a state, the multibyte string is interpreted in the state represented by the object pointed to by ps. If ps is a null pointer, a static, internal state variable used only by the mbrtowc function is used.

If the next multibyte character corresponds to the NUL wide character, the return value of the function is 0 and the state object is afterwards in the initial state. If the next n or fewer bytes form a correct multibyte character, the return value is the number of bytes starting from s that form the multibyte character. The conversion state is updated according to the bytes consumed in the conversion. In both cases the wide character (either the L'\0' or the one found in the conversion) is stored in the string pointed to by pwc if pwc is not null.

If the first n bytes of the multibyte string possibly form a valid multibyte character but there are more than n bytes needed to complete it, the return value of the function is (size_t) -2 and no value is stored. Please note that this can happen even if n has a value greater than or equal to MB_CUR_MAX since the input might contain redundant shift sequences.

If the first n bytes of the multibyte string cannot possibly form a valid multibyte character, no value is stored, the global variable errno is set to the value EILSEQ, and the function returns (size_t) -1. The conversion state is afterwards undefined.

mbrtowc was introduced in Amendment 1 to ISO C90 and is declared in wchar.h.

Use of mbrtowc is straightforward. A function that copies a multibyte string into a wide character string while at the same time converting all lowercase characters into uppercase could look like this (this is not the final version, just an example; it has no error checking, and sometimes leaks memory):

```
wchar_t *
mbstouwcs (const char *s)
{
  size_t len = strlen (s);
  wchar_t *result = malloc ((len + 1) * sizeof (wchar_t));
  wchar_t *wcp = result;
  wchar_t tmp[1];
```

```
      mbstate_t state;
      size_t nbytes;

      memset (&state, '\0', sizeof (state));
      while ((nbytes = mbrtowc (tmp, s, len, &state)) > 0)
        {
          if (nbytes >= (size_t) -2)
            /* Invalid input string.  */
            return NULL;
          *wcp++ = towupper (tmp[0]);
          len -= nbytes;
          s += nbytes;
        }
      return result;
    }
```

The use of `mbrtowc` should be clear. A single wide character is stored in *tmp[0]*, and the number of consumed bytes is stored in the variable *nbytes*. If the conversion is successful, the uppercase variant of the wide character is stored in the *result* array and the pointer to the input string and the number of available bytes is adjusted.

The only non-obvious thing about `mbrtowc` might be the way memory is allocated for the result. The above code uses the fact that there can never be more wide characters in the converted results than there are bytes in the multibyte input string. This method yields a pessimistic guess about the size of the result, and if many wide character strings have to be constructed this way or if the strings are long, the extra memory required to be allocated because the input string contains multibyte characters might be significant. The allocated memory block can be resized to the correct size before returning it, but a better solution might be to allocate just the right amount of space for the result right away. Unfortunately there is no function to compute the length of the wide character string directly from the multibyte string. There is, however, a function that does part of the work.

size_t mbrlen (*const char *restrict **s**, size_t **n**, mbstate_t *ps*)   [Function]
   Preliminary: | MT-Unsafe race:mbrlen/!ps | AS-Unsafe corrupt heap lock dlopen | AC-Unsafe corrupt lock mem fd | See Section 1.2.2.1 [POSIX Safety Concepts], page 2.

   The `mbrlen` function ("multibyte restartable length") computes the number of at most *n* bytes starting at *s*, which form the next valid and complete multibyte character.

   If the next multibyte character corresponds to the NUL wide character, the return value is 0. If the next *n* bytes form a valid multibyte character, the number of bytes belonging to this multibyte character byte sequence is returned.

   If the first *n* bytes possibly form a valid multibyte character but the character is incomplete, the return value is (`size_t`) -2. Otherwise the multibyte character sequence is invalid and the return value is (`size_t`) -1.

   The multibyte sequence is interpreted in the state represented by the object pointed to by *ps*. If *ps* is a null pointer, a state object local to `mbrlen` is used.

   `mbrlen` was introduced in Amendment 1 to ISO C90 and is declared in `wchar.h`.

The attentive reader now will note that `mbrlen` can be implemented as
```
mbrtowc (NULL, s, n, ps != NULL ? ps : &internal)
```

This is true and in fact is mentioned in the official specification. How can this function be used to determine the length of the wide character string created from a multibyte character string? It is not directly usable, but we can define a function `mbslen` using it:

```
size_t
mbslen (const char *s)
{
  mbstate_t state;
  size_t result = 0;
  size_t nbytes;
  memset (&state, '\0', sizeof (state));
  while ((nbytes = mbrlen (s, MB_LEN_MAX, &state)) > 0)
    {
      if (nbytes >= (size_t) -2)
        /* Something is wrong.  */
        return (size_t) -1;
      s += nbytes;
      ++result;
    }
  return result;
}
```

This function simply calls `mbrlen` for each multibyte character in the string and counts the number of function calls. Please note that we here use `MB_LEN_MAX` as the size argument in the `mbrlen` call. This is acceptable since a) this value is larger than the length of the longest multibyte character sequence and b) we know that the string *s* ends with a NUL byte, which cannot be part of any other multibyte character sequence but the one representing the NUL wide character. Therefore, the `mbrlen` function will never read invalid memory.

Now that this function is available (just to make this clear, this function is *not* part of the GNU C Library) we can compute the number of wide character required to store the converted multibyte character string *s* using

```
wcs_bytes = (mbslen (s) + 1) * sizeof (wchar_t);
```

Please note that the `mbslen` function is quite inefficient. The implementation of `mbstouwcs` with `mbslen` would have to perform the conversion of the multibyte character input string twice, and this conversion might be quite expensive. So it is necessary to think about the consequences of using the easier but imprecise method before doing the work twice.

`size_t` **wcrtomb** (*char *restrict* **s**, *wchar_t* **wc**, *mbstate_t *restrict* **ps**)   [Function]
     Preliminary: | MT-Unsafe race:wcrtomb/!ps | AS-Unsafe corrupt heap lock dlopen | AC-Unsafe corrupt lock mem fd | See Section 1.2.2.1 [POSIX Safety Concepts], page 2.

     The **wcrtomb** function ("wide character restartable to multibyte") converts a single wide character into a multibyte string corresponding to that wide character.

     If *s* is a null pointer, the function resets the state stored in the objects pointed to by *ps* (or the internal `mbstate_t` object) to the initial state. This can also be achieved by a call like this:

```
wcrtombs (temp_buf, L'\0', ps)
```

     since, if *s* is a null pointer, **wcrtomb** performs as if it writes into an internal buffer, which is guaranteed to be large enough.

If *wc* is the NUL wide character, `wcrtomb` emits, if necessary, a shift sequence to get the state *ps* into the initial state followed by a single NUL byte, which is stored in the string *s*.

Otherwise a byte sequence (possibly including shift sequences) is written into the string *s*. This only happens if *wc* is a valid wide character (i.e., it has a multibyte representation in the character set selected by locale of the `LC_CTYPE` category). If *wc* is no valid wide character, nothing is stored in the strings *s*, `errno` is set to `EILSEQ`, the conversion state in *ps* is undefined and the return value is `(size_t) -1`.

If no error occurred the function returns the number of bytes stored in the string *s*. This includes all bytes representing shift sequences.

One word about the interface of the function: there is no parameter specifying the length of the array *s*. Instead the function assumes that there are at least `MB_CUR_MAX` bytes available since this is the maximum length of any byte sequence representing a single character. So the caller has to make sure that there is enough space available, otherwise buffer overruns can occur.

`wcrtomb` was introduced in Amendment 1 to ISO C90 and is declared in `wchar.h`.

Using `wcrtomb` is as easy as using `mbrtowc`. The following example appends a wide character string to a multibyte character string. Again, the code is not really useful (or correct), it is simply here to demonstrate the use and some problems.

```
char *
mbscatwcs (char *s, size_t len, const wchar_t *ws)
{
  mbstate_t state;
  /* Find the end of the existing string.  */
  char *wp = strchr (s, '\0');
  len -= wp - s;
  memset (&state, '\0', sizeof (state));
  do
    {
      size_t nbytes;
      if (len < MB_CUR_LEN)
        {
          /* We cannot guarantee that the next
             character fits into the buffer, so
             return an error.  */
          errno = E2BIG;
          return NULL;
        }
      nbytes = wcrtomb (wp, *ws, &state);
      if (nbytes == (size_t) -1)
        /* Error in the conversion.  */
        return NULL;
      len -= nbytes;
      wp += nbytes;
    }
  while (*ws++ != L'\0');
  return s;
}
```

First the function has to find the end of the string currently in the array *s*. The `strchr` call does this very efficiently since a requirement for multibyte character representations is that the NUL byte is never used except to represent itself (and in this context, the end of the string).

After initializing the state object the loop is entered where the first task is to make sure there is enough room in the array *s*. We abort if there are not at least `MB_CUR_LEN` bytes available. This is not always optimal but we have no other choice. We might have less than `MB_CUR_LEN` bytes available but the next multibyte character might also be only one byte long. At the time the `wcrtomb` call returns it is too late to decide whether the buffer was large enough. If this solution is unsuitable, there is a very slow but more accurate solution.

```
  ...
if (len < MB_CUR_LEN)
  {
    mbstate_t temp_state;
    memcpy (&temp_state, &state, sizeof (state));
    if (wcrtomb (NULL, *ws, &temp_state) > len)
      {
        /* We cannot guarantee that the next
           character fits into the buffer, so
           return an error.  */
        errno = E2BIG;
        return NULL;
      }
  }
  ...
```

Here we perform the conversion that might overflow the buffer so that we are afterwards in the position to make an exact decision about the buffer size. Please note the `NULL` argument for the destination buffer in the new `wcrtomb` call; since we are not interested in the converted text at this point, this is a nice way to express this. The most unusual thing about this piece of code certainly is the duplication of the conversion state object, but if a change of the state is necessary to emit the next multibyte character, we want to have the same shift state change performed in the real conversion. Therefore, we have to preserve the initial shift state information.

There are certainly many more and even better solutions to this problem. This example is only provided for educational purposes.

6.3.4 Converting Multibyte and Wide Character Strings

The functions described in the previous section only convert a single character at a time. Most operations to be performed in real-world programs include strings and therefore the ISO C standard also defines conversions on entire strings. However, the defined set of functions is quite limited; therefore, the GNU C Library contains a few extensions that can help in some important situations.

size_t mbsrtowcs (*wchar_t *restrict* **dst**, *const char **restrict* **src**,   [Function]
          size_t **len**, *mbstate_t *restrict* **ps**)

> Preliminary: | MT-Unsafe race:mbsrtowcs/!ps | AS-Unsafe corrupt heap lock dlopen | AC-Unsafe corrupt lock mem fd | See Section 1.2.2.1 [POSIX Safety Concepts], page 2.

> The `mbsrtowcs` function ("multibyte string restartable to wide character string") converts a NUL-terminated multibyte character string at `*src` into an equivalent wide character string, including the NUL wide character at the end. The conversion

is started using the state information from the object pointed to by *ps* or from an internal object of `mbsrtowcs` if *ps* is a null pointer. Before returning, the state object is updated to match the state after the last converted character. The state is the initial state if the terminating NUL byte is reached and converted.

If *dst* is not a null pointer, the result is stored in the array pointed to by *dst*; otherwise, the conversion result is not available since it is stored in an internal buffer.

If *len* wide characters are stored in the array *dst* before reaching the end of the input string, the conversion stops and *len* is returned. If *dst* is a null pointer, *len* is never checked.

Another reason for a premature return from the function call is if the input string contains an invalid multibyte sequence. In this case the global variable `errno` is set to `EILSEQ` and the function returns (`size_t`) `-1`.

In all other cases the function returns the number of wide characters converted during this call. If *dst* is not null, `mbsrtowcs` stores in the pointer pointed to by *src* either a null pointer (if the NUL byte in the input string was reached) or the address of the byte following the last converted multibyte character.

`mbsrtowcs` was introduced in Amendment 1 to ISO C90 and is declared in `wchar.h`.

The definition of the `mbsrtowcs` function has one important limitation. The requirement that *dst* has to be a NUL-terminated string provides problems if one wants to convert buffers with text. A buffer is normally no collection of NUL-terminated strings but instead a continuous collection of lines, separated by newline characters. Now assume that a function to convert one line from a buffer is needed. Since the line is not NUL-terminated, the source pointer cannot directly point into the unmodified text buffer. This means, either one inserts the NUL byte at the appropriate place for the time of the `mbsrtowcs` function call (which is not doable for a read-only buffer or in a multi-threaded application) or one copies the line in an extra buffer where it can be terminated by a NUL byte. Note that it is not in general possible to limit the number of characters to convert by setting the parameter *len* to any specific value. Since it is not known how many bytes each multibyte character sequence is in length, one can only guess.

There is still a problem with the method of NUL-terminating a line right after the newline character, which could lead to very strange results. As said in the description of the `mbsrtowcs` function above the conversion state is guaranteed to be in the initial shift state after processing the NUL byte at the end of the input string. But this NUL byte is not really part of the text (i.e., the conversion state after the newline in the original text could be something different than the initial shift state and therefore the first character of the next line is encoded using this state). But the state in question is never accessible to the user since the conversion stops after the NUL byte (which resets the state). Most stateful character sets in use today require that the shift state after a newline be the initial state–but this is not a strict guarantee. Therefore, simply NUL-terminating a piece of a running text is not always an adequate solution and, therefore, should never be used in generally used code.

The generic conversion interface (see Section 6.5 [Generic Charset Conversion], page 148) does not have this limitation (it simply works on buffers, not strings), and the GNU C Library contains a set of functions that take additional parameters specifying the maximal number of bytes that are consumed from the input string. This way the problem of `mbsrtowcs`'s example above could be solved by determining the line length and passing this length to the function.

`size_t wcsrtombs` (*char *restrict* **dst**, *const wchar_t **restrict* **src**,   [Function]
         size_t **len**, *mbstate_t *restrict* **ps**)

> Preliminary: | MT-Unsafe race:wcsrtombs/!ps | AS-Unsafe corrupt heap lock dlopen
> | AC-Unsafe corrupt lock mem fd | See Section 1.2.2.1 [POSIX Safety Concepts],
> page 2.

> The `wcsrtombs` function ("wide character string restartable to multibyte string") converts the NUL-terminated wide character string at *src* into an equivalent multibyte character string and stores the result in the array pointed to by *dst*. The NUL wide character is also converted. The conversion starts in the state described in the object pointed to by *ps* or by a state object locally to `wcsrtombs` in case *ps* is a null pointer. If *dst* is a null pointer, the conversion is performed as usual but the result is not available. If all characters of the input string were successfully converted and if *dst* is not a null pointer, the pointer pointed to by *src* gets assigned a null pointer.

> If one of the wide characters in the input string has no valid multibyte character equivalent, the conversion stops early, sets the global variable `errno` to `EILSEQ`, and returns (`size_t`) `-1`.

> Another reason for a premature stop is if *dst* is not a null pointer and the next converted character would require more than *len* bytes in total to the array *dst*. In this case (and if *dest* is not a null pointer) the pointer pointed to by *src* is assigned a value pointing to the wide character right after the last one successfully converted.

> Except in the case of an encoding error the return value of the `wcsrtombs` function is the number of bytes in all the multibyte character sequences stored in *dst*. Before returning the state in the object pointed to by *ps* (or the internal object in case *ps* is a null pointer) is updated to reflect the state after the last conversion. The state is the initial shift state in case the terminating NUL wide character was converted.

> The `wcsrtombs` function was introduced in Amendment 1 to ISO C90 and is declared in `wchar.h`.

The restriction mentioned above for the `mbsrtowcs` function applies here also. There is no possibility of directly controlling the number of input characters. One has to place the NUL wide character at the correct place or control the consumed input indirectly via the available output array size (the *len* parameter).

`size_t mbsnrtowcs` (*wchar_t *restrict* **dst**, *const char **restrict* **src**,   [Function]
         size_t **nmc**, *size_t* **len**, *mbstate_t *restrict* **ps**)

> Preliminary: | MT-Unsafe race:mbsnrtowcs/!ps | AS-Unsafe corrupt heap lock
> dlopen | AC-Unsafe corrupt lock mem fd | See Section 1.2.2.1 [POSIX Safety
> Concepts], page 2.

> The `mbsnrtowcs` function is very similar to the `mbsrtowcs` function. All the parameters are the same except for *nmc*, which is new. The return value is the same as for `mbsrtowcs`.

> This new parameter specifies how many bytes at most can be used from the multibyte character string. In other words, the multibyte character string *src* need not be

NUL-terminated. But if a NUL byte is found within the *nmc* first bytes of the string, the conversion stops here.

This function is a GNU extension. It is meant to work around the problems mentioned above. Now it is possible to convert a buffer with multibyte character text piece for piece without having to care about inserting NUL bytes and the effect of NUL bytes on the conversion state.

A function to convert a multibyte string into a wide character string and display it could be written like this (this is not a really useful example):

```
void
showmbs (const char *src, FILE *fp)
{
  mbstate_t state;
  int cnt = 0;
  memset (&state, '\0', sizeof (state));
  while (1)
    {
      wchar_t linebuf[100];
      const char *endp = strchr (src, '\n');
      size_t n;

      /* Exit if there is no more line.  */
      if (endp == NULL)
        break;

      n = mbsnrtowcs (linebuf, &src, endp - src, 99, &state);
      linebuf[n] = L'\0';
      fprintf (fp, "line %d: \"%S\"\n", linebuf);
    }
}
```

There is no problem with the state after a call to `mbsnrtowcs`. Since we don't insert characters in the strings that were not in there right from the beginning and we use *state* only for the conversion of the given buffer, there is no problem with altering the state.

size_t wcsnrtombs (*char *restrict* **dst**, *const wchar_t **restrict* **src**,   [Function]
     size_t **nwc**, *size_t* **len**, *mbstate_t *restrict* **ps**)
     Preliminary: | MT-Unsafe race:wcsnrtombs/!ps | AS-Unsafe corrupt heap lock dlopen | AC-Unsafe corrupt lock mem fd | See Section 1.2.2.1 [POSIX Safety Concepts], page 2.

     The `wcsnrtombs` function implements the conversion from wide character strings to multibyte character strings. It is similar to `wcsrtombs` but, just like `mbsnrtowcs`, it takes an extra parameter, which specifies the length of the input string.

     No more than *nwc* wide characters from the input string *src* are converted. If the input string contains a NUL wide character in the first *nwc* characters, the conversion stops at this place.

     The `wcsnrtombs` function is a GNU extension and just like `mbsnrtowcs` helps in situations where no NUL-terminated input strings are available.

6.3.5 A Complete Multibyte Conversion Example

The example programs given in the last sections are only brief and do not contain all the error checking, etc. Presented here is a complete and documented example. It features the `mbrtowc` function but it should be easy to derive versions using the other functions.

```c
int
file_mbsrtowcs (int input, int output)
{
  /* Note the use of MB_LEN_MAX.
     MB_CUR_MAX cannot portably be used here.  */
  char buffer[BUFSIZ + MB_LEN_MAX];
  mbstate_t state;
  int filled = 0;
  int eof = 0;

  /* Initialize the state.  */
  memset (&state, '\0', sizeof (state));

  while (!eof)
    {
      ssize_t nread;
      ssize_t nwrite;
      char *inp = buffer;
      wchar_t outbuf[BUFSIZ];
      wchar_t *outp = outbuf;

      /* Fill up the buffer from the input file.  */
      nread = read (input, buffer + filled, BUFSIZ);
      if (nread < 0)
        {
          perror ("read");
          return 0;
        }
      /* If we reach end of file, make a note to read no more. */
      if (nread == 0)
        eof = 1;

      /* filled is now the number of bytes in buffer. */
      filled += nread;

      /* Convert those bytes to wide characters–as many as we can. */
      while (1)
        {
          size_t thislen = mbrtowc (outp, inp, filled, &state);
          /* Stop converting at invalid character;
             this can mean we have read just the first part
             of a valid character.  */
          if (thislen == (size_t) -1)
            break;
          /* We want to handle embedded NUL bytes
             but the return value is 0.  Correct this.  */
          if (thislen == 0)
            thislen = 1;
          /* Advance past this character. */
          inp += thislen;
          filled -= thislen;
          ++outp;
        }
```

```
/* Write the wide characters we just made.  */
nwrite = write (output, outbuf,
                (outp - outbuf) * sizeof (wchar_t));
if (nwrite < 0)
  {
    perror ("write");
    return 0;
  }

/* See if we have a real invalid character. */
if ((eof && filled > 0) || filled >= MB_CUR_MAX)
  {
    error (0, 0, "invalid multibyte character");
    return 0;
  }

/* If any characters must be carried forward,
   put them at the beginning of buffer. */
if (filled > 0)
  memmove (buffer, inp, filled);
}

return 1;
}
```

6.4 Non-reentrant Conversion Function

The functions described in the previous chapter are defined in Amendment 1 to ISO C90, but the original ISO C90 standard also contained functions for character set conversion. The reason that these original functions are not described first is that they are almost entirely useless.

The problem is that all the conversion functions described in the original ISO C90 use a local state. Using a local state implies that multiple conversions at the same time (not only when using threads) cannot be done, and that you cannot first convert single characters and then strings since you cannot tell the conversion functions which state to use.

These original functions are therefore usable only in a very limited set of situations. One must complete converting the entire string before starting a new one, and each string/text must be converted with the same function (there is no problem with the library itself; it is guaranteed that no library function changes the state of any of these functions). **For the above reasons it is highly requested that the functions described in the previous section be used in place of non-reentrant conversion functions.**

6.4.1 Non-reentrant Conversion of Single Characters

int mbtowc (wchar_t *restrict **result**, const char *restrict **string**, size_t   [Function]
    size)

> Preliminary: | MT-Unsafe race | AS-Unsafe corrupt heap lock dlopen | AC-Unsafe corrupt lock mem fd | See Section 1.2.2.1 [POSIX Safety Concepts], page 2.

> The mbtowc ("multibyte to wide character") function when called with non-null *string* converts the first multibyte character beginning at *string* to its corresponding wide character code. It stores the result in *result*.

`mbtowc` never examines more than *size* bytes. (The idea is to supply for *size* the number of bytes of data you have in hand.)

`mbtowc` with non-null *string* distinguishes three possibilities: the first *size* bytes at *string* start with valid multibyte characters, they start with an invalid byte sequence or just part of a character, or *string* points to an empty string (a null character).

For a valid multibyte character, `mbtowc` converts it to a wide character and stores that in **result*, and returns the number of bytes in that character (always at least 1 and never more than *size*).

For an invalid byte sequence, `mbtowc` returns −1. For an empty string, it returns 0, also storing '\0' in **result*.

If the multibyte character code uses shift characters, then `mbtowc` maintains and updates a shift state as it scans. If you call `mbtowc` with a null pointer for *string*, that initializes the shift state to its standard initial value. It also returns nonzero if the multibyte character code in use actually has a shift state. See Section 6.4.3 [States in Non-reentrant Functions], page 147.

int `wctomb` (*char* *`string`, *wchar_t* `wchar`)   [Function]
 Preliminary: | MT-Unsafe race | AS-Unsafe corrupt heap lock dlopen | AC-Unsafe corrupt lock mem fd | See Section 1.2.2.1 [POSIX Safety Concepts], page 2.

The `wctomb` ("wide character to multibyte") function converts the wide character code *wchar* to its corresponding multibyte character sequence, and stores the result in bytes starting at *string*. At most `MB_CUR_MAX` characters are stored.

`wctomb` with non-null *string* distinguishes three possibilities for *wchar*: a valid wide character code (one that can be translated to a multibyte character), an invalid code, and L'\0'.

Given a valid code, `wctomb` converts it to a multibyte character, storing the bytes starting at *string*. Then it returns the number of bytes in that character (always at least 1 and never more than `MB_CUR_MAX`).

If *wchar* is an invalid wide character code, `wctomb` returns −1. If *wchar* is L'\0', it returns 0, also storing '\0' in **string*.

If the multibyte character code uses shift characters, then `wctomb` maintains and updates a shift state as it scans. If you call `wctomb` with a null pointer for *string*, that initializes the shift state to its standard initial value. It also returns nonzero if the multibyte character code in use actually has a shift state. See Section 6.4.3 [States in Non-reentrant Functions], page 147.

Calling this function with a *wchar* argument of zero when *string* is not null has the side-effect of reinitializing the stored shift state *as well as* storing the multibyte character '\0' and returning 0.

Similar to `mbrlen` there is also a non-reentrant function that computes the length of a multibyte character. It can be defined in terms of `mbtowc`.

int `mblen` (*const char* *`string`, *size_t* `size`)   [Function]
 Preliminary: | MT-Unsafe race | AS-Unsafe corrupt heap lock dlopen | AC-Unsafe corrupt lock mem fd | See Section 1.2.2.1 [POSIX Safety Concepts], page 2.

The `mblen` function with a non-null *string* argument returns the number of bytes that make up the multibyte character beginning at *string*, never examining more than *size* bytes. (The idea is to supply for *size* the number of bytes of data you have in hand.)

The return value of `mblen` distinguishes three possibilities: the first *size* bytes at *string* start with valid multibyte characters, they start with an invalid byte sequence or just part of a character, or *string* points to an empty string (a null character).

For a valid multibyte character, `mblen` returns the number of bytes in that character (always at least 1 and never more than *size*). For an invalid byte sequence, `mblen` returns −1. For an empty string, it returns 0.

If the multibyte character code uses shift characters, then `mblen` maintains and updates a shift state as it scans. If you call `mblen` with a null pointer for *string*, that initializes the shift state to its standard initial value. It also returns a nonzero value if the multibyte character code in use actually has a shift state. See Section 6.4.3 [States in Non-reentrant Functions], page 147.

The function `mblen` is declared in `stdlib.h`.

6.4.2 Non-reentrant Conversion of Strings

For convenience the ISO C90 standard also defines functions to convert entire strings instead of single characters. These functions suffer from the same problems as their reentrant counterparts from Amendment 1 to ISO C90; see Section 6.3.4 [Converting Multibyte and Wide Character Strings], page 139.

`size_t mbstowcs` (*wchar_t *wstring, const char *string, size_t size*)   [Function]
Preliminary: | MT-Safe | AS-Unsafe corrupt heap lock dlopen | AC-Unsafe corrupt lock mem fd | See Section 1.2.2.1 [POSIX Safety Concepts], page 2.

The `mbstowcs` ("multibyte string to wide character string") function converts the null-terminated string of multibyte characters *string* to an array of wide character codes, storing not more than *size* wide characters into the array beginning at *wstring*. The terminating null character counts towards the size, so if *size* is less than the actual number of wide characters resulting from *string*, no terminating null character is stored.

The conversion of characters from *string* begins in the initial shift state.

If an invalid multibyte character sequence is found, the `mbstowcs` function returns a value of −1. Otherwise, it returns the number of wide characters stored in the array *wstring*. This number does not include the terminating null character, which is present if the number is less than *size*.

Here is an example showing how to convert a string of multibyte characters, allocating enough space for the result.

```
wchar_t *
mbstowcs_alloc (const char *string)
{
  size_t size = strlen (string) + 1;
  wchar_t *buf = xmalloc (size * sizeof (wchar_t));

  size = mbstowcs (buf, string, size);
  if (size == (size_t) -1)
    return NULL;
```

```
            buf = xrealloc (buf, (size + 1) * sizeof (wchar_t));
            return buf;
        }
```

size_t wcstombs (*char *string, const wchar_t *wstring, size_t size*) [Function]
Preliminary: | MT-Safe | AS-Unsafe corrupt heap lock dlopen | AC-Unsafe corrupt lock mem fd | See Section 1.2.2.1 [POSIX Safety Concepts], page 2.

The wcstombs ("wide character string to multibyte string") function converts the null-terminated wide character array *wstring* into a string containing multibyte characters, storing not more than *size* bytes starting at *string*, followed by a terminating null character if there is room. The conversion of characters begins in the initial shift state.

The terminating null character counts towards the size, so if *size* is less than or equal to the number of bytes needed in *wstring*, no terminating null character is stored.

If a code that does not correspond to a valid multibyte character is found, the wcstombs function returns a value of −1. Otherwise, the return value is the number of bytes stored in the array *string*. This number does not include the terminating null character, which is present if the number is less than *size*.

6.4.3 States in Non-reentrant Functions

In some multibyte character codes, the *meaning* of any particular byte sequence is not fixed; it depends on what other sequences have come earlier in the same string. Typically there are just a few sequences that can change the meaning of other sequences; these few are called *shift sequences* and we say that they set the *shift state* for other sequences that follow.

To illustrate shift state and shift sequences, suppose we decide that the sequence 0200 (just one byte) enters Japanese mode, in which pairs of bytes in the range from 0240 to 0377 are single characters, while 0201 enters Latin-1 mode, in which single bytes in the range from 0240 to 0377 are characters, and interpreted according to the ISO Latin-1 character set. This is a multibyte code that has two alternative shift states ("Japanese mode" and "Latin-1 mode"), and two shift sequences that specify particular shift states.

When the multibyte character code in use has shift states, then mblen, mbtowc, and wctomb must maintain and update the current shift state as they scan the string. To make this work properly, you must follow these rules:

- Before starting to scan a string, call the function with a null pointer for the multibyte character address—for example, mblen (NULL, 0). This initializes the shift state to its standard initial value.

- Scan the string one character at a time, in order. Do not "back up" and rescan characters already scanned, and do not intersperse the processing of different strings.

Here is an example of using mblen following these rules:

```
void
scan_string (char *s)
{
  int length = strlen (s);

  /* Initialize shift state.  */
  mblen (NULL, 0);
```

```
while (1)
  {
    int thischar = mblen (s, length);
    /* Deal with end of string and invalid characters.  */
    if (thischar == 0)
      break;
    if (thischar == -1)
      {
        error ("invalid multibyte character");
        break;
      }
    /* Advance past this character.  */
    s += thischar;
    length -= thischar;
  }
}
```

The functions `mblen`, `mbtowc` and `wctomb` are not reentrant when using a multibyte code that uses a shift state. However, no other library functions call these functions, so you don't have to worry that the shift state will be changed mysteriously.

6.5 Generic Charset Conversion

The conversion functions mentioned so far in this chapter all had in common that they operate on character sets that are not directly specified by the functions. The multibyte encoding used is specified by the currently selected locale for the `LC_CTYPE` category. The wide character set is fixed by the implementation (in the case of the GNU C Library it is always UCS-4 encoded ISO 10646.

This has of course several problems when it comes to general character conversion:

- For every conversion where neither the source nor the destination character set is the character set of the locale for the `LC_CTYPE` category, one has to change the `LC_CTYPE` locale using `setlocale`.

  Changing the `LC_CTYPE` locale introduces major problems for the rest of the programs since several more functions (e.g., the character classification functions, see Section 4.1 [Classification of Characters], page 77) use the `LC_CTYPE` category.

- Parallel conversions to and from different character sets are not possible since the `LC_CTYPE` selection is global and shared by all threads.

- If neither the source nor the destination character set is the character set used for `wchar_t` representation, there is at least a two-step process necessary to convert a text using the functions above. One would have to select the source character set as the multibyte encoding, convert the text into a `wchar_t` text, select the destination character set as the multibyte encoding, and convert the wide character text to the multibyte (= destination) character set.

  Even if this is possible (which is not guaranteed) it is a very tiring work. Plus it suffers from the other two raised points even more due to the steady changing of the locale.

The XPG2 standard defines a completely new set of functions, which has none of these limitations. They are not at all coupled to the selected locales, and they have no constraints on the character sets selected for source and destination. Only the set of available conversions limits them. The standard does not specify that any conversion at all must be available. Such availability is a measure of the quality of the implementation.

In the following text first the interface to `iconv` and then the conversion function, will be described. Comparisons with other implementations will show what obstacles stand in the way of portable applications. Finally, the implementation is described in so far as might interest the advanced user who wants to extend conversion capabilities.

6.5.1 Generic Character Set Conversion Interface

This set of functions follows the traditional cycle of using a resource: open–use–close. The interface consists of three functions, each of which implements one step.

Before the interfaces are described it is necessary to introduce a data type. Just like other open–use–close interfaces the functions introduced here work using handles and the `iconv.h` header defines a special type for the handles used.

`iconv_t`   [Data Type]

> This data type is an abstract type defined in `iconv.h`. The user must not assume anything about the definition of this type; it must be completely opaque.
>
> Objects of this type can get assigned handles for the conversions using the `iconv` functions. The objects themselves need not be freed, but the conversions for which the handles stand for have to.

The first step is the function to create a handle.

`iconv_t iconv_open` (*const char *tocode, const char *fromcode*)   [Function]

> Preliminary: | MT-Safe locale | AS-Unsafe corrupt heap lock dlopen | AC-Unsafe corrupt lock mem fd | See Section 1.2.2.1 [POSIX Safety Concepts], page 2.
>
> The `iconv_open` function has to be used before starting a conversion. The two parameters this function takes determine the source and destination character set for the conversion, and if the implementation has the possibility to perform such a conversion, the function returns a handle.
>
> If the wanted conversion is not available, the `iconv_open` function returns `(iconv_t) -1`. In this case the global variable `errno` can have the following values:
>
> `EMFILE`   The process already has `OPEN_MAX` file descriptors open.
>
> `ENFILE`   The system limit of open file is reached.
>
> `ENOMEM`   Not enough memory to carry out the operation.
>
> `EINVAL`   The conversion from *fromcode* to *tocode* is not supported.
>
> It is not possible to use the same descriptor in different threads to perform independent conversions. The data structures associated with the descriptor include information about the conversion state. This must not be messed up by using it in different conversions.
>
> An `iconv` descriptor is like a file descriptor as for every use a new descriptor must be created. The descriptor does not stand for all of the conversions from *fromset* to *toset*.
>
> The GNU C Library implementation of `iconv_open` has one significant extension to other implementations. To ease the extension of the set of available conversions, the implementation allows storing the necessary files with data and code in an arbitrary

number of directories. How this extension must be written will be explained below (see Section 6.5.4 [The `iconv` Implementation in the GNU C Library], page 155). Here it is only important to say that all directories mentioned in the `GCONV_PATH` environment variable are considered only if they contain a file `gconv-modules`. These directories need not necessarily be created by the system administrator. In fact, this extension is introduced to help users writing and using their own, new conversions. Of course, this does not work for security reasons in SUID binaries; in this case only the system directory is considered and this normally is *prefix/lib/gconv*. The `GCONV_PATH` environment variable is examined exactly once at the first call of the `iconv_open` function. Later modifications of the variable have no effect.

The `iconv_open` function was introduced early in the X/Open Portability Guide, version 2. It is supported by all commercial Unices as it is required for the Unix branding. However, the quality and completeness of the implementation varies widely. The `iconv_open` function is declared in `iconv.h`.

The `iconv` implementation can associate large data structure with the handle returned by `iconv_open`. Therefore, it is crucial to free all the resources once all conversions are carried out and the conversion is not needed anymore.

int iconv_close (*iconv_t cd*) [Function]
> Preliminary: | MT-Safe | AS-Unsafe corrupt heap lock dlopen | AC-Unsafe corrupt lock mem | See Section 1.2.2.1 [POSIX Safety Concepts], page 2.
>
> The `iconv_close` function frees all resources associated with the handle *cd*, which must have been returned by a successful call to the `iconv_open` function.
>
> If the function call was successful the return value is 0. Otherwise it is −1 and `errno` is set appropriately. Defined error are:
>
> EBADF   The conversion descriptor is invalid.
>
> The `iconv_close` function was introduced together with the rest of the `iconv` functions in XPG2 and is declared in `iconv.h`.

The standard defines only one actual conversion function. This has, therefore, the most general interface: it allows conversion from one buffer to another. Conversion from a file to a buffer, vice versa, or even file to file can be implemented on top of it.

size_t iconv (*iconv_t cd, char **inbuf, size_t *inbytesleft, char [Function] ***outbuf, size_t *outbytesleft*)**
> Preliminary: | MT-Safe race:cd | AS-Safe | AC-Unsafe corrupt | See Section 1.2.2.1 [POSIX Safety Concepts], page 2.
>
> The `iconv` function converts the text in the input buffer according to the rules associated with the descriptor *cd* and stores the result in the output buffer. It is possible to call the function for the same text several times in a row since for stateful character sets the necessary state information is kept in the data structures associated with the descriptor.
>
> The input buffer is specified by **inbuf* and it contains **inbytesleft* bytes. The extra indirection is necessary for communicating the used input back to the caller (see below). It is important to note that the buffer pointer is of type **char** and the length is measured in bytes even if the input text is encoded in wide characters.

The output buffer is specified in a similar way. *outbuf* points to the beginning of the buffer with at least *outbytesleft* bytes room for the result. The buffer pointer again is of type `char` and the length is measured in bytes. If *outbuf* or *outbuf* is a null pointer, the conversion is performed but no output is available.

If *inbuf* is a null pointer, the `iconv` function performs the necessary action to put the state of the conversion into the initial state. This is obviously a no-op for non-stateful encodings, but if the encoding has a state, such a function call might put some byte sequences in the output buffer, which perform the necessary state changes. The next call with *inbuf* not being a null pointer then simply goes on from the initial state. It is important that the programmer never makes any assumption as to whether the conversion has to deal with states. Even if the input and output character sets are not stateful, the implementation might still have to keep states. This is due to the implementation chosen for the GNU C Library as it is described below. Therefore an `iconv` call to reset the state should always be performed if some protocol requires this for the output text.

The conversion stops for one of three reasons. The first is that all characters from the input buffer are converted. This actually can mean two things: either all bytes from the input buffer are consumed or there are some bytes at the end of the buffer that possibly can form a complete character but the input is incomplete. The second reason for a stop is that the output buffer is full. And the third reason is that the input contains invalid characters.

In all of these cases the buffer pointers after the last successful conversion, for input and output buffer, are stored in *inbuf* and *outbuf*, and the available room in each buffer is stored in *inbytesleft* and *outbytesleft*.

Since the character sets selected in the `iconv_open` call can be almost arbitrary, there can be situations where the input buffer contains valid characters, which have no identical representation in the output character set. The behavior in this situation is undefined. The *current* behavior of the GNU C Library in this situation is to return with an error immediately. This certainly is not the most desirable solution; therefore, future versions will provide better ones, but they are not yet finished.

If all input from the input buffer is successfully converted and stored in the output buffer, the function returns the number of non-reversible conversions performed. In all other cases the return value is (`size_t`) `-1` and `errno` is set appropriately. In such cases the value pointed to by *inbytesleft* is nonzero.

EILSEQ   The conversion stopped because of an invalid byte sequence in the input. After the call, *inbuf* points at the first byte of the invalid byte sequence.

E2BIG   The conversion stopped because it ran out of space in the output buffer.

EINVAL   The conversion stopped because of an incomplete byte sequence at the end of the input buffer.

EBADF   The *cd* argument is invalid.

The `iconv` function was introduced in the XPG2 standard and is declared in the `iconv.h` header.

The definition of the `iconv` function is quite good overall. It provides quite flexible functionality. The only problems lie in the boundary cases, which are incomplete byte sequences at the end of the input buffer and invalid input. A third problem, which is not really a design problem, is the way conversions are selected. The standard does not say anything about the legitimate names, a minimal set of available conversions. We will see how this negatively impacts other implementations, as demonstrated below.

6.5.2 A complete `iconv` example

The example below features a solution for a common problem. Given that one knows the internal encoding used by the system for `wchar_t` strings, one often is in the position to read text from a file and store it in wide character buffers. One can do this using `mbsrtowcs`, but then we run into the problems discussed above.

```
int
file2wcs (int fd, const char *charset, wchar_t *outbuf, size_t avail)
{
  char inbuf[BUFSIZ];
  size_t insize = 0;
  char *wrptr = (char *) outbuf;
  int result = 0;
  iconv_t cd;

  cd = iconv_open ("WCHAR_T", charset);
  if (cd == (iconv_t) -1)
    {
      /* Something went wrong.  */
      if (errno == EINVAL)
        error (0, 0, "conversion from '%s' to wchar_t not available",
               charset);
      else
        perror ("iconv_open");

      /* Terminate the output string.  */
      *outbuf = L'\0';

      return -1;
    }

  while (avail > 0)
    {
      size_t nread;
      size_t nconv;
      char *inptr = inbuf;

      /* Read more input.  */
      nread = read (fd, inbuf + insize, sizeof (inbuf) - insize);
      if (nread == 0)
        {
          /* When we come here the file is completely read.
             This still could mean there are some unused
             characters in the inbuf.  Put them back.  */
          if (lseek (fd, -insize, SEEK_CUR) == -1)
            result = -1;

          /* Now write out the byte sequence to get into the
             initial state if this is necessary.  */
```

```
        iconv (cd, NULL, NULL, &wrptr, &avail);

        break;
      }
    insize += nread;

    /* Do the conversion.  */
    nconv = iconv (cd, &inptr, &insize, &wrptr, &avail);
    if (nconv == (size_t) -1)
      {
        /* Not everything went right.  It might only be
           an unfinished byte sequence at the end of the
           buffer.  Or it is a real problem.  */
        if (errno == EINVAL)
          /* This is harmless.  Simply move the unused
             bytes to the beginning of the buffer so that
             they can be used in the next round.  */
          memmove (inbuf, inptr, insize);
        else
          {
            /* It is a real problem.  Maybe we ran out of
               space in the output buffer or we have invalid
               input.  In any case back the file pointer to
               the position of the last processed byte.  */
            lseek (fd, -insize, SEEK_CUR);
            result = -1;
            break;
          }
      }
  }

/* Terminate the output string.  */
if (avail >= sizeof (wchar_t))
  *((wchar_t *) wrptr) = L'\0';

if (iconv_close (cd) != 0)
  perror ("iconv_close");

return (wchar_t *) wrptr - outbuf;
}
```

This example shows the most important aspects of using the `iconv` functions. It shows how successive calls to `iconv` can be used to convert large amounts of text. The user does not have to care about stateful encodings as the functions take care of everything.

An interesting point is the case where `iconv` returns an error and `errno` is set to `EINVAL`. This is not really an error in the transformation. It can happen whenever the input character set contains byte sequences of more than one byte for some character and texts are not processed in one piece. In this case there is a chance that a multibyte sequence is cut. The caller can then simply read the remainder of the takes and feed the offending bytes together with new character from the input to `iconv` and continue the work. The internal state kept in the descriptor is *not* unspecified after such an event as is the case with the conversion functions from the ISO C standard.

The example also shows the problem of using wide character strings with `iconv`. As explained in the description of the `iconv` function above, the function always takes a pointer to a **char** array and the available space is measured in bytes. In the example, the output buffer is a wide character buffer; therefore, we use a local variable *wrptr* of type **char ***, which is used in the `iconv` calls.

This looks rather innocent but can lead to problems on platforms that have tight restriction on alignment. Therefore the caller of `iconv` has to make sure that the pointers passed are suitable for access of characters from the appropriate character set. Since, in the above case, the input parameter to the function is a `wchar_t` pointer, this is the case (unless the user violates alignment when computing the parameter). But in other situations, especially when writing generic functions where one does not know what type of character set one uses and, therefore, treats text as a sequence of bytes, it might become tricky.

6.5.3 Some Details about other `iconv` Implementations

This is not really the place to discuss the `iconv` implementation of other systems but it is necessary to know a bit about them to write portable programs. The above mentioned problems with the specification of the `iconv` functions can lead to portability issues.

The first thing to notice is that, due to the large number of character sets in use, it is certainly not practical to encode the conversions directly in the C library. Therefore, the conversion information must come from files outside the C library. This is usually done in one or both of the following ways:

- The C library contains a set of generic conversion functions that can read the needed conversion tables and other information from data files. These files get loaded when necessary.

  This solution is problematic as it requires a great deal of effort to apply to all character sets (potentially an infinite set). The differences in the structure of the different character sets is so large that many different variants of the table-processing functions must be developed. In addition, the generic nature of these functions make them slower than specifically implemented functions.

- The C library only contains a framework that can dynamically load object files and execute the conversion functions contained therein.

  This solution provides much more flexibility. The C library itself contains only very little code and therefore reduces the general memory footprint. Also, with a documented interface between the C library and the loadable modules it is possible for third parties to extend the set of available conversion modules. A drawback of this solution is that dynamic loading must be available.

Some implementations in commercial Unices implement a mixture of these possibilities; the majority implement only the second solution. Using loadable modules moves the code out of the library itself and keeps the door open for extensions and improvements, but this design is also limiting on some platforms since not many platforms support dynamic loading in statically linked programs. On platforms without this capability it is therefore not possible to use this interface in statically linked programs. The GNU C Library has, on ELF platforms, no problems with dynamic loading in these situations; therefore, this point is moot. The danger is that one gets acquainted with this situation and forgets about the restrictions on other systems.

A second thing to know about other `iconv` implementations is that the number of available conversions is often very limited. Some implementations provide, in the standard release (not special international or developer releases), at most 100 to 200 conversion possibilities. This does not mean 200 different character sets are supported; for example, conversions from one character set to a set of 10 others might count as 10 conversions. Together with the other direction this makes 20 conversion possibilities used up by one character set. One can imagine the thin coverage these platform provide. Some Unix vendors even provide only a handful of conversions, which renders them useless for almost all uses.

This directly leads to a third and probably the most problematic point. The way the `iconv` conversion functions are implemented on all known Unix systems and the availability of the conversion functions from character set $\mathcal{A}$ to $\mathcal{B}$ and the conversion from $\mathcal{B}$ to $\mathcal{C}$ does *not* imply that the conversion from $\mathcal{A}$ to $\mathcal{C}$ is available.

This might not seem unreasonable and problematic at first, but it is a quite big problem as one will notice shortly after hitting it. To show the problem we assume to write a program that has to convert from $\mathcal{A}$ to $\mathcal{C}$. A call like

```
cd = iconv_open ("C", "A");
```

fails according to the assumption above. But what does the program do now? The conversion is necessary; therefore, simply giving up is not an option.

This is a nuisance. The `iconv` function should take care of this. But how should the program proceed from here on? If it tries to convert to character set $\mathcal{B}$, first the two `iconv_open` calls

```
cd1 = iconv_open ("B", "A");
```

and

```
cd2 = iconv_open ("C", "B");
```

will succeed, but how to find $\mathcal{B}$?

Unfortunately, the answer is: there is no general solution. On some systems guessing might help. On those systems most character sets can convert to and from UTF-8 encoded ISO 10646 or Unicode text. Beside this only some very system-specific methods can help. Since the conversion functions come from loadable modules and these modules must be stored somewhere in the filesystem, one *could* try to find them and determine from the available file which conversions are available and whether there is an indirect route from $\mathcal{A}$ to $\mathcal{C}$.

This example shows one of the design errors of `iconv` mentioned above. It should at least be possible to determine the list of available conversion programmatically so that if `iconv_open` says there is no such conversion, one could make sure this also is true for indirect routes.

6.5.4 The `iconv` Implementation in the GNU C Library

After reading about the problems of `iconv` implementations in the last section it is certainly good to note that the implementation in the GNU C Library has none of the problems mentioned above. What follows is a step-by-step analysis of the points raised above. The evaluation is based on the current state of the development (as of January 1999). The development of the `iconv` functions is not complete, but basic functionality has solidified.

The GNU C Library's `iconv` implementation uses shared loadable modules to implement the conversions. A very small number of conversions are built into the library itself but these are only rather trivial conversions.

All the benefits of loadable modules are available in the GNU C Library implementation. This is especially appealing since the interface is well documented (see below), and it, therefore, is easy to write new conversion modules. The drawback of using loadable objects is not a problem in the GNU C Library, at least on ELF systems. Since the library is able to load shared objects even in statically linked binaries, static linking need not be forbidden in case one wants to use `iconv`.

The second mentioned problem is the number of supported conversions. Currently, the GNU C Library supports more than 150 character sets. The way the implementation is designed the number of supported conversions is greater than 22350 (150 times 149). If any conversion from or to a character set is missing, it can be added easily.

Particularly impressive as it may be, this high number is due to the fact that the GNU C Library implementation of `iconv` does not have the third problem mentioned above (i.e., whenever there is a conversion from a character set A to B and from B to C it is always possible to convert from A to C directly). If the `iconv_open` returns an error and sets `errno` to `EINVAL`, there is no known way, directly or indirectly, to perform the wanted conversion.

Triangulation is achieved by providing for each character set a conversion from and to UCS-4 encoded ISO 10646. Using ISO 10646 as an intermediate representation it is possible to *triangulate* (i.e., convert with an intermediate representation).

There is no inherent requirement to provide a conversion to ISO 10646 for a new character set, and it is also possible to provide other conversions where neither source nor destination character set is ISO 10646. The existing set of conversions is simply meant to cover all conversions that might be of interest.

All currently available conversions use the triangulation method above, making conversion run unnecessarily slow. If, for example, somebody often needs the conversion from ISO-2022-JP to EUC-JP, a quicker solution would involve direct conversion between the two character sets, skipping the input to ISO 10646 first. The two character sets of interest are much more similar to each other than to ISO 10646.

In such a situation one easily can write a new conversion and provide it as a better alternative. The GNU C Library `iconv` implementation would automatically use the module implementing the conversion if it is specified to be more efficient.

6.5.4.1 Format of `gconv-modules` files

All information about the available conversions comes from a file named `gconv-modules`, which can be found in any of the directories along the `GCONV_PATH`. The `gconv-modules` files are line-oriented text files, where each of the lines has one of the following formats:

- If the first non-whitespace character is a `#` the line contains only comments and is ignored.
- Lines starting with `alias` define an alias name for a character set. Two more words are expected on the line. The first word defines the alias name, and the second defines the original name of the character set. The effect is that it is possible to use the alias name in the *fromset* or *toset* parameters of `iconv_open` and achieve the same result as when using the real character set name.

  This is quite important as a character set has often many different names. There is normally an official name but this need not correspond to the most popular name. Beside this many character sets have special names that are somehow constructed. For example, all character sets specified by the ISO have an alias of the form `ISO-IR-`*nnn* where *nnn* is the registration number. This allows programs that know about the registration number to construct character set names and use them in `iconv_open` calls. More on the available names and aliases follows below.

- Lines starting with `module` introduce an available conversion module. These lines must contain three or four more words.

  The first word specifies the source character set, the second word the destination character set of conversion implemented in this module, and the third word is the name of the loadable module. The filename is constructed by appending the usual shared object suffix (normally `.so`) and this file is then supposed to be found in the same directory the `gconv-modules` file is in. The last word on the line, which is optional, is a numeric value representing the cost of the conversion. If this word is missing, a cost of 1 is assumed. The numeric value itself does not matter that much; what counts are the relative values of the sums of costs for all possible conversion paths. Below is a more precise description of the use of the cost value.

Returning to the example above where one has written a module to directly convert from ISO-2022-JP to EUC-JP and back. All that has to be done is to put the new module, let its name be ISO2022JP-EUCJP.so, in a directory and add a file `gconv-modules` with the following content in the same directory:

```
module  ISO-2022-JP//   EUC-JP//        ISO2022JP-EUCJP    1
module  EUC-JP//         ISO-2022-JP//   ISO2022JP-EUCJP    1
```

To see why this is sufficient, it is necessary to understand how the conversion used by `iconv` (and described in the descriptor) is selected. The approach to this problem is quite simple.

At the first call of the `iconv_open` function the program reads all available `gconv-modules` files and builds up two tables: one containing all the known aliases and another that contains the information about the conversions and which shared object implements them.

6.5.4.2 Finding the conversion path in `iconv`

The set of available conversions form a directed graph with weighted edges. The weights on the edges are the costs specified in the `gconv-modules` files. The `iconv_open` function uses an algorithm suitable for search for the best path in such a graph and so constructs a list of conversions that must be performed in succession to get the transformation from the source to the destination character set.

Explaining why the above `gconv-modules` files allows the `iconv` implementation to resolve the specific ISO-2022-JP to EUC-JP conversion module instead of the conversion coming with the library itself is straightforward. Since the latter conversion takes two steps (from ISO-2022-JP to ISO 10646 and then from ISO 10646 to EUC-JP), the cost is $1 + 1 = 2$. The above `gconv-modules` file, however, specifies that the new conversion modules can perform this conversion with only the cost of 1.

A mysterious item about the `gconv-modules` file above (and also the file coming with the GNU C Library) are the names of the character sets specified in the `module` lines. Why do almost all the names end in `//`? And this is not all: the names can actually be regular expressions. At this point in time this mystery should not be revealed, unless you have the relevant spell-casting materials: ashes from an original DOS 6.2 boot disk burnt in effigy, a crucifix blessed by St. Emacs, assorted herbal roots from Central America, sand from Cebu, etc. Sorry! **The part of the implementation where this is used is not yet finished. For now please simply follow the existing examples. It'll become clearer once it is. –drepper**

A last remark about the `gconv-modules` is about the names not ending with `//`. A character set named `INTERNAL` is often mentioned. From the discussion above and the chosen name it should have become clear that this is the name for the representation used in the intermediate step of the triangulation. We have said that this is UCS-4 but actually that is not quite right. The UCS-4 specification also includes the specification of the byte ordering used. Since a UCS-4 value consists of four bytes, a stored value is affected by byte ordering. The internal representation is *not* the same as UCS-4 in case the byte ordering of the processor (or at least the running process) is not the same as the one required for UCS-4. This is done for performance reasons as one does not want to perform unnecessary byte-swapping operations if one is not interested in actually seeing the result in UCS-4. To avoid trouble with endianness, the internal representation consistently is named `INTERNAL` even on big-endian systems where the representations are identical.

6.5.4.3 `iconv` module data structures

So far this section has described how modules are located and considered to be used. What remains to be described is the interface of the modules so that one can write new ones. This section describes the interface as it is in use in January 1999. The interface will change a bit in the future but, with luck, only in an upwardly compatible way.

The definitions necessary to write new modules are publicly available in the non-standard header `gconv.h`. The following text, therefore, describes the definitions from this header file. First, however, it is necessary to get an overview.

From the perspective of the user of `iconv` the interface is quite simple: the `iconv_open` function returns a handle that can be used in calls to `iconv`, and finally the handle is freed with a call to `iconv_close`. The problem is that the handle has to be able to represent the possibly long sequences of conversion steps and also the state of each conversion since the handle is all that is passed to the `iconv` function. Therefore, the data structures are really the elements necessary to understanding the implementation.

We need two different kinds of data structures. The first describes the conversion and the second describes the state etc. There are really two type definitions like this in `gconv.h`.

`struct __gconv_step`   [Data type]
>   This data structure describes one conversion a module can perform. For each function in a loaded module with conversion functions there is exactly one object of this type. This object is shared by all users of the conversion (i.e., this object does not contain any information corresponding to an actual conversion; it only describes the conversion itself).

```
struct __gconv_loaded_object *__shlib_handle
const char *__modname
int __counter
```
> All these elements of the structure are used internally in the C library to coordinate loading and unloading the shared. One must not expect any of the other elements to be available or initialized.

```
const char *__from_name
const char *__to_name
```
> `__from_name` and `__to_name` contain the names of the source and destination character sets. They can be used to identify the actual conversion to be carried out since one module might implement conversions for more than one character set and/or direction.

```
gconv_fct __fct
gconv_init_fct __init_fct
gconv_end_fct __end_fct
```
> These elements contain pointers to the functions in the loadable module. The interface will be explained below.

```
int __min_needed_from
int __max_needed_from
int __min_needed_to
int __max_needed_to;
```
> These values have to be supplied in the init function of the module. The `__min_needed_from` value specifies how many bytes a character of the source character set at least needs. The `__max_needed_from` specifies the maximum value that also includes possible shift sequences.
>
> The `__min_needed_to` and `__max_needed_to` values serve the same purpose as `__min_needed_from` and `__max_needed_from` but this time for the destination character set.
>
> It is crucial that these values be accurate since otherwise the conversion functions will have problems or not work at all.

```
int __stateful
```
> This element must also be initialized by the init function. `int __stateful` is nonzero if the source character set is stateful. Otherwise it is zero.

```
void *__data
```
> This element can be used freely by the conversion functions in the module. `void *__data` can be used to communicate extra information from one call to another. `void *__data` need not be initialized if not needed at all. If `void *__data` element is assigned a pointer to dynamically allocated memory (presumably in the init function) it has to be made sure that the end function deallocates the memory. Otherwise the application will leak memory.
>
> It is important to be aware that this data structure is shared by all users of this specification conversion and therefore the `__data` element must not contain data specific to one specific use of the conversion function.

`struct __gconv_step_data`   [Data type]
>   This is the data structure that contains the information specific to each use of the conversion functions.

>   `char *__outbuf`
>   `char *__outbufend`
>>   These elements specify the output buffer for the conversion step. The `__outbuf` element points to the beginning of the buffer, and `__outbufend` points to the byte following the last byte in the buffer. The conversion function must not assume anything about the size of the buffer but it can be safely assumed the there is room for at least one complete character in the output buffer.

>>   Once the conversion is finished, if the conversion is the last step, the `__outbuf` element must be modified to point after the last byte written into the buffer to signal how much output is available. If this conversion step is not the last one, the element must not be modified. The `__outbufend` element must not be modified.

>   `int __is_last`
>>   This element is nonzero if this conversion step is the last one. This information is necessary for the recursion. See the description of the conversion function internals below. This element must never be modified.

>   `int __invocation_counter`
>>   The conversion function can use this element to see how many calls of the conversion function already happened. Some character sets require a certain prolog when generating output, and by comparing this value with zero, one can find out whether it is the first call and whether, therefore, the prolog should be emitted. This element must never be modified.

>   `int __internal_use`
>>   This element is another one rarely used but needed in certain situations. It is assigned a nonzero value in case the conversion functions are used to implement `mbsrtowcs` et.al. (i.e., the function is not used directly through the `iconv` interface).

>>   This sometimes makes a difference as it is expected that the `iconv` functions are used to translate entire texts while the `mbsrtowcs` functions are normally used only to convert single strings and might be used multiple times to convert entire texts.

>>   But in this situation we would have problem complying with some rules of the character set specification. Some character sets require a prolog, which must appear exactly once for an entire text. If a number of `mbsrtowcs` calls are used to convert the text, only the first call must add the prolog. However, because there is no communication between the different calls of `mbsrtowcs`, the conversion functions have no possibility to find this out. The situation is different for sequences of `iconv` calls since the handle allows access to the needed information.

>>   The `int __internal_use` element is mostly used together with `__invocation_counter` as follows:

```
if (!data->__internal_use
    && data->__invocation_counter == 0)
/* Emit prolog.  */
    ...
```

This element must never be modified.

`mbstate_t *__statep`

> The `__statep` element points to an object of type `mbstate_t` (see Section 6.3.2 [Representing the state of the conversion], page 132). The conversion of a stateful character set must use the object pointed to by `__statep` to store information about the conversion state. The `__statep` element itself must never be modified.

`mbstate_t __state`

> This element must *never* be used directly. It is only part of this structure to have the needed space allocated.

6.5.4.4 `iconv` module interfaces

With the knowledge about the data structures we now can describe the conversion function itself. To understand the interface a bit of knowledge is necessary about the functionality in the C library that loads the objects with the conversions.

It is often the case that one conversion is used more than once (i.e., there are several `iconv_open` calls for the same set of character sets during one program run). The `mbsrtowcs` et.al. functions in the GNU C Library also use the `iconv` functionality, which increases the number of uses of the same functions even more.

Because of this multiple use of conversions, the modules do not get loaded exclusively for one conversion. Instead a module once loaded can be used by an arbitrary number of `iconv` or `mbsrtowcs` calls at the same time. The splitting of the information between conversion- function-specific information and conversion data makes this possible. The last section showed the two data structures used to do this.

This is of course also reflected in the interface and semantics of the functions that the modules must provide. There are three functions that must have the following names:

`gconv_init`

> The `gconv_init` function initializes the conversion function specific data structure. This very same object is shared by all conversions that use this conversion and, therefore, no state information about the conversion itself must be stored in here. If a module implements more than one conversion, the `gconv_init` function will be called multiple times.

`gconv_end`

> The `gconv_end` function is responsible for freeing all resources allocated by the `gconv_init` function. If there is nothing to do, this function can be missing. Special care must be taken if the module implements more than one conversion and the `gconv_init` function does not allocate the same resources for all conversions.

`gconv` This is the actual conversion function. It is called to convert one block of text. It gets passed the conversion step information initialized by `gconv_init` and the conversion data, specific to this use of the conversion functions.

There are three data types defined for the three module interface functions and these define the interface.

int (*__gconv_init_fct) (*struct __gconv_step **)   [Data type]
> This specifies the interface of the initialization function of the module. It is called exactly once for each conversion the module implements.

> As explained in the description of the **struct __gconv_step** data structure above the initialization function has to initialize parts of it.

__min_needed_from
__max_needed_from
__min_needed_to
__max_needed_to
> > These elements must be initialized to the exact numbers of the minimum and maximum number of bytes used by one character in the source and destination character sets, respectively. If the characters all have the same size, the minimum and maximum values are the same.

__stateful
> > This element must be initialized to a nonzero value if the source character set is stateful. Otherwise it must be zero.

> If the initialization function needs to communicate some information to the conversion function, this communication can happen using the **__data** element of the **__gconv_step** structure. But since this data is shared by all the conversions, it must not be modified by the conversion function. The example below shows how this can be used.

```
#define MIN_NEEDED_FROM         1
#define MAX_NEEDED_FROM         4
#define MIN_NEEDED_TO           4
#define MAX_NEEDED_TO           4

int
gconv_init (struct __gconv_step *step)
{
  /* Determine which direction.  */
  struct iso2022jp_data *new_data;
  enum direction dir = illegal_dir;
  enum variant var = illegal_var;
  int result;

  if (__strcasecmp (step->__from_name, "ISO-2022-JP//") == 0)
    {
      dir = from_iso2022jp;
      var = iso2022jp;
    }
  else if (__strcasecmp (step->__to_name, "ISO-2022-JP//") == 0)
    {
      dir = to_iso2022jp;
      var = iso2022jp;
    }
  else if (__strcasecmp (step->__from_name, "ISO-2022-JP-2//") == 0)
    {
      dir = from_iso2022jp;
      var = iso2022jp2;
```

```
        }
      else if (__strcasecmp (step->__to_name, "ISO-2022-JP-2//") == 0)
        {
          dir = to_iso2022jp;
          var = iso2022jp2;
        }

    result = __GCONV_NOCONV;
    if (dir != illegal_dir)
      {
        new_data = (struct iso2022jp_data *)
          malloc (sizeof (struct iso2022jp_data));

        result = __GCONV_NOMEM;
        if (new_data != NULL)
          {
            new_data->dir = dir;
            new_data->var = var;
            step->__data = new_data;

            if (dir == from_iso2022jp)
              {
                step->__min_needed_from = MIN_NEEDED_FROM;
                step->__max_needed_from = MAX_NEEDED_FROM;
                step->__min_needed_to = MIN_NEEDED_TO;
                step->__max_needed_to = MAX_NEEDED_TO;
              }
            else
              {
                step->__min_needed_from = MIN_NEEDED_TO;
                step->__max_needed_from = MAX_NEEDED_TO;
                step->__min_needed_to = MIN_NEEDED_FROM;
                step->__max_needed_to = MAX_NEEDED_FROM + 2;
              }

            /* Yes, this is a stateful encoding.  */
            step->__stateful = 1;

            result = __GCONV_OK;
          }
      }

    return result;
  }
```

The function first checks which conversion is wanted. The module from which this function is taken implements four different conversions; which one is selected can be determined by comparing the names. The comparison should always be done without paying attention to the case.

Next, a data structure, which contains the necessary information about which conversion is selected, is allocated. The data structure struct iso2022jp_data is locally defined since, outside the module, this data is not used at all. Please note that if all four conversions this modules supports are requested there are four data blocks.

One interesting thing is the initialization of the __min_ and __max_ elements of the step data object. A single ISO-2022-JP character can consist of one to four bytes. Therefore the MIN_NEEDED_FROM and MAX_NEEDED_FROM macros are defined this way.

The output is always the INTERNAL character set (aka UCS-4) and therefore each character consists of exactly four bytes. For the conversion from INTERNAL to ISO-2022-JP we have to take into account that escape sequences might be necessary to switch the character sets. Therefore the __max_needed_to element for this direction gets assigned MAX_NEEDED_FROM + 2. This takes into account the two bytes needed for the escape sequences to single the switching. The asymmetry in the maximum values for the two directions can be explained easily: when reading ISO-2022-JP text, escape sequences can be handled alone (i.e., it is not necessary to process a real character since the effect of the escape sequence can be recorded in the state information). The situation is different for the other direction. Since it is in general not known which character comes next, one cannot emit escape sequences to change the state in advance. This means the escape sequences that have to be emitted together with the next character. Therefore one needs more room than only for the character itself.

The possible return values of the initialization function are:

__GCONV_OK
> The initialization succeeded

__GCONV_NOCONV
> The requested conversion is not supported in the module. This can happen if the gconv-modules file has errors.

__GCONV_NOMEM
> Memory required to store additional information could not be allocated.

The function called before the module is unloaded is significantly easier. It often has nothing at all to do; in which case it can be left out completely.

void (*__gconv_end_fct) (*struct gconv_step* *)*   [Data type]
> The task of this function is to free all resources allocated in the initialization function. Therefore only the __data element of the object pointed to by the argument is of interest. Continuing the example from the initialization function, the finalization function looks like this:
>
> ```
> void
> gconv_end (struct __gconv_step *data)
> {
>   free (data->__data);
> }
> ```

The most important function is the conversion function itself, which can get quite complicated for complex character sets. But since this is not of interest here, we will only describe a possible skeleton for the conversion function.

int (*__gconv_fct) (*struct __gconv_step* *, struct __gconv_step_data*   [Data type]
> *, const char* *, const char* *, size_t* *, int*)
> The conversion function can be called for two basic reason: to convert text or to reset the state. From the description of the iconv function it can be seen why the flushing mode is necessary. What mode is selected is determined by the sixth argument, an integer. This argument being nonzero means that flushing is selected.
>
> Common to both modes is where the output buffer can be found. The information about this buffer is stored in the conversion step data. A pointer to this information

is passed as the second argument to this function. The description of the **struct __gconv_step_data** structure has more information on the conversion step data.

What has to be done for flushing depends on the source character set. If the source character set is not stateful, nothing has to be done. Otherwise the function has to emit a byte sequence to bring the state object into the initial state. Once this all happened the other conversion modules in the chain of conversions have to get the same chance. Whether another step follows can be determined from the **__is_last** element of the step data structure to which the first parameter points.

The more interesting mode is when actual text has to be converted. The first step in this case is to convert as much text as possible from the input buffer and store the result in the output buffer. The start of the input buffer is determined by the third argument, which is a pointer to a pointer variable referencing the beginning of the buffer. The fourth argument is a pointer to the byte right after the last byte in the buffer.

The conversion has to be performed according to the current state if the character set is stateful. The state is stored in an object pointed to by the **__statep** element of the step data (second argument). Once either the input buffer is empty or the output buffer is full the conversion stops. At this point, the pointer variable referenced by the third parameter must point to the byte following the last processed byte (i.e., if all of the input is consumed, this pointer and the fourth parameter have the same value).

What now happens depends on whether this step is the last one. If it is the last step, the only thing that has to be done is to update the **__outbuf** element of the step data structure to point after the last written byte. This update gives the caller the information on how much text is available in the output buffer. In addition, the variable pointed to by the fifth parameter, which is of type **size_t**, must be incremented by the number of characters (*not bytes*) that were converted in a non-reversible way. Then, the function can return.

In case the step is not the last one, the later conversion functions have to get a chance to do their work. Therefore, the appropriate conversion function has to be called. The information about the functions is stored in the conversion data structures, passed as the first parameter. This information and the step data are stored in arrays, so the next element in both cases can be found by simple pointer arithmetic:

```
int
gconv (struct __gconv_step *step, struct __gconv_step_data *data,
       const char **inbuf, const char *inbufend, size_t *written,
       int do_flush)
{
  struct __gconv_step *next_step = step + 1;
  struct __gconv_step_data *next_data = data + 1;
  ...
```

The **next_step** pointer references the next step information and **next_data** the next data record. The call of the next function therefore will look similar to this:

```
next_step->__fct (next_step, next_data, &outerr, outbuf,
                  written, 0)
```

But this is not yet all. Once the function call returns the conversion function might have some more to do. If the return value of the function is **__GCONV_EMPTY_INPUT**, more room is available in the output buffer. Unless the input buffer is empty the conversion, functions start all over again and process the rest of the input buffer. If the return value is not `__GCONV_EMPTY_INPUT`, something went wrong and we have to recover from this.

A requirement for the conversion function is that the input buffer pointer (the third argument) always point to the last character that was put in converted form into the output buffer. This is trivially true after the conversion performed in the current step, but if the conversion functions deeper downstream stop prematurely, not all characters from the output buffer are consumed and, therefore, the input buffer pointers must be backed off to the right position.

Correcting the input buffers is easy to do if the input and output character sets have a fixed width for all characters. In this situation we can compute how many characters are left in the output buffer and, therefore, can correct the input buffer pointer appropriately with a similar computation. Things are getting tricky if either character set has characters represented with variable length byte sequences, and it gets even more complicated if the conversion has to take care of the state. In these cases the conversion has to be performed once again, from the known state before the initial conversion (i.e., if necessary the state of the conversion has to be reset and the conversion loop has to be executed again). The difference now is that it is known how much input must be created, and the conversion can stop before converting the first unused character. Once this is done the input buffer pointers must be updated again and the function can return.

One final thing should be mentioned. If it is necessary for the conversion to know whether it is the first invocation (in case a prolog has to be emitted), the conversion function should increment the `__invocation_counter` element of the step data structure just before returning to the caller. See the description of the **struct __ gconv_step_data** structure above for more information on how this can be used.

The return value must be one of the following values:

`__GCONV_EMPTY_INPUT`

> All input was consumed and there is room left in the output buffer.

`__GCONV_FULL_OUTPUT`

> No more room in the output buffer. In case this is not the last step this value is propagated down from the call of the next conversion function in the chain.

`__GCONV_INCOMPLETE_INPUT`

> The input buffer is not entirely empty since it contains an incomplete character sequence.

The following example provides a framework for a conversion function. In case a new conversion has to be written the holes in this implementation have to be filled and that is it.

```
int
gconv (struct __gconv_step *step, struct __gconv_step_data *data,
       const char **inbuf, const char *inbufend, size_t *written,
       int do_flush)
  {
```

```
struct __gconv_step *next_step = step + 1;
struct __gconv_step_data *next_data = data + 1;
gconv_fct fct = next_step->__fct;
int status;

/* If the function is called with no input this means we have
   to reset to the initial state.  The possibly partly
   converted input is dropped.  */
if (do_flush)
  {
    status = __GCONV_OK;

    /* Possible emit a byte sequence which put the state object
       into the initial state.  */

    /* Call the steps down the chain if there are any but only
       if we successfully emitted the escape sequence.  */
    if (status == __GCONV_OK && ! data->__is_last)
      status = fct (next_step, next_data, NULL, NULL,
                    written, 1);
  }
else
  {
    /* We preserve the initial values of the pointer variables.  */
    const char *inptr = *inbuf;
    char *outbuf = data->__outbuf;
    char *outend = data->__outbufend;
    char *outptr;

    do
      {
        /* Remember the start value for this round.  */
        inptr = *inbuf;
        /* The outbuf buffer is empty.  */
        outptr = outbuf;

        /* For stateful encodings the state must be safe here.  */

        /* Run the conversion loop.  status is set
           appropriately afterwards.  */

        /* If this is the last step, leave the loop.  There is
           nothing we can do.  */
        if (data->__is_last)
          {
            /* Store information about how many bytes are
               available.  */
            data->__outbuf = outbuf;

            /* If any non-reversible conversions were performed,
               add the number to *written.  */

            break;
          }

        /* Write out all output that was produced.  */
        if (outbuf > outptr)
          {
```

```
                    const char *outerr = data->__outbuf;
                    int result;

                    result = fct (next_step, next_data, &outerr,
                                  outbuf, written, 0);

                    if (result != __GCONV_EMPTY_INPUT)
                      {
                        if (outerr != outbuf)
                          {
                            /* Reset the input buffer pointer.  We
                               document here the complex case.  */
                            size_t nstatus;

                            /* Reload the pointers.  */
                            *inbuf = inptr;
                            outbuf = outptr;

                            /* Possibly reset the state.  */

                            /* Redo the conversion, but this time
                               the end of the output buffer is at
                               outerr.  */
                          }

                        /* Change the status.  */
                        status = result;
                      }
                    else
                      /* All the output is consumed, we can make
                         another run if everything was ok.  */
                      if (status == __GCONV_FULL_OUTPUT)
                        status = __GCONV_OK;
                  }
              while (status == __GCONV_OK);

              /* We finished one use of this step.  */
              ++data->__invocation_counter;
            }

      return status;
    }
```

This information should be sufficient to write new modules. Anybody doing so should also take a look at the available source code in the GNU C Library sources. It contains many examples of working and optimized modules.

7 Locales and Internationalization

Different countries and cultures have varying conventions for how to communicate. These conventions range from very simple ones, such as the format for representing dates and times, to very complex ones, such as the language spoken.

Internationalization of software means programming it to be able to adapt to the user's favorite conventions. In ISO C, internationalization works by means of *locales*. Each locale specifies a collection of conventions, one convention for each purpose. The user chooses a set of conventions by specifying a locale (via environment variables).

All programs inherit the chosen locale as part of their environment. Provided the programs are written to obey the choice of locale, they will follow the conventions preferred by the user.

7.1 What Effects a Locale Has

Each locale specifies conventions for several purposes, including the following:

- What multibyte character sequences are valid, and how they are interpreted (see Chapter 6 [Character Set Handling], page 127).

- Classification of which characters in the local character set are considered alphabetic, and upper- and lower-case conversion conventions (see Chapter 4 [Character Handling], page 77).

- The collating sequence for the local language and character set (see Section 5.6 [Collation Functions], page 106).

- Formatting of numbers and currency amounts (see Section 7.7.1.1 [Generic Numeric Formatting Parameters], page 175).

- Formatting of dates and times (see Section 21.4.5 [Formatting Calendar Time], page 608).

- What language to use for output, including error messages (see Chapter 8 [Message Translation], page 188).

- What language to use for user answers to yes-or-no questions (see Section 7.9 [Yes-or-No Questions], page 187).

- What language to use for more complex user input. (The C library doesn't yet help you implement this.)

Some aspects of adapting to the specified locale are handled automatically by the library subroutines. For example, all your program needs to do in order to use the collating sequence of the chosen locale is to use `strcoll` or `strxfrm` to compare strings.

Other aspects of locales are beyond the comprehension of the library. For example, the library can't automatically translate your program's output messages into other languages. The only way you can support output in the user's favorite language is to program this more or less by hand. The C library provides functions to handle translations for multiple languages easily.

This chapter discusses the mechanism by which you can modify the current locale. The effects of the current locale on specific library functions are discussed in more detail in the descriptions of those functions.

7.2 Choosing a Locale

The simplest way for the user to choose a locale is to set the environment variable `LANG`. This specifies a single locale to use for all purposes. For example, a user could specify a hypothetical locale named 'espana-castellano' to use the standard conventions of most of Spain.

The set of locales supported depends on the operating system you are using, and so do their names, except that the standard locale called 'C' or 'POSIX' always exist. See Section 7.6 [Locale Names], page 173.

In order to force the system to always use the default locale, the user can set the `LC_ALL` environment variable to 'C'.

A user also has the option of specifying different locales for different purposes—in effect, choosing a mixture of multiple locales. See Section 7.3 [Locale Categories], page 170.

For example, the user might specify the locale 'espana-castellano' for most purposes, but specify the locale 'usa-english' for currency formatting. This might make sense if the user is a Spanish-speaking American, working in Spanish, but representing monetary amounts in US dollars.

Note that both locales 'espana-castellano' and 'usa-english', like all locales, would include conventions for all of the purposes to which locales apply. However, the user can choose to use each locale for a particular subset of those purposes.

7.3 Locale Categories

The purposes that locales serve are grouped into *categories*, so that a user or a program can choose the locale for each category independently. Here is a table of categories; each name is both an environment variable that a user can set, and a macro name that you can use as the first argument to `setlocale`.

The contents of the environment variable (or the string in the second argument to `setlocale`) has to be a valid locale name. See Section 7.6 [Locale Names], page 173.

LC_COLLATE
> This category applies to collation of strings (functions `strcoll` and `strxfrm`); see Section 5.6 [Collation Functions], page 106.

LC_CTYPE   This category applies to classification and conversion of characters, and to multi-byte and wide characters; see Chapter 4 [Character Handling], page 77, and Chapter 6 [Character Set Handling], page 127.

LC_MONETARY
> This category applies to formatting monetary values; see Section 7.7.1.1 [Generic Numeric Formatting Parameters], page 175.

LC_NUMERIC
> This category applies to formatting numeric values that are not monetary; see Section 7.7.1.1 [Generic Numeric Formatting Parameters], page 175.

LC_TIME   This category applies to formatting date and time values; see Section 21.4.5 [Formatting Calendar Time], page 608.

LC_MESSAGES

> This category applies to selecting the language used in the user interface for message translation (see Section 8.2 [The Uniforum approach to Message Translation], page 197; see Section 8.1 [X/Open Message Catalog Handling], page 188) and contains regular expressions for affirmative and negative responses.

LC_ALL   This is not a category; it is only a macro that you can use with `setlocale` to set a single locale for all purposes. Setting this environment variable overwrites all selections by the other `LC_*` variables or `LANG`.

LANG   If this environment variable is defined, its value specifies the locale to use for all purposes except as overridden by the variables above.

When developing the message translation functions it was felt that the functionality provided by the variables above is not sufficient. For example, it should be possible to specify more than one locale name. Take a Swedish user who better speaks German than English, and a program whose messages are output in English by default. It should be possible to specify that the first choice of language is Swedish, the second German, and if this also fails to use English. This is possible with the variable `LANGUAGE`. For further description of this GNU extension see Section 8.2.1.6 [User influence on `gettext`], page 208.

7.4 How Programs Set the Locale

A C program inherits its locale environment variables when it starts up. This happens automatically. However, these variables do not automatically control the locale used by the library functions, because ISO C says that all programs start by default in the standard 'C' locale. To use the locales specified by the environment, you must call `setlocale`. Call it as follows:

```
setlocale (LC_ALL, "");
```

to select a locale based on the user choice of the appropriate environment variables.

You can also use `setlocale` to specify a particular locale, for general use or for a specific category.

The symbols in this section are defined in the header file `locale.h`.

char * setlocale (*int* category, *const char *locale*)   [Function]
> Preliminary: | MT-Unsafe const:locale env | AS-Unsafe init lock heap corrupt | AC-Unsafe init corrupt lock mem fd | See Section 1.2.2.1 [POSIX Safety Concepts], page 2.

> The function `setlocale` sets the current locale for category *category* to *locale*.

> If *category* is `LC_ALL`, this specifies the locale for all purposes. The other possible values of *category* specify an single purpose (see Section 7.3 [Locale Categories], page 170).

> You can also use this function to find out the current locale by passing a null pointer as the *locale* argument. In this case, `setlocale` returns a string that is the name of the locale currently selected for category *category*.

> The string returned by `setlocale` can be overwritten by subsequent calls, so you should make a copy of the string (see Section 5.4 [Copying and Concatenation],

page 91) if you want to save it past any further calls to `setlocale`. (The standard library is guaranteed never to call `setlocale` itself.)

You should not modify the string returned by `setlocale`. It might be the same string that was passed as an argument in a previous call to `setlocale`. One requirement is that the *category* must be the same in the call the string was returned and the one when the string is passed in as *locale* parameter.

When you read the current locale for category `LC_ALL`, the value encodes the entire combination of selected locales for all categories. If you specify the same "locale name" with `LC_ALL` in a subsequent call to `setlocale`, it restores the same combination of locale selections.

To be sure you can use the returned string encoding the currently selected locale at a later time, you must make a copy of the string. It is not guaranteed that the returned pointer remains valid over time.

When the *locale* argument is not a null pointer, the string returned by `setlocale` reflects the newly-modified locale.

If you specify an empty string for *locale*, this means to read the appropriate environment variable and use its value to select the locale for *category*.

If a nonempty string is given for *locale*, then the locale of that name is used if possible.

The effective locale name (either the second argument to `setlocale`, or if the argument is an empty string, the name obtained from the process environment) must be valid locale name. See Section 7.6 [Locale Names], page 173.

If you specify an invalid locale name, `setlocale` returns a null pointer and leaves the current locale unchanged.

Here is an example showing how you might use `setlocale` to temporarily switch to a new locale.

```
#include <stddef.h>
#include <locale.h>
#include <stdlib.h>
#include <string.h>

void
with_other_locale (char *new_locale,
                    void (*subroutine) (int),
                    int argument)
{
  char *old_locale, *saved_locale;

  /* Get the name of the current locale.  */
  old_locale = setlocale (LC_ALL, NULL);

  /* Copy the name so it won't be clobbered by setlocale. */
  saved_locale = strdup (old_locale);
  if (saved_locale == NULL)
    fatal ("Out of memory");

  /* Now change the locale and do some stuff with it. */
  setlocale (LC_ALL, new_locale);
  (*subroutine) (argument);
```

```
            /* Restore the original locale. */
            setlocale (LC_ALL, saved_locale);
            free (saved_locale);
        }
```

Portability Note: Some ISO C systems may define additional locale categories, and future versions of the library will do so. For portability, assume that any symbol beginning with 'LC_' might be defined in `locale.h`.

7.5 Standard Locales

The only locale names you can count on finding on all operating systems are these three standard ones:

`"C"`   This is the standard C locale. The attributes and behavior it provides are specified in the ISO C standard. When your program starts up, it initially uses this locale by default.

`"POSIX"`   This is the standard POSIX locale. Currently, it is an alias for the standard C locale.

`""`   The empty name says to select a locale based on environment variables. See Section 7.3 [Locale Categories], page 170.

Defining and installing named locales is normally a responsibility of the system administrator at your site (or the person who installed the GNU C Library). It is also possible for the user to create private locales. All this will be discussed later when describing the tool to do so.

If your program needs to use something other than the 'C' locale, it will be more portable if you use whatever locale the user specifies with the environment, rather than trying to specify some non-standard locale explicitly by name. Remember, different machines might have different sets of locales installed.

7.6 Locale Names

The following command prints a list of locales supported by the system:

```
            locale -a
```

Portability Note: With the notable exception of the standard locale names 'C' and 'POSIX', locale names are system-specific.

Most locale names follow XPG syntax and consist of up to four parts:

```
    language[_territory[.codeset]][@modifier]
```

Beside the first part, all of them are allowed to be missing. If the full specified locale is not found, less specific ones are looked for. The various parts will be stripped off, in the following order:

1. codeset

2. normalized codeset

3. territory

4. modifier

For example, the locale name 'de_AT.iso885915@euro' denotes a German-language locale for use in Austria, using the ISO-8859-15 (Latin-9) character set, and with the Euro as the currency symbol.

In addition to locale names which follow XPG syntax, systems may provide aliases such as 'german'. Both categories of names must not contain the slash character '/'.

If the locale name starts with a slash '/', it is treated as a path relative to the configured locale directories; see LOCPATH below. The specified path must not contain a component '..', or the name is invalid, and setlocale will fail.

Portability Note: POSIX suggests that if a locale name starts with a slash '/', it is resolved as an absolute path. However, the GNU C Library treats it as a relative path under the directories listed in LOCPATH (or the default locale directory if LOCPATH is unset).

Locale names which are longer than an implementation-defined limit are invalid and cause setlocale to fail.

As a special case, locale names used with LC_ALL can combine several locales, reflecting different locale settings for different categories. For example, you might want to use a U.S. locale with ISO A4 paper format, so you set LANG to 'en_US.UTF-8', and LC_PAPER to 'de_DE.UTF-8'. In this case, the LC_ALL-style combined locale name is

```
LC_CTYPE=en_US.UTF-8;LC_TIME=en_US.UTF-8;LC_PAPER=de_DE.UTF-8;...
```

followed by other category settings not shown here.

The path used for finding locale data can be set using the LOCPATH environment variable. This variable lists the directories in which to search for locale definitions, separated by a colon ':'.

The default path for finding locale data is system specific. A typical value for the LOCPATH default is:

```
/usr/share/locale
```

The value of LOCPATH is ignored by privileged programs for security reasons, and only the default directory is used.

7.7 Accessing Locale Information

There are several ways to access locale information. The simplest way is to let the C library itself do the work. Several of the functions in this library implicitly access the locale data, and use what information is provided by the currently selected locale. This is how the locale model is meant to work normally.

As an example take the strftime function, which is meant to nicely format date and time information (see Section 21.4.5 [Formatting Calendar Time], page 608). Part of the standard information contained in the LC_TIME category is the names of the months. Instead of requiring the programmer to take care of providing the translations the strftime function does this all by itself. %A in the format string is replaced by the appropriate weekday name of the locale currently selected by LC_TIME. This is an easy example, and wherever possible functions do things automatically in this way.

But there are quite often situations when there is simply no function to perform the task, or it is simply not possible to do the work automatically. For these cases it is necessary to access the information in the locale directly. To do this the C library provides two functions: localeconv and nl_langinfo. The former is part of ISO C and therefore portable, but has a brain-damaged interface. The second is part of the Unix interface and is portable in as far as the system follows the Unix standards.

7.7.1 `localeconv`: **It is portable but ...**

Together with the `setlocale` function the ISO C people invented the `localeconv` function. It is a masterpiece of poor design. It is expensive to use, not extendable, and not generally usable as it provides access to only `LC_MONETARY` and `LC_NUMERIC` related information. Nevertheless, if it is applicable to a given situation it should be used since it is very portable. The function `strfmon` formats monetary amounts according to the selected locale using this information.

`struct lconv * localeconv (`*void*`)` [Function]

> Preliminary: | MT-Unsafe race:localeconv locale | AS-Unsafe | AC-Safe | See Section 1.2.2.1 [POSIX Safety Concepts], page 2.
>
> The `localeconv` function returns a pointer to a structure whose components contain information about how numeric and monetary values should be formatted in the current locale.
>
> You should not modify the structure or its contents. The structure might be overwritten by subsequent calls to `localeconv`, or by calls to `setlocale`, but no other function in the library overwrites this value.

`struct lconv` [Data Type]

> `localeconv`'s return value is of this data type. Its elements are described in the following subsections.

If a member of the structure `struct lconv` has type `char`, and the value is `CHAR_MAX`, it means that the current locale has no value for that parameter.

7.7.1.1 Generic Numeric Formatting Parameters

These are the standard members of `struct lconv`; there may be others.

`char *decimal_point`
`char *mon_decimal_point`

> These are the decimal-point separators used in formatting non-monetary and monetary quantities, respectively. In the 'C' locale, the value of `decimal_point` is `"."`, and the value of `mon_decimal_point` is `""`.

`char *thousands_sep`
`char *mon_thousands_sep`

> These are the separators used to delimit groups of digits to the left of the decimal point in formatting non-monetary and monetary quantities, respectively. In the 'C' locale, both members have a value of `""` (the empty string).

`char *grouping`
`char *mon_grouping`

> These are strings that specify how to group the digits to the left of the decimal point. `grouping` applies to non-monetary quantities and `mon_grouping` applies to monetary quantities. Use either `thousands_sep` or `mon_thousands_sep` to separate the digit groups.

Each member of these strings is to be interpreted as an integer value of type **char**. Successive numbers (from left to right) give the sizes of successive groups (from right to left, starting at the decimal point.) The last member is either 0, in which case the previous member is used over and over again for all the remaining groups, or **CHAR_MAX**, in which case there is no more grouping—or, put another way, any remaining digits form one large group without separators.

For example, if **grouping** is "\04\03\02", the correct grouping for the number 123456787654321 is '12', '34', '56', '78', '765', '4321'. This uses a group of 4 digits at the end, preceded by a group of 3 digits, preceded by groups of 2 digits (as many as needed). With a separator of ',', the number would be printed as '12,34,56,78,765,4321'.

A value of "\03" indicates repeated groups of three digits, as normally used in the U.S.

In the standard 'C' locale, both **grouping** and **mon_grouping** have a value of "". This value specifies no grouping at all.

char int_frac_digits
char frac_digits

> These are small integers indicating how many fractional digits (to the right of the decimal point) should be displayed in a monetary value in international and local formats, respectively. (Most often, both members have the same value.)
>
> In the standard 'C' locale, both of these members have the value **CHAR_MAX**, meaning "unspecified". The ISO standard doesn't say what to do when you find this value; we recommend printing no fractional digits. (This locale also specifies the empty string for **mon_decimal_point**, so printing any fractional digits would be confusing!)

7.7.1.2 Printing the Currency Symbol

These members of the **struct lconv** structure specify how to print the symbol to identify a monetary value—the international analog of '$' for US dollars.

Each country has two standard currency symbols. The *local currency symbol* is used commonly within the country, while the *international currency symbol* is used internationally to refer to that country's currency when it is necessary to indicate the country unambiguously.

For example, many countries use the dollar as their monetary unit, and when dealing with international currencies it's important to specify that one is dealing with (say) Canadian dollars instead of U.S. dollars or Australian dollars. But when the context is known to be Canada, there is no need to make this explicit—dollar amounts are implicitly assumed to be in Canadian dollars.

char *currency_symbol

> The local currency symbol for the selected locale.
>
> In the standard 'C' locale, this member has a value of "" (the empty string), meaning "unspecified". The ISO standard doesn't say what to do when you find this value; we recommend you simply print the empty string as you would print any other string pointed to by this variable.

`char *int_curr_symbol`

> The international currency symbol for the selected locale.
>
> The value of `int_curr_symbol` should normally consist of a three-letter abbreviation determined by the international standard *ISO 4217 Codes for the Representation of Currency and Funds*, followed by a one-character separator (often a space).
>
> In the standard 'C' locale, this member has a value of `""` (the empty string), meaning "unspecified". We recommend you simply print the empty string as you would print any other string pointed to by this variable.

`char p_cs_precedes`
`char n_cs_precedes`
`char int_p_cs_precedes`
`char int_n_cs_precedes`

> These members are 1 if the `currency_symbol` or `int_curr_symbol` strings should precede the value of a monetary amount, or 0 if the strings should follow the value. The `p_cs_precedes` and `int_p_cs_precedes` members apply to positive amounts (or zero), and the `n_cs_precedes` and `int_n_cs_precedes` members apply to negative amounts.
>
> In the standard 'C' locale, all of these members have a value of `CHAR_MAX`, meaning "unspecified". The ISO standard doesn't say what to do when you find this value. We recommend printing the currency symbol before the amount, which is right for most countries. In other words, treat all nonzero values alike in these members.
>
> The members with the `int_` prefix apply to the `int_curr_symbol` while the other two apply to `currency_symbol`.

`char p_sep_by_space`
`char n_sep_by_space`
`char int_p_sep_by_space`
`char int_n_sep_by_space`

> These members are 1 if a space should appear between the `currency_symbol` or `int_curr_symbol` strings and the amount, or 0 if no space should appear. The `p_sep_by_space` and `int_p_sep_by_space` members apply to positive amounts (or zero), and the `n_sep_by_space` and `int_n_sep_by_space` members apply to negative amounts.
>
> In the standard 'C' locale, all of these members have a value of `CHAR_MAX`, meaning "unspecified". The ISO standard doesn't say what you should do when you find this value; we suggest you treat it as 1 (print a space). In other words, treat all nonzero values alike in these members.
>
> The members with the `int_` prefix apply to the `int_curr_symbol` while the other two apply to `currency_symbol`. There is one specialty with the `int_curr_symbol`, though. Since all legal values contain a space at the end the string one either printf this space (if the currency symbol must appear in front and must be separated) or one has to avoid printing this character at all (especially when at the end of the string).

7.7.1.3 Printing the Sign of a Monetary Amount

These members of the `struct lconv` structure specify how to print the sign (if any) of a monetary value.

`char *positive_sign`
`char *negative_sign`

> These are strings used to indicate positive (or zero) and negative monetary quantities, respectively.
>
> In the standard 'C' locale, both of these members have a value of `""` (the empty string), meaning "unspecified".
>
> The ISO standard doesn't say what to do when you find this value; we recommend printing `positive_sign` as you find it, even if it is empty. For a negative value, print `negative_sign` as you find it unless both it and `positive_sign` are empty, in which case print '-' instead. (Failing to indicate the sign at all seems rather unreasonable.)

`char p_sign_posn`
`char n_sign_posn`
`char int_p_sign_posn`
`char int_n_sign_posn`

> These members are small integers that indicate how to position the sign for nonnegative and negative monetary quantities, respectively. (The string used by the sign is what was specified with `positive_sign` or `negative_sign`.) The possible values are as follows:
>
> 0   The currency symbol and quantity should be surrounded by parentheses.
>
> 1   Print the sign string before the quantity and currency symbol.
>
> 2   Print the sign string after the quantity and currency symbol.
>
> 3   Print the sign string right before the currency symbol.
>
> 4   Print the sign string right after the currency symbol.
>
> `CHAR_MAX`   "Unspecified". Both members have this value in the standard 'C' locale.
>
> The ISO standard doesn't say what you should do when the value is `CHAR_MAX`. We recommend you print the sign after the currency symbol.
>
> The members with the `int_` prefix apply to the `int_curr_symbol` while the other two apply to `currency_symbol`.

7.7.2 Pinpoint Access to Locale Data

When writing the X/Open Portability Guide the authors realized that the `localeconv` function is not enough to provide reasonable access to locale information. The information which was meant to be available in the locale (as later specified in the POSIX.1 standard) requires more ways to access it. Therefore the `nl_langinfo` function was introduced.

char * nl_langinfo (*nl_item* **item**)   [Function]
> Preliminary: | MT-Safe locale | AS-Safe | AC-Safe | See Section 1.2.2.1 [POSIX Safety Concepts], page 2.
>
> The nl_langinfo function can be used to access individual elements of the locale categories. Unlike the localeconv function, which returns all the information, nl_langinfo lets the caller select what information it requires. This is very fast and it is not a problem to call this function multiple times.
>
> A second advantage is that in addition to the numeric and monetary formatting information, information from the LC_TIME and LC_MESSAGES categories is available.
>
> The type nl_type is defined in nl_types.h. The argument *item* is a numeric value defined in the header langinfo.h. The X/Open standard defines the following values:
>
> CODESET   nl_langinfo returns a string with the name of the coded character set used in the selected locale.
>
> ABDAY_1
> ABDAY_2
> ABDAY_3
> ABDAY_4
> ABDAY_5
> ABDAY_6
> ABDAY_7   nl_langinfo returns the abbreviated weekday name. ABDAY_1 corresponds to Sunday.
>
> DAY_1
> DAY_2
> DAY_3
> DAY_4
> DAY_5
> DAY_6
> DAY_7   Similar to ABDAY_1 etc., but here the return value is the unabbreviated weekday name.
>
> ABMON_1
> ABMON_2
> ABMON_3
> ABMON_4
> ABMON_5
> ABMON_6
> ABMON_7
> ABMON_8
> ABMON_9
> ABMON_10
> ABMON_11
> ABMON_12   The return value is abbreviated name of the month. ABMON_1 corresponds to January.

```
MON_1
MON_2
MON_3
MON_4
MON_5
MON_6
MON_7
MON_8
MON_9
MON_10
MON_11
MON_12
```
Similar to `ABMON_1` etc., but here the month names are not abbreviated. Here the first value `MON_1` also corresponds to January.

`AM_STR`

`PM_STR`   The return values are strings which can be used in the representation of time as an hour from 1 to 12 plus an am/pm specifier.

Note that in locales which do not use this time representation these strings might be empty, in which case the am/pm format cannot be used at all.

`D_T_FMT`   The return value can be used as a format string for **strftime** to represent time and date in a locale-specific way.

`D_FMT`   The return value can be used as a format string for **strftime** to represent a date in a locale-specific way.

`T_FMT`   The return value can be used as a format string for **strftime** to represent time in a locale-specific way.

`T_FMT_AMPM`

The return value can be used as a format string for **strftime** to represent time in the am/pm format.

Note that if the am/pm format does not make any sense for the selected locale, the return value might be the same as the one for `T_FMT`.

`ERA`   The return value represents the era used in the current locale.

Most locales do not define this value. An example of a locale which does define this value is the Japanese one. In Japan, the traditional representation of dates includes the name of the era corresponding to the then-emperor's reign.

Normally it should not be necessary to use this value directly. Specifying the E modifier in their format strings causes the **strftime** functions to use this information. The format of the returned string is not specified, and therefore you should not assume knowledge of it on different systems.

`ERA_YEAR`   The return value gives the year in the relevant era of the locale. As for `ERA` it should not be necessary to use this value directly.

`ERA_D_T_FMT`

This return value can be used as a format string for **strftime** to represent dates and times in a locale-specific era-based way.

ERA_D_FMT

> This return value can be used as a format string for `strftime` to represent a date in a locale-specific era-based way.

ERA_T_FMT

> This return value can be used as a format string for `strftime` to represent time in a locale-specific era-based way.

ALT_DIGITS

> The return value is a representation of up to 100 values used to represent the values 0 to 99. As for `ERA` this value is not intended to be used directly, but instead indirectly through the `strftime` function. When the modifier `O` is used in a format which would otherwise use numerals to represent hours, minutes, seconds, weekdays, months, or weeks, the appropriate value for the locale is used instead.

INT_CURR_SYMBOL

> The same as the value returned by `localeconv` in the `int_curr_symbol` element of the `struct lconv`.

CURRENCY_SYMBOL
CRNCYSTR The same as the value returned by `localeconv` in the `currency_symbol` element of the `struct lconv`.

> `CRNCYSTR` is a deprecated alias still required by Unix98.

MON_DECIMAL_POINT

> The same as the value returned by `localeconv` in the `mon_decimal_point` element of the `struct lconv`.

MON_THOUSANDS_SEP

> The same as the value returned by `localeconv` in the `mon_thousands_sep` element of the `struct lconv`.

MON_GROUPING

> The same as the value returned by `localeconv` in the `mon_grouping` element of the `struct lconv`.

POSITIVE_SIGN

> The same as the value returned by `localeconv` in the `positive_sign` element of the `struct lconv`.

NEGATIVE_SIGN

> The same as the value returned by `localeconv` in the `negative_sign` element of the `struct lconv`.

INT_FRAC_DIGITS

> The same as the value returned by `localeconv` in the `int_frac_digits` element of the `struct lconv`.

FRAC_DIGITS

> The same as the value returned by `localeconv` in the `frac_digits` element of the `struct lconv`.

P_CS_PRECEDES

> The same as the value returned by `localeconv` in the `p_cs_precedes` element of the **struct lconv**.

P_SEP_BY_SPACE

> The same as the value returned by `localeconv` in the `p_sep_by_space` element of the **struct lconv**.

N_CS_PRECEDES

> The same as the value returned by `localeconv` in the `n_cs_precedes` element of the **struct lconv**.

N_SEP_BY_SPACE

> The same as the value returned by `localeconv` in the `n_sep_by_space` element of the **struct lconv**.

P_SIGN_POSN

> The same as the value returned by `localeconv` in the `p_sign_posn` element of the **struct lconv**.

N_SIGN_POSN

> The same as the value returned by `localeconv` in the `n_sign_posn` element of the **struct lconv**.

INT_P_CS_PRECEDES

> The same as the value returned by `localeconv` in the `int_p_cs_precedes` element of the **struct lconv**.

INT_P_SEP_BY_SPACE

> The same as the value returned by `localeconv` in the `int_p_sep_by_space` element of the **struct lconv**.

INT_N_CS_PRECEDES

> The same as the value returned by `localeconv` in the `int_n_cs_precedes` element of the **struct lconv**.

INT_N_SEP_BY_SPACE

> The same as the value returned by `localeconv` in the `int_n_sep_by_space` element of the **struct lconv**.

INT_P_SIGN_POSN

> The same as the value returned by `localeconv` in the `int_p_sign_posn` element of the **struct lconv**.

INT_N_SIGN_POSN

> The same as the value returned by `localeconv` in the `int_n_sign_posn` element of the **struct lconv**.

DECIMAL_POINT
RADIXCHAR

> The same as the value returned by `localeconv` in the `decimal_point` element of the **struct lconv**.
>
> The name `RADIXCHAR` is a deprecated alias still used in Unix98.

THOUSANDS_SEP

THOUSEP   The same as the value returned by `localeconv` in the `thousands_sep`
            element of the `struct lconv`.

            The name `THOUSEP` is a deprecated alias still used in Unix98.

GROUPING   The same as the value returned by `localeconv` in the `grouping` element
            of the `struct lconv`.

YESEXPR   The return value is a regular expression which can be used with the
            `regex` function to recognize a positive response to a yes/no question.
            The GNU C Library provides the `rpmatch` function for easier handling
            in applications.

NOEXPR   The return value is a regular expression which can be used with the `regex`
            function to recognize a negative response to a yes/no question.

YESSTR   The return value is a locale-specific translation of the positive response
            to a yes/no question.

            Using this value is deprecated since it is a very special case of message
            translation, and is better handled by the message translation functions
            (see Chapter 8 [Message Translation], page 188).

            The use of this symbol is deprecated. Instead message translation should
            be used.

NOSTR   The return value is a locale-specific translation of the negative response
            to a yes/no question. What is said for `YESSTR` is also true here.

            The use of this symbol is deprecated. Instead message translation should
            be used.

The file `langinfo.h` defines a lot more symbols but none of them is official. Using
them is not portable, and the format of the return values might change. Therefore
we recommended you not use them.

Note that the return value for any valid argument can be used for in all situations
(with the possible exception of the am/pm time formatting codes). If the user has not
selected any locale for the appropriate category, `nl_langinfo` returns the information
from the "C" locale. It is therefore possible to use this function as shown in the
example below.

If the argument *item* is not valid, a pointer to an empty string is returned.

An example of `nl_langinfo` usage is a function which has to print a given date and
time in a locale-specific way. At first one might think that, since `strftime` internally uses
the locale information, writing something like the following is enough:

```
size_t
i18n_time_n_data (char *s, size_t len, const struct tm *tp)
{
  return strftime (s, len, "%X %D", tp);
}
```

The format contains no weekday or month names and therefore is internationally usable.
Wrong! The output produced is something like `"hh:mm:ss MM/DD/YY"`. This format is only
recognizable in the USA. Other countries use different formats. Therefore the function
should be rewritten like this:

```
size_t
i18n_time_n_data (char *s, size_t len, const struct tm *tp)
{
  return strftime (s, len, nl_langinfo (D_T_FMT), tp);
}
```

Now it uses the date and time format of the locale selected when the program runs. If the user selects the locale correctly there should never be a misunderstanding over the time and date format.

7.8 A dedicated function to format numbers

We have seen that the structure returned by `localeconv` as well as the values given to `nl_langinfo` allow you to retrieve the various pieces of locale-specific information to format numbers and monetary amounts. We have also seen that the underlying rules are quite complex.

Therefore the X/Open standards introduce a function which uses such locale information, making it easier for the user to format numbers according to these rules.

`ssize_t strfmon` (*char *s, size_t maxsize, const char *format, ...*)   [Function]
Preliminary: | MT-Safe locale | AS-Unsafe heap | AC-Unsafe mem | See Section 1.2.2.1 [POSIX Safety Concepts], page 2.

The `strfmon` function is similar to the `strftime` function in that it takes a buffer, its size, a format string, and values to write into the buffer as text in a form specified by the format string. Like `strftime`, the function also returns the number of bytes written into the buffer.

There are two differences: `strfmon` can take more than one argument, and, of course, the format specification is different. Like `strftime`, the format string consists of normal text, which is output as is, and format specifiers, which are indicated by a '%'. Immediately after the '%', you can optionally specify various flags and formatting information before the main formatting character, in a similar way to `printf`:

- Immediately following the '%' there can be one or more of the following flags:

  '=*f*'   The single byte character *f* is used for this field as the numeric fill character. By default this character is a space character. Filling with this character is only performed if a left precision is specified. It is not just to fill to the given field width.

  '^'   The number is printed without grouping the digits according to the rules of the current locale. By default grouping is enabled.

  '+', '('   At most one of these flags can be used. They select which format to represent the sign of a currency amount. By default, and if '+' is given, the locale equivalent of +/− is used. If '(' is given, negative amounts are enclosed in parentheses. The exact format is determined by the values of the `LC_MONETARY` category of the locale selected at program runtime.

  '!'   The output will not contain the currency symbol.

  '−'   The output will be formatted left-justified instead of right-justified if it does not fill the entire field width.

The next part of a specification is an optional field width. If no width is specified 0 is taken. During output, the function first determines how much space is required. If it requires at least as many characters as given by the field width, it is output using as much space as necessary. Otherwise, it is extended to use the full width by filling with the space character. The presence or absence of the '-' flag determines the side at which such padding occurs. If present, the spaces are added at the right making the output left-justified, and vice versa.

So far the format looks familiar, being similar to the `printf` and `strftime` formats. However, the next two optional fields introduce something new. The first one is a '#' character followed by a decimal digit string. The value of the digit string specifies the number of *digit* positions to the left of the decimal point (or equivalent). This does *not* include the grouping character when the '^' flag is not given. If the space needed to print the number does not fill the whole width, the field is padded at the left side with the fill character, which can be selected using the '=' flag and by default is a space. For example, if the field width is selected as 6 and the number is 123, the fill character is '*' the result will be '***123'.

The second optional field starts with a '.' (period) and consists of another decimal digit string. Its value describes the number of characters printed after the decimal point. The default is selected from the current locale (`frac_digits`, `int_frac_digits`, see see Section 7.7.1.1 [Generic Numeric Formatting Parameters], page 175). If the exact representation needs more digits than given by the field width, the displayed value is rounded. If the number of fractional digits is selected to be zero, no decimal point is printed.

As a GNU extension, the `strfmon` implementation in the GNU C Library allows an optional 'L' next as a format modifier. If this modifier is given, the argument is expected to be a `long double` instead of a `double` value.

Finally, the last component is a format specifier. There are three specifiers defined:

'i'   Use the locale's rules for formatting an international currency value.

'n'   Use the locale's rules for formatting a national currency value.

'%'   Place a '%' in the output. There must be no flag, width specifier or modifier given, only '%%' is allowed.

As for `printf`, the function reads the format string from left to right and uses the values passed to the function following the format string. The values are expected to be either of type `double` or `long double`, depending on the presence of the modifier 'L'. The result is stored in the buffer pointed to by *s*. At most *maxsize* characters are stored.

The return value of the function is the number of characters stored in *s*, including the terminating `NULL` byte. If the number of characters stored would exceed *maxsize*, the function returns −1 and the content of the buffer *s* is unspecified. In this case `errno` is set to `E2BIG`.

A few examples should make clear how the function works. It is assumed that all the following pieces of code are executed in a program which uses the USA locale (`en_US`). The simplest form of the format is this:

```
strfmon (buf, 100, "@%n@%n@%n@", 123.45, -567.89, 12345.678);
```

The output produced is

```
"@$123.45@-$567.89@$12,345.68@"
```

We can notice several things here. First, the widths of the output numbers are different. We have not specified a width in the format string, and so this is no wonder. Second, the third number is printed using thousands separators. The thousands separator for the en_US locale is a comma. The number is also rounded. .678 is rounded to .68 since the format does not specify a precision and the default value in the locale is 2. Finally, note that the national currency symbol is printed since '%n' was used, not 'i'. The next example shows how we can align the output.

```
strfmon (buf, 100, "@%=*11n@%=*11n@%=*11n@", 123.45, -567.89, 12345.678);
```

The output this time is:

```
"@     $123.45@    -$567.89@ $12,345.68@"
```

Two things stand out. Firstly, all fields have the same width (eleven characters) since this is the width given in the format and since no number required more characters to be printed. The second important point is that the fill character is not used. This is correct since the white space was not used to achieve a precision given by a '#' modifier, but instead to fill to the given width. The difference becomes obvious if we now add a width specification.

```
strfmon (buf, 100, "@%=*11#5n@%=*11#5n@%=*11#5n@",
        123.45, -567.89, 12345.678);
```

The output is

```
"@ $***123.45@-$***567.89@ $12,456.68@"
```

Here we can see that all the currency symbols are now aligned, and that the space between the currency sign and the number is filled with the selected fill character. Note that although the width is selected to be 5 and 123.45 has three digits left of the decimal point, the space is filled with three asterisks. This is correct since, as explained above, the width does not include the positions used to store thousands separators. One last example should explain the remaining functionality.

```
strfmon (buf, 100, "@%=0(16#5.3i@%=0(16#5.3i@%=0(16#5.3i@",
        123.45, -567.89, 12345.678);
```

This rather complex format string produces the following output:

```
"@ USD 000123,450 @(USD 000567.890)@ USD 12,345.678 @"
```

The most noticeable change is the alternative way of representing negative numbers. In financial circles this is often done using parentheses, and this is what the '(' flag selected. The fill character is now '0'. Note that this '0' character is not regarded as a numeric zero, and therefore the first and second numbers are not printed using a thousands separator. Since we used the format specifier 'i' instead of 'n', the international form of the currency symbol is used. This is a four letter string, in this case "USD ". The last point is that since the precision right of the decimal point is selected to be three, the first and second numbers are printed with an extra zero at the end and the third number is printed without rounding.

7.9 Yes-or-No Questions

Some non GUI programs ask a yes-or-no question. If the messages (especially the questions) are translated into foreign languages, be sure that you localize the answers too. It would be very bad habit to ask a question in one language and request the answer in another, often English.

The GNU C Library contains `rpmatch` to give applications easy access to the corresponding locale definitions.

---

int **rpmatch** (*const char *response*)   [Function]

> Preliminary: | MT-Safe locale | AS-Unsafe corrupt heap lock dlopen | AC-Unsafe corrupt lock mem fd | See Section 1.2.2.1 [POSIX Safety Concepts], page 2.
>
> The function `rpmatch` checks the string in *response* whether or not it is a correct yes-or-no answer and if yes, which one. The check uses the `YESEXPR` and `NOEXPR` data in the `LC_MESSAGES` category of the currently selected locale. The return value is as follows:
>
> 1   The user entered an affirmative answer.
>
> 0   The user entered a negative answer.
>
> -1   The answer matched neither the `YESEXPR` nor the `NOEXPR` regular expression.
>
> This function is not standardized but available beside in the GNU C Library at least also in the IBM AIX library.

This function would normally be used like this:

```
...
/* Use a safe default.  */
_Bool doit = false;

fputs (gettext ("Do you really want to do this? "), stdout);
fflush (stdout);
/* Prepare the getline call.  */
line = NULL;
len = 0;
while (getline (&line, &len, stdin) >= 0)
  {
    /* Check the response.  */
    int res = rpmatch (line);
    if (res >= 0)
      {
        /* We got a definitive answer.  */
        if (res > 0)
          doit = true;
        break;
      }
  }
/* Free what getline allocated.  */
free (line);
```

Note that the loop continues until a read error is detected or until a definitive (positive or negative) answer is read.

8 Message Translation

The program's interface with the user should be designed to ease the user's task. One way to ease the user's task is to use messages in whatever language the user prefers.

Printing messages in different languages can be implemented in different ways. One could add all the different languages in the source code and choose among the variants every time a message has to be printed. This is certainly not a good solution since extending the set of languages is cumbersome (the code must be changed) and the code itself can become really big with dozens of message sets.

A better solution is to keep the message sets for each language in separate files which are loaded at runtime depending on the language selection of the user.

The GNU C Library provides two different sets of functions to support message translation. The problem is that neither of the interfaces is officially defined by the POSIX standard. The `catgets` family of functions is defined in the X/Open standard but this is derived from industry decisions and therefore not necessarily based on reasonable decisions.

As mentioned above the message catalog handling provides easy extendibility by using external data files which contain the message translations. I.e., these files contain for each of the messages used in the program a translation for the appropriate language. So the tasks of the message handling functions are

- locate the external data file with the appropriate translations
- load the data and make it possible to address the messages
- map a given key to the translated message

The two approaches mainly differ in the implementation of this last step. Decisions made in the last step influence the rest of the design.

8.1 X/Open Message Catalog Handling

The `catgets` functions are based on the simple scheme:

> Associate every message to translate in the source code with a unique identifier.
> To retrieve a message from a catalog file solely the identifier is used.

This means for the author of the program that s/he will have to make sure the meaning of the identifier in the program code and in the message catalogs are always the same.

Before a message can be translated the catalog file must be located. The user of the program must be able to guide the responsible function to find whatever catalog the user wants. This is separated from what the programmer had in mind.

All the types, constants and functions for the `catgets` functions are defined/declared in the `nl_types.h` header file.

8.1.1 The catgets function family

`nl_catd catopen` (*const char* *`cat_name`, *int* `flag`)   [Function]

> Preliminary: | MT-Safe env | AS-Unsafe heap | AC-Unsafe mem | See Section 1.2.2.1 [POSIX Safety Concepts], page 2.

The `catopen` function tries to locate the message data file names *cat_name* and loads it when found. The return value is of an opaque type and can be used in calls to the other functions to refer to this loaded catalog.

The return value is (`nl_catd`) `-1` in case the function failed and no catalog was loaded. The global variable *errno* contains a code for the error causing the failure. But even if the function call succeeded this does not mean that all messages can be translated.

Locating the catalog file must happen in a way which lets the user of the program influence the decision. It is up to the user to decide about the language to use and sometimes it is useful to use alternate catalog files. All this can be specified by the user by setting some environment variables.

The first problem is to find out where all the message catalogs are stored. Every program could have its own place to keep all the different files but usually the catalog files are grouped by languages and the catalogs for all programs are kept in the same place.

To tell the `catopen` function where the catalog for the program can be found the user can set the environment variable `NLSPATH` to a value which describes her/his choice. Since this value must be usable for different languages and locales it cannot be a simple string. Instead it is a format string (similar to `printf`'s). An example is

    /usr/share/locale/%L/%N:/usr/share/locale/%L/LC_MESSAGES/%N

First one can see that more than one directory can be specified (with the usual syntax of separating them by colons). The next things to observe are the format string, `%L` and `%N` in this case. The `catopen` function knows about several of them and the replacement for all of them is of course different.

`%N`   This format element is substituted with the name of the catalog file. This is the value of the *cat_name* argument given to `catgets`.

`%L`   This format element is substituted with the name of the currently selected locale for translating messages. How this is determined is explained below.

`%l`   (This is the lowercase ell.) This format element is substituted with the language element of the locale name. The string describing the selected locale is expected to have the form `lang[_terr[.codeset]]` and this format uses the first part *lang*.

`%t`   This format element is substituted by the territory part *terr* of the name of the currently selected locale. See the explanation of the format above.

`%c`   This format element is substituted by the codeset part *codeset* of the name of the currently selected locale. See the explanation of the format above.

`%%`   Since `%` is used in a meta character there must be a way to express the `%` character in the result itself. Using `%%` does this just like it works for `printf`.

Using `NLSPATH` allows arbitrary directories to be searched for message catalogs while still allowing different languages to be used. If the `NLSPATH` environment variable is not set, the default value is

```
prefix/share/locale/%L/%N:prefix/share/locale/%L/LC_MESSAGES/%N
```

where *prefix* is given to `configure` while installing the GNU C Library (this value is in many cases `/usr` or the empty string).

The remaining problem is to decide which must be used. The value decides about the substitution of the format elements mentioned above. First of all the user can specify a path in the message catalog name (i.e., the name contains a slash character). In this situation the `NLSPATH` environment variable is not used. The catalog must exist as specified in the program, perhaps relative to the current working directory. This situation in not desirable and catalogs names never should be written this way. Beside this, this behavior is not portable to all other platforms providing the `catgets` interface.

Otherwise the values of environment variables from the standard environment are examined (see Section 25.4.2 [Standard Environment Variables], page 741). Which variables are examined is decided by the *flag* parameter of `catopen`. If the value is `NL_CAT_LOCALE` (which is defined in `nl_types.h`) then the `catopen` function use the name of the locale currently selected for the `LC_MESSAGES` category.

If *flag* is zero the `LANG` environment variable is examined. This is a left-over from the early days where the concept of the locales had not even reached the level of POSIX locales.

The environment variable and the locale name should have a value of the form `lang[_terr[.codeset]]` as explained above. If no environment variable is set the "C" locale is used which prevents any translation.

The return value of the function is in any case a valid string. Either it is a translation from a message catalog or it is the same as the *string* parameter. So a piece of code to decide whether a translation actually happened must look like this:

```
{
  char *trans = catgets (desc, set, msg, input_string);
  if (trans == input_string)
    {
      /* Something went wrong.  */
    }
}
```

When an error occurred the global variable *errno* is set to

EBADF   The catalog does not exist.

ENOMSG   The set/message tuple does not name an existing element in the message catalog.

While it sometimes can be useful to test for errors programs normally will avoid any test. If the translation is not available it is no big problem if the original, untranslated message is printed. Either the user understands this as well or s/he will look for the reason why the messages are not translated.

Please note that the currently selected locale does not depend on a call to the `setlocale` function. It is not necessary that the locale data files for this locale exist and calling `setlocale` succeeds. The `catopen` function directly reads the values of the environment variables.

char * catgets (*nl_catd* **catalog_desc**, *int* **set**, *int* **message**, *const*   [Function]
    char ***string**)
> Preliminary: | MT-Safe | AS-Safe | AC-Safe | See Section 1.2.2.1 [POSIX Safety
> Concepts], page 2.
>
> The function `catgets` has to be used to access the massage catalog previously opened
> using the `catopen` function. The *catalog_desc* parameter must be a value previously
> returned by `catopen`.
>
> The next two parameters, *set* and *message*, reflect the internal organization of the
> message catalog files. This will be explained in detail below. For now it is interesting
> to know that a catalog can consists of several set and the messages in each thread
> are individually numbered using numbers. Neither the set number nor the message
> number must be consecutive. They can be arbitrarily chosen. But each message
> (unless equal to another one) must have its own unique pair of set and message
> number.
>
> Since it is not guaranteed that the message catalog for the language selected by
> the user exists the last parameter *string* helps to handle this case gracefully. If no
> matching string can be found *string* is returned. This means for the programmer that
>
> - the *string* parameters should contain reasonable text (this also helps to under-
>   stand the program seems otherwise there would be no hint on the string which
>   is expected to be returned.
>
> - all *string* arguments should be written in the same language.

It is somewhat uncomfortable to write a program using the `catgets` functions if no
supporting functionality is available. Since each set/message number tuple must be unique
the programmer must keep lists of the messages at the same time the code is written. And
the work between several people working on the same project must be coordinated. We
will see some how these problems can be relaxed a bit (see Section 8.1.4 [How to use the
`catgets` interface], page 194).

int catclose (*nl_catd* **catalog_desc**)   [Function]
> Preliminary: | MT-Safe | AS-Unsafe heap | AC-Unsafe corrupt mem | See
> Section 1.2.2.1 [POSIX Safety Concepts], page 2.
>
> The `catclose` function can be used to free the resources associated with a message
> catalog which previously was opened by a call to `catopen`. If the resources can be
> successfully freed the function returns 0. Otherwise it return −1 and the global
> variable *errno* is set. Errors can occur if the catalog descriptor *catalog_desc* is not
> valid in which case *errno* is set to `EBADF`.

8.1.2 Format of the message catalog files

The only reasonable way the translate all the messages of a function and store the result in
a message catalog file which can be read by the `catopen` function is to write all the message
text to the translator and let her/him translate them all. I.e., we must have a file with
entries which associate the set/message tuple with a specific translation. This file format is
specified in the X/Open standard and is as follows:

- Lines containing only whitespace characters or empty lines are ignored.

- Lines which contain as the first non-whitespace character a $ followed by a whitespace character are comment and are also ignored.

- If a line contains as the first non-whitespace characters the sequence $set followed by a whitespace character an additional argument is required to follow. This argument can either be:

  - a number. In this case the value of this number determines the set to which the following messages are added.

  - an identifier consisting of alphanumeric characters plus the underscore character. In this case the set get automatically a number assigned. This value is one added to the largest set number which so far appeared.

    How to use the symbolic names is explained in section Section 8.1.4 [How to use the catgets interface], page 194.

    It is an error if a symbol name appears more than once. All following messages are placed in a set with this number.

- If a line contains as the first non-whitespace characters the sequence $delset followed by a whitespace character an additional argument is required to follow. This argument can either be:

  - a number. In this case the value of this number determines the set which will be deleted.

  - an identifier consisting of alphanumeric characters plus the underscore character. This symbolic identifier must match a name for a set which previously was defined. It is an error if the name is unknown.

  In both cases all messages in the specified set will be removed. They will not appear in the output. But if this set is later again selected with a $set command again messages could be added and these messages will appear in the output.

- If a line contains after leading whitespaces the sequence $quote, the quoting character used for this input file is changed to the first non-whitespace character following the $quote. If no non-whitespace character is present before the line ends quoting is disable.

  By default no quoting character is used. In this mode strings are terminated with the first unescaped line break. If there is a $quote sequence present newline need not be escaped. Instead a string is terminated with the first unescaped appearance of the quote character.

  A common usage of this feature would be to set the quote character to ". Then any appearance of the " in the strings must be escaped using the backslash (i.e., \" must be written).

- Any other line must start with a number or an alphanumeric identifier (with the underscore character included). The following characters (starting after the first whitespace character) will form the string which gets associated with the currently selected set and the message number represented by the number and identifier respectively.

  If the start of the line is a number the message number is obvious. It is an error if the same message number already appeared for this set.

  If the leading token was an identifier the message number gets automatically assigned. The value is the current maximum messages number for this set plus one. It is an error if the identifier was already used for a message in this set. It is OK to reuse the identifier for a message in another thread. How to use the symbolic identifiers will be explained below (see Section 8.1.4 [How to use the `catgets` interface], page 194). There is one limitation with the identifier: it must not be `Set`. The reason will be explained below.

The text of the messages can contain escape characters. The usual bunch of characters known from the ISO C language are recognized (`\n`, `\t`, `\v`, `\b`, `\r`, `\f`, `\\`, and `\nnn`, where *nnn* is the octal coding of a character code).

Important: The handling of identifiers instead of numbers for the set and messages is a GNU extension. Systems strictly following the X/Open specification do not have this feature. An example for a message catalog file is this:

```
$ This is a leading comment.
$quote "

$set SetOne
1 Message with ID 1.
two "  Message with ID \"two\", which gets the value 2 assigned"

$set SetTwo
$ Since the last set got the number 1 assigned this set has number 2.
4000 "The numbers can be arbitrary, they need not start at one."
```

This small example shows various aspects:

- Lines 1 and 9 are comments since they start with `$` followed by a whitespace.

- The quoting character is set to `"`. Otherwise the quotes in the message definition would have to be left away and in this case the message with the identifier `two` would loose its leading whitespace.

- Mixing numbered messages with message having symbolic names is no problem and the numbering happens automatically.

While this file format is pretty easy it is not the best possible for use in a running program. The `catopen` function would have to parser the file and handle syntactic errors gracefully. This is not so easy and the whole process is pretty slow. Therefore the `catgets` functions expect the data in another more compact and ready-to-use file format. There is a special program `gencat` which is explained in detail in the next section.

Files in this other format are not human readable. To be easy to use by programs it is a binary file. But the format is byte order independent so translation files can be shared by systems of arbitrary architecture (as long as they use the GNU C Library).

Details about the binary file format are not important to know since these files are always created by the `gencat` program. The sources of the GNU C Library also provide the sources for the `gencat` program and so the interested reader can look through these source files to learn about the file format.

8.1.3 Generate Message Catalogs files

The `gencat` program is specified in the X/Open standard and the GNU implementation follows this specification and so processes all correctly formed input files. Additionally some extension are implemented which help to work in a more reasonable way with the `catgets` functions.

The `gencat` program can be invoked in two ways:

> `'gencat [Option]... [Output-File [Input-File]...]'`

This is the interface defined in the X/Open standard. If no *Input-File* parameter is given input will be read from standard input. Multiple input files will be read as if they are concatenated. If *Output-File* is also missing, the output will be written to standard output. To provide the interface one is used to from other programs a second interface is provided.

> `'gencat [Option]... -o Output-File [Input-File]...'`

The option '`-o`' is used to specify the output file and all file arguments are used as input files.

Beside this one can use - or `/dev/stdin` for *Input-File* to denote the standard input. Corresponding one can use - and `/dev/stdout` for *Output-File* to denote standard output. Using - as a file name is allowed in X/Open while using the device names is a GNU extension.

The `gencat` program works by concatenating all input files and then **merge** the resulting collection of message sets with a possibly existing output file. This is done by removing all messages with set/message number tuples matching any of the generated messages from the output file and then adding all the new messages. To regenerate a catalog file while ignoring the old contents therefore requires to remove the output file if it exists. If the output is written to standard output no merging takes place.

The following table shows the options understood by the `gencat` program. The X/Open standard does not specify any option for the program so all of these are GNU extensions.

'`-V`'
'`--version`'
> Print the version information and exit.

'`-h`'
'`--help`'   Print a usage message listing all available options, then exit successfully.

'`--new`'   Do never merge the new messages from the input files with the old content of the output files. The old content of the output file is discarded.

'`-H`'
'`--header=name`'
> This option is used to emit the symbolic names given to sets and messages in the input files for use in the program. Details about how to use this are given in the next section. The *name* parameter to this option specifies the name of the output file. It will contain a number of C preprocessor `#define`s to associate a name with a number.
>
> Please note that the generated file only contains the symbols from the input files. If the output is merged with the previous content of the output file the possibly existing symbols from the file(s) which generated the old output files are not in the generated header file.

8.1.4 How to use the `catgets` interface

The `catgets` functions can be used in two different ways. By following slavishly the X/Open specs and not relying on the extension and by using the GNU extensions. We will take a look at the former method first to understand the benefits of extensions.

8.1.4.1 Not using symbolic names

Since the X/Open format of the message catalog files does not allow symbol names we have to work with numbers all the time. When we start writing a program we have to replace all appearances of translatable strings with something like

```
catgets (catdesc, set, msg, "string")
```

catgets is retrieved from a call to **catopen** which is normally done once at the program start. The **"string"** is the string we want to translate. The problems start with the set and message numbers.

In a bigger program several programmers usually work at the same time on the program and so coordinating the number allocation is crucial. Though no two different strings must be indexed by the same tuple of numbers it is highly desirable to reuse the numbers for equal strings with equal translations (please note that there might be strings which are equal in one language but have different translations due to difference contexts).

The allocation process can be relaxed a bit by different set numbers for different parts of the program. So the number of developers who have to coordinate the allocation can be reduced. But still lists must be keep track of the allocation and errors can easily happen. These errors cannot be discovered by the compiler or the **catgets** functions. Only the user of the program might see wrong messages printed. In the worst cases the messages are so irritating that they cannot be recognized as wrong. Think about the translations for **"true"** and **"false"** being exchanged. This could result in a disaster.

8.1.4.2 Using symbolic names

The problems mentioned in the last section derive from the fact that:

1. the numbers are allocated once and due to the possibly frequent use of them it is difficult to change a number later.

2. the numbers do not allow to guess anything about the string and therefore collisions can easily happen.

By constantly using symbolic names and by providing a method which maps the string content to a symbolic name (however this will happen) one can prevent both problems above. The cost of this is that the programmer has to write a complete message catalog file while s/he is writing the program itself.

This is necessary since the symbolic names must be mapped to numbers before the program sources can be compiled. In the last section it was described how to generate a header containing the mapping of the names. E.g., for the example message file given in the last section we could call the **gencat** program as follow (assume **ex.msg** contains the sources).

```
gencat -H ex.h -o ex.cat ex.msg
```

This generates a header file with the following content:

```
#define SetTwoSet 0x2    /* ex.msg:8 */

#define SetOneSet 0x1    /* ex.msg:4 */
#define SetOnetwo 0x2    /* ex.msg:6 */
```

As can be seen the various symbols given in the source file are mangled to generate unique identifiers and these identifiers get numbers assigned. Reading the source file and knowing about the rules will allow to predict the content of the header file (it is deterministic) but this is not necessary. The gencat program can take care for everything. All the programmer has to do is to put the generated header file in the dependency list of the source files of her/his project and to add a rules to regenerate the header of any of the input files change.

One word about the symbol mangling. Every symbol consists of two parts: the name of the message set plus the name of the message or the special string Set. So SetOnetwo means this macro can be used to access the translation with identifier two in the message set SetOne.

The other names denote the names of the message sets. The special string Set is used in the place of the message identifier.

If in the code the second string of the set SetOne is used the C code should look like this:

```
catgets (catdesc, SetOneSet, SetOnetwo,
         "  Message with ID \"two\", which gets the value 2 assigned")
```

Writing the function this way will allow to change the message number and even the set number without requiring any change in the C source code. (The text of the string is normally not the same; this is only for this example.)

8.1.4.3 How does to this allow to develop

To illustrate the usual way to work with the symbolic version numbers here is a little example. Assume we want to write the very complex and famous greeting program. We start by writing the code as usual:

```
#include <stdio.h>
int
main (void)
{
  printf ("Hello, world!\n");
  return 0;
}
```

Now we want to internationalize the message and therefore replace the message with whatever the user wants.

```
#include <nl_types.h>
#include <stdio.h>
#include "msgnrs.h"
int
main (void)
{
  nl_catd catdesc = catopen ("hello.cat", NL_CAT_LOCALE);
  printf (catgets (catdesc, SetMainSet, SetMainHello,
                   "Hello, world!\n"));
  catclose (catdesc);
  return 0;
}
```

We see how the catalog object is opened and the returned descriptor used in the other function calls. It is not really necessary to check for failure of any of the functions since even in these situations the functions will behave reasonable. They simply will be return a translation.

What remains unspecified here are the constants SetMainSet and SetMainHello. These are the symbolic names describing the message. To get the actual definitions which match the information in the catalog file we have to create the message catalog source file and process it using the `gencat` program.

```
$ Messages for the famous greeting program.
$quote "

$set Main
Hello "Hallo, Welt!\n"
```

Now we can start building the program (assume the message catalog source file is named `hello.msg` and the program source file `hello.c`):

```
% gencat -H msgnrs.h -o hello.cat hello.msg
% cat msgnrs.h
#define MainSet 0x1     /* hello.msg:4 */
#define MainHello 0x1   /* hello.msg:5 */
% gcc -o hello hello.c -I.
% cp hello.cat /usr/share/locale/de/LC_MESSAGES
% echo $LC_ALL
de
% ./hello
Hallo, Welt!
%
```

The call of the `gencat` program creates the missing header file `msgnrs.h` as well as the message catalog binary. The former is used in the compilation of `hello.c` while the later is placed in a directory in which the `catopen` function will try to locate it. Please check the `LC_ALL` environment variable and the default path for `catopen` presented in the description above.

8.2 The Uniforum approach to Message Translation

Sun Microsystems tried to standardize a different approach to message translation in the Uniforum group. There never was a real standard defined but still the interface was used in Sun's operating systems. Since this approach fits better in the development process of free software it is also used throughout the GNU project and the GNU `gettext` package provides support for this outside the GNU C Library.

The code of the `libintl` from GNU `gettext` is the same as the code in the GNU C Library. So the documentation in the GNU `gettext` manual is also valid for the functionality here. The following text will describe the library functions in detail. But the numerous helper programs are not described in this manual. Instead people should read the GNU `gettext` manual (see Section "GNU gettext utilities" in *Native Language Support Library and Tools*). We will only give a short overview.

Though the `catgets` functions are available by default on more systems the `gettext` interface is at least as portable as the former. The GNU `gettext` package can be used wherever the functions are not available.

8.2.1 The gettext family of functions

The paradigms underlying the `gettext` approach to message translations is different from that of the `catgets` functions the basic functionally is equivalent. There are functions of the following categories:

8.2.1.1 What has to be done to translate a message?

The `gettext` functions have a very simple interface. The most basic function just takes the string which shall be translated as the argument and it returns the translation. This is fundamentally different from the `catgets` approach where an extra key is necessary and the original string is only used for the error case.

If the string which has to be translated is the only argument this of course means the string itself is the key. I.e., the translation will be selected based on the original string. The message catalogs must therefore contain the original strings plus one translation for any such string. The task of the `gettext` function is it to compare the argument string with the available strings in the catalog and return the appropriate translation. Of course this process is optimized so that this process is not more expensive than an access using an atomic key like in `catgets`.

The `gettext` approach has some advantages but also some disadvantages. Please see the GNU `gettext` manual for a detailed discussion of the pros and cons.

All the definitions and declarations for `gettext` can be found in the `libintl.h` header file. On systems where these functions are not part of the C library they can be found in a separate library named `libintl.a` (or accordingly different for shared libraries).

char * gettext (*const char *msgid*)   [Function]
    Preliminary: | MT-Safe env | AS-Unsafe corrupt heap lock dlopen | AC-Unsafe corrupt lock fd mem | See Section 1.2.2.1 [POSIX Safety Concepts], page 2.

    The `gettext` function searches the currently selected message catalogs for a string which is equal to *msgid*. If there is such a string available it is returned. Otherwise the argument string *msgid* is returned.

    Please note that although the return value is `char *` the returned string must not be changed. This broken type results from the history of the function and does not reflect the way the function should be used.

    Please note that above we wrote "message catalogs" (plural). This is a specialty of the GNU implementation of these functions and we will say more about this when we talk about the ways message catalogs are selected (see Section 8.2.1.2 [How to determine which catalog to be used], page 200).

    The `gettext` function does not modify the value of the global *errno* variable. This is necessary to make it possible to write something like

```
printf (gettext ("Operation failed: %m\n"));
```

    Here the *errno* value is used in the `printf` function while processing the `%m` format element and if the `gettext` function would change this value (it is called before `printf` is called) we would get a wrong message.

    So there is no easy way to detect a missing message catalog beside comparing the argument string with the result. But it is normally the task of the user to react on missing catalogs. The program cannot guess when a message catalog is really necessary since for a user who speaks the language the program was developed in does not need any translation.

The remaining two functions to access the message catalog add some functionality to select a message catalog which is not the default one. This is important if parts of the program are developed independently. Every part can have its own message catalog and all of them can be used at the same time. The C library itself is an example: internally it uses the `gettext` functions but since it must not depend on a currently selected default message catalog it must specify all ambiguous information.

char * dgettext (*const char *domainname, const char *msgid*)   [Function]
> Preliminary: | MT-Safe env | AS-Unsafe corrupt heap lock dlopen | AC-Unsafe corrupt lock fd mem | See Section 1.2.2.1 [POSIX Safety Concepts], page 2.

> The `dgettext` functions acts just like the `gettext` function. It only takes an additional first argument *domainname* which guides the selection of the message catalogs which are searched for the translation. If the *domainname* parameter is the null pointer the `dgettext` function is exactly equivalent to `gettext` since the default value for the domain name is used.

> As for `gettext` the return value type is `char *` which is an anachronism. The returned string must never be modified.

char * dcgettext (*const char *domainname, const char *msgid, int*   [Function]
>   *category*)
> Preliminary: | MT-Safe env | AS-Unsafe corrupt heap lock dlopen | AC-Unsafe corrupt lock fd mem | See Section 1.2.2.1 [POSIX Safety Concepts], page 2.

> The `dcgettext` adds another argument to those which `dgettext` takes. This argument *category* specifies the last piece of information needed to localize the message catalog. I.e., the domain name and the locale category exactly specify which message catalog has to be used (relative to a given directory, see below).

> The `dgettext` function can be expressed in terms of `dcgettext` by using

```
dcgettext (domain, string, LC_MESSAGES)
```

> instead of

```
dgettext (domain, string)
```

> This also shows which values are expected for the third parameter. One has to use the available selectors for the categories available in `locale.h`. Normally the available values are `LC_CTYPE`, `LC_COLLATE`, `LC_MESSAGES`, `LC_MONETARY`, `LC_NUMERIC`, and `LC_TIME`. Please note that `LC_ALL` must not be used and even though the names might suggest this, there is no relation to the environments variables of this name.

> The `dcgettext` function is only implemented for compatibility with other systems which have `gettext` functions. There is not really any situation where it is necessary (or useful) to use a different value but `LC_MESSAGES` in for the *category* parameter. We are dealing with messages here and any other choice can only be irritating.

> As for `gettext` the return value type is `char *` which is an anachronism. The returned string must never be modified.

When using the three functions above in a program it is a frequent case that the *msgid* argument is a constant string. So it is worth to optimize this case. Thinking shortly about this one will realize that as long as no new message catalog is loaded the translation of a message will not change. This optimization is actually implemented by the `gettext`, `dgettext` and `dcgettext` functions.

8.2.1.2 How to determine which catalog to be used

The functions to retrieve the translations for a given message have a remarkable simple interface. But to provide the user of the program still the opportunity to select exactly the translation s/he wants and also to provide the programmer the possibility to influence the way to locate the search for catalogs files there is a quite complicated underlying mechanism which controls all this. The code is complicated the use is easy.

Basically we have two different tasks to perform which can also be performed by the `catgets` functions:

1. Locate the set of message catalogs. There are a number of files for different languages and which all belong to the package. Usually they are all stored in the filesystem below a certain directory.

   There can be arbitrary many packages installed and they can follow different guidelines for the placement of their files.

2. Relative to the location specified by the package the actual translation files must be searched, based on the wishes of the user. I.e., for each language the user selects the program should be able to locate the appropriate file.

This is the functionality required by the specifications for `gettext` and this is also what the `catgets` functions are able to do. But there are some problems unresolved:

- The language to be used can be specified in several different ways. There is no generally accepted standard for this and the user always expects the program understand what s/he means. E.g., to select the German translation one could write `de`, `german`, or `deutsch` and the program should always react the same.

- Sometimes the specification of the user is too detailed. If s/he, e.g., specifies `de_DE.ISO-8859-1` which means German, spoken in Germany, coded using the ISO 8859-1 character set there is the possibility that a message catalog matching this exactly is not available. But there could be a catalog matching `de` and if the character set used on the machine is always ISO 8859-1 there is no reason why this later message catalog should not be used. (We call this *message inheritance*.)

- If a catalog for a wanted language is not available it is not always the second best choice to fall back on the language of the developer and simply not translate any message. Instead a user might be better able to read the messages in another language and so the user of the program should be able to define a precedence order of languages.

We can divide the configuration actions in two parts: the one is performed by the programmer, the other by the user. We will start with the functions the programmer can use since the user configuration will be based on this.

As the functions described in the last sections already mention separate sets of messages can be selected by a *domain name*. This is a simple string which should be unique for each program part with uses a separate domain. It is possible to use in one program arbitrary many domains at the same time. E.g., the GNU C Library itself uses a domain named `libc` while the program using the C Library could use a domain named `foo`. The important point is that at any time exactly one domain is active. This is controlled with the following function.

char * textdomain (*const char *domainname*)   [Function]

Preliminary: | MT-Safe | AS-Unsafe lock heap | AC-Unsafe lock mem | See Section 1.2.2.1 [POSIX Safety Concepts], page 2.

The `textdomain` function sets the default domain, which is used in all future `gettext` calls, to *domainname*. Please note that `dgettext` and `dcgettext` calls are not influenced if the *domainname* parameter of these functions is not the null pointer.

Before the first call to `textdomain` the default domain is `messages`. This is the name specified in the specification of the `gettext` API. This name is as good as any other name. No program should ever really use a domain with this name since this can only lead to problems.

The function returns the value which is from now on taken as the default domain. If the system went out of memory the returned value is `NULL` and the global variable *errno* is set to `ENOMEM`. Despite the return value type being `char *` the return string must not be changed. It is allocated internally by the `textdomain` function.

If the *domainname* parameter is the null pointer no new default domain is set. Instead the currently selected default domain is returned.

If the *domainname* parameter is the empty string the default domain is reset to its initial value, the domain with the name `messages`. This possibility is questionable to use since the domain `messages` really never should be used.

char * bindtextdomain (*const char *domainname, const char*   [Function]
    dirname)

Preliminary: | MT-Safe | AS-Unsafe heap | AC-Unsafe mem | See Section 1.2.2.1 [POSIX Safety Concepts], page 2.

The `bindtextdomain` function can be used to specify the directory which contains the message catalogs for domain *domainname* for the different languages. To be correct, this is the directory where the hierarchy of directories is expected. Details are explained below.

For the programmer it is important to note that the translations which come with the program have be placed in a directory hierarchy starting at, say, `/foo/bar`. Then the program should make a `bindtextdomain` call to bind the domain for the current program to this directory. So it is made sure the catalogs are found. A correctly running program does not depend on the user setting an environment variable.

The `bindtextdomain` function can be used several times and if the *domainname* argument is different the previously bound domains will not be overwritten.

If the program which wish to use `bindtextdomain` at some point of time use the `chdir` function to change the current working directory it is important that the *dirname* strings ought to be an absolute pathname. Otherwise the addressed directory might vary with the time.

If the *dirname* parameter is the null pointer `bindtextdomain` returns the currently selected directory for the domain with the name *domainname*.

The `bindtextdomain` function returns a pointer to a string containing the name of the selected directory name. The string is allocated internally in the function and must not be changed by the user. If the system went out of core during the execution of `bindtextdomain` the return value is `NULL` and the global variable *errno* is set accordingly.

8.2.1.3 Additional functions for more complicated situations

The functions of the `gettext` family described so far (and all the `catgets` functions as well) have one problem in the real world which have been neglected completely in all existing approaches. What is meant here is the handling of plural forms.

Looking through Unix source code before the time anybody thought about internationalization (and, sadly, even afterwards) one can often find code similar to the following:

```
printf ("%d file%s deleted", n, n == 1 ? "" : "s");
```

After the first complaints from people internationalizing the code people either completely avoided formulations like this or used strings like `"file(s)"`. Both look unnatural and should be avoided. First tries to solve the problem correctly looked like this:

```
if (n == 1)
  printf ("%d file deleted", n);
else
  printf ("%d files deleted", n);
```

But this does not solve the problem. It helps languages where the plural form of a noun is not simply constructed by adding an 's' but that is all. Once again people fell into the trap of believing the rules their language is using are universal. But the handling of plural forms differs widely between the language families. There are two things we can differ between (and even inside language families);

- The form how plural forms are build differs. This is a problem with language which have many irregularities. German, for instance, is a drastic case. Though English and German are part of the same language family (Germanic), the almost regular forming of plural noun forms (appending an 's') is hardly found in German.

- The number of plural forms differ. This is somewhat surprising for those who only have experiences with Romanic and Germanic languages since here the number is the same (there are two).

  But other language families have only one form or many forms. More information on this in an extra section.

The consequence of this is that application writers should not try to solve the problem in their code. This would be localization since it is only usable for certain, hardcoded language environments. Instead the extended `gettext` interface should be used.

These extra functions are taking instead of the one key string two strings and a numerical argument. The idea behind this is that using the numerical argument and the first string as a key, the implementation can select using rules specified by the translator the right plural form. The two string arguments then will be used to provide a return value in case no message catalog is found (similar to the normal `gettext` behavior). In this case the rules for Germanic language is used and it is assumed that the first string argument is the singular form, the second the plural form.

This has the consequence that programs without language catalogs can display the correct strings only if the program itself is written using a Germanic language. This is a limitation but since the GNU C Library (as well as the GNU `gettext` package) are written as part of the GNU package and the coding standards for the GNU project require program being written in English, this solution nevertheless fulfills its purpose.

char * **ngettext** (*const char *msgid1, const char *msgid2, unsigned*   [Function]
  long int n)

> Preliminary: | MT-Safe env | AS-Unsafe corrupt heap lock dlopen | AC-Unsafe corrupt lock fd mem | See Section 1.2.2.1 [POSIX Safety Concepts], page 2.

> The **ngettext** function is similar to the **gettext** function as it finds the message catalogs in the same way. But it takes two extra arguments. The *msgid1* parameter must contain the singular form of the string to be converted. It is also used as the key for the search in the catalog. The *msgid2* parameter is the plural form. The parameter *n* is used to determine the plural form. If no message catalog is found *msgid1* is returned if **n == 1**, otherwise **msgid2**.

> An example for the us of this function is:

```
printf (ngettext ("%d file removed", "%d files removed", n), n);
```

> Please note that the numeric value *n* has to be passed to the **printf** function as well. It is not sufficient to pass it only to **ngettext**.

char * **dngettext** (*const char *domain, const char *msgid1, const char*   [Function]
  *msgid2, unsigned long int n)

> Preliminary: | MT-Safe env | AS-Unsafe corrupt heap lock dlopen | AC-Unsafe corrupt lock fd mem | See Section 1.2.2.1 [POSIX Safety Concepts], page 2.

> The **dngettext** is similar to the **dgettext** function in the way the message catalog is selected. The difference is that it takes two extra parameter to provide the correct plural form. These two parameters are handled in the same way **ngettext** handles them.

char * **dcngettext** (*const char *domain, const char *msgid1, const*   [Function]
  char *msgid2, unsigned long int n, int **category**)

> Preliminary: | MT-Safe env | AS-Unsafe corrupt heap lock dlopen | AC-Unsafe corrupt lock fd mem | See Section 1.2.2.1 [POSIX Safety Concepts], page 2.

> The **dcngettext** is similar to the **dcgettext** function in the way the message catalog is selected. The difference is that it takes two extra parameter to provide the correct plural form. These two parameters are handled in the same way **ngettext** handles them.

The problem of plural forms

A description of the problem can be found at the beginning of the last section. Now there is the question how to solve it. Without the input of linguists (which was not available) it was not possible to determine whether there are only a few different forms in which plural forms are formed or whether the number can increase with every new supported language.

Therefore the solution implemented is to allow the translator to specify the rules of how to select the plural form. Since the formula varies with every language this is the only viable solution except for hardcoding the information in the code (which still would require the possibility of extensions to not prevent the use of new languages). The details are explained in the GNU **gettext** manual. Here only a bit of information is provided.

The information about the plural form selection has to be stored in the header entry (the one with the empty (**msgid** string). It looks like this:

```
Plural-Forms: nplurals=2; plural=n == 1 ? 0 : 1;
```

The `nplurals` value must be a decimal number which specifies how many different plural forms exist for this language. The string following `plural` is an expression which is using the C language syntax. Exceptions are that no negative number are allowed, numbers must be decimal, and the only variable allowed is `n`. This expression will be evaluated whenever one of the functions `ngettext`, `dngettext`, or `dcngettext` is called. The numeric value passed to these functions is then substituted for all uses of the variable `n` in the expression. The resulting value then must be greater or equal to zero and smaller than the value given as the value of `nplurals`.

The following rules are known at this point. The language with families are listed. But this does not necessarily mean the information can be generalized for the whole family (as can be easily seen in the table below).[1]

Only one form:

> Some languages only require one single form. There is no distinction between the singular and plural form. An appropriate header entry would look like this:

```
Plural-Forms: nplurals=1; plural=0;
```

Languages with this property include:

Finno-Ugric family
> Hungarian

Asian family
> Japanese, Korean

Turkic/Altaic family
> Turkish

Two forms, singular used for one only

> This is the form used in most existing programs since it is what English is using. A header entry would look like this:

```
Plural-Forms: nplurals=2; plural=n != 1;
```

(Note: this uses the feature of C expressions that boolean expressions have to value zero or one.)

Languages with this property include:

Germanic family
> Danish, Dutch, English, German, Norwegian, Swedish

Finno-Ugric family
> Estonian, Finnish

Latin/Greek family
> Greek

Semitic family
> Hebrew

Romance family
> Italian, Portuguese, Spanish

---

[1] Additions are welcome. Send appropriate information to `bug-glibc-manual@gnu.org`.

Artificial   Esperanto

Two forms, singular used for zero and one

Exceptional case in the language family. The header entry would be:

```
Plural-Forms: nplurals=2; plural=n>1;
```

Languages with this property include:

Romanic family

French, Brazilian Portuguese

Three forms, special case for zero

The header entry would be:

```
Plural-Forms: nplurals=3; plural=n%10==1 && n%100!=11 ? 0 : n != 0 ? 1 : 2;
```

Languages with this property include:

Baltic family

Latvian

Three forms, special cases for one and two

The header entry would be:

```
Plural-Forms: nplurals=3; plural=n==1 ? 0 : n==2 ? 1 : 2;
```

Languages with this property include:

Celtic   Gaeilge (Irish)

Three forms, special case for numbers ending in 1[2-9]

The header entry would look like this:

```
Plural-Forms: nplurals=3; \
    plural=n%10==1 && n%100!=11 ? 0 : \
        n%10>=2 && (n%100<10 || n%100>=20) ? 1 : 2;
```

Languages with this property include:

Baltic family

Lithuanian

Three forms, special cases for numbers ending in 1 and 2, 3, 4, except those ending in 1[1-4]

The header entry would look like this:

```
Plural-Forms: nplurals=3; \
    plural=n%100/10==1 ? 2 : n%10==1 ? 0 : (n+9)%10>3 ? 2 : 1;
```

Languages with this property include:

Slavic family

Croatian, Czech, Russian, Ukrainian

Three forms, special cases for 1 and 2, 3, 4

The header entry would look like this:

```
Plural-Forms: nplurals=3; \
    plural=(n==1) ? 1 : (n>=2 && n<=4) ? 2 : 0;
```

Languages with this property include:

Slavic family

Slovak

Three forms, special case for one and some numbers ending in 2, 3, or 4
>   The header entry would look like this:

```
Plural-Forms: nplurals=3; \
        plural=n==1 ? 0 : \
                n%10>=2 && n%10<=4 && (n%100<10 || n%100>=20) ? 1 : 2;
```

>   Languages with this property include:
>
> Slavic family
>> Polish

Four forms, special case for one and all numbers ending in 02, 03, or 04
>   The header entry would look like this:

```
Plural-Forms: nplurals=4; \
        plural=n%100==1 ? 0 : n%100==2 ? 1 : n%100==3 || n%100==4 ? 2 : 3;
```

>   Languages with this property include:
>
> Slavic family
>> Slovenian

8.2.1.4 How to specify the output character set `gettext` uses

`gettext` not only looks up a translation in a message catalog. It also converts the translation on the fly to the desired output character set. This is useful if the user is working in a different character set than the translator who created the message catalog, because it avoids distributing variants of message catalogs which differ only in the character set.

The output character set is, by default, the value of `nl_langinfo (CODESET)`, which depends on the `LC_CTYPE` part of the current locale. But programs which store strings in a locale independent way (e.g. UTF-8) can request that `gettext` and related functions return the translations in that encoding, by use of the `bind_textdomain_codeset` function.

Note that the *msgid* argument to `gettext` is not subject to character set conversion. Also, when `gettext` does not find a translation for *msgid*, it returns *msgid* unchanged – independently of the current output character set. It is therefore recommended that all *msgid*s be US-ASCII strings.

`char * bind_textdomain_codeset` (*const char *domainname, const*   [Function]
>   *char *codeset*)
>
>   Preliminary: | MT-Safe | AS-Unsafe heap | AC-Unsafe mem | See Section 1.2.2.1 [POSIX Safety Concepts], page 2.
>
>   The `bind_textdomain_codeset` function can be used to specify the output character set for message catalogs for domain *domainname*. The *codeset* argument must be a valid codeset name which can be used for the `iconv_open` function, or a null pointer.
>
>   If the *codeset* parameter is the null pointer, `bind_textdomain_codeset` returns the currently selected codeset for the domain with the name *domainname*. It returns `NULL` if no codeset has yet been selected.
>
>   The `bind_textdomain_codeset` function can be used several times. If used multiple times with the same *domainname* argument, the later call overrides the settings made by the earlier one.
>
>   The `bind_textdomain_codeset` function returns a pointer to a string containing the name of the selected codeset. The string is allocated internally in the function and

must not be changed by the user. If the system went out of core during the execution of `bind_textdomain_codeset`, the return value is `NULL` and the global variable *errno* is set accordingly.

8.2.1.5 How to use gettext in GUI programs

One place where the `gettext` functions, if used normally, have big problems is within programs with graphical user interfaces (GUIs). The problem is that many of the strings which have to be translated are very short. They have to appear in pull-down menus which restricts the length. But strings which are not containing entire sentences or at least large fragments of a sentence may appear in more than one situation in the program but might have different translations. This is especially true for the one-word strings which are frequently used in GUI programs.

As a consequence many people say that the `gettext` approach is wrong and instead `catgets` should be used which indeed does not have this problem. But there is a very simple and powerful method to handle these kind of problems with the `gettext` functions.

As an example consider the following fictional situation. A GUI program has a menu bar with the following entries:

```
+------------+------------+------------------------------------------+
| File       | Printer    |                                          |
+------------+------------+------------------------------------------+
| Open       | | Select   |
| New        | | Open     |
+----------+ | Connect  |
             +----------+
```

To have the strings `File`, `Printer`, `Open`, `New`, `Select`, and `Connect` translated there has to be at some point in the code a call to a function of the `gettext` family. But in two places the string passed into the function would be `Open`. The translations might not be the same and therefore we are in the dilemma described above.

One solution to this problem is to artificially enlengthen the strings to make them unambiguous. But what would the program do if no translation is available? The enlengthened string is not what should be printed. So we should use a little bit modified version of the functions.

To enlengthen the strings a uniform method should be used. E.g., in the example above the strings could be chosen as

```
Menu|File
Menu|Printer
Menu|File|Open
Menu|File|New
Menu|Printer|Select
Menu|Printer|Open
Menu|Printer|Connect
```

Now all the strings are different and if now instead of `gettext` the following little wrapper function is used, everything works just fine:

```c
char *
sgettext (const char *msgid)
{
  char *msgval = gettext (msgid);
  if (msgval == msgid)
    msgval = strrchr (msgid, '|') + 1;
```

```
        return msgval;
    }
```

What this little function does is to recognize the case when no translation is available. This can be done very efficiently by a pointer comparison since the return value is the input value. If there is no translation we know that the input string is in the format we used for the Menu entries and therefore contains a | character. We simply search for the last occurrence of this character and return a pointer to the character following it. That's it!

If one now consistently uses the enlengthened string form and replaces the **gettext** calls with calls to **sgettext** (this is normally limited to very few places in the GUI implementation) then it is possible to produce a program which can be internationalized.

With advanced compilers (such as GNU C) one can write the **sgettext** functions as an inline function or as a macro like this:

```
#define sgettext(msgid) \
  ({ const char *__msgid = (msgid);              \
     char *__msgstr = gettext (__msgid);         \
     if (__msgval == __msgid)                    \
       __msgval = strrchr (__msgid, '|') + 1;  \
     __msgval; })
```

The other **gettext** functions (**dgettext**, **dcgettext** and the **ngettext** equivalents) can and should have corresponding functions as well which look almost identical, except for the parameters and the call to the underlying function.

Now there is of course the question why such functions do not exist in the GNU C Library? There are two parts of the answer to this question.

- They are easy to write and therefore can be provided by the project they are used in. This is not an answer by itself and must be seen together with the second part which is:

- There is no way the C library can contain a version which can work everywhere. The problem is the selection of the character to separate the prefix from the actual string in the enlenghtened string. The examples above used | which is a quite good choice because it resembles a notation frequently used in this context and it also is a character not often used in message strings.

  But what if the character is used in message strings. Or if the chose character is not available in the character set on the machine one compiles (e.g., | is not required to exist for ISO C; this is why the **iso646.h** file exists in ISO C programming environments).

There is only one more comment to make left. The wrapper function above require that the translations strings are not enlengthened themselves. This is only logical. There is no need to disambiguate the strings (since they are never used as keys for a search) and one also saves quite some memory and disk space by doing this.

8.2.1.6 User influence on gettext

The last sections described what the programmer can do to internationalize the messages of the program. But it is finally up to the user to select the message s/he wants to see. S/He must understand them.

The POSIX locale model uses the environment variables LC_COLLATE, LC_CTYPE, LC_MESSAGES, LC_MONETARY, LC_NUMERIC, and LC_TIME to select the locale which is to be used.

This way the user can influence lots of functions. As we mentioned above the `gettext` functions also take advantage of this.

To understand how this happens it is necessary to take a look at the various components of the filename which gets computed to locate a message catalog. It is composed as follows:

```
dir_name/locale/LC_category/domain_name.mo
```

The default value for *dir_name* is system specific. It is computed from the value given as the prefix while configuring the C library. This value normally is `/usr` or `/`. For the former the complete *dir_name* is:

```
/usr/share/locale
```

We can use `/usr/share` since the `.mo` files containing the message catalogs are system independent, so all systems can use the same files. If the program executed the `bindtextdomain` function for the message domain that is currently handled, the `dir_name` component is exactly the value which was given to the function as the second parameter. I.e., `bindtextdomain` allows overwriting the only system dependent and fixed value to make it possible to address files anywhere in the filesystem.

The *category* is the name of the locale category which was selected in the program code. For `gettext` and `dgettext` this is always `LC_MESSAGES`, for `dcgettext` this is selected by the value of the third parameter. As said above it should be avoided to ever use a category other than `LC_MESSAGES`.

The *locale* component is computed based on the category used. Just like for the `setlocale` function here comes the user selection into the play. Some environment variables are examined in a fixed order and the first environment variable set determines the return value of the lookup process. In detail, for the category `LC_xxx` the following variables in this order are examined:

`LANGUAGE`

`LC_ALL`

`LC_xxx`

`LANG`

This looks very familiar. With the exception of the `LANGUAGE` environment variable this is exactly the lookup order the `setlocale` function uses. But why introducing the `LANGUAGE` variable?

The reason is that the syntax of the values these variables can have is different to what is expected by the `setlocale` function. If we would set `LC_ALL` to a value following the extended syntax that would mean the `setlocale` function will never be able to use the value of this variable as well. An additional variable removes this problem plus we can select the language independently of the locale setting which sometimes is useful.

While for the `LC_xxx` variables the value should consist of exactly one specification of a locale the `LANGUAGE` variable's value can consist of a colon separated list of locale names. The attentive reader will realize that this is the way we manage to implement one of our additional demands above: we want to be able to specify an ordered list of language.

Back to the constructed filename we have only one component missing. The *domain_name* part is the name which was either registered using the `textdomain` function or which was given to `dgettext` or `dcgettext` as the first parameter. Now it becomes obvious that a good choice for the domain name in the program code is a string which is closely related to the program/package name. E.g., for the GNU C Library the domain name is `libc`.

A limit piece of example code should show how the programmer is supposed to work:

```
{
  setlocale (LC_ALL, "");
  textdomain ("test-package");
  bindtextdomain ("test-package", "/usr/local/share/locale");
  puts (gettext ("Hello, world!"));
}
```

At the program start the default domain is `messages`, and the default locale is `"C"`. The `setlocale` call sets the locale according to the user's environment variables; remember that correct functioning of `gettext` relies on the correct setting of the `LC_MESSAGES` locale (for looking up the message catalog) and of the `LC_CTYPE` locale (for the character set conversion). The `textdomain` call changes the default domain to `test-package`. The `bindtextdomain` call specifies that the message catalogs for the domain `test-package` can be found below the directory `/usr/local/share/locale`.

If now the user set in her/his environment the variable `LANGUAGE` to `de` the `gettext` function will try to use the translations from the file

```
/usr/local/share/locale/de/LC_MESSAGES/test-package.mo
```

From the above descriptions it should be clear which component of this filename is determined by which source.

In the above example we assumed that the `LANGUAGE` environment variable to `de`. This might be an appropriate selection but what happens if the user wants to use `LC_ALL` because of the wider usability and here the required value is `de_DE.ISO-8859-1`? We already mentioned above that a situation like this is not infrequent. E.g., a person might prefer reading a dialect and if this is not available fall back on the standard language.

The `gettext` functions know about situations like this and can handle them gracefully. The functions recognize the format of the value of the environment variable. It can split the value is different pieces and by leaving out the only or the other part it can construct new values. This happens of course in a predictable way. To understand this one must know the format of the environment variable value. There is one more or less standardized form, originally from the X/Open specification:

```
language[_territory[.codeset]][@modifier]
```

Less specific locale names will be stripped of in the order of the following list:

1. `codeset`
2. `normalized codeset`
3. `territory`
4. `modifier`

The `language` field will never be dropped for obvious reasons.

The only new thing is the `normalized codeset` entry. This is another goodie which is introduced to help reducing the chaos which derives from the inability of the people to standardize the names of character sets. Instead of ISO-8859-1 one can often see 8859-1, 88591, iso8859-1, or iso_8859-1. The `normalized codeset` value is generated from the user-provided character set name by applying the following rules:

1. Remove all characters beside numbers and letters.

2. Fold letters to lowercase.

3. If the same only contains digits prepend the string `"iso"`.

So all of the above name will be normalized to `iso88591`. This allows the program user much more freely choosing the locale name.

Even this extended functionality still does not help to solve the problem that completely different names can be used to denote the same locale (e.g., `de` and `german`). To be of help in this situation the locale implementation and also the `gettext` functions know about aliases.

The file `/usr/share/locale/locale.alias` (replace `/usr` with whatever prefix you used for configuring the C library) contains a mapping of alternative names to more regular names. The system manager is free to add new entries to fill her/his own needs. The selected locale from the environment is compared with the entries in the first column of this file ignoring the case. If they match the value of the second column is used instead for the further handling.

In the description of the format of the environment variables we already mentioned the character set as a factor in the selection of the message catalog. In fact, only catalogs which contain text written using the character set of the system/program can be used (directly; there will come a solution for this some day). This means for the user that s/he will always have to take care for this. If in the collection of the message catalogs there are files for the same language but coded using different character sets the user has to be careful.

8.2.2 Programs to handle message catalogs for `gettext`

The GNU C Library does not contain the source code for the programs to handle message catalogs for the `gettext` functions. As part of the GNU project the GNU gettext package contains everything the developer needs. The functionality provided by the tools in this package by far exceeds the abilities of the `gencat` program described above for the `catgets` functions.

There is a program `msgfmt` which is the equivalent program to the `gencat` program. It generates from the human-readable and -editable form of the message catalog a binary file which can be used by the `gettext` functions. But there are several more programs available.

The `xgettext` program can be used to automatically extract the translatable messages from a source file. I.e., the programmer need not take care of the translations and the list of messages which have to be translated. S/He will simply wrap the translatable string in calls to `gettext` et.al and the rest will be done by `xgettext`. This program has a lot of options which help to customize the output or help to understand the input better.

Other programs help to manage the development cycle when new messages appear in the source files or when a new translation of the messages appears. Here it should only be noted that using all the tools in GNU gettext it is possible to *completely* automate the handling of message catalogs. Beside marking the translatable strings in the source code and generating the translations the developers do not have anything to do themselves.

9 Searching and Sorting

This chapter describes functions for searching and sorting arrays of arbitrary objects. You pass the appropriate comparison function to be applied as an argument, along with the size of the objects in the array and the total number of elements.

9.1 Defining the Comparison Function

In order to use the sorted array library functions, you have to describe how to compare the elements of the array.

To do this, you supply a comparison function to compare two elements of the array. The library will call this function, passing as arguments pointers to two array elements to be compared. Your comparison function should return a value the way `strcmp` (see Section 5.5 [String/Array Comparison], page 102) does: negative if the first argument is "less" than the second, zero if they are "equal", and positive if the first argument is "greater".

Here is an example of a comparison function which works with an array of numbers of type `double`:

```
int
compare_doubles (const void *a, const void *b)
{
  const double *da = (const double *) a;
  const double *db = (const double *) b;

  return (*da > *db) - (*da < *db);
}
```

The header file `stdlib.h` defines a name for the data type of comparison functions. This type is a GNU extension.

```
int comparison_fn_t (const void *, const void *);
```

9.2 Array Search Function

Generally searching for a specific element in an array means that potentially all elements must be checked. The GNU C Library contains functions to perform linear search. The prototypes for the following two functions can be found in `search.h`.

void * lfind (*const void *key, const void *base, size_t *nmemb, size_t*   [Function]
      size, comparison_fn_t **compar**)

Preliminary: | MT-Safe | AS-Safe | AC-Safe | See Section 1.2.2.1 [POSIX Safety Concepts], page 2.

The `lfind` function searches in the array with *nmemb elements of *size* bytes pointed to by *base* for an element which matches the one pointed to by *key*. The function pointed to by *compar* is used decide whether two elements match.

The return value is a pointer to the matching element in the array starting at *base* if it is found. If no matching element is available `NULL` is returned.

The mean runtime of this function is *nmemb/2. This function should only be used if elements often get added to or deleted from the array in which case it might not be useful to sort the array before searching.

void * lsearch (*const void *key, void *base, size_t *nmemb, size_t*   [Function]
    size, comparison_fn_t **compar**)

    Preliminary: | MT-Safe | AS-Safe | AC-Safe | See Section 1.2.2.1 [POSIX Safety Concepts], page 2.

    The **lsearch** function is similar to the **lfind** function. It searches the given array for an element and returns it if found. The difference is that if no matching element is found the **lsearch** function adds the object pointed to by *key* (with a size of *size* bytes) at the end of the array and it increments the value of *nmemb* to reflect this addition.

    This means for the caller that if it is not sure that the array contains the element one is searching for the memory allocated for the array starting at *base* must have room for at least *size* more bytes. If one is sure the element is in the array it is better to use **lfind** so having more room in the array is always necessary when calling **lsearch**.

To search a sorted array for an element matching the key, use the **bsearch** function. The prototype for this function is in the header file **stdlib.h**.

void * bsearch (*const void *key, const void *array, size_t* **count**,   [Function]
    size_t **size**, *comparison_fn_t* **compare**)

    Preliminary: | MT-Safe | AS-Safe | AC-Safe | See Section 1.2.2.1 [POSIX Safety Concepts], page 2.

    The **bsearch** function searches the sorted array *array* for an object that is equivalent to *key*. The array contains *count* elements, each of which is of size *size* bytes.

    The *compare* function is used to perform the comparison. This function is called with two pointer arguments and should return an integer less than, equal to, or greater than zero corresponding to whether its first argument is considered less than, equal to, or greater than its second argument. The elements of the *array* must already be sorted in ascending order according to this comparison function.

    The return value is a pointer to the matching array element, or a null pointer if no match is found. If the array contains more than one element that matches, the one that is returned is unspecified.

    This function derives its name from the fact that it is implemented using the binary search algorithm.

9.3 Array Sort Function

To sort an array using an arbitrary comparison function, use the **qsort** function. The prototype for this function is in **stdlib.h**.

void qsort (*void *array, size_t* **count**, *size_t* **size**, *comparison_fn_t*   [Function]
    compare)

    Preliminary: | MT-Safe | AS-Safe | AC-Unsafe corrupt | See Section 1.2.2.1 [POSIX Safety Concepts], page 2.

    The **qsort** function sorts the array *array*. The array contains *count* elements, each of which is of size *size*.

    The *compare* function is used to perform the comparison on the array elements. This function is called with two pointer arguments and should return an integer less than, equal to, or greater than zero corresponding to whether its first argument is considered less than, equal to, or greater than its second argument.

Warning: If two objects compare as equal, their order after sorting is unpredictable. That is to say, the sorting is not stable. This can make a difference when the comparison considers only part of the elements. Two elements with the same sort key may differ in other respects.

Although the object addresses passed to the comparison function lie within the array, they need not correspond with the original locations of those objects because the sorting algorithm may swap around objects in the array before making some comparisons. The only way to perform a stable sort with `qsort` is to first augment the objects with a monotonic counter of some kind.

Here is a simple example of sorting an array of doubles in numerical order, using the comparison function defined above (see Section 9.1 [Defining the Comparison Function], page 212):

```
{
  double *array;
  int size;
  ...
  qsort (array, size, sizeof (double), compare_doubles);
}
```

The `qsort` function derives its name from the fact that it was originally implemented using the "quick sort" algorithm.

The implementation of `qsort` in this library might not be an in-place sort and might thereby use an extra amount of memory to store the array.

9.4 Searching and Sorting Example

Here is an example showing the use of `qsort` and `bsearch` with an array of structures. The objects in the array are sorted by comparing their `name` fields with the `strcmp` function. Then, we can look up individual objects based on their names.

```
#include <stdlib.h>
#include <stdio.h>
#include <string.h>

/* Define an array of critters to sort. */

struct critter
  {
    const char *name;
    const char *species;
  };

struct critter muppets[] =
  {
    {"Kermit", "frog"},
    {"Piggy", "pig"},
    {"Gonzo", "whatever"},
    {"Fozzie", "bear"},
    {"Sam", "eagle"},
    {"Robin", "frog"},
```

```
      {"Animal", "animal"},
      {"Camilla", "chicken"},
      {"Sweetums", "monster"},
      {"Dr. Strangepork", "pig"},
      {"Link Hogthrob", "pig"},
      {"Zoot", "human"},
      {"Dr. Bunsen Honeydew", "human"},
      {"Beaker", "human"},
      {"Swedish Chef", "human"}
  };

int count = sizeof (muppets) / sizeof (struct critter);



/* This is the comparison function used for sorting and searching. */

int
critter_cmp (const void *v1, const void *v2)
{
  const struct critter *c1 = v1;
  const struct critter *c2 = v2;

  return strcmp (c1->name, c2->name);
}



/* Print information about a critter. */

void
print_critter (const struct critter *c)
{
  printf ("%s, the %s\n", c->name, c->species);
}



/* Do the lookup into the sorted array. */

void
find_critter (const char *name)
{
  struct critter target, *result;
  target.name = name;
  result = bsearch (&target, muppets, count, sizeof (struct critter),
                    critter_cmp);
  if (result)
    print_critter (result);
  else
    printf ("Couldn't find %s.\n", name);
}

/* Main program. */

int
main (void)
{
  int i;
```

```
for (i = 0; i < count; i++)
  print_critter (&muppets[i]);
printf ("\n");

qsort (muppets, count, sizeof (struct critter), critter_cmp);

for (i = 0; i < count; i++)
  print_critter (&muppets[i]);
printf ("\n");

find_critter ("Kermit");
find_critter ("Gonzo");
find_critter ("Janice");

return 0;
}
```

The output from this program looks like:

```
Kermit, the frog
Piggy, the pig
Gonzo, the whatever
Fozzie, the bear
Sam, the eagle
Robin, the frog
Animal, the animal
Camilla, the chicken
Sweetums, the monster
Dr. Strangepork, the pig
Link Hogthrob, the pig
Zoot, the human
Dr. Bunsen Honeydew, the human
Beaker, the human
Swedish Chef, the human

Animal, the animal
Beaker, the human
Camilla, the chicken
Dr. Bunsen Honeydew, the human
Dr. Strangepork, the pig
Fozzie, the bear
Gonzo, the whatever
Kermit, the frog
Link Hogthrob, the pig
Piggy, the pig
Robin, the frog
Sam, the eagle
Swedish Chef, the human
Sweetums, the monster
Zoot, the human

Kermit, the frog
Gonzo, the whatever
Couldn't find Janice.
```

9.5 The hsearch function.

The functions mentioned so far in this chapter are for searching in a sorted or unsorted array. There are other methods to organize information which later should be searched.

The costs of insert, delete and search differ. One possible implementation is using hashing tables. The following functions are declared in the header file `search.h`.

`int hcreate (size_t nel)`   [Function]

> Preliminary: | MT-Unsafe race:hsearch | AS-Unsafe heap | AC-Unsafe corrupt mem | See Section 1.2.2.1 [POSIX Safety Concepts], page 2.

> The `hcreate` function creates a hashing table which can contain at least *nel* elements. There is no possibility to grow this table so it is necessary to choose the value for *nel* wisely. The method used to implement this function might make it necessary to make the number of elements in the hashing table larger than the expected maximal number of elements. Hashing tables usually work inefficiently if they are filled 80% or more. The constant access time guaranteed by hashing can only be achieved if few collisions exist. See Knuth's "The Art of Computer Programming, Part 3: Searching and Sorting" for more information.

> The weakest aspect of this function is that there can be at most one hashing table used through the whole program. The table is allocated in local memory out of control of the programmer. As an extension the GNU C Library provides an additional set of functions with a reentrant interface which provide a similar interface but which allow to keep arbitrarily many hashing tables.

> It is possible to use more than one hashing table in the program run if the former table is first destroyed by a call to `hdestroy`.

> The function returns a non-zero value if successful. If it return zero something went wrong. This could either mean there is already a hashing table in use or the program runs out of memory.

`void hdestroy (void)`   [Function]

> Preliminary: | MT-Unsafe race:hsearch | AS-Unsafe heap | AC-Unsafe corrupt mem | See Section 1.2.2.1 [POSIX Safety Concepts], page 2.

> The `hdestroy` function can be used to free all the resources allocated in a previous call of `hcreate`. After a call to this function it is again possible to call `hcreate` and allocate a new table with possibly different size.

> It is important to remember that the elements contained in the hashing table at the time `hdestroy` is called are *not* freed by this function. It is the responsibility of the program code to free those strings (if necessary at all). Freeing all the element memory is not possible without extra, separately kept information since there is no function to iterate through all available elements in the hashing table. If it is really necessary to free a table and all elements the programmer has to keep a list of all table elements and before calling `hdestroy` s/he has to free all element's data using this list. This is a very unpleasant mechanism and it also shows that this kind of hashing tables is mainly meant for tables which are created once and used until the end of the program run.

Entries of the hashing table and keys for the search are defined using this type:

`struct ENTRY`   [Data type]

> Both elements of this structure are pointers to zero-terminated strings. This is a limiting restriction of the functionality of the `hsearch` functions. They can only be

used for data sets which use the NUL character always and solely to terminate the records. It is not possible to handle general binary data.

char *key Pointer to a zero-terminated string of characters describing the key for the search or the element in the hashing table.

char *data

Pointer to a zero-terminated string of characters describing the data. If the functions will be called only for searching an existing entry this element might stay undefined since it is not used.

ENTRY * hsearch (*ENTRY item*, *ACTION action*)   [Function]
Preliminary: | MT-Unsafe race:hsearch | AS-Unsafe | AC-Unsafe corrupt/action==ENTER | See Section 1.2.2.1 [POSIX Safety Concepts], page 2.

To search in a hashing table created using `hcreate` the `hsearch` function must be used. This function can perform simple search for an element (if *action* has the `FIND`) or it can alternatively insert the key element into the hashing table. Entries are never replaced.

The key is denoted by a pointer to an object of type `ENTRY`. For locating the corresponding position in the hashing table only the `key` element of the structure is used.

If an entry with matching key is found the *action* parameter is irrelevant. The found entry is returned. If no matching entry is found and the *action* parameter has the value `FIND` the function returns a `NULL` pointer. If no entry is found and the *action* parameter has the value `ENTER` a new entry is added to the hashing table which is initialized with the parameter *item*. A pointer to the newly added entry is returned.

As mentioned before the hashing table used by the functions described so far is global and there can be at any time at most one hashing table in the program. A solution is to use the following functions which are a GNU extension. All have in common that they operate on a hashing table which is described by the content of an object of the type `struct hsearch_data`. This type should be treated as opaque, none of its members should be changed directly.

int hcreate_r (*size_t nel*, *struct hsearch_data *htab*)   [Function]
Preliminary: | MT-Safe race:htab | AS-Unsafe heap | AC-Unsafe corrupt mem | See Section 1.2.2.1 [POSIX Safety Concepts], page 2.

The `hcreate_r` function initializes the object pointed to by *htab* to contain a hashing table with at least *nel* elements. So this function is equivalent to the `hcreate` function except that the initialized data structure is controlled by the user.

This allows having more than one hashing table at one time. The memory necessary for the `struct hsearch_data` object can be allocated dynamically. It must be initialized with zero before calling this function.

The return value is non-zero if the operation was successful. If the return value is zero, something went wrong, which probably means the programs ran out of memory.

void hdestroy_r (*struct hsearch_data *htab*)   [Function]

> Preliminary: | MT-Safe race:htab | AS-Unsafe heap | AC-Unsafe corrupt mem | See Section 1.2.2.1 [POSIX Safety Concepts], page 2.

> The **hdestroy_r** function frees all resources allocated by the **hcreate_r** function for this very same object *htab*. As for **hdestroy** it is the programs responsibility to free the strings for the elements of the table.

int hsearch_r (*ENTRY item, ACTION action, ENTRY **retval,*   [Function]
    struct hsearch_data *htab)

> Preliminary: | MT-Safe race:htab | AS-Safe | AC-Unsafe corrupt/action==ENTER | See Section 1.2.2.1 [POSIX Safety Concepts], page 2.

> The **hsearch_r** function is equivalent to **hsearch**. The meaning of the first two arguments is identical. But instead of operating on a single global hashing table the function works on the table described by the object pointed to by *htab* (which is initialized by a call to **hcreate_r**).

> Another difference to **hcreate** is that the pointer to the found entry in the table is not the return value of the functions. It is returned by storing it in a pointer variables pointed to by the *retval* parameter. The return value of the function is an integer value indicating success if it is non-zero and failure if it is zero. In the latter case the global variable *errno* signals the reason for the failure.

> ENOMEM   The table is filled and **hsearch_r** was called with a so far unknown key and *action* set to **ENTER**.

> ESRCH   The *action* parameter is **FIND** and no corresponding element is found in the table.

9.6 The `tsearch` function.

Another common form to organize data for efficient search is to use trees. The **tsearch** function family provides a nice interface to functions to organize possibly large amounts of data by providing a mean access time proportional to the logarithm of the number of elements. The GNU C Library implementation even guarantees that this bound is never exceeded even for input data which cause problems for simple binary tree implementations.

The functions described in the chapter are all described in the System V and X/Open specifications and are therefore quite portable.

In contrast to the **hsearch** functions the **tsearch** functions can be used with arbitrary data and not only zero-terminated strings.

The **tsearch** functions have the advantage that no function to initialize data structures is necessary. A simple pointer of type **void *** initialized to **NULL** is a valid tree and can be extended or searched. The prototypes for these functions can be found in the header file **search.h**.

void * tsearch (*const void *key, void **rootp, comparison_fn_t*   [Function]
    compar)

> Preliminary: | MT-Safe race:rootp | AS-Unsafe heap | AC-Unsafe corrupt mem | See Section 1.2.2.1 [POSIX Safety Concepts], page 2.

The `tsearch` function searches in the tree pointed to by *`rootp`* for an element matching *key*. The function pointed to by *compar* is used to determine whether two elements match. See Section 9.1 [Defining the Comparison Function], page 212, for a specification of the functions which can be used for the *compar* parameter.

If the tree does not contain a matching entry the *key* value will be added to the tree. `tsearch` does not make a copy of the object pointed to by *key* (how could it since the size is unknown). Instead it adds a reference to this object which means the object must be available as long as the tree data structure is used.

The tree is represented by a pointer to a pointer since it is sometimes necessary to change the root node of the tree. So it must not be assumed that the variable pointed to by *rootp* has the same value after the call. This also shows that it is not safe to call the `tsearch` function more than once at the same time using the same tree. It is no problem to run it more than once at a time on different trees.

The return value is a pointer to the matching element in the tree. If a new element was created the pointer points to the new data (which is in fact *key*). If an entry had to be created and the program ran out of space `NULL` is returned.

void * **tfind** (*const void *key*, *void *const* ***rootp**, *comparison_fn_t*   [Function]
     compar)

Preliminary: | MT-Safe race:rootp | AS-Safe | AC-Safe | See Section 1.2.2.1 [POSIX Safety Concepts], page 2.

The `tfind` function is similar to the `tsearch` function. It locates an element matching the one pointed to by *key* and returns a pointer to this element. But if no matching element is available no new element is entered (note that the *rootp* parameter points to a constant pointer). Instead the function returns `NULL`.

Another advantage of the `tsearch` function in contrast to the `hsearch` functions is that there is an easy way to remove elements.

void * **tdelete** (*const void *key*, *void* ****rootp**, *comparison_fn_t*   [Function]
     compar)

Preliminary: | MT-Safe race:rootp | AS-Unsafe heap | AC-Unsafe corrupt mem | See Section 1.2.2.1 [POSIX Safety Concepts], page 2.

To remove a specific element matching *key* from the tree `tdelete` can be used. It locates the matching element using the same method as `tfind`. The corresponding element is then removed and a pointer to the parent of the deleted node is returned by the function. If there is no matching entry in the tree nothing can be deleted and the function returns `NULL`. If the root of the tree is deleted `tdelete` returns some unspecified value not equal to `NULL`.

void **tdestroy** (*void *vroot*, *__free_fn_t* **freefct**)   [Function]

Preliminary: | MT-Safe | AS-Unsafe heap | AC-Unsafe mem | See Section 1.2.2.1 [POSIX Safety Concepts], page 2.

If the complete search tree has to be removed one can use `tdestroy`. It frees all resources allocated by the `tsearch` function to generate the tree pointed to by *vroot*.

For the data in each tree node the function *freefct* is called. The pointer to the data is passed as the argument to the function. If no such work is necessary *freefct* must point to a function doing nothing. It is called in any case.

This function is a GNU extension and not covered by the System V or X/Open specifications.

In addition to the function to create and destroy the tree data structure, there is another function which allows you to apply a function to all elements of the tree. The function must have this type:

```
void __action_fn_t (const void *nodep, VISIT value, int level);
```

The *nodep* is the data value of the current node (once given as the *key* argument to `tsearch`). *level* is a numeric value which corresponds to the depth of the current node in the tree. The root node has the depth 0 and its children have a depth of 1 and so on. The `VISIT` type is an enumeration type.

`VISIT`   [Data Type]

   The `VISIT` value indicates the status of the current node in the tree and how the function is called. The status of a node is either 'leaf' or 'internal node'. For each leaf node the function is called exactly once, for each internal node it is called three times: before the first child is processed, after the first child is processed and after both children are processed. This makes it possible to handle all three methods of tree traversal (or even a combination of them).

   `preorder`   The current node is an internal node and the function is called before the first child was processed.

   `postorder`

                The current node is an internal node and the function is called after the first child was processed.

   `endorder`   The current node is an internal node and the function is called after the second child was processed.

   `leaf`   The current node is a leaf.

`void twalk` (*const void *root*, *__action_fn_t* `action`)   [Function]
   Preliminary: | MT-Safe race:root | AS-Safe | AC-Safe | See Section 1.2.2.1 [POSIX Safety Concepts], page 2.

   For each node in the tree with a node pointed to by *root*, the `twalk` function calls the function provided by the parameter *action*. For leaf nodes the function is called exactly once with *value* set to `leaf`. For internal nodes the function is called three times, setting the *value* parameter or *action* to the appropriate value. The *level* argument for the *action* function is computed while descending the tree with increasing the value by one for the descend to a child, starting with the value 0 for the root node.

   Since the functions used for the *action* parameter to `twalk` must not modify the tree data, it is safe to run `twalk` in more than one thread at the same time, working on the same tree. It is also safe to call `tfind` in parallel. Functions which modify the tree must not be used, otherwise the behavior is undefined.

10 Pattern Matching

The GNU C Library provides pattern matching facilities for two kinds of patterns: regular expressions and file-name wildcards. The library also provides a facility for expanding variable and command references and parsing text into words in the way the shell does.

10.1 Wildcard Matching

This section describes how to match a wildcard pattern against a particular string. The result is a yes or no answer: does the string fit the pattern or not. The symbols described here are all declared in `fnmatch.h`.

`int fnmatch` (*const char *pattern*, *const char *string*, *int flags*)   [Function]

    Preliminary: | MT-Safe env locale | AS-Unsafe heap | AC-Unsafe mem | See Section 1.2.2.1 [POSIX Safety Concepts], page 2.

    This function tests whether the string *string* matches the pattern *pattern*. It returns 0 if they do match; otherwise, it returns the nonzero value `FNM_NOMATCH`. The arguments *pattern* and *string* are both strings.

    The argument *flags* is a combination of flag bits that alter the details of matching. See below for a list of the defined flags.

    In the GNU C Library, `fnmatch` might sometimes report "errors" by returning nonzero values that are not equal to `FNM_NOMATCH`.

    These are the available flags for the *flags* argument:

`FNM_FILE_NAME`

    Treat the '/' character specially, for matching file names. If this flag is set, wildcard constructs in *pattern* cannot match '/' in *string*. Thus, the only way to match '/' is with an explicit '/' in *pattern*.

`FNM_PATHNAME`

    This is an alias for `FNM_FILE_NAME`; it comes from POSIX.2. We don't recommend this name because we don't use the term "pathname" for file names.

`FNM_PERIOD`

    Treat the '.' character specially if it appears at the beginning of *string*. If this flag is set, wildcard constructs in *pattern* cannot match '.' as the first character of *string*.

    If you set both `FNM_PERIOD` and `FNM_FILE_NAME`, then the special treatment applies to '.' following '/' as well as to '.' at the beginning of *string*. (The shell uses the `FNM_PERIOD` and `FNM_FILE_NAME` flags together for matching file names.)

`FNM_NOESCAPE`

    Don't treat the '\' character specially in patterns. Normally, '\' quotes the following character, turning off its special meaning (if any) so that it matches only itself. When quoting is enabled, the pattern '\?' matches only the string '?', because the question mark in the pattern acts like an ordinary character.

    If you use `FNM_NOESCAPE`, then '\' is an ordinary character.

FNM_LEADING_DIR

> Ignore a trailing sequence of characters starting with a '/' in *string*; that is to say, test whether *string* starts with a directory name that *pattern* matches.
>
> If this flag is set, either 'foo*' or 'foobar' as a pattern would match the string 'foobar/frobozz'.

FNM_CASEFOLD

> Ignore case in comparing *string* to *pattern*.

FNM_EXTMATCH

> Recognize beside the normal patterns also the extended patterns introduced in ksh. The patterns are written in the form explained in the following table where *pattern-list* is a | separated list of patterns.
>
> **?(pattern-list)**
>
>> The pattern matches if zero or one occurrences of any of the patterns in the *pattern-list* allow matching the input string.
>
> ***(pattern-list)**
>
>> The pattern matches if zero or more occurrences of any of the patterns in the *pattern-list* allow matching the input string.
>
> **+(pattern-list)**
>
>> The pattern matches if one or more occurrences of any of the patterns in the *pattern-list* allow matching the input string.
>
> **@(pattern-list)**
>
>> The pattern matches if exactly one occurrence of any of the patterns in the *pattern-list* allows matching the input string.
>
> **!(pattern-list)**
>
>> The pattern matches if the input string cannot be matched with any of the patterns in the *pattern-list*.

10.2 Globbing

The archetypal use of wildcards is for matching against the files in a directory, and making a list of all the matches. This is called *globbing*.

You could do this using **fnmatch**, by reading the directory entries one by one and testing each one with **fnmatch**. But that would be slow (and complex, since you would have to handle subdirectories by hand).

The library provides a function **glob** to make this particular use of wildcards convenient. **glob** and the other symbols in this section are declared in **glob.h**.

10.2.1 Calling glob

The result of globbing is a vector of file names (strings). To return this vector, **glob** uses a special data type, **glob_t**, which is a structure. You pass **glob** the address of the structure, and it fills in the structure's fields to tell you about the results.

`glob_t`   [Data Type]

This data type holds a pointer to a word vector. More precisely, it records both the address of the word vector and its size. The GNU implementation contains some more fields which are non-standard extensions.

`gl_pathc`   The number of elements in the vector, excluding the initial null entries if the GLOB_DOOFFS flag is used (see gl_offs below).

`gl_pathv`   The address of the vector. This field has type `char **`.

`gl_offs`   The offset of the first real element of the vector, from its nominal address in the `gl_pathv` field. Unlike the other fields, this is always an input to `glob`, rather than an output from it.

If you use a nonzero offset, then that many elements at the beginning of the vector are left empty. (The `glob` function fills them with null pointers.)

The `gl_offs` field is meaningful only if you use the GLOB_DOOFFS flag. Otherwise, the offset is always zero regardless of what is in this field, and the first real element comes at the beginning of the vector.

`gl_closedir`
The address of an alternative implementation of the `closedir` function. It is used if the `GLOB_ALTDIRFUNC` bit is set in the flag parameter. The type of this field is `void (*) (void *)`.

This is a GNU extension.

`gl_readdir`
The address of an alternative implementation of the `readdir` function used to read the contents of a directory. It is used if the `GLOB_ALTDIRFUNC` bit is set in the flag parameter. The type of this field is `struct dirent *(*) (void *)`.

This is a GNU extension.

`gl_opendir`
The address of an alternative implementation of the `opendir` function. It is used if the `GLOB_ALTDIRFUNC` bit is set in the flag parameter. The type of this field is `void *(*) (const char *)`.

This is a GNU extension.

`gl_stat`   The address of an alternative implementation of the `stat` function to get information about an object in the filesystem. It is used if the `GLOB_ALTDIRFUNC` bit is set in the flag parameter. The type of this field is `int (*) (const char *, struct stat *)`.

This is a GNU extension.

`gl_lstat`   The address of an alternative implementation of the `lstat` function to get information about an object in the filesystems, not following symbolic links. It is used if the `GLOB_ALTDIRFUNC` bit is set in the flag parameter. The type of this field is `int (*) (const char *, struct stat *)`.

This is a GNU extension.

gl_flags   The flags used when `glob` was called. In addition, `GLOB_MAGCHAR` might be set. See Section 10.2.2 [Flags for Globbing], page 227 for more details.

This is a GNU extension.

For use in the `glob64` function `glob.h` contains another definition for a very similar type. `glob64_t` differs from `glob_t` only in the types of the members `gl_readdir`, `gl_stat`, and `gl_lstat`.

`glob64_t`   [Data Type]

This data type holds a pointer to a word vector. More precisely, it records both the address of the word vector and its size. The GNU implementation contains some more fields which are non-standard extensions.

gl_pathc   The number of elements in the vector, excluding the initial null entries if the GLOB_DOOFFS flag is used (see gl_offs below).

gl_pathv   The address of the vector. This field has type `char **`.

gl_offs   The offset of the first real element of the vector, from its nominal address in the `gl_pathv` field. Unlike the other fields, this is always an input to `glob`, rather than an output from it.

If you use a nonzero offset, then that many elements at the beginning of the vector are left empty. (The `glob` function fills them with null pointers.)

The `gl_offs` field is meaningful only if you use the GLOB_DOOFFS flag. Otherwise, the offset is always zero regardless of what is in this field, and the first real element comes at the beginning of the vector.

gl_closedir

The address of an alternative implementation of the `closedir` function. It is used if the `GLOB_ALTDIRFUNC` bit is set in the flag parameter. The type of this field is `void (*) (void *)`.

This is a GNU extension.

gl_readdir

The address of an alternative implementation of the `readdir64` function used to read the contents of a directory. It is used if the `GLOB_ALTDIRFUNC` bit is set in the flag parameter. The type of this field is `struct dirent64 *(*) (void *)`.

This is a GNU extension.

gl_opendir

The address of an alternative implementation of the `opendir` function. It is used if the `GLOB_ALTDIRFUNC` bit is set in the flag parameter. The type of this field is `void *(*) (const char *)`.

This is a GNU extension.

gl_stat   The address of an alternative implementation of the `stat64` function to get information about an object in the filesystem. It is used if the `GLOB_ALTDIRFUNC` bit is set in the flag parameter. The type of this field is `int (*) (const char *, struct stat64 *)`.

This is a GNU extension.

gl_lstat   The address of an alternative implementation of the `lstat64` function to get information about an object in the filesystems, not following symbolic links. It is used if the `GLOB_ALTDIRFUNC` bit is set in the flag parameter. The type of this field is `int (*) (const char *, struct stat64 *)`.

This is a GNU extension.

gl_flags   The flags used when `glob` was called. In addition, `GLOB_MAGCHAR` might be set. See Section 10.2.2 [Flags for Globbing], page 227 for more details.

This is a GNU extension.

`int glob (const char *pattern, int flags, int (*errfunc) (const char`   [Function]
     `*filename, int error-code), glob_t *vector-ptr)`

Preliminary: | MT-Unsafe race:utent env sig:ALRM timer locale | AS-Unsafe dlopen plugin corrupt heap lock | AC-Unsafe corrupt lock fd mem | See Section 1.2.2.1 [POSIX Safety Concepts], page 2.

The function `glob` does globbing using the pattern *pattern* in the current directory. It puts the result in a newly allocated vector, and stores the size and address of this vector into *vector-ptr*. The argument *flags* is a combination of bit flags; see Section 10.2.2 [Flags for Globbing], page 227, for details of the flags.

The result of globbing is a sequence of file names. The function `glob` allocates a string for each resulting word, then allocates a vector of type `char **` to store the addresses of these strings. The last element of the vector is a null pointer. This vector is called the *word vector*.

To return this vector, `glob` stores both its address and its length (number of elements, not counting the terminating null pointer) into *vector-ptr*.

Normally, `glob` sorts the file names alphabetically before returning them. You can turn this off with the flag `GLOB_NOSORT` if you want to get the information as fast as possible. Usually it's a good idea to let `glob` sort them—if you process the files in alphabetical order, the users will have a feel for the rate of progress that your application is making.

If `glob` succeeds, it returns 0. Otherwise, it returns one of these error codes:

GLOB_ABORTED
            There was an error opening a directory, and you used the flag `GLOB_ERR` or your specified *errfunc* returned a nonzero value. See below for an explanation of the `GLOB_ERR` flag and *errfunc*.

GLOB_NOMATCH
            The pattern didn't match any existing files. If you use the `GLOB_NOCHECK` flag, then you never get this error code, because that flag tells `glob` to *pretend* that the pattern matched at least one file.

GLOB_NOSPACE
            It was impossible to allocate memory to hold the result.

In the event of an error, `glob` stores information in *vector-ptr* about all the matches it has found so far.

It is important to notice that the `glob` function will not fail if it encounters directories or files which cannot be handled without the LFS interfaces. The implementation of `glob` is supposed to use these functions internally. This at least is the assumptions made by the Unix standard. The GNU extension of allowing the user to provide own directory handling and `stat` functions complicates things a bit. If these callback functions are used and a large file or directory is encountered `glob` *can* fail.

int glob64 (*const char *pattern*, *int flags*, *int (*errfunc)* (*const char*   [Function]
     *filename, *int error-code*), *glob64_t *vector-ptr*)

Preliminary: | MT-Unsafe race:utent env sig:ALRM timer locale | AS-Unsafe dlopen corrupt heap lock | AC-Unsafe corrupt lock fd mem | See Section 1.2.2.1 [POSIX Safety Concepts], page 2.

The `glob64` function was added as part of the Large File Summit extensions but is not part of the original LFS proposal. The reason for this is simple: it is not necessary. The necessity for a `glob64` function is added by the extensions of the GNU `glob` implementation which allows the user to provide own directory handling and `stat` functions. The `readdir` and `stat` functions do depend on the choice of _FILE_OFFSET_BITS since the definition of the types `struct dirent` and `struct stat` will change depending on the choice.

Beside this difference the `glob64` works just like `glob` in all aspects.

This function is a GNU extension.

10.2.2 Flags for Globbing

This section describes the standard flags that you can specify in the *flags* argument to `glob`. Choose the flags you want, and combine them with the C bitwise OR operator |.

Note that there are Section 10.2.3 [More Flags for Globbing], page 228 available as GNU extensions.

GLOB_APPEND

> Append the words from this expansion to the vector of words produced by previous calls to `glob`. This way you can effectively expand several words as if they were concatenated with spaces between them.
>
> In order for appending to work, you must not modify the contents of the word vector structure between calls to `glob`. And, if you set GLOB_DOOFFS in the first call to `glob`, you must also set it when you append the results.
>
> Note that the pointer stored in `gl_pathv` may no longer be valid after you call `glob` the second time, because `glob` might have relocated the vector. So always fetch `gl_pathv` from the `glob_t` structure after each `glob` call; **never** save the pointer across calls.

GLOB_DOOFFS

> Leave blank slots at the beginning of the vector of words. The `gl_offs` field says how many slots to leave. The blank slots contain null pointers.

GLOB_ERR Give up right away and report an error if there is any difficulty reading the directories that must be read in order to expand *pattern* fully. Such difficulties might include a directory in which you don't have the requisite access. Normally, **glob** tries its best to keep on going despite any errors, reading whatever directories it can.

You can exercise even more control than this by specifying an error-handler function *errfunc* when you call **glob**. If *errfunc* is not a null pointer, then **glob** doesn't give up right away when it can't read a directory; instead, it calls *errfunc* with two arguments, like this:

```
(*errfunc) (filename, error-code)
```

The argument *filename* is the name of the directory that **glob** couldn't open or couldn't read, and *error-code* is the **errno** value that was reported to **glob**.

If the error handler function returns nonzero, then **glob** gives up right away. Otherwise, it continues.

GLOB_MARK

> If the pattern matches the name of a directory, append '/' to the directory's name when returning it.

GLOB_NOCHECK

> If the pattern doesn't match any file names, return the pattern itself as if it were a file name that had been matched. (Normally, when the pattern doesn't match anything, **glob** returns that there were no matches.)

GLOB_NOESCAPE

> Don't treat the '\' character specially in patterns. Normally, '\' quotes the following character, turning off its special meaning (if any) so that it matches only itself. When quoting is enabled, the pattern '\?' matches only the string '?', because the question mark in the pattern acts like an ordinary character.
>
> If you use GLOB_NOESCAPE, then '\' is an ordinary character.
>
> **glob** does its work by calling the function **fnmatch** repeatedly. It handles the flag GLOB_NOESCAPE by turning on the FNM_NOESCAPE flag in calls to **fnmatch**.

GLOB_NOSORT

> Don't sort the file names; return them in no particular order. (In practice, the order will depend on the order of the entries in the directory.) The only reason *not* to sort is to save time.

10.2.3 More Flags for Globbing

Beside the flags described in the last section, the GNU implementation of **glob** allows a few more flags which are also defined in the **glob.h** file. Some of the extensions implement functionality which is available in modern shell implementations.

GLOB_PERIOD

> The . character (period) is treated special. It cannot be matched by wildcards. See Section 10.1 [Wildcard Matching], page 222, FNM_PERIOD.

GLOB_MAGCHAR

> The GLOB_MAGCHAR value is not to be given to **glob** in the *flags* parameter. Instead, **glob** sets this bit in the *gl_flags* element of the *glob_t* structure provided as the result if the pattern used for matching contains any wildcard character.

GLOB_ALTDIRFUNC

Instead of the using the using the normal functions for accessing the filesystem the `glob` implementation uses the user-supplied functions specified in the structure pointed to by *pglob* parameter. For more information about the functions refer to the sections about directory handling see Section 14.2 [Accessing Directories], page 379, and Section 14.9.2 [Reading the Attributes of a File], page 403.

GLOB_BRACE

If this flag is given the handling of braces in the pattern is changed. It is now required that braces appear correctly grouped. I.e., for each opening brace there must be a closing one. Braces can be used recursively. So it is possible to define one brace expression in another one. It is important to note that the range of each brace expression is completely contained in the outer brace expression (if there is one).

The string between the matching braces is separated into single expressions by splitting at , (comma) characters. The commas themselves are discarded. Please note what we said above about recursive brace expressions. The commas used to separate the subexpressions must be at the same level. Commas in brace subexpressions are not matched. They are used during expansion of the brace expression of the deeper level. The example below shows this

```
glob ("{foo/{,bar,biz},baz}", GLOB_BRACE, NULL, &result)
```

is equivalent to the sequence

```
glob ("foo/", GLOB_BRACE, NULL, &result)
glob ("foo/bar", GLOB_BRACE|GLOB_APPEND, NULL, &result)
glob ("foo/biz", GLOB_BRACE|GLOB_APPEND, NULL, &result)
glob ("baz", GLOB_BRACE|GLOB_APPEND, NULL, &result)
```

if we leave aside error handling.

GLOB_NOMAGIC

If the pattern contains no wildcard constructs (it is a literal file name), return it as the sole "matching" word, even if no file exists by that name.

GLOB_TILDE

If this flag is used the character ~ (tilde) is handled special if it appears at the beginning of the pattern. Instead of being taken verbatim it is used to represent the home directory of a known user.

If ~ is the only character in pattern or it is followed by a / (slash), the home directory of the process owner is substituted. Using `getlogin` and `getpwnam` the information is read from the system databases. As an example take user `bart` with his home directory at `/home/bart`. For him a call like

```
glob ("~/bin/*", GLOB_TILDE, NULL, &result)
```

would return the contents of the directory `/home/bart/bin`. Instead of referring to the own home directory it is also possible to name the home directory of other users. To do so one has to append the user name after the tilde character. So the contents of user `homer`'s `bin` directory can be retrieved by

```
glob ("~homer/bin/*", GLOB_TILDE, NULL, &result)
```

If the user name is not valid or the home directory cannot be determined for some reason the pattern is left untouched and itself used as the result. I.e., if in the last example `home` is not available the tilde expansion yields to `"~homer/bin/*"` and `glob` is not looking for a directory named `~homer`.

This functionality is equivalent to what is available in C-shells if the `nonomatch` flag is set.

`GLOB_TILDE_CHECK`

If this flag is used `glob` behaves like as if `GLOB_TILDE` is given. The only difference is that if the user name is not available or the home directory cannot be determined for other reasons this leads to an error. `glob` will return `GLOB_NOMATCH` instead of using the pattern itself as the name.

This functionality is equivalent to what is available in C-shells if `nonomatch` flag is not set.

`GLOB_ONLYDIR`

If this flag is used the globbing function takes this as a **hint** that the caller is only interested in directories matching the pattern. If the information about the type of the file is easily available non-directories will be rejected but no extra work will be done to determine the information for each file. I.e., the caller must still be able to filter directories out.

This functionality is only available with the GNU `glob` implementation. It is mainly used internally to increase the performance but might be useful for a user as well and therefore is documented here.

Calling `glob` will in most cases allocate resources which are used to represent the result of the function call. If the same object of type `glob_t` is used in multiple call to `glob` the resources are freed or reused so that no leaks appear. But this does not include the time when all `glob` calls are done.

`void globfree (`*`glob_t *pglob`*`)` [Function]

Preliminary: | MT-Safe | AS-Unsafe corrupt heap | AC-Unsafe corrupt mem | See Section 1.2.2.1 [POSIX Safety Concepts], page 2.

The `globfree` function frees all resources allocated by previous calls to `glob` associated with the object pointed to by *pglob*. This function should be called whenever the currently used `glob_t` typed object isn't used anymore.

`void globfree64 (`*`glob64_t *pglob`*`)` [Function]

Preliminary: | MT-Safe | AS-Unsafe corrupt lock | AC-Unsafe corrupt lock fd mem | See Section 1.2.2.1 [POSIX Safety Concepts], page 2.

This function is equivalent to `globfree` but it frees records of type `glob64_t` which were allocated by `glob64`.

10.3 Regular Expression Matching

The GNU C Library supports two interfaces for matching regular expressions. One is the standard POSIX.2 interface, and the other is what the GNU C Library has had for many years.

Both interfaces are declared in the header file `regex.h`. If you define `_POSIX_C_SOURCE`, then only the POSIX.2 functions, structures, and constants are declared.

10.3.1 POSIX Regular Expression Compilation

Before you can actually match a regular expression, you must *compile* it. This is not true compilation—it produces a special data structure, not machine instructions. But it is like ordinary compilation in that its purpose is to enable you to "execute" the pattern fast. (See Section 10.3.3 [Matching a Compiled POSIX Regular Expression], page 233, for how to use the compiled regular expression for matching.)

There is a special data type for compiled regular expressions:

`regex_t`   [Data Type]

> This type of object holds a compiled regular expression. It is actually a structure. It has just one field that your programs should look at:
>
> `re_nsub`   This field holds the number of parenthetical subexpressions in the regular expression that was compiled.
>
> There are several other fields, but we don't describe them here, because only the functions in the library should use them.

After you create a `regex_t` object, you can compile a regular expression into it by calling `regcomp`.

`int regcomp` (*regex_t *restrict* `compiled`, *const char *restrict* `pattern`,   [Function]
        int `cflags`)

> Preliminary: | MT-Safe locale | AS-Unsafe corrupt heap lock dlopen | AC-Unsafe corrupt lock mem fd | See Section 1.2.2.1 [POSIX Safety Concepts], page 2.
>
> The function `regcomp` "compiles" a regular expression into a data structure that you can use with `regexec` to match against a string. The compiled regular expression format is designed for efficient matching. `regcomp` stores it into `*compiled`.
>
> It's up to you to allocate an object of type `regex_t` and pass its address to `regcomp`.
>
> The argument *cflags* lets you specify various options that control the syntax and semantics of regular expressions. See Section 10.3.2 [Flags for POSIX Regular Expressions], page 232.
>
> If you use the flag `REG_NOSUB`, then `regcomp` omits from the compiled regular expression the information necessary to record how subexpressions actually match. In this case, you might as well pass 0 for the *matchptr* and *nmatch* arguments when you call `regexec`.
>
> If you don't use `REG_NOSUB`, then the compiled regular expression does have the capacity to record how subexpressions match. Also, `regcomp` tells you how many subexpressions *pattern* has, by storing the number in `compiled->re_nsub`. You can use that value to decide how long an array to allocate to hold information about subexpression matches.
>
> `regcomp` returns 0 if it succeeds in compiling the regular expression; otherwise, it returns a nonzero error code (see the table below). You can use `regerror` to produce an error message string describing the reason for a nonzero value; see Section 10.3.6 [POSIX Regexp Matching Cleanup], page 235.

Here are the possible nonzero values that `regcomp` can return:

`REG_BADBR`

There was an invalid '\{...\}' construct in the regular expression. A valid '\{...\}' construct must contain either a single number, or two numbers in increasing order separated by a comma.

`REG_BADPAT`

There was a syntax error in the regular expression.

`REG_BADRPT`

A repetition operator such as '?' or '*' appeared in a bad position (with no preceding subexpression to act on).

`REG_ECOLLATE`

The regular expression referred to an invalid collating element (one not defined in the current locale for string collation). See Section 7.3 [Locale Categories], page 170.

`REG_ECTYPE`

The regular expression referred to an invalid character class name.

`REG_EESCAPE`

The regular expression ended with '\'.

`REG_ESUBREG`

There was an invalid number in the '*digit*' construct.

`REG_EBRACK`

There were unbalanced square brackets in the regular expression.

`REG_EPAREN`

An extended regular expression had unbalanced parentheses, or a basic regular expression had unbalanced '\(' and '\)'.

`REG_EBRACE`

The regular expression had unbalanced '\{' and '\}'.

`REG_ERANGE`

One of the endpoints in a range expression was invalid.

`REG_ESPACE`

`regcomp` ran out of memory.

10.3.2 Flags for POSIX Regular Expressions

These are the bit flags that you can use in the *cflags* operand when compiling a regular expression with `regcomp`.

`REG_EXTENDED`

Treat the pattern as an extended regular expression, rather than as a basic regular expression.

`REG_ICASE`

Ignore case when matching letters.

REG_NOSUB
> Don't bother storing the contents of the *matches-ptr* array.

REG_NEWLINE
> Treat a newline in *string* as dividing *string* into multiple lines, so that '$' can match before the newline and '^' can match after. Also, don't permit '.' to match a newline, and don't permit '[^...]' to match a newline.
>
> Otherwise, newline acts like any other ordinary character.

10.3.3 Matching a Compiled POSIX Regular Expression

Once you have compiled a regular expression, as described in Section 10.3.1 [POSIX Regular Expression Compilation], page 231, you can match it against strings using `regexec`. A match anywhere inside the string counts as success, unless the regular expression contains anchor characters ('^' or '$').

int regexec (*const regex_t *restrict* `compiled`, *const char *restrict*   [Function]
>   `string`, *size_t* `nmatch`, *regmatch_t* `matchptr`[*restrict*], *int* `eflags`)
>
> Preliminary: | MT-Safe locale | AS-Unsafe corrupt heap lock dlopen | AC-Unsafe corrupt lock mem fd | See Section 1.2.2.1 [POSIX Safety Concepts], page 2.
>
> This function tries to match the compiled regular expression **compiled* against *string*.
>
> `regexec` returns 0 if the regular expression matches; otherwise, it returns a nonzero value. See the table below for what nonzero values mean. You can use `regerror` to produce an error message string describing the reason for a nonzero value; see Section 10.3.6 [POSIX Regexp Matching Cleanup], page 235.
>
> The argument *eflags* is a word of bit flags that enable various options.
>
> If you want to get information about what part of *string* actually matched the regular expression or its subexpressions, use the arguments *matchptr* and *nmatch*. Otherwise, pass 0 for *nmatch*, and NULL for *matchptr*. See Section 10.3.4 [Match Results with Subexpressions], page 234.

You must match the regular expression with the same set of current locales that were in effect when you compiled the regular expression.

The function `regexec` accepts the following flags in the *eflags* argument:

REG_NOTBOL
> Do not regard the beginning of the specified string as the beginning of a line; more generally, don't make any assumptions about what text might precede it.

REG_NOTEOL
> Do not regard the end of the specified string as the end of a line; more generally, don't make any assumptions about what text might follow it.

Here are the possible nonzero values that `regexec` can return:

REG_NOMATCH
> The pattern didn't match the string. This isn't really an error.

REG_ESPACE
> `regexec` ran out of memory.

10.3.4 Match Results with Subexpressions

When `regexec` matches parenthetical subexpressions of *pattern*, it records which parts of *string* they match. It returns that information by storing the offsets into an array whose elements are structures of type `regmatch_t`. The first element of the array (index 0) records the part of the string that matched the entire regular expression. Each other element of the array records the beginning and end of the part that matched a single parenthetical subexpression.

`regmatch_t`   [Data Type]

> This is the data type of the *matcharray* array that you pass to `regexec`. It contains two structure fields, as follows:
>
> `rm_so`   The offset in *string* of the beginning of a substring. Add this value to *string* to get the address of that part.
>
> `rm_eo`   The offset in *string* of the end of the substring.

`regoff_t`   [Data Type]

> `regoff_t` is an alias for another signed integer type. The fields of `regmatch_t` have type `regoff_t`.

The `regmatch_t` elements correspond to subexpressions positionally; the first element (index 1) records where the first subexpression matched, the second element records the second subexpression, and so on. The order of the subexpressions is the order in which they begin.

When you call `regexec`, you specify how long the *matchptr* array is, with the *nmatch* argument. This tells `regexec` how many elements to store. If the actual regular expression has more than *nmatch* subexpressions, then you won't get offset information about the rest of them. But this doesn't alter whether the pattern matches a particular string or not.

If you don't want `regexec` to return any information about where the subexpressions matched, you can either supply 0 for *nmatch*, or use the flag `REG_NOSUB` when you compile the pattern with `regcomp`.

10.3.5 Complications in Subexpression Matching

Sometimes a subexpression matches a substring of no characters. This happens when 'f\(o*\)' matches the string 'fum'. (It really matches just the 'f'.) In this case, both of the offsets identify the point in the string where the null substring was found. In this example, the offsets are both 1.

Sometimes the entire regular expression can match without using some of its subexpressions at all—for example, when 'ba\(na\)*' matches the string 'ba', the parenthetical subexpression is not used. When this happens, `regexec` stores -1 in both fields of the element for that subexpression.

Sometimes matching the entire regular expression can match a particular subexpression more than once—for example, when 'ba\(na\)*' matches the string 'bananana', the parenthetical subexpression matches three times. When this happens, `regexec` usually stores the offsets of the last part of the string that matched the subexpression. In the case of 'bananana', these offsets are 6 and 8.

But the last match is not always the one that is chosen. It's more accurate to say that the last *opportunity* to match is the one that takes precedence. What this means is that when one subexpression appears within another, then the results reported for the inner subexpression reflect whatever happened on the last match of the outer subexpression. For an example, consider '\(ba\(na\)*s \)*' matching the string 'bananas bas '. The last time the inner expression actually matches is near the end of the first word. But it is *considered* again in the second word, and fails to match there. **regexec** reports nonuse of the "na" subexpression.

Another place where this rule applies is when the regular expression

    \(ba\(na\)*s \|nefer\(ti\)* \)*

matches 'bananas nefertiti'. The "na" subexpression does match in the first word, but it doesn't match in the second word because the other alternative is used there. Once again, the second repetition of the outer subexpression overrides the first, and within that second repetition, the "na" subexpression is not used. So **regexec** reports nonuse of the "na" subexpression.

10.3.6 POSIX Regexp Matching Cleanup

When you are finished using a compiled regular expression, you can free the storage it uses by calling **regfree**.

void regfree (*regex_t *compiled*)   [Function]
> Preliminary: | MT-Safe | AS-Unsafe heap | AC-Unsafe mem | See Section 1.2.2.1 [POSIX Safety Concepts], page 2.
>
> Calling **regfree** frees all the storage that *compiled* points to. This includes various internal fields of the **regex_t** structure that aren't documented in this manual.
>
> **regfree** does not free the object *compiled* itself.

You should always free the space in a **regex_t** structure with **regfree** before using the structure to compile another regular expression.

When **regcomp** or **regexec** reports an error, you can use the function **regerror** to turn it into an error message string.

size_t regerror (*int errcode*, *const regex_t *restrict compiled*, *char*   [Function]
> *restrict buffer*, *size_t length*)
> Preliminary: | MT-Safe env | AS-Unsafe corrupt heap lock dlopen | AC-Unsafe corrupt lock fd mem | See Section 1.2.2.1 [POSIX Safety Concepts], page 2.
>
> This function produces an error message string for the error code *errcode*, and stores the string in *length* bytes of memory starting at *buffer*. For the *compiled* argument, supply the same compiled regular expression structure that **regcomp** or **regexec** was working with when it got the error. Alternatively, you can supply NULL for *compiled*; you will still get a meaningful error message, but it might not be as detailed.
>
> If the error message can't fit in *length* bytes (including a terminating null character), then **regerror** truncates it. The string that **regerror** stores is always null-terminated even if it has been truncated.
>
> The return value of **regerror** is the minimum length needed to store the entire error message. If this is less than *length*, then the error message was not truncated, and you can use it. Otherwise, you should call **regerror** again with a larger buffer.

Here is a function which uses `regerror`, but always dynamically allocates a buffer for the error message:

```
char *get_regerror (int errcode, regex_t *compiled)
{
  size_t length = regerror (errcode, compiled, NULL, 0);
  char *buffer = xmalloc (length);
  (void) regerror (errcode, compiled, buffer, length);
  return buffer;
}
```

10.4 Shell-Style Word Expansion

Word expansion means the process of splitting a string into *words* and substituting for variables, commands, and wildcards just as the shell does.

For example, when you write '`ls -l foo.c`', this string is split into three separate words—'`ls`', '`-l`' and '`foo.c`'. This is the most basic function of word expansion.

When you write '`ls *.c`', this can become many words, because the word '`*.c`' can be replaced with any number of file names. This is called *wildcard expansion*, and it is also a part of word expansion.

When you use '`echo $PATH`' to print your path, you are taking advantage of *variable substitution*, which is also part of word expansion.

Ordinary programs can perform word expansion just like the shell by calling the library function `wordexp`.

10.4.1 The Stages of Word Expansion

When word expansion is applied to a sequence of words, it performs the following transformations in the order shown here:

1. *Tilde expansion*: Replacement of '`~foo`' with the name of the home directory of '`foo`'.

2. Next, three different transformations are applied in the same step, from left to right:

   - *Variable substitution*: Environment variables are substituted for references such as '`$foo`'.

   - *Command substitution*: Constructs such as '``cat foo``' and the equivalent '`$(cat foo)`' are replaced with the output from the inner command.

   - *Arithmetic expansion*: Constructs such as '`$(($x-1))`' are replaced with the result of the arithmetic computation.

3. *Field splitting*: subdivision of the text into *words*.

4. *Wildcard expansion*: The replacement of a construct such as '`*.c`' with a list of '`.c`' file names. Wildcard expansion applies to an entire word at a time, and replaces that word with 0 or more file names that are themselves words.

5. *Quote removal*: The deletion of string-quotes, now that they have done their job by inhibiting the above transformations when appropriate.

For the details of these transformations, and how to write the constructs that use them, see *The BASH Manual* (to appear).

10.4.2 Calling `wordexp`

All the functions, constants and data types for word expansion are declared in the header file `wordexp.h`.

Word expansion produces a vector of words (strings). To return this vector, `wordexp` uses a special data type, `wordexp_t`, which is a structure. You pass `wordexp` the address of the structure, and it fills in the structure's fields to tell you about the results.

`wordexp_t`   [Data Type]

This data type holds a pointer to a word vector. More precisely, it records both the address of the word vector and its size.

`we_wordc`   The number of elements in the vector.

`we_wordv`   The address of the vector. This field has type `char **`.

`we_offs`   The offset of the first real element of the vector, from its nominal address in the `we_wordv` field. Unlike the other fields, this is always an input to `wordexp`, rather than an output from it.

If you use a nonzero offset, then that many elements at the beginning of the vector are left empty. (The `wordexp` function fills them with null pointers.)

The `we_offs` field is meaningful only if you use the `WRDE_DOOFFS` flag. Otherwise, the offset is always zero regardless of what is in this field, and the first real element comes at the beginning of the vector.

`int wordexp (const char *words, wordexp_t *word-vector-ptr, int`   [Function]
`    flags)`

Preliminary: | MT-Unsafe race:utent const:env env sig:ALRM timer locale | AS-Unsafe dlopen plugin i18n heap corrupt lock | AC-Unsafe corrupt lock fd mem | See Section 1.2.2.1 [POSIX Safety Concepts], page 2.

Perform word expansion on the string *words*, putting the result in a newly allocated vector, and store the size and address of this vector into *word-vector-ptr*. The argument *flags* is a combination of bit flags; see Section 10.4.3 [Flags for Word Expansion], page 238, for details of the flags.

You shouldn't use any of the characters '`|&;<>`' in the string *words* unless they are quoted; likewise for newline. If you use these characters unquoted, you will get the `WRDE_BADCHAR` error code. Don't use parentheses or braces unless they are quoted or part of a word expansion construct. If you use quotation characters '`'"`', they should come in pairs that balance.

The results of word expansion are a sequence of words. The function `wordexp` allocates a string for each resulting word, then allocates a vector of type `char **` to store the addresses of these strings. The last element of the vector is a null pointer. This vector is called the *word vector*.

To return this vector, `wordexp` stores both its address and its length (number of elements, not counting the terminating null pointer) into *word-vector-ptr*.

If `wordexp` succeeds, it returns 0. Otherwise, it returns one of these error codes:

WRDE_BADCHAR

> The input string *words* contains an unquoted invalid character such as '|'.

WRDE_BADVAL

> The input string refers to an undefined shell variable, and you used the flag `WRDE_UNDEF` to forbid such references.

WRDE_CMDSUB

> The input string uses command substitution, and you used the flag `WRDE_NOCMD` to forbid command substitution.

WRDE_NOSPACE

> It was impossible to allocate memory to hold the result. In this case, `wordexp` can store part of the results—as much as it could allocate room for.

WRDE_SYNTAX

> There was a syntax error in the input string. For example, an unmatched quoting character is a syntax error. This error code is also used to signal division by zero and overflow in arithmetic expansion.

`void wordfree` (*wordexp_t *word-vector-ptr*)   [Function]

Preliminary: | MT-Safe | AS-Unsafe corrupt heap | AC-Unsafe corrupt mem | See Section 1.2.2.1 [POSIX Safety Concepts], page 2.

Free the storage used for the word-strings and vector that **word-vector-ptr* points to. This does not free the structure **word-vector-ptr* itself—only the other data it points to.

10.4.3 Flags for Word Expansion

This section describes the flags that you can specify in the *flags* argument to `wordexp`. Choose the flags you want, and combine them with the C operator |.

WRDE_APPEND

> Append the words from this expansion to the vector of words produced by previous calls to `wordexp`. This way you can effectively expand several words as if they were concatenated with spaces between them.
>
> In order for appending to work, you must not modify the contents of the word vector structure between calls to `wordexp`. And, if you set `WRDE_DOOFFS` in the first call to `wordexp`, you must also set it when you append to the results.

WRDE_DOOFFS

> Leave blank slots at the beginning of the vector of words. The `we_offs` field says how many slots to leave. The blank slots contain null pointers.

WRDE_NOCMD

> Don't do command substitution; if the input requests command substitution, report an error.

WRDE_REUSE

> Reuse a word vector made by a previous call to `wordexp`. Instead of allocating a new vector of words, this call to `wordexp` will use the vector that already exists (making it larger if necessary).
>
> Note that the vector may move, so it is not safe to save an old pointer and use it again after calling `wordexp`. You must fetch `we_pathv` anew after each call.

WRDE_SHOWERR

> Do show any error messages printed by commands run by command substitution. More precisely, allow these commands to inherit the standard error output stream of the current process. By default, `wordexp` gives these commands a standard error stream that discards all output.

WRDE_UNDEF

> If the input refers to a shell variable that is not defined, report an error.

10.4.4 `wordexp` Example

Here is an example of using `wordexp` to expand several strings and use the results to run a shell command. It also shows the use of `WRDE_APPEND` to concatenate the expansions and of `wordfree` to free the space allocated by `wordexp`.

```
int
expand_and_execute (const char *program, const char **options)
{
  wordexp_t result;
  pid_t pid
  int status, i;

  /* Expand the string for the program to run.  */
  switch (wordexp (program, &result, 0))
    {
    case 0:  /* Successful.  */
      break;
    case WRDE_NOSPACE:
      /* If the error was WRDE_NOSPACE,
         then perhaps part of the result was allocated.  */
      wordfree (&result);
    default:                       /* Some other error.  */
      return -1;
    }

  /* Expand the strings specified for the arguments.  */
  for (i = 0; options[i] != NULL; i++)
    {
      if (wordexp (options[i], &result, WRDE_APPEND))
        {
          wordfree (&result);
          return -1;
        }
    }

  pid = fork ();
  if (pid == 0)
    {
      /* This is the child process.  Execute the command. */
      execv (result.we_wordv[0], result.we_wordv);
```

```
        exit (EXIT_FAILURE);
    }
  else if (pid < 0)
    /* The fork failed.  Report failure.  */
    status = -1;
  else
    /* This is the parent process.  Wait for the child to complete.  */
    if (waitpid (pid, &status, 0) != pid)
      status = -1;

  wordfree (&result);
  return status;
}
```

10.4.5 Details of Tilde Expansion

It's a standard part of shell syntax that you can use '~' at the beginning of a file name to stand for your own home directory. You can use '~*user*' to stand for *user*'s home directory.

Tilde expansion is the process of converting these abbreviations to the directory names that they stand for.

Tilde expansion applies to the '~' plus all following characters up to whitespace or a slash. It takes place only at the beginning of a word, and only if none of the characters to be transformed is quoted in any way.

Plain '~' uses the value of the environment variable HOME as the proper home directory name. '~' followed by a user name uses getpwname to look up that user in the user database, and uses whatever directory is recorded there. Thus, '~' followed by your own name can give different results from plain '~', if the value of HOME is not really your home directory.

10.4.6 Details of Variable Substitution

Part of ordinary shell syntax is the use of '$*variable*' to substitute the value of a shell variable into a command. This is called *variable substitution*, and it is one part of doing word expansion.

There are two basic ways you can write a variable reference for substitution:

${*variable*}

> If you write braces around the variable name, then it is completely unambiguous where the variable name ends. You can concatenate additional letters onto the end of the variable value by writing them immediately after the close brace. For example, '${foo}s' expands into 'tractors'.

$*variable*

> If you do not put braces around the variable name, then the variable name consists of all the alphanumeric characters and underscores that follow the '$'. The next punctuation character ends the variable name. Thus, '$foo-bar' refers to the variable foo and expands into 'tractor-bar'.

When you use braces, you can also use various constructs to modify the value that is substituted, or test it in various ways.

${*variable*:-*default*}

> Substitute the value of *variable*, but if that is empty or undefined, use *default* instead.

`${variable:=default}`

> Substitute the value of *variable*, but if that is empty or undefined, use *default* instead and set the variable to *default*.

`${variable:?message}`

> If *variable* is defined and not empty, substitute its value.
>
> Otherwise, print *message* as an error message on the standard error stream, and consider word expansion a failure.

`${variable:+replacement}`

> Substitute *replacement*, but only if *variable* is defined and nonempty. Otherwise, substitute nothing for this construct.

`${#variable}`

> Substitute a numeral which expresses in base ten the number of characters in the value of *variable*. '`${#foo}`' stands for '7', because '`tractor`' is seven characters.

These variants of variable substitution let you remove part of the variable's value before substituting it. The *prefix* and *suffix* are not mere strings; they are wildcard patterns, just like the patterns that you use to match multiple file names. But in this context, they match against parts of the variable value rather than against file names.

`${variable%%suffix}`

> Substitute the value of *variable*, but first discard from that variable any portion at the end that matches the pattern *suffix*.
>
> If there is more than one alternative for how to match against *suffix*, this construct uses the longest possible match.
>
> Thus, '`${foo%%r*}`' substitutes 't', because the largest match for '`r*`' at the end of '`tractor`' is '`ractor`'.

`${variable%suffix}`

> Substitute the value of *variable*, but first discard from that variable any portion at the end that matches the pattern *suffix*.
>
> If there is more than one alternative for how to match against *suffix*, this construct uses the shortest possible alternative.
>
> Thus, '`${foo%r*}`' substitutes '`tracto`', because the shortest match for '`r*`' at the end of '`tractor`' is just '`r`'.

`${variable##prefix}`

> Substitute the value of *variable*, but first discard from that variable any portion at the beginning that matches the pattern *prefix*.
>
> If there is more than one alternative for how to match against *prefix*, this construct uses the longest possible match.
>
> Thus, '`${foo##*t}`' substitutes '`or`', because the largest match for '`*t`' at the beginning of '`tractor`' is '`tract`'.

`${variable#prefix}`

> Substitute the value of *variable*, but first discard from that variable any portion at the beginning that matches the pattern *prefix*.

If there is more than one alternative for how to match against *prefix*, this construct uses the shortest possible alternative.

Thus, '`${foo#*t}`' substitutes '`ractor`', because the shortest match for '`*t`' at the beginning of '`tractor`' is just '`t`'.

11 Input/Output Overview

Most programs need to do either input (reading data) or output (writing data), or most frequently both, in order to do anything useful. The GNU C Library provides such a large selection of input and output functions that the hardest part is often deciding which function is most appropriate!

This chapter introduces concepts and terminology relating to input and output. Other chapters relating to the GNU I/O facilities are:

- Chapter 12 [Input/Output on Streams], page 248, which covers the high-level functions that operate on streams, including formatted input and output.

- Chapter 13 [Low-Level Input/Output], page 323, which covers the basic I/O and control functions on file descriptors.

- Chapter 14 [File System Interface], page 377, which covers functions for operating on directories and for manipulating file attributes such as access modes and ownership.

- Chapter 15 [Pipes and FIFOs], page 424, which includes information on the basic interprocess communication facilities.

- Chapter 16 [Sockets], page 429, which covers a more complicated interprocess communication facility with support for networking.

- Chapter 17 [Low-Level Terminal Interface], page 477, which covers functions for changing how input and output to terminals or other serial devices are processed.

11.1 Input/Output Concepts

Before you can read or write the contents of a file, you must establish a connection or communications channel to the file. This process is called *opening* the file. You can open a file for reading, writing, or both.

The connection to an open file is represented either as a stream or as a file descriptor. You pass this as an argument to the functions that do the actual read or write operations, to tell them which file to operate on. Certain functions expect streams, and others are designed to operate on file descriptors.

When you have finished reading to or writing from the file, you can terminate the connection by *closing* the file. Once you have closed a stream or file descriptor, you cannot do any more input or output operations on it.

11.1.1 Streams and File Descriptors

When you want to do input or output to a file, you have a choice of two basic mechanisms for representing the connection between your program and the file: file descriptors and streams. File descriptors are represented as objects of type `int`, while streams are represented as `FILE *` objects.

File descriptors provide a primitive, low-level interface to input and output operations. Both file descriptors and streams can represent a connection to a device (such as a terminal), or a pipe or socket for communicating with another process, as well as a normal file. But, if you want to do control operations that are specific to a particular kind of device, you must use a file descriptor; there are no facilities to use streams in this way. You must also use file descriptors if your program needs to do input or output in special modes, such as nonblocking (or polled) input (see Section 13.14 [File Status Flags], page 363).

Streams provide a higher-level interface, layered on top of the primitive file descriptor facilities. The stream interface treats all kinds of files pretty much alike—the sole exception being the three styles of buffering that you can choose (see Section 12.20 [Stream Buffering], page 309).

The main advantage of using the stream interface is that the set of functions for performing actual input and output operations (as opposed to control operations) on streams is much richer and more powerful than the corresponding facilities for file descriptors. The file descriptor interface provides only simple functions for transferring blocks of characters, but the stream interface also provides powerful formatted input and output functions (`printf` and `scanf`) as well as functions for character- and line-oriented input and output.

Since streams are implemented in terms of file descriptors, you can extract the file descriptor from a stream and perform low-level operations directly on the file descriptor. You can also initially open a connection as a file descriptor and then make a stream associated with that file descriptor.

In general, you should stick with using streams rather than file descriptors, unless there is some specific operation you want to do that can only be done on a file descriptor. If you are a beginning programmer and aren't sure what functions to use, we suggest that you concentrate on the formatted input functions (see Section 12.14 [Formatted Input], page 292) and formatted output functions (see Section 12.12 [Formatted Output], page 270).

If you are concerned about portability of your programs to systems other than GNU, you should also be aware that file descriptors are not as portable as streams. You can expect any system running ISO C to support streams, but non-GNU systems may not support file descriptors at all, or may only implement a subset of the GNU functions that operate on file descriptors. Most of the file descriptor functions in the GNU C Library are included in the POSIX.1 standard, however.

11.1.2 File Position

One of the attributes of an open file is its *file position* that keeps track of where in the file the next character is to be read or written. On GNU systems, and all POSIX.1 systems, the file position is simply an integer representing the number of bytes from the beginning of the file.

The file position is normally set to the beginning of the file when it is opened, and each time a character is read or written, the file position is incremented. In other words, access to the file is normally *sequential*.

Ordinary files permit read or write operations at any position within the file. Some other kinds of files may also permit this. Files which do permit this are sometimes referred to as *random-access* files. You can change the file position using the `fseek` function on a stream (see Section 12.18 [File Positioning], page 305) or the `lseek` function on a file descriptor (see Section 13.2 [Input and Output Primitives], page 326). If you try to change the file position on a file that doesn't support random access, you get the `ESPIPE` error.

Streams and descriptors that are opened for *append access* are treated specially for output: output to such files is *always* appended sequentially to the *end* of the file, regardless of the file position. However, the file position is still used to control where in the file reading is done.

If you think about it, you'll realize that several programs can read a given file at the same time. In order for each program to be able to read the file at its own pace, each program must have its own file pointer, which is not affected by anything the other programs do.

In fact, each opening of a file creates a separate file position. Thus, if you open a file twice even in the same program, you get two streams or descriptors with independent file positions.

By contrast, if you open a descriptor and then duplicate it to get another descriptor, these two descriptors share the same file position: changing the file position of one descriptor will affect the other.

11.2 File Names

In order to open a connection to a file, or to perform other operations such as deleting a file, you need some way to refer to the file. Nearly all files have names that are strings—even files which are actually devices such as tape drives or terminals. These strings are called *file names*. You specify the file name to say which file you want to open or operate on.

This section describes the conventions for file names and how the operating system works with them.

11.2.1 Directories

In order to understand the syntax of file names, you need to understand how the file system is organized into a hierarchy of directories.

A *directory* is a file that contains information to associate other files with names; these associations are called *links* or *directory entries*. Sometimes, people speak of "files in a directory", but in reality, a directory only contains pointers to files, not the files themselves.

The name of a file contained in a directory entry is called a *file name component*. In general, a file name consists of a sequence of one or more such components, separated by the slash character ('/'). A file name which is just one component names a file with respect to its directory. A file name with multiple components names a directory, and then a file in that directory, and so on.

Some other documents, such as the POSIX standard, use the term *pathname* for what we call a file name, and either *filename* or *pathname component* for what this manual calls a file name component. We don't use this terminology because a "path" is something completely different (a list of directories to search), and we think that "pathname" used for something else will confuse users. We always use "file name" and "file name component" (or sometimes just "component", where the context is obvious) in GNU documentation. Some macros use the POSIX terminology in their names, such as `PATH_MAX`. These macros are defined by the POSIX standard, so we cannot change their names.

You can find more detailed information about operations on directories in Chapter 14 [File System Interface], page 377.

11.2.2 File Name Resolution

A file name consists of file name components separated by slash ('/') characters. On the systems that the GNU C Library supports, multiple successive '/' characters are equivalent to a single '/' character.

The process of determining what file a file name refers to is called *file name resolution*. This is performed by examining the components that make up a file name in left-to-right order, and locating each successive component in the directory named by the previous component. Of course, each of the files that are referenced as directories must actually exist, be directories instead of regular files, and have the appropriate permissions to be accessible by the process; otherwise the file name resolution fails.

If a file name begins with a '/', the first component in the file name is located in the *root directory* of the process (usually all processes on the system have the same root directory). Such a file name is called an *absolute file name*.

Otherwise, the first component in the file name is located in the current working directory (see Section 14.1 [Working Directory], page 377). This kind of file name is called a *relative file name*.

The file name components . ("dot") and .. ("dot-dot") have special meanings. Every directory has entries for these file name components. The file name component . refers to the directory itself, while the file name component .. refers to its *parent directory* (the directory that contains the link for the directory in question). As a special case, .. in the root directory refers to the root directory itself, since it has no parent; thus /.. is the same as /.

Here are some examples of file names:

/a   The file named a, in the root directory.

/a/b   The file named b, in the directory named a in the root directory.

a   The file named a, in the current working directory.

/a/./b   This is the same as /a/b.

./a   The file named a, in the current working directory.

../a   The file named a, in the parent directory of the current working directory.

A file name that names a directory may optionally end in a '/'. You can specify a file name of / to refer to the root directory, but the empty string is not a meaningful file name. If you want to refer to the current working directory, use a file name of . or ./.

Unlike some other operating systems, GNU systems don't have any built-in support for file types (or extensions) or file versions as part of its file name syntax. Many programs and utilities use conventions for file names—for example, files containing C source code usually have names suffixed with '.c'—but there is nothing in the file system itself that enforces this kind of convention.

11.2.3 File Name Errors

Functions that accept file name arguments usually detect these `errno` error conditions relating to the file name syntax or trouble finding the named file. These errors are referred to throughout this manual as the *usual file name errors*.

EACCES   The process does not have search permission for a directory component of the file name.

ENAMETOOLONG

This error is used when either the total length of a file name is greater than `PATH_MAX`, or when an individual file name component has a length greater than `NAME_MAX`. See Section 32.6 [Limits on File System Capacity], page 850.

On GNU/Hurd systems, there is no imposed limit on overall file name length, but some file systems may place limits on the length of a component.

ENOENT   This error is reported when a file referenced as a directory component in the file name doesn't exist, or when a component is a symbolic link whose target file does not exist. See Section 14.5 [Symbolic Links], page 393.

ENOTDIR   A file that is referenced as a directory component in the file name exists, but it isn't a directory.

ELOOP   Too many symbolic links were resolved while trying to look up the file name. The system has an arbitrary limit on the number of symbolic links that may be resolved in looking up a single file name, as a primitive way to detect loops. See Section 14.5 [Symbolic Links], page 393.

11.2.4 Portability of File Names

The rules for the syntax of file names discussed in Section 11.2 [File Names], page 245, are the rules normally used by GNU systems and by other POSIX systems. However, other operating systems may use other conventions.

There are two reasons why it can be important for you to be aware of file name portability issues:

- If your program makes assumptions about file name syntax, or contains embedded literal file name strings, it is more difficult to get it to run under other operating systems that use different syntax conventions.

- Even if you are not concerned about running your program on machines that run other operating systems, it may still be possible to access files that use different naming conventions. For example, you may be able to access file systems on another computer running a different operating system over a network, or read and write disks in formats used by other operating systems.

The ISO C standard says very little about file name syntax, only that file names are strings. In addition to varying restrictions on the length of file names and what characters can validly appear in a file name, different operating systems use different conventions and syntax for concepts such as structured directories and file types or extensions. Some concepts such as file versions might be supported in some operating systems and not by others.

The POSIX.1 standard allows implementations to put additional restrictions on file name syntax, concerning what characters are permitted in file names and on the length of file name and file name component strings. However, on GNU systems, any character except the null character is permitted in a file name string, and on GNU/Hurd systems there are no limits on the length of file name strings.

12 Input/Output on Streams

This chapter describes the functions for creating streams and performing input and output operations on them. As discussed in Chapter 11 [Input/Output Overview], page 243, a stream is a fairly abstract, high-level concept representing a communications channel to a file, device, or process.

12.1 Streams

For historical reasons, the type of the C data structure that represents a stream is called FILE rather than "stream". Since most of the library functions deal with objects of type FILE *, sometimes the term *file pointer* is also used to mean "stream". This leads to unfortunate confusion over terminology in many books on C. This manual, however, is careful to use the terms "file" and "stream" only in the technical sense.

The FILE type is declared in the header file stdio.h.

FILE   [Data Type]

> This is the data type used to represent stream objects. A FILE object holds all of the internal state information about the connection to the associated file, including such things as the file position indicator and buffering information. Each stream also has error and end-of-file status indicators that can be tested with the ferror and feof functions; see Section 12.15 [End-Of-File and Errors], page 302.

FILE objects are allocated and managed internally by the input/output library functions. Don't try to create your own objects of type FILE; let the library do it. Your programs should deal only with pointers to these objects (that is, FILE * values) rather than the objects themselves.

12.2 Standard Streams

When the main function of your program is invoked, it already has three predefined streams open and available for use. These represent the "standard" input and output channels that have been established for the process.

These streams are declared in the header file stdio.h.

FILE * stdin   [Variable]

> The *standard input* stream, which is the normal source of input for the program.

FILE * stdout   [Variable]

> The *standard output* stream, which is used for normal output from the program.

FILE * stderr   [Variable]

> The *standard error* stream, which is used for error messages and diagnostics issued by the program.

On GNU systems, you can specify what files or processes correspond to these streams using the pipe and redirection facilities provided by the shell. (The primitives shells use to implement these facilities are described in Chapter 14 [File System Interface], page 377.)

Most other operating systems provide similar mechanisms, but the details of how to use them can vary.

In the GNU C Library, `stdin`, `stdout`, and `stderr` are normal variables which you can set just like any others. For example, to redirect the standard output to a file, you could do:

```
fclose (stdout);
stdout = fopen ("standard-output-file", "w");
```

Note however, that in other systems `stdin`, `stdout`, and `stderr` are macros that you cannot assign to in the normal way. But you can use `freopen` to get the effect of closing one and reopening it. See Section 12.3 [Opening Streams], page 249.

The three streams `stdin`, `stdout`, and `stderr` are not unoriented at program start (see Section 12.6 [Streams in Internationalized Applications], page 257).

12.3 Opening Streams

Opening a file with the `fopen` function creates a new stream and establishes a connection between the stream and a file. This may involve creating a new file.

Everything described in this section is declared in the header file `stdio.h`.

`FILE * fopen` (*const char *filename, const char *opentype*)   [Function]
Preliminary: | MT-Safe | AS-Unsafe heap lock | AC-Unsafe mem fd lock | See Section 1.2.2.1 [POSIX Safety Concepts], page 2.

The `fopen` function opens a stream for I/O to the file *filename*, and returns a pointer to the stream.

The *opentype* argument is a string that controls how the file is opened and specifies attributes of the resulting stream. It must begin with one of the following sequences of characters:

'r'   Open an existing file for reading only.

'w'   Open the file for writing only. If the file already exists, it is truncated to zero length. Otherwise a new file is created.

'a'   Open a file for append access; that is, writing at the end of file only. If the file already exists, its initial contents are unchanged and output to the stream is appended to the end of the file. Otherwise, a new, empty file is created.

'r+'   Open an existing file for both reading and writing. The initial contents of the file are unchanged and the initial file position is at the beginning of the file.

'w+'   Open a file for both reading and writing. If the file already exists, it is truncated to zero length. Otherwise, a new file is created.

'a+'   Open or create file for both reading and appending. If the file exists, its initial contents are unchanged. Otherwise, a new file is created. The initial file position for reading is at the beginning of the file, but output is always appended to the end of the file.

As you can see, '+' requests a stream that can do both input and output. When using such a stream, you must call `fflush` (see Section 12.20 [Stream Buffering], page 309) or a file positioning function such as `fseek` (see Section 12.18 [File Positioning], page 305) when switching from reading to writing or vice versa. Otherwise, internal buffers might not be emptied properly.

Additional characters may appear after these to specify flags for the call. Always put the mode ('r', 'w+', etc.) first; that is the only part you are guaranteed will be understood by all systems.

The GNU C Library defines additional characters for use in *opentype*:

'c'   The file is opened with cancellation in the I/O functions disabled.

'e'   The underlying file descriptor will be closed if you use any of the `exec...` functions (see Section 26.5 [Executing a File], page 752). (This is equivalent to having set `FD_CLOEXEC` on that descriptor. See Section 13.13 [File Descriptor Flags], page 361.)

'm'   The file is opened and accessed using `mmap`. This is only supported with files opened for reading.

'x'   Insist on creating a new file—if a file *filename* already exists, `fopen` fails rather than opening it. If you use 'x' you are guaranteed that you will not clobber an existing file. This is equivalent to the `O_EXCL` option to the `open` function (see Section 13.1 [Opening and Closing Files], page 323).
            The 'x' modifier is part of ISO C11.

The character 'b' in *opentype* has a standard meaning; it requests a binary stream rather than a text stream. But this makes no difference in POSIX systems (including GNU systems). If both '+' and 'b' are specified, they can appear in either order. See Section 12.17 [Text and Binary Streams], page 304.

If the *opentype* string contains the sequence `,ccs=STRING` then *STRING* is taken as the name of a coded character set and `fopen` will mark the stream as wide-oriented with appropriate conversion functions in place to convert from and to the character set *STRING*. Any other stream is opened initially unoriented and the orientation is decided with the first file operation. If the first operation is a wide character operation, the stream is not only marked as wide-oriented, also the conversion functions to convert to the coded character set used for the current locale are loaded. This will not change anymore from this point on even if the locale selected for the `LC_CTYPE` category is changed.

Any other characters in *opentype* are simply ignored. They may be meaningful in other systems.

If the open fails, `fopen` returns a null pointer.

When the sources are compiling with `_FILE_OFFSET_BITS == 64` on a 32 bit machine this function is in fact `fopen64` since the LFS interface replaces transparently the old interface.

You can have multiple streams (or file descriptors) pointing to the same file open at the same time. If you do only input, this works straightforwardly, but you must be careful if any output streams are included. See Section 13.5 [Dangers of Mixing Streams and Descriptors], page 334. This is equally true whether the streams are in one program (not usual) or in several programs (which can easily happen). It may be advantageous to use the file locking facilities to avoid simultaneous access. See Section 13.15 [File Locks], page 368.

FILE * fopen64 (*const char *filename, const char *opentype*)   [Function]
> Preliminary: | MT-Safe | AS-Unsafe heap lock | AC-Unsafe mem fd lock | See Section 1.2.2.1 [POSIX Safety Concepts], page 2.
>
> This function is similar to fopen but the stream it returns a pointer for is opened using open64. Therefore this stream can be used even on files larger than 2^31 bytes on 32 bit machines.
>
> Please note that the return type is still FILE *. There is no special FILE type for the LFS interface.
>
> If the sources are compiled with _FILE_OFFSET_BITS == 64 on a 32 bits machine this function is available under the name fopen and so transparently replaces the old interface.

int FOPEN_MAX   [Macro]
> The value of this macro is an integer constant expression that represents the minimum number of streams that the implementation guarantees can be open simultaneously. You might be able to open more than this many streams, but that is not guaranteed. The value of this constant is at least eight, which includes the three standard streams stdin, stdout, and stderr. In POSIX.1 systems this value is determined by the OPEN_MAX parameter; see Section 32.1 [General Capacity Limits], page 838. In BSD and GNU, it is controlled by the RLIMIT_NOFILE resource limit; see Section 22.2 [Limiting Resource Usage], page 632.

FILE * freopen (*const char *filename, const char *opentype, FILE*   [Function]
> *stream*)
> Preliminary: | MT-Safe | AS-Unsafe corrupt | AC-Unsafe corrupt fd | See Section 1.2.2.1 [POSIX Safety Concepts], page 2.
>
> This function is like a combination of fclose and fopen. It first closes the stream referred to by *stream*, ignoring any errors that are detected in the process. (Because errors are ignored, you should not use freopen on an output stream if you have actually done any output using the stream.) Then the file named by *filename* is opened with mode *opentype* as for fopen, and associated with the same stream object *stream*.
>
> If the operation fails, a null pointer is returned; otherwise, freopen returns *stream*.
>
> freopen has traditionally been used to connect a standard stream such as stdin with a file of your own choice. This is useful in programs in which use of a standard stream for certain purposes is hard-coded. In the GNU C Library, you can simply close the standard streams and open new ones with fopen. But other systems lack this ability, so using freopen is more portable.
>
> When the sources are compiling with _FILE_OFFSET_BITS == 64 on a 32 bit machine this function is in fact freopen64 since the LFS interface replaces transparently the old interface.

FILE * freopen64 (const char *filename, const char *opentype, FILE   [Function]
         *stream)
     Preliminary: | MT-Safe | AS-Unsafe corrupt | AC-Unsafe corrupt fd | See
     Section 1.2.2.1 [POSIX Safety Concepts], page 2.

     This function is similar to freopen. The only difference is that on 32 bit machine the
     stream returned is able to read beyond the 2^31 bytes limits imposed by the normal
     interface. It should be noted that the stream pointed to by stream need not be opened
     using fopen64 or freopen64 since its mode is not important for this function.

     If the sources are compiled with _FILE_OFFSET_BITS == 64 on a 32 bits machine this
     function is available under the name freopen and so transparently replaces the old
     interface.

In some situations it is useful to know whether a given stream is available for reading
or writing. This information is normally not available and would have to be remembered
separately. Solaris introduced a few functions to get this information from the stream
descriptor and these functions are also available in the GNU C Library.

int __freadable (FILE *stream)   [Function]
     Preliminary: | MT-Safe | AS-Safe | AC-Safe | See Section 1.2.2.1 [POSIX Safety
     Concepts], page 2.

     The __freadable function determines whether the stream stream was opened to
     allow reading. In this case the return value is nonzero. For write-only streams the
     function returns zero.

     This function is declared in stdio_ext.h.

int __fwritable (FILE *stream)   [Function]
     Preliminary: | MT-Safe | AS-Safe | AC-Safe | See Section 1.2.2.1 [POSIX Safety
     Concepts], page 2.

     The __fwritable function determines whether the stream stream was opened to
     allow writing. In this case the return value is nonzero. For read-only streams the
     function returns zero.

     This function is declared in stdio_ext.h.

For slightly different kind of problems there are two more functions. They provide even
finer-grained information.

int __freading (FILE *stream)   [Function]
     Preliminary: | MT-Safe | AS-Safe | AC-Safe | See Section 1.2.2.1 [POSIX Safety
     Concepts], page 2.

     The __freading function determines whether the stream stream was last read from
     or whether it is opened read-only. In this case the return value is nonzero, otherwise it
     is zero. Determining whether a stream opened for reading and writing was last used
     for writing allows to draw conclusions about the content about the buffer, among
     other things.

     This function is declared in stdio_ext.h.

int __fwriting (*FILE *stream*) [Function]
> Preliminary: | MT-Safe | AS-Safe | AC-Safe | See Section 1.2.2.1 [POSIX Safety Concepts], page 2.
>
> The __fwriting function determines whether the stream *stream* was last written to or whether it is opened write-only. In this case the return value is nonzero, otherwise it is zero.
>
> This function is declared in stdio_ext.h.

12.4 Closing Streams

When a stream is closed with fclose, the connection between the stream and the file is canceled. After you have closed a stream, you cannot perform any additional operations on it.

int fclose (*FILE *stream*) [Function]
> Preliminary: | MT-Safe | AS-Unsafe heap lock | AC-Unsafe lock mem fd | See Section 1.2.2.1 [POSIX Safety Concepts], page 2.
>
> This function causes *stream* to be closed and the connection to the corresponding file to be broken. Any buffered output is written and any buffered input is discarded. The fclose function returns a value of 0 if the file was closed successfully, and EOF if an error was detected.
>
> It is important to check for errors when you call fclose to close an output stream, because real, everyday errors can be detected at this time. For example, when fclose writes the remaining buffered output, it might get an error because the disk is full. Even if you know the buffer is empty, errors can still occur when closing a file if you are using NFS.
>
> The function fclose is declared in stdio.h.

To close all streams currently available the GNU C Library provides another function.

int fcloseall (*void*) [Function]
> Preliminary: | MT-Unsafe race:streams | AS-Unsafe | AC-Safe | See Section 1.2.2.1 [POSIX Safety Concepts], page 2.
>
> This function causes all open streams of the process to be closed and the connection to corresponding files to be broken. All buffered data is written and any buffered input is discarded. The fcloseall function returns a value of 0 if all the files were closed successfully, and EOF if an error was detected.
>
> This function should be used only in special situations, e.g., when an error occurred and the program must be aborted. Normally each single stream should be closed separately so that problems with individual streams can be identified. It is also problematic since the standard streams (see Section 12.2 [Standard Streams], page 248) will also be closed.
>
> The function fcloseall is declared in stdio.h.

If the main function to your program returns, or if you call the exit function (see Section 25.7.1 [Normal Termination], page 745), all open streams are automatically closed properly. If your program terminates in any other manner, such as by calling the abort function (see Section 25.7.4 [Aborting a Program], page 747) or from a fatal signal (see Chapter 24 [Signal Handling], page 661), open streams might not be closed properly. Buffered output might not be flushed and files may be incomplete. For more information on buffering of streams, see Section 12.20 [Stream Buffering], page 309.

12.5 Streams and Threads

Streams can be used in multi-threaded applications in the same way they are used in single-threaded applications. But the programmer must be aware of the possible complications. It is important to know about these also if the program one writes never use threads since the design and implementation of many stream functions is heavily influenced by the requirements added by multi-threaded programming.

The POSIX standard requires that by default the stream operations are atomic. I.e., issuing two stream operations for the same stream in two threads at the same time will cause the operations to be executed as if they were issued sequentially. The buffer operations performed while reading or writing are protected from other uses of the same stream. To do this each stream has an internal lock object which has to be (implicitly) acquired before any work can be done.

But there are situations where this is not enough and there are also situations where this is not wanted. The implicit locking is not enough if the program requires more than one stream function call to happen atomically. One example would be if an output line a program wants to generate is created by several function calls. The functions by themselves would ensure only atomicity of their own operation, but not atomicity over all the function calls. For this it is necessary to perform the stream locking in the application code.

void flockfile (*FILE *stream*)   [Function]
> Preliminary: | MT-Safe | AS-Safe | AC-Unsafe lock | See Section 1.2.2.1 [POSIX Safety Concepts], page 2.
>
> The `flockfile` function acquires the internal locking object associated with the stream *stream*. This ensures that no other thread can explicitly through `flockfile`/`ftrylockfile` or implicit through a call of a stream function lock the stream. The thread will block until the lock is acquired. An explicit call to `funlockfile` has to be used to release the lock.

int ftrylockfile (*FILE *stream*)   [Function]
> Preliminary: | MT-Safe | AS-Safe | AC-Unsafe lock | See Section 1.2.2.1 [POSIX Safety Concepts], page 2.
>
> The `ftrylockfile` function tries to acquire the internal locking object associated with the stream *stream* just like `flockfile`. But unlike `flockfile` this function does not block if the lock is not available. `ftrylockfile` returns zero if the lock was successfully acquired. Otherwise the stream is locked by another thread.

void funlockfile (*FILE *stream*)   [Function]
> Preliminary: | MT-Safe | AS-Safe | AC-Unsafe lock | See Section 1.2.2.1 [POSIX Safety Concepts], page 2.
>
> The `funlockfile` function releases the internal locking object of the stream *stream*. The stream must have been locked before by a call to `flockfile` or a successful call

of `ftrylockfile`. The implicit locking performed by the stream operations do not count. The `funlockfile` function does not return an error status and the behavior of a call for a stream which is not locked by the current thread is undefined.

The following example shows how the functions above can be used to generate an output line atomically even in multi-threaded applications (yes, the same job could be done with one `fprintf` call but it is sometimes not possible):

```
FILE *fp;
{
    ...
    flockfile (fp);
    fputs ("This is test number ", fp);
    fprintf (fp, "%d\n", test);
    funlockfile (fp)
}
```

Without the explicit locking it would be possible for another thread to use the stream *fp* after the `fputs` call return and before `fprintf` was called with the result that the number does not follow the word 'number'.

From this description it might already be clear that the locking objects in streams are no simple mutexes. Since locking the same stream twice in the same thread is allowed the locking objects must be equivalent to recursive mutexes. These mutexes keep track of the owner and the number of times the lock is acquired. The same number of `funlockfile` calls by the same threads is necessary to unlock the stream completely. For instance:

```
void
foo (FILE *fp)
{
  ftrylockfile (fp);
  fputs ("in foo\n", fp);
  /* This is very wrong!!!  */
  funlockfile (fp);
}
```

It is important here that the `funlockfile` function is only called if the `ftrylockfile` function succeeded in locking the stream. It is therefore always wrong to ignore the result of `ftrylockfile`. And it makes no sense since otherwise one would use `flockfile`. The result of code like that above is that either `funlockfile` tries to free a stream that hasn't been locked by the current thread or it frees the stream prematurely. The code should look like this:

```
void
foo (FILE *fp)
{
  if (ftrylockfile (fp) == 0)
    {
      fputs ("in foo\n", fp);
      funlockfile (fp);
    }
}
```

Now that we covered why it is necessary to have these locking it is necessary to talk about situations when locking is unwanted and what can be done. The locking operations (explicit or implicit) don't come for free. Even if a lock is not taken the cost is not zero. The operations which have to be performed require memory operations that are safe in multi-processor environments. With the many local caches involved in such systems this is quite costly. So it is best to avoid the locking completely if it is not needed – because the code in question is never used in a context where two or more threads may use a stream at a time. This can be determined most of the time for application code; for library code which can be used in many contexts one should default to be conservative and use locking.

There are two basic mechanisms to avoid locking. The first is to use the `_unlocked` variants of the stream operations. The POSIX standard defines quite a few of those and the GNU C Library adds a few more. These variants of the functions behave just like the functions with the name without the suffix except that they do not lock the stream. Using these functions is very desirable since they are potentially much faster. This is not only because the locking operation itself is avoided. More importantly, functions like `putc` and `getc` are very simple and traditionally (before the introduction of threads) were implemented as macros which are very fast if the buffer is not empty. With the addition of locking requirements these functions are no longer implemented as macros since they would expand to too much code. But these macros are still available with the same functionality under the new names `putc_unlocked` and `getc_unlocked`. This possibly huge difference of speed also suggests the use of the `_unlocked` functions even if locking is required. The difference is that the locking then has to be performed in the program:

```
void
foo (FILE *fp, char *buf)
{
  flockfile (fp);
  while (*buf != '/')
    putc_unlocked (*buf++, fp);
  funlockfile (fp);
}
```

If in this example the `putc` function would be used and the explicit locking would be missing the `putc` function would have to acquire the lock in every call, potentially many times depending on when the loop terminates. Writing it the way illustrated above allows the `putc_unlocked` macro to be used which means no locking and direct manipulation of the buffer of the stream.

A second way to avoid locking is by using a non-standard function which was introduced in Solaris and is available in the GNU C Library as well.

int __fsetlocking (*FILE *stream, int* **type**)   [Function]
> Preliminary: | MT-Safe race:stream | AS-Unsafe lock | AC-Safe | See Section 1.2.2.1 [POSIX Safety Concepts], page 2.

> The `__fsetlocking` function can be used to select whether the stream operations will implicitly acquire the locking object of the stream *stream*. By default this is done but it can be disabled and reinstated using this function. There are three values defined for the *type* parameter.

> **FSETLOCKING_INTERNAL**
> > The stream **stream** will from now on use the default internal locking. Every stream operation with exception of the `_unlocked` variants will implicitly lock the stream.

FSETLOCKING_BYCALLER

> After the `__fsetlocking` function returns the user is responsible for locking the stream. None of the stream operations will implicitly do this anymore until the state is set back to `FSETLOCKING_INTERNAL`.

FSETLOCKING_QUERY

> `__fsetlocking` only queries the current locking state of the stream. The return value will be `FSETLOCKING_INTERNAL` or `FSETLOCKING_BYCALLER` depending on the state.

The return value of `__fsetlocking` is either `FSETLOCKING_INTERNAL` or `FSETLOCKING_BYCALLER` depending on the state of the stream before the call.

This function and the values for the *type* parameter are declared in `stdio_ext.h`.

This function is especially useful when program code has to be used which is written without knowledge about the `_unlocked` functions (or if the programmer was too lazy to use them).

12.6 Streams in Internationalized Applications

ISO C90 introduced the new type `wchar_t` to allow handling larger character sets. What was missing was a possibility to output strings of `wchar_t` directly. One had to convert them into multibyte strings using `mbstowcs` (there was no `mbsrtowcs` yet) and then use the normal stream functions. While this is doable it is very cumbersome since performing the conversions is not trivial and greatly increases program complexity and size.

The Unix standard early on (I think in XPG4.2) introduced two additional format specifiers for the `printf` and `scanf` families of functions. Printing and reading of single wide characters was made possible using the `%C` specifier and wide character strings can be handled with `%S`. These modifiers behave just like `%c` and `%s` only that they expect the corresponding argument to have the wide character type and that the wide character and string are transformed into/from multibyte strings before being used.

This was a beginning but it is still not good enough. Not always is it desirable to use `printf` and `scanf`. The other, smaller and faster functions cannot handle wide characters. Second, it is not possible to have a format string for `printf` and `scanf` consisting of wide characters. The result is that format strings would have to be generated if they have to contain non-basic characters.

In the Amendment 1 to ISO C90 a whole new set of functions was added to solve the problem. Most of the stream functions got a counterpart which take a wide character or wide character string instead of a character or string respectively. The new functions operate on the same streams (like `stdout`). This is different from the model of the C++ runtime library where separate streams for wide and normal I/O are used.

Being able to use the same stream for wide and normal operations comes with a restriction: a stream can be used either for wide operations or for normal operations. Once it is decided there is no way back. Only a call to `freopen` or `freopen64` can reset the *orientation*. The orientation can be decided in three ways:

- If any of the normal character functions is used (this includes the `fread` and `fwrite` functions) the stream is marked as not wide oriented.

- If any of the wide character functions is used the stream is marked as wide oriented.

- The `fwide` function can be used to set the orientation either way.

It is important to never mix the use of wide and not wide operations on a stream. There are no diagnostics issued. The application behavior will simply be strange or the application will simply crash. The `fwide` function can help avoiding this.

`int fwide` (*FILE *stream, int mode*)   [Function]

> Preliminary: | MT-Safe | AS-Unsafe corrupt | AC-Unsafe lock | See Section 1.2.2.1 [POSIX Safety Concepts], page 2.
>
> The `fwide` function can be used to set and query the state of the orientation of the stream *stream*. If the *mode* parameter has a positive value the streams get wide oriented, for negative values narrow oriented. It is not possible to overwrite previous orientations with `fwide`. I.e., if the stream *stream* was already oriented before the call nothing is done.
>
> If *mode* is zero the current orientation state is queried and nothing is changed.
>
> The `fwide` function returns a negative value, zero, or a positive value if the stream is narrow, not at all, or wide oriented respectively.
>
> This function was introduced in Amendment 1 to ISO C90 and is declared in `wchar.h`.

It is generally a good idea to orient a stream as early as possible. This can prevent surprise especially for the standard streams `stdin`, `stdout`, and `stderr`. If some library function in some situations uses one of these streams and this use orients the stream in a different way the rest of the application expects it one might end up with hard to reproduce errors. Remember that no errors are signal if the streams are used incorrectly. Leaving a stream unoriented after creation is normally only necessary for library functions which create streams which can be used in different contexts.

When writing code which uses streams and which can be used in different contexts it is important to query the orientation of the stream before using it (unless the rules of the library interface demand a specific orientation). The following little, silly function illustrates this.

```
void
print_f (FILE *fp)
{
  if (fwide (fp, 0) > 0)
    /* Positive return value means wide orientation.  */
    fputwc (L'f', fp);
  else
    fputc ('f', fp);
}
```

Note that in this case the function `print_f` decides about the orientation of the stream if it was unoriented before (will not happen if the advise above is followed).

The encoding used for the `wchar_t` values is unspecified and the user must not make any assumptions about it. For I/O of `wchar_t` values this means that it is impossible to write these values directly to the stream. This is not what follows from the ISO C locale model either. What happens instead is that the bytes read from or written to the underlying media are first converted into the internal encoding chosen by the implementation for `wchar_t`. The external encoding is determined by the `LC_CTYPE` category of the current locale or by the 'ccs' part of the mode specification given to `fopen`, `fopen64`, `freopen`, or `freopen64`. How and when the conversion happens is unspecified and it happens invisible to the user.

Since a stream is created in the unoriented state it has at that point no conversion associated with it. The conversion which will be used is determined by the `LC_CTYPE` category selected at the time the stream is oriented. If the locales are changed at the runtime this might produce surprising results unless one pays attention. This is just another good reason to orient the stream explicitly as soon as possible, perhaps with a call to `fwide`.

12.7 Simple Output by Characters or Lines

This section describes functions for performing character- and line-oriented output.

These narrow streams functions are declared in the header file `stdio.h` and the wide stream functions in `wchar.h`.

`int fputc` (*int c, FILE *stream*)   [Function]
>   Preliminary: | MT-Safe | AS-Unsafe corrupt | AC-Unsafe corrupt lock | See Section 1.2.2.1 [POSIX Safety Concepts], page 2.
>
>   The `fputc` function converts the character *c* to type **unsigned char**, and writes it to the stream *stream*. `EOF` is returned if a write error occurs; otherwise the character *c* is returned.

`wint_t fputwc` (*wchar_t wc, FILE *stream*)   [Function]
>   Preliminary: | MT-Safe | AS-Unsafe corrupt | AC-Unsafe corrupt lock | See Section 1.2.2.1 [POSIX Safety Concepts], page 2.
>
>   The `fputwc` function writes the wide character *wc* to the stream *stream*. `WEOF` is returned if a write error occurs; otherwise the character *wc* is returned.

`int fputc_unlocked` (*int c, FILE *stream*)   [Function]
>   Preliminary: | MT-Safe race:stream | AS-Unsafe corrupt | AC-Unsafe corrupt | See Section 1.2.2.1 [POSIX Safety Concepts], page 2.
>
>   The `fputc_unlocked` function is equivalent to the `fputc` function except that it does not implicitly lock the stream.

`wint_t fputwc_unlocked` (*wchar_t wc, FILE *stream*)   [Function]
>   Preliminary: | MT-Safe race:stream | AS-Unsafe corrupt | AC-Unsafe corrupt | See Section 1.2.2.1 [POSIX Safety Concepts], page 2.
>
>   The `fputwc_unlocked` function is equivalent to the `fputwc` function except that it does not implicitly lock the stream.
>
>   This function is a GNU extension.

`int putc` (*int c, FILE *stream*)   [Function]
>   Preliminary: | MT-Safe | AS-Unsafe corrupt | AC-Unsafe corrupt lock | See Section 1.2.2.1 [POSIX Safety Concepts], page 2.
>
>   This is just like `fputc`, except that most systems implement it as a macro, making it faster. One consequence is that it may evaluate the *stream* argument more than once, which is an exception to the general rule for macros. `putc` is usually the best function to use for writing a single character.

wint_t putwc (*wchar_t wc, FILE *stream*)   [Function]
> Preliminary: | MT-Safe | AS-Unsafe corrupt | AC-Unsafe corrupt lock | See Section 1.2.2.1 [POSIX Safety Concepts], page 2.
>
> This is just like **fputwc**, except that it can be implement as a macro, making it faster. One consequence is that it may evaluate the *stream* argument more than once, which is an exception to the general rule for macros. **putwc** is usually the best function to use for writing a single wide character.

int putc_unlocked (*int c, FILE *stream*)   [Function]
> Preliminary: | MT-Safe race:stream | AS-Unsafe corrupt | AC-Unsafe corrupt | See Section 1.2.2.1 [POSIX Safety Concepts], page 2.
>
> The **putc_unlocked** function is equivalent to the **putc** function except that it does not implicitly lock the stream.

wint_t putwc_unlocked (*wchar_t wc, FILE *stream*)   [Function]
> Preliminary: | MT-Safe race:stream | AS-Unsafe corrupt | AC-Unsafe corrupt | See Section 1.2.2.1 [POSIX Safety Concepts], page 2.
>
> The **putwc_unlocked** function is equivalent to the **putwc** function except that it does not implicitly lock the stream.
>
> This function is a GNU extension.

int putchar (*int c*)   [Function]
> Preliminary: | MT-Safe | AS-Unsafe corrupt | AC-Unsafe corrupt lock | See Section 1.2.2.1 [POSIX Safety Concepts], page 2.
>
> The **putchar** function is equivalent to **putc** with **stdout** as the value of the *stream* argument.

wint_t putwchar (*wchar_t wc*)   [Function]
> Preliminary: | MT-Safe | AS-Unsafe corrupt | AC-Unsafe corrupt lock | See Section 1.2.2.1 [POSIX Safety Concepts], page 2.
>
> The **putwchar** function is equivalent to **putwc** with **stdout** as the value of the *stream* argument.

int putchar_unlocked (*int c*)   [Function]
> Preliminary: | MT-Unsafe race:stdout | AS-Unsafe corrupt | AC-Unsafe corrupt | See Section 1.2.2.1 [POSIX Safety Concepts], page 2.
>
> The **putchar_unlocked** function is equivalent to the **putchar** function except that it does not implicitly lock the stream.

wint_t putwchar_unlocked (*wchar_t wc*)   [Function]
> Preliminary: | MT-Unsafe race:stdout | AS-Unsafe corrupt | AC-Unsafe corrupt | See Section 1.2.2.1 [POSIX Safety Concepts], page 2.
>
> The **putwchar_unlocked** function is equivalent to the **putwchar** function except that it does not implicitly lock the stream.
>
> This function is a GNU extension.

int **fputs** (*const char *s, FILE *stream*) [Function]
>Preliminary: | MT-Safe | AS-Unsafe corrupt | AC-Unsafe corrupt lock | See Section 1.2.2.1 [POSIX Safety Concepts], page 2.
>
>The function **fputs** writes the string *s* to the stream *stream*. The terminating null character is not written. This function does *not* add a newline character, either. It outputs only the characters in the string.
>
>This function returns **EOF** if a write error occurs, and otherwise a non-negative value.
>
>For example:
>
>```
>fputs ("Are ", stdout);
>fputs ("you ", stdout);
>fputs ("hungry?\n", stdout);
>```
>
>outputs the text 'Are you hungry?' followed by a newline.

int **fputws** (*const wchar_t *ws, FILE *stream*) [Function]
>Preliminary: | MT-Safe | AS-Unsafe corrupt | AC-Unsafe corrupt lock | See Section 1.2.2.1 [POSIX Safety Concepts], page 2.
>
>The function **fputws** writes the wide character string *ws* to the stream *stream*. The terminating null character is not written. This function does *not* add a newline character, either. It outputs only the characters in the string.
>
>This function returns **WEOF** if a write error occurs, and otherwise a non-negative value.

int **fputs_unlocked** (*const char *s, FILE *stream*) [Function]
>Preliminary: | MT-Safe race:stream | AS-Unsafe corrupt | AC-Unsafe corrupt | See Section 1.2.2.1 [POSIX Safety Concepts], page 2.
>
>The **fputs_unlocked** function is equivalent to the **fputs** function except that it does not implicitly lock the stream.
>
>This function is a GNU extension.

int **fputws_unlocked** (*const wchar_t *ws, FILE *stream*) [Function]
>Preliminary: | MT-Safe race:stream | AS-Unsafe corrupt | AC-Unsafe corrupt | See Section 1.2.2.1 [POSIX Safety Concepts], page 2.
>
>The **fputws_unlocked** function is equivalent to the **fputws** function except that it does not implicitly lock the stream.
>
>This function is a GNU extension.

int **puts** (*const char *s*) [Function]
>Preliminary: | MT-Safe | AS-Unsafe corrupt | AC-Unsafe lock corrupt | See Section 1.2.2.1 [POSIX Safety Concepts], page 2.
>
>The **puts** function writes the string *s* to the stream **stdout** followed by a newline. The terminating null character of the string is not written. (Note that **fputs** does *not* write a newline as this function does.)
>
>**puts** is the most convenient function for printing simple messages. For example:
>
>```
>puts ("This is a message.");
>```
>
>outputs the text 'This is a message.' followed by a newline.

int putw (*int w, FILE *stream*)   [Function]

> Preliminary: | MT-Safe | AS-Unsafe corrupt | AC-Unsafe lock corrupt | See Section 1.2.2.1 [POSIX Safety Concepts], page 2.
>
> This function writes the word *w* (that is, an **int**) to *stream*. It is provided for compatibility with SVID, but we recommend you use **fwrite** instead (see Section 12.11 [Block Input/Output], page 268).

12.8 Character Input

This section describes functions for performing character-oriented input. These narrow streams functions are declared in the header file **stdio.h** and the wide character functions are declared in **wchar.h**.

These functions return an **int** or **wint_t** value (for narrow and wide stream functions respectively) that is either a character of input, or the special value **EOF/WEOF** (usually -1). For the narrow stream functions it is important to store the result of these functions in a variable of type **int** instead of **char**, even when you plan to use it only as a character. Storing **EOF** in a **char** variable truncates its value to the size of a character, so that it is no longer distinguishable from the valid character '(char) -1'. So always use an **int** for the result of **getc** and friends, and check for **EOF** after the call; once you've verified that the result is not **EOF**, you can be sure that it will fit in a 'char' variable without loss of information.

int fgetc (*FILE *stream*)   [Function]

> Preliminary: | MT-Safe | AS-Unsafe corrupt | AC-Unsafe lock corrupt | See Section 1.2.2.1 [POSIX Safety Concepts], page 2.
>
> This function reads the next character as an **unsigned char** from the stream *stream* and returns its value, converted to an **int**. If an end-of-file condition or read error occurs, **EOF** is returned instead.

wint_t fgetwc (*FILE *stream*)   [Function]

> Preliminary: | MT-Safe | AS-Unsafe corrupt | AC-Unsafe lock corrupt | See Section 1.2.2.1 [POSIX Safety Concepts], page 2.
>
> This function reads the next wide character from the stream *stream* and returns its value. If an end-of-file condition or read error occurs, **WEOF** is returned instead.

int fgetc_unlocked (*FILE *stream*)   [Function]

> Preliminary: | MT-Safe race:stream | AS-Unsafe corrupt | AC-Unsafe corrupt | See Section 1.2.2.1 [POSIX Safety Concepts], page 2.
>
> The **fgetc_unlocked** function is equivalent to the **fgetc** function except that it does not implicitly lock the stream.

wint_t fgetwc_unlocked (*FILE *stream*)   [Function]

> Preliminary: | MT-Safe race:stream | AS-Unsafe corrupt | AC-Unsafe corrupt | See Section 1.2.2.1 [POSIX Safety Concepts], page 2.
>
> The **fgetwc_unlocked** function is equivalent to the **fgetwc** function except that it does not implicitly lock the stream.
>
> This function is a GNU extension.

`int getc (FILE *stream)` [Function]

Preliminary: | MT-Safe | AS-Unsafe corrupt | AC-Unsafe lock corrupt | See Section 1.2.2.1 [POSIX Safety Concepts], page 2.

This is just like `fgetc`, except that it is permissible (and typical) for it to be implemented as a macro that evaluates the *stream* argument more than once. `getc` is often highly optimized, so it is usually the best function to use to read a single character.

`wint_t getwc (FILE *stream)` [Function]

Preliminary: | MT-Safe | AS-Unsafe corrupt | AC-Unsafe lock corrupt | See Section 1.2.2.1 [POSIX Safety Concepts], page 2.

This is just like `fgetwc`, except that it is permissible for it to be implemented as a macro that evaluates the *stream* argument more than once. `getwc` can be highly optimized, so it is usually the best function to use to read a single wide character.

`int getc_unlocked (FILE *stream)` [Function]

Preliminary: | MT-Safe race:stream | AS-Unsafe corrupt | AC-Unsafe corrupt | See Section 1.2.2.1 [POSIX Safety Concepts], page 2.

The `getc_unlocked` function is equivalent to the `getc` function except that it does not implicitly lock the stream.

`wint_t getwc_unlocked (FILE *stream)` [Function]

Preliminary: | MT-Safe race:stream | AS-Unsafe corrupt | AC-Unsafe corrupt | See Section 1.2.2.1 [POSIX Safety Concepts], page 2.

The `getwc_unlocked` function is equivalent to the `getwc` function except that it does not implicitly lock the stream.

This function is a GNU extension.

`int getchar (void)` [Function]

Preliminary: | MT-Safe | AS-Unsafe corrupt | AC-Unsafe lock corrupt | See Section 1.2.2.1 [POSIX Safety Concepts], page 2.

The `getchar` function is equivalent to `getc` with `stdin` as the value of the *stream* argument.

`wint_t getwchar (void)` [Function]

Preliminary: | MT-Safe | AS-Unsafe corrupt | AC-Unsafe lock corrupt | See Section 1.2.2.1 [POSIX Safety Concepts], page 2.

The `getwchar` function is equivalent to `getwc` with `stdin` as the value of the *stream* argument.

`int getchar_unlocked (void)` [Function]

Preliminary: | MT-Unsafe race:stdin | AS-Unsafe corrupt | AC-Unsafe corrupt | See Section 1.2.2.1 [POSIX Safety Concepts], page 2.

The `getchar_unlocked` function is equivalent to the `getchar` function except that it does not implicitly lock the stream.

`wint_t getwchar_unlocked (void)` [Function]

Preliminary: | MT-Unsafe race:stdin | AS-Unsafe corrupt | AC-Unsafe corrupt | See Section 1.2.2.1 [POSIX Safety Concepts], page 2.

The `getwchar_unlocked` function is equivalent to the `getwchar` function except that it does not implicitly lock the stream.

This function is a GNU extension.

Here is an example of a function that does input using `fgetc`. It would work just as well using `getc` instead, or using `getchar ()` instead of `fgetc (stdin)`. The code would also work the same for the wide character stream functions.

```
int
y_or_n_p (const char *question)
{
  fputs (question, stdout);
  while (1)
    {
      int c, answer;
      /* Write a space to separate answer from question. */
      fputc (' ', stdout);
      /* Read the first character of the line.
         This should be the answer character, but might not be. */
      c = tolower (fgetc (stdin));
      answer = c;
      /* Discard rest of input line. */
      while (c != '\n' && c != EOF)
        c = fgetc (stdin);
      /* Obey the answer if it was valid. */
      if (answer == 'y')
        return 1;
      if (answer == 'n')
        return 0;
      /* Answer was invalid: ask for valid answer. */
      fputs ("Please answer y or n:", stdout);
    }
}
```

`int getw (FILE *stream)`   [Function]
Preliminary: | MT-Safe | AS-Unsafe corrupt | AC-Unsafe lock corrupt | See Section 1.2.2.1 [POSIX Safety Concepts], page 2.

This function reads a word (that is, an `int`) from *stream*. It's provided for compatibility with SVID. We recommend you use `fread` instead (see Section 12.11 [Block Input/Output], page 268). Unlike `getc`, any `int` value could be a valid result. `getw` returns `EOF` when it encounters end-of-file or an error, but there is no way to distinguish this from an input word with value -1.

12.9 Line-Oriented Input

Since many programs interpret input on the basis of lines, it is convenient to have functions to read a line of text from a stream.

Standard C has functions to do this, but they aren't very safe: null characters and even (for `gets`) long lines can confuse them. So the GNU C Library provides the nonstandard `getline` function that makes it easy to read lines reliably.

Another GNU extension, `getdelim`, generalizes `getline`. It reads a delimited record, defined as everything through the next occurrence of a specified delimiter character.

All these functions are declared in `stdio.h`.

ssize_t getline (*char* ****lineptr**, *size_t* ***n**, *FILE* ***stream**)   [Function]
>   Preliminary: | MT-Safe | AS-Unsafe corrupt heap | AC-Unsafe lock corrupt mem
> | See Section 1.2.2.1 [POSIX Safety Concepts], page 2.
>
>   This function reads an entire line from *stream*, storing the text (including the new-
>   line and a terminating null character) in a buffer and storing the buffer address in
>   ***lineptr**.
>
>   Before calling **getline**, you should place in ***lineptr** the address of a buffer ***n**
>   bytes long, allocated with **malloc**. If this buffer is long enough to hold the line,
>   **getline** stores the line in this buffer. Otherwise, **getline** makes the buffer bigger
>   using **realloc**, storing the new buffer address back in ***lineptr** and the increased
>   size back in ***n**. See Section 3.2.2 [Unconstrained Allocation], page 42.
>
>   If you set ***lineptr** to a null pointer, and ***n** to zero, before the call, then **getline**
>   allocates the initial buffer for you by calling **malloc**. This buffer remains allocated
>   even if **getline** encounters errors and is unable to read any bytes.
>
>   In either case, when **getline** returns, ***lineptr** is a **char** * which points to the text
>   of the line.
>
>   When **getline** is successful, it returns the number of characters read (including
>   the newline, but not including the terminating null). This value enables you to
>   distinguish null characters that are part of the line from the null character inserted
>   as a terminator.
>
>   This function is a GNU extension, but it is the recommended way to read lines from
>   a stream. The alternative standard functions are unreliable.
>
>   If an error occurs or end of file is reached without any bytes read, **getline** returns
>   **-1**.

ssize_t getdelim (*char* ****lineptr**, *size_t* ***n**, *int* **delimiter**, *FILE*   [Function]
>   ***stream**)
>   Preliminary: | MT-Safe | AS-Unsafe corrupt heap | AC-Unsafe lock corrupt mem
> | See Section 1.2.2.1 [POSIX Safety Concepts], page 2.
>
>   This function is like **getline** except that the character which tells it to stop reading
>   is not necessarily newline. The argument *delimiter* specifies the delimiter character;
>   **getdelim** keeps reading until it sees that character (or end of file).
>
>   The text is stored in *lineptr*, including the delimiter character and a terminating null.
>   Like **getline**, **getdelim** makes *lineptr* bigger if it isn't big enough.
>
>   **getline** is in fact implemented in terms of **getdelim**, just like this:
>
>   ```
>   ssize_t
>   getline (char **lineptr, size_t *n, FILE *stream)
>   {
>     return getdelim (lineptr, n, '\n', stream);
>   }
>   ```

char * fgets (*char* ***s**, *int* **count**, *FILE* ***stream**)   [Function]
>   Preliminary: | MT-Safe | AS-Unsafe corrupt | AC-Unsafe lock corrupt | See
>   Section 1.2.2.1 [POSIX Safety Concepts], page 2.
>
>   The **fgets** function reads characters from the stream *stream* up to and including a
>   newline character and stores them in the string *s*, adding a null character to mark

the end of the string. You must supply *count* characters worth of space in *s*, but the number of characters read is at most *count* − 1. The extra character space is used to hold the null character at the end of the string.

If the system is already at end of file when you call `fgets`, then the contents of the array *s* are unchanged and a null pointer is returned. A null pointer is also returned if a read error occurs. Otherwise, the return value is the pointer *s*.

Warning: If the input data has a null character, you can't tell. So don't use `fgets` unless you know the data cannot contain a null. Don't use it to read files edited by the user because, if the user inserts a null character, you should either handle it properly or print a clear error message. We recommend using `getline` instead of `fgets`.

`wchar_t * fgetws` (*wchar_t *ws*, *int* `count`, *FILE* `*stream`)   [Function]
Preliminary: | MT-Safe | AS-Unsafe corrupt | AC-Unsafe lock corrupt | See Section 1.2.2.1 [POSIX Safety Concepts], page 2.

The `fgetws` function reads wide characters from the stream *stream* up to and including a newline character and stores them in the string *ws*, adding a null wide character to mark the end of the string. You must supply *count* wide characters worth of space in *ws*, but the number of characters read is at most *count* − 1. The extra character space is used to hold the null wide character at the end of the string.

If the system is already at end of file when you call `fgetws`, then the contents of the array *ws* are unchanged and a null pointer is returned. A null pointer is also returned if a read error occurs. Otherwise, the return value is the pointer *ws*.

Warning: If the input data has a null wide character (which are null bytes in the input stream), you can't tell. So don't use `fgetws` unless you know the data cannot contain a null. Don't use it to read files edited by the user because, if the user inserts a null character, you should either handle it properly or print a clear error message.

`char * fgets_unlocked` (*char *s*, *int* `count`, *FILE* `*stream`)   [Function]
Preliminary: | MT-Safe race:stream | AS-Unsafe corrupt | AC-Unsafe corrupt | See Section 1.2.2.1 [POSIX Safety Concepts], page 2.

The `fgets_unlocked` function is equivalent to the `fgets` function except that it does not implicitly lock the stream.

This function is a GNU extension.

`wchar_t * fgetws_unlocked` (*wchar_t *ws*, *int* `count`, *FILE* `*stream`)   [Function]
Preliminary: | MT-Safe race:stream | AS-Unsafe corrupt | AC-Unsafe corrupt | See Section 1.2.2.1 [POSIX Safety Concepts], page 2.

The `fgetws_unlocked` function is equivalent to the `fgetws` function except that it does not implicitly lock the stream.

This function is a GNU extension.

`char * gets` (*char *s*)   [Deprecated function]
Preliminary: | MT-Safe | AS-Unsafe corrupt | AC-Unsafe lock corrupt | See Section 1.2.2.1 [POSIX Safety Concepts], page 2.

The function `gets` reads characters from the stream `stdin` up to the next newline character, and stores them in the string *s*. The newline character is discarded (note that this differs from the behavior of `fgets`, which copies the newline character into the string). If `gets` encounters a read error or end-of-file, it returns a null pointer; otherwise it returns *s*.

Warning: The `gets` function is **very dangerous** because it provides no protection against overflowing the string *s*. The GNU C Library includes it for compatibility only. You should **always** use `fgets` or `getline` instead. To remind you of this, the linker (if using GNU `ld`) will issue a warning whenever you use `gets`.

12.10 Unreading

In parser programs it is often useful to examine the next character in the input stream without removing it from the stream. This is called "peeking ahead" at the input because your program gets a glimpse of the input it will read next.

Using stream I/O, you can peek ahead at input by first reading it and then *unreading* it (also called *pushing it back* on the stream). Unreading a character makes it available to be input again from the stream, by the next call to `fgetc` or other input function on that stream.

12.10.1 What Unreading Means

Here is a pictorial explanation of unreading. Suppose you have a stream reading a file that contains just six characters, the letters '`foobar`'. Suppose you have read three characters so far. The situation looks like this:

```
f  o  o  b  a  r
^
```

so the next input character will be '`b`'.

If instead of reading '`b`' you unread the letter '`o`', you get a situation like this:

```
f  o  o  b  a  r
|
    o--
    ^
```

so that the next input characters will be '`o`' and '`b`'.

If you unread '`9`' instead of '`o`', you get this situation:

```
f  o  o  b  a  r
|
    9--
    ^
```

so that the next input characters will be '`9`' and '`b`'.

12.10.2 Using `ungetc` To Do Unreading

The function to unread a character is called `ungetc`, because it reverses the action of `getc`.

int ungetc (*int c, FILE *stream*)   [Function]
  Preliminary: | MT-Safe | AS-Unsafe corrupt | AC-Unsafe lock corrupt | See Section 1.2.2.1 [POSIX Safety Concepts], page 2.

  The `ungetc` function pushes back the character *c* onto the input stream *stream*. So the next input from *stream* will read *c* before anything else.

If c is EOF, ungetc does nothing and just returns EOF. This lets you call ungetc with the return value of getc without needing to check for an error from getc.

The character that you push back doesn't have to be the same as the last character that was actually read from the stream. In fact, it isn't necessary to actually read any characters from the stream before unreading them with ungetc! But that is a strange way to write a program; usually ungetc is used only to unread a character that was just read from the same stream. The GNU C Library supports this even on files opened in binary mode, but other systems might not.

The GNU C Library only supports one character of pushback—in other words, it does not work to call ungetc twice without doing input in between. Other systems might let you push back multiple characters; then reading from the stream retrieves the characters in the reverse order that they were pushed.

Pushing back characters doesn't alter the file; only the internal buffering for the stream is affected. If a file positioning function (such as fseek, fseeko or rewind; see Section 12.18 [File Positioning], page 305) is called, any pending pushed-back characters are discarded.

Unreading a character on a stream that is at end of file clears the end-of-file indicator for the stream, because it makes the character of input available. After you read that character, trying to read again will encounter end of file.

wint_t ungetwc (*wint_t wc, FILE *stream*)   [Function]
    Preliminary: | MT-Safe | AS-Unsafe corrupt | AC-Unsafe lock corrupt | See Section 1.2.2.1 [POSIX Safety Concepts], page 2.

    The ungetwc function behaves just like ungetc just that it pushes back a wide character.

Here is an example showing the use of getc and ungetc to skip over whitespace characters. When this function reaches a non-whitespace character, it unreads that character to be seen again on the next read operation on the stream.

```
#include <stdio.h>
#include <ctype.h>

void
skip_whitespace (FILE *stream)
{
  int c;
  do
    /* No need to check for EOF because it is not
       isspace, and ungetc ignores EOF.  */
    c = getc (stream);
  while (isspace (c));
  ungetc (c, stream);
}
```

12.11 Block Input/Output

This section describes how to do input and output operations on blocks of data. You can use these functions to read and write binary data, as well as to read and write text in fixed-size blocks instead of by characters or lines.

Binary files are typically used to read and write blocks of data in the same format as is used to represent the data in a running program. In other words, arbitrary blocks of memory—not just character or string objects—can be written to a binary file, and meaningfully read in again by the same program.

Storing data in binary form is often considerably more efficient than using the formatted I/O functions. Also, for floating-point numbers, the binary form avoids possible loss of precision in the conversion process. On the other hand, binary files can't be examined or modified easily using many standard file utilities (such as text editors), and are not portable between different implementations of the language, or different kinds of computers.

These functions are declared in `stdio.h`.

`size_t fread` (*void *data, size_t* `size`, *size_t* `count`, *FILE **`stream`)   [Function]
> Preliminary: | MT-Safe | AS-Unsafe corrupt | AC-Unsafe lock corrupt | See Section 1.2.2.1 [POSIX Safety Concepts], page 2.
>
> This function reads up to *count* objects of size *size* into the array *data*, from the stream *stream*. It returns the number of objects actually read, which might be less than *count* if a read error occurs or the end of the file is reached. This function returns a value of zero (and doesn't read anything) if either *size* or *count* is zero.
>
> If `fread` encounters end of file in the middle of an object, it returns the number of complete objects read, and discards the partial object. Therefore, the stream remains at the actual end of the file.

`size_t fread_unlocked` (*void *data, size_t* `size`, *size_t* `count`, *FILE*   [Function]
>   *`stream`)
> Preliminary: | MT-Safe race:stream | AS-Unsafe corrupt | AC-Unsafe corrupt | See Section 1.2.2.1 [POSIX Safety Concepts], page 2.
>
> The `fread_unlocked` function is equivalent to the `fread` function except that it does not implicitly lock the stream.
>
> This function is a GNU extension.

`size_t fwrite` (*const void *data, size_t* `size`, *size_t* `count`, *FILE*   [Function]
>   *`stream`)
> Preliminary: | MT-Safe | AS-Unsafe corrupt | AC-Unsafe lock corrupt | See Section 1.2.2.1 [POSIX Safety Concepts], page 2.
>
> This function writes up to *count* objects of size *size* from the array *data*, to the stream *stream*. The return value is normally *count*, if the call succeeds. Any other value indicates some sort of error, such as running out of space.

`size_t fwrite_unlocked` (*const void *data, size_t* `size`, *size_t* `count`,   [Function]
>   *FILE **`stream`)
> Preliminary: | MT-Safe race:stream | AS-Unsafe corrupt | AC-Unsafe corrupt | See Section 1.2.2.1 [POSIX Safety Concepts], page 2.
>
> The `fwrite_unlocked` function is equivalent to the `fwrite` function except that it does not implicitly lock the stream.
>
> This function is a GNU extension.

12.12 Formatted Output

The functions described in this section (**printf** and related functions) provide a convenient way to perform formatted output. You call **printf** with a *format string* or *template string* that specifies how to format the values of the remaining arguments.

Unless your program is a filter that specifically performs line- or character-oriented processing, using **printf** or one of the other related functions described in this section is usually the easiest and most concise way to perform output. These functions are especially useful for printing error messages, tables of data, and the like.

12.12.1 Formatted Output Basics

The **printf** function can be used to print any number of arguments. The template string argument you supply in a call provides information not only about the number of additional arguments, but also about their types and what style should be used for printing them.

Ordinary characters in the template string are simply written to the output stream as-is, while *conversion specifications* introduced by a '%' character in the template cause subsequent arguments to be formatted and written to the output stream. For example,

```
int pct = 37;
char filename[] = "foo.txt";
printf ("Processing of '%s' is %d%% finished.\nPlease be patient.\n",
filename, pct);
```

produces output like

```
Processing of 'foo.txt' is 37% finished.
Please be patient.
```

This example shows the use of the '%d' conversion to specify that an **int** argument should be printed in decimal notation, the '%s' conversion to specify printing of a string argument, and the '%%' conversion to print a literal '%' character.

There are also conversions for printing an integer argument as an unsigned value in octal, decimal, or hexadecimal radix ('%o', '%u', or '%x', respectively); or as a character value ('%c').

Floating-point numbers can be printed in normal, fixed-point notation using the '%f' conversion or in exponential notation using the '%e' conversion. The '%g' conversion uses either '%e' or '%f' format, depending on what is more appropriate for the magnitude of the particular number.

You can control formatting more precisely by writing *modifiers* between the '%' and the character that indicates which conversion to apply. These slightly alter the ordinary behavior of the conversion. For example, most conversion specifications permit you to specify a minimum field width and a flag indicating whether you want the result left- or right-justified within the field.

The specific flags and modifiers that are permitted and their interpretation vary depending on the particular conversion. They're all described in more detail in the following sections. Don't worry if this all seems excessively complicated at first; you can almost always get reasonable free-format output without using any of the modifiers at all. The modifiers are mostly used to make the output look "prettier" in tables.

12.12.2 Output Conversion Syntax

This section provides details about the precise syntax of conversion specifications that can appear in a `printf` template string.

Characters in the template string that are not part of a conversion specification are printed as-is to the output stream. Multibyte character sequences (see Chapter 6 [Character Set Handling], page 127) are permitted in a template string.

The conversion specifications in a `printf` template string have the general form:

> % [*param-no* $] *flags width* [. *precision*] *type conversion*

or

> % [*param-no* $] *flags width* . * [*param-no* $] *type conversion*

For example, in the conversion specifier '`%-10.8ld`', the '`-`' is a flag, '`10`' specifies the field width, the precision is '`8`', the letter '`l`' is a type modifier, and '`d`' specifies the conversion style. (This particular type specifier says to print a **long int** argument in decimal notation, with a minimum of 8 digits left-justified in a field at least 10 characters wide.)

In more detail, output conversion specifications consist of an initial '`%`' character followed in sequence by:

- An optional specification of the parameter used for this format. Normally the parameters to the `printf` function are assigned to the formats in the order of appearance in the format string. But in some situations (such as message translation) this is not desirable and this extension allows an explicit parameter to be specified.

  The *param-no* parts of the format must be integers in the range of 1 to the maximum number of arguments present to the function call. Some implementations limit this number to a certainly upper bound. The exact limit can be retrieved by the following constant.

  NL_ARGMAX   [Macro]
  > The value of **NL_ARGMAX** is the maximum value allowed for the specification of a positional parameter in a `printf` call. The actual value in effect at run-time can be retrieved by using **sysconf** using the **_SC_NL_ARGMAX** parameter see Section 32.4.1 [Definition of **sysconf**], page 841.
  >
  > Some system have a quite low limit such as 9 for System V systems. The GNU C Library has no real limit.

  If any of the formats has a specification for the parameter position all of them in the format string shall have one. Otherwise the behavior is undefined.

- Zero or more *flag characters* that modify the normal behavior of the conversion specification.

- An optional decimal integer specifying the *minimum field width*. If the normal conversion produces fewer characters than this, the field is padded with spaces to the specified width. This is a *minimum* value; if the normal conversion produces more characters than this, the field is *not* truncated. Normally, the output is right-justified within the field.

  You can also specify a field width of '`*`'. This means that the next argument in the argument list (before the actual value to be printed) is used as the field width. The value must be an `int`. If the value is negative, this means to set the '-' flag (see below) and to use the absolute value as the field width.

- An optional *precision* to specify the number of digits to be written for the numeric conversions. If the precision is specified, it consists of a period ('.') followed optionally by a decimal integer (which defaults to zero if omitted).

  You can also specify a precision of '*'. This means that the next argument in the argument list (before the actual value to be printed) is used as the precision. The value must be an `int`, and is ignored if it is negative. If you specify '*' for both the field width and precision, the field width argument precedes the precision argument. Other C library versions may not recognize this syntax.

- An optional *type modifier character*, which is used to specify the data type of the corresponding argument if it differs from the default type. (For example, the integer conversions assume a type of `int`, but you can specify 'h', 'l', or 'L' for other integer types.)

- A character that specifies the conversion to be applied.

The exact options that are permitted and how they are interpreted vary between the different conversion specifiers. See the descriptions of the individual conversions for information about the particular options that they use.

With the '-Wformat' option, the GNU C compiler checks calls to `printf` and related functions. It examines the format string and verifies that the correct number and types of arguments are supplied. There is also a GNU C syntax to tell the compiler that a function you write uses a `printf`-style format string. See Section "Declaring Attributes of Functions" in *Using GNU CC*, for more information.

12.12.3 Table of Output Conversions

Here is a table summarizing what all the different conversions do:

'%d', '%i' Print an integer as a signed decimal number. See Section 12.12.4 [Integer Conversions], page 273, for details. '%d' and '%i' are synonymous for output, but are different when used with `scanf` for input (see Section 12.14.3 [Table of Input Conversions], page 294).

'%o' Print an integer as an unsigned octal number. See Section 12.12.4 [Integer Conversions], page 273, for details.

'%u' Print an integer as an unsigned decimal number. See Section 12.12.4 [Integer Conversions], page 273, for details.

'%x', '%X' Print an integer as an unsigned hexadecimal number. '%x' uses lower-case letters and '%X' uses upper-case. See Section 12.12.4 [Integer Conversions], page 273, for details.

'%f' Print a floating-point number in normal (fixed-point) notation. See Section 12.12.5 [Floating-Point Conversions], page 275, for details.

'%e', '%E' Print a floating-point number in exponential notation. '%e' uses lower-case letters and '%E' uses upper-case. See Section 12.12.5 [Floating-Point Conversions], page 275, for details.

'%g', '%G'   Print a floating-point number in either normal or exponential notation, which-
              ever is more appropriate for its magnitude. '%g' uses lower-case letters and '%G'
              uses upper-case. See Section 12.12.5 [Floating-Point Conversions], page 275, for
              details.

'%a', '%A'   Print a floating-point number in a hexadecimal fractional notation which the
              exponent to base 2 represented in decimal digits. '%a' uses lower-case letters
              and '%A' uses upper-case. See Section 12.12.5 [Floating-Point Conversions],
              page 275, for details.

'%c'   Print a single character. See Section 12.12.6 [Other Output Conversions],
              page 277.

'%C'   This is an alias for '%lc' which is supported for compatibility with the Unix
              standard.

'%s'   Print a string. See Section 12.12.6 [Other Output Conversions], page 277.

'%S'   This is an alias for '%ls' which is supported for compatibility with the Unix
              standard.

'%p'   Print the value of a pointer. See Section 12.12.6 [Other Output Conversions],
              page 277.

'%n'   Get the number of characters printed so far. See Section 12.12.6 [Other Output
              Conversions], page 277. Note that this conversion specification never produces
              any output.

'%m'   Print the string corresponding to the value of `errno`. (This is a GNU extension.)
              See Section 12.12.6 [Other Output Conversions], page 277.

'%%'   Print a literal '%' character. See Section 12.12.6 [Other Output Conversions],
              page 277.

If the syntax of a conversion specification is invalid, unpredictable things will happen,
so don't do this. If there aren't enough function arguments provided to supply values for
all the conversion specifications in the template string, or if the arguments are not of the
correct types, the results are unpredictable. If you supply more arguments than conversion
specifications, the extra argument values are simply ignored; this is sometimes useful.

12.12.4 Integer Conversions

This section describes the options for the '%d', '%i', '%o', '%u', '%x', and '%X' conversion
specifications. These conversions print integers in various formats.

The '%d' and '%i' conversion specifications both print an `int` argument as a signed
decimal number; while '%o', '%u', and '%x' print the argument as an unsigned octal, decimal,
or hexadecimal number (respectively). The '%X' conversion specification is just like '%x'
except that it uses the characters 'ABCDEF' as digits instead of 'abcdef'.

The following flags are meaningful:

'-'   Left-justify the result in the field (instead of the normal right-justification).

'+'   For the signed '%d' and '%i' conversions, print a plus sign if the value is positive.

' '

For the signed '%d' and '%i' conversions, if the result doesn't start with a plus or minus sign, prefix it with a space character instead. Since the '+' flag ensures that the result includes a sign, this flag is ignored if you supply both of them.

'#'

For the '%o' conversion, this forces the leading digit to be '0', as if by increasing the precision. For '%x' or '%X', this prefixes a leading '0x' or '0X' (respectively) to the result. This doesn't do anything useful for the '%d', '%i', or '%u' conversions. Using this flag produces output which can be parsed by the strtoul function (see Section 20.11.1 [Parsing of Integers], page 585) and scanf with the '%i' conversion (see Section 12.14.4 [Numeric Input Conversions], page 296).

'''

Separate the digits into groups as specified by the locale specified for the LC_NUMERIC category; see Section 7.7.1.1 [Generic Numeric Formatting Parameters], page 175. This flag is a GNU extension.

'0'

Pad the field with zeros instead of spaces. The zeros are placed after any indication of sign or base. This flag is ignored if the '-' flag is also specified, or if a precision is specified.

If a precision is supplied, it specifies the minimum number of digits to appear; leading zeros are produced if necessary. If you don't specify a precision, the number is printed with as many digits as it needs. If you convert a value of zero with an explicit precision of zero, then no characters at all are produced.

Without a type modifier, the corresponding argument is treated as an int (for the signed conversions '%i' and '%d') or unsigned int (for the unsigned conversions '%o', '%u', '%x', and '%X'). Recall that since printf and friends are variadic, any char and short arguments are automatically converted to int by the default argument promotions. For arguments of other integer types, you can use these modifiers:

'hh'

Specifies that the argument is a signed char or unsigned char, as appropriate. A char argument is converted to an int or unsigned int by the default argument promotions anyway, but the 'h' modifier says to convert it back to a char again.

This modifier was introduced in ISO C99.

'h'

Specifies that the argument is a short int or unsigned short int, as appropriate. A short argument is converted to an int or unsigned int by the default argument promotions anyway, but the 'h' modifier says to convert it back to a short again.

'j'

Specifies that the argument is a intmax_t or uintmax_t, as appropriate.

This modifier was introduced in ISO C99.

'l'

Specifies that the argument is a long int or unsigned long int, as appropriate. Two 'l' characters is like the 'L' modifier, below.

If used with '%c' or '%s' the corresponding parameter is considered as a wide character or wide character string respectively. This use of 'l' was introduced in Amendment 1 to ISO C90.

'L'

'll'

'q'   Specifies that the argument is a long long int. (This type is an extension
                 supported by the GNU C compiler. On systems that don't support extra-long
                 integers, this is the same as long int.)

                 The 'q' modifier is another name for the same thing, which comes from 4.4
                 BSD; a long long int is sometimes called a "quad" int.

't'   Specifies that the argument is a ptrdiff_t.

                 This modifier was introduced in ISO C99.

'z'

'Z'   Specifies that the argument is a size_t.

                 'z' was introduced in ISO C99. 'Z' is a GNU extension predating this addition
                 and should not be used in new code.

Here is an example. Using the template string:

```
"|%5d|%-5d|%+5d|%+-5d|% 5d|%05d|%5.0d|%5.2d|%d|\n"
```

to print numbers using the different options for the '%d' conversion gives results like:

```
|    0|0    |   +0|+0   |    0|00000|     |   00|0 |
|    1|1    |   +1|+1   |    1|00001|    1|   01|1 |
|   -1|-1   |   -1|-1   |   -1|-0001|   -1|  -01|-1 |
|100000|100000|+100000|+100000| 100000|100000|100000|100000|100000|
```

In particular, notice what happens in the last case where the number is too large to fit
in the minimum field width specified.

Here are some more examples showing how unsigned integers print under various format
options, using the template string:

```
"|%5u|%5o|%5x|%5X|%#5o|%#5x|%#5X|%#10.8x|\n"
```

```
|    0|    0|    0|    0|    0|    0|    0|  00000000|
|    1|    1|    1|    1|   01|  0x1|  0X1|0x00000001|
|100000|303240|186a0|186A0|0303240|0x186a0|0X186A0|0x000186a0|
```

12.12.5 Floating-Point Conversions

This section discusses the conversion specifications for floating-point numbers: the '%f',
'%e', '%E', '%g', and '%G' conversions.

The '%f' conversion prints its argument in fixed-point notation, producing output of the
form [-]$ddd.ddd$, where the number of digits following the decimal point is controlled by
the precision you specify.

The '%e' conversion prints its argument in exponential notation, producing output of
the form [-]$d.ddd$e[+|-]dd. Again, the number of digits following the decimal point is
controlled by the precision. The exponent always contains at least two digits. The '%E'
conversion is similar but the exponent is marked with the letter 'E' instead of 'e'.

The '%g' and '%G' conversions print the argument in the style of '%e' or '%E' (respectively)
if the exponent would be less than -4 or greater than or equal to the precision; otherwise
they use the '%f' style. A precision of 0, is taken as 1. Trailing zeros are removed from the
fractional portion of the result and a decimal-point character appears only if it is followed
by a digit.

The '%a' and '%A' conversions are meant for representing floating-point numbers exactly in textual form so that they can be exchanged as texts between different programs and/or machines. The numbers are represented is the form [-]0x*h*.*hhh*p[+|-]*dd*. At the left of the decimal-point character exactly one digit is print. This character is only 0 if the number is denormalized. Otherwise the value is unspecified; it is implementation dependent how many bits are used. The number of hexadecimal digits on the right side of the decimal-point character is equal to the precision. If the precision is zero it is determined to be large enough to provide an exact representation of the number (or it is large enough to distinguish two adjacent values if the FLT_RADIX is not a power of 2, see Section A.5.3.2 [Floating Point Parameters], page 888). For the '%a' conversion lower-case characters are used to represent the hexadecimal number and the prefix and exponent sign are printed as 0x and p respectively. Otherwise upper-case characters are used and 0X and P are used for the representation of prefix and exponent string. The exponent to the base of two is printed as a decimal number using at least one digit but at most as many digits as necessary to represent the value exactly.

If the value to be printed represents infinity or a NaN, the output is [-]inf or nan respectively if the conversion specifier is '%a', '%e', '%f', or '%g' and it is [-]INF or NAN respectively if the conversion is '%A', '%E', or '%G'.

The following flags can be used to modify the behavior:

'-'   Left-justify the result in the field. Normally the result is right-justified.

'+'   Always include a plus or minus sign in the result.

' '   If the result doesn't start with a plus or minus sign, prefix it with a space instead. Since the '+' flag ensures that the result includes a sign, this flag is ignored if you supply both of them.

'#'   Specifies that the result should always include a decimal point, even if no digits follow it. For the '%g' and '%G' conversions, this also forces trailing zeros after the decimal point to be left in place where they would otherwise be removed.

'''   Separate the digits of the integer part of the result into groups as specified by the locale specified for the LC_NUMERIC category; see Section 7.7.1.1 [Generic Numeric Formatting Parameters], page 175. This flag is a GNU extension.

'0'   Pad the field with zeros instead of spaces; the zeros are placed after any sign. This flag is ignored if the '-' flag is also specified.

The precision specifies how many digits follow the decimal-point character for the '%f', '%e', and '%E' conversions. For these conversions, the default precision is 6. If the precision is explicitly 0, this suppresses the decimal point character entirely. For the '%g' and '%G' conversions, the precision specifies how many significant digits to print. Significant digits are the first digit before the decimal point, and all the digits after it. If the precision is 0 or not specified for '%g' or '%G', it is treated like a value of 1. If the value being printed cannot be expressed accurately in the specified number of digits, the value is rounded to the nearest number that fits.

Without a type modifier, the floating-point conversions use an argument of type double. (By the default argument promotions, any float arguments are automatically converted to double.) The following type modifier is supported:

'L'   An uppercase 'L' specifies that the argument is a **long double**.

Here are some examples showing how numbers print using the various floating-point conversions. All of the numbers were printed using this template string:

```
"|%13.4a|%13.4f|%13.4e|%13.4g|\n"
```

Here is the output:

```
|   0x0.0000p+0|       0.0000|   0.0000e+00|            0|
|   0x1.0000p-1|       0.5000|   5.0000e-01|          0.5|
|   0x1.0000p+0|       1.0000|   1.0000e+00|            1|
|  -0x1.0000p+0|      -1.0000|  -1.0000e+00|           -1|
|   0x1.9000p+6|     100.0000|   1.0000e+02|          100|
|   0x1.f400p+9|    1000.0000|   1.0000e+03|         1000|
|  0x1.3880p+13|   10000.0000|   1.0000e+04|        1e+04|
|  0x1.81c8p+13|   12345.0000|   1.2345e+04|    1.234e+04|
|  0x1.86a0p+16|  100000.0000|   1.0000e+05|        1e+05|
|  0x1.e240p+16|  123456.0000|   1.2346e+05|    1.235e+05|
```

Notice how the '%g' conversion drops trailing zeros.

12.12.6 Other Output Conversions

This section describes miscellaneous conversions for **printf**.

The '%c' conversion prints a single character. In case there is no 'l' modifier the **int** argument is first converted to an **unsigned char**. Then, if used in a wide stream function, the character is converted into the corresponding wide character. The '-' flag can be used to specify left-justification in the field, but no other flags are defined, and no precision or type modifier can be given. For example:

```
printf ("%c%c%c%c%c", 'h', 'e', 'l', 'l', 'o');
```

prints 'hello'.

If there is a 'l' modifier present the argument is expected to be of type **wint_t**. If used in a multibyte function the wide character is converted into a multibyte character before being added to the output. In this case more than one output byte can be produced.

The '%s' conversion prints a string. If no 'l' modifier is present the corresponding argument must be of type **char *** (or **const char ***). If used in a wide stream function the string is first converted in a wide character string. A precision can be specified to indicate the maximum number of characters to write; otherwise characters in the string up to but not including the terminating null character are written to the output stream. The '-' flag can be used to specify left-justification in the field, but no other flags or type modifiers are defined for this conversion. For example:

```
printf ("%3s%-6s", "no", "where");
```

prints ' nowhere '.

If there is a 'l' modifier present the argument is expected to be of type **wchar_t** (or **const wchar_t ***).

If you accidentally pass a null pointer as the argument for a '%s' conversion, the GNU C Library prints it as '(null)'. We think this is more useful than crashing. But it's not good practice to pass a null argument intentionally.

The '%m' conversion prints the string corresponding to the error code in **errno**. See Section 2.3 [Error Messages], page 33. Thus:

```
fprintf (stderr, "can't open '%s': %m\n", filename);
```

is equivalent to:

```
fprintf (stderr, "can't open '%s': %s\n", filename, strerror (errno));
```

The '%m' conversion is a GNU C Library extension.

The '%p' conversion prints a pointer value. The corresponding argument must be of type **void ***. In practice, you can use any type of pointer.

In the GNU C Library, non-null pointers are printed as unsigned integers, as if a '%#x' conversion were used. Null pointers print as '(nil)'. (Pointers might print differently in other systems.)

For example:

```
printf ("%p", "testing");
```

prints '0x' followed by a hexadecimal number—the address of the string constant "testing". It does not print the word 'testing'.

You can supply the '-' flag with the '%p' conversion to specify left-justification, but no other flags, precision, or type modifiers are defined.

The '%n' conversion is unlike any of the other output conversions. It uses an argument which must be a pointer to an **int**, but instead of printing anything it stores the number of characters printed so far by this call at that location. The 'h' and 'l' type modifiers are permitted to specify that the argument is of type **short int *** or **long int *** instead of **int ***, but no flags, field width, or precision are permitted.

For example,

```
int nchar;
printf ("%d %s%n\n", 3, "bears", &nchar);
```

prints:

```
3 bears
```

and sets **nchar** to 7, because '3 bears' is seven characters.

The '%%' conversion prints a literal '%' character. This conversion doesn't use an argument, and no flags, field width, precision, or type modifiers are permitted.

12.12.7 Formatted Output Functions

This section describes how to call **printf** and related functions. Prototypes for these functions are in the header file **stdio.h**. Because these functions take a variable number of arguments, you *must* declare prototypes for them before using them. Of course, the easiest way to make sure you have all the right prototypes is to just include **stdio.h**.

int printf (*const char *template*, ...)   [Function]
> Preliminary: | MT-Safe locale | AS-Unsafe corrupt heap | AC-Unsafe mem lock corrupt | See Section 1.2.2.1 [POSIX Safety Concepts], page 2.

> The **printf** function prints the optional arguments under the control of the template string *template* to the stream **stdout**. It returns the number of characters printed, or a negative value if there was an output error.

int wprintf (*const wchar_t *template*, ...)   [Function]
> Preliminary: | MT-Safe locale | AS-Unsafe corrupt heap | AC-Unsafe mem lock corrupt | See Section 1.2.2.1 [POSIX Safety Concepts], page 2.

The `wprintf` function prints the optional arguments under the control of the wide template string *template* to the stream `stdout`. It returns the number of wide characters printed, or a negative value if there was an output error.

int fprintf (*FILE *stream*, *const char *template*, ...)   [Function]
Preliminary: | MT-Safe locale | AS-Unsafe corrupt heap | AC-Unsafe mem lock corrupt | See Section 1.2.2.1 [POSIX Safety Concepts], page 2.

This function is just like `printf`, except that the output is written to the stream *stream* instead of `stdout`.

int fwprintf (*FILE *stream*, *const wchar_t *template*, ...)   [Function]
Preliminary: | MT-Safe locale | AS-Unsafe corrupt heap | AC-Unsafe mem lock corrupt | See Section 1.2.2.1 [POSIX Safety Concepts], page 2.

This function is just like `wprintf`, except that the output is written to the stream *stream* instead of `stdout`.

int sprintf (*char *s*, *const char *template*, ...)   [Function]
Preliminary: | MT-Safe locale | AS-Unsafe heap | AC-Unsafe mem | See Section 1.2.2.1 [POSIX Safety Concepts], page 2.

This is like `printf`, except that the output is stored in the character array *s* instead of written to a stream. A null character is written to mark the end of the string.

The `sprintf` function returns the number of characters stored in the array *s*, not including the terminating null character.

The behavior of this function is undefined if copying takes place between objects that overlap—for example, if *s* is also given as an argument to be printed under control of the '`%s`' conversion. See Section 5.4 [Copying and Concatenation], page 91.

Warning: The `sprintf` function can be **dangerous** because it can potentially output more characters than can fit in the allocation size of the string *s*. Remember that the field width given in a conversion specification is only a *minimum* value.

To avoid this problem, you can use `snprintf` or `asprintf`, described below.

int swprintf (*wchar_t *s*, *size_t size*, *const wchar_t *template*, ...)   [Function]
Preliminary: | MT-Safe locale | AS-Unsafe heap | AC-Unsafe mem | See Section 1.2.2.1 [POSIX Safety Concepts], page 2.

This is like `wprintf`, except that the output is stored in the wide character array *ws* instead of written to a stream. A null wide character is written to mark the end of the string. The *size* argument specifies the maximum number of characters to produce. The trailing null character is counted towards this limit, so you should allocate at least *size* wide characters for the string *ws*.

The return value is the number of characters generated for the given input, excluding the trailing null. If not all output fits into the provided buffer a negative value is returned. You should try again with a bigger output string. *Note:* this is different from how `snprintf` handles this situation.

Note that the corresponding narrow stream function takes fewer parameters. `swprintf` in fact corresponds to the `snprintf` function. Since the `sprintf` function can be dangerous and should be avoided the ISO C committee refused to make the same mistake again and decided to not define a function exactly corresponding to `sprintf`.

int **snprintf** (*char *s*, *size_t size*, *const char *template*, ...)   [Function]
Preliminary: | MT-Safe locale | AS-Unsafe heap | AC-Unsafe mem | See
Section 1.2.2.1 [POSIX Safety Concepts], page 2.

The `snprintf` function is similar to `sprintf`, except that the *size* argument specifies the maximum number of characters to produce. The trailing null character is counted towards this limit, so you should allocate at least *size* characters for the string *s*. If *size* is zero, nothing, not even the null byte, shall be written and *s* may be a null pointer.

The return value is the number of characters which would be generated for the given input, excluding the trailing null. If this value is greater or equal to *size*, not all characters from the result have been stored in *s*. You should try again with a bigger output string. Here is an example of doing this:

```
/* Construct a message describing the value of a variable
   whose name is name and whose value is value. */
char *
make_message (char *name, char *value)
{
  /* Guess we need no more than 100 chars of space. */
  int size = 100;
  char *buffer = (char *) xmalloc (size);
  int nchars;
  if (buffer == NULL)
    return NULL;

  /* Try to print in the allocated space. */
  nchars = snprintf (buffer, size, "value of %s is %s",
    name, value);
  if (nchars >= size)
    {
      /* Reallocate buffer now that we know
how much space is needed. */
      size = nchars + 1;
      buffer = (char *) xrealloc (buffer, size);

      if (buffer != NULL)
/* Try again. */
snprintf (buffer, size, "value of %s is %s",
  name, value);
    }
  /* The last call worked, return the string. */
  return buffer;
}
```

In practice, it is often easier just to use `asprintf`, below.

Attention: In versions of the GNU C Library prior to 2.1 the return value is the number of characters stored, not including the terminating null; unless there was not enough space in *s* to store the result in which case -1 is returned. This was changed in order to comply with the ISO C99 standard.

12.12.8 Dynamically Allocating Formatted Output

The functions in this section do formatted output and place the results in dynamically allocated memory.

int asprintf (*char **ptr*, *const char *template*, ...)   [Function]
>   Preliminary: | MT-Safe locale | AS-Unsafe heap | AC-Unsafe mem | See Section 1.2.2.1 [POSIX Safety Concepts], page 2.
>
>   This function is similar to sprintf, except that it dynamically allocates a string (as with malloc; see Section 3.2.2 [Unconstrained Allocation], page 42) to hold the output, instead of putting the output in a buffer you allocate in advance. The *ptr* argument should be the address of a char * object, and a successful call to asprintf stores a pointer to the newly allocated string at that location.
>
>   The return value is the number of characters allocated for the buffer, or less than zero if an error occurred. Usually this means that the buffer could not be allocated.
>
>   Here is how to use asprintf to get the same result as the snprintf example, but more easily:

```
/* Construct a message describing the value of a variable
   whose name is name and whose value is value. */
char *
make_message (char *name, char *value)
{
  char *result;
  if (asprintf (&result, "value of %s is %s", name, value) < 0)
    return NULL;
  return result;
}
```

int obstack_printf (*struct obstack *obstack*, *const char *template*,   [Function]
...)
>   Preliminary: | MT-Safe race:obstack locale | AS-Unsafe corrupt heap | AC-Unsafe corrupt mem | See Section 1.2.2.1 [POSIX Safety Concepts], page 2.
>
>   This function is similar to asprintf, except that it uses the obstack *obstack* to allocate the space. See Section 3.2.4 [Obstacks], page 58.
>
>   The characters are written onto the end of the current object. To get at them, you must finish the object with obstack_finish (see Section 3.2.4.6 [Growing Objects], page 62).

12.12.9 Variable Arguments Output Functions

The functions vprintf and friends are provided so that you can define your own variadic printf-like functions that make use of the same internals as the built-in formatted output functions.

The most natural way to define such functions would be to use a language construct to say, "Call printf and pass this template plus all of my arguments after the first five." But there is no way to do this in C, and it would be hard to provide a way, since at the C language level there is no way to tell how many arguments your function received.

Since that method is impossible, we provide alternative functions, the vprintf series, which lets you pass a va_list to describe "all of my arguments after the first five."

When it is sufficient to define a macro rather than a real function, the GNU C compiler provides a way to do this much more easily with macros. For example:

```
#define myprintf(a, b, c, d, e, rest...) \
    printf (mytemplate , ## rest)
```

See Section "Variadic Macros" in *The C preprocessor*, for details. But this is limited to macros, and does not apply to real functions at all.

Before calling **vprintf** or the other functions listed in this section, you *must* call **va_start** (see Section A.2 [Variadic Functions], page 878) to initialize a pointer to the variable arguments. Then you can call **va_arg** to fetch the arguments that you want to handle yourself. This advances the pointer past those arguments.

Once your **va_list** pointer is pointing at the argument of your choice, you are ready to call **vprintf**. That argument and all subsequent arguments that were passed to your function are used by **vprintf** along with the template that you specified separately.

In some other systems, the **va_list** pointer may become invalid after the call to **vprintf**, so you must not use **va_arg** after you call **vprintf**. Instead, you should call **va_end** to retire the pointer from service. However, you can safely call **va_start** on another pointer variable and begin fetching the arguments again through that pointer. Calling **vprintf** does not destroy the argument list of your function, merely the particular pointer that you passed to it.

GNU C does not have such restrictions. You can safely continue to fetch arguments from a **va_list** pointer after passing it to **vprintf**, and **va_end** is a no-op. (Note, however, that subsequent **va_arg** calls will fetch the same arguments which **vprintf** previously used.)

Prototypes for these functions are declared in **stdio.h**.

int vprintf (*const char *template*, *va_list* **ap**)   [Function]
    Preliminary: | MT-Safe locale | AS-Unsafe corrupt heap | AC-Unsafe mem lock corrupt | See Section 1.2.2.1 [POSIX Safety Concepts], page 2.

    This function is similar to **printf** except that, instead of taking a variable number of arguments directly, it takes an argument list pointer *ap*.

int vwprintf (*const wchar_t *template*, *va_list* **ap**)   [Function]
    Preliminary: | MT-Safe locale | AS-Unsafe corrupt heap | AC-Unsafe mem lock corrupt | See Section 1.2.2.1 [POSIX Safety Concepts], page 2.

    This function is similar to **wprintf** except that, instead of taking a variable number of arguments directly, it takes an argument list pointer *ap*.

int vfprintf (*FILE *stream*, *const char *template*, *va_list* **ap**)   [Function]
    Preliminary: | MT-Safe locale | AS-Unsafe corrupt heap | AC-Unsafe mem lock corrupt | See Section 1.2.2.1 [POSIX Safety Concepts], page 2.

    This is the equivalent of **fprintf** with the variable argument list specified directly as for **vprintf**.

int vfwprintf (*FILE *stream*, *const wchar_t *template*, *va_list* **ap**)   [Function]
    Preliminary: | MT-Safe locale | AS-Unsafe corrupt heap | AC-Unsafe mem lock corrupt | See Section 1.2.2.1 [POSIX Safety Concepts], page 2.

    This is the equivalent of **fwprintf** with the variable argument list specified directly as for **vwprintf**.

int **vsprintf** (*char *s, const char *template, va_list ap*)   [Function]
> Preliminary: | MT-Safe locale | AS-Unsafe heap | AC-Unsafe mem | See Section 1.2.2.1 [POSIX Safety Concepts], page 2.
>
> This is the equivalent of **sprintf** with the variable argument list specified directly as for **vprintf**.

int **vswprintf** (*wchar_t *s, size_t size, const wchar_t *template,*   [Function]
> *va_list ap*)
> Preliminary: | MT-Safe locale | AS-Unsafe heap | AC-Unsafe mem | See Section 1.2.2.1 [POSIX Safety Concepts], page 2.
>
> This is the equivalent of **swprintf** with the variable argument list specified directly as for **vwprintf**.

int **vsnprintf** (*char *s, size_t size, const char *template, va_list ap*)   [Function]
> Preliminary: | MT-Safe locale | AS-Unsafe heap | AC-Unsafe mem | See Section 1.2.2.1 [POSIX Safety Concepts], page 2.
>
> This is the equivalent of **snprintf** with the variable argument list specified directly as for **vprintf**.

int **vasprintf** (*char **ptr, const char *template, va_list ap*)   [Function]
> Preliminary: | MT-Safe locale | AS-Unsafe heap | AC-Unsafe mem | See Section 1.2.2.1 [POSIX Safety Concepts], page 2.
>
> The **vasprintf** function is the equivalent of **asprintf** with the variable argument list specified directly as for **vprintf**.

int **obstack_vprintf** (*struct obstack *obstack, const char*   [Function]
> **template, va_list ap*)
> Preliminary: | MT-Safe race:obstack locale | AS-Unsafe corrupt heap | AC-Unsafe corrupt mem | See Section 1.2.2.1 [POSIX Safety Concepts], page 2.
>
> The **obstack_vprintf** function is the equivalent of **obstack_printf** with the variable argument list specified directly as for **vprintf**.

Here's an example showing how you might use **vfprintf**. This is a function that prints error messages to the stream **stderr**, along with a prefix indicating the name of the program (see Section 2.3 [Error Messages], page 33, for a description of **program_invocation_short_name**).

```
#include <stdio.h>
#include <stdarg.h>

void
eprintf (const char *template, ...)
{
  va_list ap;
  extern char *program_invocation_short_name;

  fprintf (stderr, "%s: ", program_invocation_short_name);
  va_start (ap, template);
  vfprintf (stderr, template, ap);
  va_end (ap);
}
```

You could call **eprintf** like this:

```
eprintf ("file '%s' does not exist\n", filename);
```

In GNU C, there is a special construct you can use to let the compiler know that a function uses a `printf`-style format string. Then it can check the number and types of arguments in each call to the function, and warn you when they do not match the format string. For example, take this declaration of `eprintf`:

```
void eprintf (const char *template, ...)
__attribute__ ((format (printf, 1, 2)));
```

This tells the compiler that `eprintf` uses a format string like `printf` (as opposed to `scanf`; see Section 12.14 [Formatted Input], page 292); the format string appears as the first argument; and the arguments to satisfy the format begin with the second. See Section "Declaring Attributes of Functions" in *Using GNU CC*, for more information.

12.12.10 Parsing a Template String

You can use the function `parse_printf_format` to obtain information about the number and types of arguments that are expected by a given template string. This function permits interpreters that provide interfaces to `printf` to avoid passing along invalid arguments from the user's program, which could cause a crash.

All the symbols described in this section are declared in the header file `printf.h`.

`size_t parse_printf_format` (*const char *template, size_t n, int*   [Function]
        *argtypes)

Preliminary: | MT-Safe locale | AS-Safe | AC-Safe | See Section 1.2.2.1 [POSIX Safety Concepts], page 2.

This function returns information about the number and types of arguments expected by the `printf` template string *template*. The information is stored in the array *argtypes*; each element of this array describes one argument. This information is encoded using the various 'PA_' macros, listed below.

The argument *n* specifies the number of elements in the array *argtypes*. This is the maximum number of elements that `parse_printf_format` will try to write.

`parse_printf_format` returns the total number of arguments required by *template*. If this number is greater than *n*, then the information returned describes only the first *n* arguments. If you want information about additional arguments, allocate a bigger array and call `parse_printf_format` again.

The argument types are encoded as a combination of a basic type and modifier flag bits.

`int PA_FLAG_MASK`   [Macro]

This macro is a bitmask for the type modifier flag bits. You can write the expression (`argtypes[i] & PA_FLAG_MASK`) to extract just the flag bits for an argument, or (`argtypes[i] & ~PA_FLAG_MASK`) to extract just the basic type code.

Here are symbolic constants that represent the basic types; they stand for integer values.

`PA_INT`   This specifies that the base type is `int`.

`PA_CHAR`   This specifies that the base type is `int`, cast to `char`.

`PA_STRING`

        This specifies that the base type is `char *`, a null-terminated string.

PA_POINTER

This specifies that the base type is `void *`, an arbitrary pointer.

PA_FLOAT   This specifies that the base type is `float`.

PA_DOUBLE

This specifies that the base type is `double`.

PA_LAST   You can define additional base types for your own programs as offsets from
`PA_LAST`. For example, if you have data types 'foo' and 'bar' with their own
specialized `printf` conversions, you could define encodings for these types as:

```
#define PA_FOO  PA_LAST
#define PA_BAR  (PA_LAST + 1)
```

Here are the flag bits that modify a basic type. They are combined with the code for
the basic type using inclusive-or.

PA_FLAG_PTR

If this bit is set, it indicates that the encoded type is a pointer to the base
type, rather than an immediate value. For example, 'PA_INT|PA_FLAG_PTR'
represents the type 'int *'.

PA_FLAG_SHORT

If this bit is set, it indicates that the base type is modified with `short`. (This
corresponds to the 'h' type modifier.)

PA_FLAG_LONG

If this bit is set, it indicates that the base type is modified with `long`. (This
corresponds to the 'l' type modifier.)

PA_FLAG_LONG_LONG

If this bit is set, it indicates that the base type is modified with `long long`.
(This corresponds to the 'L' type modifier.)

PA_FLAG_LONG_DOUBLE

This is a synonym for `PA_FLAG_LONG_LONG`, used by convention with a base
type of `PA_DOUBLE` to indicate a type of `long double`.

12.12.11 Example of Parsing a Template String

Here is an example of decoding argument types for a format string. We assume this is part
of an interpreter which contains arguments of type NUMBER, CHAR, STRING and STRUCTURE
(and perhaps others which are not valid here).

```
/* Test whether the nargs specified objects
   in the vector args are valid
   for the format string format:
   if so, return 1.
   If not, return 0 after printing an error message.  */

int
validate_args (char *format, int nargs, OBJECT *args)
{
  int *argtypes;
  int nwanted;
```

```
/* Get the information about the arguments.
   Each conversion specification must be at least two characters
   long, so there cannot be more specifications than half the
   length of the string.  */

argtypes = (int *) alloca (strlen (format) / 2 * sizeof (int));
nwanted = parse_printf_format (string, nelts, argtypes);

/* Check the number of arguments.  */
if (nwanted > nargs)
  {
    error ("too few arguments (at least %d required)", nwanted);
    return 0;
  }

/* Check the C type wanted for each argument
   and see if the object given is suitable.  */
for (i = 0; i < nwanted; i++)
  {
    int wanted;

    if (argtypes[i] & PA_FLAG_PTR)
wanted = STRUCTURE;
    else
switch (argtypes[i] & ~PA_FLAG_MASK)
  {
  case PA_INT:
  case PA_FLOAT:
  case PA_DOUBLE:
    wanted = NUMBER;
    break;
  case PA_CHAR:
    wanted = CHAR;
    break;
  case PA_STRING:
    wanted = STRING;
    break;
  case PA_POINTER:
    wanted = STRUCTURE;
    break;
  }
    if (TYPE (args[i]) != wanted)
{
  error ("type mismatch for arg number %d", i);
  return 0;
}
  }
  return 1;
}
```

12.13 Customizing `printf`

The GNU C Library lets you define your own custom conversion specifiers for `printf` template strings, to teach `printf` clever ways to print the important data structures of your program.

The way you do this is by registering the conversion with the function `register_printf_function`; see Section 12.13.1 [Registering New Conversions], page 287. One of the arguments you pass to this function is a pointer to a handler function that produces the actual output; see Section 12.13.3 [Defining the Output Handler], page 289, for information on how to write this function.

You can also install a function that just returns information about the number and type of arguments expected by the conversion specifier. See Section 12.12.10 [Parsing a Template String], page 284, for information about this.

The facilities of this section are declared in the header file `printf.h`.

Portability Note: The ability to extend the syntax of `printf` template strings is a GNU extension. ISO standard C has nothing similar.

12.13.1 Registering New Conversions

The function to register a new output conversion is `register_printf_function`, declared in `printf.h`.

int register_printf_function (*int* **spec**, *printf_function*   [Function]
       handler-function, *printf_arginfo_function* **arginfo-function**)

Preliminary: | MT-Unsafe const:printfext | AS-Unsafe heap lock | AC-Unsafe mem lock | See Section 1.2.2.1 [POSIX Safety Concepts], page 2.

This function defines the conversion specifier character *spec*. Thus, if *spec* is 'Y', it defines the conversion '%Y'. You can redefine the built-in conversions like '%s', but flag characters like '#' and type modifiers like 'l' can never be used as conversions; calling `register_printf_function` for those characters has no effect. It is advisable not to use lowercase letters, since the ISO C standard warns that additional lowercase letters may be standardized in future editions of the standard.

The *handler-function* is the function called by `printf` and friends when this conversion appears in a template string. See Section 12.13.3 [Defining the Output Handler], page 289, for information about how to define a function to pass as this argument. If you specify a null pointer, any existing handler function for *spec* is removed.

The *arginfo-function* is the function called by `parse_printf_format` when this conversion appears in a template string. See Section 12.12.10 [Parsing a Template String], page 284, for information about this.

Attention: In the GNU C Library versions before 2.0 the *arginfo-function* function did not need to be installed unless the user used the `parse_printf_format` function. This has changed. Now a call to any of the `printf` functions will call this function when this format specifier appears in the format string.

The return value is 0 on success, and -1 on failure (which occurs if *spec* is out of range).

You can redefine the standard output conversions, but this is probably not a good idea because of the potential for confusion. Library routines written by other people could break if you do this.

12.13.2 Conversion Specifier Options

If you define a meaning for '%A', what if the template contains '%+23A' or '%-#A'? To implement a sensible meaning for these, the handler when called needs to be able to get the options specified in the template.

Both the *handler-function* and *arginfo-function* accept an argument that points to a `struct printf_info`, which contains information about the options appearing in an instance of the conversion specifier. This data type is declared in the header file `printf.h`.

`struct printf_info`   [Type]

This structure is used to pass information about the options appearing in an instance of a conversion specifier in a `printf` template string to the handler and arginfo functions for that specifier. It contains the following members:

`int prec`   This is the precision specified. The value is `-1` if no precision was specified. If the precision was given as '`*`', the `printf_info` structure passed to the handler function contains the actual value retrieved from the argument list. But the structure passed to the arginfo function contains a value of `INT_MIN`, since the actual value is not known.

`int width`   This is the minimum field width specified. The value is `0` if no width was specified. If the field width was given as '`*`', the `printf_info` structure passed to the handler function contains the actual value retrieved from the argument list. But the structure passed to the arginfo function contains a value of `INT_MIN`, since the actual value is not known.

`wchar_t spec`

This is the conversion specifier character specified. It's stored in the structure so that you can register the same handler function for multiple characters, but still have a way to tell them apart when the handler function is called.

`unsigned int is_long_double`

This is a boolean that is true if the 'L', '`ll`', or '`q`' type modifier was specified. For integer conversions, this indicates `long long int`, as opposed to `long double` for floating point conversions.

`unsigned int is_char`

This is a boolean that is true if the '`hh`' type modifier was specified.

`unsigned int is_short`

This is a boolean that is true if the '`h`' type modifier was specified.

`unsigned int is_long`

This is a boolean that is true if the '`l`' type modifier was specified.

`unsigned int alt`

This is a boolean that is true if the '`#`' flag was specified.

`unsigned int space`

This is a boolean that is true if the '` `' flag was specified.

`unsigned int left`

This is a boolean that is true if the '`-`' flag was specified.

`unsigned int showsign`

This is a boolean that is true if the '`+`' flag was specified.

`unsigned int group`

> This is a boolean that is true if the '' flag was specified.

`unsigned int extra`

> This flag has a special meaning depending on the context. It could be used freely by the user-defined handlers but when called from the `printf` function this variable always contains the value 0.

`unsigned int wide`

> This flag is set if the stream is wide oriented.

`wchar_t pad`

> This is the character to use for padding the output to the minimum field width. The value is '0' if the '0' flag was specified, and ' ' otherwise.

12.13.3 Defining the Output Handler

Now let's look at how to define the handler and arginfo functions which are passed as arguments to `register_printf_function`.

Compatibility Note: The interface changed in the GNU C Library version 2.0. Previously the third argument was of type `va_list *`.

You should define your handler functions with a prototype like:

```
int function (FILE *stream, const struct printf_info *info,
    const void *const *args)
```

The *stream* argument passed to the handler function is the stream to which it should write output.

The *info* argument is a pointer to a structure that contains information about the various options that were included with the conversion in the template string. You should not modify this structure inside your handler function. See Section 12.13.2 [Conversion Specifier Options], page 287, for a description of this data structure.

The *args* is a vector of pointers to the arguments data. The number of arguments was determined by calling the argument information function provided by the user.

Your handler function should return a value just like `printf` does: it should return the number of characters it has written, or a negative value to indicate an error.

`printf_function`   [Data Type]

> This is the data type that a handler function should have.

If you are going to use `parse_printf_format` in your application, you must also define a function to pass as the *arginfo-function* argument for each new conversion you install with `register_printf_function`.

You have to define these functions with a prototype like:

```
int function (const struct printf_info *info,
    size_t n, int *argtypes)
```

The return value from the function should be the number of arguments the conversion expects. The function should also fill in no more than *n* elements of the *argtypes* array with information about the types of each of these arguments. This information is encoded using the various 'PA_' macros. (You will notice that this is the same calling convention `parse_printf_format` itself uses.)

printf_arginfo_function   [Data Type]

This type is used to describe functions that return information about the number and type of arguments used by a conversion specifier.

12.13.4 printf Extension Example

Here is an example showing how to define a **printf** handler function. This program defines a data structure called a **Widget** and defines the '%W' conversion to print information about **Widget *** arguments, including the pointer value and the name stored in the data structure. The '%W' conversion supports the minimum field width and left-justification options, but ignores everything else.

```
#include <stdio.h>
#include <stdlib.h>
#include <printf.h>

typedef struct
{
  char *name;
}
Widget;

int
print_widget (FILE *stream,
              const struct printf_info *info,
              const void *const *args)
{
  const Widget *w;
  char *buffer;
  int len;

  /* Format the output into a string. */
  w = *((const Widget **) (args[0]));
  len = asprintf (&buffer, "<Widget %p: %s>", w, w->name);
  if (len == -1)
    return -1;

  /* Pad to the minimum field width and print to the stream. */
  len = fprintf (stream, "%*s",
                 (info->left ? -info->width : info->width),
                 buffer);

  /* Clean up and return. */
  free (buffer);
  return len;
}


int
print_widget_arginfo (const struct printf_info *info, size_t n,
                      int *argtypes)
{
  /* We always take exactly one argument and this is a pointer to the
     structure.. */
  if (n > 0)
    argtypes[0] = PA_POINTER;
  return 1;
```

```
}

int
main (void)
{
  /* Make a widget to print. */
  Widget mywidget;
  mywidget.name = "mywidget";

  /* Register the print function for widgets. */
  register_printf_function ('W', print_widget, print_widget_arginfo);

  /* Now print the widget. */
  printf ("|%W|\n", &mywidget);
  printf ("|%35W|\n", &mywidget);
  printf ("|%-35W|\n", &mywidget);

  return 0;
}
```

The output produced by this program looks like:

```
|<Widget 0xffeffb7c: mywidget>|
|      <Widget 0xffeffb7c: mywidget>|
|<Widget 0xffeffb7c: mywidget>      |
```

12.13.5 Predefined `printf` Handlers

The GNU C Library also contains a concrete and useful application of the `printf` handler extension. There are two functions available which implement a special way to print floating-point numbers.

int `printf_size` (*FILE *fp*, *const struct printf_info *info*, *const void*   [Function]
       **const *args*)

Preliminary: | MT-Safe race:fp locale | AS-Unsafe corrupt heap | AC-Unsafe mem corrupt | See Section 1.2.2.1 [POSIX Safety Concepts], page 2.

Print a given floating point number as for the format `%f` except that there is a postfix character indicating the divisor for the number to make this less than 1000. There are two possible divisors: powers of 1024 or powers of 1000. Which one is used depends on the format character specified while registered this handler. If the character is of lower case, 1024 is used. For upper case characters, 1000 is used.

The postfix tag corresponds to bytes, kilobytes, megabytes, gigabytes, etc. The full table is:

low	Multiplier	From	Upper	Multiplier
␣	1		␣	1
k	$2^{10} = 1024$	kilo	K	$10^3 = 1000$
m	2^{20}	mega	M	10^6
g	2^{30}	giga	G	10^9
t	2^{40}	tera	T	10^{12}
p	2^{50}	peta	P	10^{15}
e	2^{60}	exa	E	10^{18}
z	2^{70}	zetta	Z	10^{21}
y	2^{80}	yotta	Y	10^{24}

The default precision is 3, i.e., 1024 is printed with a lower-case format character as if it were `%.3fk` and will yield `1.000k`.

Due to the requirements of `register_printf_function` we must also provide the function which returns information about the arguments.

`int printf_size_info` (*const struct printf_info *info*, *size_t n*, *int*   [Function]
    ***argtypes*)
Preliminary: | MT-Safe | AS-Safe | AC-Safe | See Section 1.2.2.1 [POSIX Safety Concepts], page 2.

This function will return in *argtypes* the information about the used parameters in the way the `vfprintf` implementation expects it. The format always takes one argument.

To use these functions both functions must be registered with a call like

```
register_printf_function ('B', printf_size, printf_size_info);
```

Here we register the functions to print numbers as powers of 1000 since the format character 'B' is an upper-case character. If we would additionally use 'b' in a line like

```
register_printf_function ('b', printf_size, printf_size_info);
```

we could also print using a power of 1024. Please note that all that is different in these two lines is the format specifier. The `printf_size` function knows about the difference between lower and upper case format specifiers.

The use of 'B' and 'b' is no coincidence. Rather it is the preferred way to use this functionality since it is available on some other systems which also use format specifiers.

12.14 Formatted Input

The functions described in this section (`scanf` and related functions) provide facilities for formatted input analogous to the formatted output facilities. These functions provide a mechanism for reading arbitrary values under the control of a *format string* or *template string*.

12.14.1 Formatted Input Basics

Calls to `scanf` are superficially similar to calls to `printf` in that arbitrary arguments are read under the control of a template string. While the syntax of the conversion specifications in the template is very similar to that for `printf`, the interpretation of the template is oriented more towards free-format input and simple pattern matching, rather than fixed-field formatting. For example, most `scanf` conversions skip over any amount of "white space" (including spaces, tabs, and newlines) in the input file, and there is no concept of precision for the numeric input conversions as there is for the corresponding output conversions. Ordinarily, non-whitespace characters in the template are expected to match characters in the input stream exactly, but a matching failure is distinct from an input error on the stream.

Another area of difference between `scanf` and `printf` is that you must remember to supply pointers rather than immediate values as the optional arguments to `scanf`; the values that are read are stored in the objects that the pointers point to. Even experienced programmers tend to forget this occasionally, so if your program is getting strange errors that seem to be related to `scanf`, you might want to double-check this.

When a *matching failure* occurs, `scanf` returns immediately, leaving the first non-matching character as the next character to be read from the stream. The normal return value from `scanf` is the number of values that were assigned, so you can use this to determine if a matching error happened before all the expected values were read.

The `scanf` function is typically used for things like reading in the contents of tables. For example, here is a function that uses `scanf` to initialize an array of `double`:

```
void
readarray (double *array, int n)
{
  int i;
  for (i=0; i<n; i++)
    if (scanf (" %lf", &(array[i])) != 1)
      invalid_input_error ();
}
```

The formatted input functions are not used as frequently as the formatted output functions. Partly, this is because it takes some care to use them properly. Another reason is that it is difficult to recover from a matching error.

If you are trying to read input that doesn't match a single, fixed pattern, you may be better off using a tool such as Flex to generate a lexical scanner, or Bison to generate a parser, rather than using `scanf`. For more information about these tools, see *Flex: The Lexical Scanner Generator*, and *The Bison Reference Manual*.

12.14.2 Input Conversion Syntax

A `scanf` template string is a string that contains ordinary multibyte characters interspersed with conversion specifications that start with '%'.

Any whitespace character (as defined by the `isspace` function; see Section 4.1 [Classification of Characters], page 77) in the template causes any number of whitespace characters in the input stream to be read and discarded. The whitespace characters that are matched need not be exactly the same whitespace characters that appear in the template string. For example, write ' , ' in the template to recognize a comma with optional whitespace before and after.

Other characters in the template string that are not part of conversion specifications must match characters in the input stream exactly; if this is not the case, a matching failure occurs.

The conversion specifications in a `scanf` template string have the general form:

> % *flags width type conversion*

In more detail, an input conversion specification consists of an initial '%' character followed in sequence by:

- An optional *flag character* '*', which says to ignore the text read for this specification. When `scanf` finds a conversion specification that uses this flag, it reads input as directed by the rest of the conversion specification, but it discards this input, does not use a pointer argument, and does not increment the count of successful assignments.

- An optional flag character 'a' (valid with string conversions only) which requests allocation of a buffer long enough to store the string in. (This is a GNU extension.) See Section 12.14.6 [Dynamically Allocating String Conversions], page 299.

- An optional decimal integer that specifies the *maximum field width*. Reading of characters from the input stream stops either when this maximum is reached or when a non-matching character is found, whichever happens first. Most conversions discard initial whitespace characters (those that don't are explicitly documented), and these discarded characters don't count towards the maximum field width. String input conversions store a null character to mark the end of the input; the maximum field width does not include this terminator.

- An optional *type modifier character*. For example, you can specify a type modifier of '1' with integer conversions such as '%d' to specify that the argument is a pointer to a `long int` rather than a pointer to an `int`.

- A character that specifies the conversion to be applied.

The exact options that are permitted and how they are interpreted vary between the different conversion specifiers. See the descriptions of the individual conversions for information about the particular options that they allow.

With the '-Wformat' option, the GNU C compiler checks calls to `scanf` and related functions. It examines the format string and verifies that the correct number and types of arguments are supplied. There is also a GNU C syntax to tell the compiler that a function you write uses a `scanf`-style format string. See Section "Declaring Attributes of Functions" in *Using GNU CC*, for more information.

12.14.3 Table of Input Conversions

Here is a table that summarizes the various conversion specifications:

'%d' Matches an optionally signed integer written in decimal. See Section 12.14.4 [Numeric Input Conversions], page 296.

'%i' Matches an optionally signed integer in any of the formats that the C language defines for specifying an integer constant. See Section 12.14.4 [Numeric Input Conversions], page 296.

'%o' Matches an unsigned integer written in octal radix. See Section 12.14.4 [Numeric Input Conversions], page 296.

'%u' Matches an unsigned integer written in decimal radix. See Section 12.14.4 [Numeric Input Conversions], page 296.

'%x', '%X' Matches an unsigned integer written in hexadecimal radix. See Section 12.14.4 [Numeric Input Conversions], page 296.

'%e', '%f', '%g', '%E', '%G'
      Matches an optionally signed floating-point number. See Section 12.14.4 [Numeric Input Conversions], page 296.

'%s'

> Matches a string containing only non-whitespace characters. See Section 12.14.5 [String Input Conversions], page 297. The presence of the 'l' modifier determines whether the output is stored as a wide character string or a multibyte string. If '%s' is used in a wide character function the string is converted as with multiple calls to `wcrtomb` into a multibyte string. This means that the buffer must provide room for `MB_CUR_MAX` bytes for each wide character read. In case '%ls' is used in a multibyte function the result is converted into wide characters as with multiple calls of `mbrtowc` before being stored in the user provided buffer.

'%S'

> This is an alias for '%ls' which is supported for compatibility with the Unix standard.

'%['

> Matches a string of characters that belong to a specified set. See Section 12.14.5 [String Input Conversions], page 297. The presence of the 'l' modifier determines whether the output is stored as a wide character string or a multibyte string. If '%[' is used in a wide character function the string is converted as with multiple calls to `wcrtomb` into a multibyte string. This means that the buffer must provide room for `MB_CUR_MAX` bytes for each wide character read. In case '%l[' is used in a multibyte function the result is converted into wide characters as with multiple calls of `mbrtowc` before being stored in the user provided buffer.

'%c'

> Matches a string of one or more characters; the number of characters read is controlled by the maximum field width given for the conversion. See Section 12.14.5 [String Input Conversions], page 297.
>
> If the '%c' is used in a wide stream function the read value is converted from a wide character to the corresponding multibyte character before storing it. Note that this conversion can produce more than one byte of output and therefore the provided buffer be large enough for up to `MB_CUR_MAX` bytes for each character. If '%lc' is used in a multibyte function the input is treated as a multibyte sequence (and not bytes) and the result is converted as with calls to `mbrtowc`.

'%C'

> This is an alias for '%lc' which is supported for compatibility with the Unix standard.

'%p'

> Matches a pointer value in the same implementation-defined format used by the '%p' output conversion for `printf`. See Section 12.14.7 [Other Input Conversions], page 299.

'%n'

> This conversion doesn't read any characters; it records the number of characters read so far by this call. See Section 12.14.7 [Other Input Conversions], page 299.

'%%'

> This matches a literal '%' character in the input stream. No corresponding argument is used. See Section 12.14.7 [Other Input Conversions], page 299.

If the syntax of a conversion specification is invalid, the behavior is undefined. If there aren't enough function arguments provided to supply addresses for all the conversion specifications in the template strings that perform assignments, or if the arguments are not of the correct types, the behavior is also undefined. On the other hand, extra arguments are simply ignored.

12.14.4 Numeric Input Conversions

This section describes the scanf conversions for reading numeric values.

The '%d' conversion matches an optionally signed integer in decimal radix. The syntax that is recognized is the same as that for the strtol function (see Section 20.11.1 [Parsing of Integers], page 585) with the value 10 for the *base* argument.

The '%i' conversion matches an optionally signed integer in any of the formats that the C language defines for specifying an integer constant. The syntax that is recognized is the same as that for the strtol function (see Section 20.11.1 [Parsing of Integers], page 585) with the value 0 for the *base* argument. (You can print integers in this syntax with printf by using the '#' flag character with the '%x', '%o', or '%d' conversion. See Section 12.12.4 [Integer Conversions], page 273.)

For example, any of the strings '10', '0xa', or '012' could be read in as integers under the '%i' conversion. Each of these specifies a number with decimal value 10.

The '%o', '%u', and '%x' conversions match unsigned integers in octal, decimal, and hexadecimal radices, respectively. The syntax that is recognized is the same as that for the strtoul function (see Section 20.11.1 [Parsing of Integers], page 585) with the appropriate value (8, 10, or 16) for the *base* argument.

The '%X' conversion is identical to the '%x' conversion. They both permit either uppercase or lowercase letters to be used as digits.

The default type of the corresponding argument for the %d and %i conversions is int *, and unsigned int * for the other integer conversions. You can use the following type modifiers to specify other sizes of integer:

'hh'   Specifies that the argument is a signed char * or unsigned char *.

            This modifier was introduced in ISO C99.

'h'   Specifies that the argument is a short int * or unsigned short int *.

'j'   Specifies that the argument is a intmax_t * or uintmax_t *.

            This modifier was introduced in ISO C99.

'l'   Specifies that the argument is a long int * or unsigned long int *. Two 'l' characters is like the 'L' modifier, below.

            If used with '%c' or '%s' the corresponding parameter is considered as a pointer to a wide character or wide character string respectively. This use of 'l' was introduced in Amendment 1 to ISO C90.

'll'

'L'

'q'   Specifies that the argument is a long long int * or unsigned long long int *. (The long long type is an extension supported by the GNU C compiler. For systems that don't provide extra-long integers, this is the same as long int.)

            The 'q' modifier is another name for the same thing, which comes from 4.4 BSD; a long long int is sometimes called a "quad" int.

't'   Specifies that the argument is a ptrdiff_t *.

            This modifier was introduced in ISO C99.

'z'   Specifies that the argument is a `size_t *`.

             This modifier was introduced in ISO C99.

All of the '%e', '%f', '%g', '%E', and '%G' input conversions are interchangeable. They all match an optionally signed floating point number, in the same syntax as for the `strtod` function (see Section 20.11.2 [Parsing of Floats], page 589).

For the floating-point input conversions, the default argument type is `float *`. (This is different from the corresponding output conversions, where the default type is `double`; remember that `float` arguments to `printf` are converted to `double` by the default argument promotions, but `float *` arguments are not promoted to `double *`.) You can specify other sizes of float using these type modifiers:

'l'   Specifies that the argument is of type `double *`.

'L'   Specifies that the argument is of type `long double *`.

For all the above number parsing formats there is an additional optional flag '''. When this flag is given the `scanf` function expects the number represented in the input string to be formatted according to the grouping rules of the currently selected locale (see Section 7.7.1.1 [Generic Numeric Formatting Parameters], page 175).

If the "C" or "POSIX" locale is selected there is no difference. But for a locale which specifies values for the appropriate fields in the locale the input must have the correct form in the input. Otherwise the longest prefix with a correct form is processed.

12.14.5 String Input Conversions

This section describes the `scanf` input conversions for reading string and character values: '%s', '%S', '%[', '%c', and '%C'.

You have two options for how to receive the input from these conversions:

- Provide a buffer to store it in. This is the default. You should provide an argument of type `char *` or `wchar_t *` (the latter of the 'l' modifier is present).

  Warning: To make a robust program, you must make sure that the input (plus its terminating null) cannot possibly exceed the size of the buffer you provide. In general, the only way to do this is to specify a maximum field width one less than the buffer size. **If you provide the buffer, always specify a maximum field width to prevent overflow.**

- Ask `scanf` to allocate a big enough buffer, by specifying the 'a' flag character. This is a GNU extension. You should provide an argument of type `char **` for the buffer address to be stored in. See Section 12.14.6 [Dynamically Allocating String Conversions], page 299.

The '%c' conversion is the simplest: it matches a fixed number of characters, always. The maximum field width says how many characters to read; if you don't specify the maximum, the default is 1. This conversion doesn't append a null character to the end of the text it reads. It also does not skip over initial whitespace characters. It reads precisely the next n characters, and fails if it cannot get that many. Since there is always a maximum field width with '%c' (whether specified, or 1 by default), you can always prevent overflow by making the buffer long enough.

If the format is '%lc' or '%C' the function stores wide characters which are converted using the conversion determined at the time the stream was opened from the external byte stream. The number of bytes read from the medium is limited by `MB_CUR_LEN * n` but at most n wide character get stored in the output string.

The '`%s`' conversion matches a string of non-whitespace characters. It skips and discards initial whitespace, but stops when it encounters more whitespace after having read something. It stores a null character at the end of the text that it reads.

For example, reading the input:

        hello, world

with the conversion '`%10c`' produces "` hello, wo`", but reading the same input with the conversion '`%10s`' produces "`hello,`".

Warning: If you do not specify a field width for '`%s`', then the number of characters read is limited only by where the next whitespace character appears. This almost certainly means that invalid input can make your program crash—which is a bug.

The '`%ls`' and '`%S`' format are handled just like '`%s`' except that the external byte sequence is converted using the conversion associated with the stream to wide characters with their own encoding. A width or precision specified with the format do not directly determine how many bytes are read from the stream since they measure wide characters. But an upper limit can be computed by multiplying the value of the width or precision by `MB_CUR_MAX`.

To read in characters that belong to an arbitrary set of your choice, use the '`%[`' conversion. You specify the set between the '`[`' character and a following '`]`' character, using the same syntax used in regular expressions for explicit sets of characters. As special cases:

- A literal '`]`' character can be specified as the first character of the set.

- An embedded '`-`' character (that is, one that is not the first or last character of the set) is used to specify a range of characters.

- If a caret character '`^`' immediately follows the initial '`[`', then the set of allowed input characters is the everything *except* the characters listed.

The '`%[`' conversion does not skip over initial whitespace characters.

Note that the *character class* syntax available in character sets that appear inside regular expressions (such as '`[:alpha:]`') is *not* available in the '`%[`' conversion.

Here are some examples of '`%[`' conversions and what they mean:

'`%25[1234567890]`'
        Matches a string of up to 25 digits.

'`%25[][]`'   Matches a string of up to 25 square brackets.

'`%25[^ \f\n\r\t\v]`'
        Matches a string up to 25 characters long that doesn't contain any of the standard whitespace characters. This is slightly different from '`%s`', because if the input begins with a whitespace character, '`%[`' reports a matching failure while '`%s`' simply discards the initial whitespace.

'`%25[a-z]`'
        Matches up to 25 lowercase characters.

As for '`%c`' and '`%s`' the '`%[`' format is also modified to produce wide characters if the '`l`' modifier is present. All what is said about '`%ls`' above is true for '`%l[`'.

One more reminder: the '%s' and '%[' conversions are **dangerous** if you don't specify a maximum width or use the 'a' flag, because input too long would overflow whatever buffer you have provided for it. No matter how long your buffer is, a user could supply input that is longer. A well-written program reports invalid input with a comprehensible error message, not with a crash.

12.14.6 Dynamically Allocating String Conversions

A GNU extension to formatted input lets you safely read a string with no maximum size. Using this feature, you don't supply a buffer; instead, scanf allocates a buffer big enough to hold the data and gives you its address. To use this feature, write 'a' as a flag character, as in '%as' or '%a[0-9a-z]'.

The pointer argument you supply for where to store the input should have type char **. The scanf function allocates a buffer and stores its address in the word that the argument points to. You should free the buffer with free when you no longer need it.

Here is an example of using the 'a' flag with the '%[...]' conversion specification to read a "variable assignment" of the form 'variable = value'.

```
{
  char *variable, *value;

  if (2 > scanf ("%a[a-zA-Z0-9] = %a[^\n]\n",
&variable, &value))
    {
      invalid_input_error ();
      return 0;
    }

  ...
}
```

12.14.7 Other Input Conversions

This section describes the miscellaneous input conversions.

The '%p' conversion is used to read a pointer value. It recognizes the same syntax used by the '%p' output conversion for printf (see Section 12.12.6 [Other Output Conversions], page 277); that is, a hexadecimal number just as the '%x' conversion accepts. The corresponding argument should be of type void **; that is, the address of a place to store a pointer.

The resulting pointer value is not guaranteed to be valid if it was not originally written during the same program execution that reads it in.

The '%n' conversion produces the number of characters read so far by this call. The corresponding argument should be of type int *. This conversion works in the same way as the '%n' conversion for printf; see Section 12.12.6 [Other Output Conversions], page 277, for an example.

The '%n' conversion is the only mechanism for determining the success of literal matches or conversions with suppressed assignments. If the '%n' follows the locus of a matching failure, then no value is stored for it since scanf returns before processing the '%n'. If you store -1 in that argument slot before calling scanf, the presence of -1 after scanf indicates an error occurred before the '%n' was reached.

Finally, the '%%' conversion matches a literal '%' character in the input stream, without using an argument. This conversion does not permit any flags, field width, or type modifier to be specified.

12.14.8 Formatted Input Functions

Here are the descriptions of the functions for performing formatted input. Prototypes for these functions are in the header file `stdio.h`.

`int scanf (const char *template, ...)`   [Function]

> Preliminary: | MT-Safe locale | AS-Unsafe corrupt heap | AC-Unsafe mem lock corrupt | See Section 1.2.2.1 [POSIX Safety Concepts], page 2.
>
> The `scanf` function reads formatted input from the stream `stdin` under the control of the template string *template*. The optional arguments are pointers to the places which receive the resulting values.
>
> The return value is normally the number of successful assignments. If an end-of-file condition is detected before any matches are performed, including matches against whitespace and literal characters in the template, then `EOF` is returned.

`int wscanf (const wchar_t *template, ...)`   [Function]

> Preliminary: | MT-Safe locale | AS-Unsafe corrupt heap | AC-Unsafe mem lock corrupt | See Section 1.2.2.1 [POSIX Safety Concepts], page 2.
>
> The `wscanf` function reads formatted input from the stream `stdin` under the control of the template string *template*. The optional arguments are pointers to the places which receive the resulting values.
>
> The return value is normally the number of successful assignments. If an end-of-file condition is detected before any matches are performed, including matches against whitespace and literal characters in the template, then `WEOF` is returned.

`int fscanf (FILE *stream, const char *template, ...)`   [Function]

> Preliminary: | MT-Safe locale | AS-Unsafe corrupt heap | AC-Unsafe mem lock corrupt | See Section 1.2.2.1 [POSIX Safety Concepts], page 2.
>
> This function is just like `scanf`, except that the input is read from the stream *stream* instead of `stdin`.

`int fwscanf (FILE *stream, const wchar_t *template, ...)`   [Function]

> Preliminary: | MT-Safe locale | AS-Unsafe corrupt heap | AC-Unsafe mem lock corrupt | See Section 1.2.2.1 [POSIX Safety Concepts], page 2.
>
> This function is just like `wscanf`, except that the input is read from the stream *stream* instead of `stdin`.

`int sscanf (const char *s, const char *template, ...)`   [Function]

> Preliminary: | MT-Safe locale | AS-Unsafe heap | AC-Unsafe mem | See Section 1.2.2.1 [POSIX Safety Concepts], page 2.
>
> This is like `scanf`, except that the characters are taken from the null-terminated string *s* instead of from a stream. Reaching the end of the string is treated as an end-of-file condition.

The behavior of this function is undefined if copying takes place between objects that overlap—for example, if *s* is also given as an argument to receive a string read under control of the '%s', '%S', or '%[' conversion.

int swscanf (*const wchar_t *ws, const wchar_t *template, ...*)   [Function]
Preliminary: | MT-Safe locale | AS-Unsafe heap | AC-Unsafe mem | See Section 1.2.2.1 [POSIX Safety Concepts], page 2.

This is like wscanf, except that the characters are taken from the null-terminated string *ws* instead of from a stream. Reaching the end of the string is treated as an end-of-file condition.

The behavior of this function is undefined if copying takes place between objects that overlap—for example, if *ws* is also given as an argument to receive a string read under control of the '%s', '%S', or '%[' conversion.

12.14.9 Variable Arguments Input Functions

The functions vscanf and friends are provided so that you can define your own variadic scanf-like functions that make use of the same internals as the built-in formatted output functions. These functions are analogous to the vprintf series of output functions. See Section 12.12.9 [Variable Arguments Output Functions], page 281, for important information on how to use them.

Portability Note: The functions listed in this section were introduced in ISO C99 and were before available as GNU extensions.

int vscanf (*const char *template,* va_list ap)   [Function]
Preliminary: | MT-Safe locale | AS-Unsafe corrupt heap | AC-Unsafe mem lock corrupt | See Section 1.2.2.1 [POSIX Safety Concepts], page 2.

This function is similar to scanf, but instead of taking a variable number of arguments directly, it takes an argument list pointer *ap* of type va_list (see Section A.2 [Variadic Functions], page 878).

int vwscanf (*const wchar_t *template,* va_list ap)   [Function]
Preliminary: | MT-Safe locale | AS-Unsafe corrupt heap | AC-Unsafe mem lock corrupt | See Section 1.2.2.1 [POSIX Safety Concepts], page 2.

This function is similar to wscanf, but instead of taking a variable number of arguments directly, it takes an argument list pointer *ap* of type va_list (see Section A.2 [Variadic Functions], page 878).

int vfscanf (*FILE *stream, const char *template,* va_list ap)   [Function]
Preliminary: | MT-Safe locale | AS-Unsafe corrupt heap | AC-Unsafe mem lock corrupt | See Section 1.2.2.1 [POSIX Safety Concepts], page 2.

This is the equivalent of fscanf with the variable argument list specified directly as for vscanf.

int vfwscanf (*FILE *stream, const wchar_t *template,* va_list ap)   [Function]
Preliminary: | MT-Safe locale | AS-Unsafe corrupt heap | AC-Unsafe mem lock corrupt | See Section 1.2.2.1 [POSIX Safety Concepts], page 2.

This is the equivalent of fwscanf with the variable argument list specified directly as for vwscanf.

int vsscanf (*const char *s, const char *template, va_list ap*)   [Function]

> Preliminary: | MT-Safe locale | AS-Unsafe heap | AC-Unsafe mem | See Section 1.2.2.1 [POSIX Safety Concepts], page 2.
>
> This is the equivalent of `sscanf` with the variable argument list specified directly as for `vscanf`.

int vswscanf (*const wchar_t *s, const wchar_t *template, va_list ap*)   [Function]

> Preliminary: | MT-Safe locale | AS-Unsafe heap | AC-Unsafe mem | See Section 1.2.2.1 [POSIX Safety Concepts], page 2.
>
> This is the equivalent of `swscanf` with the variable argument list specified directly as for `vwscanf`.

In GNU C, there is a special construct you can use to let the compiler know that a function uses a `scanf`-style format string. Then it can check the number and types of arguments in each call to the function, and warn you when they do not match the format string. For details, see Section "Declaring Attributes of Functions" in *Using GNU CC*.

12.15 End-Of-File and Errors

Many of the functions described in this chapter return the value of the macro `EOF` to indicate unsuccessful completion of the operation. Since `EOF` is used to report both end of file and random errors, it's often better to use the `feof` function to check explicitly for end of file and `ferror` to check for errors. These functions check indicators that are part of the internal state of the stream object, indicators set if the appropriate condition was detected by a previous I/O operation on that stream.

int EOF   [Macro]

> This macro is an integer value that is returned by a number of narrow stream functions to indicate an end-of-file condition, or some other error situation. With the GNU C Library, `EOF` is `-1`. In other libraries, its value may be some other negative number.
>
> This symbol is declared in `stdio.h`.

int WEOF   [Macro]

> This macro is an integer value that is returned by a number of wide stream functions to indicate an end-of-file condition, or some other error situation. With the GNU C Library, `WEOF` is `-1`. In other libraries, its value may be some other negative number.
>
> This symbol is declared in `wchar.h`.

int feof (*FILE *stream*)   [Function]

> Preliminary: | MT-Safe | AS-Safe | AC-Unsafe lock | See Section 1.2.2.1 [POSIX Safety Concepts], page 2.
>
> The `feof` function returns nonzero if and only if the end-of-file indicator for the stream *stream* is set.
>
> This symbol is declared in `stdio.h`.

int feof_unlocked (*FILE *stream*)   [Function]

> Preliminary: | MT-Safe | AS-Safe | AC-Safe | See Section 1.2.2.1 [POSIX Safety Concepts], page 2.

The `feof_unlocked` function is equivalent to the `feof` function except that it does not implicitly lock the stream.

This function is a GNU extension.

This symbol is declared in `stdio.h`.

`int ferror (FILE *stream)`   [Function]
    Preliminary: | MT-Safe | AS-Safe | AC-Unsafe lock | See Section 1.2.2.1 [POSIX Safety Concepts], page 2.

    The `ferror` function returns nonzero if and only if the error indicator for the stream *stream* is set, indicating that an error has occurred on a previous operation on the stream.

    This symbol is declared in `stdio.h`.

`int ferror_unlocked (FILE *stream)`   [Function]
    Preliminary: | MT-Safe | AS-Safe | AC-Safe | See Section 1.2.2.1 [POSIX Safety Concepts], page 2.

    The `ferror_unlocked` function is equivalent to the `ferror` function except that it does not implicitly lock the stream.

    This function is a GNU extension.

    This symbol is declared in `stdio.h`.

In addition to setting the error indicator associated with the stream, the functions that operate on streams also set `errno` in the same way as the corresponding low-level functions that operate on file descriptors. For example, all of the functions that perform output to a stream—such as `fputc`, `printf`, and `fflush`—are implemented in terms of `write`, and all of the `errno` error conditions defined for `write` are meaningful for these functions. For more information about the descriptor-level I/O functions, see Chapter 13 [Low-Level Input/Output], page 323.

12.16 Recovering from errors

You may explicitly clear the error and EOF flags with the `clearerr` function.

`void clearerr (FILE *stream)`   [Function]
    Preliminary: | MT-Safe | AS-Safe | AC-Unsafe lock | See Section 1.2.2.1 [POSIX Safety Concepts], page 2.

    This function clears the end-of-file and error indicators for the stream *stream*.

    The file positioning functions (see Section 12.18 [File Positioning], page 305) also clear the end-of-file indicator for the stream.

`void clearerr_unlocked (FILE *stream)`   [Function]
    Preliminary: | MT-Safe race:stream | AS-Safe | AC-Safe | See Section 1.2.2.1 [POSIX Safety Concepts], page 2.

    The `clearerr_unlocked` function is equivalent to the `clearerr` function except that it does not implicitly lock the stream.

    This function is a GNU extension.

Note that it is *not* correct to just clear the error flag and retry a failed stream operation. After a failed write, any number of characters since the last buffer flush may have been committed to the file, while some buffered data may have been discarded. Merely retrying can thus cause lost or repeated data.

A failed read may leave the file pointer in an inappropriate position for a second try. In both cases, you should seek to a known position before retrying.

Most errors that can happen are not recoverable — a second try will always fail again in the same way. So usually it is best to give up and report the error to the user, rather than install complicated recovery logic.

One important exception is `EINTR` (see Section 24.5 [Primitives Interrupted by Signals], page 687). Many stream I/O implementations will treat it as an ordinary error, which can be quite inconvenient. You can avoid this hassle by installing all signals with the `SA_RESTART` flag.

For similar reasons, setting nonblocking I/O on a stream's file descriptor is not usually advisable.

12.17 Text and Binary Streams

GNU systems and other POSIX-compatible operating systems organize all files as uniform sequences of characters. However, some other systems make a distinction between files containing text and files containing binary data, and the input and output facilities of ISO C provide for this distinction. This section tells you how to write programs portable to such systems.

When you open a stream, you can specify either a *text stream* or a *binary stream*. You indicate that you want a binary stream by specifying the 'b' modifier in the *opentype* argument to `fopen`; see Section 12.3 [Opening Streams], page 249. Without this option, `fopen` opens the file as a text stream.

Text and binary streams differ in several ways:

- The data read from a text stream is divided into *lines* which are terminated by newline ('\n') characters, while a binary stream is simply a long series of characters. A text stream might on some systems fail to handle lines more than 254 characters long (including the terminating newline character).

- On some systems, text files can contain only printing characters, horizontal tab characters, and newlines, and so text streams may not support other characters. However, binary streams can handle any character value.

- Space characters that are written immediately preceding a newline character in a text stream may disappear when the file is read in again.

- More generally, there need not be a one-to-one mapping between characters that are read from or written to a text stream, and the characters in the actual file.

Since a binary stream is always more capable and more predictable than a text stream, you might wonder what purpose text streams serve. Why not simply always use binary streams? The answer is that on these operating systems, text and binary streams use different file formats, and the only way to read or write "an ordinary file of text" that can work with other text-oriented programs is through a text stream.

In the GNU C Library, and on all POSIX systems, there is no difference between text streams and binary streams. When you open a stream, you get the same kind of stream regardless of whether you ask for binary. This stream can handle any file content, and has none of the restrictions that text streams sometimes have.

12.18 File Positioning

The *file position* of a stream describes where in the file the stream is currently reading or writing. I/O on the stream advances the file position through the file. On GNU systems, the file position is represented as an integer, which counts the number of bytes from the beginning of the file. See Section 11.1.2 [File Position], page 244.

During I/O to an ordinary disk file, you can change the file position whenever you wish, so as to read or write any portion of the file. Some other kinds of files may also permit this. Files which support changing the file position are sometimes referred to as *random-access* files.

You can use the functions in this section to examine or modify the file position indicator associated with a stream. The symbols listed below are declared in the header file `stdio.h`.

long int ftell (*FILE *stream*)   [Function]
> Preliminary: | MT-Safe | AS-Unsafe corrupt | AC-Unsafe lock corrupt | See Section 1.2.2.1 [POSIX Safety Concepts], page 2.
>
> This function returns the current file position of the stream *stream*.
>
> This function can fail if the stream doesn't support file positioning, or if the file position can't be represented in a `long int`, and possibly for other reasons as well. If a failure occurs, a value of `-1` is returned.

off_t ftello (*FILE *stream*)   [Function]
> Preliminary: | MT-Safe | AS-Unsafe corrupt | AC-Unsafe lock corrupt | See Section 1.2.2.1 [POSIX Safety Concepts], page 2.
>
> The `ftello` function is similar to `ftell`, except that it returns a value of type `off_t`. Systems which support this type use it to describe all file positions, unlike the POSIX specification which uses a long int. The two are not necessarily the same size. Therefore, using ftell can lead to problems if the implementation is written on top of a POSIX compliant low-level I/O implementation, and using `ftello` is preferable whenever it is available.
>
> If this function fails it returns (`off_t`) `-1`. This can happen due to missing support for file positioning or internal errors. Otherwise the return value is the current file position.
>
> The function is an extension defined in the Unix Single Specification version 2.
>
> When the sources are compiled with `_FILE_OFFSET_BITS == 64` on a 32 bit system this function is in fact `ftello64`. I.e., the LFS interface transparently replaces the old interface.

off64_t ftello64 (*FILE *stream*)   [Function]
> Preliminary: | MT-Safe | AS-Unsafe corrupt | AC-Unsafe lock corrupt | See Section 1.2.2.1 [POSIX Safety Concepts], page 2.

This function is similar to **ftello** with the only difference that the return value is of type **off64_t**. This also requires that the stream *stream* was opened using either **fopen64**, **freopen64**, or **tmpfile64** since otherwise the underlying file operations to position the file pointer beyond the 2^31 bytes limit might fail.

If the sources are compiled with **_FILE_OFFSET_BITS == 64** on a 32 bits machine this function is available under the name **ftello** and so transparently replaces the old interface.

int fseek (*FILE *stream, long int offset, int whence*)						[Function]
Preliminary: | MT-Safe | AS-Unsafe corrupt | AC-Unsafe lock corrupt | See Section 1.2.2.1 [POSIX Safety Concepts], page 2.

The **fseek** function is used to change the file position of the stream *stream*. The value of *whence* must be one of the constants **SEEK_SET**, **SEEK_CUR**, or **SEEK_END**, to indicate whether the *offset* is relative to the beginning of the file, the current file position, or the end of the file, respectively.

This function returns a value of zero if the operation was successful, and a nonzero value to indicate failure. A successful call also clears the end-of-file indicator of *stream* and discards any characters that were "pushed back" by the use of **ungetc**.

fseek either flushes any buffered output before setting the file position or else remembers it so it will be written later in its proper place in the file.

int fseeko (*FILE *stream, off_t offset, int whence*)						[Function]
Preliminary: | MT-Safe | AS-Unsafe corrupt | AC-Unsafe lock corrupt | See Section 1.2.2.1 [POSIX Safety Concepts], page 2.

This function is similar to **fseek** but it corrects a problem with **fseek** in a system with POSIX types. Using a value of type **long int** for the offset is not compatible with POSIX. **fseeko** uses the correct type **off_t** for the *offset* parameter.

For this reason it is a good idea to prefer **ftello** whenever it is available since its functionality is (if different at all) closer the underlying definition.

The functionality and return value is the same as for **fseek**.

The function is an extension defined in the Unix Single Specification version 2.

When the sources are compiled with **_FILE_OFFSET_BITS == 64** on a 32 bit system this function is in fact **fseeko64**. I.e., the LFS interface transparently replaces the old interface.

int fseeko64 (*FILE *stream, off64_t offset, int whence*)						[Function]
Preliminary: | MT-Safe | AS-Unsafe corrupt | AC-Unsafe lock corrupt | See Section 1.2.2.1 [POSIX Safety Concepts], page 2.

This function is similar to **fseeko** with the only difference that the *offset* parameter is of type **off64_t**. This also requires that the stream *stream* was opened using either **fopen64**, **freopen64**, or **tmpfile64** since otherwise the underlying file operations to position the file pointer beyond the 2^31 bytes limit might fail.

If the sources are compiled with **_FILE_OFFSET_BITS == 64** on a 32 bits machine this function is available under the name **fseeko** and so transparently replaces the old interface.

Portability Note: In non-POSIX systems, `ftell`, `ftello`, `fseek` and `fseeko` might work reliably only on binary streams. See Section 12.17 [Text and Binary Streams], page 304.

The following symbolic constants are defined for use as the *whence* argument to `fseek`. They are also used with the `lseek` function (see Section 13.2 [Input and Output Primitives], page 326) and to specify offsets for file locks (see Section 13.11 [Control Operations on Files], page 359).

`int SEEK_SET`   [Macro]

> This is an integer constant which, when used as the *whence* argument to the `fseek` or `fseeko` function, specifies that the offset provided is relative to the beginning of the file.

`int SEEK_CUR`   [Macro]

> This is an integer constant which, when used as the *whence* argument to the `fseek` or `fseeko` function, specifies that the offset provided is relative to the current file position.

`int SEEK_END`   [Macro]

> This is an integer constant which, when used as the *whence* argument to the `fseek` or `fseeko` function, specifies that the offset provided is relative to the end of the file.

`void rewind (FILE *stream)`   [Function]

> Preliminary: | MT-Safe | AS-Unsafe corrupt | AC-Unsafe lock corrupt | See Section 1.2.2.1 [POSIX Safety Concepts], page 2.
>
> The `rewind` function positions the stream *stream* at the beginning of the file. It is equivalent to calling `fseek` or `fseeko` on the *stream* with an *offset* argument of 0L and a *whence* argument of `SEEK_SET`, except that the return value is discarded and the error indicator for the stream is reset.

These three aliases for the 'SEEK_...' constants exist for the sake of compatibility with older BSD systems. They are defined in two different header files: `fcntl.h` and `sys/file.h`.

`L_SET`   An alias for `SEEK_SET`.

`L_INCR`   An alias for `SEEK_CUR`.

`L_XTND`   An alias for `SEEK_END`.

12.19 Portable File-Position Functions

On GNU systems, the file position is truly a character count. You can specify any character count value as an argument to `fseek` or `fseeko` and get reliable results for any random access file. However, some ISO C systems do not represent file positions in this way.

On some systems where text streams truly differ from binary streams, it is impossible to represent the file position of a text stream as a count of characters from the beginning of the file. For example, the file position on some systems must encode both a record offset within the file, and a character offset within the record.

As a consequence, if you want your programs to be portable to these systems, you must observe certain rules:

- The value returned from `ftell` on a text stream has no predictable relationship to the number of characters you have read so far. The only thing you can rely on is that you can use it subsequently as the *offset* argument to `fseek` or `fseeko` to move back to the same file position.

- In a call to `fseek` or `fseeko` on a text stream, either the *offset* must be zero, or *whence* must be `SEEK_SET` and the *offset* must be the result of an earlier call to `ftell` on the same stream.

- The value of the file position indicator of a text stream is undefined while there are characters that have been pushed back with `ungetc` that haven't been read or discarded. See Section 12.10 [Unreading], page 267.

But even if you observe these rules, you may still have trouble for long files, because `ftell` and `fseek` use a `long int` value to represent the file position. This type may not have room to encode all the file positions in a large file. Using the `ftello` and `fseeko` functions might help here since the `off_t` type is expected to be able to hold all file position values but this still does not help to handle additional information which must be associated with a file position.

So if you do want to support systems with peculiar encodings for the file positions, it is better to use the functions `fgetpos` and `fsetpos` instead. These functions represent the file position using the data type `fpos_t`, whose internal representation varies from system to system.

These symbols are declared in the header file `stdio.h`.

`fpos_t`   [Data Type]
> This is the type of an object that can encode information about the file position of a stream, for use by the functions `fgetpos` and `fsetpos`.
>
> In the GNU C Library, `fpos_t` is an opaque data structure that contains internal data to represent file offset and conversion state information. In other systems, it might have a different internal representation.
>
> When compiling with `_FILE_OFFSET_BITS == 64` on a 32 bit machine this type is in fact equivalent to `fpos64_t` since the LFS interface transparently replaces the old interface.

`fpos64_t`   [Data Type]
> This is the type of an object that can encode information about the file position of a stream, for use by the functions `fgetpos64` and `fsetpos64`.
>
> In the GNU C Library, `fpos64_t` is an opaque data structure that contains internal data to represent file offset and conversion state information. In other systems, it might have a different internal representation.

`int fgetpos (FILE *stream, fpos_t *position)`   [Function]
> Preliminary: | MT-Safe | AS-Unsafe corrupt | AC-Unsafe lock corrupt | See Section 1.2.2.1 [POSIX Safety Concepts], page 2.
>
> This function stores the value of the file position indicator for the stream *stream* in the `fpos_t` object pointed to by *position*. If successful, `fgetpos` returns zero; otherwise it returns a nonzero value and stores an implementation-defined positive value in `errno`.

When the sources are compiled with `_FILE_OFFSET_BITS` == 64 on a 32 bit system the function is in fact `fgetpos64`. I.e., the LFS interface transparently replaces the old interface.

`int fgetpos64 (FILE *stream, fpos64_t *position)`   [Function]
Preliminary: | MT-Safe | AS-Unsafe corrupt | AC-Unsafe lock corrupt | See Section 1.2.2.1 [POSIX Safety Concepts], page 2.

This function is similar to `fgetpos` but the file position is returned in a variable of type `fpos64_t` to which *position* points.

If the sources are compiled with `_FILE_OFFSET_BITS` == 64 on a 32 bits machine this function is available under the name `fgetpos` and so transparently replaces the old interface.

`int fsetpos (FILE *stream, const fpos_t *position)`   [Function]
Preliminary: | MT-Safe | AS-Unsafe corrupt | AC-Unsafe lock corrupt | See Section 1.2.2.1 [POSIX Safety Concepts], page 2.

This function sets the file position indicator for the stream *stream* to the position *position*, which must have been set by a previous call to `fgetpos` on the same stream. If successful, `fsetpos` clears the end-of-file indicator on the stream, discards any characters that were "pushed back" by the use of `ungetc`, and returns a value of zero. Otherwise, `fsetpos` returns a nonzero value and stores an implementation-defined positive value in `errno`.

When the sources are compiled with `_FILE_OFFSET_BITS` == 64 on a 32 bit system the function is in fact `fsetpos64`. I.e., the LFS interface transparently replaces the old interface.

`int fsetpos64 (FILE *stream, const fpos64_t *position)`   [Function]
Preliminary: | MT-Safe | AS-Unsafe corrupt | AC-Unsafe lock corrupt | See Section 1.2.2.1 [POSIX Safety Concepts], page 2.

This function is similar to `fsetpos` but the file position used for positioning is provided in a variable of type `fpos64_t` to which *position* points.

If the sources are compiled with `_FILE_OFFSET_BITS` == 64 on a 32 bits machine this function is available under the name `fsetpos` and so transparently replaces the old interface.

12.20 Stream Buffering

Characters that are written to a stream are normally accumulated and transmitted asynchronously to the file in a block, instead of appearing as soon as they are output by the application program. Similarly, streams often retrieve input from the host environment in blocks rather than on a character-by-character basis. This is called *buffering*.

If you are writing programs that do interactive input and output using streams, you need to understand how buffering works when you design the user interface to your program. Otherwise, you might find that output (such as progress or prompt messages) doesn't appear when you intended it to, or displays some other unexpected behavior.

This section deals only with controlling when characters are transmitted between the stream and the file or device, and *not* with how things like echoing, flow control, and the like are handled on specific classes of devices. For information on common control operations on terminal devices, see Chapter 17 [Low-Level Terminal Interface], page 477.

You can bypass the stream buffering facilities altogether by using the low-level input and output functions that operate on file descriptors instead. See Chapter 13 [Low-Level Input/Output], page 323.

12.20.1 Buffering Concepts

There are three different kinds of buffering strategies:

- Characters written to or read from an *unbuffered* stream are transmitted individually to or from the file as soon as possible.
- Characters written to a *line buffered* stream are transmitted to the file in blocks when a newline character is encountered.
- Characters written to or read from a *fully buffered* stream are transmitted to or from the file in blocks of arbitrary size.

Newly opened streams are normally fully buffered, with one exception: a stream connected to an interactive device such as a terminal is initially line buffered. See Section 12.20.3 [Controlling Which Kind of Buffering], page 311, for information on how to select a different kind of buffering. Usually the automatic selection gives you the most convenient kind of buffering for the file or device you open.

The use of line buffering for interactive devices implies that output messages ending in a newline will appear immediately—which is usually what you want. Output that doesn't end in a newline might or might not show up immediately, so if you want them to appear immediately, you should flush buffered output explicitly with `fflush`, as described in Section 12.20.2 [Flushing Buffers], page 310.

12.20.2 Flushing Buffers

Flushing output on a buffered stream means transmitting all accumulated characters to the file. There are many circumstances when buffered output on a stream is flushed automatically:

- When you try to do output and the output buffer is full.
- When the stream is closed. See Section 12.4 [Closing Streams], page 253.
- When the program terminates by calling `exit`. See Section 25.7.1 [Normal Termination], page 745.
- When a newline is written, if the stream is line buffered.
- Whenever an input operation on *any* stream actually reads data from its file.

If you want to flush the buffered output at another time, call `fflush`, which is declared in the header file `stdio.h`.

`int fflush (FILE *stream)` [Function]
> Preliminary: | MT-Safe | AS-Unsafe corrupt | AC-Unsafe lock corrupt | See Section 1.2.2.1 [POSIX Safety Concepts], page 2.
>
> This function causes any buffered output on *stream* to be delivered to the file. If *stream* is a null pointer, then `fflush` causes buffered output on *all* open output streams to be flushed.
>
> This function returns `EOF` if a write error occurs, or zero otherwise.

`int fflush_unlocked (FILE *stream)`   [Function]

> Preliminary: | MT-Safe race:stream | AS-Unsafe corrupt | AC-Unsafe corrupt | See Section 1.2.2.1 [POSIX Safety Concepts], page 2.
>
> The `fflush_unlocked` function is equivalent to the `fflush` function except that it does not implicitly lock the stream.

The `fflush` function can be used to flush all streams currently opened. While this is useful in some situations it does often more than necessary since it might be done in situations when terminal input is required and the program wants to be sure that all output is visible on the terminal. But this means that only line buffered streams have to be flushed. Solaris introduced a function especially for this. It was always available in the GNU C Library in some form but never officially exported.

`void _flushlbf (void)`   [Function]

> Preliminary: | MT-Safe | AS-Unsafe corrupt | AC-Unsafe lock corrupt | See Section 1.2.2.1 [POSIX Safety Concepts], page 2.
>
> The `_flushlbf` function flushes all line buffered streams currently opened.
>
> This function is declared in the `stdio_ext.h` header.

Compatibility Note: Some brain-damaged operating systems have been known to be so thoroughly fixated on line-oriented input and output that flushing a line buffered stream causes a newline to be written! Fortunately, this "feature" seems to be becoming less common. You do not need to worry about this with the GNU C Library.

In some situations it might be useful to not flush the output pending for a stream but instead simply forget it. If transmission is costly and the output is not needed anymore this is valid reasoning. In this situation a non-standard function introduced in Solaris and available in the GNU C Library can be used.

`void __fpurge (FILE *stream)`   [Function]

> Preliminary: | MT-Safe race:stream | AS-Unsafe corrupt | AC-Unsafe corrupt | See Section 1.2.2.1 [POSIX Safety Concepts], page 2.
>
> The `__fpurge` function causes the buffer of the stream *stream* to be emptied. If the stream is currently in read mode all input in the buffer is lost. If the stream is in output mode the buffered output is not written to the device (or whatever other underlying storage) and the buffer the cleared.
>
> This function is declared in `stdio_ext.h`.

12.20.3 Controlling Which Kind of Buffering

After opening a stream (but before any other operations have been performed on it), you can explicitly specify what kind of buffering you want it to have using the `setvbuf` function.

The facilities listed in this section are declared in the header file `stdio.h`.

`int setvbuf (FILE *stream, char *buf, int mode, size_t size)`   [Function]

> Preliminary: | MT-Safe | AS-Unsafe corrupt | AC-Unsafe lock corrupt | See Section 1.2.2.1 [POSIX Safety Concepts], page 2.

This function is used to specify that the stream *stream* should have the buffering mode *mode*, which can be either `_IOFBF` (for full buffering), `_IOLBF` (for line buffering), or `_IONBF` (for unbuffered input/output).

If you specify a null pointer as the *buf* argument, then `setvbuf` allocates a buffer itself using `malloc`. This buffer will be freed when you close the stream.

Otherwise, *buf* should be a character array that can hold at least *size* characters. You should not free the space for this array as long as the stream remains open and this array remains its buffer. You should usually either allocate it statically, or `malloc` (see Section 3.2.2 [Unconstrained Allocation], page 42) the buffer. Using an automatic array is not a good idea unless you close the file before exiting the block that declares the array.

While the array remains a stream buffer, the stream I/O functions will use the buffer for their internal purposes. You shouldn't try to access the values in the array directly while the stream is using it for buffering.

The `setvbuf` function returns zero on success, or a nonzero value if the value of *mode* is not valid or if the request could not be honored.

int _IOFBF   [Macro]

The value of this macro is an integer constant expression that can be used as the *mode* argument to the `setvbuf` function to specify that the stream should be fully buffered.

int _IOLBF   [Macro]

The value of this macro is an integer constant expression that can be used as the *mode* argument to the `setvbuf` function to specify that the stream should be line buffered.

int _IONBF   [Macro]

The value of this macro is an integer constant expression that can be used as the *mode* argument to the `setvbuf` function to specify that the stream should be unbuffered.

int BUFSIZ   [Macro]

The value of this macro is an integer constant expression that is good to use for the *size* argument to `setvbuf`. This value is guaranteed to be at least **256**.

The value of BUFSIZ is chosen on each system so as to make stream I/O efficient. So it is a good idea to use BUFSIZ as the size for the buffer when you call `setvbuf`.

Actually, you can get an even better value to use for the buffer size by means of the `fstat` system call: it is found in the `st_blksize` field of the file attributes. See Section 14.9.1 [The meaning of the File Attributes], page 399.

Sometimes people also use BUFSIZ as the allocation size of buffers used for related purposes, such as strings used to receive a line of input with `fgets` (see Section 12.8 [Character Input], page 262). There is no particular reason to use BUFSIZ for this instead of any other integer, except that it might lead to doing I/O in chunks of an efficient size.

void setbuf (*FILE *stream*, *char *buf*)   [Function]

Preliminary: | MT-Safe | AS-Unsafe corrupt | AC-Unsafe lock corrupt | See Section 1.2.2.1 [POSIX Safety Concepts], page 2.

If *buf* is a null pointer, the effect of this function is equivalent to calling `setvbuf` with a *mode* argument of `_IONBF`. Otherwise, it is equivalent to calling `setvbuf` with *buf*, and a *mode* of `_IOFBF` and a *size* argument of `BUFSIZ`.

The `setbuf` function is provided for compatibility with old code; use `setvbuf` in all new programs.

`void setbuffer` (*FILE *stream, char *buf, size_t size*)   [Function]
    Preliminary: | MT-Safe | AS-Unsafe corrupt | AC-Unsafe lock corrupt | See Section 1.2.2.1 [POSIX Safety Concepts], page 2.

    If *buf* is a null pointer, this function makes *stream* unbuffered. Otherwise, it makes *stream* fully buffered using *buf* as the buffer. The *size* argument specifies the length of *buf*.

    This function is provided for compatibility with old BSD code. Use `setvbuf` instead.

`void setlinebuf` (*FILE *stream*)   [Function]
    Preliminary: | MT-Safe | AS-Unsafe corrupt | AC-Unsafe lock corrupt | See Section 1.2.2.1 [POSIX Safety Concepts], page 2.

    This function makes *stream* be line buffered, and allocates the buffer for you.

    This function is provided for compatibility with old BSD code. Use `setvbuf` instead.

It is possible to query whether a given stream is line buffered or not using a non-standard function introduced in Solaris and available in the GNU C Library.

`int __flbf` (*FILE *stream*)   [Function]
    Preliminary: | MT-Safe | AS-Safe | AC-Safe | See Section 1.2.2.1 [POSIX Safety Concepts], page 2.

    The `__flbf` function will return a nonzero value in case the stream *stream* is line buffered. Otherwise the return value is zero.

    This function is declared in the `stdio_ext.h` header.

Two more extensions allow to determine the size of the buffer and how much of it is used. These functions were also introduced in Solaris.

`size_t __fbufsize` (*FILE *stream*)   [Function]
    Preliminary: | MT-Safe race:stream | AS-Unsafe corrupt | AC-Safe | See Section 1.2.2.1 [POSIX Safety Concepts], page 2.

    The `__fbufsize` function return the size of the buffer in the stream *stream*. This value can be used to optimize the use of the stream.

    This function is declared in the `stdio_ext.h` header.

`size_t __fpending` (*FILE *stream*)   [Function]
    Preliminary: | MT-Safe race:stream | AS-Unsafe corrupt | AC-Safe | See Section 1.2.2.1 [POSIX Safety Concepts], page 2.

    The `__fpending` function returns the number of bytes currently in the output buffer. For wide-oriented stream the measuring unit is wide characters. This function should not be used on buffers in read mode or opened read-only.

    This function is declared in the `stdio_ext.h` header.

12.21 Other Kinds of Streams

The GNU C Library provides ways for you to define additional kinds of streams that do not necessarily correspond to an open file.

One such type of stream takes input from or writes output to a string. These kinds of streams are used internally to implement the `sprintf` and `sscanf` functions. You can also create such a stream explicitly, using the functions described in Section 12.21.1 [String Streams], page 314.

More generally, you can define streams that do input/output to arbitrary objects using functions supplied by your program. This protocol is discussed in Section 12.21.2 [Programming Your Own Custom Streams], page 316.

Portability Note: The facilities described in this section are specific to GNU. Other systems or C implementations might or might not provide equivalent functionality.

12.21.1 String Streams

The `fmemopen` and `open_memstream` functions allow you to do I/O to a string or memory buffer. These facilities are declared in `stdio.h`.

FILE * fmemopen (*void *buf, size_t* `size`, *const char *opentype*)   [Function]
> Preliminary: | MT-Safe | AS-Unsafe heap lock | AC-Unsafe mem lock | See Section 1.2.2.1 [POSIX Safety Concepts], page 2.
>
> This function opens a stream that allows the access specified by the *opentype* argument, that reads from or writes to the buffer specified by the argument *buf*. This array must be at least *size* bytes long.
>
> If you specify a null pointer as the *buf* argument, `fmemopen` dynamically allocates an array *size* bytes long (as with `malloc`; see Section 3.2.2 [Unconstrained Allocation], page 42). This is really only useful if you are going to write things to the buffer and then read them back in again, because you have no way of actually getting a pointer to the buffer (for this, try `open_memstream`, below). The buffer is freed when the stream is closed.
>
> The argument *opentype* is the same as in `fopen` (see Section 12.3 [Opening Streams], page 249). If the *opentype* specifies append mode, then the initial file position is set to the first null character in the buffer. Otherwise the initial file position is at the beginning of the buffer.
>
> When a stream open for writing is flushed or closed, a null character (zero byte) is written at the end of the buffer if it fits. You should add an extra byte to the *size* argument to account for this. Attempts to write more than *size* bytes to the buffer result in an error.
>
> For a stream open for reading, null characters (zero bytes) in the buffer do not count as "end of file". Read operations indicate end of file only when the file position advances past *size* bytes. So, if you want to read characters from a null-terminated string, you should supply the length of the string as the *size* argument.

Here is an example of using `fmemopen` to create a stream for reading from a string:

```
#include <stdio.h>
```

```
static char buffer[] = "foobar";

int
main (void)
{
  int ch;
  FILE *stream;

  stream = fmemopen (buffer, strlen (buffer), "r");
  while ((ch = fgetc (stream)) != EOF)
    printf ("Got %c\n", ch);
  fclose (stream);

  return 0;
}
```

This program produces the following output:

```
Got f
Got o
Got o
Got b
Got a
Got r
```

FILE * open_memstream (*char **ptr*, *size_t *sizeloc*)   [Function]
   Preliminary: | MT-Safe | AS-Unsafe heap | AC-Unsafe mem | See Section 1.2.2.1
   [POSIX Safety Concepts], page 2.

   This function opens a stream for writing to a buffer. The buffer is allocated dynamically and grown as necessary, using **malloc**. After you've closed the stream, this
   buffer is your responsibility to clean up using **free** or **realloc**. See Section 3.2.2
   [Unconstrained Allocation], page 42.

   When the stream is closed with **fclose** or flushed with **fflush**, the locations *ptr* and
   sizeloc are updated to contain the pointer to the buffer and its size. The values thus
   stored remain valid only as long as no further output on the stream takes place. If
   you do more output, you must flush the stream again to store new values before you
   use them again.

   A null character is written at the end of the buffer. This null character is *not* included
   in the size value stored at *sizeloc*.

   You can move the stream's file position with **fseek** or **fseeko** (see Section 12.18 [File
   Positioning], page 305). Moving the file position past the end of the data already
   written fills the intervening space with zeroes.

   Here is an example of using **open_memstream**:

```
#include <stdio.h>

int
main (void)
{
  char *bp;
  size_t size;
  FILE *stream;
```

```
        stream = open_memstream (&bp, &size);
        fprintf (stream, "hello");
        fflush (stream);
        printf ("buf = '%s', size = %d\n", bp, size);
        fprintf (stream, ", world");
        fclose (stream);
        printf ("buf = '%s', size = %d\n", bp, size);

        return 0;
    }
```

This program produces the following output:

```
buf = 'hello', size = 5
buf = 'hello, world', size = 12
```

12.21.2 Programming Your Own Custom Streams

This section describes how you can make a stream that gets input from an arbitrary data source or writes output to an arbitrary data sink programmed by you. We call these *custom streams*. The functions and types described here are all GNU extensions.

12.21.2.1 Custom Streams and Cookies

Inside every custom stream is a special object called the *cookie*. This is an object supplied by you which records where to fetch or store the data read or written. It is up to you to define a data type to use for the cookie. The stream functions in the library never refer directly to its contents, and they don't even know what the type is; they record its address with type void *.

To implement a custom stream, you must specify *how* to fetch or store the data in the specified place. You do this by defining *hook functions* to read, write, change "file position", and close the stream. All four of these functions will be passed the stream's cookie so they can tell where to fetch or store the data. The library functions don't know what's inside the cookie, but your functions will know.

When you create a custom stream, you must specify the cookie pointer, and also the four hook functions stored in a structure of type cookie_io_functions_t.

These facilities are declared in stdio.h.

cookie_io_functions_t   [Data Type]
> This is a structure type that holds the functions that define the communications protocol between the stream and its cookie. It has the following members:
>
> cookie_read_function_t *read
>> This is the function that reads data from the cookie. If the value is a null pointer instead of a function, then read operations on this stream always return EOF.
>
> cookie_write_function_t *write
>> This is the function that writes data to the cookie. If the value is a null pointer instead of a function, then data written to the stream is discarded.
>
> cookie_seek_function_t *seek
>> This is the function that performs the equivalent of file positioning on the cookie. If the value is a null pointer instead of a function, calls to fseek

or `fseeko` on this stream can only seek to locations within the buffer; any attempt to seek outside the buffer will return an `ESPIPE` error.

`cookie_close_function_t *close`

This function performs any appropriate cleanup on the cookie when closing the stream. If the value is a null pointer instead of a function, nothing special is done to close the cookie when the stream is closed.

`FILE * fopencookie (`*void *cookie, const char **`opentype,`   [Function]
        cookie_io_functions_t `io-functions)`

Preliminary: | MT-Safe | AS-Unsafe heap lock | AC-Unsafe mem lock | See Section 1.2.2.1 [POSIX Safety Concepts], page 2.

This function actually creates the stream for communicating with the *cookie* using the functions in the *io-functions* argument. The *opentype* argument is interpreted as for `fopen`; see Section 12.3 [Opening Streams], page 249. (But note that the "truncate on open" option is ignored.) The new stream is fully buffered.

The `fopencookie` function returns the newly created stream, or a null pointer in case of an error.

12.21.2.2 Custom Stream Hook Functions

Here are more details on how you should define the four hook functions that a custom stream needs.

You should define the function to read data from the cookie as:

    `ssize_t` *reader* `(void *`*cookie*`, char *`*buffer*`, size_t` *size*`)`

This is very similar to the **read** function; see Section 13.2 [Input and Output Primitives], page 326. Your function should transfer up to *size* bytes into the *buffer*, and return the number of bytes read, or zero to indicate end-of-file. You can return a value of −1 to indicate an error.

You should define the function to write data to the cookie as:

    `ssize_t` *writer* `(void *`*cookie*`, const char *`*buffer*`, size_t` *size*`)`

This is very similar to the **write** function; see Section 13.2 [Input and Output Primitives], page 326. Your function should transfer up to *size* bytes from the buffer, and return the number of bytes written. You can return a value of 0 to indicate an error. You must not return any negative value.

You should define the function to perform seek operations on the cookie as:

    `int` *seeker* `(void *`*cookie*`, off64_t *`*position*`, int` *whence*`)`

For this function, the *position* and *whence* arguments are interpreted as for `fgetpos`; see Section 12.19 [Portable File-Position Functions], page 307.

After doing the seek operation, your function should store the resulting file position relative to the beginning of the file in *position*. Your function should return a value of 0 on success and −1 to indicate an error.

You should define the function to do cleanup operations on the cookie appropriate for closing the stream as:

    `int` *cleaner* `(void *`*cookie*`)`

Your function should return −1 to indicate an error, and 0 otherwise.

`cookie_read_function_t`   [Data Type]
>   This is the data type that the read function for a custom stream should have. If you declare the function as shown above, this is the type it will have.

`cookie_write_function_t`   [Data Type]
>   The data type of the write function for a custom stream.

`cookie_seek_function_t`   [Data Type]
>   The data type of the seek function for a custom stream.

`cookie_close_function_t`   [Data Type]
>   The data type of the close function for a custom stream.

12.22 Formatted Messages

On systems which are based on System V messages of programs (especially the system tools) are printed in a strict form using the `fmtmsg` function. The uniformity sometimes helps the user to interpret messages and the strictness tests of the `fmtmsg` function ensure that the programmer follows some minimal requirements.

12.22.1 Printing Formatted Messages

Messages can be printed to standard error and/or to the console. To select the destination the programmer can use the following two values, bitwise OR combined if wanted, for the *classification* parameter of `fmtmsg`:

`MM_PRINT`   Display the message in standard error.

`MM_CONSOLE`
>   Display the message on the system console.

The erroneous piece of the system can be signalled by exactly one of the following values which also is bitwise ORed with the *classification* parameter to `fmtmsg`:

`MM_HARD`   The source of the condition is some hardware.

`MM_SOFT`   The source of the condition is some software.

`MM_FIRM`   The source of the condition is some firmware.

A third component of the *classification* parameter to `fmtmsg` can describe the part of the system which detects the problem. This is done by using exactly one of the following values:

`MM_APPL`   The erroneous condition is detected by the application.

`MM_UTIL`   The erroneous condition is detected by a utility.

`MM_OPSYS`   The erroneous condition is detected by the operating system.

A last component of *classification* can signal the results of this message. Exactly one of the following values can be used:

`MM_RECOVER`
>   It is a recoverable error.

`MM_NRECOV`
>   It is a non-recoverable error.

int fmtmsg (*long int* **classification**, *const char *label, int*   [Function]
        severity, *const char *text, const char *action, const char *tag*)
   Preliminary: | MT-Safe | AS-Unsafe lock | AC-Safe | See Section 1.2.2.1 [POSIX
   Safety Concepts], page 2.

   Display a message described by its parameters on the device(s) specified in the *classification* parameter. The *label* parameter identifies the source of the message. The
   string should consist of two colon separated parts where the first part has not more
   than 10 and the second part not more than 14 characters. The *text* parameter describes the condition of the error, the *action* parameter possible steps to recover from
   the error and the *tag* parameter is a reference to the online documentation where
   more information can be found. It should contain the *label* value and a unique identification number.

   Each of the parameters can be a special value which means this value is to be omitted.
   The symbolic names for these values are:

   MM_NULLLBL
              Ignore *label* parameter.

   MM_NULLSEV
              Ignore *severity* parameter.

   MM_NULLMC
              Ignore *classification* parameter. This implies that nothing is actually
              printed.

   MM_NULLTXT
              Ignore *text* parameter.

   MM_NULLACT
              Ignore *action* parameter.

   MM_NULLTAG
              Ignore *tag* parameter.

   There is another way certain fields can be omitted from the output to standard error.
   This is described below in the description of environment variables influencing the
   behavior.

   The *severity* parameter can have one of the values in the following table:

   MM_NOSEV   Nothing is printed, this value is the same as MM_NULLSEV.

   MM_HALT   This value is printed as HALT.

   MM_ERROR   This value is printed as ERROR.

   MM_WARNING
              This value is printed as WARNING.

   MM_INFO   This value is printed as INFO.

   The numeric value of these five macros are between 0 and 4. Using the environment variable SEV_LEVEL or using the **addseverity** function one can add more
   severity levels with their corresponding string to print. This is described below (see
   Section 12.22.2 [Adding Severity Classes], page 320).

   If no parameter is ignored the output looks like this:

```
label: severity-string: text
TO FIX: action tag
```

The colons, new line characters and the TO FIX string are inserted if necessary, i.e., if the corresponding parameter is not ignored.

This function is specified in the X/Open Portability Guide. It is also available on all systems derived from System V.

The function returns the value MM_OK if no error occurred. If only the printing to standard error failed, it returns MM_NOMSG. If printing to the console fails, it returns MM_NOCON. If nothing is printed MM_NOTOK is returned. Among situations where all outputs fail this last value is also returned if a parameter value is incorrect.

There are two environment variables which influence the behavior of fmtmsg. The first is MSGVERB. It is used to control the output actually happening on standard error (*not* the console output). Each of the five fields can explicitly be enabled. To do this the user has to put the MSGVERB variable with a format like the following in the environment before calling the fmtmsg function the first time:

```
MSGVERB=keyword[:keyword[:...]]
```

Valid *keyword*s are label, severity, text, action, and tag. If the environment variable is not given or is the empty string, a not supported keyword is given or the value is somehow else invalid, no part of the message is masked out.

The second environment variable which influences the behavior of fmtmsg is SEV_LEVEL. This variable and the change in the behavior of fmtmsg is not specified in the X/Open Portability Guide. It is available in System V systems, though. It can be used to introduce new severity levels. By default, only the five severity levels described above are available. Any other numeric value would make fmtmsg print nothing.

If the user puts SEV_LEVEL with a format like

```
SEV_LEVEL=[description[:description[:...]]]
```

in the environment of the process before the first call to fmtmsg, where *description* has a value of the form

```
severity-keyword,level,printstring
```

The *severity-keyword* part is not used by fmtmsg but it has to be present. The *level* part is a string representation of a number. The numeric value must be a number greater than 4. This value must be used in the *severity* parameter of fmtmsg to select this class. It is not possible to overwrite any of the predefined classes. The *printstring* is the string printed when a message of this class is processed by fmtmsg (see above, fmtsmg does not print the numeric value but instead the string representation).

12.22.2 Adding Severity Classes

There is another possibility to introduce severity classes besides using the environment variable SEV_LEVEL. This simplifies the task of introducing new classes in a running program. One could use the setenv or putenv function to set the environment variable, but this is toilsome.

int addseverity (*int severity, const char *string*)   [Function]
    Preliminary: | MT-Safe | AS-Unsafe heap lock | AC-Unsafe lock mem | See Section 1.2.2.1 [POSIX Safety Concepts], page 2.

This function allows the introduction of new severity classes which can be addressed by the *severity* parameter of the `fmtmsg` function. The *severity* parameter of `addseverity` must match the value for the parameter with the same name of `fmtmsg`, and *string* is the string printed in the actual messages instead of the numeric value.

If *string* is `NULL` the severity class with the numeric value according to *severity* is removed.

It is not possible to overwrite or remove one of the default severity classes. All calls to `addseverity` with *severity* set to one of the values for the default classes will fail.

The return value is `MM_OK` if the task was successfully performed. If the return value is `MM_NOTOK` something went wrong. This could mean that no more memory is available or a class is not available when it has to be removed.

This function is not specified in the X/Open Portability Guide although the `fmtsmg` function is. It is available on System V systems.

12.22.3 How to use `fmtmsg` and `addseverity`

Here is a simple example program to illustrate the use of the both functions described in this section.

```
#include <fmtmsg.h>

int
main (void)
{
  addseverity (5, "NOTE2");
  fmtmsg (MM_PRINT, "only1field", MM_INFO, "text2", "action2", "tag2");
  fmtmsg (MM_PRINT, "UX:cat", 5, "invalid syntax", "refer to manual",
          "UX:cat:001");
  fmtmsg (MM_PRINT, "label:foo", 6, "text", "action", "tag");
  return 0;
}
```

The second call to `fmtmsg` illustrates a use of this function as it usually occurs on System V systems, which heavily use this function. It seems worthwhile to give a short explanation here of how this system works on System V. The value of the *label* field (`UX:cat`) says that the error occurred in the Unix program `cat`. The explanation of the error follows and the value for the *action* parameter is `"refer to manual"`. One could be more specific here, if necessary. The *tag* field contains, as proposed above, the value of the string given for the *label* parameter, and additionally a unique ID (`001` in this case). For a GNU environment this string could contain a reference to the corresponding node in the Info page for the program.

Running this program without specifying the `MSGVERB` and `SEV_LEVEL` function produces the following output:

```
UX:cat: NOTE2: invalid syntax
TO FIX: refer to manual UX:cat:001
```

We see the different fields of the message and how the extra glue (the colons and the `TO FIX` string) are printed. But only one of the three calls to `fmtmsg` produced output. The first call does not print anything because the *label* parameter is not in the correct form. The string must contain two fields, separated by a colon (see Section 12.22.1 [Printing Formatted

Messages], page 318). The third `fmtmsg` call produced no output since the class with the numeric value 6 is not defined. Although a class with numeric value 5 is also not defined by default, the call to `addseverity` introduces it and the second call to `fmtmsg` produces the above output.

When we change the environment of the program to contain `SEV_LEVEL=XXX,6,NOTE` when running it we get a different result:

```
UX:cat: NOTE2: invalid syntax
TO FIX: refer to manual UX:cat:001
label:foo: NOTE: text
TO FIX: action tag
```

Now the third call to `fmtmsg` produced some output and we see how the string `NOTE` from the environment variable appears in the message.

Now we can reduce the output by specifying which fields we are interested in. If we additionally set the environment variable `MSGVERB` to the value `severity:label:action` we get the following output:

```
UX:cat: NOTE2
TO FIX: refer to manual
label:foo: NOTE
TO FIX: action
```

I.e., the output produced by the *text* and the *tag* parameters to `fmtmsg` vanished. Please also note that now there is no colon after the `NOTE` and `NOTE2` strings in the output. This is not necessary since there is no more output on this line because the text is missing.

13 Low-Level Input/Output

This chapter describes functions for performing low-level input/output operations on file descriptors. These functions include the primitives for the higher-level I/O functions described in Chapter 12 [Input/Output on Streams], page 248, as well as functions for performing low-level control operations for which there are no equivalents on streams.

Stream-level I/O is more flexible and usually more convenient; therefore, programmers generally use the descriptor-level functions only when necessary. These are some of the usual reasons:

- For reading binary files in large chunks.

- For reading an entire file into core before parsing it.

- To perform operations other than data transfer, which can only be done with a descriptor. (You can use `fileno` to get the descriptor corresponding to a stream.)

- To pass descriptors to a child process. (The child can create its own stream to use a descriptor that it inherits, but cannot inherit a stream directly.)

13.1 Opening and Closing Files

This section describes the primitives for opening and closing files using file descriptors. The `open` and `creat` functions are declared in the header file `fcntl.h`, while `close` is declared in `unistd.h`.

int **open** (*const char *filename*, *int* **flags**[, *mode_t* **mode**])   [Function]
Preliminary: | MT-Safe | AS-Safe | AC-Safe fd | See Section 1.2.2.1 [POSIX Safety Concepts], page 2.

The `open` function creates and returns a new file descriptor for the file named by *filename*. Initially, the file position indicator for the file is at the beginning of the file. The argument *mode* (see Section 14.9.5 [The Mode Bits for Access Permission], page 408) is used only when a file is created, but it doesn't hurt to supply the argument in any case.

The *flags* argument controls how the file is to be opened. This is a bit mask; you create the value by the bitwise OR of the appropriate parameters (using the '|' operator in C). See Section 13.14 [File Status Flags], page 363, for the parameters available.

The normal return value from `open` is a non-negative integer file descriptor. In the case of an error, a value of −1 is returned instead. In addition to the usual file name errors (see Section 11.2.3 [File Name Errors], page 246), the following `errno` error conditions are defined for this function:

EACCES   The file exists but is not readable/writable as requested by the *flags* argument, the file does not exist and the directory is unwritable so it cannot be created.

EEXIST   Both `O_CREAT` and `O_EXCL` are set, and the named file already exists.

EINTR   The `open` operation was interrupted by a signal. See Section 24.5 [Primitives Interrupted by Signals], page 687.

EISDIR   The *flags* argument specified write access, and the file is a directory.

EMFILE	The process has too many files open. The maximum number of file descriptors is controlled by the `RLIMIT_NOFILE` resource limit; see Section 22.2 [Limiting Resource Usage], page 632.
ENFILE	The entire system, or perhaps the file system which contains the directory, cannot support any additional open files at the moment. (This problem cannot happen on GNU/Hurd systems.)
ENOENT	The named file does not exist, and `O_CREAT` is not specified.
ENOSPC	The directory or file system that would contain the new file cannot be extended, because there is no disk space left.
ENXIO	`O_NONBLOCK` and `O_WRONLY` are both set in the *flags* argument, the file named by *filename* is a FIFO (see Chapter 15 [Pipes and FIFOs], page 424), and no process has the file open for reading.
EROFS	The file resides on a read-only file system and any of `O_WRONLY`, `O_RDWR`, and `O_TRUNC` are set in the *flags* argument, or `O_CREAT` is set and the file does not already exist.

If on a 32 bit machine the sources are translated with `_FILE_OFFSET_BITS == 64` the function **open** returns a file descriptor opened in the large file mode which enables the file handling functions to use files up to 2^63 bytes in size and offset from -2^63 to 2^63. This happens transparently for the user since all of the lowlevel file handling functions are equally replaced.

This function is a cancellation point in multi-threaded programs. This is a problem if the thread allocates some resources (like memory, file descriptors, semaphores or whatever) at the time **open** is called. If the thread gets canceled these resources stay allocated until the program ends. To avoid this calls to **open** should be protected using cancellation handlers.

The **open** function is the underlying primitive for the **fopen** and **freopen** functions, that create streams.

int **open64** (*const char *filename*, *int flags*[, *mode_t mode*])   [Function]
> Preliminary: | MT-Safe | AS-Safe | AC-Safe fd | See Section 1.2.2.1 [POSIX Safety Concepts], page 2.
>
> This function is similar to **open**. It returns a file descriptor which can be used to access the file named by *filename*. The only difference is that on 32 bit systems the file is opened in the large file mode. I.e., file length and file offsets can exceed 31 bits.
>
> When the sources are translated with `_FILE_OFFSET_BITS == 64` this function is actually available under the name **open**. I.e., the new, extended API using 64 bit file sizes and offsets transparently replaces the old API.

int **creat** (*const char *filename*, *mode_t mode*)   [Obsolete function]
> Preliminary: | MT-Safe | AS-Safe | AC-Safe fd | See Section 1.2.2.1 [POSIX Safety Concepts], page 2.
>
> This function is obsolete. The call:
>
>   creat (filename, mode)
>
> is equivalent to:

```
open (filename, O_WRONLY | O_CREAT | O_TRUNC, mode)
```

If on a 32 bit machine the sources are translated with `_FILE_OFFSET_BITS == 64` the function `creat` returns a file descriptor opened in the large file mode which enables the file handling functions to use files up to 2^63 in size and offset from -2^63 to 2^63. This happens transparently for the user since all of the lowlevel file handling functions are equally replaced.

int **creat64** (*const char *filename*, *mode_t mode*)   [Obsolete function]
Preliminary: | MT-Safe | AS-Safe | AC-Safe fd | See Section 1.2.2.1 [POSIX Safety Concepts], page 2.

This function is similar to `creat`. It returns a file descriptor which can be used to access the file named by *filename*. The only the difference is that on 32 bit systems the file is opened in the large file mode. I.e., file length and file offsets can exceed 31 bits.

To use this file descriptor one must not use the normal operations but instead the counterparts named *64, e.g., `read64`.

When the sources are translated with `_FILE_OFFSET_BITS == 64` this function is actually available under the name `open`. I.e., the new, extended API using 64 bit file sizes and offsets transparently replaces the old API.

int **close** (*int filedes*)   [Function]
Preliminary: | MT-Safe | AS-Safe | AC-Safe fd | See Section 1.2.2.1 [POSIX Safety Concepts], page 2.

The function `close` closes the file descriptor *filedes*. Closing a file has the following consequences:

- The file descriptor is deallocated.

- Any record locks owned by the process on the file are unlocked.

- When all file descriptors associated with a pipe or FIFO have been closed, any unread data is discarded.

This function is a cancellation point in multi-threaded programs. This is a problem if the thread allocates some resources (like memory, file descriptors, semaphores or whatever) at the time `close` is called. If the thread gets canceled these resources stay allocated until the program ends. To avoid this, calls to `close` should be protected using cancellation handlers.

The normal return value from `close` is 0; a value of -1 is returned in case of failure. The following `errno` error conditions are defined for this function:

EBADF   The *filedes* argument is not a valid file descriptor.

EINTR   The `close` call was interrupted by a signal. See Section 24.5 [Primitives
               Interrupted by Signals], page 687. Here is an example of how to handle
               EINTR properly:

```
TEMP_FAILURE_RETRY (close (desc));
```

```
ENOSPC
EIO
EDQUOT     When the file is accessed by NFS, these errors from write can some-
           times not be detected until close. See Section 13.2 [Input and Output
           Primitives], page 326, for details on their meaning.
```

Please note that there is *no* separate close64 function. This is not necessary since this function does not determine nor depend on the mode of the file. The kernel which performs the close operation knows which mode the descriptor is used for and can handle this situation.

To close a stream, call fclose (see Section 12.4 [Closing Streams], page 253) instead of trying to close its underlying file descriptor with close. This flushes any buffered output and updates the stream object to indicate that it is closed.

13.2 Input and Output Primitives

This section describes the functions for performing primitive input and output operations on file descriptors: read, write, and lseek. These functions are declared in the header file unistd.h.

ssize_t   [Data Type]
  This data type is used to represent the sizes of blocks that can be read or written in a single operation. It is similar to size_t, but must be a signed type.

ssize_t read (*int filedes*, *void *buffer*, *size_t size*)   [Function]
  Preliminary: | MT-Safe | AS-Safe | AC-Safe | See Section 1.2.2.1 [POSIX Safety Concepts], page 2.

  The read function reads up to *size* bytes from the file with descriptor *filedes*, storing the results in the *buffer*. (This is not necessarily a character string, and no terminating null character is added.)

  The return value is the number of bytes actually read. This might be less than *size*; for example, if there aren't that many bytes left in the file or if there aren't that many bytes immediately available. The exact behavior depends on what kind of file it is. Note that reading less than *size* bytes is not an error.

  A value of zero indicates end-of-file (except if the value of the *size* argument is also zero). This is not considered an error. If you keep calling read while at end-of-file, it will keep returning zero and doing nothing else.

  If read returns at least one character, there is no way you can tell whether end-of-file was reached. But if you did reach the end, the next read will return zero.

  In case of an error, read returns −1. The following errno error conditions are defined for this function:

EAGAIN   Normally, when no input is immediately available, read waits for some
           input. But if the O_NONBLOCK flag is set for the file (see Section 13.14
           [File Status Flags], page 363), read returns immediately without reading
           any data, and reports this error.

Compatibility Note: Most versions of BSD Unix use a different error code for this: EWOULDBLOCK. In the GNU C Library, EWOULDBLOCK is an alias for EAGAIN, so it doesn't matter which name you use.

On some systems, reading a large amount of data from a character special file can also fail with EAGAIN if the kernel cannot find enough physical memory to lock down the user's pages. This is limited to devices that transfer with direct memory access into the user's memory, which means it does not include terminals, since they always use separate buffers inside the kernel. This problem never happens on GNU/Hurd systems.

Any condition that could result in EAGAIN can instead result in a successful **read** which returns fewer bytes than requested. Calling **read** again immediately would result in EAGAIN.

EBADF   The *filedes* argument is not a valid file descriptor, or is not open for reading.

EINTR   **read** was interrupted by a signal while it was waiting for input. See Section 24.5 [Primitives Interrupted by Signals], page 687. A signal will not necessary cause **read** to return EINTR; it may instead result in a successful **read** which returns fewer bytes than requested.

EIO   For many devices, and for disk files, this error code indicates a hardware error.

            EIO also occurs when a background process tries to read from the controlling terminal, and the normal action of stopping the process by sending it a SIGTTIN signal isn't working. This might happen if the signal is being blocked or ignored, or because the process group is orphaned. See Chapter 28 [Job Control], page 763, for more information about job control, and Chapter 24 [Signal Handling], page 661, for information about signals.

EINVAL   In some systems, when reading from a character or block device, position and size offsets must be aligned to a particular block size. This error indicates that the offsets were not properly aligned.

Please note that there is no function named **read64**. This is not necessary since this function does not directly modify or handle the possibly wide file offset. Since the kernel handles this state internally, the **read** function can be used for all cases.

This function is a cancellation point in multi-threaded programs. This is a problem if the thread allocates some resources (like memory, file descriptors, semaphores or whatever) at the time **read** is called. If the thread gets canceled these resources stay allocated until the program ends. To avoid this, calls to **read** should be protected using cancellation handlers.

The **read** function is the underlying primitive for all of the functions that read from streams, such as **fgetc**.

ssize_t pread (*int* `filedes`, *void* `*buffer`, *size_t* `size`, *off_t* `offset`)   [Function]
        Preliminary: | MT-Safe | AS-Safe | AC-Safe | See Section 1.2.2.1 [POSIX Safety Concepts], page 2.

The **pread** function is similar to the **read** function. The first three arguments are identical, and the return values and error codes also correspond.

The difference is the fourth argument and its handling. The data block is not read from the current position of the file descriptor **filedes**. Instead the data is read from the file starting at position *offset*. The position of the file descriptor itself is not affected by the operation. The value is the same as before the call.

When the source file is compiled with _FILE_OFFSET_BITS == 64 the **pread** function is in fact **pread64** and the type **off_t** has 64 bits, which makes it possible to handle files up to 2^63 bytes in length.

The return value of **pread** describes the number of bytes read. In the error case it returns -1 like **read** does and the error codes are also the same, with these additions:

EINVAL   The value given for *offset* is negative and therefore illegal.

ESPIPE   The file descriptor *filedes* is associate with a pipe or a FIFO and this device does not allow positioning of the file pointer.

The function is an extension defined in the Unix Single Specification version 2.

ssize_t pread64 (*int* **filedes**, *void* ***buffer**, *size_t* **size**, *off64_t*   [Function]
      offset)
Preliminary: | MT-Safe | AS-Safe | AC-Safe | See Section 1.2.2.1 [POSIX Safety Concepts], page 2.

This function is similar to the **pread** function. The difference is that the *offset* parameter is of type **off64_t** instead of **off_t** which makes it possible on 32 bit machines to address files larger than 2^31 bytes and up to 2^63 bytes. The file descriptor **filedes** must be opened using **open64** since otherwise the large offsets possible with **off64_t** will lead to errors with a descriptor in small file mode.

When the source file is compiled with _FILE_OFFSET_BITS == 64 on a 32 bit machine this function is actually available under the name **pread** and so transparently replaces the 32 bit interface.

ssize_t write (*int* **filedes**, *const void* ***buffer**, *size_t* **size**)   [Function]
Preliminary: | MT-Safe | AS-Safe | AC-Safe | See Section 1.2.2.1 [POSIX Safety Concepts], page 2.

The **write** function writes up to *size* bytes from *buffer* to the file with descriptor *filedes*. The data in *buffer* is not necessarily a character string and a null character is output like any other character.

The return value is the number of bytes actually written. This may be *size*, but can always be smaller. Your program should always call **write** in a loop, iterating until all the data is written.

Once **write** returns, the data is enqueued to be written and can be read back right away, but it is not necessarily written out to permanent storage immediately. You can use **fsync** when you need to be sure your data has been permanently stored before continuing. (It is more efficient for the system to batch up consecutive writes and do them all at once when convenient. Normally they will always be written to disk within a minute or less.) Modern systems provide another function **fdatasync** which guarantees integrity only for the file data and is therefore faster. You can use the O_FSYNC open mode to make write always store the data to disk before returning; see Section 13.14.3 [I/O Operating Modes], page 366.

In the case of an error, write returns −1. The following errno error conditions are defined for this function:

EAGAIN   Normally, write blocks until the write operation is complete. But if the O_NONBLOCK flag is set for the file (see Section 13.11 [Control Operations on Files], page 359), it returns immediately without writing any data and reports this error. An example of a situation that might cause the process to block on output is writing to a terminal device that supports flow control, where output has been suspended by receipt of a STOP character.

            Compatibility Note: Most versions of BSD Unix use a different error code for this: EWOULDBLOCK. In the GNU C Library, EWOULDBLOCK is an alias for EAGAIN, so it doesn't matter which name you use.

            On some systems, writing a large amount of data from a character special file can also fail with EAGAIN if the kernel cannot find enough physical memory to lock down the user's pages. This is limited to devices that transfer with direct memory access into the user's memory, which means it does not include terminals, since they always use separate buffers inside the kernel. This problem does not arise on GNU/Hurd systems.

EBADF   The *filedes* argument is not a valid file descriptor, or is not open for writing.

EFBIG   The size of the file would become larger than the implementation can support.

EINTR   The write operation was interrupted by a signal while it was blocked waiting for completion. A signal will not necessarily cause write to return EINTR; it may instead result in a successful write which writes fewer bytes than requested. See Section 24.5 [Primitives Interrupted by Signals], page 687.

EIO   For many devices, and for disk files, this error code indicates a hardware error.

ENOSPC   The device containing the file is full.

EPIPE   This error is returned when you try to write to a pipe or FIFO that isn't open for reading by any process. When this happens, a SIGPIPE signal is also sent to the process; see Chapter 24 [Signal Handling], page 661.

EINVAL   In some systems, when writing to a character or block device, position and size offsets must be aligned to a particular block size. This error indicates that the offsets were not properly aligned.

Unless you have arranged to prevent EINTR failures, you should check errno after each failing call to write, and if the error was EINTR, you should simply repeat the call. See Section 24.5 [Primitives Interrupted by Signals], page 687. The easy way to do this is with the macro TEMP_FAILURE_RETRY, as follows:

```
nbytes = TEMP_FAILURE_RETRY (write (desc, buffer, count));
```

Please note that there is no function named **write64**. This is not necessary since this function does not directly modify or handle the possibly wide file offset. Since the kernel handles this state internally the **write** function can be used for all cases.

This function is a cancellation point in multi-threaded programs. This is a problem if the thread allocates some resources (like memory, file descriptors, semaphores or whatever) at the time **write** is called. If the thread gets canceled these resources stay allocated until the program ends. To avoid this, calls to **write** should be protected using cancellation handlers.

The **write** function is the underlying primitive for all of the functions that write to streams, such as **fputc**.

ssize_t pwrite (*int* **filedes**, *const void* ***buffer**, *size_t* **size**, *off_t*   [Function]
     offset)

Preliminary: | MT-Safe | AS-Safe | AC-Safe | See Section 1.2.2.1 [POSIX Safety Concepts], page 2.

The **pwrite** function is similar to the **write** function. The first three arguments are identical, and the return values and error codes also correspond.

The difference is the fourth argument and its handling. The data block is not written to the current position of the file descriptor **filedes**. Instead the data is written to the file starting at position *offset*. The position of the file descriptor itself is not affected by the operation. The value is the same as before the call.

When the source file is compiled with **_FILE_OFFSET_BITS == 64** the **pwrite** function is in fact **pwrite64** and the type **off_t** has 64 bits, which makes it possible to handle files up to 2^63 bytes in length.

The return value of **pwrite** describes the number of written bytes. In the error case it returns -1 like **write** does and the error codes are also the same, with these additions:

EINVAL   The value given for *offset* is negative and therefore illegal.

ESPIPE   The file descriptor *filedes* is associated with a pipe or a FIFO and this device does not allow positioning of the file pointer.

The function is an extension defined in the Unix Single Specification version 2.

ssize_t pwrite64 (*int* **filedes**, *const void* ***buffer**, *size_t* **size**,   [Function]
     off64_t **offset**)

Preliminary: | MT-Safe | AS-Safe | AC-Safe | See Section 1.2.2.1 [POSIX Safety Concepts], page 2.

This function is similar to the **pwrite** function. The difference is that the *offset* parameter is of type **off64_t** instead of **off_t** which makes it possible on 32 bit machines to address files larger than 2^31 bytes and up to 2^63 bytes. The file descriptor **filedes** must be opened using **open64** since otherwise the large offsets possible with **off64_t** will lead to errors with a descriptor in small file mode.

When the source file is compiled using **_FILE_OFFSET_BITS == 64** on a 32 bit machine this function is actually available under the name **pwrite** and so transparently replaces the 32 bit interface.

13.3 Setting the File Position of a Descriptor

Just as you can set the file position of a stream with **fseek**, you can set the file position of a descriptor with **lseek**. This specifies the position in the file for the next **read** or **write** operation. See Section 12.18 [File Positioning], page 305, for more information on the file position and what it means.

To read the current file position value from a descriptor, use **lseek** (*desc*, 0, SEEK_CUR).

off_t lseek (*int* **filedes**, *off_t* **offset**, *int* **whence**)   [Function]
    Preliminary: | MT-Safe | AS-Safe | AC-Safe | See Section 1.2.2.1 [POSIX Safety Concepts], page 2.

    The **lseek** function is used to change the file position of the file with descriptor *filedes*.

    The *whence* argument specifies how the *offset* should be interpreted, in the same way as for the **fseek** function, and it must be one of the symbolic constants SEEK_SET, SEEK_CUR, or SEEK_END.

    SEEK_SET   Specifies that *offset* is a count of characters from the beginning of the file.

    SEEK_CUR   Specifies that *offset* is a count of characters from the current file position. This count may be positive or negative.

    SEEK_END   Specifies that *offset* is a count of characters from the end of the file. A negative count specifies a position within the current extent of the file; a positive count specifies a position past the current end. If you set the position past the current end, and actually write data, you will extend the file with zeros up to that position.

    The return value from **lseek** is normally the resulting file position, measured in bytes from the beginning of the file. You can use this feature together with SEEK_CUR to read the current file position.

    If you want to append to the file, setting the file position to the current end of file with SEEK_END is not sufficient. Another process may write more data after you seek but before you write, extending the file so the position you write onto clobbers their data. Instead, use the O_APPEND operating mode; see Section 13.14.3 [I/O Operating Modes], page 366.

    You can set the file position past the current end of the file. This does not by itself make the file longer; **lseek** never changes the file. But subsequent output at that position will extend the file. Characters between the previous end of file and the new position are filled with zeros. Extending the file in this way can create a "hole": the blocks of zeros are not actually allocated on disk, so the file takes up less space than it appears to; it is then called a "sparse file".

    If the file position cannot be changed, or the operation is in some way invalid, **lseek** returns a value of −1. The following **errno** error conditions are defined for this function:

    EBADF   The *filedes* is not a valid file descriptor.

    EINVAL   The *whence* argument value is not valid, or the resulting file offset is not valid. A file offset is invalid.

ESPIPE The *filedes* corresponds to an object that cannot be positioned, such as a pipe, FIFO or terminal device. (POSIX.1 specifies this error only for pipes and FIFOs, but on GNU systems, you always get ESPIPE if the object is not seekable.)

When the source file is compiled with _FILE_OFFSET_BITS == 64 the lseek function is in fact lseek64 and the type off_t has 64 bits which makes it possible to handle files up to 2^63 bytes in length.

This function is a cancellation point in multi-threaded programs. This is a problem if the thread allocates some resources (like memory, file descriptors, semaphores or whatever) at the time lseek is called. If the thread gets canceled these resources stay allocated until the program ends. To avoid this calls to lseek should be protected using cancellation handlers.

The lseek function is the underlying primitive for the fseek, fseeko, ftell, ftello and rewind functions, which operate on streams instead of file descriptors.

off64_t lseek64 (*int* `filedes`, *off64_t* `offset`, *int* `whence`)   [Function]
Preliminary: | MT-Safe | AS-Safe | AC-Safe | See Section 1.2.2.1 [POSIX Safety Concepts], page 2.

This function is similar to the lseek function. The difference is that the *offset* parameter is of type off64_t instead of off_t which makes it possible on 32 bit machines to address files larger than 2^31 bytes and up to 2^63 bytes. The file descriptor **filedes** must be opened using **open64** since otherwise the large offsets possible with off64_t will lead to errors with a descriptor in small file mode.

When the source file is compiled with _FILE_OFFSET_BITS == 64 on a 32 bits machine this function is actually available under the name lseek and so transparently replaces the 32 bit interface.

You can have multiple descriptors for the same file if you open the file more than once, or if you duplicate a descriptor with **dup**. Descriptors that come from separate calls to **open** have independent file positions; using lseek on one descriptor has no effect on the other. For example,

```
{
  int d1, d2;
  char buf[4];
  d1 = open ("foo", O_RDONLY);
  d2 = open ("foo", O_RDONLY);
  lseek (d1, 1024, SEEK_SET);
  read (d2, buf, 4);
}
```

will read the first four characters of the file **foo**. (The error-checking code necessary for a real program has been omitted here for brevity.)

By contrast, descriptors made by duplication share a common file position with the original descriptor that was duplicated. Anything which alters the file position of one of the duplicates, including reading or writing data, affects all of them alike. Thus, for example,

```
{
  int d1, d2, d3;
  char buf1[4], buf2[4];
  d1 = open ("foo", O_RDONLY);
```

```
    d2 = dup (d1);
    d3 = dup (d2);
    lseek (d3, 1024, SEEK_SET);
    read (d1, buf1, 4);
    read (d2, buf2, 4);
}
```

will read four characters starting with the 1024'th character of `foo`, and then four more characters starting with the 1028'th character.

`off_t`   [Data Type]

> This is a signed integer type used to represent file sizes. In the GNU C Library, this type is no narrower than `int`.
>
> If the source is compiled with `_FILE_OFFSET_BITS == 64` this type is transparently replaced by `off64_t`.

`off64_t`   [Data Type]

> This type is used similar to `off_t`. The difference is that even on 32 bit machines, where the `off_t` type would have 32 bits, `off64_t` has 64 bits and so is able to address files up to 2^63 bytes in length.
>
> When compiling with `_FILE_OFFSET_BITS == 64` this type is available under the name `off_t`.

These aliases for the 'SEEK_...' constants exist for the sake of compatibility with older BSD systems. They are defined in two different header files: `fcntl.h` and `sys/file.h`.

`L_SET`   An alias for `SEEK_SET`.

`L_INCR`   An alias for `SEEK_CUR`.

`L_XTND`   An alias for `SEEK_END`.

13.4 Descriptors and Streams

Given an open file descriptor, you can create a stream for it with the `fdopen` function. You can get the underlying file descriptor for an existing stream with the `fileno` function. These functions are declared in the header file `stdio.h`.

`FILE * fdopen` (*int* `filedes`, *const char* `*opentype`)   [Function]

> Preliminary: | MT-Safe | AS-Unsafe heap lock | AC-Unsafe mem lock | See Section 1.2.2.1 [POSIX Safety Concepts], page 2.
>
> The `fdopen` function returns a new stream for the file descriptor *filedes*.
>
> The *opentype* argument is interpreted in the same way as for the `fopen` function (see Section 12.3 [Opening Streams], page 249), except that the 'b' option is not permitted; this is because GNU systems make no distinction between text and binary files. Also, `"w"` and `"w+"` do not cause truncation of the file; these have an effect only when opening a file, and in this case the file has already been opened. You must make sure that the *opentype* argument matches the actual mode of the open file descriptor.
>
> The return value is the new stream. If the stream cannot be created (for example, if the modes for the file indicated by the file descriptor do not permit the access specified by the *opentype* argument), a null pointer is returned instead.

In some other systems, **fdopen** may fail to detect that the modes for file descriptor do not permit the access specified by **opentype**. The GNU C Library always checks for this.

For an example showing the use of the **fdopen** function, see Section 15.1 [Creating a Pipe], page 424.

int fileno (*FILE *stream*)   [Function]
    Preliminary: | MT-Safe | AS-Safe | AC-Safe | See Section 1.2.2.1 [POSIX Safety Concepts], page 2.

    This function returns the file descriptor associated with the stream *stream*. If an error is detected (for example, if the *stream* is not valid) or if *stream* does not do I/O to a file, **fileno** returns −1.

int fileno_unlocked (*FILE *stream*)   [Function]
    Preliminary: | MT-Safe | AS-Safe | AC-Safe | See Section 1.2.2.1 [POSIX Safety Concepts], page 2.

    The **fileno_unlocked** function is equivalent to the **fileno** function except that it does not implicitly lock the stream if the state is **FSETLOCKING_INTERNAL**.

    This function is a GNU extension.

There are also symbolic constants defined in **unistd.h** for the file descriptors belonging to the standard streams **stdin**, **stdout**, and **stderr**; see Section 12.2 [Standard Streams], page 248.

STDIN_FILENO
        This macro has value 0, which is the file descriptor for standard input.

STDOUT_FILENO
        This macro has value 1, which is the file descriptor for standard output.

STDERR_FILENO
        This macro has value 2, which is the file descriptor for standard error output.

13.5 Dangers of Mixing Streams and Descriptors

You can have multiple file descriptors and streams (let's call both streams and descriptors "channels" for short) connected to the same file, but you must take care to avoid confusion between channels. There are two cases to consider: *linked* channels that share a single file position value, and *independent* channels that have their own file positions.

It's best to use just one channel in your program for actual data transfer to any given file, except when all the access is for input. For example, if you open a pipe (something you can only do at the file descriptor level), either do all I/O with the descriptor, or construct a stream from the descriptor with **fdopen** and then do all I/O with the stream.

13.5.1 Linked Channels

Channels that come from a single opening share the same file position; we call them *linked* channels. Linked channels result when you make a stream from a descriptor using **fdopen**, when you get a descriptor from a stream with **fileno**, when you copy a descriptor with dup or dup2, and when descriptors are inherited during fork. For files that don't support random access, such as terminals and pipes, *all* channels are effectively linked. On random-access files, all append-type output streams are effectively linked to each other.

If you have been using a stream for I/O (or have just opened the stream), and you want to do I/O using another channel (either a stream or a descriptor) that is linked to it, you must first *clean up* the stream that you have been using. See Section 13.5.3 [Cleaning Streams], page 335.

Terminating a process, or executing a new program in the process, destroys all the streams in the process. If descriptors linked to these streams persist in other processes, their file positions become undefined as a result. To prevent this, you must clean up the streams before destroying them.

13.5.2 Independent Channels

When you open channels (streams or descriptors) separately on a seekable file, each channel has its own file position. These are called *independent channels*.

The system handles each channel independently. Most of the time, this is quite predictable and natural (especially for input): each channel can read or write sequentially at its own place in the file. However, if some of the channels are streams, you must take these precautions:

- You should clean an output stream after use, before doing anything else that might read or write from the same part of the file.

- You should clean an input stream before reading data that may have been modified using an independent channel. Otherwise, you might read obsolete data that had been in the stream's buffer.

If you do output to one channel at the end of the file, this will certainly leave the other independent channels positioned somewhere before the new end. You cannot reliably set their file positions to the new end of file before writing, because the file can always be extended by another process between when you set the file position and when you write the data. Instead, use an append-type descriptor or stream; they always output at the current end of the file. In order to make the end-of-file position accurate, you must clean the output channel you were using, if it is a stream.

It's impossible for two channels to have separate file pointers for a file that doesn't support random access. Thus, channels for reading or writing such files are always linked, never independent. Append-type channels are also always linked. For these channels, follow the rules for linked channels; see Section 13.5.1 [Linked Channels], page 334.

13.5.3 Cleaning Streams

You can use fflush to clean a stream in most cases.

You can skip the fflush if you know the stream is already clean. A stream is clean whenever its buffer is empty. For example, an unbuffered stream is always clean. An input stream that is at end-of-file is clean. A line-buffered stream is clean when the last character output was a newline. However, a just-opened input stream might not be clean, as its input buffer might not be empty.

There is one case in which cleaning a stream is impossible on most systems. This is when the stream is doing input from a file that is not random-access. Such streams typically read ahead, and when the file is not random access, there is no way to give back the excess data already read. When an input stream reads from a random-access file, `fflush` does clean the stream, but leaves the file pointer at an unpredictable place; you must set the file pointer before doing any further I/O.

Closing an output-only stream also does `fflush`, so this is a valid way of cleaning an output stream.

You need not clean a stream before using its descriptor for control operations such as setting terminal modes; these operations don't affect the file position and are not affected by it. You can use any descriptor for these operations, and all channels are affected simultaneously. However, text already "output" to a stream but still buffered by the stream will be subject to the new terminal modes when subsequently flushed. To make sure "past" output is covered by the terminal settings that were in effect at the time, flush the output streams for that terminal before setting the modes. See Section 17.4 [Terminal Modes], page 479.

13.6 Fast Scatter-Gather I/O

Some applications may need to read or write data to multiple buffers, which are separated in memory. Although this can be done easily enough with multiple calls to `read` and `write`, it is inefficient because there is overhead associated with each kernel call.

Instead, many platforms provide special high-speed primitives to perform these *scatter-gather* operations in a single kernel call. The GNU C Library will provide an emulation on any system that lacks these primitives, so they are not a portability threat. They are defined in `sys/uio.h`.

These functions are controlled with arrays of `iovec` structures, which describe the location and size of each buffer.

`struct iovec`   [Data Type]
> The `iovec` structure describes a buffer. It contains two fields:
>
> `void *iov_base`
> > Contains the address of a buffer.
>
> `size_t iov_len`
> > Contains the length of the buffer.

`ssize_t readv (int filedes, const struct iovec *vector, int count)`   [Function]
> Preliminary: | MT-Safe | AS-Unsafe heap | AC-Unsafe mem | See Section 1.2.2.1 [POSIX Safety Concepts], page 2.
>
> The `readv` function reads data from *filedes* and scatters it into the buffers described in *vector*, which is taken to be *count* structures long. As each buffer is filled, data is sent to the next.
>
> Note that `readv` is not guaranteed to fill all the buffers. It may stop at any point, for the same reasons `read` would.
>
> The return value is a count of bytes (*not* buffers) read, 0 indicating end-of-file, or −1 indicating an error. The possible errors are the same as in `read`.

`ssize_t writev` (*int* `filedes`, *const struct iovec* `*vector`, *int* `count`)   [Function]
> Preliminary: | MT-Safe | AS-Unsafe heap | AC-Unsafe mem | See Section 1.2.2.1
> [POSIX Safety Concepts], page 2.
>
> The `writev` function gathers data from the buffers described in *vector*, which is taken
> to be *count* structures long, and writes them to `filedes`. As each buffer is written,
> it moves on to the next.
>
> Like `readv`, `writev` may stop midstream under the same conditions `write` would.
>
> The return value is a count of bytes written, or −1 indicating an error. The possible
> errors are the same as in `write`.

Note that if the buffers are small (under about 1kB), high-level streams may be easier to
use than these functions. However, `readv` and `writev` are more efficient when the individual
buffers themselves (as opposed to the total output), are large. In that case, a high-level
stream would not be able to cache the data effectively.

13.7 Memory-mapped I/O

On modern operating systems, it is possible to *mmap* (pronounced "em-map") a file to a
region of memory. When this is done, the file can be accessed just like an array in the
program.

This is more efficient than `read` or `write`, as only the regions of the file that a program
actually accesses are loaded. Accesses to not-yet-loaded parts of the mmapped region are
handled in the same way as swapped out pages.

Since mmapped pages can be stored back to their file when physical memory is low, it
is possible to mmap files orders of magnitude larger than both the physical memory *and*
swap space. The only limit is address space. The theoretical limit is 4GB on a 32-bit
machine - however, the actual limit will be smaller since some areas will be reserved for
other purposes. If the LFS interface is used the file size on 32-bit systems is not limited to
2GB (offsets are signed which reduces the addressable area of 4GB by half); the full 64-bit
are available.

Memory mapping only works on entire pages of memory. Thus, addresses for mapping
must be page-aligned, and length values will be rounded up. To determine the size of a
page the machine uses one should use

```
size_t page_size = (size_t) sysconf (_SC_PAGESIZE);
```

These functions are declared in `sys/mman.h`.

`void * mmap` (*void* `*address`, *size_t* `length`, *int* `protect`, *int* `flags`, *int*   [Function]
        `filedes`, *off_t* `offset`)
> Preliminary: | MT-Safe | AS-Safe | AC-Safe | See Section 1.2.2.1 [POSIX Safety
> Concepts], page 2.
>
> The `mmap` function creates a new mapping, connected to bytes (*offset*) to (*offset* +
> *length* - 1) in the file open on *filedes*. A new reference for the file specified by *filedes*
> is created, which is not removed by closing the file.
>
> *address* gives a preferred starting address for the mapping. `NULL` expresses no prefer-
> ence. Any previous mapping at that address is automatically removed. The address
> you give may still be changed, unless you use the `MAP_FIXED` flag.

protect contains flags that control what kind of access is permitted. They include `PROT_READ`, `PROT_WRITE`, and `PROT_EXEC`, which permit reading, writing, and execution, respectively. Inappropriate access will cause a segfault (see Section 24.2.1 [Program Error Signals], page 663).

Note that most hardware designs cannot support write permission without read permission, and many do not distinguish read and execute permission. Thus, you may receive wider permissions than you ask for, and mappings of write-only files may be denied even if you do not use `PROT_READ`.

flags contains flags that control the nature of the map. One of `MAP_SHARED` or `MAP_PRIVATE` must be specified.

They include:

`MAP_PRIVATE`

> This specifies that writes to the region should never be written back to the attached file. Instead, a copy is made for the process, and the region will be swapped normally if memory runs low. No other process will see the changes.

> Since private mappings effectively revert to ordinary memory when written to, you must have enough virtual memory for a copy of the entire mmapped region if you use this mode with `PROT_WRITE`.

`MAP_SHARED`

> This specifies that writes to the region will be written back to the file. Changes made will be shared immediately with other processes mmaping the same file.

> Note that actual writing may take place at any time. You need to use `msync`, described below, if it is important that other processes using conventional I/O get a consistent view of the file.

`MAP_FIXED`

> This forces the system to use the exact mapping address specified in *address* and fail if it can't.

`MAP_ANONYMOUS`
`MAP_ANON`   This flag tells the system to create an anonymous mapping, not connected to a file. *filedes* and *off* are ignored, and the region is initialized with zeros.

> Anonymous maps are used as the basic primitive to extend the heap on some systems. They are also useful to share data between multiple tasks without creating a file.

> On some systems using private anonymous mmaps is more efficient than using `malloc` for large blocks. This is not an issue with the GNU C Library, as the included `malloc` automatically uses `mmap` where appropriate.

`mmap` returns the address of the new mapping, or `MAP_FAILED` for an error.

Possible errors include:

`EINVAL`

> Either *address* was unusable, or inconsistent *flags* were given.

EACCES

> *filedes* was not open for the type of access specified in *protect*.

ENOMEM

> Either there is not enough memory for the operation, or the process is out of address space.

ENODEV

> This file is of a type that doesn't support mapping.

ENOEXEC

> The file is on a filesystem that doesn't support mapping.

void * **mmap64** (*void *address, size_t length, int protect, int flags,*   [Function]
> *int filedes, off64_t offset*)
> Preliminary: | MT-Safe | AS-Safe | AC-Safe | See Section 1.2.2.1 [POSIX Safety Concepts], page 2.

> The **mmap64** function is equivalent to the **mmap** function but the *offset* parameter is of type **off64_t**. On 32-bit systems this allows the file associated with the *filedes* descriptor to be larger than 2GB. *filedes* must be a descriptor returned from a call to **open64** or **fopen64** and **freopen64** where the descriptor is retrieved with **fileno**.

> When the sources are translated with **_FILE_OFFSET_BITS == 64** this function is actually available under the name **mmap**. I.e., the new, extended API using 64 bit file sizes and offsets transparently replaces the old API.

int **munmap** (*void *addr, size_t length*)   [Function]
> Preliminary: | MT-Safe | AS-Safe | AC-Safe | See Section 1.2.2.1 [POSIX Safety Concepts], page 2.

> **munmap** removes any memory maps from (*addr*) to (*addr + length*). *length* should be the length of the mapping.

> It is safe to unmap multiple mappings in one command, or include unmapped space in the range. It is also possible to unmap only part of an existing mapping. However, only entire pages can be removed. If *length* is not an even number of pages, it will be rounded up.

> It returns 0 for success and −1 for an error.

> One error is possible:

EINVAL   The memory range given was outside the user mmap range or wasn't page aligned.

int **msync** (*void *address, size_t length, int flags*)   [Function]
> Preliminary: | MT-Safe | AS-Safe | AC-Safe | See Section 1.2.2.1 [POSIX Safety Concepts], page 2.

> When using shared mappings, the kernel can write the file at any time before the mapping is removed. To be certain data has actually been written to the file and will be accessible to non-memory-mapped I/O, it is necessary to use this function.

It operates on the region *address* to (*address* + *length*). It may be used on part of a mapping or multiple mappings, however the region given should not contain any unmapped space.

flags can contain some options:

MS_SYNC

> This flag makes sure the data is actually written *to disk*. Normally `msync` only makes sure that accesses to a file with conventional I/O reflect the recent changes.

MS_ASYNC

> This tells `msync` to begin the synchronization, but not to wait for it to complete.

`msync` returns 0 for success and −1 for error. Errors include:

EINVAL   An invalid region was given, or the *flags* were invalid.

EFAULT   There is no existing mapping in at least part of the given region.

void * mremap (*void *address*, *size_t* **length**, *size_t* **new_length**, *int*   [Function]
        flag)
Preliminary: | MT-Safe | AS-Safe | AC-Safe | See Section 1.2.2.1 [POSIX Safety Concepts], page 2.

This function can be used to change the size of an existing memory area. *address* and *length* must cover a region entirely mapped in the same `mmap` statement. A new mapping with the same characteristics will be returned with the length *new_length*.

One option is possible, `MREMAP_MAYMOVE`. If it is given in *flags*, the system may remove the existing mapping and create a new one of the desired length in another location.

The address of the resulting mapping is returned, or −1. Possible error codes include:

EFAULT   There is no existing mapping in at least part of the original region, or the
            region covers two or more distinct mappings.

EINVAL   The address given is misaligned or inappropriate.

EAGAIN   The region has pages locked, and if extended it would exceed the process's
            resource limit for locked pages. See Section 22.2 [Limiting Resource Us-
            age], page 632.

ENOMEM   The region is private writable, and insufficient virtual memory is available
            to extend it. Also, this error will occur if `MREMAP_MAYMOVE` is not given
            and the extension would collide with another mapped region.

This function is only available on a few systems. Except for performing optional optimizations one should not rely on this function.

Not all file descriptors may be mapped. Sockets, pipes, and most devices only allow sequential access and do not fit into the mapping abstraction. In addition, some regular files may not be mmapable, and older kernels may not support mapping at all. Thus, programs using `mmap` should have a fallback method to use should it fail. See Section "Mmap" in *GNU Coding Standards*.

int madvise (*void *addr*, *size_t length*, *int advice*)   [Function]
>   Preliminary: | MT-Safe | AS-Safe | AC-Safe | See Section 1.2.2.1 [POSIX Safety
>   Concepts], page 2.
>
>   This function can be used to provide the system with *advice* about the intended usage
>   patterns of the memory region starting at *addr* and extending *length* bytes.
>
>   The valid BSD values for *advice* are:
>
>   MADV_NORMAL
>>   The region should receive no further special treatment.
>
>   MADV_RANDOM
>>   The region will be accessed via random page references. The kernel should
>>   page-in the minimal number of pages for each page fault.
>
>   MADV_SEQUENTIAL
>>   The region will be accessed via sequential page references. This may
>>   cause the kernel to aggressively read-ahead, expecting further sequential
>>   references after any page fault within this region.
>
>   MADV_WILLNEED
>>   The region will be needed. The pages within this region may be pre-
>>   faulted in by the kernel.
>
>   MADV_DONTNEED
>>   The region is no longer needed. The kernel may free these pages, causing
>>   any changes to the pages to be lost, as well as swapped out pages to be
>>   discarded.
>
>   The POSIX names are slightly different, but with the same meanings:
>
>   POSIX_MADV_NORMAL
>>   This corresponds with BSD's MADV_NORMAL.
>
>   POSIX_MADV_RANDOM
>>   This corresponds with BSD's MADV_RANDOM.
>
>   POSIX_MADV_SEQUENTIAL
>>   This corresponds with BSD's MADV_SEQUENTIAL.
>
>   POSIX_MADV_WILLNEED
>>   This corresponds with BSD's MADV_WILLNEED.
>
>   POSIX_MADV_DONTNEED
>>   This corresponds with BSD's MADV_DONTNEED.
>
>   madvise returns 0 for success and −1 for error. Errors include:
>
>   EINVAL   An invalid region was given, or the *advice* was invalid.
>
>   EFAULT   There is no existing mapping in at least part of the given region.

int shm_open (*const char *name*, *int oflag*, *mode_t mode*)   [Function]
>   Preliminary: | MT-Safe locale | AS-Unsafe init heap lock | AC-Unsafe lock mem fd
> | See Section 1.2.2.1 [POSIX Safety Concepts], page 2.

This function returns a file descriptor that can be used to allocate shared memory via mmap. Unrelated processes can use same *name* to create or open existing shared memory objects.

A *name* argument specifies the shared memory object to be opened. In the GNU C Library it must be a string smaller than `NAME_MAX` bytes starting with an optional slash but containing no other slashes.

The semantics of *oflag* and *mode* arguments is same as in `open`.

`shm_open` returns the file descriptor on success or −1 on error. On failure `errno` is set.

int shm_unlink (*const char *name*)   [Function]
> Preliminary: | MT-Safe locale | AS-Unsafe init heap lock | AC-Unsafe lock mem fd | See Section 1.2.2.1 [POSIX Safety Concepts], page 2.
>
> This function is inverse of `shm_open` and removes the object with the given *name* previously created by `shm_open`.
>
> `shm_unlink` returns 0 on success or −1 on error. On failure `errno` is set.

13.8 Waiting for Input or Output

Sometimes a program needs to accept input on multiple input channels whenever input arrives. For example, some workstations may have devices such as a digitizing tablet, function button box, or dial box that are connected via normal asynchronous serial interfaces; good user interface style requires responding immediately to input on any device. Another example is a program that acts as a server to several other processes via pipes or sockets.

You cannot normally use `read` for this purpose, because this blocks the program until input is available on one particular file descriptor; input on other channels won't wake it up. You could set nonblocking mode and poll each file descriptor in turn, but this is very inefficient.

A better solution is to use the `select` function. This blocks the program until input or output is ready on a specified set of file descriptors, or until a timer expires, whichever comes first. This facility is declared in the header file `sys/types.h`.

In the case of a server socket (see Section 16.9.2 [Listening for Connections], page 457), we say that "input" is available when there are pending connections that could be accepted (see Section 16.9.3 [Accepting Connections], page 457). `accept` for server sockets blocks and interacts with `select` just as `read` does for normal input.

The file descriptor sets for the `select` function are specified as `fd_set` objects. Here is the description of the data type and some macros for manipulating these objects.

fd_set   [Data Type]
> The `fd_set` data type represents file descriptor sets for the `select` function. It is actually a bit array.

int FD_SETSIZE   [Macro]
> The value of this macro is the maximum number of file descriptors that a `fd_set` object can hold information about. On systems with a fixed maximum number, `FD_SETSIZE` is at least that number. On some systems, including GNU, there is no

absolute limit on the number of descriptors open, but this macro still has a constant value which controls the number of bits in an `fd_set`; if you get a file descriptor with a value as high as `FD_SETSIZE`, you cannot put that descriptor into an `fd_set`.

void **FD_ZERO** (*fd_set *set*)   [Macro]
> Preliminary: | MT-Safe race:set | AS-Safe | AC-Safe | See Section 1.2.2.1 [POSIX Safety Concepts], page 2.
>
> This macro initializes the file descriptor set *set* to be the empty set.

void **FD_SET** (*int **filedes**, fd_set *set*)   [Macro]
> Preliminary: | MT-Safe race:set | AS-Safe | AC-Safe | See Section 1.2.2.1 [POSIX Safety Concepts], page 2.
>
> This macro adds *filedes* to the file descriptor set *set*.
>
> The *filedes* parameter must not have side effects since it is evaluated more than once.

void **FD_CLR** (*int **filedes**, fd_set *set*)   [Macro]
> Preliminary: | MT-Safe race:set | AS-Safe | AC-Safe | See Section 1.2.2.1 [POSIX Safety Concepts], page 2.
>
> This macro removes *filedes* from the file descriptor set *set*.
>
> The *filedes* parameter must not have side effects since it is evaluated more than once.

int **FD_ISSET** (*int **filedes**, const fd_set *set*)   [Macro]
> Preliminary: | MT-Safe race:set | AS-Safe | AC-Safe | See Section 1.2.2.1 [POSIX Safety Concepts], page 2.
>
> This macro returns a nonzero value (true) if *filedes* is a member of the file descriptor set *set*, and zero (false) otherwise.
>
> The *filedes* parameter must not have side effects since it is evaluated more than once.

Next, here is the description of the **select** function itself.

int **select** (*int **nfds**, fd_set ***read-fds**, fd_set ***write-fds**, fd_set*   [Function]
> ****except-fds**, struct timeval ***timeout**)
> Preliminary: | MT-Safe race:read-fds race:write-fds race:except-fds | AS-Safe | AC-Safe | See Section 1.2.2.1 [POSIX Safety Concepts], page 2.
>
> The **select** function blocks the calling process until there is activity on any of the specified sets of file descriptors, or until the timeout period has expired.
>
> The file descriptors specified by the *read-fds* argument are checked to see if they are ready for reading; the *write-fds* file descriptors are checked to see if they are ready for writing; and the *except-fds* file descriptors are checked for exceptional conditions. You can pass a null pointer for any of these arguments if you are not interested in checking for that kind of condition.
>
> A file descriptor is considered ready for reading if a **read** call will not block. This usually includes the read offset being at the end of the file or there is an error to report. A server socket is considered ready for reading if there is a pending connection which can be accepted with **accept**; see Section 16.9.3 [Accepting Connections], page 457. A client socket is ready for writing when its connection is fully established; see Section 16.9.1 [Making a Connection], page 456.

"Exceptional conditions" does not mean errors—errors are reported immediately when an erroneous system call is executed, and do not constitute a state of the descriptor. Rather, they include conditions such as the presence of an urgent message on a socket. (See Chapter 16 [Sockets], page 429, for information on urgent messages.)

The **select** function checks only the first *nfds* file descriptors. The usual thing is to pass **FD_SETSIZE** as the value of this argument.

The *timeout* specifies the maximum time to wait. If you pass a null pointer for this argument, it means to block indefinitely until one of the file descriptors is ready. Otherwise, you should provide the time in **struct timeval** format; see Section 21.4.2 [High-Resolution Calendar], page 600. Specify zero as the time (a **struct timeval** containing all zeros) if you want to find out which descriptors are ready without waiting if none are ready.

The normal return value from **select** is the total number of ready file descriptors in all of the sets. Each of the argument sets is overwritten with information about the descriptors that are ready for the corresponding operation. Thus, to see if a particular descriptor *desc* has input, use **FD_ISSET (*desc, read-fds*)** after **select** returns.

If **select** returns because the timeout period expires, it returns a value of zero.

Any signal will cause **select** to return immediately. So if your program uses signals, you can't rely on **select** to keep waiting for the full time specified. If you want to be sure of waiting for a particular amount of time, you must check for **EINTR** and repeat the **select** with a newly calculated timeout based on the current time. See the example below. See also Section 24.5 [Primitives Interrupted by Signals], page 687.

If an error occurs, **select** returns **-1** and does not modify the argument file descriptor sets. The following **errno** error conditions are defined for this function:

EBADF   One of the file descriptor sets specified an invalid file descriptor.

EINTR   The operation was interrupted by a signal. See Section 24.5 [Primitives Interrupted by Signals], page 687.

EINVAL   The *timeout* argument is invalid; one of the components is negative or too large.

Portability Note: The **select** function is a BSD Unix feature.

Here is an example showing how you can use **select** to establish a timeout period for reading from a file descriptor. The **input_timeout** function blocks the calling process until input is available on the file descriptor, or until the timeout period expires.

```
#include <errno.h>
#include <stdio.h>
#include <unistd.h>
#include <sys/types.h>
#include <sys/time.h>

int
input_timeout (int filedes, unsigned int seconds)
{
  fd_set set;
  struct timeval timeout;
```

```
   /* Initialize the file descriptor set. */
   FD_ZERO (&set);
   FD_SET (filedes, &set);

   /* Initialize the timeout data structure. */
   timeout.tv_sec = seconds;
   timeout.tv_usec = 0;

   /* select returns 0 if timeout, 1 if input available, -1 if error. */
   return TEMP_FAILURE_RETRY (select (FD_SETSIZE,
                                      &set, NULL, NULL,
                                      &timeout));
}

int
main (void)
{
  fprintf (stderr, "select returned %d.\n",
           input_timeout (STDIN_FILENO, 5));
  return 0;
}
```

There is another example showing the use of **select** to multiplex input from multiple sockets in Section 16.9.7 [Byte Stream Connection Server Example], page 462.

13.9 Synchronizing I/O operations

In most modern operating systems, the normal I/O operations are not executed synchronously. I.e., even if a **write** system call returns, this does not mean the data is actually written to the media, e.g., the disk.

In situations where synchronization points are necessary, you can use special functions which ensure that all operations finish before they return.

void sync (*void*)   [Function]
    Preliminary: | MT-Safe | AS-Safe | AC-Safe | See Section 1.2.2.1 [POSIX Safety Concepts], page 2.

    A call to this function will not return as long as there is data which has not been written to the device. All dirty buffers in the kernel will be written and so an overall consistent system can be achieved (if no other process in parallel writes data).

    A prototype for **sync** can be found in **unistd.h**.

Programs more often want to ensure that data written to a given file is committed, rather than all data in the system. For this, **sync** is overkill.

int fsync (*int fildes*)   [Function]
    Preliminary: | MT-Safe | AS-Safe | AC-Safe | See Section 1.2.2.1 [POSIX Safety Concepts], page 2.

    The **fsync** function can be used to make sure all data associated with the open file *fildes* is written to the device associated with the descriptor. The function call does not return unless all actions have finished.

    A prototype for **fsync** can be found in **unistd.h**.

This function is a cancellation point in multi-threaded programs. This is a problem if the thread allocates some resources (like memory, file descriptors, semaphores or whatever) at the time `fsync` is called. If the thread gets canceled these resources stay allocated until the program ends. To avoid this, calls to `fsync` should be protected using cancellation handlers.

The return value of the function is zero if no error occurred. Otherwise it is −1 and the global variable *errno* is set to the following values:

EBADF   The descriptor *fildes* is not valid.

EINVAL   No synchronization is possible since the system does not implement this.

Sometimes it is not even necessary to write all data associated with a file descriptor. E.g., in database files which do not change in size it is enough to write all the file content data to the device. Meta-information, like the modification time etc., are not that important and leaving such information uncommitted does not prevent a successful recovering of the file in case of a problem.

`int fdatasync (int fildes)`   [Function]
Preliminary: | MT-Safe | AS-Safe | AC-Safe | See Section 1.2.2.1 [POSIX Safety Concepts], page 2.

When a call to the `fdatasync` function returns, it is ensured that all of the file data is written to the device. For all pending I/O operations, the parts guaranteeing data integrity finished.

Not all systems implement the `fdatasync` operation. On systems missing this functionality `fdatasync` is emulated by a call to `fsync` since the performed actions are a superset of those required by `fdatasync`.

The prototype for `fdatasync` is in `unistd.h`.

The return value of the function is zero if no error occurred. Otherwise it is −1 and the global variable *errno* is set to the following values:

EBADF   The descriptor *fildes* is not valid.

EINVAL   No synchronization is possible since the system does not implement this.

13.10 Perform I/O Operations in Parallel

The POSIX.1b standard defines a new set of I/O operations which can significantly reduce the time an application spends waiting at I/O. The new functions allow a program to initiate one or more I/O operations and then immediately resume normal work while the I/O operations are executed in parallel. This functionality is available if the `unistd.h` file defines the symbol `_POSIX_ASYNCHRONOUS_IO`.

These functions are part of the library with realtime functions named `librt`. They are not actually part of the `libc` binary. The implementation of these functions can be done using support in the kernel (if available) or using an implementation based on threads at userlevel. In the latter case it might be necessary to link applications with the thread library `libpthread` in addition to `librt`.

All AIO operations operate on files which were opened previously. There might be arbitrarily many operations running for one file. The asynchronous I/O operations are controlled using a data structure named **struct aiocb** (*AIO control block*). It is defined in **aio.h** as follows.

struct aiocb   [Data Type]

The POSIX.1b standard mandates that the **struct aiocb** structure contains at least the members described in the following table. There might be more elements which are used by the implementation, but depending upon these elements is not portable and is highly deprecated.

int aio_fildes

This element specifies the file descriptor to be used for the operation. It must be a legal descriptor, otherwise the operation will fail.

The device on which the file is opened must allow the seek operation. I.e., it is not possible to use any of the AIO operations on devices like terminals where an **lseek** call would lead to an error.

off_t aio_offset

This element specifies the offset in the file at which the operation (input or output) is performed. Since the operations are carried out in arbitrary order and more than one operation for one file descriptor can be started, one cannot expect a current read/write position of the file descriptor.

volatile void *aio_buf

This is a pointer to the buffer with the data to be written or the place where the read data is stored.

size_t aio_nbytes

This element specifies the length of the buffer pointed to by **aio_buf**.

int aio_reqprio

If the platform has defined **_POSIX_PRIORITIZED_IO** and **_POSIX_PRIORITY_SCHEDULING**, the AIO requests are processed based on the current scheduling priority. The **aio_reqprio** element can then be used to lower the priority of the AIO operation.

struct sigevent aio_sigevent

This element specifies how the calling process is notified once the operation terminates. If the **sigev_notify** element is **SIGEV_NONE**, no notification is sent. If it is **SIGEV_SIGNAL**, the signal determined by **sigev_signo** is sent. Otherwise, **sigev_notify** must be **SIGEV_THREAD**. In this case, a thread is created which starts executing the function pointed to by **sigev_notify_function**.

int aio_lio_opcode

This element is only used by the **lio_listio** and **lio_listio64** functions. Since these functions allow an arbitrary number of operations to start at once, and each operation can be input or output (or nothing), the information must be stored in the control block. The possible values are:

LIO_READ Start a read operation. Read from the file at position aio_offset and store the next aio_nbytes bytes in the buffer pointed to by aio_buf.

LIO_WRITE

Start a write operation. Write aio_nbytes bytes starting at aio_buf into the file starting at position aio_offset.

LIO_NOP Do nothing for this control block. This value is useful sometimes when an array of struct aiocb values contains holes, i.e., some of the values must not be handled although the whole array is presented to the lio_listio function.

When the sources are compiled using _FILE_OFFSET_BITS == 64 on a 32 bit machine, this type is in fact struct aiocb64, since the LFS interface transparently replaces the struct aiocb definition.

For use with the AIO functions defined in the LFS, there is a similar type defined which replaces the types of the appropriate members with larger types but otherwise is equivalent to struct aiocb. Particularly, all member names are the same.

struct aiocb64 [Data Type]

int aio_fildes

This element specifies the file descriptor which is used for the operation. It must be a legal descriptor since otherwise the operation fails for obvious reasons.

The device on which the file is opened must allow the seek operation. I.e., it is not possible to use any of the AIO operations on devices like terminals where an lseek call would lead to an error.

off64_t aio_offset

This element specifies at which offset in the file the operation (input or output) is performed. Since the operation are carried in arbitrary order and more than one operation for one file descriptor can be started, one cannot expect a current read/write position of the file descriptor.

volatile void *aio_buf

This is a pointer to the buffer with the data to be written or the place where the read data is stored.

size_t aio_nbytes

This element specifies the length of the buffer pointed to by aio_buf.

int aio_reqprio

If for the platform _POSIX_PRIORITIZED_IO and _POSIX_PRIORITY_SCHEDULING are defined the AIO requests are processed based on the current scheduling priority. The aio_reqprio element can then be used to lower the priority of the AIO operation.

struct sigevent aio_sigevent

This element specifies how the calling process is notified once the operation terminates. If the sigev_notify, element is SIGEV_NONE no notification is sent. If it is SIGEV_SIGNAL, the signal determined by sigev_signo is sent. Otherwise, `sigev_notify` must be `SIGEV_THREAD` in which case a thread which starts executing the function pointed to by `sigev_notify_function`.

`int aio_lio_opcode`
> This element is only used by the `lio_listio` and [`lio_listio64` functions. Since these functions allow an arbitrary number of operations to start at once, and since each operation can be input or output (or nothing), the information must be stored in the control block. See the description of `struct aiocb` for a description of the possible values.

When the sources are compiled using `_FILE_OFFSET_BITS` == 64 on a 32 bit machine, this type is available under the name `struct aiocb64`, since the LFS transparently replaces the old interface.

13.10.1 Asynchronous Read and Write Operations

`int aio_read` (*struct aiocb *aiocbp*)   [Function]
> Preliminary: | MT-Safe | AS-Unsafe lock heap | AC-Unsafe lock mem | See Section 1.2.2.1 [POSIX Safety Concepts], page 2.

This function initiates an asynchronous read operation. It immediately returns after the operation was enqueued or when an error was encountered.

The first `aiocbp->aio_nbytes` bytes of the file for which `aiocbp->aio_fildes` is a descriptor are written to the buffer starting at `aiocbp->aio_buf`. Reading starts at the absolute position `aiocbp->aio_offset` in the file.

If prioritized I/O is supported by the platform the `aiocbp->aio_reqprio` value is used to adjust the priority before the request is actually enqueued.

The calling process is notified about the termination of the read request according to the `aiocbp->aio_sigevent` value.

When `aio_read` returns, the return value is zero if no error occurred that can be found before the process is enqueued. If such an early error is found, the function returns −1 and sets `errno` to one of the following values:

`EAGAIN`
> The request was not enqueued due to (temporarily) exceeded resource limitations.

`ENOSYS`
> The `aio_read` function is not implemented.

`EBADF`
> The `aiocbp->aio_fildes` descriptor is not valid. This condition need not be recognized before enqueueing the request and so this error might also be signaled asynchronously.

`EINVAL`
> The `aiocbp->aio_offset` or `aiocbp->aio_reqpiro` value is invalid. This condition need not be recognized before enqueueing the request and so this error might also be signaled asynchronously.

If `aio_read` returns zero, the current status of the request can be queried using `aio_error` and `aio_return` functions. As long as the value returned by `aio_error` is `EINPROGRESS` the operation has not yet completed. If `aio_error` returns zero, the operation successfully terminated, otherwise the value is to be interpreted as an error code. If the function terminated, the result of the operation can be obtained using a call to `aio_return`. The returned value is the same as an equivalent call to `read` would have returned. Possible error codes returned by `aio_error` are:

EBADF   The `aiocbp->aio_fildes` descriptor is not valid.

ECANCELED

            The operation was canceled before the operation was finished (see Section 13.10.4 [Cancellation of AIO Operations], page 356)

EINVAL   The `aiocbp->aio_offset` value is invalid.

When the sources are compiled with `_FILE_OFFSET_BITS == 64` this function is in fact `aio_read64` since the LFS interface transparently replaces the normal implementation.

int `aio_read64` (*struct aiocb64 *aiocbp*)   [Function]
      Preliminary: | MT-Safe | AS-Unsafe lock heap | AC-Unsafe lock mem | See Section 1.2.2.1 [POSIX Safety Concepts], page 2.

      This function is similar to the `aio_read` function. The only difference is that on 32 bit machines, the file descriptor should be opened in the large file mode. Internally, `aio_read64` uses functionality equivalent to `lseek64` (see Section 13.3 [Setting the File Position of a Descriptor], page 331) to position the file descriptor correctly for the reading, as opposed to `lseek` functionality used in `aio_read`.

      When the sources are compiled with `_FILE_OFFSET_BITS == 64`, this function is available under the name `aio_read` and so transparently replaces the interface for small files on 32 bit machines.

To write data asynchronously to a file, there exists an equivalent pair of functions with a very similar interface.

int `aio_write` (*struct aiocb *aiocbp*)   [Function]
      Preliminary: | MT-Safe | AS-Unsafe lock heap | AC-Unsafe lock mem | See Section 1.2.2.1 [POSIX Safety Concepts], page 2.

      This function initiates an asynchronous write operation. The function call immediately returns after the operation was enqueued or if before this happens an error was encountered.

      The first `aiocbp->aio_nbytes` bytes from the buffer starting at `aiocbp->aio_buf` are written to the file for which `aiocbp->aio_fildes` is a descriptor, starting at the absolute position `aiocbp->aio_offset` in the file.

      If prioritized I/O is supported by the platform, the `aiocbp->aio_reqprio` value is used to adjust the priority before the request is actually enqueued.

      The calling process is notified about the termination of the read request according to the `aiocbp->aio_sigevent` value.

      When `aio_write` returns, the return value is zero if no error occurred that can be found before the process is enqueued. If such an early error is found the function returns −1 and sets `errno` to one of the following values.

EAGAIN   The request was not enqueued due to (temporarily) exceeded resource limitations.

ENOSYS   The `aio_write` function is not implemented.

EBADF   The `aiocbp->aio_fildes` descriptor is not valid. This condition may not be recognized before enqueueing the request, and so this error might also be signaled asynchronously.

EINVAL   The `aiocbp->aio_offset` or `aiocbp->aio_reqprio` value is invalid. This condition may not be recognized before enqueueing the request and so this error might also be signaled asynchronously.

In the case `aio_write` returns zero, the current status of the request can be queried using `aio_error` and `aio_return` functions. As long as the value returned by `aio_error` is `EINPROGRESS` the operation has not yet completed. If `aio_error` returns zero, the operation successfully terminated, otherwise the value is to be interpreted as an error code. If the function terminated, the result of the operation can be get using a call to `aio_return`. The returned value is the same as an equivalent call to `read` would have returned. Possible error codes returned by `aio_error` are:

EBADF   The `aiocbp->aio_fildes` descriptor is not valid.

ECANCELED

              The operation was canceled before the operation was finished. (see Section 13.10.4 [Cancellation of AIO Operations], page 356)

EINVAL   The `aiocbp->aio_offset` value is invalid.

When the sources are compiled with `_FILE_OFFSET_BITS == 64`, this function is in fact `aio_write64` since the LFS interface transparently replaces the normal implementation.

`int aio_write64 (struct aiocb64 *aiocbp)`   [Function]
Preliminary: | MT-Safe | AS-Unsafe lock heap | AC-Unsafe lock mem | See Section 1.2.2.1 [POSIX Safety Concepts], page 2.

This function is similar to the `aio_write` function. The only difference is that on 32 bit machines the file descriptor should be opened in the large file mode. Internally `aio_write64` uses functionality equivalent to `lseek64` (see Section 13.3 [Setting the File Position of a Descriptor], page 331) to position the file descriptor correctly for the writing, as opposed to `lseek` functionality used in `aio_write`.

When the sources are compiled with `_FILE_OFFSET_BITS == 64`, this function is available under the name `aio_write` and so transparently replaces the interface for small files on 32 bit machines.

Besides these functions with the more or less traditional interface, POSIX.1b also defines a function which can initiate more than one operation at a time, and which can handle freely mixed read and write operations. It is therefore similar to a combination of `readv` and `writev`.

`int lio_listio (int mode, struct aiocb *const list[], int nent, struct`   [Function]
`        sigevent *sig)`
Preliminary: | MT-Safe | AS-Unsafe lock heap | AC-Unsafe lock mem | See Section 1.2.2.1 [POSIX Safety Concepts], page 2.

The `lio_listio` function can be used to enqueue an arbitrary number of read and write requests at one time. The requests can all be meant for the same file, all for different files or every solution in between.

`lio_listio` gets the *nent* requests from the array pointed to by *list*. The operation to be performed is determined by the `aio_lio_opcode` member in each element of *list*. If this field is `LIO_READ` a read operation is enqueued, similar to a call of `aio_read` for this element of the array (except that the way the termination is signalled is different, as we will see below). If the `aio_lio_opcode` member is `LIO_WRITE` a write operation is enqueued. Otherwise the `aio_lio_opcode` must be `LIO_NOP` in which case this element of *list* is simply ignored. This "operation" is useful in situations where one has a fixed array of `struct aiocb` elements from which only a few need to be handled at a time. Another situation is where the `lio_listio` call was canceled before all requests are processed (see Section 13.10.4 [Cancellation of AIO Operations], page 356) and the remaining requests have to be reissued.

The other members of each element of the array pointed to by `list` must have values suitable for the operation as described in the documentation for `aio_read` and `aio_write` above.

The *mode* argument determines how `lio_listio` behaves after having enqueued all the requests. If *mode* is `LIO_WAIT` it waits until all requests terminated. Otherwise *mode* must be `LIO_NOWAIT` and in this case the function returns immediately after having enqueued all the requests. In this case the caller gets a notification of the termination of all requests according to the *sig* parameter. If *sig* is `NULL` no notification is send. Otherwise a signal is sent or a thread is started, just as described in the description for `aio_read` or `aio_write`.

If *mode* is `LIO_WAIT`, the return value of `lio_listio` is 0 when all requests completed successfully. Otherwise the function return -1 and `errno` is set accordingly. To find out which request or requests failed one has to use the `aio_error` function on all the elements of the array *list*.

In case *mode* is `LIO_NOWAIT`, the function returns 0 if all requests were enqueued correctly. The current state of the requests can be found using `aio_error` and `aio_return` as described above. If `lio_listio` returns -1 in this mode, the global variable `errno` is set accordingly. If a request did not yet terminate, a call to `aio_error` returns `EINPROGRESS`. If the value is different, the request is finished and the error value (or 0) is returned and the result of the operation can be retrieved using `aio_return`.

Possible values for `errno` are:

EAGAIN   The resources necessary to queue all the requests are not available at the moment. The error status for each element of *list* must be checked to determine which request failed.

Another reason could be that the system wide limit of AIO requests is exceeded. This cannot be the case for the implementation on GNU systems since no arbitrary limits exist.

EINVAL   The *mode* parameter is invalid or *nent* is larger than `AIO_LISTIO_MAX`.

EIO   One or more of the request's I/O operations failed. The error status of each request should be checked to determine which one failed.

ENOSYS   The `lio_listio` function is not supported.

If the *mode* parameter is `LIO_NOWAIT` and the caller cancels a request, the error status for this request returned by `aio_error` is `ECANCELED`.

When the sources are compiled with `_FILE_OFFSET_BITS == 64`, this function is in fact `lio_listio64` since the LFS interface transparently replaces the normal implementation.

int **lio_listio64** (*int* **mode**, *struct aiocb64 *const* **list**[], *int* **nent**,   [Function]
        *struct sigevent *****sig***)

Preliminary: | MT-Safe | AS-Unsafe lock heap | AC-Unsafe lock mem | See Section 1.2.2.1 [POSIX Safety Concepts], page 2.

This function is similar to the `lio_listio` function. The only difference is that on 32 bit machines, the file descriptor should be opened in the large file mode. Internally, `lio_listio64` uses functionality equivalent to `lseek64` (see Section 13.3 [Setting the File Position of a Descriptor], page 331) to position the file descriptor correctly for the reading or writing, as opposed to `lseek` functionality used in `lio_listio`.

When the sources are compiled with `_FILE_OFFSET_BITS == 64`, this function is available under the name `lio_listio` and so transparently replaces the interface for small files on 32 bit machines.

13.10.2 Getting the Status of AIO Operations

As already described in the documentation of the functions in the last section, it must be possible to get information about the status of an I/O request. When the operation is performed truly asynchronously (as with `aio_read` and `aio_write` and with `lio_listio` when the mode is `LIO_NOWAIT`), one sometimes needs to know whether a specific request already terminated and if so, what the result was. The following two functions allow you to get this kind of information.

int **aio_error** (*const struct aiocb ****aiocbp*)   [Function]

Preliminary: | MT-Safe | AS-Safe | AC-Safe | See Section 1.2.2.1 [POSIX Safety Concepts], page 2.

This function determines the error state of the request described by the **struct aiocb** variable pointed to by *aiocbp*. If the request has not yet terminated the value returned is always `EINPROGRESS`. Once the request has terminated the value `aio_error` returns is either 0 if the request completed successfully or it returns the value which would be stored in the **errno** variable if the request would have been done using **read**, **write**, or **fsync**.

The function can return `ENOSYS` if it is not implemented. It could also return `EINVAL` if the *aiocbp* parameter does not refer to an asynchronous operation whose return status is not yet known.

When the sources are compiled with `_FILE_OFFSET_BITS == 64` this function is in fact `aio_error64` since the LFS interface transparently replaces the normal implementation.

int **aio_error64** (*const struct aiocb64 ****aiocbp*)   [Function]

Preliminary: | MT-Safe | AS-Safe | AC-Safe | See Section 1.2.2.1 [POSIX Safety Concepts], page 2.

This function is similar to `aio_error` with the only difference that the argument is a reference to a variable of type `struct aiocb64`.

When the sources are compiled with `_FILE_OFFSET_BITS == 64` this function is available under the name `aio_error` and so transparently replaces the interface for small files on 32 bit machines.

`ssize_t aio_return (struct aiocb *aiocbp)`   [Function]
> Preliminary: | MT-Safe | AS-Safe | AC-Safe | See Section 1.2.2.1 [POSIX Safety Concepts], page 2.
>
> This function can be used to retrieve the return status of the operation carried out by the request described in the variable pointed to by *aiocbp*. As long as the error status of this request as returned by `aio_error` is `EINPROGRESS` the return of this function is undefined.
>
> Once the request is finished this function can be used exactly once to retrieve the return value. Following calls might lead to undefined behavior. The return value itself is the value which would have been returned by the `read`, `write`, or `fsync` call.
>
> The function can return `ENOSYS` if it is not implemented. It could also return `EINVAL` if the *aiocbp* parameter does not refer to an asynchronous operation whose return status is not yet known.
>
> When the sources are compiled with `_FILE_OFFSET_BITS == 64` this function is in fact `aio_return64` since the LFS interface transparently replaces the normal implementation.

`ssize_t aio_return64 (struct aiocb64 *aiocbp)`   [Function]
> Preliminary: | MT-Safe | AS-Safe | AC-Safe | See Section 1.2.2.1 [POSIX Safety Concepts], page 2.
>
> This function is similar to `aio_return` with the only difference that the argument is a reference to a variable of type `struct aiocb64`.
>
> When the sources are compiled with `_FILE_OFFSET_BITS == 64` this function is available under the name `aio_return` and so transparently replaces the interface for small files on 32 bit machines.

13.10.3 Getting into a Consistent State

When dealing with asynchronous operations it is sometimes necessary to get into a consistent state. This would mean for AIO that one wants to know whether a certain request or a group of request were processed. This could be done by waiting for the notification sent by the system after the operation terminated, but this sometimes would mean wasting resources (mainly computation time). Instead POSIX.1b defines two functions which will help with most kinds of consistency.

The `aio_fsync` and `aio_fsync64` functions are only available if the symbol `_POSIX_SYNCHRONIZED_IO` is defined in `unistd.h`.

`int aio_fsync (int op, struct aiocb *aiocbp)`   [Function]
> Preliminary: | MT-Safe | AS-Unsafe lock heap | AC-Unsafe lock mem | See Section 1.2.2.1 [POSIX Safety Concepts], page 2.

Calling this function forces all I/O operations operating queued at the time of the function call operating on the file descriptor `aiocbp->aio_fildes` into the synchronized I/O completion state (see Section 13.9 [Synchronizing I/O operations], page 345). The `aio_fsync` function returns immediately but the notification through the method described in `aiocbp->aio_sigevent` will happen only after all requests for this file descriptor have terminated and the file is synchronized. This also means that requests for this very same file descriptor which are queued after the synchronization request are not affected.

If *op* is `O_DSYNC` the synchronization happens as with a call to `fdatasync`. Otherwise *op* should be `O_SYNC` and the synchronization happens as with `fsync`.

As long as the synchronization has not happened, a call to `aio_error` with the reference to the object pointed to by *aiocbp* returns `EINPROGRESS`. Once the synchronization is done `aio_error` return 0 if the synchronization was not successful. Otherwise the value returned is the value to which the `fsync` or `fdatasync` function would have set the `errno` variable. In this case nothing can be assumed about the consistency for the data written to this file descriptor.

The return value of this function is 0 if the request was successfully enqueued. Otherwise the return value is −1 and `errno` is set to one of the following values:

`EAGAIN`   The request could not be enqueued due to temporary lack of resources.

`EBADF`   The file descriptor `aiocbp->aio_fildes` is not valid.

`EINVAL`   The implementation does not support I/O synchronization or the *op* parameter is other than `O_DSYNC` and `O_SYNC`.

`ENOSYS`   This function is not implemented.

When the sources are compiled with `_FILE_OFFSET_BITS == 64` this function is in fact `aio_fsync64` since the LFS interface transparently replaces the normal implementation.

`int aio_fsync64` (*int op, struct aiocb64 *`aiocbp`)   [Function]
Preliminary: | MT-Safe | AS-Unsafe lock heap | AC-Unsafe lock mem | See Section 1.2.2.1 [POSIX Safety Concepts], page 2.

This function is similar to `aio_fsync` with the only difference that the argument is a reference to a variable of type `struct aiocb64`.

When the sources are compiled with `_FILE_OFFSET_BITS == 64` this function is available under the name `aio_fsync` and so transparently replaces the interface for small files on 32 bit machines.

Another method of synchronization is to wait until one or more requests of a specific set terminated. This could be achieved by the `aio_*` functions to notify the initiating process about the termination but in some situations this is not the ideal solution. In a program which constantly updates clients somehow connected to the server it is not always the best solution to go round robin since some connections might be slow. On the other hand letting the `aio_*` function notify the caller might also be not the best solution since whenever the process works on preparing data for on client it makes no sense to be interrupted by a notification since the new client will not be handled before the current client is served. For situations like this `aio_suspend` should be used.

int aio_suspend (*const struct aiocb *const* `list[]`, *int* **nent**, *const*   [Function]
    *struct timespec ****timeout***)

Preliminary: | MT-Safe | AS-Unsafe lock | AC-Unsafe lock | See Section 1.2.2.1
[POSIX Safety Concepts], page 2.

When calling this function, the calling thread is suspended until at least one of the
requests pointed to by the *nent* elements of the array *list* has completed. If any of
the requests has already completed at the time `aio_suspend` is called, the function
returns immediately. Whether a request has terminated or not is determined by
comparing the error status of the request with `EINPROGRESS`. If an element of *list* is
`NULL`, the entry is simply ignored.

If no request has finished, the calling process is suspended. If *timeout* is `NULL`, the
process is not woken until a request has finished. If *timeout* is not `NULL`, the process
remains suspended at least as long as specified in *timeout*. In this case, `aio_suspend`
returns with an error.

The return value of the function is 0 if one or more requests from the *list* have
terminated. Otherwise the function returns −1 and `errno` is set to one of the following
values:

`EAGAIN`   None of the requests from the *list* completed in the time specified by
             timeout.

`EINTR`   A signal interrupted the `aio_suspend` function. This signal might also
             be sent by the AIO implementation while signalling the termination of
             one of the requests.

`ENOSYS`   The `aio_suspend` function is not implemented.

When the sources are compiled with `_FILE_OFFSET_BITS == 64` this function is in
fact `aio_suspend64` since the LFS interface transparently replaces the normal implementation.

int aio_suspend64 (*const struct aiocb64 *const* `list[]`, *int* **nent**, *const*   [Function]
        *struct timespec ****timeout***)

Preliminary: | MT-Safe | AS-Unsafe lock | AC-Unsafe lock | See Section 1.2.2.1
[POSIX Safety Concepts], page 2.

This function is similar to `aio_suspend` with the only difference that the argument
is a reference to a variable of type `struct aiocb64`.

When the sources are compiled with `_FILE_OFFSET_BITS == 64` this function is available under the name `aio_suspend` and so transparently replaces the interface for
small files on 32 bit machines.

13.10.4 Cancellation of AIO Operations

When one or more requests are asynchronously processed, it might be useful in some situations to cancel a selected operation, e.g., if it becomes obvious that the written data
is no longer accurate and would have to be overwritten soon. As an example, assume an
application, which writes data in files in a situation where new incoming data would have
to be written in a file which will be updated by an enqueued request. The POSIX AIO
implementation provides such a function, but this function is not capable of forcing the

cancellation of the request. It is up to the implementation to decide whether it is possible
to cancel the operation or not. Therefore using this function is merely a hint.

int aio_cancel (*int **fildes**, struct aiocb ***aiocbp**)   [Function]
    Preliminary: | MT-Safe | AS-Unsafe lock heap | AC-Unsafe lock mem | See
    Section 1.2.2.1 [POSIX Safety Concepts], page 2.

    The **aio_cancel** function can be used to cancel one or more outstanding requests.
    If the *aiocbp* parameter is **NULL**, the function tries to cancel all of the outstanding
    requests which would process the file descriptor *fildes* (i.e., whose **aio_fildes** member
    is *fildes*). If *aiocbp* is not **NULL**, **aio_cancel** attempts to cancel the specific request
    pointed to by *aiocbp*.

    For requests which were successfully canceled, the normal notification about the ter-
    mination of the request should take place. I.e., depending on the **struct sigevent**
    object which controls this, nothing happens, a signal is sent or a thread is started.
    If the request cannot be canceled, it terminates the usual way after performing the
    operation.

    After a request is successfully canceled, a call to **aio_error** with a reference to this
    request as the parameter will return **ECANCELED** and a call to **aio_return** will re-
    turn −1. If the request wasn't canceled and is still running the error status is still
    EINPROGRESS.

    The return value of the function is **AIO_CANCELED** if there were requests which haven't
    terminated and which were successfully canceled. If there is one or more requests left
    which couldn't be canceled, the return value is **AIO_NOTCANCELED**. In this case **aio_**
    error must be used to find out which of the, perhaps multiple, requests (in *aiocbp*
    is **NULL**) weren't successfully canceled. If all requests already terminated at the time
    aio_cancel is called the return value is **AIO_ALLDONE**.

    If an error occurred during the execution of **aio_cancel** the function returns −1 and
    sets **errno** to one of the following values.

    EBADF   The file descriptor *fildes* is not valid.

    ENOSYS   **aio_cancel** is not implemented.

    When the sources are compiled with **_FILE_OFFSET_BITS == 64**, this function is in
    fact **aio_cancel64** since the LFS interface transparently replaces the normal imple-
    mentation.

int aio_cancel64 (*int **fildes**, struct aiocb64 ***aiocbp**)   [Function]
    Preliminary: | MT-Safe | AS-Unsafe lock heap | AC-Unsafe lock mem | See
    Section 1.2.2.1 [POSIX Safety Concepts], page 2.

    This function is similar to **aio_cancel** with the only difference that the argument is
    a reference to a variable of type **struct aiocb64**.

    When the sources are compiled with **_FILE_OFFSET_BITS == 64**, this function is avail-
    able under the name **aio_cancel** and so transparently replaces the interface for small
    files on 32 bit machines.

13.10.5 How to optimize the AIO implementation

The POSIX standard does not specify how the AIO functions are implemented. They could be system calls, but it is also possible to emulate them at userlevel.

At the point of this writing, the available implementation is a userlevel implementation which uses threads for handling the enqueued requests. While this implementation requires making some decisions about limitations, hard limitations are something which is best avoided in the GNU C Library. Therefore, the GNU C Library provides a means for tuning the AIO implementation according to the individual use.

struct aioinit   [Data Type]

This data type is used to pass the configuration or tunable parameters to the implementation. The program has to initialize the members of this struct and pass it to the implementation using the **aio_init** function.

int aio_threads

This member specifies the maximal number of threads which may be used at any one time.

int aio_num

This number provides an estimate on the maximal number of simultaneously enqueued requests.

int aio_locks

Unused.

int aio_usedba

Unused.

int aio_debug

Unused.

int aio_numusers

Unused.

int aio_reserved[2]

Unused.

void aio_init (*const struct aioinit *init*)   [Function]

Preliminary: | MT-Safe | AS-Unsafe lock | AC-Unsafe lock | See Section 1.2.2.1 [POSIX Safety Concepts], page 2.

This function must be called before any other AIO function. Calling it is completely voluntary, as it is only meant to help the AIO implementation perform better.

Before calling the **aio_init**, function the members of a variable of type **struct aioinit** must be initialized. Then a reference to this variable is passed as the parameter to **aio_init** which itself may or may not pay attention to the hints.

The function has no return value and no error cases are defined. It is a extension which follows a proposal from the SGI implementation in Irix 6. It is not covered by POSIX.1b or Unix98.

13.11 Control Operations on Files

This section describes how you can perform various other operations on file descriptors, such as inquiring about or setting flags describing the status of the file descriptor, manipulating record locks, and the like. All of these operations are performed by the function fcntl.

The second argument to the fcntl function is a command that specifies which operation to perform. The function and macros that name various flags that are used with it are declared in the header file fcntl.h. Many of these flags are also used by the open function; see Section 13.1 [Opening and Closing Files], page 323.

int fcntl (*int filedes*, *int command*, ...)   [Function]
    Preliminary: | MT-Safe | AS-Safe | AC-Safe | See Section 1.2.2.1 [POSIX Safety Concepts], page 2.

    The fcntl function performs the operation specified by *command* on the file descriptor *filedes*. Some commands require additional arguments to be supplied. These additional arguments and the return value and error conditions are given in the detailed descriptions of the individual commands.

    Briefly, here is a list of what the various commands are.

    F_DUPFD   Duplicate the file descriptor (return another file descriptor pointing to the same open file). See Section 13.12 [Duplicating Descriptors], page 360.

    F_GETFD   Get flags associated with the file descriptor. See Section 13.13 [File Descriptor Flags], page 361.

    F_SETFD   Set flags associated with the file descriptor. See Section 13.13 [File Descriptor Flags], page 361.

    F_GETFL   Get flags associated with the open file. See Section 13.14 [File Status Flags], page 363.

    F_SETFL   Set flags associated with the open file. See Section 13.14 [File Status Flags], page 363.

    F_GETLK   Test a file lock. See Section 13.15 [File Locks], page 368.

    F_SETLK   Set or clear a file lock. See Section 13.15 [File Locks], page 368.

    F_SETLKW   Like F_SETLK, but wait for completion. See Section 13.15 [File Locks], page 368.

    F_OFD_GETLK

               Test an open file description lock. See Section 13.16 [Open File Description Locks], page 371. Specific to Linux.

    F_OFD_SETLK

               Set or clear an open file description lock. See Section 13.16 [Open File Description Locks], page 371. Specific to Linux.

    F_OFD_SETLKW

               Like F_OFD_SETLK, but block until lock is acquired. See Section 13.16 [Open File Description Locks], page 371. Specific to Linux.

F_GETOWN   Get process or process group ID to receive SIGIO signals.   See
            Section 13.18 [Interrupt-Driven Input], page 375.

F_SETOWN   Set process or process group ID to receive SIGIO signals. See Section 13.18
            [Interrupt-Driven Input], page 375.

This function is a cancellation point in multi-threaded programs. This is a problem
if the thread allocates some resources (like memory, file descriptors, semaphores or
whatever) at the time fcntl is called. If the thread gets canceled these resources stay
allocated until the program ends. To avoid this calls to fcntl should be protected
using cancellation handlers.

13.12 Duplicating Descriptors

You can *duplicate* a file descriptor, or allocate another file descriptor that refers to the same
open file as the original. Duplicate descriptors share one file position and one set of file
status flags (see Section 13.14 [File Status Flags], page 363), but each has its own set of file
descriptor flags (see Section 13.13 [File Descriptor Flags], page 361).

The major use of duplicating a file descriptor is to implement *redirection* of input or
output: that is, to change the file or pipe that a particular file descriptor corresponds to.

You can perform this operation using the fcntl function with the F_DUPFD command,
but there are also convenient functions dup and dup2 for duplicating descriptors.

The fcntl function and flags are declared in fcntl.h, while prototypes for dup and
dup2 are in the header file unistd.h.

int dup (*int old*)   [Function]
    Preliminary: | MT-Safe | AS-Safe | AC-Safe | See Section 1.2.2.1 [POSIX Safety
    Concepts], page 2.

    This function copies descriptor *old* to the first available descriptor number (the first
    number not currently open). It is equivalent to fcntl (*old*, F_DUPFD, 0).

int dup2 (*int old, int new*)   [Function]
    Preliminary: | MT-Safe | AS-Safe | AC-Safe | See Section 1.2.2.1 [POSIX Safety
    Concepts], page 2.

    This function copies the descriptor *old* to descriptor number *new*.

    If *old* is an invalid descriptor, then dup2 does nothing; it does not close *new*. Other-
    wise, the new duplicate of *old* replaces any previous meaning of descriptor *new*, as if
    new were closed first.

    If *old* and *new* are different numbers, and *old* is a valid descriptor number, then dup2
    is equivalent to:

```
close (new);
fcntl (old, F_DUPFD, new)
```

    However, dup2 does this atomically; there is no instant in the middle of calling dup2
    at which *new* is closed and not yet a duplicate of *old*.

int F_DUPFD   [Macro]
    This macro is used as the *command* argument to fcntl, to copy the file descriptor
    given as the first argument.

    The form of the call in this case is:

```
fcntl (old, F_DUPFD, next-filedes)
```

The *next-filedes* argument is of type `int` and specifies that the file descriptor returned should be the next available one greater than or equal to this value.

The return value from `fcntl` with this command is normally the value of the new file descriptor. A return value of −1 indicates an error. The following `errno` error conditions are defined for this command:

`EBADF`   The *old* argument is invalid.

`EINVAL`   The *next-filedes* argument is invalid.

`EMFILE`   There are no more file descriptors available—your program is already using the maximum. In BSD and GNU, the maximum is controlled by a resource limit that can be changed; see Section 22.2 [Limiting Resource Usage], page 632, for more information about the `RLIMIT_NOFILE` limit.

`ENFILE` is not a possible error code for `dup2` because `dup2` does not create a new opening of a file; duplicate descriptors do not count toward the limit which `ENFILE` indicates. `EMFILE` is possible because it refers to the limit on distinct descriptor numbers in use in one process.

Here is an example showing how to use `dup2` to do redirection. Typically, redirection of the standard streams (like `stdin`) is done by a shell or shell-like program before calling one of the `exec` functions (see Section 26.5 [Executing a File], page 752) to execute a new program in a child process. When the new program is executed, it creates and initializes the standard streams to point to the corresponding file descriptors, before its `main` function is invoked.

So, to redirect standard input to a file, the shell could do something like:

```
pid = fork ();
if (pid == 0)
  {
    char *filename;
    char *program;
    int file;
    ...
    file = TEMP_FAILURE_RETRY (open (filename, O_RDONLY));
    dup2 (file, STDIN_FILENO);
    TEMP_FAILURE_RETRY (close (file));
    execv (program, NULL);
  }
```

There is also a more detailed example showing how to implement redirection in the context of a pipeline of processes in Section 28.6.3 [Launching Jobs], page 768.

13.13 File Descriptor Flags

File descriptor flags are miscellaneous attributes of a file descriptor. These flags are associated with particular file descriptors, so that if you have created duplicate file descriptors from a single opening of a file, each descriptor has its own set of flags.

Currently there is just one file descriptor flag: `FD_CLOEXEC`, which causes the descriptor to be closed if you use any of the `exec...` functions (see Section 26.5 [Executing a File], page 752).

The symbols in this section are defined in the header file `fcntl.h`.

int F_GETFD [Macro]

This macro is used as the *command* argument to `fcntl`, to specify that it should return the file descriptor flags associated with the *filedes* argument.

The normal return value from `fcntl` with this command is a nonnegative number which can be interpreted as the bitwise OR of the individual flags (except that currently there is only one flag to use).

In case of an error, `fcntl` returns −1. The following `errno` error conditions are defined for this command:

EBADF   The *filedes* argument is invalid.

int F_SETFD [Macro]

This macro is used as the *command* argument to `fcntl`, to specify that it should set the file descriptor flags associated with the *filedes* argument. This requires a third `int` argument to specify the new flags, so the form of the call is:

        fcntl (*filedes*, F_SETFD, *new-flags*)

The normal return value from `fcntl` with this command is an unspecified value other than −1, which indicates an error. The flags and error conditions are the same as for the `F_GETFD` command.

The following macro is defined for use as a file descriptor flag with the `fcntl` function. The value is an integer constant usable as a bit mask value.

int FD_CLOEXEC [Macro]

This flag specifies that the file descriptor should be closed when an `exec` function is invoked; see Section 26.5 [Executing a File], page 752. When a file descriptor is allocated (as with `open` or `dup`), this bit is initially cleared on the new file descriptor, meaning that descriptor will survive into the new program after `exec`.

If you want to modify the file descriptor flags, you should get the current flags with `F_GETFD` and modify the value. Don't assume that the flags listed here are the only ones that are implemented; your program may be run years from now and more flags may exist then. For example, here is a function to set or clear the flag `FD_CLOEXEC` without altering any other flags:

```
/* Set the FD_CLOEXEC flag of desc if value is nonzero,
   or clear the flag if value is 0.
   Return 0 on success, or -1 on error with errno set. */

int
set_cloexec_flag (int desc, int value)
{
  int oldflags = fcntl (desc, F_GETFD, 0);
  /* If reading the flags failed, return error indication now. */
  if (oldflags < 0)
    return oldflags;
  /* Set just the flag we want to set. */
  if (value != 0)
    oldflags |= FD_CLOEXEC;
  else
    oldflags &= ~FD_CLOEXEC;
  /* Store modified flag word in the descriptor. */
  return fcntl (desc, F_SETFD, oldflags);
}
```

13.14 File Status Flags

File status flags are used to specify attributes of the opening of a file. Unlike the file descriptor flags discussed in Section 13.13 [File Descriptor Flags], page 361, the file status flags are shared by duplicated file descriptors resulting from a single opening of the file. The file status flags are specified with the *flags* argument to open; see Section 13.1 [Opening and Closing Files], page 323.

File status flags fall into three categories, which are described in the following sections.

- Section 13.14.1 [File Access Modes], page 363, specify what type of access is allowed to the file: reading, writing, or both. They are set by open and are returned by fcntl, but cannot be changed.

- Section 13.14.2 [Open-time Flags], page 364, control details of what open will do. These flags are not preserved after the open call.

- Section 13.14.3 [I/O Operating Modes], page 366, affect how operations such as read and write are done. They are set by open, and can be fetched or changed with fcntl.

The symbols in this section are defined in the header file fcntl.h.

13.14.1 File Access Modes

The file access modes allow a file descriptor to be used for reading, writing, or both. (On GNU/Hurd systems, they can also allow none of these, and allow execution of the file as a program.) The access modes are chosen when the file is opened, and never change.

int O_RDONLY   [Macro]
>   Open the file for read access.

int O_WRONLY   [Macro]
>   Open the file for write access.

int O_RDWR   [Macro]
>   Open the file for both reading and writing.

On GNU/Hurd systems (and not on other systems), O_RDONLY and O_WRONLY are independent bits that can be bitwise-ORed together, and it is valid for either bit to be set or clear. This means that O_RDWR is the same as O_RDONLY|O_WRONLY. A file access mode of zero is permissible; it allows no operations that do input or output to the file, but does allow other operations such as fchmod. On GNU/Hurd systems, since "read-only" or "write-only" is a misnomer, fcntl.h defines additional names for the file access modes. These names are preferred when writing GNU-specific code. But most programs will want to be portable to other POSIX.1 systems and should use the POSIX.1 names above instead.

int O_READ   [Macro]
>   Open the file for reading. Same as O_RDONLY; only defined on GNU.

int O_WRITE   [Macro]
>   Open the file for writing. Same as O_WRONLY; only defined on GNU.

int O_EXEC   [Macro]
>   Open the file for executing. Only defined on GNU.

To determine the file access mode with `fcntl`, you must extract the access mode bits from the retrieved file status flags. On GNU/Hurd systems, you can just test the `O_READ` and `O_WRITE` bits in the flags word. But in other POSIX.1 systems, reading and writing access modes are not stored as distinct bit flags. The portable way to extract the file access mode bits is with `O_ACCMODE`.

int O_ACCMODE   [Macro]

> This macro stands for a mask that can be bitwise-ANDed with the file status flag value to produce a value representing the file access mode. The mode will be `O_RDONLY`, `O_WRONLY`, or `O_RDWR`. (On GNU/Hurd systems it could also be zero, and it never includes the `O_EXEC` bit.)

13.14.2 Open-time Flags

The open-time flags specify options affecting how `open` will behave. These options are not preserved once the file is open. The exception to this is `O_NONBLOCK`, which is also an I/O operating mode and so it *is* saved. See Section 13.1 [Opening and Closing Files], page 323, for how to call `open`.

There are two sorts of options specified by open-time flags.

- *File name translation flags* affect how `open` looks up the file name to locate the file, and whether the file can be created.

- *Open-time action flags* specify extra operations that `open` will perform on the file once it is open.

Here are the file name translation flags.

int O_CREAT   [Macro]

> If set, the file will be created if it doesn't already exist.

int O_EXCL   [Macro]

> If both `O_CREAT` and `O_EXCL` are set, then `open` fails if the specified file already exists. This is guaranteed to never clobber an existing file.

int O_NONBLOCK   [Macro]

> This prevents `open` from blocking for a "long time" to open the file. This is only meaningful for some kinds of files, usually devices such as serial ports; when it is not meaningful, it is harmless and ignored. Often opening a port to a modem blocks until the modem reports carrier detection; if `O_NONBLOCK` is specified, `open` will return immediately without a carrier.
>
> Note that the `O_NONBLOCK` flag is overloaded as both an I/O operating mode and a file name translation flag. This means that specifying `O_NONBLOCK` in `open` also sets nonblocking I/O mode; see Section 13.14.3 [I/O Operating Modes], page 366. To open the file without blocking but do normal I/O that blocks, you must call `open` with `O_NONBLOCK` set and then call `fcntl` to turn the bit off.

int O_NOCTTY   [Macro]

> If the named file is a terminal device, don't make it the controlling terminal for the process. See Chapter 28 [Job Control], page 763, for information about what it means to be the controlling terminal.

On GNU/Hurd systems and 4.4 BSD, opening a file never makes it the controlling terminal and O_NOCTTY is zero. However, GNU/Linux systems and some other systems use a nonzero value for O_NOCTTY and set the controlling terminal when you open a file that is a terminal device; so to be portable, use O_NOCTTY when it is important to avoid this.

The following three file name translation flags exist only on GNU/Hurd systems.

int O_IGNORE_CTTY   [Macro]

> Do not recognize the named file as the controlling terminal, even if it refers to the process's existing controlling terminal device. Operations on the new file descriptor will never induce job control signals. See Chapter 28 [Job Control], page 763.

int O_NOLINK   [Macro]

> If the named file is a symbolic link, open the link itself instead of the file it refers to. (fstat on the new file descriptor will return the information returned by lstat on the link's name.)

int O_NOTRANS   [Macro]

> If the named file is specially translated, do not invoke the translator. Open the bare file the translator itself sees.

The open-time action flags tell **open** to do additional operations which are not really related to opening the file. The reason to do them as part of **open** instead of in separate calls is that **open** can do them *atomically*.

int O_TRUNC   [Macro]

> Truncate the file to zero length. This option is only useful for regular files, not special files such as directories or FIFOs. POSIX.1 requires that you open the file for writing to use O_TRUNC. In BSD and GNU you must have permission to write the file to truncate it, but you need not open for write access.

> This is the only open-time action flag specified by POSIX.1. There is no good reason for truncation to be done by **open**, instead of by calling **ftruncate** afterwards. The O_TRUNC flag existed in Unix before **ftruncate** was invented, and is retained for backward compatibility.

The remaining operating modes are BSD extensions. They exist only on some systems. On other systems, these macros are not defined.

int O_SHLOCK   [Macro]

> Acquire a shared lock on the file, as with **flock**. See Section 13.15 [File Locks], page 368.

> If O_CREAT is specified, the locking is done atomically when creating the file. You are guaranteed that no other process will get the lock on the new file first.

int O_EXLOCK   [Macro]

> Acquire an exclusive lock on the file, as with **flock**. See Section 13.15 [File Locks], page 368. This is atomic like O_SHLOCK.

13.14.3 I/O Operating Modes

The operating modes affect how input and output operations using a file descriptor work. These flags are set by **open** and can be fetched and changed with **fcntl**.

int O_APPEND   [Macro]

> The bit that enables append mode for the file. If set, then all **write** operations write the data at the end of the file, extending it, regardless of the current file position. This is the only reliable way to append to a file. In append mode, you are guaranteed that the data you write will always go to the current end of the file, regardless of other processes writing to the file. Conversely, if you simply set the file position to the end of file and write, then another process can extend the file after you set the file position but before you write, resulting in your data appearing someplace before the real end of file.

int O_NONBLOCK   [Macro]

> The bit that enables nonblocking mode for the file. If this bit is set, **read** requests on the file can return immediately with a failure status if there is no input immediately available, instead of blocking. Likewise, **write** requests can also return immediately with a failure status if the output can't be written immediately.

> Note that the **O_NONBLOCK** flag is overloaded as both an I/O operating mode and a file name translation flag; see Section 13.14.2 [Open-time Flags], page 364.

int O_NDELAY   [Macro]

> This is an obsolete name for **O_NONBLOCK**, provided for compatibility with BSD. It is not defined by the POSIX.1 standard.

The remaining operating modes are BSD and GNU extensions. They exist only on some systems. On other systems, these macros are not defined.

int O_ASYNC   [Macro]

> The bit that enables asynchronous input mode. If set, then **SIGIO** signals will be generated when input is available. See Section 13.18 [Interrupt-Driven Input], page 375.

> Asynchronous input mode is a BSD feature.

int O_FSYNC   [Macro]

> The bit that enables synchronous writing for the file. If set, each **write** call will make sure the data is reliably stored on disk before returning.

> Synchronous writing is a BSD feature.

int O_SYNC   [Macro]

> This is another name for **O_FSYNC**. They have the same value.

int O_NOATIME   [Macro]

> If this bit is set, **read** will not update the access time of the file. See Section 14.9.9 [File Times], page 413. This is used by programs that do backups, so that backing a file up does not count as reading it. Only the owner of the file or the superuser may use this bit.

> This is a GNU extension.

13.14.4 Getting and Setting File Status Flags

The fcntl function can fetch or change file status flags.

int F_GETFL   [Macro]

>   This macro is used as the *command* argument to fcntl, to read the file status flags
>   for the open file with descriptor *filedes*.
>
>   The normal return value from fcntl with this command is a nonnegative number
>   which can be interpreted as the bitwise OR of the individual flags. Since the file
>   access modes are not single-bit values, you can mask off other bits in the returned
>   flags with O_ACCMODE to compare them.
>
>   In case of an error, fcntl returns −1. The following **errno** error conditions are
>   defined for this command:
>
>   EBADF   The *filedes* argument is invalid.

int F_SETFL   [Macro]

>   This macro is used as the *command* argument to fcntl, to set the file status flags for
>   the open file corresponding to the *filedes* argument. This command requires a third
>   int argument to specify the new flags, so the call looks like this:
>
>   fcntl (*filedes*, F_SETFL, *new-flags*)
>
>   You can't change the access mode for the file in this way; that is, whether the file
>   descriptor was opened for reading or writing.
>
>   The normal return value from fcntl with this command is an unspecified value other
>   than −1, which indicates an error. The error conditions are the same as for the
>   F_GETFL command.

If you want to modify the file status flags, you should get the current flags with F_GETFL
and modify the value. Don't assume that the flags listed here are the only ones that are
implemented; your program may be run years from now and more flags may exist then. For
example, here is a function to set or clear the flag O_NONBLOCK without altering any other
flags:

```
/* Set the O_NONBLOCK flag of desc if value is nonzero,
   or clear the flag if value is 0.
   Return 0 on success, or -1 on error with errno set. */

int
set_nonblock_flag (int desc, int value)
{
  int oldflags = fcntl (desc, F_GETFL, 0);
  /* If reading the flags failed, return error indication now. */
  if (oldflags == -1)
    return -1;
  /* Set just the flag we want to set. */
  if (value != 0)
    oldflags |= O_NONBLOCK;
  else
    oldflags &= ~O_NONBLOCK;
  /* Store modified flag word in the descriptor. */
  return fcntl (desc, F_SETFL, oldflags);
}
```

13.15 File Locks

This section describes record locks that are associated with the process. There is also a different type of record lock that is associated with the open file description instead of the process. See Section 13.16 [Open File Description Locks], page 371.

The remaining `fcntl` commands are used to support *record locking*, which permits multiple cooperating programs to prevent each other from simultaneously accessing parts of a file in error-prone ways.

An *exclusive* or *write* lock gives a process exclusive access for writing to the specified part of the file. While a write lock is in place, no other process can lock that part of the file.

A *shared* or *read* lock prohibits any other process from requesting a write lock on the specified part of the file. However, other processes can request read locks.

The `read` and `write` functions do not actually check to see whether there are any locks in place. If you want to implement a locking protocol for a file shared by multiple processes, your application must do explicit `fcntl` calls to request and clear locks at the appropriate points.

Locks are associated with processes. A process can only have one kind of lock set for each byte of a given file. When any file descriptor for that file is closed by the process, all of the locks that process holds on that file are released, even if the locks were made using other descriptors that remain open. Likewise, locks are released when a process exits, and are not inherited by child processes created using `fork` (see Section 26.4 [Creating a Process], page 751).

When making a lock, use a `struct flock` to specify what kind of lock and where. This data type and the associated macros for the `fcntl` function are declared in the header file `fcntl.h`.

`struct flock`   [Data Type]

> This structure is used with the `fcntl` function to describe a file lock. It has these members:

> `short int l_type`
>> Specifies the type of the lock; one of `F_RDLCK`, `F_WRLCK`, or `F_UNLCK`.

> `short int l_whence`
>> This corresponds to the *whence* argument to `fseek` or `lseek`, and specifies what the offset is relative to. Its value can be one of `SEEK_SET`, `SEEK_CUR`, or `SEEK_END`.

> `off_t l_start`
>> This specifies the offset of the start of the region to which the lock applies, and is given in bytes relative to the point specified by `l_whence` member.

> `off_t l_len`
>> This specifies the length of the region to be locked. A value of 0 is treated specially; it means the region extends to the end of the file.

> `pid_t l_pid`
>> This field is the process ID (see Section 26.2 [Process Creation Concepts], page 750) of the process holding the lock. It is filled in by calling `fcntl`

with the `F_GETLK` command, but is ignored when making a lock. If the conflicting lock is an open file description lock (see Section 13.16 [Open File Description Locks], page 371), then this field will be set to −1.

int F_GETLK   [Macro]

> This macro is used as the *command* argument to `fcntl`, to specify that it should get information about a lock. This command requires a third argument of type `struct flock *` to be passed to `fcntl`, so that the form of the call is:
>
>   fcntl (filedes, F_GETLK, lockp)
>
> If there is a lock already in place that would block the lock described by the *lockp* argument, information about that lock overwrites *`*lockp`*. Existing locks are not reported if they are compatible with making a new lock as specified. Thus, you should specify a lock type of `F_WRLCK` if you want to find out about both read and write locks, or `F_RDLCK` if you want to find out about write locks only.
>
> There might be more than one lock affecting the region specified by the *lockp* argument, but `fcntl` only returns information about one of them. The `l_whence` member of the *lockp* structure is set to `SEEK_SET` and the `l_start` and `l_len` fields set to identify the locked region.
>
> If no lock applies, the only change to the *lockp* structure is to update the `l_type` to a value of `F_UNLCK`.
>
> The normal return value from `fcntl` with this command is an unspecified value other than −1, which is reserved to indicate an error. The following `errno` error conditions are defined for this command:
>
> `EBADF`   The *filedes* argument is invalid.
>
> `EINVAL`   Either the *lockp* argument doesn't specify valid lock information, or the file associated with *filedes* doesn't support locks.

int F_SETLK   [Macro]

> This macro is used as the *command* argument to `fcntl`, to specify that it should set or clear a lock. This command requires a third argument of type `struct flock *` to be passed to `fcntl`, so that the form of the call is:
>
>   fcntl (filedes, F_SETLK, lockp)
>
> If the process already has a lock on any part of the region, the old lock on that part is replaced with the new lock. You can remove a lock by specifying a lock type of `F_UNLCK`.
>
> If the lock cannot be set, `fcntl` returns immediately with a value of −1. This function does not block waiting for other processes to release locks. If `fcntl` succeeds, it return a value other than −1.
>
> The following `errno` error conditions are defined for this function:
>
> `EAGAIN`
> `EACCES`   The lock cannot be set because it is blocked by an existing lock on the file. Some systems use `EAGAIN` in this case, and other systems use `EACCES`; your program should treat them alike, after `F_SETLK`. (GNU/Linux and GNU/Hurd systems always use `EAGAIN`.)

EBADF   Either: the *filedes* argument is invalid; you requested a read lock but the
            filedes is not open for read access; or, you requested a write lock but the
            filedes is not open for write access.

EINVAL   Either the *lockp* argument doesn't specify valid lock information, or the
            file associated with *filedes* doesn't support locks.

ENOLCK   The system has run out of file lock resources; there are already too many
            file locks in place.

            Well-designed file systems never report this error, because they have no
            limitation on the number of locks. However, you must still take account
            of the possibility of this error, as it could result from network access to a
            file system on another machine.

int F_SETLKW   [Macro]
This macro is used as the *command* argument to `fcntl`, to specify that it should set
or clear a lock. It is just like the `F_SETLK` command, but causes the process to block
(or wait) until the request can be specified.

This command requires a third argument of type `struct flock *`, as for the `F_SETLK`
command.

The `fcntl` return values and errors are the same as for the `F_SETLK` command, but
these additional `errno` error conditions are defined for this command:

EINTR   The function was interrupted by a signal while it was waiting. See
            Section 24.5 [Primitives Interrupted by Signals], page 687.

EDEADLK   The specified region is being locked by another process. But that process
            is waiting to lock a region which the current process has locked, so waiting
            for the lock would result in deadlock. The system does not guarantee that
            it will detect all such conditions, but it lets you know if it notices one.

The following macros are defined for use as values for the `l_type` member of the `flock`
structure. The values are integer constants.

F_RDLCK   This macro is used to specify a read (or shared) lock.

F_WRLCK   This macro is used to specify a write (or exclusive) lock.

F_UNLCK   This macro is used to specify that the region is unlocked.

As an example of a situation where file locking is useful, consider a program that can
be run simultaneously by several different users, that logs status information to a common
file. One example of such a program might be a game that uses a file to keep track of high
scores. Another example might be a program that records usage or accounting information
for billing purposes.

Having multiple copies of the program simultaneously writing to the file could cause
the contents of the file to become mixed up. But you can prevent this kind of problem by
setting a write lock on the file before actually writing to the file.

If the program also needs to read the file and wants to make sure that the contents of
the file are in a consistent state, then it can also use a read lock. While the read lock is set,
no other process can lock that part of the file for writing.

Remember that file locks are only an *advisory* protocol for controlling access to a file. There is still potential for access to the file by programs that don't use the lock protocol.

13.16 Open File Description Locks

In contrast to process-associated record locks (see Section 13.15 [File Locks], page 368), open file description record locks are associated with an open file description rather than a process.

Using `fcntl` to apply an open file description lock on a region that already has an existing open file description lock that was created via the same file descriptor will never cause a lock conflict.

Open file description locks are also inherited by child processes across `fork`, or `clone` with `CLONE_FILES` set (see Section 26.4 [Creating a Process], page 751), along with the file descriptor.

It is important to distinguish between the open file *description* (an instance of an open file, usually created by a call to `open`) and an open file *descriptor*, which is a numeric value that refers to the open file description. The locks described here are associated with the open file *description* and not the open file *descriptor*.

Using `dup` (see Section 13.12 [Duplicating Descriptors], page 360) to copy a file descriptor does not give you a new open file description, but rather copies a reference to an existing open file description and assigns it to a new file descriptor. Thus, open file description locks set on a file descriptor cloned by `dup` will never conflict with open file description locks set on the original descriptor since they refer to the same open file description. Depending on the range and type of lock involved, the original lock may be modified by a `F_OFD_SETLK` or `F_OFD_SETLKW` command in this situation however.

Open file description locks always conflict with process-associated locks, even if acquired by the same process or on the same open file descriptor.

Open file description locks use the same `struct flock` as process-associated locks as an argument (see Section 13.15 [File Locks], page 368) and the macros for the `command` values are also declared in the header file `fcntl.h`. To use them, the macro `_GNU_SOURCE` must be defined prior to including any header file.

In contrast to process-associated locks, any `struct flock` used as an argument to open file description lock commands must have the `l_pid` value set to 0. Also, when returning information about an open file description lock in a `F_GETLK` or `F_OFD_GETLK` request, the `l_pid` field in `struct flock` will be set to -1 to indicate that the lock is not associated with a process.

When the same `struct flock` is reused as an argument to a `F_OFD_SETLK` or `F_OFD_SETLKW` request after being used for an `F_OFD_GETLK` request, it is necessary to inspect and reset the `l_pid` field to 0.

int F_OFD_GETLK   [Macro]
    This macro is used as the *command* argument to `fcntl`, to specify that it should get information about a lock. This command requires a third argument of type `struct flock *` to be passed to `fcntl`, so that the form of the call is:

```
fcntl (filedes, F_OFD_GETLK, lockp)
```

If there is a lock already in place that would block the lock described by the *lockp* argument, information about that lock is written to **lockp*. Existing locks are not reported if they are compatible with making a new lock as specified. Thus, you should specify a lock type of F_WRLCK if you want to find out about both read and write locks, or F_RDLCK if you want to find out about write locks only.

There might be more than one lock affecting the region specified by the *lockp* argument, but fcntl only returns information about one of them. Which lock is returned in this situation is undefined.

The l_whence member of the *lockp* structure are set to SEEK_SET and the l_start and l_len fields are set to identify the locked region.

If no conflicting lock exists, the only change to the *lockp* structure is to update the l_type field to the value F_UNLCK.

The normal return value from fcntl with this command is either 0 on success or −1, which indicates an error. The following errno error conditions are defined for this command:

EBADF   The *filedes* argument is invalid.

EINVAL   Either the *lockp* argument doesn't specify valid lock information, the operating system kernel doesn't support open file description locks, or the file associated with *filedes* doesn't support locks.

int F_OFD_SETLK   [Macro]

This macro is used as the *command* argument to fcntl, to specify that it should set or clear a lock. This command requires a third argument of type **struct flock *** to be passed to fcntl, so that the form of the call is:

    fcntl (*filedes*, F_OFD_SETLK, *lockp*)

If the open file already has a lock on any part of the region, the old lock on that part is replaced with the new lock. You can remove a lock by specifying a lock type of F_UNLCK.

If the lock cannot be set, fcntl returns immediately with a value of −1. This command does not wait for other tasks to release locks. If fcntl succeeds, it returns 0.

The following errno error conditions are defined for this command:

EAGAIN   The lock cannot be set because it is blocked by an existing lock on the file.

EBADF   Either: the *filedes* argument is invalid; you requested a read lock but the *filedes* is not open for read access; or, you requested a write lock but the *filedes* is not open for write access.

EINVAL   Either the *lockp* argument doesn't specify valid lock information, the operating system kernel doesn't support open file description locks, or the file associated with *filedes* doesn't support locks.

ENOLCK   The system has run out of file lock resources; there are already too many file locks in place.

Well-designed file systems never report this error, because they have no
limitation on the number of locks. However, you must still take account
of the possibility of this error, as it could result from network access to a
file system on another machine.

int **F_OFD_SETLKW**   [Macro]
This macro is used as the *command* argument to **fcntl**, to specify that it should set
or clear a lock. It is just like the **F_OFD_SETLK** command, but causes the process to
wait until the request can be completed.

This command requires a third argument of type **struct flock ***, as for the **F_OFD_
SETLK** command.

The **fcntl** return values and errors are the same as for the **F_OFD_SETLK** command,
but these additional **errno** error conditions are defined for this command:

EINTR   The function was interrupted by a signal while it was waiting. See
             Section 24.5 [Primitives Interrupted by Signals], page 687.

Open file description locks are useful in the same sorts of situations as process-associated
locks. They can also be used to synchronize file access between threads within the same
process by having each thread perform its own **open** of the file, to obtain its own open file
description.

Because open file description locks are automatically freed only upon closing the last
file descriptor that refers to the open file description, this locking mechanism avoids the
possibility that locks are inadvertently released due to a library routine opening and closing
a file without the application being aware.

As with process-associated locks, open file description locks are advisory.

13.17 Open File Description Locks Example

Here is an example of using open file description locks in a threaded program. If this
program used process-associated locks, then it would be subject to data corruption because
process-associated locks are shared by the threads inside a process, and thus cannot be used
by one thread to lock out another thread in the same process.

Proper error handling has been omitted in the following program for brevity.

```
#define _GNU_SOURCE
#include <stdio.h>
#include <sys/types.h>
#include <sys/stat.h>
#include <unistd.h>
#include <fcntl.h>
#include <pthread.h>

#define FILENAME      "/tmp/foo"
#define NUM_THREADS   3
#define ITERATIONS    5

void *
thread_start (void *arg)
{
```

```c
    int i, fd, len;
    long tid = (long) arg;
    char buf[256];
    struct flock lck = {
      .l_whence = SEEK_SET,
      .l_start = 0,
      .l_len = 1,
    };

    fd = open ("/tmp/foo", O_RDWR | O_CREAT, 0666);

    for (i = 0; i < ITERATIONS; i++)
      {
        lck.l_type = F_WRLCK;
        fcntl (fd, F_OFD_SETLKW, &lck);

        len = sprintf (buf, "%d: tid=%ld fd=%d\n", i, tid, fd);

        lseek (fd, 0, SEEK_END);
        write (fd, buf, len);
        fsync (fd);

        lck.l_type = F_UNLCK;
        fcntl (fd, F_OFD_SETLK, &lck);

        /* sleep to ensure lock is yielded to another thread */
        usleep (1);
      }
    pthread_exit (NULL);
}

int
main (int argc, char **argv)
{
  long i;
  pthread_t threads[NUM_THREADS];

  truncate (FILENAME, 0);

  for (i = 0; i < NUM_THREADS; i++)
    pthread_create (&threads[i], NULL, thread_start, (void *) i);

  pthread_exit (NULL);
  return 0;
}
```

This example creates three threads each of which loops five times, appending to the file. Access to the file is serialized via open file description locks. If we compile and run the above program, we'll end up with /tmp/foo that has 15 lines in it.

If we, however, were to replace the F_OFD_SETLK and F_OFD_SETLKW commands with their process-associated lock equivalents, the locking essentially becomes a noop since it is all done within the context of the same process. That leads to data corruption (typically manifested as missing lines) as some threads race in and overwrite the data written by others.

13.18 Interrupt-Driven Input

If you set the `O_ASYNC` status flag on a file descriptor (see Section 13.14 [File Status Flags], page 363), a `SIGIO` signal is sent whenever input or output becomes possible on that file descriptor. The process or process group to receive the signal can be selected by using the `F_SETOWN` command to the `fcntl` function. If the file descriptor is a socket, this also selects the recipient of `SIGURG` signals that are delivered when out-of-band data arrives on that socket; see Section 16.9.8 [Out-of-Band Data], page 464. (`SIGURG` is sent in any situation where `select` would report the socket as having an "exceptional condition". See Section 13.8 [Waiting for Input or Output], page 342.)

If the file descriptor corresponds to a terminal device, then `SIGIO` signals are sent to the foreground process group of the terminal. See Chapter 28 [Job Control], page 763.

The symbols in this section are defined in the header file `fcntl.h`.

int F_GETOWN [Macro]

> This macro is used as the *command* argument to `fcntl`, to specify that it should get information about the process or process group to which `SIGIO` signals are sent. (For a terminal, this is actually the foreground process group ID, which you can get using `tcgetpgrp`; see Section 28.7.3 [Functions for Controlling Terminal Access], page 780.)
>
> The return value is interpreted as a process ID; if negative, its absolute value is the process group ID.
>
> The following `errno` error condition is defined for this command:
>
> EBADF   The *filedes* argument is invalid.

int F_SETOWN [Macro]

> This macro is used as the *command* argument to `fcntl`, to specify that it should set the process or process group to which `SIGIO` signals are sent. This command requires a third argument of type `pid_t` to be passed to `fcntl`, so that the form of the call is:
>
>   `fcntl (`*filedes*`, F_SETOWN, `*pid*`)`
>
> The *pid* argument should be a process ID. You can also pass a negative number whose absolute value is a process group ID.
>
> The return value from `fcntl` with this command is −1 in case of error and some other value if successful. The following `errno` error conditions are defined for this command:
>
> EBADF   The *filedes* argument is invalid.
>
> ESRCH   There is no process or process group corresponding to *pid*.

13.19 Generic I/O Control operations

GNU systems can handle most input/output operations on many different devices and objects in terms of a few file primitives - `read`, `write` and `lseek`. However, most devices also have a few peculiar operations which do not fit into this model. Such as:

- Changing the character font used on a terminal.
- Telling a magnetic tape system to rewind or fast forward. (Since they cannot move in byte increments, `lseek` is inapplicable).

- Ejecting a disk from a drive.
- Playing an audio track from a CD-ROM drive.
- Maintaining routing tables for a network.

Although some such objects such as sockets and terminals[1] have special functions of their own, it would not be practical to create functions for all these cases.

Instead these minor operations, known as *IOCTLs*, are assigned code numbers and multiplexed through the `ioctl` function, defined in `sys/ioctl.h`. The code numbers themselves are defined in many different headers.

`int ioctl (int filedes, int command, ...)`   [Function]
   Preliminary: | MT-Safe | AS-Safe | AC-Safe | See Section 1.2.2.1 [POSIX Safety Concepts], page 2.

   The `ioctl` function performs the generic I/O operation *command* on *filedes*.

   A third argument is usually present, either a single number or a pointer to a structure. The meaning of this argument, the returned value, and any error codes depends upon the command used. Often −1 is returned for a failure.

On some systems, IOCTLs used by different devices share the same numbers. Thus, although use of an inappropriate IOCTL *usually* only produces an error, you should not attempt to use device-specific IOCTLs on an unknown device.

Most IOCTLs are OS-specific and/or only used in special system utilities, and are thus beyond the scope of this document. For an example of the use of an IOCTL, see Section 16.9.8 [Out-of-Band Data], page 464.

---

[1] Actually, the terminal-specific functions are implemented with IOCTLs on many platforms.

14 File System Interface

This chapter describes the GNU C Library's functions for manipulating files. Unlike the input and output functions (see Chapter 12 [Input/Output on Streams], page 248; see Chapter 13 [Low-Level Input/Output], page 323), these functions are concerned with operating on the files themselves rather than on their contents.

Among the facilities described in this chapter are functions for examining or modifying directories, functions for renaming and deleting files, and functions for examining and setting file attributes such as access permissions and modification times.

14.1 Working Directory

Each process has associated with it a directory, called its *current working directory* or simply *working directory*, that is used in the resolution of relative file names (see Section 11.2.2 [File Name Resolution], page 246).

When you log in and begin a new session, your working directory is initially set to the home directory associated with your login account in the system user database. You can find any user's home directory using the `getpwuid` or `getpwnam` functions; see Section 30.13 [User Database], page 810.

Users can change the working directory using shell commands like `cd`. The functions described in this section are the primitives used by those commands and by other programs for examining and changing the working directory.

Prototypes for these functions are declared in the header file `unistd.h`.

char * getcwd (*char *buffer*, *size_t* **size**)   [Function]
> Preliminary: | MT-Safe | AS-Unsafe heap | AC-Unsafe mem fd | See Section 1.2.2.1 [POSIX Safety Concepts], page 2.
>
> The `getcwd` function returns an absolute file name representing the current working directory, storing it in the character array *buffer* that you provide. The *size* argument is how you tell the system the allocation size of *buffer*.
>
> The GNU C Library version of this function also permits you to specify a null pointer for the *buffer* argument. Then `getcwd` allocates a buffer automatically, as with `malloc` (see Section 3.2.2 [Unconstrained Allocation], page 42). If the *size* is greater than zero, then the buffer is that large; otherwise, the buffer is as large as necessary to hold the result.
>
> The return value is *buffer* on success and a null pointer on failure. The following `errno` error conditions are defined for this function:
>
> EINVAL   The *size* argument is zero and *buffer* is not a null pointer.
>
> ERANGE   The *size* argument is less than the length of the working directory name. You need to allocate a bigger array and try again.
>
> EACCES   Permission to read or search a component of the file name was denied.

You could implement the behavior of GNU's `getcwd (NULL, 0)` using only the standard behavior of `getcwd`:

```
char *
gnu_getcwd ()
{
  size_t size = 100;

  while (1)
    {
      char *buffer = (char *) xmalloc (size);
      if (getcwd (buffer, size) == buffer)
        return buffer;
      free (buffer);
      if (errno != ERANGE)
        return 0;
      size *= 2;
    }
}
```

See Section 3.2.2.2 [Examples of `malloc`], page 42, for information about `xmalloc`, which is not a library function but is a customary name used in most GNU software.

char * getwd (*char *buffer*)   [Deprecated Function]

> Preliminary: | MT-Safe | AS-Unsafe heap i18n | AC-Unsafe mem fd | See Section 1.2.2.1 [POSIX Safety Concepts], page 2.

> This is similar to `getcwd`, but has no way to specify the size of the buffer. The GNU C Library provides `getwd` only for backwards compatibility with BSD.

> The *buffer* argument should be a pointer to an array at least `PATH_MAX` bytes long (see Section 32.6 [Limits on File System Capacity], page 850). On GNU/Hurd systems there is no limit to the size of a file name, so this is not necessarily enough space to contain the directory name. That is why this function is deprecated.

char * get_current_dir_name (*void*)   [Function]

> Preliminary: | MT-Safe env | AS-Unsafe heap | AC-Unsafe mem fd | See Section 1.2.2.1 [POSIX Safety Concepts], page 2.

> This `get_current_dir_name` function is basically equivalent to `getcwd (NULL, 0)`. The only difference is that the value of the `PWD` variable is returned if this value is correct. This is a subtle difference which is visible if the path described by the `PWD` value is using one or more symbol links in which case the value returned by `getcwd` can resolve the symbol links and therefore yield a different result.

> This function is a GNU extension.

int chdir (*const char *filename*)   [Function]

> Preliminary: | MT-Safe | AS-Safe | AC-Safe | See Section 1.2.2.1 [POSIX Safety Concepts], page 2.

> This function is used to set the process's working directory to *filename*.

> The normal, successful return value from `chdir` is 0. A value of -1 is returned to indicate an error. The `errno` error conditions defined for this function are the usual file name syntax errors (see Section 11.2.3 [File Name Errors], page 246), plus `ENOTDIR` if the file *filename* is not a directory.

int fchdir (*int filedes*)   [Function]

> Preliminary: | MT-Safe | AS-Safe | AC-Safe | See Section 1.2.2.1 [POSIX Safety Concepts], page 2.

This function is used to set the process's working directory to directory associated with the file descriptor *filedes*.

The normal, successful return value from **fchdir** is 0. A value of −1 is returned to indicate an error. The following **errno** error conditions are defined for this function:

EACCES   Read permission is denied for the directory named by **dirname**.

EBADF   The *filedes* argument is not a valid file descriptor.

ENOTDIR   The file descriptor *filedes* is not associated with a directory.

EINTR   The function call was interrupt by a signal.

EIO   An I/O error occurred.

14.2 Accessing Directories

The facilities described in this section let you read the contents of a directory file. This is useful if you want your program to list all the files in a directory, perhaps as part of a menu.

The **opendir** function opens a *directory stream* whose elements are directory entries. Alternatively **fdopendir** can be used which can have advantages if the program needs to have more control over the way the directory is opened for reading. This allows, for instance, to pass the **O_NOATIME** flag to **open**.

You use the **readdir** function on the directory stream to retrieve these entries, represented as **struct dirent** objects. The name of the file for each entry is stored in the **d_name** member of this structure. There are obvious parallels here to the stream facilities for ordinary files, described in Chapter 12 [Input/Output on Streams], page 248.

14.2.1 Format of a Directory Entry

This section describes what you find in a single directory entry, as you might obtain it from a directory stream. All the symbols are declared in the header file **dirent.h**.

struct dirent   [Data Type]
     This is a structure type used to return information about directory entries. It contains the following fields:

char d_name[]
               This is the null-terminated file name component. This is the only field you can count on in all POSIX systems.

ino_t d_fileno
               This is the file serial number. For BSD compatibility, you can also refer to this member as **d_ino**. On GNU/Linux and GNU/Hurd systems and most POSIX systems, for most files this the same as the **st_ino** member that **stat** will return for the file. See Section 14.9 [File Attributes], page 399.

unsigned char d_namlen
               This is the length of the file name, not including the terminating null character. Its type is **unsigned char** because that is the integer type of the appropriate size. This member is a BSD extension. The symbol **_DIRENT_HAVE_D_NAMLEN** is defined if this member is available.

`unsigned char d_type`

> This is the type of the file, possibly unknown. The following constants are defined for its value:

> `DT_UNKNOWN`
>> The type is unknown. Only some filesystems have full support to return the type of the file, others might always return this value.

> `DT_REG`   A regular file.

> `DT_DIR`   A directory.

> `DT_FIFO`   A named pipe, or FIFO. See Section 15.3 [FIFO Special Files], page 427.

> `DT_SOCK`   A local-domain socket.

> `DT_CHR`   A character device.

> `DT_BLK`   A block device.

> `DT_LNK`   A symbolic link.

> This member is a BSD extension. The symbol `_DIRENT_HAVE_D_TYPE` is defined if this member is available. On systems where it is used, it corresponds to the file type bits in the `st_mode` member of `struct stat`. If the value cannot be determine the member value is DT_UNKNOWN. These two macros convert between `d_type` values and `st_mode` values:

> `int IFTODT (mode_t mode)`   [Function]
>> Preliminary: | MT-Safe | AS-Safe | AC-Safe | See Section 1.2.2.1 [POSIX Safety Concepts], page 2.

>> This returns the `d_type` value corresponding to *mode*.

> `mode_t DTTOIF (int dtype)`   [Function]
>> Preliminary: | MT-Safe | AS-Safe | AC-Safe | See Section 1.2.2.1 [POSIX Safety Concepts], page 2.

>> This returns the `st_mode` value corresponding to *dtype*.

This structure may contain additional members in the future. Their availability is always announced in the compilation environment by a macro names `_DIRENT_HAVE_D_xxx` where *xxx* is replaced by the name of the new member. For instance, the member `d_reclen` available on some systems is announced through the macro `_DIRENT_HAVE_D_RECLEN`.

When a file has multiple names, each name has its own directory entry. The only way you can tell that the directory entries belong to a single file is that they have the same value for the `d_fileno` field.

File attributes such as size, modification times etc., are part of the file itself, not of any particular directory entry. See Section 14.9 [File Attributes], page 399.

14.2.2 Opening a Directory Stream

This section describes how to open a directory stream. All the symbols are declared in the header file dirent.h.

DIR   [Data Type]
> The DIR data type represents a directory stream.

You shouldn't ever allocate objects of the **struct dirent** or DIR data types, since the directory access functions do that for you. Instead, you refer to these objects using the pointers returned by the following functions.

DIR * opendir (*const char *dirname*)   [Function]
> Preliminary: | MT-Safe | AS-Unsafe heap | AC-Unsafe mem fd | See Section 1.2.2.1 [POSIX Safety Concepts], page 2.
>
> The opendir function opens and returns a directory stream for reading the directory whose file name is *dirname*. The stream has type DIR *.
>
> If unsuccessful, opendir returns a null pointer. In addition to the usual file name errors (see Section 11.2.3 [File Name Errors], page 246), the following **errno** error conditions are defined for this function:
>
> EACCES   Read permission is denied for the directory named by dirname.
>
> EMFILE   The process has too many files open.
>
> ENFILE   The entire system, or perhaps the file system which contains the directory, cannot support any additional open files at the moment. (This problem cannot happen on GNU/Hurd systems.)
>
> ENOMEM   Not enough memory available.
>
> The DIR type is typically implemented using a file descriptor, and the opendir function in terms of the open function. See Chapter 13 [Low-Level Input/Output], page 323. Directory streams and the underlying file descriptors are closed on exec (see Section 26.5 [Executing a File], page 752).

The directory which is opened for reading by opendir is identified by the name. In some situations this is not sufficient. Or the way opendir implicitly creates a file descriptor for the directory is not the way a program might want it. In these cases an alternative interface can be used.

DIR * fdopendir (*int fd*)   [Function]
> Preliminary: | MT-Safe | AS-Unsafe heap | AC-Unsafe mem fd | See Section 1.2.2.1 [POSIX Safety Concepts], page 2.
>
> The fdopendir function works just like opendir but instead of taking a file name and opening a file descriptor for the directory the caller is required to provide a file descriptor. This file descriptor is then used in subsequent uses of the returned directory stream object.
>
> The caller must make sure the file descriptor is associated with a directory and it allows reading.

If the `fdopendir` call returns successfully the file descriptor is now under the control of the system. It can be used in the same way the descriptor implicitly created by `opendir` can be used but the program must not close the descriptor.

In case the function is unsuccessful it returns a null pointer and the file descriptor remains to be usable by the program. The following `errno` error conditions are defined for this function:

`EBADF`   The file descriptor is not valid.

`ENOTDIR`   The file descriptor is not associated with a directory.

`EINVAL`   The descriptor does not allow reading the directory content.

`ENOMEM`   Not enough memory available.

In some situations it can be desirable to get hold of the file descriptor which is created by the `opendir` call. For instance, to switch the current working directory to the directory just read the `fchdir` function could be used. Historically the `DIR` type was exposed and programs could access the fields. This does not happen in the GNU C Library. Instead a separate function is provided to allow access.

`int dirfd (DIR *dirstream)`   [Function]
  Preliminary: | MT-Safe | AS-Safe | AC-Safe | See Section 1.2.2.1 [POSIX Safety Concepts], page 2.

  The function `dirfd` returns the file descriptor associated with the directory stream *dirstream*. This descriptor can be used until the directory is closed with `closedir`. If the directory stream implementation is not using file descriptors the return value is `-1`.

14.2.3 Reading and Closing a Directory Stream

This section describes how to read directory entries from a directory stream, and how to close the stream when you are done with it. All the symbols are declared in the header file `dirent.h`.

`struct dirent * readdir (DIR *dirstream)`   [Function]
  Preliminary: | MT-Unsafe race:dirstream | AS-Unsafe lock | AC-Unsafe lock | See Section 1.2.2.1 [POSIX Safety Concepts], page 2.

  This function reads the next entry from the directory. It normally returns a pointer to a structure containing information about the file. This structure is associated with the *dirstream* handle and can be rewritten by a subsequent call.

  Portability Note: On some systems `readdir` may not return entries for . and .., even though these are always valid file names in any directory. See Section 11.2.2 [File Name Resolution], page 246.

  If there are no more entries in the directory or an error is detected, `readdir` returns a null pointer. The following `errno` error conditions are defined for this function:

  `EBADF`   The *dirstream* argument is not valid.

  To distinguish between an end-of-directory condition or an error, you must set `errno` to zero before calling `readdir`. To avoid entering an infinite loop, you should stop reading from the directory after the first error.

In POSIX.1-2008, `readdir` is not thread-safe. In the GNU C Library implementation, it is safe to call `readdir` concurrently on different *dirstreams*, but multiple threads accessing the same *dirstream* result in undefined behavior. `readdir_r` is a fully thread-safe alternative, but suffers from poor portability (see below). It is recommended that you use `readdir`, with external locking if multiple threads access the same *dirstream*.

`int readdir_r (DIR *dirstream, struct dirent *entry, struct dirent` [Function]
`**result)`
Preliminary: | MT-Safe | AS-Unsafe lock | AC-Unsafe lock | See Section 1.2.2.1 [POSIX Safety Concepts], page 2.

This function is a version of `readdir` which performs internal locking. Like `readdir` it returns the next entry from the directory. To prevent conflicts between simultaneously running threads the result is stored inside the *entry* object.

Portability Note: It is recommended to use `readdir` instead of `readdir_r` for the following reasons:

- On systems which do not define `NAME_MAX`, it may not be possible to use `readdir_r` safely because the caller does not specify the length of the buffer for the directory entry.

- On some systems, `readdir_r` cannot read directory entries with very long names. If such a name is encountered, the GNU C Library implementation of `readdir_r` returns with an error code of `ENAMETOOLONG` after the final directory entry has been read. On other systems, `readdir_r` may return successfully, but the `d_name` member may not be NUL-terminated or may be truncated.

- POSIX-1.2008 does not guarantee that `readdir` is thread-safe, even when access to the same *dirstream* is serialized. But in current implementations (including the GNU C Library), it is safe to call `readdir` concurrently on different *dirstreams*, so there is no need to use `readdir_r` in most multi-threaded programs. In the rare case that multiple threads need to read from the same *dirstream*, it is still better to use `readdir` and external synchronization.

- It is expected that future versions of POSIX will obsolete `readdir_r` and mandate the level of thread safety for `readdir` which is provided by the GNU C Library and other implementations today.

Normally `readdir_r` returns zero and sets `*result` to *entry*. If there are no more entries in the directory or an error is detected, `readdir_r` sets `*result` to a null pointer and returns a nonzero error code, also stored in `errno`, as described for `readdir`.

It is also important to look at the definition of the `struct dirent` type. Simply passing a pointer to an object of this type for the second parameter of `readdir_r` might not be enough. Some systems don't define the `d_name` element sufficiently long. In this case the user has to provide additional space. There must be room for at least `NAME_MAX + 1` characters in the `d_name` array. Code to call `readdir_r` could look like this:

```
union
{
```

```
        struct dirent d;
        char b[offsetof (struct dirent, d_name) + NAME_MAX + 1];
    } u;

    if (readdir_r (dir, &u.d, &res) == 0)
        ...
```

To support large filesystems on 32-bit machines there are LFS variants of the last two functions.

struct dirent64 * readdir64 (*DIR *dirstream*)   [Function]
> Preliminary: | MT-Unsafe race:dirstream | AS-Unsafe lock | AC-Unsafe lock | See Section 1.2.2.1 [POSIX Safety Concepts], page 2.

> The **readdir64** function is just like the **readdir** function except that it returns a pointer to a record of type **struct dirent64**. Some of the members of this data type (notably **d_ino**) might have a different size to allow large filesystems.

> In all other aspects this function is equivalent to **readdir**.

int readdir64_r (*DIR *dirstream*, *struct dirent64 *entry*, *struct dirent64 **result*)   [Function]
> Preliminary: | MT-Safe | AS-Unsafe lock | AC-Unsafe lock | See Section 1.2.2.1 [POSIX Safety Concepts], page 2.

> The **readdir64_r** function is equivalent to the **readdir_r** function except that it takes parameters of base type **struct dirent64** instead of **struct dirent** in the second and third position. The same precautions mentioned in the documentation of **readdir_r** also apply here.

int closedir (*DIR *dirstream*)   [Function]
> Preliminary: | MT-Safe | AS-Unsafe heap lock/hurd | AC-Unsafe mem fd lock/hurd | See Section 1.2.2.1 [POSIX Safety Concepts], page 2.

> This function closes the directory stream *dirstream*. It returns 0 on success and -1 on failure.

> The following **errno** error conditions are defined for this function:

> **EBADF**   The *dirstream* argument is not valid.

14.2.4 Simple Program to List a Directory

Here's a simple program that prints the names of the files in the current working directory:

```
#include <stdio.h>
#include <sys/types.h>
#include <dirent.h>

int
main (void)
{
  DIR *dp;
  struct dirent *ep;

  dp = opendir ("./");
  if (dp != NULL)
```

```
  {
    while (ep = readdir (dp))
      puts (ep->d_name);
    (void) closedir (dp);
  }
  else
    perror ("Couldn't open the directory");

  return 0;
}
```

The order in which files appear in a directory tends to be fairly random. A more useful program would sort the entries (perhaps by alphabetizing them) before printing them; see Section 14.2.6 [Scanning the Content of a Directory], page 385, and Section 9.3 [Array Sort Function], page 213.

14.2.5 Random Access in a Directory Stream

This section describes how to reread parts of a directory that you have already read from an open directory stream. All the symbols are declared in the header file dirent.h.

void rewinddir (*DIR *dirstream*) [Function]

> Preliminary: | MT-Safe | AS-Unsafe lock | AC-Unsafe lock | See Section 1.2.2.1 [POSIX Safety Concepts], page 2.

> The rewinddir function is used to reinitialize the directory stream *dirstream*, so that if you call readdir it returns information about the first entry in the directory again. This function also notices if files have been added or removed to the directory since it was opened with opendir. (Entries for these files might or might not be returned by readdir if they were added or removed since you last called opendir or rewinddir.)

long int telldir (*DIR *dirstream*) [Function]

> Preliminary: | MT-Safe | AS-Unsafe heap/bsd lock/bsd | AC-Unsafe mem/bsd lock/bsd | See Section 1.2.2.1 [POSIX Safety Concepts], page 2.

> The telldir function returns the file position of the directory stream *dirstream*. You can use this value with seekdir to restore the directory stream to that position.

void seekdir (*DIR *dirstream*, *long int pos*) [Function]

> Preliminary: | MT-Safe | AS-Unsafe heap/bsd lock/bsd | AC-Unsafe mem/bsd lock/bsd | See Section 1.2.2.1 [POSIX Safety Concepts], page 2.

> The seekdir function sets the file position of the directory stream *dirstream* to *pos*. The value *pos* must be the result of a previous call to telldir on this particular stream; closing and reopening the directory can invalidate values returned by telldir.

14.2.6 Scanning the Content of a Directory

A higher-level interface to the directory handling functions is the scandir function. With its help one can select a subset of the entries in a directory, possibly sort them and get a list of names as the result.

`int scandir` (*const char *dir, struct dirent ***namelist, int*   [Function]
    (**selector*) (*const struct dirent **), *int* (**cmp*) (*const struct dirent **, const struct dirent ***))

    Preliminary: | MT-Safe | AS-Unsafe heap | AC-Unsafe mem fd | See Section 1.2.2.1 [POSIX Safety Concepts], page 2.

    The `scandir` function scans the contents of the directory selected by *dir*. The result in *namelist is an array of pointers to structure of type `struct dirent` which describe all selected directory entries and which is allocated using `malloc`. Instead of always getting all directory entries returned, the user supplied function *selector* can be used to decide which entries are in the result. Only the entries for which *selector* returns a non-zero value are selected.

    Finally the entries in *namelist are sorted using the user-supplied function *cmp*. The arguments passed to the *cmp* function are of type `struct dirent **`, therefore one cannot directly use the `strcmp` or `strcoll` functions; instead see the functions `alphasort` and `versionsort` below.

    The return value of the function is the number of entries placed in *namelist. If it is `-1` an error occurred (either the directory could not be opened for reading or the malloc call failed) and the global variable `errno` contains more information on the error.

As described above the fourth argument to the `scandir` function must be a pointer to a sorting function. For the convenience of the programmer the GNU C Library contains implementations of functions which are very helpful for this purpose.

`int alphasort` (*const struct dirent **a, const struct dirent **b*)   [Function]
    Preliminary: | MT-Safe locale | AS-Unsafe heap | AC-Unsafe mem | See Section 1.2.2.1 [POSIX Safety Concepts], page 2.

    The `alphasort` function behaves like the `strcoll` function (see Section 5.5 [String/Array Comparison], page 102). The difference is that the arguments are not string pointers but instead they are of type `struct dirent **`.

    The return value of `alphasort` is less than, equal to, or greater than zero depending on the order of the two entries *a* and *b*.

`int versionsort` (*const struct dirent **a, const struct dirent **b*)   [Function]
    Preliminary: | MT-Safe locale | AS-Safe | AC-Safe | See Section 1.2.2.1 [POSIX Safety Concepts], page 2.

    The `versionsort` function is like `alphasort` except that it uses the `strverscmp` function internally.

If the filesystem supports large files we cannot use the `scandir` anymore since the `dirent` structure might not able to contain all the information. The LFS provides the new type `struct dirent64`. To use this we need a new function.

`int scandir64` (*const char *dir, struct dirent64 ***namelist, int*   [Function]
    (**selector*) (*const struct dirent64 **), *int* (**cmp*) (*const struct dirent64 **, const struct dirent64 ***))

    Preliminary: | MT-Safe | AS-Unsafe heap | AC-Unsafe mem fd | See Section 1.2.2.1 [POSIX Safety Concepts], page 2.

The `scandir64` function works like the `scandir` function except that the directory entries it returns are described by elements of type `struct dirent64`. The function pointed to by *selector* is again used to select the desired entries, except that *selector* now must point to a function which takes a `struct dirent64 *` parameter.

Similarly the *cmp* function should expect its two arguments to be of type `struct dirent64 **`.

As *cmp* is now a function of a different type, the functions `alphasort` and `versionsort` cannot be supplied for that argument. Instead we provide the two replacement functions below.

`int alphasort64` (*const struct dirent64 **a, const struct dirent **b*)   [Function]
> Preliminary: | MT-Safe locale | AS-Unsafe heap | AC-Unsafe mem | See Section 1.2.2.1 [POSIX Safety Concepts], page 2.
>
> The `alphasort64` function behaves like the `strcoll` function (see Section 5.5 [String/Array Comparison], page 102). The difference is that the arguments are not string pointers but instead they are of type `struct dirent64 **`.
>
> Return value of `alphasort64` is less than, equal to, or greater than zero depending on the order of the two entries *a* and *b*.

`int versionsort64` (*const struct dirent64 **a, const struct dirent64 **b*)   [Function]
> Preliminary: | MT-Safe locale | AS-Safe | AC-Safe | See Section 1.2.2.1 [POSIX Safety Concepts], page 2.
>
> The `versionsort64` function is like `alphasort64`, excepted that it uses the `strverscmp` function internally.

It is important not to mix the use of `scandir` and the 64-bit comparison functions or vice versa. There are systems on which this works but on others it will fail miserably.

14.2.7 Simple Program to List a Directory, Mark II

Here is a revised version of the directory lister found above (see Section 14.2.4 [Simple Program to List a Directory], page 384). Using the `scandir` function we can avoid the functions which work directly with the directory contents. After the call the returned entries are available for direct use.

```
#include <stdio.h>
#include <dirent.h>

static int
one (const struct dirent *unused)
{
  return 1;
}

int
main (void)
{
  struct dirent **eps;
  int n;
```

```
      n = scandir ("./", &eps, one, alphasort);
      if (n >= 0)
        {
          int cnt;
          for (cnt = 0; cnt < n; ++cnt)
            puts (eps[cnt]->d_name);
        }
      else
        perror ("Couldn't open the directory");

      return 0;
}
```

Note the simple selector function in this example. Since we want to see all directory entries we always return 1.

14.3 Working with Directory Trees

The functions described so far for handling the files in a directory have allowed you to either retrieve the information bit by bit, or to process all the files as a group (see **scandir**). Sometimes it is useful to process whole hierarchies of directories and their contained files. The X/Open specification defines two functions to do this. The simpler form is derived from an early definition in System V systems and therefore this function is available on SVID-derived systems. The prototypes and required definitions can be found in the **ftw.h** header.

There are four functions in this family: **ftw**, **nftw** and their 64-bit counterparts **ftw64** and **nftw64**. These functions take as one of their arguments a pointer to a callback function of the appropriate type.

__ftw_func_t   [Data Type]
        int (*) (const char *, const struct stat *, int)

The type of callback functions given to the **ftw** function. The first parameter points to the file name, the second parameter to an object of type **struct stat** which is filled in for the file named in the first parameter.

The last parameter is a flag giving more information about the current file. It can have the following values:

FTW_F   The item is either a normal file or a file which does not fit into one of the following categories. This could be special files, sockets etc.

FTW_D   The item is a directory.

FTW_NS   The **stat** call failed and so the information pointed to by the second paramater is invalid.

FTW_DNR   The item is a directory which cannot be read.

FTW_SL   The item is a symbolic link. Since symbolic links are normally followed seeing this value in a **ftw** callback function means the referenced file does not exist. The situation for **nftw** is different.

               This value is only available if the program is compiled with **_XOPEN_ EXTENDED** defined before including the first header. The original SVID systems do not have symbolic links.

If the sources are compiled with _FILE_OFFSET_BITS == 64 this type is in fact __ ftw64_func_t since this mode changes struct stat to be struct stat64.

For the LFS interface and for use in the function ftw64, the header ftw.h defines another function type.

__ftw64_func_t   [Data Type]
      int (*) (const char *, const struct stat64 *, int)

This type is used just like __ftw_func_t for the callback function, but this time is called from ftw64. The second parameter to the function is a pointer to a variable of type struct stat64 which is able to represent the larger values.

__nftw_func_t   [Data Type]
      int (*) (const char *, const struct stat *, int, struct FTW *)

The first three arguments are the same as for the __ftw_func_t type. However for the third argument some additional values are defined to allow finer differentiation:

FTW_DP   The current item is a directory and all subdirectories have already been visited and reported. This flag is returned instead of FTW_D if the FTW_ DEPTH flag is passed to nftw (see below).

FTW_SLN   The current item is a stale symbolic link. The file it points to does not exist.

The last parameter of the callback function is a pointer to a structure with some extra information as described below.

If the sources are compiled with _FILE_OFFSET_BITS == 64 this type is in fact __ nftw64_func_t since this mode changes struct stat to be struct stat64.

For the LFS interface there is also a variant of this data type available which has to be used with the nftw64 function.

__nftw64_func_t   [Data Type]
      int (*) (const char *, const struct stat64 *, int, struct FTW *)

This type is used just like __nftw_func_t for the callback function, but this time is called from nftw64. The second parameter to the function is this time a pointer to a variable of type struct stat64 which is able to represent the larger values.

struct FTW   [Data Type]
The information contained in this structure helps in interpreting the name parameter and gives some information about the current state of the traversal of the directory hierarchy.

int base   The value is the offset into the string passed in the first parameter to the callback function of the beginning of the file name. The rest of the string is the path of the file. This information is especially important if the FTW_CHDIR flag was set in calling nftw since then the current directory is the one the current item is found in.

int level   Whilst processing, the code tracks how many directories down it has gone to find the current file. This nesting level starts at 0 for files in the initial directory (or is zero for the initial file if a file was passed).

int ftw (*const char *filename*, *__ftw_func_t func*, *int descriptors*)   [Function]
> Preliminary: | MT-Safe | AS-Unsafe heap | AC-Unsafe mem fd | See Section 1.2.2.1
> [POSIX Safety Concepts], page 2.
>
> The `ftw` function calls the callback function given in the parameter *func* for every
> item which is found in the directory specified by *filename* and all directories below.
> The function follows symbolic links if necessary but does not process an item twice.
> If *filename* is not a directory then it itself is the only object returned to the callback
> function.
>
> The file name passed to the callback function is constructed by taking the *filename*
> parameter and appending the names of all passed directories and then the local file
> name. So the callback function can use this parameter to access the file. `ftw` also
> calls `stat` for the file and passes that information on to the callback function. If this
> `stat` call was not successful the failure is indicated by setting the third argument of
> the callback function to `FTW_NS`. Otherwise it is set according to the description given
> in the account of `__ftw_func_t` above.
>
> The callback function is expected to return 0 to indicate that no error occurred and
> that processing should continue. If an error occurred in the callback function or
> it wants `ftw` to return immediately, the callback function can return a value other
> than 0. This is the only correct way to stop the function. The program must not
> use `setjmp` or similar techniques to continue from another place. This would leave
> resources allocated by the `ftw` function unfreed.
>
> The *descriptors* parameter to `ftw` specifies how many file descriptors it is allowed to
> consume. The function runs faster the more descriptors it can use. For each level in
> the directory hierarchy at most one descriptor is used, but for very deep ones any limit
> on open file descriptors for the process or the system may be exceeded. Moreover,
> file descriptor limits in a multi-threaded program apply to all the threads as a group,
> and therefore it is a good idea to supply a reasonable limit to the number of open
> descriptors.
>
> The return value of the `ftw` function is 0 if all callback function calls returned 0 and
> all actions performed by the `ftw` succeeded. If a function call failed (other than calling
> `stat` on an item) the function returns −1. If a callback function returns a value other
> than 0 this value is returned as the return value of `ftw`.
>
> When the sources are compiled with `_FILE_OFFSET_BITS == 64` on a 32-bit system
> this function is in fact `ftw64`, i.e., the LFS interface transparently replaces the old
> interface.

int ftw64 (*const char *filename*, *__ftw64_func_t func*, *int*   [Function]
> *descriptors*)
> Preliminary: | MT-Safe | AS-Unsafe heap | AC-Unsafe mem fd | See Section 1.2.2.1
> [POSIX Safety Concepts], page 2.
>
> This function is similar to `ftw` but it can work on filesystems with large files. File
> information is reported using a variable of type `struct stat64` which is passed by
> reference to the callback function.
>
> When the sources are compiled with `_FILE_OFFSET_BITS == 64` on a 32-bit system
> this function is available under the name `ftw` and transparently replaces the old
> implementation.

int nftw (*const char* ***filename**, *__nftw_func_t* **func**, *int* **descriptors**,   [Function]
    int **flag**)

Preliminary: | MT-Safe cwd | AS-Unsafe heap | AC-Unsafe mem fd cwd | See
Section 1.2.2.1 [POSIX Safety Concepts], page 2.

The **nftw** function works like the **ftw** functions. They call the callback function *func*
for all items found in the directory *filename* and below. At most *descriptors* file
descriptors are consumed during the **nftw** call.

One difference is that the callback function is of a different type. It is of type
struct FTW * and provides the callback function with the extra information described
above.

A second difference is that **nftw** takes a fourth argument, which is 0 or a bitwise-OR
combination of any of the following values.

FTW_PHYS   While traversing the directory symbolic links are not followed. Instead
                  symbolic links are reported using the **FTW_SL** value for the type parameter
                  to the callback function. If the file referenced by a symbolic link does not
                  exist **FTW_SLN** is returned instead.

FTW_MOUNT

                  The callback function is only called for items which are on the same
                  mounted filesystem as the directory given by the *filename* parameter to
                  nftw.

FTW_CHDIR

                  If this flag is given the current working directory is changed to the direc-
                  tory of the reported object before the callback function is called. When
                  ntfw finally returns the current directory is restored to its original value.

FTW_DEPTH

                  If this option is specified then all subdirectories and files within them
                  are processed before processing the top directory itself (depth-first pro-
                  cessing). This also means the type flag given to the callback function is
                  FTW_DP and not **FTW_D**.

FTW_ACTIONRETVAL

                  If this option is specified then return values from callbacks are handled
                  differently. If the callback returns **FTW_CONTINUE**, walking continues nor-
                  mally. **FTW_STOP** means walking stops and **FTW_STOP** is returned to the
                  caller. If **FTW_SKIP_SUBTREE** is returned by the callback with **FTW_D** ar-
                  gument, the subtree is skipped and walking continues with next sibling
                  of the directory. If **FTW_SKIP_SIBLINGS** is returned by the callback, all
                  siblings of the current entry are skipped and walking continues in its par-
                  ent. No other return values should be returned from the callbacks if this
                  option is set. This option is a GNU extension.

The return value is computed in the same way as for **ftw**. **nftw** returns 0 if no
failures occurred and all callback functions returned 0. In case of internal errors, such
as memory problems, the return value is −1 and *errno* is set accordingly. If the return
value of a callback invocation was non-zero then that value is returned.

When the sources are compiled with _FILE_OFFSET_BITS == 64 on a 32-bit system this function is in fact **nftw64**, i.e., the LFS interface transparently replaces the old interface.

int **nftw64** (*const char *filename, __nftw64_func_t* **func**, *int*   [Function]
       descriptors, *int* **flag**)

Preliminary: | MT-Safe cwd | AS-Unsafe heap | AC-Unsafe mem fd cwd | See Section 1.2.2.1 [POSIX Safety Concepts], page 2.

This function is similar to **nftw** but it can work on filesystems with large files. File information is reported using a variable of type **struct stat64** which is passed by reference to the callback function.

When the sources are compiled with _FILE_OFFSET_BITS == 64 on a 32-bit system this function is available under the name **nftw** and transparently replaces the old implementation.

14.4 Hard Links

In POSIX systems, one file can have many names at the same time. All of the names are equally real, and no one of them is preferred to the others.

To add a name to a file, use the **link** function. (The new name is also called a *hard link* to the file.) Creating a new link to a file does not copy the contents of the file; it simply makes a new name by which the file can be known, in addition to the file's existing name or names.

One file can have names in several directories, so the organization of the file system is not a strict hierarchy or tree.

In most implementations, it is not possible to have hard links to the same file in multiple file systems. **link** reports an error if you try to make a hard link to the file from another file system when this cannot be done.

The prototype for the **link** function is declared in the header file **unistd.h**.

int **link** (*const char *oldname, const char *newname*)   [Function]

Preliminary: | MT-Safe | AS-Safe | AC-Safe | See Section 1.2.2.1 [POSIX Safety Concepts], page 2.

The **link** function makes a new link to the existing file named by *oldname*, under the new name *newname*.

This function returns a value of 0 if it is successful and −1 on failure. In addition to the usual file name errors (see Section 11.2.3 [File Name Errors], page 246) for both *oldname* and *newname*, the following **errno** error conditions are defined for this function:

EACCES   You are not allowed to write to the directory in which the new link is to be written.

EEXIST   There is already a file named *newname*. If you want to replace this link with a new link, you must remove the old link explicitly first.

EMLINK   There are already too many links to the file named by *oldname*. (The maximum number of links to a file is **LINK_MAX**; see Section 32.6 [Limits on File System Capacity], page 850.)

ENOENT   The file named by *oldname* doesn't exist. You can't make a link to a file
             that doesn't exist.

ENOSPC   The directory or file system that would contain the new link is full and
             cannot be extended.

EPERM   On GNU/Linux and GNU/Hurd systems and some others, you cannot
             make links to directories. Many systems allow only privileged users to do
             so. This error is used to report the problem.

EROFS   The directory containing the new link can't be modified because it's on
             a read-only file system.

EXDEV   The directory specified in *newname* is on a different file system than the
             existing file.

EIO   A hardware error occurred while trying to read or write the to filesystem.

14.5 Symbolic Links

GNU systems support *soft links* or *symbolic links*. This is a kind of "file" that is essentially
a pointer to another file name. Unlike hard links, symbolic links can be made to directories
or across file systems with no restrictions. You can also make a symbolic link to a name
which is not the name of any file. (Opening this link will fail until a file by that name is
created.) Likewise, if the symbolic link points to an existing file which is later deleted, the
symbolic link continues to point to the same file name even though the name no longer
names any file.

The reason symbolic links work the way they do is that special things happen when you
try to open the link. The `open` function realizes you have specified the name of a link, reads
the file name contained in the link, and opens that file name instead. The `stat` function
likewise operates on the file that the symbolic link points to, instead of on the link itself.

By contrast, other operations such as deleting or renaming the file operate on the link
itself. The functions `readlink` and `lstat` also refrain from following symbolic links, because
their purpose is to obtain information about the link. `link`, the function that makes a hard
link, does too. It makes a hard link to the symbolic link, which one rarely wants.

Some systems have for some functions operating on files have a limit on how many
symbolic links are followed when resolving a path name. The limit if it exists is published
in the `sys/param.h` header file.

`int MAXSYMLINKS`   [Macro]
     The macro `MAXSYMLINKS` specifies how many symlinks some function will follow before
     returning `ELOOP`. Not all functions behave the same and this value is not the same a
     that returned for `_SC_SYMLOOP` by `sysconf`. In fact, the `sysconf` result can indicate
     that there is no fixed limit although `MAXSYMLINKS` exists and has a finite value.

Prototypes for most of the functions listed in this section are in `unistd.h`.

`int symlink` (*const char *oldname, const char *newname*)   [Function]
     Preliminary: | MT-Safe | AS-Safe | AC-Safe | See Section 1.2.2.1 [POSIX Safety
     Concepts], page 2.

The `symlink` function makes a symbolic link to *oldname* named *newname*.

The normal return value from `symlink` is 0. A return value of −1 indicates an error. In addition to the usual file name syntax errors (see Section 11.2.3 [File Name Errors], page 246), the following `errno` error conditions are defined for this function:

EEXIST   There is already an existing file named *newname*.

EROFS   The file *newname* would exist on a read-only file system.

ENOSPC   The directory or file system cannot be extended to make the new link.

EIO   A hardware error occurred while reading or writing data on the disk.

`ssize_t readlink` (*const char *filename, char *buffer, size_t size*)   [Function]
Preliminary: | MT-Safe | AS-Safe | AC-Safe | See Section 1.2.2.1 [POSIX Safety Concepts], page 2.

The `readlink` function gets the value of the symbolic link *filename*. The file name that the link points to is copied into *buffer*. This file name string is *not* null-terminated; `readlink` normally returns the number of characters copied. The *size* argument specifies the maximum number of characters to copy, usually the allocation size of *buffer*.

If the return value equals *size*, you cannot tell whether or not there was room to return the entire name. So make a bigger buffer and call `readlink` again. Here is an example:

```
char *
readlink_malloc (const char *filename)
{
  int size = 100;
  char *buffer = NULL;

  while (1)
    {
      buffer = (char *) xrealloc (buffer, size);
      int nchars = readlink (filename, buffer, size);
      if (nchars < 0)
        {
          free (buffer);
          return NULL;
        }
      if (nchars < size)
        return buffer;
      size *= 2;
    }
}
```

A value of −1 is returned in case of error. In addition to the usual file name errors (see Section 11.2.3 [File Name Errors], page 246), the following `errno` error conditions are defined for this function:

EINVAL   The named file is not a symbolic link.

EIO   A hardware error occurred while reading or writing data on the disk.

In some situations it is desirable to resolve all the symbolic links to get the real name of a file where no prefix names a symbolic link which is followed and no filename in the path is . or ... This is for instance desirable if files have to be compare in which case different names can refer to the same inode.

char * canonicalize_file_name (*const char *name*)   [Function]
Preliminary: | MT-Safe | AS-Unsafe heap | AC-Unsafe mem fd | See Section 1.2.2.1 [POSIX Safety Concepts], page 2.

The `canonicalize_file_name` function returns the absolute name of the file named by *name* which contains no ., .. components nor any repeated path separators (/) or symlinks. The result is passed back as the return value of the function in a block of memory allocated with `malloc`. If the result is not used anymore the memory should be freed with a call to `free`.

If any of the path components is missing the function returns a NULL pointer. This is also what is returned if the length of the path reaches or exceeds `PATH_MAX` characters. In any case `errno` is set accordingly.

ENAMETOOLONG
            The resulting path is too long. This error only occurs on systems which have a limit on the file name length.

EACCES   At least one of the path components is not readable.

ENOENT   The input file name is empty.

ENOENT   At least one of the path components does not exist.

ELOOP   More than `MAXSYMLINKS` many symlinks have been followed.

This function is a GNU extension and is declared in `stdlib.h`.

The Unix standard includes a similar function which differs from `canonicalize_file_name` in that the user has to provide the buffer where the result is placed in.

char * realpath (*const char *restrict name, char *restrict resolved*)   [Function]
Preliminary: | MT-Safe | AS-Unsafe heap | AC-Unsafe mem fd | See Section 1.2.2.1 [POSIX Safety Concepts], page 2.

A call to `realpath` where the *resolved* parameter is `NULL` behaves exactly like `canonicalize_file_name`. The function allocates a buffer for the file name and returns a pointer to it. If *resolved* is not `NULL` it points to a buffer into which the result is copied. It is the callers responsibility to allocate a buffer which is large enough. On systems which define `PATH_MAX` this means the buffer must be large enough for a pathname of this size. For systems without limitations on the pathname length the requirement cannot be met and programs should not call `realpath` with anything but `NULL` for the second parameter.

One other difference is that the buffer *resolved* (if nonzero) will contain the part of the path component which does not exist or is not readable if the function returns `NULL` and `errno` is set to `EACCES` or `ENOENT`.

This function is declared in `stdlib.h`.

The advantage of using this function is that it is more widely available. The drawback is that it reports failures for long path on systems which have no limits on the file name length.

14.6 Deleting Files

You can delete a file with `unlink` or `remove`.

Deletion actually deletes a file name. If this is the file's only name, then the file is deleted as well. If the file has other remaining names (see Section 14.4 [Hard Links], page 392), it remains accessible under those names.

`int unlink (const char *filename)`   [Function]

> Preliminary: | MT-Safe | AS-Safe | AC-Safe | See Section 1.2.2.1 [POSIX Safety Concepts], page 2.

> The `unlink` function deletes the file name *filename*. If this is a file's sole name, the file itself is also deleted. (Actually, if any process has the file open when this happens, deletion is postponed until all processes have closed the file.)

> The function `unlink` is declared in the header file `unistd.h`.

> This function returns 0 on successful completion, and -1 on error. In addition to the usual file name errors (see Section 11.2.3 [File Name Errors], page 246), the following `errno` error conditions are defined for this function:

> EACCES
> > Write permission is denied for the directory from which the file is to be removed, or the directory has the sticky bit set and you do not own the file.

> EBUSY
> > This error indicates that the file is being used by the system in such a way that it can't be unlinked. For example, you might see this error if the file name specifies the root directory or a mount point for a file system.

> ENOENT
> > The file name to be deleted doesn't exist.

> EPERM
> > On some systems `unlink` cannot be used to delete the name of a directory, or at least can only be used this way by a privileged user. To avoid such problems, use `rmdir` to delete directories. (On GNU/Linux and GNU/Hurd systems `unlink` can never delete the name of a directory.)

> EROFS
> > The directory containing the file name to be deleted is on a read-only file system and can't be modified.

`int rmdir (const char *filename)`   [Function]

> Preliminary: | MT-Safe | AS-Safe | AC-Safe | See Section 1.2.2.1 [POSIX Safety Concepts], page 2.

> The `rmdir` function deletes a directory. The directory must be empty before it can be removed; in other words, it can only contain entries for . and ...

> In most other respects, `rmdir` behaves like `unlink`. There are two additional `errno` error conditions defined for `rmdir`:

> ENOTEMPTY
> EEXIST   The directory to be deleted is not empty.

> These two error codes are synonymous; some systems use one, and some use the other. GNU/Linux and GNU/Hurd systems always use `ENOTEMPTY`.

> The prototype for this function is declared in the header file `unistd.h`.

`int remove (const char *filename)`   [Function]
> Preliminary: | MT-Safe | AS-Safe | AC-Safe | See Section 1.2.2.1 [POSIX Safety
> Concepts], page 2.
>
> This is the ISO C function to remove a file. It works like `unlink` for files and like
> `rmdir` for directories. `remove` is declared in `stdio.h`.

14.7 Renaming Files

The `rename` function is used to change a file's name.

`int rename (const char *oldname, const char *newname)`   [Function]
> Preliminary: | MT-Safe | AS-Safe | AC-Safe | See Section 1.2.2.1 [POSIX Safety
> Concepts], page 2.
>
> The `rename` function renames the file *oldname* to *newname*. The file formerly acces-
> sible under the name *oldname* is afterwards accessible as *newname* instead. (If the
> file had any other names aside from *oldname*, it continues to have those names.)
>
> The directory containing the name *newname* must be on the same file system as the
> directory containing the name *oldname*.
>
> One special case for `rename` is when *oldname* and *newname* are two names for the
> same file. The consistent way to handle this case is to delete *oldname*. However,
> in this case POSIX requires that `rename` do nothing and report success—which is
> inconsistent. We don't know what your operating system will do.
>
> If *oldname* is not a directory, then any existing file named *newname* is removed during
> the renaming operation. However, if *newname* is the name of a directory, `rename` fails
> in this case.
>
> If *oldname* is a directory, then either *newname* must not exist or it must name a
> directory that is empty. In the latter case, the existing directory named *newname* is
> deleted first. The name *newname* must not specify a subdirectory of the directory
> `oldname` which is being renamed.
>
> One useful feature of `rename` is that the meaning of *newname* changes "atomically"
> from any previously existing file by that name to its new meaning (i.e., the file that
> was called *oldname*). There is no instant at which *newname* is non-existent "in
> between" the old meaning and the new meaning. If there is a system crash during
> the operation, it is possible for both names to still exist; but *newname* will always be
> intact if it exists at all.
>
> If `rename` fails, it returns `-1`. In addition to the usual file name errors (see
> Section 11.2.3 [File Name Errors], page 246), the following `errno` error conditions
> are defined for this function:
>
> EACCES   One of the directories containing *newname* or *oldname* refuses write per-
>   mission; or *newname* and *oldname* are directories and write permission
>   is refused for one of them.
>
> EBUSY   A directory named by *oldname* or *newname* is being used by the system in
>   a way that prevents the renaming from working. This includes directories
>   that are mount points for filesystems, and directories that are the current
>   working directories of processes.

```
ENOTEMPTY
```
EEXIST   The directory *newname* isn't empty. GNU/Linux and GNU/Hurd systems always return `ENOTEMPTY` for this, but some other systems return `EEXIST`.

EINVAL   *oldname* is a directory that contains *newname*.

EISDIR   *newname* is a directory but the *oldname* isn't.

EMLINK   The parent directory of *newname* would have too many links (entries).

ENOENT   The file *oldname* doesn't exist.

ENOSPC   The directory that would contain *newname* has no room for another entry, and there is no space left in the file system to expand it.

EROFS   The operation would involve writing to a directory on a read-only file system.

EXDEV   The two file names *newname* and *oldname* are on different file systems.

14.8 Creating Directories

Directories are created with the `mkdir` function. (There is also a shell command `mkdir` which does the same thing.)

int mkdir (*const char *filename*, *mode_t mode*)   [Function]
Preliminary: | MT-Safe | AS-Safe | AC-Safe | See Section 1.2.2.1 [POSIX Safety Concepts], page 2.

The `mkdir` function creates a new, empty directory with name *filename*.

The argument *mode* specifies the file permissions for the new directory file. See Section 14.9.5 [The Mode Bits for Access Permission], page 408, for more information about this.

A return value of 0 indicates successful completion, and −1 indicates failure. In addition to the usual file name syntax errors (see Section 11.2.3 [File Name Errors], page 246), the following `errno` error conditions are defined for this function:

EACCES   Write permission is denied for the parent directory in which the new directory is to be added.

EEXIST   A file named *filename* already exists.

EMLINK   The parent directory has too many links (entries).

          Well-designed file systems never report this error, because they permit more links than your disk could possibly hold. However, you must still take account of the possibility of this error, as it could result from network access to a file system on another machine.

ENOSPC   The file system doesn't have enough room to create the new directory.

EROFS   The parent directory of the directory being created is on a read-only file system and cannot be modified.

To use this function, your program should include the header file `sys/stat.h`.

14.9 File Attributes

When you issue an 'ls -l' shell command on a file, it gives you information about the size of the file, who owns it, when it was last modified, etc. These are called the *file attributes*, and are associated with the file itself and not a particular one of its names.

This section contains information about how you can inquire about and modify the attributes of a file.

14.9.1 The meaning of the File Attributes

When you read the attributes of a file, they come back in a structure called **struct stat**. This section describes the names of the attributes, their data types, and what they mean. For the functions to read the attributes of a file, see Section 14.9.2 [Reading the Attributes of a File], page 403.

The header file **sys/stat.h** declares all the symbols defined in this section.

struct stat   [Data Type]

> The **stat** structure type is used to return information about the attributes of a file. It contains at least the following members:
>
> **mode_t st_mode**
>> Specifies the mode of the file. This includes file type information (see Section 14.9.3 [Testing the Type of a File], page 404) and the file permission bits (see Section 14.9.5 [The Mode Bits for Access Permission], page 408).
>
> **ino_t st_ino**
>> The file serial number, which distinguishes this file from all other files on the same device.
>
> **dev_t st_dev**
>> Identifies the device containing the file. The **st_ino** and **st_dev**, taken together, uniquely identify the file. The **st_dev** value is not necessarily consistent across reboots or system crashes, however.
>
> **nlink_t st_nlink**
>> The number of hard links to the file. This count keeps track of how many directories have entries for this file. If the count is ever decremented to zero, then the file itself is discarded as soon as no process still holds it open. Symbolic links are not counted in the total.
>
> **uid_t st_uid**
>> The user ID of the file's owner. See Section 14.9.4 [File Owner], page 406.
>
> **gid_t st_gid**
>> The group ID of the file. See Section 14.9.4 [File Owner], page 406.
>
> **off_t st_size**
>> This specifies the size of a regular file in bytes. For files that are really devices this field isn't usually meaningful. For symbolic links this specifies the length of the file name the link refers to.

`time_t st_atime`
> This is the last access time for the file. See Section 14.9.9 [File Times], page 413.

`unsigned long int st_atime_usec`
> This is the fractional part of the last access time for the file. See Section 14.9.9 [File Times], page 413.

`time_t st_mtime`
> This is the time of the last modification to the contents of the file. See Section 14.9.9 [File Times], page 413.

`unsigned long int st_mtime_usec`
> This is the fractional part of the time of the last modification to the contents of the file. See Section 14.9.9 [File Times], page 413.

`time_t st_ctime`
> This is the time of the last modification to the attributes of the file. See Section 14.9.9 [File Times], page 413.

`unsigned long int st_ctime_usec`
> This is the fractional part of the time of the last modification to the attributes of the file. See Section 14.9.9 [File Times], page 413.

`blkcnt_t st_blocks`
> This is the amount of disk space that the file occupies, measured in units of 512-byte blocks.
>
> The number of disk blocks is not strictly proportional to the size of the file, for two reasons: the file system may use some blocks for internal record keeping; and the file may be sparse—it may have "holes" which contain zeros but do not actually take up space on the disk.
>
> You can tell (approximately) whether a file is sparse by comparing this value with `st_size`, like this:
>
>> `(st.st_blocks * 512 < st.st_size)`
>
> This test is not perfect because a file that is just slightly sparse might not be detected as sparse at all. For practical applications, this is not a problem.

`unsigned int st_blksize`
> The optimal block size for reading of writing this file, in bytes. You might use this size for allocating the buffer space for reading of writing the file. (This is unrelated to `st_blocks`.)

The extensions for the Large File Support (LFS) require, even on 32-bit machines, types which can handle file sizes up to 2^63. Therefore a new definition of **struct stat** is necessary.

struct stat64   [Data Type]
> The members of this type are the same and have the same names as those in **struct stat**. The only difference is that the members **st_ino**, **st_size**, and **st_blocks** have a different type to support larger values.

`mode_t st_mode`

> Specifies the mode of the file. This includes file type information (see Section 14.9.3 [Testing the Type of a File], page 404) and the file permission bits (see Section 14.9.5 [The Mode Bits for Access Permission], page 408).

`ino64_t st_ino`

> The file serial number, which distinguishes this file from all other files on the same device.

`dev_t st_dev`

> Identifies the device containing the file. The `st_ino` and `st_dev`, taken together, uniquely identify the file. The `st_dev` value is not necessarily consistent across reboots or system crashes, however.

`nlink_t st_nlink`

> The number of hard links to the file. This count keeps track of how many directories have entries for this file. If the count is ever decremented to zero, then the file itself is discarded as soon as no process still holds it open. Symbolic links are not counted in the total.

`uid_t st_uid`

> The user ID of the file's owner. See Section 14.9.4 [File Owner], page 406.

`gid_t st_gid`

> The group ID of the file. See Section 14.9.4 [File Owner], page 406.

`off64_t st_size`

> This specifies the size of a regular file in bytes. For files that are really devices this field isn't usually meaningful. For symbolic links this specifies the length of the file name the link refers to.

`time_t st_atime`

> This is the last access time for the file. See Section 14.9.9 [File Times], page 413.

`unsigned long int st_atime_usec`

> This is the fractional part of the last access time for the file. See Section 14.9.9 [File Times], page 413.

`time_t st_mtime`

> This is the time of the last modification to the contents of the file. See Section 14.9.9 [File Times], page 413.

`unsigned long int st_mtime_usec`

> This is the fractional part of the time of the last modification to the contents of the file. See Section 14.9.9 [File Times], page 413.

`time_t st_ctime`

> This is the time of the last modification to the attributes of the file. See Section 14.9.9 [File Times], page 413.

`unsigned long int st_ctime_usec`

> This is the fractional part of the time of the last modification to the attributes of the file. See Section 14.9.9 [File Times], page 413.

`blkcnt64_t st_blocks`
> This is the amount of disk space that the file occupies, measured in units of 512-byte blocks.

`unsigned int st_blksize`
> The optimal block size for reading of writing this file, in bytes. You might use this size for allocating the buffer space for reading of writing the file. (This is unrelated to `st_blocks`.)

Some of the file attributes have special data type names which exist specifically for those attributes. (They are all aliases for well-known integer types that you know and love.) These typedef names are defined in the header file `sys/types.h` as well as in `sys/stat.h`. Here is a list of them.

`mode_t`   [Data Type]
> This is an integer data type used to represent file modes. In the GNU C Library, this is an unsigned type no narrower than `unsigned int`.

`ino_t`   [Data Type]
> This is an unsigned integer type used to represent file serial numbers. (In Unix jargon, these are sometimes called *inode numbers*.) In the GNU C Library, this type is no narrower than `unsigned int`.
>
> If the source is compiled with `_FILE_OFFSET_BITS == 64` this type is transparently replaced by `ino64_t`.

`ino64_t`   [Data Type]
> This is an unsigned integer type used to represent file serial numbers for the use in LFS. In the GNU C Library, this type is no narrower than `unsigned int`.
>
> When compiling with `_FILE_OFFSET_BITS == 64` this type is available under the name `ino_t`.

`dev_t`   [Data Type]
> This is an arithmetic data type used to represent file device numbers. In the GNU C Library, this is an integer type no narrower than `int`.

`nlink_t`   [Data Type]
> This is an integer type used to represent file link counts.

`blkcnt_t`   [Data Type]
> This is a signed integer type used to represent block counts. In the GNU C Library, this type is no narrower than `int`.
>
> If the source is compiled with `_FILE_OFFSET_BITS == 64` this type is transparently replaced by `blkcnt64_t`.

`blkcnt64_t`   [Data Type]
> This is a signed integer type used to represent block counts for the use in LFS. In the GNU C Library, this type is no narrower than `int`.
>
> When compiling with `_FILE_OFFSET_BITS == 64` this type is available under the name `blkcnt_t`.

14.9.2 Reading the Attributes of a File

To examine the attributes of files, use the functions `stat`, `fstat` and `lstat`. They return the attribute information in a `struct stat` object. All three functions are declared in the header file `sys/stat.h`.

`int stat (const char *filename, struct stat *buf)`   [Function]
> Preliminary: | MT-Safe | AS-Safe | AC-Safe | See Section 1.2.2.1 [POSIX Safety Concepts], page 2.
>
> The `stat` function returns information about the attributes of the file named by *filename* in the structure pointed to by *buf*.
>
> If *filename* is the name of a symbolic link, the attributes you get describe the file that the link points to. If the link points to a nonexistent file name, then `stat` fails reporting a nonexistent file.
>
> The return value is 0 if the operation is successful, or -1 on failure. In addition to the usual file name errors (see Section 11.2.3 [File Name Errors], page 246, the following `errno` error conditions are defined for this function:
>
> ENOENT   The file named by *filename* doesn't exist.
>
> When the sources are compiled with `_FILE_OFFSET_BITS == 64` this function is in fact `stat64` since the LFS interface transparently replaces the normal implementation.

`int stat64 (const char *filename, struct stat64 *buf)`   [Function]
> Preliminary: | MT-Safe | AS-Safe | AC-Safe | See Section 1.2.2.1 [POSIX Safety Concepts], page 2.
>
> This function is similar to `stat` but it is also able to work on files larger than 2^31 bytes on 32-bit systems. To be able to do this the result is stored in a variable of type `struct stat64` to which *buf* must point.
>
> When the sources are compiled with `_FILE_OFFSET_BITS == 64` this function is available under the name `stat` and so transparently replaces the interface for small files on 32-bit machines.

`int fstat (int filedes, struct stat *buf)`   [Function]
> Preliminary: | MT-Safe | AS-Safe | AC-Safe | See Section 1.2.2.1 [POSIX Safety Concepts], page 2.
>
> The `fstat` function is like `stat`, except that it takes an open file descriptor as an argument instead of a file name. See Chapter 13 [Low-Level Input/Output], page 323.
>
> Like `stat`, `fstat` returns 0 on success and -1 on failure. The following `errno` error conditions are defined for `fstat`:
>
> EBADF   The *filedes* argument is not a valid file descriptor.
>
> When the sources are compiled with `_FILE_OFFSET_BITS == 64` this function is in fact `fstat64` since the LFS interface transparently replaces the normal implementation.

`int fstat64 (int filedes, struct stat64 *buf)`   [Function]
> Preliminary: | MT-Safe | AS-Safe | AC-Safe | See Section 1.2.2.1 [POSIX Safety Concepts], page 2.

This function is similar to **fstat** but is able to work on large files on 32-bit platforms. For large files the file descriptor *filedes* should be obtained by **open64** or **creat64**. The *buf* pointer points to a variable of type **struct stat64** which is able to represent the larger values.

When the sources are compiled with **_FILE_OFFSET_BITS == 64** this function is available under the name **fstat** and so transparently replaces the interface for small files on 32-bit machines.

int lstat (*const char *filename*, *struct stat *buf*)   [Function]
    Preliminary: | MT-Safe | AS-Safe | AC-Safe | See Section 1.2.2.1 [POSIX Safety Concepts], page 2.

    The **lstat** function is like **stat**, except that it does not follow symbolic links. If *filename* is the name of a symbolic link, **lstat** returns information about the link itself; otherwise **lstat** works like **stat**. See Section 14.5 [Symbolic Links], page 393.

    When the sources are compiled with **_FILE_OFFSET_BITS == 64** this function is in fact **lstat64** since the LFS interface transparently replaces the normal implementation.

int lstat64 (*const char *filename*, *struct stat64 *buf*)   [Function]
    Preliminary: | MT-Safe | AS-Safe | AC-Safe | See Section 1.2.2.1 [POSIX Safety Concepts], page 2.

    This function is similar to **lstat** but it is also able to work on files larger than 2^31 bytes on 32-bit systems. To be able to do this the result is stored in a variable of type **struct stat64** to which *buf* must point.

    When the sources are compiled with **_FILE_OFFSET_BITS == 64** this function is available under the name **lstat** and so transparently replaces the interface for small files on 32-bit machines.

14.9.3 Testing the Type of a File

The *file mode*, stored in the **st_mode** field of the file attributes, contains two kinds of information: the file type code, and the access permission bits. This section discusses only the type code, which you can use to tell whether the file is a directory, socket, symbolic link, and so on. For details about access permissions see Section 14.9.5 [The Mode Bits for Access Permission], page 408.

There are two ways you can access the file type information in a file mode. Firstly, for each file type there is a *predicate macro* which examines a given file mode and returns whether it is of that type or not. Secondly, you can mask out the rest of the file mode to leave just the file type code, and compare this against constants for each of the supported file types.

All of the symbols listed in this section are defined in the header file **sys/stat.h**.

The following predicate macros test the type of a file, given the value *m* which is the **st_mode** field returned by **stat** on that file:

int S_ISDIR (*mode_t m*)   [Macro]
    Preliminary: | MT-Safe | AS-Safe | AC-Safe | See Section 1.2.2.1 [POSIX Safety Concepts], page 2.

    This macro returns non-zero if the file is a directory.

`int S_ISCHR` (*mode_t m*)   [Macro]
> Preliminary: | MT-Safe | AS-Safe | AC-Safe | See Section 1.2.2.1 [POSIX Safety
> Concepts], page 2.
>
> This macro returns non-zero if the file is a character special file (a device like a
> terminal).

`int S_ISBLK` (*mode_t m*)   [Macro]
> Preliminary: | MT-Safe | AS-Safe | AC-Safe | See Section 1.2.2.1 [POSIX Safety
> Concepts], page 2.
>
> This macro returns non-zero if the file is a block special file (a device like a disk).

`int S_ISREG` (*mode_t m*)   [Macro]
> Preliminary: | MT-Safe | AS-Safe | AC-Safe | See Section 1.2.2.1 [POSIX Safety
> Concepts], page 2.
>
> This macro returns non-zero if the file is a regular file.

`int S_ISFIFO` (*mode_t m*)   [Macro]
> Preliminary: | MT-Safe | AS-Safe | AC-Safe | See Section 1.2.2.1 [POSIX Safety
> Concepts], page 2.
>
> This macro returns non-zero if the file is a FIFO special file, or a pipe. See Chapter 15
> [Pipes and FIFOs], page 424.

`int S_ISLNK` (*mode_t m*)   [Macro]
> Preliminary: | MT-Safe | AS-Safe | AC-Safe | See Section 1.2.2.1 [POSIX Safety
> Concepts], page 2.
>
> This macro returns non-zero if the file is a symbolic link. See Section 14.5 [Symbolic
> Links], page 393.

`int S_ISSOCK` (*mode_t m*)   [Macro]
> Preliminary: | MT-Safe | AS-Safe | AC-Safe | See Section 1.2.2.1 [POSIX Safety
> Concepts], page 2.
>
> This macro returns non-zero if the file is a socket. See Chapter 16 [Sockets], page 429.

An alternate non-POSIX method of testing the file type is supported for compatibility
with BSD. The mode can be bitwise AND-ed with `S_IFMT` to extract the file type code, and
compared to the appropriate constant. For example,

    S_ISCHR (mode)

is equivalent to:

    ((mode & S_IFMT) == S_IFCHR)

`int S_IFMT`   [Macro]
> This is a bit mask used to extract the file type code from a mode value.

These are the symbolic names for the different file type codes:

`S_IFDIR`   This is the file type constant of a directory file.

`S_IFCHR`   This is the file type constant of a character-oriented device file.

`S_IFBLK`   This is the file type constant of a block-oriented device file.

`S_IFREG`   This is the file type constant of a regular file.

`S_IFLNK`   This is the file type constant of a symbolic link.

`S_IFSOCK`   This is the file type constant of a socket.

`S_IFIFO`   This is the file type constant of a FIFO or pipe.

The POSIX.1b standard introduced a few more objects which possibly can be implemented as object in the filesystem. These are message queues, semaphores, and shared memory objects. To allow differentiating these objects from other files the POSIX standard introduces three new test macros. But unlike the other macros it does not take the value of the `st_mode` field as the parameter. Instead they expect a pointer to the whole `struct stat` structure.

int **S_TYPEISMQ** (*struct stat *s*)   [Macro]
> Preliminary: | MT-Safe | AS-Safe | AC-Safe | See Section 1.2.2.1 [POSIX Safety Concepts], page 2.
>
> If the system implement POSIX message queues as distinct objects and the file is a message queue object, this macro returns a non-zero value. In all other cases the result is zero.

int **S_TYPEISSEM** (*struct stat *s*)   [Macro]
> Preliminary: | MT-Safe | AS-Safe | AC-Safe | See Section 1.2.2.1 [POSIX Safety Concepts], page 2.
>
> If the system implement POSIX semaphores as distinct objects and the file is a semaphore object, this macro returns a non-zero value. In all other cases the result is zero.

int **S_TYPEISSHM** (*struct stat *s*)   [Macro]
> Preliminary: | MT-Safe | AS-Safe | AC-Safe | See Section 1.2.2.1 [POSIX Safety Concepts], page 2.
>
> If the system implement POSIX shared memory objects as distinct objects and the file is a shared memory object, this macro returns a non-zero value. In all other cases the result is zero.

14.9.4 File Owner

Every file has an *owner* which is one of the registered user names defined on the system. Each file also has a *group* which is one of the defined groups. The file owner can often be useful for showing you who edited the file (especially when you edit with GNU Emacs), but its main purpose is for access control.

The file owner and group play a role in determining access because the file has one set of access permission bits for the owner, another set that applies to users who belong to the file's group, and a third set of bits that applies to everyone else. See Section 14.9.6 [How Your Access to a File is Decided], page 409, for the details of how access is decided based on this data.

When a file is created, its owner is set to the effective user ID of the process that creates it (see Section 30.2 [The Persona of a Process], page 791). The file's group ID may be set to either the effective group ID of the process, or the group ID of the directory that contains the file, depending on the system where the file is stored. When you access a remote file system, it behaves according to its own rules, not according to the system your program is running on. Thus, your program must be prepared to encounter either kind of behavior no matter what kind of system you run it on.

You can change the owner and/or group owner of an existing file using the `chown` function. This is the primitive for the `chown` and `chgrp` shell commands.

The prototype for this function is declared in `unistd.h`.

int chown (*const char *filename, uid_t owner, gid_t group*)   [Function]
> Preliminary: | MT-Safe | AS-Safe | AC-Safe | See Section 1.2.2.1 [POSIX Safety Concepts], page 2.
>
> The `chown` function changes the owner of the file *filename* to *owner*, and its group owner to *group*.
>
> Changing the owner of the file on certain systems clears the set-user-ID and set-group-ID permission bits. (This is because those bits may not be appropriate for the new owner.) Other file permission bits are not changed.
>
> The return value is `0` on success and `-1` on failure. In addition to the usual file name errors (see Section 11.2.3 [File Name Errors], page 246), the following `errno` error conditions are defined for this function:
>
> EPERM
> > This process lacks permission to make the requested change.
> >
> > Only privileged users or the file's owner can change the file's group. On most file systems, only privileged users can change the file owner; some file systems allow you to change the owner if you are currently the owner. When you access a remote file system, the behavior you encounter is determined by the system that actually holds the file, not by the system your program is running on.
> >
> > See Section 32.7 [Optional Features in File Support], page 851, for information about the `_POSIX_CHOWN_RESTRICTED` macro.
>
> EROFS
> > The file is on a read-only file system.

int fchown (*int filedes, uid_t owner, gid_t group*)   [Function]
> Preliminary: | MT-Safe | AS-Safe | AC-Safe | See Section 1.2.2.1 [POSIX Safety Concepts], page 2.
>
> This is like `chown`, except that it changes the owner of the open file with descriptor *filedes*.
>
> The return value from `fchown` is `0` on success and `-1` on failure. The following `errno` error codes are defined for this function:
>
> EBADF
> > The *filedes* argument is not a valid file descriptor.
>
> EINVAL
> > The *filedes* argument corresponds to a pipe or socket, not an ordinary file.
>
> EPERM
> > This process lacks permission to make the requested change. For details see `chmod` above.
>
> EROFS
> > The file resides on a read-only file system.

14.9.5 The Mode Bits for Access Permission

The *file mode*, stored in the `st_mode` field of the file attributes, contains two kinds of information: the file type code, and the access permission bits. This section discusses only the access permission bits, which control who can read or write the file. See Section 14.9.3 [Testing the Type of a File], page 404, for information about the file type code.

All of the symbols listed in this section are defined in the header file `sys/stat.h`.

These symbolic constants are defined for the file mode bits that control access permission for the file:

S_IRUSR

S_IREAD   Read permission bit for the owner of the file. On many systems this bit is 0400. `S_IREAD` is an obsolete synonym provided for BSD compatibility.

S_IWUSR

S_IWRITE   Write permission bit for the owner of the file. Usually 0200. `S_IWRITE` is an obsolete synonym provided for BSD compatibility.

S_IXUSR

S_IEXEC   Execute (for ordinary files) or search (for directories) permission bit for the owner of the file. Usually 0100. `S_IEXEC` is an obsolete synonym provided for BSD compatibility.

S_IRWXU   This is equivalent to '(S_IRUSR | S_IWUSR | S_IXUSR)'.

S_IRGRP   Read permission bit for the group owner of the file. Usually 040.

S_IWGRP   Write permission bit for the group owner of the file. Usually 020.

S_IXGRP   Execute or search permission bit for the group owner of the file. Usually 010.

S_IRWXG   This is equivalent to '(S_IRGRP | S_IWGRP | S_IXGRP)'.

S_IROTH   Read permission bit for other users. Usually 04.

S_IWOTH   Write permission bit for other users. Usually 02.

S_IXOTH   Execute or search permission bit for other users. Usually 01.

S_IRWXO   This is equivalent to '(S_IROTH | S_IWOTH | S_IXOTH)'.

S_ISUID   This is the set-user-ID on execute bit, usually 04000. See Section 30.4 [How an Application Can Change Persona], page 792.

S_ISGID   This is the set-group-ID on execute bit, usually 02000. See Section 30.4 [How an Application Can Change Persona], page 792.

S_ISVTX   This is the *sticky* bit, usually 01000.

For a directory it gives permission to delete a file in that directory only if you own that file. Ordinarily, a user can either delete all the files in a directory or cannot delete any of them (based on whether the user has write permission for the directory). The same restriction applies—you must have both write permission for the directory and own the file you want to delete. The one exception is that the owner of the directory can delete any file in the directory, no matter who owns it (provided the owner has given himself write permission for the directory). This is commonly used for the /tmp directory, where anyone may create files but not delete files created by other users.

Originally the sticky bit on an executable file modified the swapping policies of the system. Normally, when a program terminated, its pages in core were immediately freed and reused. If the sticky bit was set on the executable file, the system kept the pages in core for a while as if the program were still running. This was advantageous for a program likely to be run many times in succession. This usage is obsolete in modern systems. When a program terminates, its pages always remain in core as long as there is no shortage of memory in the system. When the program is next run, its pages will still be in core if no shortage arose since the last run.

On some modern systems where the sticky bit has no useful meaning for an executable file, you cannot set the bit at all for a non-directory. If you try, chmod fails with EFTYPE; see Section 14.9.7 [Assigning File Permissions], page 410.

Some systems (particularly SunOS) have yet another use for the sticky bit. If the sticky bit is set on a file that is *not* executable, it means the opposite: never cache the pages of this file at all. The main use of this is for the files on an NFS server machine which are used as the swap area of diskless client machines. The idea is that the pages of the file will be cached in the client's memory, so it is a waste of the server's memory to cache them a second time. With this usage the sticky bit also implies that the filesystem may fail to record the file's modification time onto disk reliably (the idea being that no-one cares for a swap file).

This bit is only available on BSD systems (and those derived from them). Therefore one has to use the _GNU_SOURCE feature select macro, or not define any feature test macros, to get the definition (see Section 1.3.4 [Feature Test Macros], page 15).

The actual bit values of the symbols are listed in the table above so you can decode file mode values when debugging your programs. These bit values are correct for most systems, but they are not guaranteed.

Warning: Writing explicit numbers for file permissions is bad practice. Not only is it not portable, it also requires everyone who reads your program to remember what the bits mean. To make your program clean use the symbolic names.

14.9.6 How Your Access to a File is Decided

Recall that the operating system normally decides access permission for a file based on the effective user and group IDs of the process and its supplementary group IDs, together with the file's owner, group and permission bits. These concepts are discussed in detail in Section 30.2 [The Persona of a Process], page 791.

If the effective user ID of the process matches the owner user ID of the file, then permissions for read, write, and execute/search are controlled by the corresponding "user" (or "owner") bits. Likewise, if any of the effective group ID or supplementary group IDs of the process matches the group owner ID of the file, then permissions are controlled by the "group" bits. Otherwise, permissions are controlled by the "other" bits.

Privileged users, like 'root', can access any file regardless of its permission bits. As a special case, for a file to be executable even by a privileged user, at least one of its execute bits must be set.

14.9.7 Assigning File Permissions

The primitive functions for creating files (for example, open or mkdir) take a *mode* argument, which specifies the file permissions to give the newly created file. This mode is modified by the process's *file creation mask*, or *umask*, before it is used.

The bits that are set in the file creation mask identify permissions that are always to be disabled for newly created files. For example, if you set all the "other" access bits in the mask, then newly created files are not accessible at all to processes in the "other" category, even if the *mode* argument passed to the create function would permit such access. In other words, the file creation mask is the complement of the ordinary access permissions you want to grant.

Programs that create files typically specify a *mode* argument that includes all the permissions that make sense for the particular file. For an ordinary file, this is typically read and write permission for all classes of users. These permissions are then restricted as specified by the individual user's own file creation mask.

To change the permission of an existing file given its name, call chmod. This function uses the specified permission bits and ignores the file creation mask.

In normal use, the file creation mask is initialized by the user's login shell (using the umask shell command), and inherited by all subprocesses. Application programs normally don't need to worry about the file creation mask. It will automatically do what it is supposed to do.

When your program needs to create a file and bypass the umask for its access permissions, the easiest way to do this is to use fchmod after opening the file, rather than changing the umask. In fact, changing the umask is usually done only by shells. They use the umask function.

The functions in this section are declared in sys/stat.h.

mode_t umask (*mode_t mask*)   [Function]

> Preliminary: | MT-Safe | AS-Safe | AC-Safe | See Section 1.2.2.1 [POSIX Safety Concepts], page 2.
>
> The umask function sets the file creation mask of the current process to *mask*, and returns the previous value of the file creation mask.
>
> Here is an example showing how to read the mask with umask without changing it permanently:
>
> ```
> mode_t
> read_umask (void)
> {
>   mode_t mask = umask (0);
>   umask (mask);
>   return mask;
> }
> ```
>
> However, on GNU/Hurd systems it is better to use getumask if you just want to read the mask value, because it is reentrant.

`mode_t getumask (void)`   [Function]
> Preliminary: | MT-Safe | AS-Safe | AC-Safe | See Section 1.2.2.1 [POSIX Safety Concepts], page 2.
>
> Return the current value of the file creation mask for the current process. This function is a GNU extension and is only available on GNU/Hurd systems.

`int chmod (const char *filename, mode_t mode)`   [Function]
> Preliminary: | MT-Safe | AS-Safe | AC-Safe | See Section 1.2.2.1 [POSIX Safety Concepts], page 2.
>
> The `chmod` function sets the access permission bits for the file named by *filename* to *mode*.
>
> If *filename* is a symbolic link, `chmod` changes the permissions of the file pointed to by the link, not those of the link itself.
>
> This function returns 0 if successful and -1 if not. In addition to the usual file name errors (see Section 11.2.3 [File Name Errors], page 246), the following `errno` error conditions are defined for this function:
>
> `ENOENT`   The named file doesn't exist.
>
> `EPERM`   This process does not have permission to change the access permissions of this file. Only the file's owner (as judged by the effective user ID of the process) or a privileged user can change them.
>
> `EROFS`   The file resides on a read-only file system.
>
> `EFTYPE`   *mode* has the `S_ISVTX` bit (the "sticky bit") set, and the named file is not a directory. Some systems do not allow setting the sticky bit on non-directory files, and some do (and only some of those assign a useful meaning to the bit for non-directory files).
>
> > You only get `EFTYPE` on systems where the sticky bit has no useful meaning for non-directory files, so it is always safe to just clear the bit in *mode* and call `chmod` again. See Section 14.9.5 [The Mode Bits for Access Permission], page 408, for full details on the sticky bit.

`int fchmod (int filedes, mode_t mode)`   [Function]
> Preliminary: | MT-Safe | AS-Safe | AC-Safe | See Section 1.2.2.1 [POSIX Safety Concepts], page 2.
>
> This is like `chmod`, except that it changes the permissions of the currently open file given by *filedes*.
>
> The return value from `fchmod` is 0 on success and -1 on failure. The following `errno` error codes are defined for this function:
>
> `EBADF`   The *filedes* argument is not a valid file descriptor.
>
> `EINVAL`   The *filedes* argument corresponds to a pipe or socket, or something else that doesn't really have access permissions.
>
> `EPERM`   This process does not have permission to change the access permissions of this file. Only the file's owner (as judged by the effective user ID of the process) or a privileged user can change them.
>
> `EROFS`   The file resides on a read-only file system.

14.9.8 Testing Permission to Access a File

In some situations it is desirable to allow programs to access files or devices even if this is not possible with the permissions granted to the user. One possible solution is to set the setuid-bit of the program file. If such a program is started the *effective* user ID of the process is changed to that of the owner of the program file. So to allow write access to files like /etc/passwd, which normally can be written only by the super-user, the modifying program will have to be owned by root and the setuid-bit must be set.

But beside the files the program is intended to change the user should not be allowed to access any file to which s/he would not have access anyway. The program therefore must explicitly check whether *the user* would have the necessary access to a file, before it reads or writes the file.

To do this, use the function access, which checks for access permission based on the process's *real* user ID rather than the effective user ID. (The setuid feature does not alter the real user ID, so it reflects the user who actually ran the program.)

There is another way you could check this access, which is easy to describe, but very hard to use. This is to examine the file mode bits and mimic the system's own access computation. This method is undesirable because many systems have additional access control features; your program cannot portably mimic them, and you would not want to try to keep track of the diverse features that different systems have. Using access is simple and automatically does whatever is appropriate for the system you are using.

access is *only* only appropriate to use in setuid programs. A non-setuid program will always use the effective ID rather than the real ID.

The symbols in this section are declared in unistd.h.

int access (*const char *filename, int how*)   [Function]
    Preliminary: | MT-Safe | AS-Safe | AC-Safe | See Section 1.2.2.1 [POSIX Safety Concepts], page 2.

    The access function checks to see whether the file named by *filename* can be accessed in the way specified by the *how* argument. The *how* argument either can be the bitwise OR of the flags R_OK, W_OK, X_OK, or the existence test F_OK.

    This function uses the *real* user and group IDs of the calling process, rather than the *effective* IDs, to check for access permission. As a result, if you use the function from a setuid or setgid program (see Section 30.4 [How an Application Can Change Persona], page 792), it gives information relative to the user who actually ran the program.

    The return value is 0 if the access is permitted, and -1 otherwise. (In other words, treated as a predicate function, access returns true if the requested access is *denied*.)

    In addition to the usual file name errors (see Section 11.2.3 [File Name Errors], page 246), the following errno error conditions are defined for this function:

    EACCES   The access specified by *how* is denied.

    ENOENT   The file doesn't exist.

    EROFS   Write permission was requested for a file on a read-only file system.

These macros are defined in the header file `unistd.h` for use as the *how* argument to the `access` function. The values are integer constants.

int R_OK   [Macro]
>   Flag meaning test for read permission.

int W_OK   [Macro]
>   Flag meaning test for write permission.

int X_OK   [Macro]
>   Flag meaning test for execute/search permission.

int F_OK   [Macro]
>   Flag meaning test for existence of the file.

14.9.9 File Times

Each file has three time stamps associated with it: its access time, its modification time, and its attribute modification time. These correspond to the `st_atime`, `st_mtime`, and `st_ctime` members of the `stat` structure; see Section 14.9 [File Attributes], page 399.

All of these times are represented in calendar time format, as `time_t` objects. This data type is defined in `time.h`. For more information about representation and manipulation of time values, see Section 21.4 [Calendar Time], page 599.

Reading from a file updates its access time attribute, and writing updates its modification time. When a file is created, all three time stamps for that file are set to the current time. In addition, the attribute change time and modification time fields of the directory that contains the new entry are updated.

Adding a new name for a file with the `link` function updates the attribute change time field of the file being linked, and both the attribute change time and modification time fields of the directory containing the new name. These same fields are affected if a file name is deleted with `unlink`, `remove` or `rmdir`. Renaming a file with `rename` affects only the attribute change time and modification time fields of the two parent directories involved, and not the times for the file being renamed.

Changing the attributes of a file (for example, with `chmod`) updates its attribute change time field.

You can also change some of the time stamps of a file explicitly using the `utime` function—all except the attribute change time. You need to include the header file `utime.h` to use this facility.

struct utimbuf   [Data Type]
>   The `utimbuf` structure is used with the `utime` function to specify new access and modification times for a file. It contains the following members:
>
>   time_t actime
>   >   This is the access time for the file.
>
>   time_t modtime
>   >   This is the modification time for the file.

`int utime` (*const char *filename, const struct utimbuf *times*)   [Function]
> Preliminary: | MT-Safe | AS-Safe | AC-Safe | See Section 1.2.2.1 [POSIX Safety Concepts], page 2.
>
> This function is used to modify the file times associated with the file named *filename*.
>
> If *times* is a null pointer, then the access and modification times of the file are set to the current time. Otherwise, they are set to the values from the `actime` and `modtime` members (respectively) of the `utimbuf` structure pointed to by *times*.
>
> The attribute modification time for the file is set to the current time in either case (since changing the time stamps is itself a modification of the file attributes).
>
> The `utime` function returns `0` if successful and `-1` on failure. In addition to the usual file name errors (see Section 11.2.3 [File Name Errors], page 246), the following `errno` error conditions are defined for this function:
>
> EACCES   There is a permission problem in the case where a null pointer was passed as the *times* argument. In order to update the time stamp on the file, you must either be the owner of the file, have write permission for the file, or be a privileged user.
>
> ENOENT   The file doesn't exist.
>
> EPERM   If the *times* argument is not a null pointer, you must either be the owner of the file or be a privileged user.
>
> EROFS   The file lives on a read-only file system.

Each of the three time stamps has a corresponding microsecond part, which extends its resolution. These fields are called `st_atime_usec`, `st_mtime_usec`, and `st_ctime_usec`; each has a value between 0 and 999,999, which indicates the time in microseconds. They correspond to the `tv_usec` field of a `timeval` structure; see Section 21.4.2 [High-Resolution Calendar], page 600.

The `utimes` function is like `utime`, but also lets you specify the fractional part of the file times. The prototype for this function is in the header file `sys/time.h`.

`int utimes` (*const char *filename, const struct timeval tvp*[2])   [Function]
> Preliminary: | MT-Safe | AS-Safe | AC-Safe | See Section 1.2.2.1 [POSIX Safety Concepts], page 2.
>
> This function sets the file access and modification times of the file *filename*. The new file access time is specified by `tvp[0]`, and the new modification time by `tvp[1]`. Similar to `utime`, if *tvp* is a null pointer then the access and modification times of the file are set to the current time. This function comes from BSD.
>
> The return values and error conditions are the same as for the `utime` function.

`int lutimes` (*const char *filename, const struct timeval tvp*[2])   [Function]
> Preliminary: | MT-Safe | AS-Safe | AC-Safe | See Section 1.2.2.1 [POSIX Safety Concepts], page 2.
>
> This function is like `utimes`, except that it does not follow symbolic links. If *filename* is the name of a symbolic link, `lutimes` sets the file access and modification times of the symbolic link special file itself (as seen by `lstat`; see Section 14.5 [Symbolic

Links], page 393) while `utimes` sets the file access and modification times of the file the symbolic link refers to. This function comes from FreeBSD, and is not available on all platforms (if not available, it will fail with `ENOSYS`).

The return values and error conditions are the same as for the `utime` function.

`int futimes (int fd, const struct timeval tvp[2])`   [Function]
Preliminary: | MT-Safe | AS-Safe | AC-Safe | See Section 1.2.2.1 [POSIX Safety Concepts], page 2.

This function is like `utimes`, except that it takes an open file descriptor as an argument instead of a file name. See Chapter 13 [Low-Level Input/Output], page 323. This function comes from FreeBSD, and is not available on all platforms (if not available, it will fail with `ENOSYS`).

Like `utimes`, `futimes` returns 0 on success and -1 on failure. The following `errno` error conditions are defined for `futimes`:

`EACCES`   There is a permission problem in the case where a null pointer was passed as the *times* argument. In order to update the time stamp on the file, you must either be the owner of the file, have write permission for the file, or be a privileged user.

`EBADF`   The *filedes* argument is not a valid file descriptor.

`EPERM`   If the *times* argument is not a null pointer, you must either be the owner of the file or be a privileged user.

`EROFS`   The file lives on a read-only file system.

14.9.10 File Size

Normally file sizes are maintained automatically. A file begins with a size of 0 and is automatically extended when data is written past its end. It is also possible to empty a file completely by an `open` or `fopen` call.

However, sometimes it is necessary to *reduce* the size of a file. This can be done with the `truncate` and `ftruncate` functions. They were introduced in BSD Unix. `ftruncate` was later added to POSIX.1.

Some systems allow you to extend a file (creating holes) with these functions. This is useful when using memory-mapped I/O (see Section 13.7 [Memory-mapped I/O], page 337), where files are not automatically extended. However, it is not portable but must be implemented if `mmap` allows mapping of files (i.e., `_POSIX_MAPPED_FILES` is defined).

Using these functions on anything other than a regular file gives *undefined* results. On many systems, such a call will appear to succeed, without actually accomplishing anything.

`int truncate (const char *filename, off_t length)`   [Function]
Preliminary: | MT-Safe | AS-Safe | AC-Safe | See Section 1.2.2.1 [POSIX Safety Concepts], page 2.

The `truncate` function changes the size of *filename* to *length*. If *length* is shorter than the previous length, data at the end will be lost. The file must be writable by the user to perform this operation.

If *length* is longer, holes will be added to the end. However, some systems do not support this feature and will leave the file unchanged.

When the source file is compiled with `_FILE_OFFSET_BITS == 64` the `truncate` function is in fact `truncate64` and the type `off_t` has 64 bits which makes it possible to handle files up to 2^63 bytes in length.

The return value is 0 for success, or −1 for an error. In addition to the usual file name errors, the following errors may occur:

EACCES   The file is a directory or not writable.

EINVAL   *length* is negative.

EFBIG   The operation would extend the file beyond the limits of the operating system.

EIO   A hardware I/O error occurred.

EPERM   The file is "append-only" or "immutable".

EINTR   The operation was interrupted by a signal.

int truncate64 (*const char *name, off64_t* **length**)   [Function]
Preliminary: | MT-Safe | AS-Safe | AC-Safe | See Section 1.2.2.1 [POSIX Safety Concepts], page 2.

This function is similar to the `truncate` function. The difference is that the *length* argument is 64 bits wide even on 32 bits machines, which allows the handling of files with sizes up to 2^63 bytes.

When the source file is compiled with `_FILE_OFFSET_BITS == 64` on a 32 bits machine this function is actually available under the name `truncate` and so transparently replaces the 32 bits interface.

int ftruncate (*int fd, off_t* **length**)   [Function]
Preliminary: | MT-Safe | AS-Safe | AC-Safe | See Section 1.2.2.1 [POSIX Safety Concepts], page 2.

This is like `truncate`, but it works on a file descriptor *fd* for an opened file instead of a file name to identify the object. The file must be opened for writing to successfully carry out the operation.

The POSIX standard leaves it implementation defined what happens if the specified new *length* of the file is bigger than the original size. The `ftruncate` function might simply leave the file alone and do nothing or it can increase the size to the desired size. In this later case the extended area should be zero-filled. So using `ftruncate` is no reliable way to increase the file size but if it is possible it is probably the fastest way. The function also operates on POSIX shared memory segments if these are implemented by the system.

`ftruncate` is especially useful in combination with `mmap`. Since the mapped region must have a fixed size one cannot enlarge the file by writing something beyond the last mapped page. Instead one has to enlarge the file itself and then remap the file with the new size. The example below shows how this works.

When the source file is compiled with _FILE_OFFSET_BITS == 64 the `ftruncate` function is in fact `ftruncate64` and the type `off_t` has 64 bits which makes it possible to handle files up to 2^63 bytes in length.

The return value is 0 for success, or −1 for an error. The following errors may occur:

EBADF   *fd* does not correspond to an open file.

EACCES   *fd* is a directory or not open for writing.

EINVAL   *length* is negative.

EFBIG   The operation would extend the file beyond the limits of the operating system.

EIO   A hardware I/O error occurred.

EPERM   The file is "append-only" or "immutable".

EINTR   The operation was interrupted by a signal.

`int ftruncate64` (*int id, off64_t length*)   [Function]
Preliminary: | MT-Safe | AS-Safe | AC-Safe | See Section 1.2.2.1 [POSIX Safety Concepts], page 2.

This function is similar to the `ftruncate` function. The difference is that the *length* argument is 64 bits wide even on 32 bits machines which allows the handling of files with sizes up to 2^63 bytes.

When the source file is compiled with _FILE_OFFSET_BITS == 64 on a 32 bits machine this function is actually available under the name `ftruncate` and so transparently replaces the 32 bits interface.

As announced here is a little example of how to use `ftruncate` in combination with `mmap`:

```
int fd;
void *start;
size_t len;

int
add (off_t at, void *block, size_t size)
{
  if (at + size > len)
    {
      /* Resize the file and remap.  */
      size_t ps = sysconf (_SC_PAGESIZE);
      size_t ns = (at + size + ps - 1) & ~(ps - 1);
      void *np;
      if (ftruncate (fd, ns) < 0)
        return -1;
      np = mmap (NULL, ns, PROT_READ|PROT_WRITE, MAP_SHARED, fd, 0);
      if (np == MAP_FAILED)
        return -1;
      start = np;
      len = ns;
    }
  memcpy ((char *) start + at, block, size);
  return 0;
```

```
}
```

The function `add` writes a block of memory at an arbitrary position in the file. If the current size of the file is too small it is extended. Note the it is extended by a round number of pages. This is a requirement of `mmap`. The program has to keep track of the real size, and when it has finished a final `ftruncate` call should set the real size of the file.

14.9.11 Storage Allocation

Most file systems support allocating large files in a non-contiguous fashion: the file is split into *fragments* which are allocated sequentially, but the fragments themselves can be scattered across the disk. File systems generally try to avoid such fragmentation because it decreases performance, but if a file gradually increases in size, there might be no other option than to fragment it. In addition, many file systems support *sparse files* with *holes*: regions of null bytes for which no backing storage has been allocated by the file system. When the holes are finally overwritten with data, fragmentation can occur as well.

Explicit allocation of storage for yet-unwritten parts of the file can help the system to avoid fragmentation. Additionally, if storage pre-allocation fails, it is possible to report the out-of-disk error early, often without filling up the entire disk. However, due to deduplication, copy-on-write semantics, and file compression, such pre-allocation may not reliably prevent the out-of-disk-space error from occurring later. Checking for write errors is still required, and writes to memory-mapped regions created with `mmap` can still result in `SIGBUS`.

`int posix_fallocate` (*int fd, off_t offset, off_t length*)   [Function]
   Preliminary: | MT-Safe | AS-Safe | AC-Safe | See Section 1.2.2.1 [POSIX Safety Concepts], page 2.

   Allocate backing store for the region of *length* bytes starting at byte *offset* in the file for the descriptor *fd*. The file length is increased to '`length + offset`' if necessary.

   fd must be a regular file opened for writing, or `EBADF` is returned. If there is insufficient disk space to fulfill the allocation request, `ENOSPC` is returned.

   Note: If `fallocate` is not available (because the file system does not support it), `posix_fallocate` is emulated, which has the following drawbacks:

   - It is very inefficient because all file system blocks in the requested range need to be examined (even if they have been allocated before) and potentially rewritten. In contrast, with proper `fallocate` support (see below), the file system can examine the internal file allocation data structures and eliminate holes directly, maybe even using unwritten extents (which are pre-allocated but uninitialized on disk).

   - There is a race condition if another thread or process modifies the underlying file in the to-be-allocated area. Non-null bytes could be overwritten with null bytes.

   - If *fd* has been opened with the `O_APPEND` flag, the function will fail with an `errno` value of `EBADF`.

   - If *length* is zero, `ftruncate` is used to increase the file size as requested, without allocating file system blocks. There is a race condition which means that `ftruncate` can accidentally truncate the file if it has been extended concurrently.

   On Linux, if an application does not benefit from emulation or if the emulation is harmful due to its inherent race conditions, the application can use the Linux-specific fallocate function, with a zero flag argument. For the `fallocate` function, the GNU C Library does not perform allocation emulation if the file system does not support allocation. Instead, an `EOPNOTSUPP` is returned to the caller.

int posix_fallocate64 (*int* `fd`, *off64_t* `length`, *off64_t* `offset`)   [Function]
> Preliminary: | MT-Safe | AS-Safe | AC-Safe | See Section 1.2.2.1 [POSIX Safety Concepts], page 2.
>
> This function is a variant of `posix_fallocate64` which accepts 64-bit file offsets on all platforms.

14.10 Making Special Files

The `mknod` function is the primitive for making special files, such as files that correspond to devices. The GNU C Library includes this function for compatibility with BSD.

The prototype for `mknod` is declared in `sys/stat.h`.

int mknod (*const char* `*filename`, *mode_t* `mode`, *dev_t* `dev`)   [Function]
> Preliminary: | MT-Safe | AS-Safe | AC-Safe | See Section 1.2.2.1 [POSIX Safety Concepts], page 2.
>
> The `mknod` function makes a special file with name *filename*. The *mode* specifies the mode of the file, and may include the various special file bits, such as `S_IFCHR` (for a character special file) or `S_IFBLK` (for a block special file). See Section 14.9.3 [Testing the Type of a File], page 404.
>
> The *dev* argument specifies which device the special file refers to. Its exact interpretation depends on the kind of special file being created.
>
> The return value is 0 on success and -1 on error. In addition to the usual file name errors (see Section 11.2.3 [File Name Errors], page 246), the following `errno` error conditions are defined for this function:
>
> EPERM   The calling process is not privileged. Only the superuser can create special files.
>
> ENOSPC   The directory or file system that would contain the new file is full and cannot be extended.
>
> EROFS   The directory containing the new file can't be modified because it's on a read-only file system.
>
> EEXIST   There is already a file named *filename*. If you want to replace this file, you must remove the old file explicitly first.

14.11 Temporary Files

If you need to use a temporary file in your program, you can use the `tmpfile` function to open it. Or you can use the `tmpnam` (better: `tmpnam_r`) function to provide a name for a temporary file and then you can open it in the usual way with `fopen`.

The `tempnam` function is like `tmpnam` but lets you choose what directory temporary files will go in, and something about what their file names will look like. Important for multi-threaded programs is that `tempnam` is reentrant, while `tmpnam` is not since it returns a pointer to a static buffer.

These facilities are declared in the header file `stdio.h`.

FILE * tmpfile (*void*)   [Function]
>   Preliminary: | MT-Safe | AS-Unsafe heap lock | AC-Unsafe mem fd lock | See
>   Section 1.2.2.1 [POSIX Safety Concepts], page 2.
>
>   This function creates a temporary binary file for update mode, as if by calling `fopen`
>   with mode `"wb+"`. The file is deleted automatically when it is closed or when the
>   program terminates. (On some other ISO C systems the file may fail to be deleted if
>   the program terminates abnormally).
>
>   This function is reentrant.
>
>   When the sources are compiled with `_FILE_OFFSET_BITS == 64` on a 32-bit system
>   this function is in fact `tmpfile64`, i.e., the LFS interface transparently replaces the
>   old interface.

FILE * tmpfile64 (*void*)   [Function]
>   Preliminary: | MT-Safe | AS-Unsafe heap lock | AC-Unsafe mem fd lock | See
>   Section 1.2.2.1 [POSIX Safety Concepts], page 2.
>
>   This function is similar to `tmpfile`, but the stream it returns a pointer to was opened
>   using `tmpfile64`. Therefore this stream can be used for files larger than 2^31 bytes on
>   32-bit machines.
>
>   Please note that the return type is still `FILE *`. There is no special `FILE` type for the
>   LFS interface.
>
>   If the sources are compiled with `_FILE_OFFSET_BITS == 64` on a 32 bits machine this
>   function is available under the name `tmpfile` and so transparently replaces the old
>   interface.

char * tmpnam (*char *result*)   [Function]
>   Preliminary: | MT-Unsafe race:tmpnam/!result | AS-Unsafe | AC-Safe | See
>   Section 1.2.2.1 [POSIX Safety Concepts], page 2.
>
>   This function constructs and returns a valid file name that does not refer to any
>   existing file. If the *result* argument is a null pointer, the return value is a pointer to
>   an internal static string, which might be modified by subsequent calls and therefore
>   makes this function non-reentrant. Otherwise, the *result* argument should be a pointer
>   to an array of at least `L_tmpnam` characters, and the result is written into that array.
>
>   It is possible for `tmpnam` to fail if you call it too many times without removing
>   previously-created files. This is because the limited length of the temporary file names
>   gives room for only a finite number of different names. If `tmpnam` fails it returns a
>   null pointer.
>
>   **Warning:** Between the time the pathname is constructed and the file is created an-
>   other process might have created a file with the same name using `tmpnam`, leading to
>   a possible security hole. The implementation generates names which can hardly be
>   predicted, but when opening the file you should use the `O_EXCL` flag. Using `tmpfile`
>   or `mkstemp` is a safe way to avoid this problem.

char * tmpnam_r (*char *result*)   [Function]
>   Preliminary: | MT-Safe | AS-Safe | AC-Safe | See Section 1.2.2.1 [POSIX Safety
>   Concepts], page 2.

This function is nearly identical to the **tmpnam** function, except that if *result* is a null pointer it returns a null pointer.

This guarantees reentrancy because the non-reentrant situation of **tmpnam** cannot happen here.

Warning: This function has the same security problems as **tmpnam**.

int L_tmpnam   [Macro]

> The value of this macro is an integer constant expression that represents the minimum size of a string large enough to hold a file name generated by the **tmpnam** function.

int TMP_MAX   [Macro]

> The macro **TMP_MAX** is a lower bound for how many temporary names you can create with **tmpnam**. You can rely on being able to call **tmpnam** at least this many times before it might fail saying you have made too many temporary file names.
>
> With the GNU C Library, you can create a very large number of temporary file names. If you actually created the files, you would probably run out of disk space before you ran out of names. Some other systems have a fixed, small limit on the number of temporary files. The limit is never less than **25**.

char * tempnam (*const char *dir, const char *prefix*)   [Function]

> Preliminary: | MT-Safe env | AS-Unsafe heap | AC-Unsafe mem | See Section 1.2.2.1 [POSIX Safety Concepts], page 2.
>
> This function generates a unique temporary file name. If *prefix* is not a null pointer, up to five characters of this string are used as a prefix for the file name. The return value is a string newly allocated with **malloc**, so you should release its storage with **free** when it is no longer needed.
>
> Because the string is dynamically allocated this function is reentrant.
>
> The directory prefix for the temporary file name is determined by testing each of the following in sequence. The directory must exist and be writable.
>
> - The environment variable **TMPDIR**, if it is defined. For security reasons this only happens if the program is not SUID or SGID enabled.
> - The *dir* argument, if it is not a null pointer.
> - The value of the **P_tmpdir** macro.
> - The directory **/tmp**.
>
> This function is defined for SVID compatibility.
>
> **Warning:** Between the time the pathname is constructed and the file is created another process might have created a file with the same name using **tempnam**, leading to a possible security hole. The implementation generates names which can hardly be predicted, but when opening the file you should use the **O_EXCL** flag. Using **tmpfile** or **mkstemp** is a safe way to avoid this problem.

char * P_tmpdir   [SVID Macro]

> This macro is the name of the default directory for temporary files.

Older Unix systems did not have the functions just described. Instead they used `mktemp` and `mkstemp`. Both of these functions work by modifying a file name template string you pass. The last six characters of this string must be 'XXXXXX'. These six 'X's are replaced with six characters which make the whole string a unique file name. Usually the template string is something like '/tmp/*prefix*XXXXXX', and each program uses a unique *prefix*.

NB: Because `mktemp` and `mkstemp` modify the template string, you *must not* pass string constants to them. String constants are normally in read-only storage, so your program would crash when `mktemp` or `mkstemp` tried to modify the string. These functions are declared in the header file `stdlib.h`.

char * mktemp (*char *template*)   [Function]
> Preliminary: | MT-Safe | AS-Safe | AC-Safe | See Section 1.2.2.1 [POSIX Safety Concepts], page 2.
>
> The `mktemp` function generates a unique file name by modifying *template* as described above. If successful, it returns *template* as modified. If `mktemp` cannot find a unique file name, it makes *template* an empty string and returns that. If *template* does not end with 'XXXXXX', `mktemp` returns a null pointer.
>
> **Warning:** Between the time the pathname is constructed and the file is created another process might have created a file with the same name using `mktemp`, leading to a possible security hole. The implementation generates names which can hardly be predicted, but when opening the file you should use the `O_EXCL` flag. Using `mkstemp` is a safe way to avoid this problem.

int mkstemp (*char *template*)   [Function]
> Preliminary: | MT-Safe | AS-Safe | AC-Safe fd | See Section 1.2.2.1 [POSIX Safety Concepts], page 2.
>
> The `mkstemp` function generates a unique file name just as `mktemp` does, but it also opens the file for you with **open** (see Section 13.1 [Opening and Closing Files], page 323). If successful, it modifies *template* in place and returns a file descriptor for that file open for reading and writing. If `mkstemp` cannot create a uniquely-named file, it returns −1. If *template* does not end with 'XXXXXX', `mkstemp` returns −1 and does not modify *template*.
>
> The file is opened using mode 0600. If the file is meant to be used by other users this mode must be changed explicitly.

Unlike `mktemp`, `mkstemp` is actually guaranteed to create a unique file that cannot possibly clash with any other program trying to create a temporary file. This is because it works by calling **open** with the `O_EXCL` flag, which says you want to create a new file and get an error if the file already exists.

char * mkdtemp (*char *template*)   [Function]
> Preliminary: | MT-Safe | AS-Safe | AC-Safe | See Section 1.2.2.1 [POSIX Safety Concepts], page 2.
>
> The `mkdtemp` function creates a directory with a unique name. If it succeeds, it overwrites *template* with the name of the directory, and returns *template*. As with `mktemp` and `mkstemp`, *template* should be a string ending with 'XXXXXX'.

If `mkdtemp` cannot create an uniquely named directory, it returns `NULL` and sets *errno* appropriately. If *template* does not end with 'XXXXXX', `mkdtemp` returns `NULL` and does not modify *template*. *errno* will be set to `EINVAL` in this case.

The directory is created using mode `0700`.

The directory created by `mkdtemp` cannot clash with temporary files or directories created by other users. This is because directory creation always works like `open` with `O_EXCL`. See Section 14.8 [Creating Directories], page 398.

The `mkdtemp` function comes from OpenBSD.

15 Pipes and FIFOs

A *pipe* is a mechanism for interprocess communication; data written to the pipe by one process can be read by another process. The data is handled in a first-in, first-out (FIFO) order. The pipe has no name; it is created for one use and both ends must be inherited from the single process which created the pipe.

A *FIFO special file* is similar to a pipe, but instead of being an anonymous, temporary connection, a FIFO has a name or names like any other file. Processes open the FIFO by name in order to communicate through it.

A pipe or FIFO has to be open at both ends simultaneously. If you read from a pipe or FIFO file that doesn't have any processes writing to it (perhaps because they have all closed the file, or exited), the read returns end-of-file. Writing to a pipe or FIFO that doesn't have a reading process is treated as an error condition; it generates a `SIGPIPE` signal, and fails with error code `EPIPE` if the signal is handled or blocked.

Neither pipes nor FIFO special files allow file positioning. Both reading and writing operations happen sequentially; reading from the beginning of the file and writing at the end.

15.1 Creating a Pipe

The primitive for creating a pipe is the `pipe` function. This creates both the reading and writing ends of the pipe. It is not very useful for a single process to use a pipe to talk to itself. In typical use, a process creates a pipe just before it forks one or more child processes (see Section 26.4 [Creating a Process], page 751). The pipe is then used for communication either between the parent or child processes, or between two sibling processes.

The `pipe` function is declared in the header file `unistd.h`.

int pipe (*int filedes*[2])   [Function]
> Preliminary: | MT-Safe | AS-Safe | AC-Safe fd | See Section 1.2.2.1 [POSIX Safety Concepts], page 2.
>
> The `pipe` function creates a pipe and puts the file descriptors for the reading and writing ends of the pipe (respectively) into `filedes[0]` and `filedes[1]`.
>
> An easy way to remember that the input end comes first is that file descriptor `0` is standard input, and file descriptor `1` is standard output.
>
> If successful, `pipe` returns a value of `0`. On failure, `-1` is returned. The following `errno` error conditions are defined for this function:
>
> `EMFILE`   The process has too many files open.
>
> `ENFILE`   There are too many open files in the entire system. See Section 2.2 [Error Codes], page 23, for more information about `ENFILE`. This error never occurs on GNU/Hurd systems.

Here is an example of a simple program that creates a pipe. This program uses the `fork` function (see Section 26.4 [Creating a Process], page 751) to create a child process. The parent process writes data to the pipe, which is read by the child process.

```
#include <sys/types.h>
#include <unistd.h>
#include <stdio.h>
#include <stdlib.h>

/* Read characters from the pipe and echo them to stdout. */

void
read_from_pipe (int file)
{
  FILE *stream;
  int c;
  stream = fdopen (file, "r");
  while ((c = fgetc (stream)) != EOF)
    putchar (c);
  fclose (stream);
}

/* Write some random text to the pipe. */

void
write_to_pipe (int file)
{
  FILE *stream;
  stream = fdopen (file, "w");
  fprintf (stream, "hello, world!\n");
  fprintf (stream, "goodbye, world!\n");
  fclose (stream);
}

int
main (void)
{
  pid_t pid;
  int mypipe[2];

  /* Create the pipe. */
  if (pipe (mypipe))
    {
      fprintf (stderr, "Pipe failed.\n");
      return EXIT_FAILURE;
    }

  /* Create the child process. */
  pid = fork ();
  if (pid == (pid_t) 0)
    {
      /* This is the child process.
      Close other end first. */
      close (mypipe[1]);
      read_from_pipe (mypipe[0]);
      return EXIT_SUCCESS;
    }
  else if (pid < (pid_t) 0)
    {
      /* The fork failed. */
      fprintf (stderr, "Fork failed.\n");
```

```
          return EXIT_FAILURE;
        }
     else
        {
          /* This is the parent process.
          Close other end first. */
          close (mypipe[0]);
          write_to_pipe (mypipe[1]);
          return EXIT_SUCCESS;
        }
  }
```

15.2 Pipe to a Subprocess

A common use of pipes is to send data to or receive data from a program being run as a subprocess. One way of doing this is by using a combination of pipe (to create the pipe), fork (to create the subprocess), dup2 (to force the subprocess to use the pipe as its standard input or output channel), and exec (to execute the new program). Or, you can use popen and pclose.

The advantage of using popen and pclose is that the interface is much simpler and easier to use. But it doesn't offer as much flexibility as using the low-level functions directly.

FILE * popen (*const char *command*, *const char *mode*)   [Function]
> Preliminary: | MT-Safe | AS-Unsafe heap corrupt | AC-Unsafe corrupt lock fd mem
> | See Section 1.2.2.1 [POSIX Safety Concepts], page 2.
>
> The popen function is closely related to the system function; see Section 26.1 [Running a Command], page 749. It executes the shell command *command* as a subprocess. However, instead of waiting for the command to complete, it creates a pipe to the subprocess and returns a stream that corresponds to that pipe.
>
> If you specify a *mode* argument of "r", you can read from the stream to retrieve data from the standard output channel of the subprocess. The subprocess inherits its standard input channel from the parent process.
>
> Similarly, if you specify a *mode* argument of "w", you can write to the stream to send data to the standard input channel of the subprocess. The subprocess inherits its standard output channel from the parent process.
>
> In the event of an error popen returns a null pointer. This might happen if the pipe or stream cannot be created, if the subprocess cannot be forked, or if the program cannot be executed.

int pclose (*FILE *stream*)   [Function]
> Preliminary: | MT-Safe | AS-Unsafe heap plugin corrupt lock | AC-Unsafe corrupt lock fd mem | See Section 1.2.2.1 [POSIX Safety Concepts], page 2.
>
> The pclose function is used to close a stream created by popen. It waits for the child process to terminate and returns its status value, as for the system function.

Here is an example showing how to use popen and pclose to filter output through another program, in this case the paging program more.

```
#include <stdio.h>
```

```
#include <stdlib.h>

void
write_data (FILE * stream)
{
  int i;
  for (i = 0; i < 100; i++)
    fprintf (stream, "%d\n", i);
  if (ferror (stream))
    {
      fprintf (stderr, "Output to stream failed.\n");
      exit (EXIT_FAILURE);
    }
}

int
main (void)
{
  FILE *output;

  output = popen ("more", "w");
  if (!output)
    {
      fprintf (stderr,
               "incorrect parameters or too many files.\n");
      return EXIT_FAILURE;
    }
  write_data (output);
  if (pclose (output) != 0)
    {
      fprintf (stderr,
               "Could not run more or other error.\n");
    }
  return EXIT_SUCCESS;
}
```

15.3 FIFO Special Files

A FIFO special file is similar to a pipe, except that it is created in a different way. Instead of being an anonymous communications channel, a FIFO special file is entered into the file system by calling `mkfifo`.

Once you have created a FIFO special file in this way, any process can open it for reading or writing, in the same way as an ordinary file. However, it has to be open at both ends simultaneously before you can proceed to do any input or output operations on it. Opening a FIFO for reading normally blocks until some other process opens the same FIFO for writing, and vice versa.

The `mkfifo` function is declared in the header file `sys/stat.h`.

int mkfifo (*const char *filename, mode_t mode*)   [Function]
    Preliminary: | MT-Safe | AS-Safe | AC-Safe | See Section 1.2.2.1 [POSIX Safety Concepts], page 2.

    The `mkfifo` function makes a FIFO special file with name *filename*. The *mode* argument is used to set the file's permissions; see Section 14.9.7 [Assigning File Permissions], page 410.

The normal, successful return value from `mkfifo` is 0. In the case of an error, `-1` is returned. In addition to the usual file name errors (see Section 11.2.3 [File Name Errors], page 246), the following `errno` error conditions are defined for this function:

`EEXIST`   The named file already exists.

`ENOSPC`   The directory or file system cannot be extended.

`EROFS`   The directory that would contain the file resides on a read-only file system.

15.4 Atomicity of Pipe I/O

Reading or writing pipe data is *atomic* if the size of data written is not greater than `PIPE_BUF`. This means that the data transfer seems to be an instantaneous unit, in that nothing else in the system can observe a state in which it is partially complete. Atomic I/O may not begin right away (it may need to wait for buffer space or for data), but once it does begin it finishes immediately.

Reading or writing a larger amount of data may not be atomic; for example, output data from other processes sharing the descriptor may be interspersed. Also, once `PIPE_BUF` characters have been written, further writes will block until some characters are read.

See Section 32.6 [Limits on File System Capacity], page 850, for information about the `PIPE_BUF` parameter.

16 Sockets

This chapter describes the GNU facilities for interprocess communication using sockets.

A *socket* is a generalized interprocess communication channel. Like a pipe, a socket is represented as a file descriptor. Unlike pipes sockets support communication between unrelated processes, and even between processes running on different machines that communicate over a network. Sockets are the primary means of communicating with other machines; telnet, rlogin, ftp, talk and the other familiar network programs use sockets.

Not all operating systems support sockets. In the GNU C Library, the header file sys/socket.h exists regardless of the operating system, and the socket functions always exist, but if the system does not really support sockets these functions always fail.

Incomplete: We do not currently document the facilities for broadcast messages or for configuring Internet interfaces. The reentrant functions and some newer functions that are related to IPv6 aren't documented either so far.

16.1 Socket Concepts

When you create a socket, you must specify the style of communication you want to use and the type of protocol that should implement it. The *communication style* of a socket defines the user-level semantics of sending and receiving data on the socket. Choosing a communication style specifies the answers to questions such as these:

- **What are the units of data transmission?** Some communication styles regard the data as a sequence of bytes with no larger structure; others group the bytes into records (which are known in this context as *packets*).

- **Can data be lost during normal operation?** Some communication styles guarantee that all the data sent arrives in the order it was sent (barring system or network crashes); other styles occasionally lose data as a normal part of operation, and may sometimes deliver packets more than once or in the wrong order.

  Designing a program to use unreliable communication styles usually involves taking precautions to detect lost or misordered packets and to retransmit data as needed.

- **Is communication entirely with one partner?** Some communication styles are like a telephone call—you make a *connection* with one remote socket and then exchange data freely. Other styles are like mailing letters—you specify a destination address for each message you send.

You must also choose a *namespace* for naming the socket. A socket name ("address") is meaningful only in the context of a particular namespace. In fact, even the data type to use for a socket name may depend on the namespace. Namespaces are also called "domains", but we avoid that word as it can be confused with other usage of the same term. Each namespace has a symbolic name that starts with 'PF_'. A corresponding symbolic name starting with 'AF_' designates the address format for that namespace.

Finally you must choose the *protocol* to carry out the communication. The protocol determines what low-level mechanism is used to transmit and receive data. Each protocol is valid for a particular namespace and communication style; a namespace is sometimes called a *protocol family* because of this, which is why the namespace names start with 'PF_'.

The rules of a protocol apply to the data passing between two programs, perhaps on different computers; most of these rules are handled by the operating system and you need not know about them. What you do need to know about protocols is this:

- In order to have communication between two sockets, they must specify the *same* protocol.

- Each protocol is meaningful with particular style/namespace combinations and cannot be used with inappropriate combinations. For example, the TCP protocol fits only the byte stream style of communication and the Internet namespace.

- For each combination of style and namespace there is a *default protocol*, which you can request by specifying 0 as the protocol number. And that's what you should normally do—use the default.

Throughout the following description at various places variables/parameters to denote sizes are required. And here the trouble starts. In the first implementations the type of these variables was simply `int`. On most machines at that time an `int` was 32 bits wide, which created a *de facto* standard requiring 32-bit variables. This is important since references to variables of this type are passed to the kernel.

Then the POSIX people came and unified the interface with the words "all size values are of type `size_t`". On 64-bit machines `size_t` is 64 bits wide, so pointers to variables were no longer possible.

The Unix98 specification provides a solution by introducing a type `socklen_t`. This type is used in all of the cases that POSIX changed to use `size_t`. The only requirement of this type is that it be an unsigned type of at least 32 bits. Therefore, implementations which require that references to 32-bit variables be passed can be as happy as implementations which use 64-bit values.

16.2 Communication Styles

The GNU C Library includes support for several different kinds of sockets, each with different characteristics. This section describes the supported socket types. The symbolic constants listed here are defined in `sys/socket.h`.

`int SOCK_STREAM`   [Macro]

> The `SOCK_STREAM` style is like a pipe (see Chapter 15 [Pipes and FIFOs], page 424). It operates over a connection with a particular remote socket and transmits data reliably as a stream of bytes.
>
> Use of this style is covered in detail in Section 16.9 [Using Sockets with Connections], page 455.

`int SOCK_DGRAM`   [Macro]

> The `SOCK_DGRAM` style is used for sending individually-addressed packets unreliably. It is the diametrical opposite of `SOCK_STREAM`.
>
> Each time you write data to a socket of this kind, that data becomes one packet. Since `SOCK_DGRAM` sockets do not have connections, you must specify the recipient address with each packet.
>
> The only guarantee that the system makes about your requests to transmit data is that it will try its best to deliver each packet you send. It may succeed with the sixth

packet after failing with the fourth and fifth packets; the seventh packet may arrive before the sixth, and may arrive a second time after the sixth.

The typical use for SOCK_DGRAM is in situations where it is acceptable to simply re-send a packet if no response is seen in a reasonable amount of time.

See Section 16.10 [Datagram Socket Operations], page 467, for detailed information about how to use datagram sockets.

int SOCK_RAW   [Macro]
    This style provides access to low-level network protocols and interfaces. Ordinary user programs usually have no need to use this style.

16.3 Socket Addresses

The name of a socket is normally called an *address*. The functions and symbols for dealing with socket addresses were named inconsistently, sometimes using the term "name" and sometimes using "address". You can regard these terms as synonymous where sockets are concerned.

A socket newly created with the socket function has no address. Other processes can find it for communication only if you give it an address. We call this *binding* the address to the socket, and the way to do it is with the bind function.

You need be concerned with the address of a socket if other processes are to find it and start communicating with it. You can specify an address for other sockets, but this is usually pointless; the first time you send data from a socket, or use it to initiate a connection, the system assigns an address automatically if you have not specified one.

Occasionally a client needs to specify an address because the server discriminates based on address; for example, the rsh and rlogin protocols look at the client's socket address and only bypass password checking if it is less than IPPORT_RESERVED (see Section 16.6.3 [Internet Ports], page 447).

The details of socket addresses vary depending on what namespace you are using. See Section 16.5 [The Local Namespace], page 435, or Section 16.6 [The Internet Namespace], page 437, for specific information.

Regardless of the namespace, you use the same functions bind and getsockname to set and examine a socket's address. These functions use a phony data type, struct sockaddr *, to accept the address. In practice, the address lives in a structure of some other data type appropriate to the address format you are using, but you cast its address to struct sockaddr * when you pass it to bind.

16.3.1 Address Formats

The functions bind and getsockname use the generic data type struct sockaddr * to represent a pointer to a socket address. You can't use this data type effectively to interpret an address or construct one; for that, you must use the proper data type for the socket's namespace.

Thus, the usual practice is to construct an address of the proper namespace-specific type, then cast a pointer to struct sockaddr * when you call bind or getsockname.

The one piece of information that you can get from the **struct sockaddr** data type is the *address format designator*. This tells you which data type to use to understand the address fully.

The symbols in this section are defined in the header file **sys/socket.h**.

struct sockaddr   [Data Type]

The **struct sockaddr** type itself has the following members:

short int sa_family

> This is the code for the address format of this address. It identifies the format of the data which follows.

char sa_data[14]

> This is the actual socket address data, which is format-dependent. Its length also depends on the format, and may well be more than 14. The length 14 of **sa_data** is essentially arbitrary.

Each address format has a symbolic name which starts with 'AF_'. Each of them corresponds to a 'PF_' symbol which designates the corresponding namespace. Here is a list of address format names:

AF_LOCAL   This designates the address format that goes with the local namespace. (**PF_LOCAL** is the name of that namespace.) See Section 16.5.2 [Details of Local Namespace], page 435, for information about this address format.

AF_UNIX   This is a synonym for **AF_LOCAL**. Although **AF_LOCAL** is mandated by POSIX.1g, **AF_UNIX** is portable to more systems. **AF_UNIX** was the traditional name stemming from BSD, so even most POSIX systems support it. It is also the name of choice in the Unix98 specification. (The same is true for **PF_UNIX** vs. **PF_LOCAL**).

AF_FILE   This is another synonym for **AF_LOCAL**, for compatibility. (**PF_FILE** is likewise a synonym for **PF_LOCAL**.)

AF_INET   This designates the address format that goes with the Internet namespace. (**PF_INET** is the name of that namespace.) See Section 16.6.1 [Internet Socket Address Formats], page 438.

AF_INET6   This is similar to **AF_INET**, but refers to the IPv6 protocol. (**PF_INET6** is the name of the corresponding namespace.)

AF_UNSPEC

> This designates no particular address format. It is used only in rare cases, such as to clear out the default destination address of a "connected" datagram socket. See Section 16.10.1 [Sending Datagrams], page 467.
>
> The corresponding namespace designator symbol **PF_UNSPEC** exists for completeness, but there is no reason to use it in a program.

sys/socket.h defines symbols starting with 'AF_' for many different kinds of networks, most or all of which are not actually implemented. We will document those that really work as we receive information about how to use them.

16.3.2 Setting the Address of a Socket

Use the `bind` function to assign an address to a socket. The prototype for `bind` is in the header file `sys/socket.h`. For examples of use, see Section 16.5.3 [Example of Local-Namespace Sockets], page 436, or see Section 16.6.7 [Internet Socket Example], page 452.

int bind (*int* `socket`, *struct sockaddr *addr, socklen_t* `length`)   [Function]
> Preliminary: | MT-Safe | AS-Safe | AC-Safe | See Section 1.2.2.1 [POSIX Safety Concepts], page 2.
>
> The `bind` function assigns an address to the socket *socket*. The *addr* and *length* arguments specify the address; the detailed format of the address depends on the namespace. The first part of the address is always the format designator, which specifies a namespace, and says that the address is in the format of that namespace.
>
> The return value is `0` on success and `-1` on failure. The following `errno` error conditions are defined for this function:
>
> EBADF   The *socket* argument is not a valid file descriptor.
>
> ENOTSOCK   The descriptor *socket* is not a socket.
>
> EADDRNOTAVAIL
> > The specified address is not available on this machine.
>
> EADDRINUSE
> > Some other socket is already using the specified address.
>
> EINVAL   The socket *socket* already has an address.
>
> EACCES   You do not have permission to access the requested address. (In the Internet domain, only the super-user is allowed to specify a port number in the range 0 through `IPPORT_RESERVED` minus one; see Section 16.6.3 [Internet Ports], page 447.)
>
> Additional conditions may be possible depending on the particular namespace of the socket.

16.3.3 Reading the Address of a Socket

Use the function `getsockname` to examine the address of an Internet socket. The prototype for this function is in the header file `sys/socket.h`.

int getsockname (*int* `socket`, *struct sockaddr *addr, socklen_t* `*length-ptr`)   [Function]
> Preliminary: | MT-Safe | AS-Safe | AC-Safe mem/hurd | See Section 1.2.2.1 [POSIX Safety Concepts], page 2.
>
> The `getsockname` function returns information about the address of the socket *socket* in the locations specified by the *addr* and *length-ptr* arguments. Note that the *length-ptr* is a pointer; you should initialize it to be the allocation size of *addr*, and on return it contains the actual size of the address data.
>
> The format of the address data depends on the socket namespace. The length of the information is usually fixed for a given namespace, so normally you can know exactly how much space is needed and can provide that much. The usual practice is

to allocate a place for the value using the proper data type for the socket's namespace, then cast its address to `struct sockaddr *` to pass it to `getsockname`.

The return value is 0 on success and -1 on error. The following `errno` error conditions are defined for this function:

EBADF   The *socket* argument is not a valid file descriptor.

ENOTSOCK   The descriptor *socket* is not a socket.

ENOBUFS   There are not enough internal buffers available for the operation.

You can't read the address of a socket in the file namespace. This is consistent with the rest of the system; in general, there's no way to find a file's name from a descriptor for that file.

16.4 Interface Naming

Each network interface has a name. This usually consists of a few letters that relate to the type of interface, which may be followed by a number if there is more than one interface of that type. Examples might be `lo` (the loopback interface) and `eth0` (the first Ethernet interface).

Although such names are convenient for humans, it would be clumsy to have to use them whenever a program needs to refer to an interface. In such situations an interface is referred to by its *index*, which is an arbitrarily-assigned small positive integer.

The following functions, constants and data types are declared in the header file `net/if.h`.

size_t IFNAMSIZ   [Constant]
> This constant defines the maximum buffer size needed to hold an interface name, including its terminating zero byte.

unsigned int if_nametoindex (*const char *ifname*)   [Function]
> Preliminary: | MT-Safe | AS-Unsafe lock | AC-Unsafe lock fd | See Section 1.2.2.1 [POSIX Safety Concepts], page 2.

> This function yields the interface index corresponding to a particular name. If no interface exists with the name given, it returns 0.

char * if_indextoname (*unsigned int **ifindex**, char *ifname*)   [Function]
> Preliminary: | MT-Safe | AS-Unsafe lock | AC-Unsafe lock fd | See Section 1.2.2.1 [POSIX Safety Concepts], page 2.

> This function maps an interface index to its corresponding name. The returned name is placed in the buffer pointed to by `ifname`, which must be at least `IFNAMSIZ` bytes in length. If the index was invalid, the function's return value is a null pointer, otherwise it is `ifname`.

struct if_nameindex   [Data Type]
> This data type is used to hold the information about a single interface. It has the following members:

> **unsigned int if_index;**
> > This is the interface index.

`char *if_name`
> This is the null-terminated index name.

`struct if_nameindex * if_nameindex (`*void*`)` [Function]
> Preliminary: | MT-Safe | AS-Unsafe heap lock/hurd | AC-Unsafe lock/hurd fd mem | See Section 1.2.2.1 [POSIX Safety Concepts], page 2.
>
> This function returns an array of `if_nameindex` structures, one for every interface that is present. The end of the list is indicated by a structure with an interface of 0 and a null name pointer. If an error occurs, this function returns a null pointer.
>
> The returned structure must be freed with `if_freenameindex` after use.

`void if_freenameindex (`*struct if_nameindex *ptr*`)` [Function]
> Preliminary: | MT-Safe | AS-Unsafe heap | AC-Unsafe mem | See Section 1.2.2.1 [POSIX Safety Concepts], page 2.
>
> This function frees the structure returned by an earlier call to `if_nameindex`.

16.5 The Local Namespace

This section describes the details of the local namespace, whose symbolic name (required when you create a socket) is `PF_LOCAL`. The local namespace is also known as "Unix domain sockets". Another name is file namespace since socket addresses are normally implemented as file names.

16.5.1 Local Namespace Concepts

In the local namespace socket addresses are file names. You can specify any file name you want as the address of the socket, but you must have write permission on the directory containing it. It's common to put these files in the `/tmp` directory.

One peculiarity of the local namespace is that the name is only used when opening the connection; once open the address is not meaningful and may not exist.

Another peculiarity is that you cannot connect to such a socket from another machine—not even if the other machine shares the file system which contains the name of the socket. You can see the socket in a directory listing, but connecting to it never succeeds. Some programs take advantage of this, such as by asking the client to send its own process ID, and using the process IDs to distinguish between clients. However, we recommend you not use this method in protocols you design, as we might someday permit connections from other machines that mount the same file systems. Instead, send each new client an identifying number if you want it to have one.

After you close a socket in the local namespace, you should delete the file name from the file system. Use `unlink` or `remove` to do this; see Section 14.6 [Deleting Files], page 396.

The local namespace supports just one protocol for any communication style; it is protocol number `0`.

16.5.2 Details of Local Namespace

To create a socket in the local namespace, use the constant `PF_LOCAL` as the *namespace* argument to `socket` or `socketpair`. This constant is defined in `sys/socket.h`.

int PF_LOCAL [Macro]

This designates the local namespace, in which socket addresses are local names, and its associated family of protocols. PF_Local is the macro used by Posix.1g.

int PF_UNIX [Macro]

This is a synonym for PF_LOCAL, for compatibility's sake.

int PF_FILE [Macro]

This is a synonym for PF_LOCAL, for compatibility's sake.

The structure for specifying socket names in the local namespace is defined in the header file sys/un.h:

struct sockaddr_un [Data Type]

This structure is used to specify local namespace socket addresses. It has the following members:

short int sun_family

This identifies the address family or format of the socket address. You should store the value AF_LOCAL to designate the local namespace. See Section 16.3 [Socket Addresses], page 431.

char sun_path[108]

This is the file name to use.

Incomplete: Why is 108 a magic number? RMS suggests making this a zero-length array and tweaking the following example to use alloca to allocate an appropriate amount of storage based on the length of the filename.

You should compute the *length* parameter for a socket address in the local namespace as the sum of the size of the sun_family component and the string length (*not* the allocation size!) of the file name string. This can be done using the macro SUN_LEN:

int SUN_LEN (*struct sockaddr_un * ptr*) [Macro]

Preliminary: | MT-Safe | AS-Safe | AC-Safe | See Section 1.2.2.1 [POSIX Safety Concepts], page 2.

The macro computes the length of socket address in the local namespace.

16.5.3 Example of Local-Namespace Sockets

Here is an example showing how to create and name a socket in the local namespace.

```
#include <stddef.h>
#include <stdio.h>
#include <errno.h>
#include <stdlib.h>
#include <string.h>
#include <sys/socket.h>
#include <sys/un.h>

int
make_named_socket (const char *filename)
```

```
{
  struct sockaddr_un name;
  int sock;
  size_t size;

  /* Create the socket. */
  sock = socket (PF_LOCAL, SOCK_DGRAM, 0);
  if (sock < 0)
    {
      perror ("socket");
      exit (EXIT_FAILURE);
    }

  /* Bind a name to the socket. */
  name.sun_family = AF_LOCAL;
  strncpy (name.sun_path, filename, sizeof (name.sun_path));
  name.sun_path[sizeof (name.sun_path) - 1] = '\0';

  /* The size of the address is
     the offset of the start of the filename,
     plus its length (not including the terminating null byte).
     Alternatively you can just do:
     size = SUN_LEN (&name);
  */
  size = (offsetof (struct sockaddr_un, sun_path)
          + strlen (name.sun_path));

  if (bind (sock, (struct sockaddr *) &name, size) < 0)
    {
      perror ("bind");
      exit (EXIT_FAILURE);
    }

  return sock;
}
```

16.6 The Internet Namespace

This section describes the details of the protocols and socket naming conventions used in the Internet namespace.

Originally the Internet namespace used only IP version 4 (IPv4). With the growing number of hosts on the Internet, a new protocol with a larger address space was necessary: IP version 6 (IPv6). IPv6 introduces 128-bit addresses (IPv4 has 32-bit addresses) and other features, and will eventually replace IPv4.

To create a socket in the IPv4 Internet namespace, use the symbolic name `PF_INET` of this namespace as the *namespace* argument to `socket` or `socketpair`. For IPv6 addresses you need the macro `PF_INET6`. These macros are defined in `sys/socket.h`.

int PF_INET   [Macro]
　　　This designates the IPv4 Internet namespace and associated family of protocols.

int PF_INET6   [Macro]
　　　This designates the IPv6 Internet namespace and associated family of protocols.

A socket address for the Internet namespace includes the following components:

- The address of the machine you want to connect to. Internet addresses can be specified in several ways; these are discussed in Section 16.6.1 [Internet Socket Address Formats], page 438, Section 16.6.2 [Host Addresses], page 439 and Section 16.6.2.4 [Host Names], page 443.

- A port number for that machine. See Section 16.6.3 [Internet Ports], page 447.

You must ensure that the address and port number are represented in a canonical format called *network byte order*. See Section 16.6.5 [Byte Order Conversion], page 449, for information about this.

16.6.1 Internet Socket Address Formats

In the Internet namespace, for both IPv4 (`AF_INET`) and IPv6 (`AF_INET6`), a socket address consists of a host address and a port on that host. In addition, the protocol you choose serves effectively as a part of the address because local port numbers are meaningful only within a particular protocol.

The data types for representing socket addresses in the Internet namespace are defined in the header file `netinet/in.h`.

`struct sockaddr_in`   [Data Type]

This is the data type used to represent socket addresses in the Internet namespace. It has the following members:

`sa_family_t sin_family`

This identifies the address family or format of the socket address. You should store the value `AF_INET` in this member. See Section 16.3 [Socket Addresses], page 431.

`struct in_addr sin_addr`

This is the Internet address of the host machine. See Section 16.6.2 [Host Addresses], page 439, and Section 16.6.2.4 [Host Names], page 443, for how to get a value to store here.

`unsigned short int sin_port`

This is the port number. See Section 16.6.3 [Internet Ports], page 447.

When you call `bind` or `getsockname`, you should specify `sizeof (struct sockaddr_in)` as the *length* parameter if you are using an IPv4 Internet namespace socket address.

`struct sockaddr_in6`   [Data Type]

This is the data type used to represent socket addresses in the IPv6 namespace. It has the following members:

`sa_family_t sin6_family`

This identifies the address family or format of the socket address. You should store the value of `AF_INET6` in this member. See Section 16.3 [Socket Addresses], page 431.

`struct in6_addr sin6_addr`

This is the IPv6 address of the host machine. See Section 16.6.2 [Host Addresses], page 439, and Section 16.6.2.4 [Host Names], page 443, for how to get a value to store here.

`uint32_t sin6_flowinfo`
> This is a currently unimplemented field.

`uint16_t sin6_port`
> This is the port number. See Section 16.6.3 [Internet Ports], page 447.

16.6.2 Host Addresses

Each computer on the Internet has one or more *Internet addresses*, numbers which identify that computer among all those on the Internet. Users typically write IPv4 numeric host addresses as sequences of four numbers, separated by periods, as in '`128.52.46.32`', and IPv6 numeric host addresses as sequences of up to eight numbers separated by colons, as in '`5f03:1200:836f:c100::1`'.

Each computer also has one or more *host names*, which are strings of words separated by periods, as in '`www.gnu.org`'.

Programs that let the user specify a host typically accept both numeric addresses and host names. To open a connection a program needs a numeric address, and so must convert a host name to the numeric address it stands for.

16.6.2.1 Internet Host Addresses

An IPv4 Internet host address is a number containing four bytes of data. Historically these are divided into two parts, a *network number* and a *local network address number* within that network. In the mid-1990s classless addresses were introduced which changed this behavior. Since some functions implicitly expect the old definitions, we first describe the class-based network and will then describe classless addresses. IPv6 uses only classless addresses and therefore the following paragraphs don't apply.

The class-based IPv4 network number consists of the first one, two or three bytes; the rest of the bytes are the local address.

IPv4 network numbers are registered with the Network Information Center (NIC), and are divided into three classes—A, B and C. The local network address numbers of individual machines are registered with the administrator of the particular network.

Class A networks have single-byte numbers in the range 0 to 127. There are only a small number of Class A networks, but they can each support a very large number of hosts. Medium-sized Class B networks have two-byte network numbers, with the first byte in the range 128 to 191. Class C networks are the smallest; they have three-byte network numbers, with the first byte in the range 192-255. Thus, the first 1, 2, or 3 bytes of an Internet address specify a network. The remaining bytes of the Internet address specify the address within that network.

The Class A network 0 is reserved for broadcast to all networks. In addition, the host number 0 within each network is reserved for broadcast to all hosts in that network. These uses are obsolete now but for compatibility reasons you shouldn't use network 0 and host number 0.

The Class A network 127 is reserved for loopback; you can always use the Internet address '`127.0.0.1`' to refer to the host machine.

Since a single machine can be a member of multiple networks, it can have multiple Internet host addresses. However, there is never supposed to be more than one machine with the same host address.

There are four forms of the *standard numbers-and-dots notation* for Internet addresses:

a.b.c.d   This specifies all four bytes of the address individually and is the commonly used representation.

a.b.c   The last part of the address, *c*, is interpreted as a 2-byte quantity. This is useful for specifying host addresses in a Class B network with network address number *a.b*.

a.b   The last part of the address, *b*, is interpreted as a 3-byte quantity. This is useful for specifying host addresses in a Class A network with network address number *a*.

a   If only one part is given, this corresponds directly to the host address number.

Within each part of the address, the usual C conventions for specifying the radix apply. In other words, a leading '0x' or '0X' implies hexadecimal radix; a leading '0' implies octal; and otherwise decimal radix is assumed.

Classless Addresses

IPv4 addresses (and IPv6 addresses also) are now considered classless; the distinction between classes A, B and C can be ignored. Instead an IPv4 host address consists of a 32-bit address and a 32-bit mask. The mask contains set bits for the network part and cleared bits for the host part. The network part is contiguous from the left, with the remaining bits representing the host. As a consequence, the netmask can simply be specified as the number of set bits. Classes A, B and C are just special cases of this general rule. For example, class A addresses have a netmask of '255.0.0.0' or a prefix length of 8.

Classless IPv4 network addresses are written in numbers-and-dots notation with the prefix length appended and a slash as separator. For example the class A network 10 is written as '10.0.0.0/8'.

IPv6 Addresses

IPv6 addresses contain 128 bits (IPv4 has 32 bits) of data. A host address is usually written as eight 16-bit hexadecimal numbers that are separated by colons. Two colons are used to abbreviate strings of consecutive zeros. For example, the IPv6 loopback address '0:0:0:0:0:0:0:1' can just be written as '::1'.

16.6.2.2 Host Address Data Type

IPv4 Internet host addresses are represented in some contexts as integers (type uint32_t). In other contexts, the integer is packaged inside a structure of type struct in_addr. It would be better if the usage were made consistent, but it is not hard to extract the integer from the structure or put the integer into a structure.

You will find older code that uses unsigned long int for IPv4 Internet host addresses instead of uint32_t or struct in_addr. Historically unsigned long int was a 32-bit number but with 64-bit machines this has changed. Using unsigned long int might break the code if it is used on machines where this type doesn't have 32 bits. uint32_t is specified by Unix98 and guaranteed to have 32 bits.

IPv6 Internet host addresses have 128 bits and are packaged inside a structure of type struct in6_addr.

The following basic definitions for Internet addresses are declared in the header file netinet/in.h:

struct in_addr   [Data Type]

This data type is used in certain contexts to contain an IPv4 Internet host address. It has just one field, named **s_addr**, which records the host address number as an uint32_t.

uint32_t INADDR_LOOPBACK   [Macro]

You can use this constant to stand for "the address of this machine," instead of finding its actual address. It is the IPv4 Internet address '127.0.0.1', which is usually called 'localhost'. This special constant saves you the trouble of looking up the address of your own machine. Also, the system usually implements INADDR_LOOPBACK specially, avoiding any network traffic for the case of one machine talking to itself.

uint32_t INADDR_ANY   [Macro]

You can use this constant to stand for "any incoming address" when binding to an address. See Section 16.3.2 [Setting the Address of a Socket], page 433. This is the usual address to give in the **sin_addr** member of **struct sockaddr_in** when you want to accept Internet connections.

uint32_t INADDR_BROADCAST   [Macro]

This constant is the address you use to send a broadcast message.

uint32_t INADDR_NONE   [Macro]

This constant is returned by some functions to indicate an error.

struct in6_addr   [Data Type]

This data type is used to store an IPv6 address. It stores 128 bits of data, which can be accessed (via a union) in a variety of ways.

struct in6_addr in6addr_loopback   [Constant]

This constant is the IPv6 address '::1', the loopback address. See above for a description of what this means. The macro IN6ADDR_LOOPBACK_INIT is provided to allow you to initialize your own variables to this value.

struct in6_addr in6addr_any   [Constant]

This constant is the IPv6 address '::', the unspecified address. See above for a description of what this means. The macro IN6ADDR_ANY_INIT is provided to allow you to initialize your own variables to this value.

16.6.2.3 Host Address Functions

These additional functions for manipulating Internet addresses are declared in the header file arpa/inet.h. They represent Internet addresses in network byte order, and network numbers and local-address-within-network numbers in host byte order. See Section 16.6.5 [Byte Order Conversion], page 449, for an explanation of network and host byte order.

int inet_aton (*const char *name, struct in_addr *addr*)   [Function]

Preliminary: | MT-Safe locale | AS-Safe | AC-Safe | See Section 1.2.2.1 [POSIX Safety Concepts], page 2.

This function converts the IPv4 Internet host address *name* from the standard numbers-and-dots notation into binary data and stores it in the **struct in_addr** that *addr* points to. **inet_aton** returns nonzero if the address is valid, zero if not.

uint32_t inet_addr (*const char* ***name***)   [Function]
Preliminary: | MT-Safe locale | AS-Safe | AC-Safe | See Section 1.2.2.1 [POSIX Safety Concepts], page 2.

This function converts the IPv4 Internet host address *name* from the standard numbers-and-dots notation into binary data. If the input is not valid, **inet_addr** returns **INADDR_NONE**. This is an obsolete interface to **inet_aton**, described immediately above. It is obsolete because **INADDR_NONE** is a valid address (255.255.255.255), and **inet_aton** provides a cleaner way to indicate error return.

uint32_t inet_network (*const char* ***name***)   [Function]
Preliminary: | MT-Safe locale | AS-Safe | AC-Safe | See Section 1.2.2.1 [POSIX Safety Concepts], page 2.

This function extracts the network number from the address *name*, given in the standard numbers-and-dots notation. The returned address is in host order. If the input is not valid, **inet_network** returns **-1**.

The function works only with traditional IPv4 class A, B and C network types. It doesn't work with classless addresses and shouldn't be used anymore.

char * inet_ntoa (*struct in_addr* ***addr***)   [Function]
Preliminary: | MT-Safe locale | AS-Unsafe race | AC-Safe | See Section 1.2.2.1 [POSIX Safety Concepts], page 2.

This function converts the IPv4 Internet host address *addr* to a string in the standard numbers-and-dots notation. The return value is a pointer into a statically-allocated buffer. Subsequent calls will overwrite the same buffer, so you should copy the string if you need to save it.

In multi-threaded programs each thread has an own statically-allocated buffer. But still subsequent calls of **inet_ntoa** in the same thread will overwrite the result of the last call.

Instead of **inet_ntoa** the newer function **inet_ntop** which is described below should be used since it handles both IPv4 and IPv6 addresses.

struct in_addr inet_makeaddr (*uint32_t* ***net***, *uint32_t* ***local***)   [Function]
Preliminary: | MT-Safe | AS-Safe | AC-Safe | See Section 1.2.2.1 [POSIX Safety Concepts], page 2.

This function makes an IPv4 Internet host address by combining the network number *net* with the local-address-within-network number *local*.

uint32_t inet_lnaof (*struct in_addr* ***addr***)   [Function]
Preliminary: | MT-Safe | AS-Safe | AC-Safe | See Section 1.2.2.1 [POSIX Safety Concepts], page 2.

This function returns the local-address-within-network part of the Internet host address *addr*.

The function works only with traditional IPv4 class A, B and C network types. It doesn't work with classless addresses and shouldn't be used anymore.

`uint32_t inet_netof` (*struct in_addr* `addr`)   [Function]

> Preliminary: | MT-Safe | AS-Safe | AC-Safe | See Section 1.2.2.1 [POSIX Safety Concepts], page 2.

> This function returns the network number part of the Internet host address *addr*.

> The function works only with traditional IPv4 class A, B and C network types. It doesn't work with classless addresses and shouldn't be used anymore.

`int inet_pton` (*int* `af`, *const char* `*cp`, *void* `*buf`)   [Function]

> Preliminary: | MT-Safe locale | AS-Safe | AC-Safe | See Section 1.2.2.1 [POSIX Safety Concepts], page 2.

> This function converts an Internet address (either IPv4 or IPv6) from presentation (textual) to network (binary) format. *af* should be either `AF_INET` or `AF_INET6`, as appropriate for the type of address being converted. *cp* is a pointer to the input string, and *buf* is a pointer to a buffer for the result. It is the caller's responsibility to make sure the buffer is large enough.

`const char * inet_ntop` (*int* `af`, *const void* `*cp`, *char* `*buf`, *socklen_t* `len`)   [Function]

> Preliminary: | MT-Safe locale | AS-Safe | AC-Safe | See Section 1.2.2.1 [POSIX Safety Concepts], page 2.

> This function converts an Internet address (either IPv4 or IPv6) from network (binary) to presentation (textual) form. *af* should be either `AF_INET` or `AF_INET6`, as appropriate. *cp* is a pointer to the address to be converted. *buf* should be a pointer to a buffer to hold the result, and *len* is the length of this buffer. The return value from the function will be this buffer address.

16.6.2.4 Host Names

Besides the standard numbers-and-dots notation for Internet addresses, you can also refer to a host by a symbolic name. The advantage of a symbolic name is that it is usually easier to remember. For example, the machine with Internet address '158.121.106.19' is also known as 'alpha.gnu.org'; and other machines in the 'gnu.org' domain can refer to it simply as 'alpha'.

Internally, the system uses a database to keep track of the mapping between host names and host numbers. This database is usually either the file **/etc/hosts** or an equivalent provided by a name server. The functions and other symbols for accessing this database are declared in **netdb.h**. They are BSD features, defined unconditionally if you include **netdb.h**.

`struct hostent`   [Data Type]

> This data type is used to represent an entry in the hosts database. It has the following members:

> `char *h_name`
>> This is the "official" name of the host.

> `char **h_aliases`
>> These are alternative names for the host, represented as a null-terminated vector of strings.

int h_addrtype
>   This is the host address type; in practice, its value is always either AF_
>   INET or AF_INET6, with the latter being used for IPv6 hosts. In principle
>   other kinds of addresses could be represented in the database as well as
>   Internet addresses; if this were done, you might find a value in this field
>   other than AF_INET or AF_INET6. See Section 16.3 [Socket Addresses],
>   page 431.

int h_length
>   This is the length, in bytes, of each address.

char **h_addr_list
>   This is the vector of addresses for the host. (Recall that the host might
>   be connected to multiple networks and have different addresses on each
>   one.) The vector is terminated by a null pointer.

char *h_addr
>   This is a synonym for h_addr_list[0]; in other words, it is the first host
>   address.

As far as the host database is concerned, each address is just a block of memory h_
length bytes long. But in other contexts there is an implicit assumption that you can
convert IPv4 addresses to a struct in_addr or an uint32_t. Host addresses in a struct
hostent structure are always given in network byte order; see Section 16.6.5 [Byte Order
Conversion], page 449.

You can use gethostbyname, gethostbyname2 or gethostbyaddr to search the hosts
database for information about a particular host. The information is returned in a statically-
allocated structure; you must copy the information if you need to save it across calls. You
can also use getaddrinfo and getnameinfo to obtain this information.

struct hostent * gethostbyname (*const char *name*)   [Function]
>   Preliminary: | MT-Unsafe race:hostbyname env locale | AS-Unsafe dlopen plugin
>   corrupt heap lock | AC-Unsafe lock corrupt mem fd | See Section 1.2.2.1 [POSIX
>   Safety Concepts], page 2.

>   The gethostbyname function returns information about the host named *name*. If the
>   lookup fails, it returns a null pointer.

struct hostent * gethostbyname2 (*const char *name*, *int af*)   [Function]
>   Preliminary: | MT-Unsafe race:hostbyname2 env locale | AS-Unsafe dlopen plugin
>   corrupt heap lock | AC-Unsafe lock corrupt mem fd | See Section 1.2.2.1 [POSIX
>   Safety Concepts], page 2.

>   The gethostbyname2 function is like gethostbyname, but allows the caller to specify
>   the desired address family (e.g. AF_INET or AF_INET6) of the result.

struct hostent * gethostbyaddr (*const void *addr*, *socklen_t*   [Function]
>   *length*, *int format*)
>   Preliminary: | MT-Unsafe race:hostbyaddr env locale | AS-Unsafe dlopen plugin
>   corrupt heap lock | AC-Unsafe lock corrupt mem fd | See Section 1.2.2.1 [POSIX
>   Safety Concepts], page 2.

The `gethostbyaddr` function returns information about the host with Internet address *addr*. The parameter *addr* is not really a pointer to char - it can be a pointer to an IPv4 or an IPv6 address. The *length* argument is the size (in bytes) of the address at *addr*. *format* specifies the address format; for an IPv4 Internet address, specify a value of `AF_INET`; for an IPv6 Internet address, use `AF_INET6`.

If the lookup fails, `gethostbyaddr` returns a null pointer.

If the name lookup by `gethostbyname` or `gethostbyaddr` fails, you can find out the reason by looking at the value of the variable `h_errno`. (It would be cleaner design for these functions to set `errno`, but use of `h_errno` is compatible with other systems.)

Here are the error codes that you may find in `h_errno`:

`HOST_NOT_FOUND`

> No such host is known in the database.

`TRY_AGAIN`

> This condition happens when the name server could not be contacted. If you try again later, you may succeed then.

`NO_RECOVERY`

> A non-recoverable error occurred.

`NO_ADDRESS`

> The host database contains an entry for the name, but it doesn't have an associated Internet address.

The lookup functions above all have one in common: they are not reentrant and therefore unusable in multi-threaded applications. Therefore provides the GNU C Library a new set of functions which can be used in this context.

int **gethostbyname_r** (*const char *restrict* **name**, *struct hostent *restrict*   [Function]
> **result_buf**, *char *restrict* **buf**, *size_t* **buflen**, *struct hostent **restrict*
> **result**, *int *restrict* **h_errnop**)

> Preliminary: | MT-Safe env locale | AS-Unsafe dlopen plugin corrupt heap lock | AC-Unsafe lock corrupt mem fd | See Section 1.2.2.1 [POSIX Safety Concepts], page 2.

> The `gethostbyname_r` function returns information about the host named *name*. The caller must pass a pointer to an object of type `struct hostent` in the *result_buf* parameter. In addition the function may need extra buffer space and the caller must pass an pointer and the size of the buffer in the *buf* and *buflen* parameters.

> A pointer to the buffer, in which the result is stored, is available in `*result` after the function call successfully returned. The buffer passed as the *buf* parameter can be freed only once the caller has finished with the result hostent struct, or has copied it including all the other memory that it points to. If an error occurs or if no entry is found, the pointer `*result` is a null pointer. Success is signalled by a zero return value. If the function failed the return value is an error number. In addition to the errors defined for `gethostbyname` it can also be `ERANGE`. In this case the call should be repeated with a larger buffer. Additional error information is not stored in the global variable `h_errno` but instead in the object pointed to by *h_errnop*.

> Here's a small example:

```
                  struct hostent *
                  gethostname (char *host)
                  {
                    struct hostent *hostbuf, *hp;
                    size_t hstbuflen;
                    char *tmphstbuf;
                    int res;
                    int herr;

                    hostbuf = malloc (sizeof (struct hostent));
                    hstbuflen = 1024;
                    tmphstbuf = malloc (hstbuflen);

                    while ((res = gethostbyname_r (host, hostbuf, tmphstbuf, hstbuflen,
                                            &hp, &herr)) == ERANGE)
                      {
                        /* Enlarge the buffer.  */
                        hstbuflen *= 2;
                        tmphstbuf = realloc (tmphstbuf, hstbuflen);
                      }

                    free (tmphstbuf);
                    /*  Check for errors.  */
                    if (res || hp == NULL)
                      return NULL;
                    return hp;
                  }
```

int **gethostbyname2_r** (*const char* ***name***, *int* ***af***, *struct hostent*   [Function]
      *restrict ***result_buf***, *char* *restrict ***buf***, *size_t* ***buflen***, *struct hostent*
      restrict ***result*, *int* *restrict ***h_errnop***)

    Preliminary: | MT-Safe env locale | AS-Unsafe dlopen plugin corrupt heap lock
    | AC-Unsafe lock corrupt mem fd | See Section 1.2.2.1 [POSIX Safety Concepts],
    page 2.

    The **gethostbyname2_r** function is like **gethostbyname_r**, but allows the caller to
    specify the desired address family (e.g. **AF_INET** or **AF_INET6**) for the result.

int **gethostbyaddr_r** (*const void* ***addr***, *socklen_t* ***length***, *int* ***format***,   [Function]
      struct hostent *restrict ***result_buf***, *char* *restrict ***buf***, *size_t* ***buflen***, *struct*
      hostent **restrict ***result***, *int* *restrict ***h_errnop***)

    Preliminary: | MT-Safe env locale | AS-Unsafe dlopen plugin corrupt heap lock
    | AC-Unsafe lock corrupt mem fd | See Section 1.2.2.1 [POSIX Safety Concepts],
    page 2.

    The **gethostbyaddr_r** function returns information about the host with Internet
    address *addr*. The parameter *addr* is not really a pointer to char - it can be a pointer
    to an IPv4 or an IPv6 address. The *length* argument is the size (in bytes) of the
    address at *addr*. *format* specifies the address format; for an IPv4 Internet address,
    specify a value of **AF_INET**; for an IPv6 Internet address, use **AF_INET6**.

    Similar to the **gethostbyname_r** function, the caller must provide buffers for the
    result and memory used internally. In case of success the function returns zero.
    Otherwise the value is an error number where **ERANGE** has the special meaning that
    the caller-provided buffer is too small.

You can also scan the entire hosts database one entry at a time using **sethostent**, **gethostent** and **endhostent**. Be careful when using these functions because they are not reentrant.

void sethostent (*int stayopen*)   [Function]
> Preliminary: | MT-Unsafe race:hostent env locale | AS-Unsafe dlopen plugin heap lock | AC-Unsafe corrupt lock fd mem | See Section 1.2.2.1 [POSIX Safety Concepts], page 2.
>
> This function opens the hosts database to begin scanning it. You can then call **gethostent** to read the entries.
>
> If the *stayopen* argument is nonzero, this sets a flag so that subsequent calls to **gethostbyname** or **gethostbyaddr** will not close the database (as they usually would). This makes for more efficiency if you call those functions several times, by avoiding reopening the database for each call.

struct hostent * gethostent (*void*)   [Function]
> Preliminary: | MT-Unsafe race:hostent race:hostentbuf env locale | AS-Unsafe dlopen plugin heap lock | AC-Unsafe corrupt lock fd mem | See Section 1.2.2.1 [POSIX Safety Concepts], page 2.
>
> This function returns the next entry in the hosts database. It returns a null pointer if there are no more entries.

void endhostent (*void*)   [Function]
> Preliminary: | MT-Unsafe race:hostent env locale | AS-Unsafe dlopen plugin heap lock | AC-Unsafe corrupt lock fd mem | See Section 1.2.2.1 [POSIX Safety Concepts], page 2.
>
> This function closes the hosts database.

16.6.3 Internet Ports

A socket address in the Internet namespace consists of a machine's Internet address plus a *port number* which distinguishes the sockets on a given machine (for a given protocol). Port numbers range from 0 to 65,535.

Port numbers less than **IPPORT_RESERVED** are reserved for standard servers, such as **finger** and **telnet**. There is a database that keeps track of these, and you can use the **getservbyname** function to map a service name onto a port number; see Section 16.6.4 [The Services Database], page 448.

If you write a server that is not one of the standard ones defined in the database, you must choose a port number for it. Use a number greater than **IPPORT_USERRESERVED**; such numbers are reserved for servers and won't ever be generated automatically by the system. Avoiding conflicts with servers being run by other users is up to you.

When you use a socket without specifying its address, the system generates a port number for it. This number is between **IPPORT_RESERVED** and **IPPORT_USERRESERVED**.

On the Internet, it is actually legitimate to have two different sockets with the same port number, as long as they never both try to communicate with the same socket address (host address plus port number). You shouldn't duplicate a port number except in special circumstances where a higher-level protocol requires it. Normally, the system won't let you do it; **bind** normally insists on distinct port numbers. To reuse a port number, you must set the socket option **SO_REUSEADDR**. See Section 16.12.2 [Socket-Level Options], page 473.

These macros are defined in the header file **netinet/in.h**.

int IPPORT_RESERVED [Macro]

> Port numbers less than **IPPORT_RESERVED** are reserved for superuser use.

int IPPORT_USERRESERVED [Macro]

> Port numbers greater than or equal to **IPPORT_USERRESERVED** are reserved for explicit use; they will never be allocated automatically.

16.6.4 The Services Database

The database that keeps track of "well-known" services is usually either the file **/etc/services** or an equivalent from a name server. You can use these utilities, declared in **netdb.h**, to access the services database.

struct servent [Data Type]

> This data type holds information about entries from the services database. It has the following members:
>
> **char *s_name**
>> This is the "official" name of the service.
>
> **char **s_aliases**
>> These are alternate names for the service, represented as an array of strings. A null pointer terminates the array.
>
> **int s_port**
>> This is the port number for the service. Port numbers are given in network byte order; see Section 16.6.5 [Byte Order Conversion], page 449.
>
> **char *s_proto**
>> This is the name of the protocol to use with this service. See Section 16.6.6 [Protocols Database], page 450.

To get information about a particular service, use the **getservbyname** or **getservbyport** functions. The information is returned in a statically-allocated structure; you must copy the information if you need to save it across calls.

struct servent * getservbyname (*const char *name, const char* [Function]
> *proto*)

> Preliminary: | MT-Unsafe race:servbyname locale | AS-Unsafe dlopen plugin heap lock | AC-Unsafe corrupt lock fd mem | See Section 1.2.2.1 [POSIX Safety Concepts], page 2.
>
> The **getservbyname** function returns information about the service named *name* using protocol *proto*. If it can't find such a service, it returns a null pointer.
>
> This function is useful for servers as well as for clients; servers use it to determine which port they should listen on (see Section 16.9.2 [Listening for Connections], page 457).

`struct servent * getservbyport (`*int* `port,` *const char* `*proto)`   [Function]
> Preliminary: | MT-Unsafe race:servbyport locale | AS-Unsafe dlopen plugin heap
> lock | AC-Unsafe corrupt lock fd mem | See Section 1.2.2.1 [POSIX Safety Concepts],
> page 2.
>
> The `getservbyport` function returns information about the service at port *port* using
> protocol *proto*. If it can't find such a service, it returns a null pointer.

You can also scan the services database using `setservent`, `getservent` and `endservent`.
Be careful when using these functions because they are not reentrant.

`void setservent (`*int* `stayopen)`   [Function]
> Preliminary: | MT-Unsafe race:servent locale | AS-Unsafe dlopen plugin heap lock
> | AC-Unsafe corrupt lock fd mem | See Section 1.2.2.1 [POSIX Safety Concepts],
> page 2.
>
> This function opens the services database to begin scanning it.
>
> If the *stayopen* argument is nonzero, this sets a flag so that subsequent calls to
> `getservbyname` or `getservbyport` will not close the database (as they usually would).
> This makes for more efficiency if you call those functions several times, by avoiding
> reopening the database for each call.

`struct servent * getservent (`*void*`)`   [Function]
> Preliminary: | MT-Unsafe race:servent race:serventbuf locale | AS-Unsafe dlopen
> plugin heap lock | AC-Unsafe corrupt lock fd mem | See Section 1.2.2.1 [POSIX
> Safety Concepts], page 2.
>
> This function returns the next entry in the services database. If there are no more
> entries, it returns a null pointer.

`void endservent (`*void*`)`   [Function]
> Preliminary: | MT-Unsafe race:servent locale | AS-Unsafe dlopen plugin heap lock
> | AC-Unsafe corrupt lock fd mem | See Section 1.2.2.1 [POSIX Safety Concepts],
> page 2.
>
> This function closes the services database.

16.6.5 Byte Order Conversion

Different kinds of computers use different conventions for the ordering of bytes within a
word. Some computers put the most significant byte within a word first (this is called
"big-endian" order), and others put it last ("little-endian" order).

So that machines with different byte order conventions can communicate, the Internet
protocols specify a canonical byte order convention for data transmitted over the network.
This is known as *network byte order*.

When establishing an Internet socket connection, you must make sure that the data
in the `sin_port` and `sin_addr` members of the `sockaddr_in` structure are represented in
network byte order. If you are encoding integer data in the messages sent through the socket,
you should convert this to network byte order too. If you don't do this, your program may
fail when running on or talking to other kinds of machines.

If you use `getservbyname` and `gethostbyname` or `inet_addr` to get the port number and host address, the values are already in network byte order, and you can copy them directly into the `sockaddr_in` structure.

Otherwise, you have to convert the values explicitly. Use `htons` and `ntohs` to convert values for the `sin_port` member. Use `htonl` and `ntohl` to convert IPv4 addresses for the `sin_addr` member. (Remember, `struct in_addr` is equivalent to `uint32_t`.) These functions are declared in `netinet/in.h`.

`uint16_t htons` (*uint16_t* `hostshort`)   [Function]
> Preliminary: | MT-Safe | AS-Safe | AC-Safe | See Section 1.2.2.1 [POSIX Safety Concepts], page 2.
>
> This function converts the `uint16_t` integer *hostshort* from host byte order to network byte order.

`uint16_t ntohs` (*uint16_t* `netshort`)   [Function]
> Preliminary: | MT-Safe | AS-Safe | AC-Safe | See Section 1.2.2.1 [POSIX Safety Concepts], page 2.
>
> This function converts the `uint16_t` integer *netshort* from network byte order to host byte order.

`uint32_t htonl` (*uint32_t* `hostlong`)   [Function]
> Preliminary: | MT-Safe | AS-Safe | AC-Safe | See Section 1.2.2.1 [POSIX Safety Concepts], page 2.
>
> This function converts the `uint32_t` integer *hostlong* from host byte order to network byte order.
>
> This is used for IPv4 Internet addresses.

`uint32_t ntohl` (*uint32_t* `netlong`)   [Function]
> Preliminary: | MT-Safe | AS-Safe | AC-Safe | See Section 1.2.2.1 [POSIX Safety Concepts], page 2.
>
> This function converts the `uint32_t` integer *netlong* from network byte order to host byte order.
>
> This is used for IPv4 Internet addresses.

16.6.6 Protocols Database

The communications protocol used with a socket controls low-level details of how data are exchanged. For example, the protocol implements things like checksums to detect errors in transmissions, and routing instructions for messages. Normal user programs have little reason to mess with these details directly.

The default communications protocol for the Internet namespace depends on the communication style. For stream communication, the default is TCP ("transmission control protocol"). For datagram communication, the default is UDP ("user datagram protocol"). For reliable datagram communication, the default is RDP ("reliable datagram protocol"). You should nearly always use the default.

Internet protocols are generally specified by a name instead of a number. The network protocols that a host knows about are stored in a database. This is usually either derived from the file /etc/protocols, or it may be an equivalent provided by a name server. You look up the protocol number associated with a named protocol in the database using the getprotobyname function.

Here are detailed descriptions of the utilities for accessing the protocols database. These are declared in netdb.h.

struct protoent   [Data Type]

This data type is used to represent entries in the network protocols database. It has the following members:

char *p_name

This is the official name of the protocol.

char **p_aliases

These are alternate names for the protocol, specified as an array of strings. The last element of the array is a null pointer.

int p_proto

This is the protocol number (in host byte order); use this member as the *protocol* argument to socket.

You can use getprotobyname and getprotobynumber to search the protocols database for a specific protocol. The information is returned in a statically-allocated structure; you must copy the information if you need to save it across calls.

struct protoent * getprotobyname (*const char *name*)   [Function]

Preliminary: | MT-Unsafe race:protobyname locale | AS-Unsafe dlopen plugin heap lock | AC-Unsafe corrupt lock fd mem | See Section 1.2.2.1 [POSIX Safety Concepts], page 2.

The getprotobyname function returns information about the network protocol named *name*. If there is no such protocol, it returns a null pointer.

struct protoent * getprotobynumber (*int protocol*)   [Function]

Preliminary: | MT-Unsafe race:protobynumber locale | AS-Unsafe dlopen plugin heap lock | AC-Unsafe corrupt lock fd mem | See Section 1.2.2.1 [POSIX Safety Concepts], page 2.

The getprotobynumber function returns information about the network protocol with number *protocol*. If there is no such protocol, it returns a null pointer.

You can also scan the whole protocols database one protocol at a time by using setprotoent, getprotoent and endprotoent. Be careful when using these functions because they are not reentrant.

void setprotoent (*int stayopen*)   [Function]

Preliminary: | MT-Unsafe race:protoent locale | AS-Unsafe dlopen plugin heap lock | AC-Unsafe corrupt lock fd mem | See Section 1.2.2.1 [POSIX Safety Concepts], page 2.

This function opens the protocols database to begin scanning it.

If the *stayopen* argument is nonzero, this sets a flag so that subsequent calls to getprotobyname or getprotobynumber will not close the database (as they usually would). This makes for more efficiency if you call those functions several times, by avoiding reopening the database for each call.

struct protoent * getprotoent (*void*)   [Function]

Preliminary: | MT-Unsafe race:protoent race:protoentbuf locale | AS-Unsafe dlopen plugin heap lock | AC-Unsafe corrupt lock fd mem | See Section 1.2.2.1 [POSIX Safety Concepts], page 2.

This function returns the next entry in the protocols database. It returns a null pointer if there are no more entries.

void endprotoent (*void*)   [Function]

Preliminary: | MT-Unsafe race:protoent locale | AS-Unsafe dlopen plugin heap lock | AC-Unsafe corrupt lock fd mem | See Section 1.2.2.1 [POSIX Safety Concepts], page 2.

This function closes the protocols database.

16.6.7 Internet Socket Example

Here is an example showing how to create and name a socket in the Internet namespace. The newly created socket exists on the machine that the program is running on. Rather than finding and using the machine's Internet address, this example specifies `INADDR_ANY` as the host address; the system replaces that with the machine's actual address.

```
#include <stdio.h>
#include <stdlib.h>
#include <sys/socket.h>
#include <netinet/in.h>

int
make_socket (uint16_t port)
{
  int sock;
  struct sockaddr_in name;

  /* Create the socket. */
  sock = socket (PF_INET, SOCK_STREAM, 0);
  if (sock < 0)
    {
      perror ("socket");
      exit (EXIT_FAILURE);
    }

  /* Give the socket a name. */
  name.sin_family = AF_INET;
  name.sin_port = htons (port);
  name.sin_addr.s_addr = htonl (INADDR_ANY);
  if (bind (sock, (struct sockaddr *) &name, sizeof (name)) < 0)
    {
      perror ("bind");
      exit (EXIT_FAILURE);
    }

  return sock;
}
```

Here is another example, showing how you can fill in a `sockaddr_in` structure, given a host name string and a port number:

```
#include <stdio.h>
#include <stdlib.h>
#include <sys/socket.h>
#include <netinet/in.h>
#include <netdb.h>

void
init_sockaddr (struct sockaddr_in *name,
               const char *hostname,
               uint16_t port)
{
  struct hostent *hostinfo;

  name->sin_family = AF_INET;
  name->sin_port = htons (port);
  hostinfo = gethostbyname (hostname);
  if (hostinfo == NULL)
    {
      fprintf (stderr, "Unknown host %s.\n", hostname);
      exit (EXIT_FAILURE);
    }
  name->sin_addr = *(struct in_addr *) hostinfo->h_addr;
}
```

16.7 Other Namespaces

Certain other namespaces and associated protocol families are supported but not documented yet because they are not often used. `PF_NS` refers to the Xerox Network Software protocols. `PF_ISO` stands for Open Systems Interconnect. `PF_CCITT` refers to protocols from CCITT. `socket.h` defines these symbols and others naming protocols not actually implemented.

`PF_IMPLINK` is used for communicating between hosts and Internet Message Processors. For information on this and `PF_ROUTE`, an occasionally-used local area routing protocol, see the GNU Hurd Manual (to appear in the future).

16.8 Opening and Closing Sockets

This section describes the actual library functions for opening and closing sockets. The same functions work for all namespaces and connection styles.

16.8.1 Creating a Socket

The primitive for creating a socket is the `socket` function, declared in `sys/socket.h`.

int socket (*int* `namespace`, *int* `style`, *int* `protocol`)   [Function]
    Preliminary: | MT-Safe | AS-Safe | AC-Safe fd | See Section 1.2.2.1 [POSIX Safety Concepts], page 2.

    This function creates a socket and specifies communication style *style*, which should be one of the socket styles listed in Section 16.2 [Communication Styles], page 430. The *namespace* argument specifies the namespace; it must be `PF_LOCAL` (see Section 16.5

[The Local Namespace], page 435) or `PF_INET` (see Section 16.6 [The Internet Namespace], page 437). *protocol* designates the specific protocol (see Section 16.1 [Socket Concepts], page 429); zero is usually right for *protocol*.

The return value from `socket` is the file descriptor for the new socket, or `-1` in case of error. The following `errno` error conditions are defined for this function:

`EPROTONOSUPPORT`
> The *protocol* or *style* is not supported by the *namespace* specified.

`EMFILE` The process already has too many file descriptors open.

`ENFILE` The system already has too many file descriptors open.

`EACCES` The process does not have the privilege to create a socket of the specified *style* or *protocol*.

`ENOBUFS` The system ran out of internal buffer space.

The file descriptor returned by the `socket` function supports both read and write operations. However, like pipes, sockets do not support file positioning operations.

For examples of how to call the `socket` function, see Section 16.5.3 [Example of Local-Namespace Sockets], page 436, or Section 16.6.7 [Internet Socket Example], page 452.

16.8.2 Closing a Socket

When you have finished using a socket, you can simply close its file descriptor with `close`; see Section 13.1 [Opening and Closing Files], page 323. If there is still data waiting to be transmitted over the connection, normally `close` tries to complete this transmission. You can control this behavior using the `SO_LINGER` socket option to specify a timeout period; see Section 16.12 [Socket Options], page 472.

You can also shut down only reception or transmission on a connection by calling `shutdown`, which is declared in `sys/socket.h`.

`int shutdown (int socket, int how)`   [Function]
> Preliminary: | MT-Safe | AS-Safe | AC-Safe | See Section 1.2.2.1 [POSIX Safety Concepts], page 2.
>
> The `shutdown` function shuts down the connection of socket *socket*. The argument *how* specifies what action to perform:
>
> 0   Stop receiving data for this socket. If further data arrives, reject it.
>
> 1   Stop trying to transmit data from this socket. Discard any data waiting to be sent. Stop looking for acknowledgement of data already sent; don't retransmit it if it is lost.
>
> 2   Stop both reception and transmission.
>
> The return value is `0` on success and `-1` on failure. The following `errno` error conditions are defined for this function:
>
> `EBADF`   *socket* is not a valid file descriptor.
>
> `ENOTSOCK` *socket* is not a socket.
>
> `ENOTCONN` *socket* is not connected.

16.8.3 Socket Pairs

A *socket pair* consists of a pair of connected (but unnamed) sockets. It is very similar to a pipe and is used in much the same way. Socket pairs are created with the `socketpair` function, declared in `sys/socket.h`. A socket pair is much like a pipe; the main difference is that the socket pair is bidirectional, whereas the pipe has one input-only end and one output-only end (see Chapter 15 [Pipes and FIFOs], page 424).

`int socketpair` (*int* `namespace`, *int* `style`, *int* `protocol`, *int*   [Function]
     `filedes`[2])

> Preliminary: | MT-Safe | AS-Safe | AC-Safe fd | See Section 1.2.2.1 [POSIX Safety Concepts], page 2.
>
> This function creates a socket pair, returning the file descriptors in `filedes`[0] and `filedes`[1]. The socket pair is a full-duplex communications channel, so that both reading and writing may be performed at either end.
>
> The *namespace*, *style* and *protocol* arguments are interpreted as for the `socket` function. *style* should be one of the communication styles listed in Section 16.2 [Communication Styles], page 430. The *namespace* argument specifies the namespace, which must be `AF_LOCAL` (see Section 16.5 [The Local Namespace], page 435); *protocol* specifies the communications protocol, but zero is the only meaningful value.
>
> If *style* specifies a connectionless communication style, then the two sockets you get are not *connected*, strictly speaking, but each of them knows the other as the default destination address, so they can send packets to each other.
>
> The `socketpair` function returns 0 on success and -1 on failure. The following `errno` error conditions are defined for this function:
>
> `EMFILE`   The process has too many file descriptors open.
>
> `EAFNOSUPPORT`
> > The specified namespace is not supported.
>
> `EPROTONOSUPPORT`
> > The specified protocol is not supported.
>
> `EOPNOTSUPP`
> > The specified protocol does not support the creation of socket pairs.

16.9 Using Sockets with Connections

The most common communication styles involve making a connection to a particular other socket, and then exchanging data with that socket over and over. Making a connection is asymmetric; one side (the *client*) acts to request a connection, while the other side (the *server*) makes a socket and waits for the connection request.

- Section 16.9.1 [Making a Connection], page 456, describes what the client program must do to initiate a connection with a server.

- Section 16.9.2 [Listening for Connections], page 457 and Section 16.9.3 [Accepting Connections], page 457 describe what the server program must do to wait for and act upon connection requests from clients.

- Section 16.9.5 [Transferring Data], page 459, describes how data are transferred through the connected socket.

16.9.1 Making a Connection

In making a connection, the client makes a connection while the server waits for and accepts the connection. Here we discuss what the client program must do with the **connect** function, which is declared in **sys/socket.h**.

int connect (*int socket*, *struct sockaddr ***addr**, *socklen_t **length***)   [Function]
> Preliminary: | MT-Safe | AS-Safe | AC-Safe | See Section 1.2.2.1 [POSIX Safety Concepts], page 2.

> The **connect** function initiates a connection from the socket with file descriptor *socket* to the socket whose address is specified by the *addr* and *length* arguments. (This socket is typically on another machine, and it must be already set up as a server.) See Section 16.3 [Socket Addresses], page 431, for information about how these arguments are interpreted.

> Normally, **connect** waits until the server responds to the request before it returns. You can set nonblocking mode on the socket *socket* to make **connect** return immediately without waiting for the response. See Section 13.14 [File Status Flags], page 363, for information about nonblocking mode.

> The normal return value from **connect** is 0. If an error occurs, **connect** returns -1. The following **errno** error conditions are defined for this function:

> EBADF   The socket *socket* is not a valid file descriptor.

> ENOTSOCK   File descriptor *socket* is not a socket.

> EADDRNOTAVAIL
> > The specified address is not available on the remote machine.

> EAFNOSUPPORT
> > The namespace of the *addr* is not supported by this socket.

> EISCONN   The socket *socket* is already connected.

> ETIMEDOUT
> > The attempt to establish the connection timed out.

> ECONNREFUSED
> > The server has actively refused to establish the connection.

> ENETUNREACH
> > The network of the given *addr* isn't reachable from this host.

> EADDRINUSE
> > The socket address of the given *addr* is already in use.

> EINPROGRESS
> > The socket *socket* is non-blocking and the connection could not be established immediately. You can determine when the connection is completely established with **select**; see Section 13.8 [Waiting for Input or Output], page 342. Another **connect** call on the same socket, before the connection is completely established, will fail with **EALREADY**.

> EALREADY   The socket *socket* is non-blocking and already has a pending connection in progress (see **EINPROGRESS** above).

This function is defined as a cancellation point in multi-threaded programs, so one has to be prepared for this and make sure that allocated resources (like memory, files descriptors, semaphores or whatever) are freed even if the thread is canceled.

16.9.2 Listening for Connections

Now let us consider what the server process must do to accept connections on a socket. First it must use the `listen` function to enable connection requests on the socket, and then accept each incoming connection with a call to `accept` (see Section 16.9.3 [Accepting Connections], page 457). Once connection requests are enabled on a server socket, the `select` function reports when the socket has a connection ready to be accepted (see Section 13.8 [Waiting for Input or Output], page 342).

The `listen` function is not allowed for sockets using connectionless communication styles.

You can write a network server that does not even start running until a connection to it is requested. See Section 16.11.1 [`inetd` Servers], page 471.

In the Internet namespace, there are no special protection mechanisms for controlling access to a port; any process on any machine can make a connection to your server. If you want to restrict access to your server, make it examine the addresses associated with connection requests or implement some other handshaking or identification protocol.

In the local namespace, the ordinary file protection bits control who has access to connect to the socket.

`int listen (int socket, int n)`   [Function]
> Preliminary: | MT-Safe | AS-Safe | AC-Safe fd | See Section 1.2.2.1 [POSIX Safety Concepts], page 2.
>
> The `listen` function enables the socket *socket* to accept connections, thus making it a server socket.
>
> The argument *n* specifies the length of the queue for pending connections. When the queue fills, new clients attempting to connect fail with `ECONNREFUSED` until the server calls `accept` to accept a connection from the queue.
>
> The `listen` function returns 0 on success and -1 on failure. The following `errno` error conditions are defined for this function:
>
> `EBADF`   The argument *socket* is not a valid file descriptor.
>
> `ENOTSOCK`   The argument *socket* is not a socket.
>
> `EOPNOTSUPP`
> > The socket *socket* does not support this operation.

16.9.3 Accepting Connections

When a server receives a connection request, it can complete the connection by accepting the request. Use the function `accept` to do this.

A socket that has been established as a server can accept connection requests from multiple clients. The server's original socket *does not become part of the connection*; instead, `accept` makes a new socket which participates in the connection. `accept` returns the descriptor for this socket. The server's original socket remains available for listening for further connection requests.

The number of pending connection requests on a server socket is finite. If connection requests arrive from clients faster than the server can act upon them, the queue can fill up and additional requests are refused with an `ECONNREFUSED` error. You can specify the maximum length of this queue as an argument to the `listen` function, although the system may also impose its own internal limit on the length of this queue.

`int accept` (*int* `socket`, *struct sockaddr* `*addr`, *socklen_t* `*length_ptr`)　　[Function]
> Preliminary: | MT-Safe | AS-Safe | AC-Safe fd | See Section 1.2.2.1 [POSIX Safety Concepts], page 2.
>
> This function is used to accept a connection request on the server socket *socket*.
>
> The `accept` function waits if there are no connections pending, unless the socket *socket* has nonblocking mode set. (You can use `select` to wait for a pending connection, with a nonblocking socket.) See Section 13.14 [File Status Flags], page 363, for information about nonblocking mode.
>
> The *addr* and *length-ptr* arguments are used to return information about the name of the client socket that initiated the connection. See Section 16.3 [Socket Addresses], page 431, for information about the format of the information.
>
> Accepting a connection does not make *socket* part of the connection. Instead, it creates a new socket which becomes connected. The normal return value of `accept` is the file descriptor for the new socket.
>
> After `accept`, the original socket *socket* remains open and unconnected, and continues listening until you close it. You can accept further connections with *socket* by calling `accept` again.
>
> If an error occurs, `accept` returns `-1`. The following `errno` error conditions are defined for this function:
>
> `EBADF`　　The *socket* argument is not a valid file descriptor.
>
> `ENOTSOCK`　　The descriptor *socket* argument is not a socket.
>
> `EOPNOTSUPP`
> > The descriptor *socket* does not support this operation.
>
> `EWOULDBLOCK`
> > *socket* has nonblocking mode set, and there are no pending connections immediately available.
>
> This function is defined as a cancellation point in multi-threaded programs, so one has to be prepared for this and make sure that allocated resources (like memory, files descriptors, semaphores or whatever) are freed even if the thread is canceled.

The `accept` function is not allowed for sockets using connectionless communication styles.

16.9.4 Who is Connected to Me?

int getpeername (*int* `socket`, *struct sockaddr* `*addr`, *socklen_t*   [Function]
     `*length-ptr`)

> Preliminary: | MT-Safe | AS-Safe | AC-Safe | See Section 1.2.2.1 [POSIX Safety
> Concepts], page 2.
>
> The `getpeername` function returns the address of the socket that *socket* is connected
> to; it stores the address in the memory space specified by *addr* and *length-ptr*. It
> stores the length of the address in *`*length-ptr`*.
>
> See Section 16.3 [Socket Addresses], page 431, for information about the format of
> the address. In some operating systems, `getpeername` works only for sockets in the
> Internet domain.
>
> The return value is 0 on success and -1 on error. The following `errno` error conditions
> are defined for this function:
>
> EBADF   The argument *socket* is not a valid file descriptor.
>
> ENOTSOCK   The descriptor *socket* is not a socket.
>
> ENOTCONN   The socket *socket* is not connected.
>
> ENOBUFS   There are not enough internal buffers available.

16.9.5 Transferring Data

Once a socket has been connected to a peer, you can use the ordinary **read** and **write**
operations (see Section 13.2 [Input and Output Primitives], page 326) to transfer data. A
socket is a two-way communications channel, so read and write operations can be performed
at either end.

There are also some I/O modes that are specific to socket operations. In order to specify
these modes, you must use the **recv** and **send** functions instead of the more generic **read**
and **write** functions. The **recv** and **send** functions take an additional argument which you
can use to specify various flags to control special I/O modes. For example, you can specify
the `MSG_OOB` flag to read or write out-of-band data, the `MSG_PEEK` flag to peek at input, or
the `MSG_DONTROUTE` flag to control inclusion of routing information on output.

16.9.5.1 Sending Data

The **send** function is declared in the header file **sys/socket.h**. If your *flags* argument is
zero, you can just as well use **write** instead of **send**; see Section 13.2 [Input and Output
Primitives], page 326. If the socket was connected but the connection has broken, you get
a `SIGPIPE` signal for any use of **send** or **write** (see Section 24.2.7 [Miscellaneous Signals],
page 670).

ssize_t send (*int* `socket`, *const void* `*buffer`, *size_t* `size`, *int* `flags`)   [Function]

> Preliminary: | MT-Safe | AS-Safe | AC-Safe | See Section 1.2.2.1 [POSIX Safety
> Concepts], page 2.
>
> The **send** function is like **write**, but with the additional flags *flags*. The possible
> values of *flags* are described in Section 16.9.5.3 [Socket Data Options], page 461.
>
> This function returns the number of bytes transmitted, or -1 on failure. If the socket
> is nonblocking, then **send** (like **write**) can return after sending just part of the data.

See Section 13.14 [File Status Flags], page 363, for information about nonblocking mode.

Note, however, that a successful return value merely indicates that the message has been sent without error, not necessarily that it has been received without error.

The following **errno** error conditions are defined for this function:

EBADF   The *socket* argument is not a valid file descriptor.

EINTR   The operation was interrupted by a signal before any data was sent. See Section 24.5 [Primitives Interrupted by Signals], page 687.

ENOTSOCK   The descriptor *socket* is not a socket.

EMSGSIZE   The socket type requires that the message be sent atomically, but the message is too large for this to be possible.

EWOULDBLOCK
                 Nonblocking mode has been set on the socket, and the write operation would block. (Normally **send** blocks until the operation can be completed.)

ENOBUFS   There is not enough internal buffer space available.

ENOTCONN   You never connected this socket.

EPIPE   This socket was connected but the connection is now broken. In this case, **send** generates a **SIGPIPE** signal first; if that signal is ignored or blocked, or if its handler returns, then **send** fails with **EPIPE**.

This function is defined as a cancellation point in multi-threaded programs, so one has to be prepared for this and make sure that allocated resources (like memory, files descriptors, semaphores or whatever) are freed even if the thread is canceled.

16.9.5.2 Receiving Data

The **recv** function is declared in the header file **sys/socket.h**. If your *flags* argument is zero, you can just as well use **read** instead of **recv**; see Section 13.2 [Input and Output Primitives], page 326.

ssize_t recv (*int* **socket**, *void* ***buffer**, *size_t* **size**, *int* **flags**)   [Function]
    Preliminary: | MT-Safe | AS-Safe | AC-Safe | See Section 1.2.2.1 [POSIX Safety Concepts], page 2.

    The **recv** function is like **read**, but with the additional flags *flags*. The possible values of *flags* are described in Section 16.9.5.3 [Socket Data Options], page 461.

    If nonblocking mode is set for *socket*, and no data are available to be read, **recv** fails immediately rather than waiting. See Section 13.14 [File Status Flags], page 363, for information about nonblocking mode.

    This function returns the number of bytes received, or −1 on failure. The following **errno** error conditions are defined for this function:

    EBADF   The *socket* argument is not a valid file descriptor.

    ENOTSOCK   The descriptor *socket* is not a socket.

EWOULDBLOCK
>Nonblocking mode has been set on the socket, and the read operation would block. (Normally, `recv` blocks until there is input available to be read.)

EINTR   The operation was interrupted by a signal before any data was read. See Section 24.5 [Primitives Interrupted by Signals], page 687.

ENOTCONN   You never connected this socket.

This function is defined as a cancellation point in multi-threaded programs, so one has to be prepared for this and make sure that allocated resources (like memory, files descriptors, semaphores or whatever) are freed even if the thread is canceled.

16.9.5.3 Socket Data Options

The *flags* argument to `send` and `recv` is a bit mask. You can bitwise-OR the values of the following macros together to obtain a value for this argument. All are defined in the header file `sys/socket.h`.

int MSG_OOB   [Macro]
>Send or receive out-of-band data. See Section 16.9.8 [Out-of-Band Data], page 464.

int MSG_PEEK   [Macro]
>Look at the data but don't remove it from the input queue. This is only meaningful with input functions such as `recv`, not with `send`.

int MSG_DONTROUTE   [Macro]
>Don't include routing information in the message. This is only meaningful with output operations, and is usually only of interest for diagnostic or routing programs. We don't try to explain it here.

16.9.6 Byte Stream Socket Example

Here is an example client program that makes a connection for a byte stream socket in the Internet namespace. It doesn't do anything particularly interesting once it has connected to the server; it just sends a text string to the server and exits.

This program uses `init_sockaddr` to set up the socket address; see Section 16.6.7 [Internet Socket Example], page 452.

```
#include <stdio.h>
#include <errno.h>
#include <stdlib.h>
#include <unistd.h>
#include <sys/types.h>
#include <sys/socket.h>
#include <netinet/in.h>
#include <netdb.h>

#define PORT            5555
#define MESSAGE         "Yow!!! Are we having fun yet?!?"
#define SERVERHOST      "www.gnu.org"

void
```

```
write_to_server (int filedes)
{
  int nbytes;

  nbytes = write (filedes, MESSAGE, strlen (MESSAGE) + 1);
  if (nbytes < 0)
    {
      perror ("write");
      exit (EXIT_FAILURE);
    }
}


int
main (void)
{
  extern void init_sockaddr (struct sockaddr_in *name,
                             const char *hostname,
                             uint16_t port);
  int sock;
  struct sockaddr_in servername;

  /* Create the socket. */
  sock = socket (PF_INET, SOCK_STREAM, 0);
  if (sock < 0)
    {
      perror ("socket (client)");
      exit (EXIT_FAILURE);
    }

  /* Connect to the server. */
  init_sockaddr (&servername, SERVERHOST, PORT);
  if (0 > connect (sock,
                   (struct sockaddr *) &servername,
                   sizeof (servername)))
    {
      perror ("connect (client)");
      exit (EXIT_FAILURE);
    }

  /* Send data to the server. */
  write_to_server (sock);
  close (sock);
  exit (EXIT_SUCCESS);
}
```

16.9.7 Byte Stream Connection Server Example

The server end is much more complicated. Since we want to allow multiple clients to be connected to the server at the same time, it would be incorrect to wait for input from a single client by simply calling **read** or **recv**. Instead, the right thing to do is to use **select** (see Section 13.8 [Waiting for Input or Output], page 342) to wait for input on all of the open sockets. This also allows the server to deal with additional connection requests.

This particular server doesn't do anything interesting once it has gotten a message from a client. It does close the socket for that client when it detects an end-of-file condition (resulting from the client shutting down its end of the connection).

This program uses `make_socket` to set up the socket address; see Section 16.6.7 [Internet Socket Example], page 452.

```
#include <stdio.h>
#include <errno.h>
#include <stdlib.h>
#include <unistd.h>
#include <sys/types.h>
#include <sys/socket.h>
#include <netinet/in.h>
#include <netdb.h>

#define PORT    5555
#define MAXMSG  512

int
read_from_client (int filedes)
{
  char buffer[MAXMSG];
  int nbytes;

  nbytes = read (filedes, buffer, MAXMSG);
  if (nbytes < 0)
    {
      /* Read error. */
      perror ("read");
      exit (EXIT_FAILURE);
    }
  else if (nbytes == 0)
    /* End-of-file. */
    return -1;
  else
    {
      /* Data read. */
      fprintf (stderr, "Server: got message: '%s'\n", buffer);
      return 0;
    }
}

int
main (void)
{
  extern int make_socket (uint16_t port);
  int sock;
  fd_set active_fd_set, read_fd_set;
  int i;
  struct sockaddr_in clientname;
  size_t size;

  /* Create the socket and set it up to accept connections. */
  sock = make_socket (PORT);
  if (listen (sock, 1) < 0)
    {
      perror ("listen");
      exit (EXIT_FAILURE);
    }

  /* Initialize the set of active sockets. */
```

```
FD_ZERO (&active_fd_set);
FD_SET (sock, &active_fd_set);

while (1)
  {
    /* Block until input arrives on one or more active sockets. */
    read_fd_set = active_fd_set;
    if (select (FD_SETSIZE, &read_fd_set, NULL, NULL, NULL) < 0)
      {
        perror ("select");
        exit (EXIT_FAILURE);
      }

    /* Service all the sockets with input pending. */
    for (i = 0; i < FD_SETSIZE; ++i)
      if (FD_ISSET (i, &read_fd_set))
        {
          if (i == sock)
            {
              /* Connection request on original socket. */
              int new;
              size = sizeof (clientname);
              new = accept (sock,
                            (struct sockaddr *) &clientname,
                            &size);
              if (new < 0)
                {
                  perror ("accept");
                  exit (EXIT_FAILURE);
                }
              fprintf (stderr,
                       "Server: connect from host %s, port %hd.\n",
                       inet_ntoa (clientname.sin_addr),
                       ntohs (clientname.sin_port));
              FD_SET (new, &active_fd_set);
            }
          else
            {
              /* Data arriving on an already-connected socket. */
              if (read_from_client (i) < 0)
                {
                  close (i);
                  FD_CLR (i, &active_fd_set);
                }
            }
        }
  }
}
```

16.9.8 Out-of-Band Data

Streams with connections permit *out-of-band* data that is delivered with higher priority than ordinary data. Typically the reason for sending out-of-band data is to send notice of an exceptional condition. To send out-of-band data use **send**, specifying the flag `MSG_OOB` (see Section 16.9.5.1 [Sending Data], page 459).

Out-of-band data are received with higher priority because the receiving process need not read it in sequence; to read the next available out-of-band data, use **recv** with the

MSG_OOB flag (see Section 16.9.5.2 [Receiving Data], page 460). Ordinary read operations do not read out-of-band data; they read only ordinary data.

When a socket finds that out-of-band data are on their way, it sends a SIGURG signal to the owner process or process group of the socket. You can specify the owner using the F_SETOWN command to the fcntl function; see Section 13.18 [Interrupt-Driven Input], page 375. You must also establish a handler for this signal, as described in Chapter 24 [Signal Handling], page 661, in order to take appropriate action such as reading the out-of-band data.

Alternatively, you can test for pending out-of-band data, or wait until there is out-of-band data, using the select function; it can wait for an exceptional condition on the socket. See Section 13.8 [Waiting for Input or Output], page 342, for more information about select.

Notification of out-of-band data (whether with SIGURG or with select) indicates that out-of-band data are on the way; the data may not actually arrive until later. If you try to read the out-of-band data before it arrives, recv fails with an EWOULDBLOCK error.

Sending out-of-band data automatically places a "mark" in the stream of ordinary data, showing where in the sequence the out-of-band data "would have been". This is useful when the meaning of out-of-band data is "cancel everything sent so far". Here is how you can test, in the receiving process, whether any ordinary data was sent before the mark:

```
success = ioctl (socket, SIOCATMARK, &atmark);
```

The integer variable *atmark* is set to a nonzero value if the socket's read pointer has reached the "mark".

Here's a function to discard any ordinary data preceding the out-of-band mark:

```
int
discard_until_mark (int socket)
{
  while (1)
    {
      /* This is not an arbitrary limit; any size will do.  */
      char buffer[1024];
      int atmark, success;

      /* If we have reached the mark, return.  */
      success = ioctl (socket, SIOCATMARK, &atmark);
      if (success < 0)
        perror ("ioctl");
      if (result)
        return;

      /* Otherwise, read a bunch of ordinary data and discard it.
         This is guaranteed not to read past the mark
         if it starts before the mark.  */
      success = read (socket, buffer, sizeof buffer);
      if (success < 0)
        perror ("read");
    }
}
```

If you don't want to discard the ordinary data preceding the mark, you may need to read some of it anyway, to make room in internal system buffers for the out-of-band data. If you try to read out-of-band data and get an EWOULDBLOCK error, try reading some ordinary data (saving it so that you can use it when you want it) and see if that makes room. Here is an example:

```
struct buffer
{
  char *buf;
  int size;
  struct buffer *next;
};

/* Read the out-of-band data from SOCKET and return it
   as a 'struct buffer', which records the address of the data
   and its size.

   It may be necessary to read some ordinary data
   in order to make room for the out-of-band data.
   If so, the ordinary data are saved as a chain of buffers
   found in the 'next' field of the value.   */

struct buffer *
read_oob (int socket)
{
  struct buffer *tail = 0;
  struct buffer *list = 0;

  while (1)
    {
      /* This is an arbitrary limit.
         Does anyone know how to do this without a limit?   */
#define BUF_SZ 1024
      char *buf = (char *) xmalloc (BUF_SZ);
      int success;
      int atmark;

      /* Try again to read the out-of-band data.   */
      success = recv (socket, buf, BUF_SZ, MSG_OOB);
      if (success >= 0)
        {
          /* We got it, so return it.   */
          struct buffer *link
            = (struct buffer *) xmalloc (sizeof (struct buffer));
          link->buf = buf;
          link->size = success;
          link->next = list;
          return link;
        }

      /* If we fail, see if we are at the mark.   */
      success = ioctl (socket, SIOCATMARK, &atmark);
      if (success < 0)
        perror ("ioctl");
      if (atmark)
        {
          /* At the mark; skipping past more ordinary data cannot help.
             So just wait a while.   */
          sleep (1);
          continue;
        }
```

```
        /* Otherwise, read a bunch of ordinary data and save it.
           This is guaranteed not to read past the mark
           if it starts before the mark.  */
        success = read (socket, buf, BUF_SZ);
        if (success < 0)
          perror ("read");

        /* Save this data in the buffer list.  */
        {
          struct buffer *link
            = (struct buffer *) xmalloc (sizeof (struct buffer));
          link->buf = buf;
          link->size = success;

          /* Add the new link to the end of the list.  */
          if (tail)
            tail->next = link;
          else
            list = link;
          tail = link;
        }
      }
  }
```

16.10 Datagram Socket Operations

This section describes how to use communication styles that don't use connections (styles
`SOCK_DGRAM` and `SOCK_RDM`). Using these styles, you group data into packets and each packet
is an independent communication. You specify the destination for each packet individually.

Datagram packets are like letters: you send each one independently with its own destination address, and they may arrive in the wrong order or not at all.

The `listen` and `accept` functions are not allowed for sockets using connectionless communication styles.

16.10.1 Sending Datagrams

The normal way of sending data on a datagram socket is by using the `sendto` function,
declared in `sys/socket.h`.

You can call `connect` on a datagram socket, but this only specifies a default destination
for further data transmission on the socket. When a socket has a default destination you can
use `send` (see Section 16.9.5.1 [Sending Data], page 459) or even `write` (see Section 13.2
[Input and Output Primitives], page 326) to send a packet there. You can cancel the
default destination by calling `connect` using an address format of `AF_UNSPEC` in the *addr*
argument. See Section 16.9.1 [Making a Connection], page 456, for more information about
the `connect` function.

ssize_t sendto (int *socket*, const void **buffer*, size_t *size*, int   [Function]
        flags, struct sockaddr **addr*, socklen_t *length*)
    Preliminary: | MT-Safe | AS-Safe | AC-Safe | See Section 1.2.2.1 [POSIX Safety
    Concepts], page 2.

The `sendto` function transmits the data in the *buffer* through the socket *socket* to the destination address specified by the *addr* and *length* arguments. The *size* argument specifies the number of bytes to be transmitted.

The *flags* are interpreted the same way as for `send`; see Section 16.9.5.3 [Socket Data Options], page 461.

The return value and error conditions are also the same as for `send`, but you cannot rely on the system to detect errors and report them; the most common error is that the packet is lost or there is no-one at the specified address to receive it, and the operating system on your machine usually does not know this.

It is also possible for one call to `sendto` to report an error owing to a problem related to a previous call.

This function is defined as a cancellation point in multi-threaded programs, so one has to be prepared for this and make sure that allocated resources (like memory, files descriptors, semaphores or whatever) are freed even if the thread is canceled.

16.10.2 Receiving Datagrams

The `recvfrom` function reads a packet from a datagram socket and also tells you where it was sent from. This function is declared in `sys/socket.h`.

ssize_t recvfrom (*int* `socket`, *void* `*buffer`, *size_t* `size`, *int* `flags`,   [Function]
   struct sockaddr `*addr`, *socklen_t* `*length-ptr`)
Preliminary: | MT-Safe | AS-Safe | AC-Safe | See Section 1.2.2.1 [POSIX Safety Concepts], page 2.

The `recvfrom` function reads one packet from the socket *socket* into the buffer *buffer*. The *size* argument specifies the maximum number of bytes to be read.

If the packet is longer than *size* bytes, then you get the first *size* bytes of the packet and the rest of the packet is lost. There's no way to read the rest of the packet. Thus, when you use a packet protocol, you must always know how long a packet to expect.

The *addr* and *length-ptr* arguments are used to return the address where the packet came from. See Section 16.3 [Socket Addresses], page 431. For a socket in the local domain the address information won't be meaningful, since you can't read the address of such a socket (see Section 16.5 [The Local Namespace], page 435). You can specify a null pointer as the *addr* argument if you are not interested in this information.

The *flags* are interpreted the same way as for `recv` (see Section 16.9.5.3 [Socket Data Options], page 461). The return value and error conditions are also the same as for `recv`.

This function is defined as a cancellation point in multi-threaded programs, so one has to be prepared for this and make sure that allocated resources (like memory, files descriptors, semaphores or whatever) are freed even if the thread is canceled.

You can use plain `recv` (see Section 16.9.5.2 [Receiving Data], page 460) instead of `recvfrom` if you don't need to find out who sent the packet (either because you know where it should come from or because you treat all possible senders alike). Even `read` can be used if you don't want to specify *flags* (see Section 13.2 [Input and Output Primitives], page 326).

16.10.3 Datagram Socket Example

Here is a set of example programs that send messages over a datagram stream in the local namespace. Both the client and server programs use the `make_named_socket` function that was presented in Section 16.5.3 [Example of Local-Namespace Sockets], page 436, to create and name their sockets.

First, here is the server program. It sits in a loop waiting for messages to arrive, bouncing each message back to the sender. Obviously this isn't a particularly useful program, but it does show the general ideas involved.

```
#include <stdio.h>
#include <errno.h>
#include <stdlib.h>
#include <sys/socket.h>
#include <sys/un.h>

#define SERVER  "/tmp/serversocket"
#define MAXMSG  512

int
main (void)
{
  int sock;
  char message[MAXMSG];
  struct sockaddr_un name;
  size_t size;
  int nbytes;

  /* Remove the filename first, it's ok if the call fails */
  unlink (SERVER);

  /* Make the socket, then loop endlessly. */
  sock = make_named_socket (SERVER);
  while (1)
    {
      /* Wait for a datagram. */
      size = sizeof (name);
      nbytes = recvfrom (sock, message, MAXMSG, 0,
                         (struct sockaddr *) & name, &size);
      if (nbytes < 0)
        {
          perror ("recfrom (server)");
          exit (EXIT_FAILURE);
        }

      /* Give a diagnostic message. */
      fprintf (stderr, "Server: got message: %s\n", message);

      /* Bounce the message back to the sender. */
      nbytes = sendto (sock, message, nbytes, 0,
                       (struct sockaddr *) & name, size);
      if (nbytes < 0)
        {
          perror ("sendto (server)");
          exit (EXIT_FAILURE);
        }
    }
}
```

```
        }
```

16.10.4 Example of Reading Datagrams

Here is the client program corresponding to the server above.

It sends a datagram to the server and then waits for a reply. Notice that the socket for the client (as well as for the server) in this example has to be given a name. This is so that the server can direct a message back to the client. Since the socket has no associated connection state, the only way the server can do this is by referencing the name of the client.

```c
#include <stdio.h>
#include <errno.h>
#include <unistd.h>
#include <stdlib.h>
#include <sys/socket.h>
#include <sys/un.h>

#define SERVER  "/tmp/serversocket"
#define CLIENT  "/tmp/mysocket"
#define MAXMSG  512
#define MESSAGE "Yow!!! Are we having fun yet?!?"

int
main (void)
{
  extern int make_named_socket (const char *name);
  int sock;
  char message[MAXMSG];
  struct sockaddr_un name;
  size_t size;
  int nbytes;

  /* Make the socket. */
  sock = make_named_socket (CLIENT);

  /* Initialize the server socket address. */
  name.sun_family = AF_LOCAL;
  strcpy (name.sun_path, SERVER);
  size = strlen (name.sun_path) + sizeof (name.sun_family);

  /* Send the datagram. */
  nbytes = sendto (sock, MESSAGE, strlen (MESSAGE) + 1, 0,
                   (struct sockaddr *) & name, size);
  if (nbytes < 0)
    {
      perror ("sendto (client)");
      exit (EXIT_FAILURE);
    }

  /* Wait for a reply. */
  nbytes = recvfrom (sock, message, MAXMSG, 0, NULL, 0);
  if (nbytes < 0)
    {
      perror ("recfrom (client)");
      exit (EXIT_FAILURE);
    }
```

```
    /* Print a diagnostic message. */
    fprintf (stderr, "Client: got message: %s\n", message);

    /* Clean up. */
    remove (CLIENT);
    close (sock);
}
```

Keep in mind that datagram socket communications are unreliable. In this example, the client program waits indefinitely if the message never reaches the server or if the server's response never comes back. It's up to the user running the program to kill and restart it if desired. A more automatic solution could be to use `select` (see Section 13.8 [Waiting for Input or Output], page 342) to establish a timeout period for the reply, and in case of timeout either re-send the message or shut down the socket and exit.

16.11 The `inetd` Daemon

We've explained above how to write a server program that does its own listening. Such a server must already be running in order for anyone to connect to it.

Another way to provide a service on an Internet port is to let the daemon program `inetd` do the listening. `inetd` is a program that runs all the time and waits (using `select`) for messages on a specified set of ports. When it receives a message, it accepts the connection (if the socket style calls for connections) and then forks a child process to run the corresponding server program. You specify the ports and their programs in the file `/etc/inetd.conf`.

16.11.1 `inetd` Servers

Writing a server program to be run by `inetd` is very simple. Each time someone requests a connection to the appropriate port, a new server process starts. The connection already exists at this time; the socket is available as the standard input descriptor and as the standard output descriptor (descriptors 0 and 1) in the server process. Thus the server program can begin reading and writing data right away. Often the program needs only the ordinary I/O facilities; in fact, a general-purpose filter program that knows nothing about sockets can work as a byte stream server run by `inetd`.

You can also use `inetd` for servers that use connectionless communication styles. For these servers, `inetd` does not try to accept a connection since no connection is possible. It just starts the server program, which can read the incoming datagram packet from descriptor 0. The server program can handle one request and then exit, or you can choose to write it to keep reading more requests until no more arrive, and then exit. You must specify which of these two techniques the server uses when you configure `inetd`.

16.11.2 Configuring `inetd`

The file `/etc/inetd.conf` tells `inetd` which ports to listen to and what server programs to run for them. Normally each entry in the file is one line, but you can split it onto multiple lines provided all but the first line of the entry start with whitespace. Lines that start with '#' are comments.

Here are two standard entries in `/etc/inetd.conf`:

```
ftp stream tcp nowait root /libexec/ftpd ftpd
talk dgram udp wait root /libexec/talkd talkd
```

An entry has this format:

```
service style protocol wait username program arguments
```

The *service* field says which service this program provides. It should be the name of a service defined in `/etc/services`. `inetd` uses *service* to decide which port to listen on for this entry.

The fields *style* and *protocol* specify the communication style and the protocol to use for the listening socket. The style should be the name of a communication style, converted to lower case and with 'SOCK_' deleted—for example, 'stream' or 'dgram'. *protocol* should be one of the protocols listed in `/etc/protocols`. The typical protocol names are 'tcp' for byte stream connections and 'udp' for unreliable datagrams.

The *wait* field should be either 'wait' or 'nowait'. Use 'wait' if *style* is a connectionless style and the server, once started, handles multiple requests as they come in. Use 'nowait' if `inetd` should start a new process for each message or request that comes in. If *style* uses connections, then *wait* **must** be 'nowait'.

user is the user name that the server should run as. `inetd` runs as root, so it can set the user ID of its children arbitrarily. It's best to avoid using 'root' for *user* if you can; but some servers, such as Telnet and FTP, read a username and password themselves. These servers need to be root initially so they can log in as commanded by the data coming over the network.

program together with *arguments* specifies the command to run to start the server. *program* should be an absolute file name specifying the executable file to run. *arguments* consists of any number of whitespace-separated words, which become the command-line arguments of *program*. The first word in *arguments* is argument zero, which should by convention be the program name itself (sans directories).

If you edit `/etc/inetd.conf`, you can tell `inetd` to reread the file and obey its new contents by sending the `inetd` process the `SIGHUP` signal. You'll have to use `ps` to determine the process ID of the `inetd` process as it is not fixed.

16.12 Socket Options

This section describes how to read or set various options that modify the behavior of sockets and their underlying communications protocols.

When you are manipulating a socket option, you must specify which *level* the option pertains to. This describes whether the option applies to the socket interface, or to a lower-level communications protocol interface.

16.12.1 Socket Option Functions

Here are the functions for examining and modifying socket options. They are declared in `sys/socket.h`.

int getsockopt (*int* `socket`, *int* `level`, *int* `optname`, *void* `*optval`,   [Function]
        socklen_t `*optlen-ptr`)

> Preliminary: | MT-Safe | AS-Safe | AC-Safe | See Section 1.2.2.1 [POSIX Safety Concepts], page 2.
>
> The `getsockopt` function gets information about the value of option *optname* at level *level* for socket *socket*.

The option value is stored in a buffer that *optval* points to. Before the call, you should supply in *optlen-ptr* the size of this buffer; on return, it contains the number of bytes of information actually stored in the buffer.

Most options interpret the *optval* buffer as a single `int` value.

The actual return value of `getsockopt` is 0 on success and `-1` on failure. The following `errno` error conditions are defined:

`EBADF`   The *socket* argument is not a valid file descriptor.

`ENOTSOCK`   The descriptor *socket* is not a socket.

`ENOPROTOOPT`
          The *optname* doesn't make sense for the given *level*.

`int setsockopt` (*int* `socket`, *int* `level`, *int* `optname`, *const void*   [Function]
          optval, socklen_t `optlen`)
          Preliminary: | MT-Safe | AS-Safe | AC-Safe | See Section 1.2.2.1 [POSIX Safety Concepts], page 2.

          This function is used to set the socket option *optname* at level *level* for socket *socket*. The value of the option is passed in the buffer *optval* of size *optlen*.

          The return value and error codes for `setsockopt` are the same as for `getsockopt`.

16.12.2 Socket-Level Options

`int SOL_SOCKET`   [Constant]
          Use this constant as the *level* argument to `getsockopt` or `setsockopt` to manipulate the socket-level options described in this section.

Here is a table of socket-level option names; all are defined in the header file `sys/socket.h`.

`SO_DEBUG`
          This option toggles recording of debugging information in the underlying protocol modules. The value has type `int`; a nonzero value means "yes".

`SO_REUSEADDR`
          This option controls whether `bind` (see Section 16.3.2 [Setting the Address of a Socket], page 433) should permit reuse of local addresses for this socket. If you enable this option, you can actually have two sockets with the same Internet port number; but the system won't allow you to use the two identically-named sockets in a way that would confuse the Internet. The reason for this option is that some higher-level Internet protocols, including FTP, require you to keep reusing the same port number.

          The value has type `int`; a nonzero value means "yes".

`SO_KEEPALIVE`
          This option controls whether the underlying protocol should periodically transmit messages on a connected socket. If the peer fails to respond to these messages, the connection is considered broken. The value has type `int`; a nonzero value means "yes".

SO_DONTROUTE

> This option controls whether outgoing messages bypass the normal message routing facilities. If set, messages are sent directly to the network interface instead. The value has type `int`; a nonzero value means "yes".

SO_LINGER

> This option specifies what should happen when the socket of a type that promises reliable delivery still has untransmitted messages when it is closed; see Section 16.8.2 [Closing a Socket], page 454. The value has type `struct linger`.

> **struct linger**   [Data Type]
>> This structure type has the following members:

>> **int l_onoff**
>>> This field is interpreted as a boolean. If nonzero, `close` blocks until the data are transmitted or the timeout period has expired.

>> **int l_linger**
>>> This specifies the timeout period, in seconds.

SO_BROADCAST

> This option controls whether datagrams may be broadcast from the socket. The value has type `int`; a nonzero value means "yes".

SO_OOBINLINE

> If this option is set, out-of-band data received on the socket is placed in the normal input queue. This permits it to be read using `read` or `recv` without specifying the `MSG_OOB` flag. See Section 16.9.8 [Out-of-Band Data], page 464. The value has type `int`; a nonzero value means "yes".

SO_SNDBUF

> This option gets or sets the size of the output buffer. The value is a `size_t`, which is the size in bytes.

SO_RCVBUF

> This option gets or sets the size of the input buffer. The value is a `size_t`, which is the size in bytes.

SO_STYLE
SO_TYPE This option can be used with `getsockopt` only. It is used to get the socket's communication style. `SO_TYPE` is the historical name, and `SO_STYLE` is the preferred name in GNU. The value has type `int` and its value designates a communication style; see Section 16.2 [Communication Styles], page 430.

SO_ERROR

> This option can be used with `getsockopt` only. It is used to reset the error status of the socket. The value is an `int`, which represents the previous error status.

16.13 Networks Database

Many systems come with a database that records a list of networks known to the system developer. This is usually kept either in the file /etc/networks or in an equivalent from a name server. This data base is useful for routing programs such as **route**, but it is not useful for programs that simply communicate over the network. We provide functions to access this database, which are declared in **netdb.h**.

struct netent   [Data Type]

>   This data type is used to represent information about entries in the networks database. It has the following members:

>   **char *n_name**
>
>   >   This is the "official" name of the network.

>   **char **n_aliases**
>
>   >   These are alternative names for the network, represented as a vector of strings. A null pointer terminates the array.

>   **int n_addrtype**
>
>   >   This is the type of the network number; this is always equal to **AF_INET** for Internet networks.

>   **unsigned long int n_net**
>
>   >   This is the network number. Network numbers are returned in host byte order; see Section 16.6.5 [Byte Order Conversion], page 449.

Use the **getnetbyname** or **getnetbyaddr** functions to search the networks database for information about a specific network. The information is returned in a statically-allocated structure; you must copy the information if you need to save it.

struct netent * getnetbyname (*const char *name*)   [Function]

>   Preliminary: | MT-Unsafe race:netbyname env locale | AS-Unsafe dlopen plugin heap lock | AC-Unsafe corrupt lock fd mem | See Section 1.2.2.1 [POSIX Safety Concepts], page 2.

>   The **getnetbyname** function returns information about the network named *name*. It returns a null pointer if there is no such network.

struct netent * getnetbyaddr (*uint32_t net*, *int type*)   [Function]

>   Preliminary: | MT-Unsafe race:netbyaddr locale | AS-Unsafe dlopen plugin heap lock | AC-Unsafe corrupt lock fd mem | See Section 1.2.2.1 [POSIX Safety Concepts], page 2.

>   The **getnetbyaddr** function returns information about the network of type *type* with number *net*. You should specify a value of **AF_INET** for the *type* argument for Internet networks.

>   **getnetbyaddr** returns a null pointer if there is no such network.

You can also scan the networks database using **setnetent**, **getnetent** and **endnetent**. Be careful when using these functions because they are not reentrant.

void setnetent (*int* *stayopen*) [Function]

> Preliminary: | MT-Unsafe race:netent env locale | AS-Unsafe dlopen plugin heap lock | AC-Unsafe corrupt lock fd mem | See Section 1.2.2.1 [POSIX Safety Concepts], page 2.

> This function opens and rewinds the networks database.

> If the *stayopen* argument is nonzero, this sets a flag so that subsequent calls to **getnetbyname** or **getnetbyaddr** will not close the database (as they usually would). This makes for more efficiency if you call those functions several times, by avoiding reopening the database for each call.

struct netent * getnetent (*void*) [Function]

> Preliminary: | MT-Unsafe race:netent race:netentbuf env locale | AS-Unsafe dlopen plugin heap lock | AC-Unsafe corrupt lock fd mem | See Section 1.2.2.1 [POSIX Safety Concepts], page 2.

> This function returns the next entry in the networks database. It returns a null pointer if there are no more entries.

void endnetent (*void*) [Function]

> Preliminary: | MT-Unsafe race:netent env locale | AS-Unsafe dlopen plugin heap lock | AC-Unsafe corrupt lock fd mem | See Section 1.2.2.1 [POSIX Safety Concepts], page 2.

> This function closes the networks database.

17 Low-Level Terminal Interface

This chapter describes functions that are specific to terminal devices. You can use these functions to do things like turn off input echoing; set serial line characteristics such as line speed and flow control; and change which characters are used for end-of-file, command-line editing, sending signals, and similar control functions.

Most of the functions in this chapter operate on file descriptors. See Chapter 13 [Low-Level Input/Output], page 323, for more information about what a file descriptor is and how to open a file descriptor for a terminal device.

17.1 Identifying Terminals

The functions described in this chapter only work on files that correspond to terminal devices. You can find out whether a file descriptor is associated with a terminal by using the `isatty` function.

Prototypes for the functions in this section are declared in the header file `unistd.h`.

int **isatty** (*int filedes*)   [Function]
> Preliminary: | MT-Safe | AS-Safe | AC-Safe | See Section 1.2.2.1 [POSIX Safety Concepts], page 2.
>
> This function returns 1 if *filedes* is a file descriptor associated with an open terminal device, and 0 otherwise.

If a file descriptor is associated with a terminal, you can get its associated file name using the `ttyname` function. See also the `ctermid` function, described in Section 28.7.1 [Identifying the Controlling Terminal], page 778.

char * **ttyname** (*int filedes*)   [Function]
> Preliminary: | MT-Unsafe race:ttyname | AS-Unsafe heap lock | AC-Unsafe lock fd mem | See Section 1.2.2.1 [POSIX Safety Concepts], page 2.
>
> If the file descriptor *filedes* is associated with a terminal device, the `ttyname` function returns a pointer to a statically-allocated, null-terminated string containing the file name of the terminal file. The value is a null pointer if the file descriptor isn't associated with a terminal, or the file name cannot be determined.

int **ttyname_r** (*int filedes*, *char *buf*, *size_t len*)   [Function]
> Preliminary: | MT-Safe | AS-Unsafe heap | AC-Unsafe mem fd | See Section 1.2.2.1 [POSIX Safety Concepts], page 2.
>
> The `ttyname_r` function is similar to the `ttyname` function except that it places its result into the user-specified buffer starting at *buf* with length *len*.
>
> The normal return value from `ttyname_r` is 0. Otherwise an error number is returned to indicate the error. The following `errno` error conditions are defined for this function:
>
> EBADF   The *filedes* argument is not a valid file descriptor.
>
> ENOTTY   The *filedes* is not associated with a terminal.
>
> ERANGE   The buffer length *len* is too small to store the string to be returned.

17.2 I/O Queues

Many of the remaining functions in this section refer to the input and output queues of a terminal device. These queues implement a form of buffering *within the kernel* independent of the buffering implemented by I/O streams (see Chapter 12 [Input/Output on Streams], page 248).

The *terminal input queue* is also sometimes referred to as its *typeahead buffer*. It holds the characters that have been received from the terminal but not yet read by any process.

The size of the input queue is described by the `MAX_INPUT` and `_POSIX_MAX_INPUT` parameters; see Section 32.6 [Limits on File System Capacity], page 850. You are guaranteed a queue size of at least `MAX_INPUT`, but the queue might be larger, and might even dynamically change size. If input flow control is enabled by setting the `IXOFF` input mode bit (see Section 17.4.4 [Input Modes], page 482), the terminal driver transmits STOP and START characters to the terminal when necessary to prevent the queue from overflowing. Otherwise, input may be lost if it comes in too fast from the terminal. In canonical mode, all input stays in the queue until a newline character is received, so the terminal input queue can fill up when you type a very long line. See Section 17.3 [Two Styles of Input: Canonical or Not], page 478.

The *terminal output queue* is like the input queue, but for output; it contains characters that have been written by processes, but not yet transmitted to the terminal. If output flow control is enabled by setting the `IXON` input mode bit (see Section 17.4.4 [Input Modes], page 482), the terminal driver obeys START and STOP characters sent by the terminal to stop and restart transmission of output.

Clearing the terminal input queue means discarding any characters that have been received but not yet read. Similarly, clearing the terminal output queue means discarding any characters that have been written but not yet transmitted.

17.3 Two Styles of Input: Canonical or Not

POSIX systems support two basic modes of input: canonical and noncanonical.

In *canonical input processing* mode, terminal input is processed in lines terminated by newline (`'\n'`), EOF, or EOL characters. No input can be read until an entire line has been typed by the user, and the `read` function (see Section 13.2 [Input and Output Primitives], page 326) returns at most a single line of input, no matter how many bytes are requested.

In canonical input mode, the operating system provides input editing facilities: some characters are interpreted specially to perform editing operations within the current line of text, such as ERASE and KILL. See Section 17.4.9.1 [Characters for Input Editing], page 490.

The constants `_POSIX_MAX_CANON` and `MAX_CANON` parameterize the maximum number of bytes which may appear in a single line of canonical input. See Section 32.6 [Limits on File System Capacity], page 850. You are guaranteed a maximum line length of at least `MAX_CANON` bytes, but the maximum might be larger, and might even dynamically change size.

In *noncanonical input processing* mode, characters are not grouped into lines, and ERASE and KILL processing is not performed. The granularity with which bytes are read in noncanonical input mode is controlled by the MIN and TIME settings. See Section 17.4.10 [Noncanonical Input], page 494.

Most programs use canonical input mode, because this gives the user a way to edit input line by line. The usual reason to use noncanonical mode is when the program accepts single-character commands or provides its own editing facilities.

The choice of canonical or noncanonical input is controlled by the ICANON flag in the c_lflag member of struct termios. See Section 17.4.7 [Local Modes], page 486.

17.4 Terminal Modes

This section describes the various terminal attributes that control how input and output are done. The functions, data structures, and symbolic constants are all declared in the header file termios.h.

Don't confuse terminal attributes with file attributes. A device special file which is associated with a terminal has file attributes as described in Section 14.9 [File Attributes], page 399. These are unrelated to the attributes of the terminal device itself, which are discussed in this section.

17.4.1 Terminal Mode Data Types

The entire collection of attributes of a terminal is stored in a structure of type struct termios. This structure is used with the functions tcgetattr and tcsetattr to read and set the attributes.

struct termios   [Data Type]
    Structure that records all the I/O attributes of a terminal. The structure includes at least the following members:

    tcflag_t c_iflag
            A bit mask specifying flags for input modes; see Section 17.4.4 [Input Modes], page 482.

    tcflag_t c_oflag
            A bit mask specifying flags for output modes; see Section 17.4.5 [Output Modes], page 484.

    tcflag_t c_cflag
            A bit mask specifying flags for control modes; see Section 17.4.6 [Control Modes], page 485.

    tcflag_t c_lflag
            A bit mask specifying flags for local modes; see Section 17.4.7 [Local Modes], page 486.

    cc_t c_cc[NCCS]
            An array specifying which characters are associated with various control functions; see Section 17.4.9 [Special Characters], page 490.

    The struct termios structure also contains members which encode input and output transmission speeds, but the representation is not specified. See Section 17.4.8 [Line Speed], page 489, for how to examine and store the speed values.

The following sections describe the details of the members of the **struct termios** structure.

tcflag_t   [Data Type]

> This is an unsigned integer type used to represent the various bit masks for terminal flags.

cc_t   [Data Type]

> This is an unsigned integer type used to represent characters associated with various terminal control functions.

int NCCS   [Macro]

> The value of this macro is the number of elements in the **c_cc** array.

17.4.2 Terminal Mode Functions

int tcgetattr (*int* **filedes**, *struct termios* ***termios-p**)   [Function]

> Preliminary: | MT-Safe | AS-Safe | AC-Safe | See Section 1.2.2.1 [POSIX Safety Concepts], page 2.
>
> This function is used to examine the attributes of the terminal device with file descriptor *filedes*. The attributes are returned in the structure that *termios-p* points to.
>
> If successful, **tcgetattr** returns 0. A return value of −1 indicates an error. The following **errno** error conditions are defined for this function:
>
> **EBADF**   The *filedes* argument is not a valid file descriptor.
>
> **ENOTTY**   The *filedes* is not associated with a terminal.

int tcsetattr (*int* **filedes**, *int* **when**, *const struct termios*   [Function]
    *termios-p)

> Preliminary: | MT-Safe | AS-Safe | AC-Safe | See Section 1.2.2.1 [POSIX Safety Concepts], page 2.
>
> This function sets the attributes of the terminal device with file descriptor *filedes*. The new attributes are taken from the structure that *termios-p* points to.
>
> The *when* argument specifies how to deal with input and output already queued. It can be one of the following values:
>
> **TCSANOW**   Make the change immediately.
>
> **TCSADRAIN**
>
>> Make the change after waiting until all queued output has been written. You should usually use this option when changing parameters that affect output.
>
> **TCSAFLUSH**
>
>> This is like **TCSADRAIN**, but also discards any queued input.
>
> **TCSASOFT**   This is a flag bit that you can add to any of the above alternatives. Its meaning is to inhibit alteration of the state of the terminal hardware. It

is a BSD extension; it is only supported on BSD systems and GNU/Hurd systems.

Using `TCSASOFT` is exactly the same as setting the `CIGNORE` bit in the `c_cflag` member of the structure *termios-p* points to. See Section 17.4.6 [Control Modes], page 485, for a description of `CIGNORE`.

If this function is called from a background process on its controlling terminal, normally all processes in the process group are sent a `SIGTTOU` signal, in the same way as if the process were trying to write to the terminal. The exception is if the calling process itself is ignoring or blocking `SIGTTOU` signals, in which case the operation is performed and no signal is sent. See Chapter 28 [Job Control], page 763.

If successful, `tcsetattr` returns 0. A return value of −1 indicates an error. The following `errno` error conditions are defined for this function:

`EBADF`   The *filedes* argument is not a valid file descriptor.

`ENOTTY`   The *filedes* is not associated with a terminal.

`EINVAL`   Either the value of the `when` argument is not valid, or there is something wrong with the data in the *termios-p* argument.

Although `tcgetattr` and `tcsetattr` specify the terminal device with a file descriptor, the attributes are those of the terminal device itself and not of the file descriptor. This means that the effects of changing terminal attributes are persistent; if another process opens the terminal file later on, it will see the changed attributes even though it doesn't have anything to do with the open file descriptor you originally specified in changing the attributes.

Similarly, if a single process has multiple or duplicated file descriptors for the same terminal device, changing the terminal attributes affects input and output to all of these file descriptors. This means, for example, that you can't open one file descriptor or stream to read from a terminal in the normal line-buffered, echoed mode; and simultaneously have another file descriptor for the same terminal that you use to read from it in single-character, non-echoed mode. Instead, you have to explicitly switch the terminal back and forth between the two modes.

17.4.3 Setting Terminal Modes Properly

When you set terminal modes, you should call `tcgetattr` first to get the current modes of the particular terminal device, modify only those modes that you are really interested in, and store the result with `tcsetattr`.

It's a bad idea to simply initialize a **struct termios** structure to a chosen set of attributes and pass it directly to `tcsetattr`. Your program may be run years from now, on systems that support members not documented in this manual. The way to avoid setting these members to unreasonable values is to avoid changing them.

What's more, different terminal devices may require different mode settings in order to function properly. So you should avoid blindly copying attributes from one terminal device to another.

When a member contains a collection of independent flags, as the `c_iflag`, `c_oflag` and `c_cflag` members do, even setting the entire member is a bad idea, because particular operating systems have their own flags. Instead, you should start with the current value of the member and alter only the flags whose values matter in your program, leaving any other flags unchanged.

Here is an example of how to set one flag (`ISTRIP`) in the **struct termios** structure while properly preserving all the other data in the structure:

```
int
set_istrip (int desc, int value)
{
  struct termios settings;
  int result;

  result = tcgetattr (desc, &settings);
  if (result < 0)
    {
      perror ("error in tcgetattr");
      return 0;
    }
  settings.c_iflag &= ~ISTRIP;
  if (value)
    settings.c_iflag |= ISTRIP;
  result = tcsetattr (desc, TCSANOW, &settings);
  if (result < 0)
    {
      perror ("error in tcsetattr");
      return 0;
    }
  return 1;
}
```

17.4.4 Input Modes

This section describes the terminal attribute flags that control fairly low-level aspects of input processing: handling of parity errors, break signals, flow control, and RET and LFD characters.

All of these flags are bits in the `c_iflag` member of the **struct termios** structure. The member is an integer, and you change flags using the operators &, | and ^. Don't try to specify the entire value for `c_iflag`—instead, change only specific flags and leave the rest untouched (see Section 17.4.3 [Setting Terminal Modes Properly], page 481).

tcflag_t INPCK   [Macro]

If this bit is set, input parity checking is enabled. If it is not set, no checking at all is done for parity errors on input; the characters are simply passed through to the application.

Parity checking on input processing is independent of whether parity detection and generation on the underlying terminal hardware is enabled; see Section 17.4.6 [Control Modes], page 485. For example, you could clear the INPCK input mode flag and set the PARENB control mode flag to ignore parity errors on input, but still generate parity on output.

If this bit is set, what happens when a parity error is detected depends on whether the IGNPAR or PARMRK bits are set. If neither of these bits are set, a byte with a parity error is passed to the application as a '\0' character.

`tcflag_t IGNPAR`   [Macro]

> If this bit is set, any byte with a framing or parity error is ignored. This is only useful if `INPCK` is also set.

`tcflag_t PARMRK`   [Macro]

> If this bit is set, input bytes with parity or framing errors are marked when passed to the program. This bit is meaningful only when `INPCK` is set and `IGNPAR` is not set.
>
> The way erroneous bytes are marked is with two preceding bytes, 377 and 0. Thus, the program actually reads three bytes for one erroneous byte received from the terminal.
>
> If a valid byte has the value 0377, and `ISTRIP` (see below) is not set, the program might confuse it with the prefix that marks a parity error. So a valid byte 0377 is passed to the program as two bytes, 0377 0377, in this case.

`tcflag_t ISTRIP`   [Macro]

> If this bit is set, valid input bytes are stripped to seven bits; otherwise, all eight bits are available for programs to read.

`tcflag_t IGNBRK`   [Macro]

> If this bit is set, break conditions are ignored.
>
> A *break condition* is defined in the context of asynchronous serial data transmission as a series of zero-value bits longer than a single byte.

`tcflag_t BRKINT`   [Macro]

> If this bit is set and `IGNBRK` is not set, a break condition clears the terminal input and output queues and raises a `SIGINT` signal for the foreground process group associated with the terminal.
>
> If neither `BRKINT` nor `IGNBRK` are set, a break condition is passed to the application as a single '\0' character if `PARMRK` is not set, or otherwise as a three-character sequence '\377', '\0', '\0'.

`tcflag_t IGNCR`   [Macro]

> If this bit is set, carriage return characters ('\r') are discarded on input. Discarding carriage return may be useful on terminals that send both carriage return and linefeed when you type the `RET` key.

`tcflag_t ICRNL`   [Macro]

> If this bit is set and `IGNCR` is not set, carriage return characters ('\r') received as input are passed to the application as newline characters ('\n').

`tcflag_t INLCR`   [Macro]

> If this bit is set, newline characters ('\n') received as input are passed to the application as carriage return characters ('\r').

`tcflag_t IXOFF`   [Macro]

> If this bit is set, start/stop control on input is enabled. In other words, the computer sends STOP and START characters as necessary to prevent input from coming in faster than programs are reading it. The idea is that the actual terminal hardware that is generating the input data responds to a STOP character by suspending transmission, and to a START character by resuming transmission. See Section 17.4.9.3 [Special Characters for Flow Control], page 493.

`tcflag_t IXON`   [Macro]

> If this bit is set, start/stop control on output is enabled. In other words, if the computer receives a STOP character, it suspends output until a START character is received. In this case, the STOP and START characters are never passed to the application program. If this bit is not set, then START and STOP can be read as ordinary characters. See Section 17.4.9.3 [Special Characters for Flow Control], page 493.

`tcflag_t IXANY`   [Macro]

> If this bit is set, any input character restarts output when output has been suspended with the STOP character. Otherwise, only the START character restarts output.
>
> This is a BSD extension; it exists only on BSD systems and GNU/Linux and GNU/Hurd systems.

`tcflag_t IMAXBEL`   [Macro]

> If this bit is set, then filling up the terminal input buffer sends a BEL character (code 007) to the terminal to ring the bell.
>
> This is a BSD extension.

17.4.5 Output Modes

This section describes the terminal flags and fields that control how output characters are translated and padded for display. All of these are contained in the `c_oflag` member of the **struct termios** structure.

The `c_oflag` member itself is an integer, and you change the flags and fields using the operators &, |, and ^. Don't try to specify the entire value for `c_oflag`—instead, change only specific flags and leave the rest untouched (see Section 17.4.3 [Setting Terminal Modes Properly], page 481).

`tcflag_t OPOST`   [Macro]

> If this bit is set, output data is processed in some unspecified way so that it is displayed appropriately on the terminal device. This typically includes mapping newline characters (`'\n'`) onto carriage return and linefeed pairs.
>
> If this bit isn't set, the characters are transmitted as-is.

The following three bits are effective only if `OPOST` is set.

`tcflag_t ONLCR`   [Macro]

> If this bit is set, convert the newline character on output into a pair of characters, carriage return followed by linefeed.

`tcflag_t OXTABS`   [Macro]

> If this bit is set, convert tab characters on output into the appropriate number of spaces to emulate a tab stop every eight columns. This bit exists only on BSD systems and GNU/Hurd systems; on GNU/Linux systems it is available as `XTABS`.

`tcflag_t ONOEOT`   [Macro]

> If this bit is set, discard `C-d` characters (code 004) on output. These characters cause many dial-up terminals to disconnect. This bit exists only on BSD systems and GNU/Hurd systems.

17.4.6 Control Modes

This section describes the terminal flags and fields that control parameters usually associated with asynchronous serial data transmission. These flags may not make sense for other kinds of terminal ports (such as a network connection pseudo-terminal). All of these are contained in the `c_cflag` member of the **struct termios** structure.

The `c_cflag` member itself is an integer, and you change the flags and fields using the operators `&`, `|`, and `^`. Don't try to specify the entire value for `c_cflag`—instead, change only specific flags and leave the rest untouched (see Section 17.4.3 [Setting Terminal Modes Properly], page 481).

`tcflag_t CLOCAL`   [Macro]
> If this bit is set, it indicates that the terminal is connected "locally" and that the modem status lines (such as carrier detect) should be ignored.
>
> On many systems if this bit is not set and you call **open** without the `O_NONBLOCK` flag set, **open** blocks until a modem connection is established.
>
> If this bit is not set and a modem disconnect is detected, a `SIGHUP` signal is sent to the controlling process group for the terminal (if it has one). Normally, this causes the process to exit; see Chapter 24 [Signal Handling], page 661. Reading from the terminal after a disconnect causes an end-of-file condition, and writing causes an `EIO` error to be returned. The terminal device must be closed and reopened to clear the condition.

`tcflag_t HUPCL`   [Macro]
> If this bit is set, a modem disconnect is generated when all processes that have the terminal device open have either closed the file or exited.

`tcflag_t CREAD`   [Macro]
> If this bit is set, input can be read from the terminal. Otherwise, input is discarded when it arrives.

`tcflag_t CSTOPB`   [Macro]
> If this bit is set, two stop bits are used. Otherwise, only one stop bit is used.

`tcflag_t PARENB`   [Macro]
> If this bit is set, generation and detection of a parity bit are enabled. See Section 17.4.4 [Input Modes], page 482, for information on how input parity errors are handled.
>
> If this bit is not set, no parity bit is added to output characters, and input characters are not checked for correct parity.

`tcflag_t PARODD`   [Macro]
> This bit is only useful if `PARENB` is set. If `PARODD` is set, odd parity is used, otherwise even parity is used.

The control mode flags also includes a field for the number of bits per character. You can use the `CSIZE` macro as a mask to extract the value, like this: `settings.c_cflag & CSIZE`.

`tcflag_t CSIZE`   [Macro]
> This is a mask for the number of bits per character.

`tcflag_t CS5` [Macro]
> This specifies five bits per byte.

`tcflag_t CS6` [Macro]
> This specifies six bits per byte.

`tcflag_t CS7` [Macro]
> This specifies seven bits per byte.

`tcflag_t CS8` [Macro]
> This specifies eight bits per byte.

The following four bits are BSD extensions; these exist only on BSD systems and GNU/Hurd systems.

`tcflag_t CCTS_OFLOW` [Macro]
> If this bit is set, enable flow control of output based on the CTS wire (RS232 protocol).

`tcflag_t CRTS_IFLOW` [Macro]
> If this bit is set, enable flow control of input based on the RTS wire (RS232 protocol).

`tcflag_t MDMBUF` [Macro]
> If this bit is set, enable carrier-based flow control of output.

`tcflag_t CIGNORE` [Macro]
> If this bit is set, it says to ignore the control modes and line speed values entirely. This is only meaningful in a call to `tcsetattr`.
>
> The `c_cflag` member and the line speed values returned by `cfgetispeed` and `cfgetospeed` will be unaffected by the call. `CIGNORE` is useful if you want to set all the software modes in the other members, but leave the hardware details in `c_cflag` unchanged. (This is how the `TCSASOFT` flag to `tcsettattr` works.)
>
> This bit is never set in the structure filled in by `tcgetattr`.

17.4.7 Local Modes

This section describes the flags for the `c_lflag` member of the **struct termios** structure. These flags generally control higher-level aspects of input processing than the input modes flags described in Section 17.4.4 [Input Modes], page 482, such as echoing, signals, and the choice of canonical or noncanonical input.

The `c_lflag` member itself is an integer, and you change the flags and fields using the operators &, |, and ^. Don't try to specify the entire value for `c_lflag`—instead, change only specific flags and leave the rest untouched (see Section 17.4.3 [Setting Terminal Modes Properly], page 481).

`tcflag_t ICANON` [Macro]
> This bit, if set, enables canonical input processing mode. Otherwise, input is processed in noncanonical mode. See Section 17.3 [Two Styles of Input: Canonical or Not], page 478.

`tcflag_t ECHO` [Macro]
> If this bit is set, echoing of input characters back to the terminal is enabled.

tcflag_t ECHOE   [Macro]

If this bit is set, echoing indicates erasure of input with the ERASE character by erasing the last character in the current line from the screen. Otherwise, the character erased is re-echoed to show what has happened (suitable for a printing terminal).

This bit only controls the display behavior; the `ICANON` bit by itself controls actual recognition of the ERASE character and erasure of input, without which `ECHOE` is simply irrelevant.

tcflag_t ECHOPRT   [Macro]

This bit is like `ECHOE`, enables display of the ERASE character in a way that is geared to a hardcopy terminal. When you type the ERASE character, a '\' character is printed followed by the first character erased. Typing the ERASE character again just prints the next character erased. Then, the next time you type a normal character, a '/' character is printed before the character echoes.

This is a BSD extension, and exists only in BSD systems and GNU/Linux and GNU/Hurd systems.

tcflag_t ECHOK   [Macro]

This bit enables special display of the KILL character by moving to a new line after echoing the KILL character normally. The behavior of `ECHOKE` (below) is nicer to look at.

If this bit is not set, the KILL character echoes just as it would if it were not the KILL character. Then it is up to the user to remember that the KILL character has erased the preceding input; there is no indication of this on the screen.

This bit only controls the display behavior; the `ICANON` bit by itself controls actual recognition of the KILL character and erasure of input, without which `ECHOK` is simply irrelevant.

tcflag_t ECHOKE   [Macro]

This bit is similar to `ECHOK`. It enables special display of the KILL character by erasing on the screen the entire line that has been killed. This is a BSD extension, and exists only in BSD systems and GNU/Linux and GNU/Hurd systems.

tcflag_t ECHONL   [Macro]

If this bit is set and the `ICANON` bit is also set, then the newline ('\n') character is echoed even if the `ECHO` bit is not set.

tcflag_t ECHOCTL   [Macro]

If this bit is set and the `ECHO` bit is also set, echo control characters with '^' followed by the corresponding text character. Thus, control-A echoes as '^A'. This is usually the preferred mode for interactive input, because echoing a control character back to the terminal could have some undesired effect on the terminal.

This is a BSD extension, and exists only in BSD systems and GNU/Linux and GNU/Hurd systems.

tcflag_t ISIG   [Macro]

This bit controls whether the INTR, QUIT, and SUSP characters are recognized. The functions associated with these characters are performed if and only if this bit is set.

Being in canonical or noncanonical input mode has no affect on the interpretation of these characters.

You should use caution when disabling recognition of these characters. Programs that cannot be interrupted interactively are very user-unfriendly. If you clear this bit, your program should provide some alternate interface that allows the user to interactively send the signals associated with these characters, or to escape from the program.

See Section 17.4.9.2 [Characters that Cause Signals], page 492.

`tcflag_t IEXTEN`   [Macro]

POSIX.1 gives `IEXTEN` implementation-defined meaning, so you cannot rely on this interpretation on all systems.

On BSD systems and GNU/Linux and GNU/Hurd systems, it enables the LNEXT and DISCARD characters. See Section 17.4.9.4 [Other Special Characters], page 494.

`tcflag_t NOFLSH`   [Macro]

Normally, the INTR, QUIT, and SUSP characters cause input and output queues for the terminal to be cleared. If this bit is set, the queues are not cleared.

`tcflag_t TOSTOP`   [Macro]

If this bit is set and the system supports job control, then `SIGTTOU` signals are generated by background processes that attempt to write to the terminal. See Section 28.4 [Access to the Controlling Terminal], page 764.

The following bits are BSD extensions; they exist only on BSD systems and GNU/Hurd systems.

`tcflag_t ALTWERASE`   [Macro]

This bit determines how far the WERASE character should erase. The WERASE character erases back to the beginning of a word; the question is, where do words begin?

If this bit is clear, then the beginning of a word is a nonwhitespace character following a whitespace character. If the bit is set, then the beginning of a word is an alphanumeric character or underscore following a character which is none of those.

See Section 17.4.9.1 [Characters for Input Editing], page 490, for more information about the WERASE character.

`tcflag_t FLUSHO`   [Macro]

This is the bit that toggles when the user types the DISCARD character. While this bit is set, all output is discarded. See Section 17.4.9.4 [Other Special Characters], page 494.

`tcflag_t NOKERNINFO`   [Macro]

Setting this bit disables handling of the STATUS character. See Section 17.4.9.4 [Other Special Characters], page 494.

`tcflag_t PENDIN`   [Macro]

If this bit is set, it indicates that there is a line of input that needs to be reprinted. Typing the REPRINT character sets this bit; the bit remains set until reprinting is finished. See Section 17.4.9.1 [Characters for Input Editing], page 490.

17.4.8 Line Speed

The terminal line speed tells the computer how fast to read and write data on the terminal.

If the terminal is connected to a real serial line, the terminal speed you specify actually controls the line—if it doesn't match the terminal's own idea of the speed, communication does not work. Real serial ports accept only certain standard speeds. Also, particular hardware may not support even all the standard speeds. Specifying a speed of zero hangs up a dialup connection and turns off modem control signals.

If the terminal is not a real serial line (for example, if it is a network connection), then the line speed won't really affect data transmission speed, but some programs will use it to determine the amount of padding needed. It's best to specify a line speed value that matches the actual speed of the actual terminal, but you can safely experiment with different values to vary the amount of padding.

There are actually two line speeds for each terminal, one for input and one for output. You can set them independently, but most often terminals use the same speed for both directions.

The speed values are stored in the **struct termios** structure, but don't try to access them in the **struct termios** structure directly. Instead, you should use the following functions to read and store them:

speed_t cfgetospeed (*const struct termios *termios-p*)   [Function]
> Preliminary: | MT-Safe | AS-Safe | AC-Safe | See Section 1.2.2.1 [POSIX Safety Concepts], page 2.
>
> This function returns the output line speed stored in the structure **termios-p*.

speed_t cfgetispeed (*const struct termios *termios-p*)   [Function]
> Preliminary: | MT-Safe | AS-Safe | AC-Safe | See Section 1.2.2.1 [POSIX Safety Concepts], page 2.
>
> This function returns the input line speed stored in the structure **termios-p*.

int cfsetospeed (*struct termios *termios-p, speed_t speed*)   [Function]
> Preliminary: | MT-Safe | AS-Safe | AC-Safe | See Section 1.2.2.1 [POSIX Safety Concepts], page 2.
>
> This function stores *speed* in **termios-p* as the output speed. The normal return value is 0; a value of −1 indicates an error. If *speed* is not a speed, **cfsetospeed** returns −1.

int cfsetispeed (*struct termios *termios-p, speed_t speed*)   [Function]
> Preliminary: | MT-Safe | AS-Safe | AC-Safe | See Section 1.2.2.1 [POSIX Safety Concepts], page 2.
>
> This function stores *speed* in **termios-p* as the input speed. The normal return value is 0; a value of −1 indicates an error. If *speed* is not a speed, **cfsetospeed** returns −1.

int cfsetspeed (*struct termios *termios-p, speed_t speed*)   [Function]
> Preliminary: | MT-Safe | AS-Safe | AC-Safe | See Section 1.2.2.1 [POSIX Safety Concepts], page 2.

This function stores *speed* in *termios-p* as both the input and output speeds. The normal return value is 0; a value of −1 indicates an error. If *speed* is not a speed, cfsetspeed returns −1. This function is an extension in 4.4 BSD.

speed_t [Data Type]

The speed_t type is an unsigned integer data type used to represent line speeds.

The functions cfsetospeed and cfsetispeed report errors only for speed values that the system simply cannot handle. If you specify a speed value that is basically acceptable, then those functions will succeed. But they do not check that a particular hardware device can actually support the specified speeds—in fact, they don't know which device you plan to set the speed for. If you use tcsetattr to set the speed of a particular device to a value that it cannot handle, tcsetattr returns −1.

Portability note: In the GNU C Library, the functions above accept speeds measured in bits per second as input, and return speed values measured in bits per second. Other libraries require speeds to be indicated by special codes. For POSIX.1 portability, you must use one of the following symbols to represent the speed; their precise numeric values are system-dependent, but each name has a fixed meaning: B110 stands for 110 bps, B300 for 300 bps, and so on. There is no portable way to represent any speed but these, but these are the only speeds that typical serial lines can support.

```
B0    B50    B75    B110   B134    B150   B200
B300  B600   B1200  B1800  B2400   B4800
B9600 B19200 B38400 B57600 B115200
B230400 B460800
```

BSD defines two additional speed symbols as aliases: EXTA is an alias for B19200 and EXTB is an alias for B38400. These aliases are obsolete.

17.4.9 Special Characters

In canonical input, the terminal driver recognizes a number of special characters which perform various control functions. These include the ERASE character (usually DEL) for editing input, and other editing characters. The INTR character (normally C-c) for sending a SIGINT signal, and other signal-raising characters, may be available in either canonical or noncanonical input mode. All these characters are described in this section.

The particular characters used are specified in the c_cc member of the struct termios structure. This member is an array; each element specifies the character for a particular role. Each element has a symbolic constant that stands for the index of that element—for example, VINTR is the index of the element that specifies the INTR character, so storing '=' in termios.c_cc[VINTR] specifies '=' as the INTR character.

On some systems, you can disable a particular special character function by specifying the value _POSIX_VDISABLE for that role. This value is unequal to any possible character code. See Section 32.7 [Optional Features in File Support], page 851, for more information about how to tell whether the operating system you are using supports _POSIX_VDISABLE.

17.4.9.1 Characters for Input Editing

These special characters are active only in canonical input mode. See Section 17.3 [Two Styles of Input: Canonical or Not], page 478.

`int VEOF`   [Macro]

> This is the subscript for the EOF character in the special control character array.
> `termios.c_cc[VEOF]` holds the character itself.
>
> The EOF character is recognized only in canonical input mode. It acts as a line
> terminator in the same way as a newline character, but if the EOF character is typed
> at the beginning of a line it causes **read** to return a byte count of zero, indicating
> end-of-file. The EOF character itself is discarded.
>
> Usually, the EOF character is *C-d*.

`int VEOL`   [Macro]

> This is the subscript for the EOL character in the special control character array.
> `termios.c_cc[VEOL]` holds the character itself.
>
> The EOL character is recognized only in canonical input mode. It acts as a line
> terminator, just like a newline character. The EOL character is not discarded; it is
> read as the last character in the input line.
>
> You don't need to use the EOL character to make RET end a line. Just set the ICRNL
> flag. In fact, this is the default state of affairs.

`int VEOL2`   [Macro]

> This is the subscript for the EOL2 character in the special control character array.
> `termios.c_cc[VEOL2]` holds the character itself.
>
> The EOL2 character works just like the EOL character (see above), but it can be a
> different character. Thus, you can specify two characters to terminate an input line,
> by setting EOL to one of them and EOL2 to the other.
>
> The EOL2 character is a BSD extension; it exists only on BSD systems and
> GNU/Linux and GNU/Hurd systems.

`int VERASE`   [Macro]

> This is the subscript for the ERASE character in the special control character array.
> `termios.c_cc[VERASE]` holds the character itself.
>
> The ERASE character is recognized only in canonical input mode. When the user
> types the erase character, the previous character typed is discarded. (If the terminal
> generates multibyte character sequences, this may cause more than one byte of input
> to be discarded.) This cannot be used to erase past the beginning of the current line
> of text. The ERASE character itself is discarded.
>
> Usually, the ERASE character is `DEL`.

`int VWERASE`   [Macro]

> This is the subscript for the WERASE character in the special control character array.
> `termios.c_cc[VWERASE]` holds the character itself.
>
> The WERASE character is recognized only in canonical mode. It erases an entire
> word of prior input, and any whitespace after it; whitespace characters before the
> word are not erased.
>
> The definition of a "word" depends on the setting of the `ALTWERASE` mode; see
> Section 17.4.7 [Local Modes], page 486.

If the **ALTWERASE** mode is not set, a word is defined as a sequence of any characters except space or tab.

If the **ALTWERASE** mode is set, a word is defined as a sequence of characters containing only letters, numbers, and underscores, optionally followed by one character that is not a letter, number, or underscore.

The WERASE character is usually `C-w`.

This is a BSD extension.

---

int VKILL   [Macro]

This is the subscript for the KILL character in the special control character array. `termios.c_cc[VKILL]` holds the character itself.

The KILL character is recognized only in canonical input mode. When the user types the kill character, the entire contents of the current line of input are discarded. The kill character itself is discarded too.

The KILL character is usually `C-u`.

---

int VREPRINT   [Macro]

This is the subscript for the REPRINT character in the special control character array. `termios.c_cc[VREPRINT]` holds the character itself.

The REPRINT character is recognized only in canonical mode. It reprints the current input line. If some asynchronous output has come while you are typing, this lets you see the line you are typing clearly again.

The REPRINT character is usually `C-r`.

This is a BSD extension.

17.4.9.2 Characters that Cause Signals

These special characters may be active in either canonical or noncanonical input mode, but only when the `ISIG` flag is set (see Section 17.4.7 [Local Modes], page 486).

---

int VINTR   [Macro]

This is the subscript for the INTR character in the special control character array. `termios.c_cc[VINTR]` holds the character itself.

The INTR (interrupt) character raises a **SIGINT** signal for all processes in the foreground job associated with the terminal. The INTR character itself is then discarded. See Chapter 24 [Signal Handling], page 661, for more information about signals.

Typically, the INTR character is `C-c`.

---

int VQUIT   [Macro]

This is the subscript for the QUIT character in the special control character array. `termios.c_cc[VQUIT]` holds the character itself.

The QUIT character raises a **SIGQUIT** signal for all processes in the foreground job associated with the terminal. The QUIT character itself is then discarded. See Chapter 24 [Signal Handling], page 661, for more information about signals.

Typically, the QUIT character is `C-\`.

`int VSUSP`   [Macro]

> This is the subscript for the SUSP character in the special control character array. *termios*.c_cc`[VSUSP]` holds the character itself.
>
> The SUSP (suspend) character is recognized only if the implementation supports job control (see Chapter 28 [Job Control], page 763). It causes a `SIGTSTP` signal to be sent to all processes in the foreground job associated with the terminal. The SUSP character itself is then discarded. See Chapter 24 [Signal Handling], page 661, for more information about signals.
>
> Typically, the SUSP character is *C-z*.

Few applications disable the normal interpretation of the SUSP character. If your program does this, it should provide some other mechanism for the user to stop the job. When the user invokes this mechanism, the program should send a `SIGTSTP` signal to the process group of the process, not just to the process itself. See Section 24.6.2 [Signaling Another Process], page 689.

`int VDSUSP`   [Macro]

> This is the subscript for the DSUSP character in the special control character array. *termios*.c_cc`[VDSUSP]` holds the character itself.
>
> The DSUSP (suspend) character is recognized only if the implementation supports job control (see Chapter 28 [Job Control], page 763). It sends a `SIGTSTP` signal, like the SUSP character, but not right away—only when the program tries to read it as input. Not all systems with job control support DSUSP; only BSD-compatible systems (including GNU/Hurd systems).
>
> See Chapter 24 [Signal Handling], page 661, for more information about signals.
>
> Typically, the DSUSP character is *C-y*.

17.4.9.3 Special Characters for Flow Control

These special characters may be active in either canonical or noncanonical input mode, but their use is controlled by the flags `IXON` and `IXOFF` (see Section 17.4.4 [Input Modes], page 482).

`int VSTART`   [Macro]

> This is the subscript for the START character in the special control character array. *termios*.c_cc`[VSTART]` holds the character itself.
>
> The START character is used to support the `IXON` and `IXOFF` input modes. If `IXON` is set, receiving a START character resumes suspended output; the START character itself is discarded. If `IXANY` is set, receiving any character at all resumes suspended output; the resuming character is not discarded unless it is the START character. `IXOFF` is set, the system may also transmit START characters to the terminal.
>
> The usual value for the START character is *C-q*. You may not be able to change this value—the hardware may insist on using *C-q* regardless of what you specify.

`int VSTOP`   [Macro]

> This is the subscript for the STOP character in the special control character array. *termios*.c_cc`[VSTOP]` holds the character itself.

The STOP character is used to support the `IXON` and `IXOFF` input modes. If `IXON` is set, receiving a STOP character causes output to be suspended; the STOP character itself is discarded. If `IXOFF` is set, the system may also transmit STOP characters to the terminal, to prevent the input queue from overflowing.

The usual value for the STOP character is *C-s*. You may not be able to change this value—the hardware may insist on using *C-s* regardless of what you specify.

17.4.9.4 Other Special Characters

int VLNEXT   [Macro]

This is the subscript for the LNEXT character in the special control character array. `termios.c_cc[VLNEXT]` holds the character itself.

The LNEXT character is recognized only when `IEXTEN` is set, but in both canonical and noncanonical mode. It disables any special significance of the next character the user types. Even if the character would normally perform some editing function or generate a signal, it is read as a plain character. This is the analogue of the *C-q* command in Emacs. "LNEXT" stands for "literal next."

The LNEXT character is usually *C-v*.

This character is available on BSD systems and GNU/Linux and GNU/Hurd systems.

int VDISCARD   [Macro]

This is the subscript for the DISCARD character in the special control character array. `termios.c_cc[VDISCARD]` holds the character itself.

The DISCARD character is recognized only when `IEXTEN` is set, but in both canonical and noncanonical mode. Its effect is to toggle the discard-output flag. When this flag is set, all program output is discarded. Setting the flag also discards all output currently in the output buffer. Typing any other character resets the flag.

This character is available on BSD systems and GNU/Linux and GNU/Hurd systems.

int VSTATUS   [Macro]

This is the subscript for the STATUS character in the special control character array. `termios.c_cc[VSTATUS]` holds the character itself.

The STATUS character's effect is to print out a status message about how the current process is running.

The STATUS character is recognized only in canonical mode, and only if `NOKERNINFO` is not set.

This character is available only on BSD systems and GNU/Hurd systems.

17.4.10 Noncanonical Input

In noncanonical input mode, the special editing characters such as ERASE and KILL are ignored. The system facilities for the user to edit input are disabled in noncanonical mode, so that all input characters (unless they are special for signal or flow-control purposes) are passed to the application program exactly as typed. It is up to the application program to give the user ways to edit the input, if appropriate.

Noncanonical mode offers special parameters called MIN and TIME for controlling whether and how long to wait for input to be available. You can even use them to avoid ever waiting—to return immediately with whatever input is available, or with no input.

The MIN and TIME are stored in elements of the c_cc array, which is a member of the **struct termios** structure. Each element of this array has a particular role, and each element has a symbolic constant that stands for the index of that element. VMIN and VMAX are the names for the indices in the array of the MIN and TIME slots.

int VMIN   [Macro]
> This is the subscript for the MIN slot in the c_cc array. Thus, *termios.c_cc[VMIN]* is the value itself.
>
> The MIN slot is only meaningful in noncanonical input mode; it specifies the minimum number of bytes that must be available in the input queue in order for **read** to return.

int VTIME   [Macro]
> This is the subscript for the TIME slot in the c_cc array. Thus, *termios.c_cc[VTIME]* is the value itself.
>
> The TIME slot is only meaningful in noncanonical input mode; it specifies how long to wait for input before returning, in units of 0.1 seconds.

The MIN and TIME values interact to determine the criterion for when **read** should return; their precise meanings depend on which of them are nonzero. There are four possible cases:

- Both TIME and MIN are nonzero.

  In this case, TIME specifies how long to wait after each input character to see if more input arrives. After the first character received, **read** keeps waiting until either MIN bytes have arrived in all, or TIME elapses with no further input.

  read always blocks until the first character arrives, even if TIME elapses first. **read** can return more than MIN characters if more than MIN happen to be in the queue.

- Both MIN and TIME are zero.

  In this case, **read** always returns immediately with as many characters as are available in the queue, up to the number requested. If no input is immediately available, **read** returns a value of zero.

- MIN is zero but TIME has a nonzero value.

  In this case, **read** waits for time TIME for input to become available; the availability of a single byte is enough to satisfy the read request and cause **read** to return. When it returns, it returns as many characters as are available, up to the number requested. If no input is available before the timer expires, **read** returns a value of zero.

- TIME is zero but MIN has a nonzero value.

  In this case, **read** waits until at least MIN bytes are available in the queue. At that time, **read** returns as many characters as are available, up to the number requested. **read** can return more than MIN characters if more than MIN happen to be in the queue.

What happens if MIN is 50 and you ask to read just 10 bytes? Normally, **read** waits until there are 50 bytes in the buffer (or, more generally, the wait condition described above is satisfied), and then reads 10 of them, leaving the other 40 buffered in the operating system for a subsequent call to **read**.

Portability note: On some systems, the MIN and TIME slots are actually the same as the EOF and EOL slots. This causes no serious problem because the MIN and TIME slots are used only in noncanonical input and the EOF and EOL slots are used only in canonical input, but it isn't very clean. The GNU C Library allocates separate slots for these uses.

void cfmakeraw (*struct termios *termios-p*)   [Function]
> Preliminary: | MT-Safe | AS-Safe | AC-Safe | See Section 1.2.2.1 [POSIX Safety Concepts], page 2.
>
> This function provides an easy way to set up **termios-p* for what has traditionally been called "raw mode" in BSD. This uses noncanonical input, and turns off most processing to give an unmodified channel to the terminal.
>
> It does exactly this:

```
termios-p->c_iflag &= ~(IGNBRK|BRKINT|PARMRK|ISTRIP
                        |INLCR|IGNCR|ICRNL|IXON);
termios-p->c_oflag &= ~OPOST;
termios-p->c_lflag &= ~(ECHO|ECHONL|ICANON|ISIG|IEXTEN);
termios-p->c_cflag &= ~(CSIZE|PARENB);
termios-p->c_cflag |= CS8;
```

17.5 BSD Terminal Modes

The usual way to get and set terminal modes is with the functions described in Section 17.4 [Terminal Modes], page 479. However, on some systems you can use the BSD-derived functions in this section to do some of the same thing. On many systems, these functions do not exist. Even with the GNU C Library, the functions simply fail with **errno** = **ENOSYS** with many kernels, including Linux.

The symbols used in this section are declared in **sgtty.h**.

struct sgttyb   [Data Type]
> This structure is an input or output parameter list for **gtty** and **stty**.
>
> **char sg_ispeed**
>> Line speed for input
>
> **char sg_ospeed**
>> Line speed for output
>
> **char sg_erase**
>> Erase character
>
> **char sg_kill**
>> Kill character
>
> **int sg_flags**
>> Various flags

int gtty (*int filedes*, *struct sgttyb *attributes*)   [Function]
> Preliminary: | MT-Safe | AS-Safe | AC-Safe | See Section 1.2.2.1 [POSIX Safety Concepts], page 2.

This function gets the attributes of a terminal.

gtty sets *attributes to describe the terminal attributes of the terminal which is open with file descriptor filedes.

int stty (int *filedes*, const struct sgttyb **attributes**)   [Function]
Preliminary: | MT-Safe | AS-Safe | AC-Safe | See Section 1.2.2.1 [POSIX Safety Concepts], page 2.

This function sets the attributes of a terminal.

stty sets the terminal attributes of the terminal which is open with file descriptor filedes to those described by *filedes.

17.6 Line Control Functions

These functions perform miscellaneous control actions on terminal devices. As regards terminal access, they are treated like doing output: if any of these functions is used by a background process on its controlling terminal, normally all processes in the process group are sent a SIGTTOU signal. The exception is if the calling process itself is ignoring or blocking SIGTTOU signals, in which case the operation is performed and no signal is sent. See Chapter 28 [Job Control], page 763.

int tcsendbreak (int *filedes*, int *duration*)   [Function]
Preliminary: | MT-Unsafe race:tcattr(filedes)/bsd | AS-Unsafe | AC-Unsafe corrupt/bsd | See Section 1.2.2.1 [POSIX Safety Concepts], page 2.

This function generates a break condition by transmitting a stream of zero bits on the terminal associated with the file descriptor filedes. The duration of the break is controlled by the *duration* argument. If zero, the duration is between 0.25 and 0.5 seconds. The meaning of a nonzero value depends on the operating system.

This function does nothing if the terminal is not an asynchronous serial data port.

The return value is normally zero. In the event of an error, a value of −1 is returned. The following errno error conditions are defined for this function:

EBADF   The filedes is not a valid file descriptor.

ENOTTY   The filedes is not associated with a terminal device.

int tcdrain (int *filedes*)   [Function]
Preliminary: | MT-Safe | AS-Safe | AC-Safe | See Section 1.2.2.1 [POSIX Safety Concepts], page 2.

The tcdrain function waits until all queued output to the terminal filedes has been transmitted.

This function is a cancellation point in multi-threaded programs. This is a problem if the thread allocates some resources (like memory, file descriptors, semaphores or whatever) at the time tcdrain is called. If the thread gets canceled these resources stay allocated until the program ends. To avoid this calls to tcdrain should be protected using cancellation handlers.

The return value is normally zero. In the event of an error, a value of −1 is returned. The following errno error conditions are defined for this function:

EBADF   The *filedes* is not a valid file descriptor.

ENOTTY   The *filedes* is not associated with a terminal device.

EINTR   The operation was interrupted by delivery of a signal. See Section 24.5 [Primitives Interrupted by Signals], page 687.

`int tcflush (`*int* `filedes,` *int* `queue)`   [Function]
> Preliminary: | MT-Safe | AS-Safe | AC-Safe | See Section 1.2.2.1 [POSIX Safety Concepts], page 2.

> The `tcflush` function is used to clear the input and/or output queues associated with the terminal file *filedes*. The *queue* argument specifies which queue(s) to clear, and can be one of the following values:

> TCIFLUSH
>> Clear any input data received, but not yet read.

> TCOFLUSH
>> Clear any output data written, but not yet transmitted.

> TCIOFLUSH
>> Clear both queued input and output.

> The return value is normally zero. In the event of an error, a value of −1 is returned. The following `errno` error conditions are defined for this function:

> EBADF   The *filedes* is not a valid file descriptor.

> ENOTTY   The *filedes* is not associated with a terminal device.

> EINVAL   A bad value was supplied as the *queue* argument.

> It is unfortunate that this function is named `tcflush`, because the term "flush" is normally used for quite another operation—waiting until all output is transmitted—and using it for discarding input or output would be confusing. Unfortunately, the name `tcflush` comes from POSIX and we cannot change it.

`int tcflow (`*int* `filedes,` *int* `action)`   [Function]
> Preliminary: | MT-Unsafe race:tcattr(filedes)/bsd | AS-Unsafe | AC-Safe | See Section 1.2.2.1 [POSIX Safety Concepts], page 2.

> The `tcflow` function is used to perform operations relating to XON/XOFF flow control on the terminal file specified by *filedes*.

> The *action* argument specifies what operation to perform, and can be one of the following values:

> TCOOFF   Suspend transmission of output.

> TCOON   Restart transmission of output.

> TCIOFF   Transmit a STOP character.

> TCION   Transmit a START character.

For more information about the STOP and START characters, see Section 17.4.9 [Special Characters], page 490.

The return value is normally zero. In the event of an error, a value of −1 is returned. The following `errno` error conditions are defined for this function:

EBADF   The *filedes* is not a valid file descriptor.

ENOTTY   The *filedes* is not associated with a terminal device.

EINVAL   A bad value was supplied as the *action* argument.

17.7 Noncanonical Mode Example

Here is an example program that shows how you can set up a terminal device to read single characters in noncanonical input mode, without echo.

```
#include <unistd.h>
#include <stdio.h>
#include <stdlib.h>
#include <termios.h>

/* Use this variable to remember original terminal attributes. */

struct termios saved_attributes;

void
reset_input_mode (void)
{
  tcsetattr (STDIN_FILENO, TCSANOW, &saved_attributes);
}

void
set_input_mode (void)
{
  struct termios tattr;
  char *name;

  /* Make sure stdin is a terminal. */
  if (!isatty (STDIN_FILENO))
    {
      fprintf (stderr, "Not a terminal.\n");
      exit (EXIT_FAILURE);
    }

  /* Save the terminal attributes so we can restore them later. */
  tcgetattr (STDIN_FILENO, &saved_attributes);
  atexit (reset_input_mode);

  /* Set the funny terminal modes. */
  tcgetattr (STDIN_FILENO, &tattr);
  tattr.c_lflag &= ~(ICANON|ECHO); /* Clear ICANON and ECHO. */
  tattr.c_cc[VMIN] = 1;
  tattr.c_cc[VTIME] = 0;
  tcsetattr (STDIN_FILENO, TCSAFLUSH, &tattr);
}

int
```

```
main (void)
{
  char c;

  set_input_mode ();

  while (1)
    {
      read (STDIN_FILENO, &c, 1);
      if (c == '\004')           /* C-d */
        break;
      else
        putchar (c);
    }

  return EXIT_SUCCESS;
}
```

This program is careful to restore the original terminal modes before exiting or terminating with a signal. It uses the **atexit** function (see Section 25.7.3 [Cleanups on Exit], page 746) to make sure this is done by **exit**.

The shell is supposed to take care of resetting the terminal modes when a process is stopped or continued; see Chapter 28 [Job Control], page 763. But some existing shells do not actually do this, so you may wish to establish handlers for job control signals that reset terminal modes. The above example does so.

17.8 Pseudo-Terminals

A *pseudo-terminal* is a special interprocess communication channel that acts like a terminal. One end of the channel is called the *master* side or *master pseudo-terminal device*, the other side is called the *slave* side. Data written to the master side is received by the slave side as if it was the result of a user typing at an ordinary terminal, and data written to the slave side is sent to the master side as if it was written on an ordinary terminal.

Pseudo terminals are the way programs like **xterm** and **emacs** implement their terminal emulation functionality.

17.8.1 Allocating Pseudo-Terminals

This subsection describes functions for allocating a pseudo-terminal, and for making this pseudo-terminal available for actual use. These functions are declared in the header file **stdlib.h**.

int getpt (*void*)   [Function]
>   Preliminary: | MT-Safe | AS-Safe | AC-Safe fd | See Section 1.2.2.1 [POSIX Safety Concepts], page 2.
>
>   The **getpt** function returns a new file descriptor for the next available master pseudo-terminal. The normal return value from **getpt** is a non-negative integer file descriptor. In the case of an error, a value of −1 is returned instead. The following **errno** conditions are defined for this function:
>
>   ENOENT   There are no free master pseudo-terminals available.
>
>   This function is a GNU extension.

`int grantpt (int filedes)`   [Function]

Preliminary: | MT-Safe locale | AS-Unsafe dlopen plugin heap lock | AC-Unsafe corrupt lock fd mem | See Section 1.2.2.1 [POSIX Safety Concepts], page 2.

The `grantpt` function changes the ownership and access permission of the slave pseudo-terminal device corresponding to the master pseudo-terminal device associated with the file descriptor *filedes*. The owner is set from the real user ID of the calling process (see Section 30.2 [The Persona of a Process], page 791), and the group is set to a special group (typically *tty*) or from the real group ID of the calling process. The access permission is set such that the file is both readable and writable by the owner and only writable by the group.

On some systems this function is implemented by invoking a special `setuid` root program (see Section 30.4 [How an Application Can Change Persona], page 792). As a consequence, installing a signal handler for the `SIGCHLD` signal (see Section 24.2.5 [Job Control Signals], page 668) may interfere with a call to `grantpt`.

The normal return value from `grantpt` is 0; a value of −1 is returned in case of failure. The following `errno` error conditions are defined for this function:

EBADF   The *filedes* argument is not a valid file descriptor.

EINVAL   The *filedes* argument is not associated with a master pseudo-terminal device.

EACCES   The slave pseudo-terminal device corresponding to the master associated with *filedes* could not be accessed.

`int unlockpt (int filedes)`   [Function]

Preliminary: | MT-Safe | AS-Unsafe heap/bsd | AC-Unsafe mem fd | See Section 1.2.2.1 [POSIX Safety Concepts], page 2.

The `unlockpt` function unlocks the slave pseudo-terminal device corresponding to the master pseudo-terminal device associated with the file descriptor *filedes*. On many systems, the slave can only be opened after unlocking, so portable applications should always call `unlockpt` before trying to open the slave.

The normal return value from `unlockpt` is 0; a value of −1 is returned in case of failure. The following `errno` error conditions are defined for this function:

EBADF   The *filedes* argument is not a valid file descriptor.

EINVAL   The *filedes* argument is not associated with a master pseudo-terminal device.

`char * ptsname (int filedes)`   [Function]

Preliminary: | MT-Unsafe race:ptsname | AS-Unsafe heap/bsd | AC-Unsafe mem fd | See Section 1.2.2.1 [POSIX Safety Concepts], page 2.

If the file descriptor *filedes* is associated with a master pseudo-terminal device, the `ptsname` function returns a pointer to a statically-allocated, null-terminated string containing the file name of the associated slave pseudo-terminal file. This string might be overwritten by subsequent calls to `ptsname`.

int ptsname_r (*int filedes*, *char *buf*, *size_t len*)   [Function]
     Preliminary: | MT-Safe | AS-Unsafe heap/bsd | AC-Unsafe mem fd | See
     Section 1.2.2.1 [POSIX Safety Concepts], page 2.

     The `ptsname_r` function is similar to the `ptsname` function except that it places its
     result into the user-specified buffer starting at *buf* with length *len*.

     This function is a GNU extension.

Portability Note: On System V derived systems, the file returned by the `ptsname` and
`ptsname_r` functions may be STREAMS-based, and therefore require additional processing
after opening before it actually behaves as a pseudo terminal.

     Typical usage of these functions is illustrated by the following example:

```
int
open_pty_pair (int *amaster, int *aslave)
{
  int master, slave;
  char *name;

  master = getpt ();
  if (master < 0)
    return 0;

  if (grantpt (master) < 0 || unlockpt (master) < 0)
    goto close_master;
  name = ptsname (master);
  if (name == NULL)
    goto close_master;

  slave = open (name, O_RDWR);
  if (slave == -1)
    goto close_master;

  if (isastream (slave))
    {
      if (ioctl (slave, I_PUSH, "ptem") < 0
          || ioctl (slave, I_PUSH, "ldterm") < 0)
        goto close_slave;
    }

  *amaster = master;
  *aslave = slave;
  return 1;

close_slave:
  close (slave);

close_master:
  close (master);
  return 0;
}
```

17.8.2 Opening a Pseudo-Terminal Pair

These functions, derived from BSD, are available in the separate `libutil` library, and
declared in `pty.h`.

int openpty (*int* ***amaster**, *int* ***aslave**, *char* ***name**, *const struct*   [Function]
          termios ***termp**, *const struct winsize* ***winp**)

Preliminary: | MT-Safe locale | AS-Unsafe dlopen plugin heap lock | AC-Unsafe
corrupt lock fd mem | See Section 1.2.2.1 [POSIX Safety Concepts], page 2.

This function allocates and opens a pseudo-terminal pair, returning the file descriptor
for the master in **amaster*, and the file descriptor for the slave in **aslave*. If the
argument *name* is not a null pointer, the file name of the slave pseudo-terminal device
is stored in ***name**. If *termp* is not a null pointer, the terminal attributes of the slave
are set to the ones specified in the structure that *termp* points to (see Section 17.4
[Terminal Modes], page 479). Likewise, if the *winp* is not a null pointer, the screen
size of the slave is set to the values specified in the structure that *winp* points to.

The normal return value from **openpty** is 0; a value of −1 is returned in case of failure.
The following **errno** conditions are defined for this function:

ENOENT   There are no free pseudo-terminal pairs available.

Warning: Using the **openpty** function with *name* not set to NULL is **very dangerous**
because it provides no protection against overflowing the string *name*. You should
use the **ttyname** function on the file descriptor returned in **slave* to find out the file
name of the slave pseudo-terminal device instead.

int forkpty (*int* ***amaster**, *char* ***name**, *const struct termios* ***termp**,   [Function]
          const struct winsize ***winp**)

Preliminary: | MT-Safe locale | AS-Unsafe dlopen plugin heap lock | AC-Unsafe
corrupt lock fd mem | See Section 1.2.2.1 [POSIX Safety Concepts], page 2.

This function is similar to the **openpty** function, but in addition, forks a new process (see Section 26.4 [Creating a Process], page 751) and makes the newly opened
slave pseudo-terminal device the controlling terminal (see Section 28.3 [Controlling
Terminal of a Process], page 764) for the child process.

If the operation is successful, there are then both parent and child processes and both
see **forkpty** return, but with different values: it returns a value of 0 in the child
process and returns the child's process ID in the parent process.

If the allocation of a pseudo-terminal pair or the process creation failed, **forkpty**
returns a value of −1 in the parent process.

Warning: The **forkpty** function has the same problems with respect to the *name*
argument as **openpty**.

18 Syslog

This chapter describes facilities for issuing and logging messages of system administration interest. This chapter has nothing to do with programs issuing messages to their own users or keeping private logs (One would typically do that with the facilities described in Chapter 12 [Input/Output on Streams], page 248).

Most systems have a facility called "Syslog" that allows programs to submit messages of interest to system administrators and can be configured to pass these messages on in various ways, such as printing on the console, mailing to a particular person, or recording in a log file for future reference.

A program uses the facilities in this chapter to submit such messages.

18.1 Overview of Syslog

System administrators have to deal with lots of different kinds of messages from a plethora of subsystems within each system, and usually lots of systems as well. For example, an FTP server might report every connection it gets. The kernel might report hardware failures on a disk drive. A DNS server might report usage statistics at regular intervals.

Some of these messages need to be brought to a system administrator's attention immediately. And it may not be just any system administrator – there may be a particular system administrator who deals with a particular kind of message. Other messages just need to be recorded for future reference if there is a problem. Still others may need to have information extracted from them by an automated process that generates monthly reports.

To deal with these messages, most Unix systems have a facility called "Syslog." It is generally based on a daemon called "Syslogd" Syslogd listens for messages on a Unix domain socket named `/dev/log`. Based on classification information in the messages and its configuration file (usually `/etc/syslog.conf`), Syslogd routes them in various ways. Some of the popular routings are:

- Write to the system console
- Mail to a specific user
- Write to a log file
- Pass to another daemon
- Discard

Syslogd can also handle messages from other systems. It listens on the `syslog` UDP port as well as the local socket for messages.

Syslog can handle messages from the kernel itself. But the kernel doesn't write to `/dev/log`; rather, another daemon (sometimes called "Klogd") extracts messages from the kernel and passes them on to Syslog as any other process would (and it properly identifies them as messages from the kernel).

Syslog can even handle messages that the kernel issued before Syslogd or Klogd was running. A Linux kernel, for example, stores startup messages in a kernel message ring and they are normally still there when Klogd later starts up. Assuming Syslogd is running by the time Klogd starts, Klogd then passes everything in the message ring to it.

In order to classify messages for disposition, Syslog requires any process that submits a message to it to provide two pieces of classification information with it:

facility   This identifies who submitted the message. There are a small number of facilities defined. The kernel, the mail subsystem, and an FTP server are examples of recognized facilities. For the complete list, See Section 18.2.2 [syslog, vsyslog], page 507. Keep in mind that these are essentially arbitrary classifications. "Mail subsystem" doesn't have any more meaning than the system administrator gives to it.

priority   This tells how important the content of the message is. Examples of defined priority values are: debug, informational, warning, critical. For the complete list, see Section 18.2.2 [syslog, vsyslog], page 507. Except for the fact that the priorities have a defined order, the meaning of each of these priorities is entirely determined by the system administrator.

A "facility/priority" is a number that indicates both the facility and the priority.

Warning: This terminology is not universal. Some people use "level" to refer to the priority and "priority" to refer to the combination of facility and priority. A Linux kernel has a concept of a message "level," which corresponds both to a Syslog priority and to a Syslog facility/priority (It can be both because the facility code for the kernel is zero, and that makes priority and facility/priority the same value).

The GNU C Library provides functions to submit messages to Syslog. They do it by writing to the /dev/log socket. See Section 18.2 [Submitting Syslog Messages], page 505.

The GNU C Library functions only work to submit messages to the Syslog facility on the same system. To submit a message to the Syslog facility on another system, use the socket I/O functions to write a UDP datagram to the syslog UDP port on that system. See Chapter 16 [Sockets], page 429.

18.2 Submitting Syslog Messages

The GNU C Library provides functions to submit messages to the Syslog facility:

These functions only work to submit messages to the Syslog facility on the same system. To submit a message to the Syslog facility on another system, use the socket I/O functions to write a UDP datagram to the syslog UDP port on that system. See Chapter 16 [Sockets], page 429.

18.2.1 openlog

The symbols referred to in this section are declared in the file syslog.h.

void **openlog** (*const char *ident*, *int option*, *int facility*)   [Function]
    Preliminary: | MT-Safe | AS-Unsafe lock | AC-Unsafe lock fd | See Section 1.2.2.1 [POSIX Safety Concepts], page 2.

    openlog opens or reopens a connection to Syslog in preparation for submitting messages.

    ident is an arbitrary identification string which future syslog invocations will prefix to each message. This is intended to identify the source of the message, and people conventionally set it to the name of the program that will submit the messages.

    If *ident* is NULL, or if openlog is not called, the default identification string used in Syslog messages will be the program name, taken from argv[0].

Please note that the string pointer *ident* will be retained internally by the Syslog routines. You must not free the memory that *ident* points to. It is also dangerous to pass a reference to an automatic variable since leaving the scope would mean ending the lifetime of the variable. If you want to change the *ident* string, you must call `openlog` again; overwriting the string pointed to by *ident* is not thread-safe.

You can cause the Syslog routines to drop the reference to *ident* and go back to the default string (the program name taken from argv[0]), by calling `closelog`: See Section 18.2.3 [closelog], page 509.

In particular, if you are writing code for a shared library that might get loaded and then unloaded (e.g. a PAM module), and you use `openlog`, you must call `closelog` before any point where your library might get unloaded, as in this example:

```
#include <syslog.h>

void
shared_library_function (void)
{
  openlog ("mylibrary", option, priority);

  syslog (LOG_INFO, "shared library has been invoked");

  closelog ();
}
```

Without the call to `closelog`, future invocations of `syslog` by the program using the shared library may crash, if the library gets unloaded and the memory containing the string `"mylibrary"` becomes unmapped. This is a limitation of the BSD syslog interface.

`openlog` may or may not open the `/dev/log` socket, depending on *option*. If it does, it tries to open it and connect it as a stream socket. If that doesn't work, it tries to open it and connect it as a datagram socket. The socket has the "Close on Exec" attribute, so the kernel will close it if the process performs an exec.

You don't have to use `openlog`. If you call `syslog` without having called `openlog`, `syslog` just opens the connection implicitly and uses defaults for the information in *ident* and *options*.

options is a bit string, with the bits as defined by the following single bit masks:

`LOG_PERROR`
> If on, `openlog` sets up the connection so that any `syslog` on this connection writes its message to the calling process' Standard Error stream in addition to submitting it to Syslog. If off, `syslog` does not write the message to Standard Error.

`LOG_CONS` If on, `openlog` sets up the connection so that a `syslog` on this connection that fails to submit a message to Syslog writes the message instead to system console. If off, `syslog` does not write to the system console (but of course Syslog may write messages it receives to the console).

`LOG_PID` When on, `openlog` sets up the connection so that a `syslog` on this connection inserts the calling process' Process ID (PID) into the message. When off, `openlog` does not insert the PID.

LOG_NDELAY

> When on, **openlog** opens and connects the **/dev/log** socket. When off, a future **syslog** call must open and connect the socket.
>
> **Portability note:** In early systems, the sense of this bit was exactly the opposite.

LOG_ODELAY

> This bit does nothing. It exists for backward compatibility.

If any other bit in *options* is on, the result is undefined.

facility is the default facility code for this connection. A **syslog** on this connection that specifies default facility causes this facility to be associated with the message. See **syslog** for possible values. A value of zero means the default default, which is **LOG_USER**.

If a Syslog connection is already open when you call **openlog**, **openlog** "reopens" the connection. Reopening is like opening except that if you specify zero for the default facility code, the default facility code simply remains unchanged and if you specify LOG_NDELAY and the socket is already open and connected, **openlog** just leaves it that way.

18.2.2 syslog, vsyslog

The symbols referred to in this section are declared in the file **syslog.h**.

void syslog (*int* **facility_priority**, *const char* ***format**, ...)   [Function]
> Preliminary: | MT-Safe env locale | AS-Unsafe corrupt heap lock dlopen | AC-Unsafe corrupt lock mem fd | See Section 1.2.2.1 [POSIX Safety Concepts], page 2.
>
> **syslog** submits a message to the Syslog facility. It does this by writing to the Unix domain socket **/dev/log**.
>
> **syslog** submits the message with the facility and priority indicated by *facility_priority*. The macro **LOG_MAKEPRI** generates a facility/priority from a facility and a priority, as in the following example:
>
> ```
> LOG_MAKEPRI(LOG_USER, LOG_WARNING)
> ```
>
> The possible values for the facility code are (macros):

LOG_USER   A miscellaneous user process

LOG_MAIL   Mail

LOG_DAEMON
> A miscellaneous system daemon

LOG_AUTH   Security (authorization)

LOG_SYSLOG
> Syslog

LOG_LPR   Central printer

LOG_NEWS   Network news (e.g. Usenet)

LOG_UUCP   UUCP

`LOG_CRON`   Cron and At

`LOG_AUTHPRIV`

>   Private security (authorization)

`LOG_FTP`   Ftp server

`LOG_LOCAL0`

>   Locally defined

`LOG_LOCAL1`

>   Locally defined

`LOG_LOCAL2`

>   Locally defined

`LOG_LOCAL3`

>   Locally defined

`LOG_LOCAL4`

>   Locally defined

`LOG_LOCAL5`

>   Locally defined

`LOG_LOCAL6`

>   Locally defined

`LOG_LOCAL7`

>   Locally defined

Results are undefined if the facility code is anything else.

NB: `syslog` recognizes one other facility code: that of the kernel. But you can't specify that facility code with these functions. If you try, it looks the same to `syslog` as if you are requesting the default facility. But you wouldn't want to anyway, because any program that uses the GNU C Library is not the kernel.

You can use just a priority code as *facility_priority*. In that case, `syslog` assumes the default facility established when the Syslog connection was opened. See Section 18.2.5 [Syslog Example], page 510.

The possible values for the priority code are (macros):

`LOG_EMERG`

>   The message says the system is unusable.

`LOG_ALERT`

>   Action on the message must be taken immediately.

`LOG_CRIT`   The message states a critical condition.

`LOG_ERR`   The message describes an error.

`LOG_WARNING`

>   The message is a warning.

`LOG_NOTICE`

>   The message describes a normal but important event.

LOG_INFO   The message is purely informational.

LOG_DEBUG
        The message is only for debugging purposes.

Results are undefined if the priority code is anything else.

If the process does not presently have a Syslog connection open (i.e., it did not call
`openlog`), `syslog` implicitly opens the connection the same as `openlog` would, with
the following defaults for information that would otherwise be included in an `openlog`
call: The default identification string is the program name. The default default facility
is `LOG_USER`. The default for all the connection options in *options* is as if those bits
were off. `syslog` leaves the Syslog connection open.

If the `/dev/log` socket is not open and connected, `syslog` opens and connects it, the
same as `openlog` with the `LOG_NDELAY` option would.

`syslog` leaves `/dev/log` open and connected unless its attempt to send the message
failed, in which case `syslog` closes it (with the hope that a future implicit open will
restore the Syslog connection to a usable state).

Example:

```
#include <syslog.h>
syslog (LOG_MAKEPRI(LOG_LOCAL1, LOG_ERROR),
        "Unable to make network connection to %s.  Error=%m", host);
```

void vsyslog (*int* `facility_priority`, *const char* *`format`, *va_list*   [Function]
    `arglist`)
    Preliminary: | MT-Safe env locale | AS-Unsafe corrupt heap lock dlopen | AC-Unsafe
    corrupt lock mem fd | See Section 1.2.2.1 [POSIX Safety Concepts], page 2.

    This is functionally identical to `syslog`, with the BSD style variable length argument.

18.2.3 closelog

The symbols referred to in this section are declared in the file `syslog.h`.

void closelog (*void*)   [Function]
    Preliminary: | MT-Safe | AS-Unsafe lock | AC-Unsafe lock fd | See Section 1.2.2.1
    [POSIX Safety Concepts], page 2.

    `closelog` closes the current Syslog connection, if there is one. This includes closing
    the `/dev/log` socket, if it is open. `closelog` also sets the identification string for
    Syslog messages back to the default, if `openlog` was called with a non-NULL argument
    to *ident*. The default identification string is the program name taken from argv[0].

    If you are writing shared library code that uses `openlog` to generate custom syslog
    output, you should use `closelog` to drop the GNU C Library's internal reference to
    the *ident* pointer when you are done. Please read the section on `openlog` for more
    information: See Section 18.2.1 [openlog], page 505.

    `closelog` does not flush any buffers. You do not have to call `closelog` before re-
    opening a Syslog connection with `openlog`. Syslog connections are automatically
    closed on exec or exit.

18.2.4 setlogmask

The symbols referred to in this section are declared in the file `syslog.h`.

`int setlogmask (`*`int mask`*`)`   [Function]

> Preliminary: | MT-Unsafe race:LogMask | AS-Unsafe | AC-Safe | See Section 1.2.2.1 [POSIX Safety Concepts], page 2.
>
> `setlogmask` sets a mask (the "logmask") that determines which future `syslog` calls shall be ignored. If a program has not called `setlogmask`, `syslog` doesn't ignore any calls. You can use `setlogmask` to specify that messages of particular priorities shall be ignored in the future.
>
> A `setlogmask` call overrides any previous `setlogmask` call.
>
> Note that the logmask exists entirely independently of opening and closing of Syslog connections.
>
> Setting the logmask has a similar effect to, but is not the same as, configuring Syslog. The Syslog configuration may cause Syslog to discard certain messages it receives, but the logmask causes certain messages never to get submitted to Syslog in the first place.
>
> *mask* is a bit string with one bit corresponding to each of the possible message priorities. If the bit is on, `syslog` handles messages of that priority normally. If it is off, `syslog` discards messages of that priority. Use the message priority macros described in Section 18.2.2 [syslog, vsyslog], page 507 and the `LOG_MASK` to construct an appropriate *mask* value, as in this example:
>
> ```
> LOG_MASK(LOG_EMERG) | LOG_MASK(LOG_ERROR)
> ```
>
> or
>
> ```
> ~(LOG_MASK(LOG_INFO))
> ```
>
> There is also a `LOG_UPTO` macro, which generates a mask with the bits on for a certain priority and all priorities above it:
>
> ```
> LOG_UPTO(LOG_ERROR)
> ```
>
> The unfortunate naming of the macro is due to the fact that internally, higher numbers are used for lower message priorities.

18.2.5 Syslog Example

Here is an example of `openlog`, `syslog`, and `closelog`:

This example sets the logmask so that debug and informational messages get discarded without ever reaching Syslog. So the second `syslog` in the example does nothing.

```
#include <syslog.h>

setlogmask (LOG_UPTO (LOG_NOTICE));

openlog ("exampleprog", LOG_CONS | LOG_PID | LOG_NDELAY, LOG_LOCAL1);

syslog (LOG_NOTICE, "Program started by User %d", getuid ());
syslog (LOG_INFO, "A tree falls in a forest");

closelog ();
```

Appendix I GNU Free Documentation License

Version 1.3, 3 November 2008

Copyright © 2000, 2001, 2002, 2007, 2008 Free Software Foundation, Inc.
`http://fsf.org/`

0. PREAMBLE

The purpose of this License is to make a manual, textbook, or other functional and useful document *free* in the sense of freedom: to assure everyone the effective freedom to copy and redistribute it, with or without modifying it, either commercially or non-commercially. Secondarily, this License preserves for the author and publisher a way to get credit for their work, while not being considered responsible for modifications made by others.

This License is a kind of "copyleft", which means that derivative works of the document must themselves be free in the same sense. It complements the GNU General Public License, which is a copyleft license designed for free software.

We have designed this License in order to use it for manuals for free software, because free software needs free documentation: a free program should come with manuals providing the same freedoms that the software does. But this License is not limited to software manuals; it can be used for any textual work, regardless of subject matter or whether it is published as a printed book. We recommend this License principally for works whose purpose is instruction or reference.

1. APPLICABILITY AND DEFINITIONS

This License applies to any manual or other work, in any medium, that contains a notice placed by the copyright holder saying it can be distributed under the terms of this License. Such a notice grants a world-wide, royalty-free license, unlimited in duration, to use that work under the conditions stated herein. The "Document", below, refers to any such manual or work. Any member of the public is a licensee, and is addressed as "you". You accept the license if you copy, modify or distribute the work in a way requiring permission under copyright law.

A "Modified Version" of the Document means any work containing the Document or a portion of it, either copied verbatim, or with modifications and/or translated into another language.

A "Secondary Section" is a named appendix or a front-matter section of the Document that deals exclusively with the relationship of the publishers or authors of the Document to the Document's overall subject (or to related matters) and contains nothing that could fall directly within that overall subject. (Thus, if the Document is in part a textbook of mathematics, a Secondary Section may not explain any mathematics.) The relationship could be a matter of historical connection with the subject or with related matters, or of legal, commercial, philosophical, ethical or political position regarding them.

The "Invariant Sections" are certain Secondary Sections whose titles are designated, as being those of Invariant Sections, in the notice that says that the Document is released under this License. If a section does not fit the above definition of Secondary then it is not allowed to be designated as Invariant. The Document may contain zero Invariant Sections. If the Document does not identify any Invariant Sections then there are none.

The "Cover Texts" are certain short passages of text that are listed, as Front-Cover Texts or Back-Cover Texts, in the notice that says that the Document is released under this License. A Front-Cover Text may be at most 5 words, and a Back-Cover Text may be at most 25 words.

A "Transparent" copy of the Document means a machine-readable copy, represented in a format whose specification is available to the general public, that is suitable for revising the document straightforwardly with generic text editors or (for images composed of pixels) generic paint programs or (for drawings) some widely available drawing editor, and that is suitable for input to text formatters or for automatic translation to a variety of formats suitable for input to text formatters. A copy made in an otherwise Transparent file format whose markup, or absence of markup, has been arranged to thwart or discourage subsequent modification by readers is not Transparent. An image format is not Transparent if used for any substantial amount of text. A copy that is not "Transparent" is called "Opaque".

Examples of suitable formats for Transparent copies include plain ASCII without markup, Texinfo input format, LaTeX input format, SGML or XML using a publicly available DTD, and standard-conforming simple HTML, PostScript or PDF designed for human modification. Examples of transparent image formats include PNG, XCF and JPG. Opaque formats include proprietary formats that can be read and edited only by proprietary word processors, SGML or XML for which the DTD and/or processing tools are not generally available, and the machine-generated HTML, PostScript or PDF produced by some word processors for output purposes only.

The "Title Page" means, for a printed book, the title page itself, plus such following pages as are needed to hold, legibly, the material this License requires to appear in the title page. For works in formats which do not have any title page as such, "Title Page" means the text near the most prominent appearance of the work's title, preceding the beginning of the body of the text.

The "publisher" means any person or entity that distributes copies of the Document to the public.

A section "Entitled XYZ" means a named subunit of the Document whose title either is precisely XYZ or contains XYZ in parentheses following text that translates XYZ in another language. (Here XYZ stands for a specific section name mentioned below, such as "Acknowledgements", "Dedications", "Endorsements", or "History".) To "Preserve the Title" of such a section when you modify the Document means that it remains a section "Entitled XYZ" according to this definition.

The Document may include Warranty Disclaimers next to the notice which states that this License applies to the Document. These Warranty Disclaimers are considered to be included by reference in this License, but only as regards disclaiming warranties: any other implication that these Warranty Disclaimers may have is void and has no effect on the meaning of this License.

2. VERBATIM COPYING

You may copy and distribute the Document in any medium, either commercially or noncommercially, provided that this License, the copyright notices, and the license notice saying this License applies to the Document are reproduced in all copies, and that you add no other conditions whatsoever to those of this License. You may not use technical measures to obstruct or control the reading or further copying of the copies you make or distribute. However, you may accept compensation in exchange for copies. If you distribute a large enough number of copies you must also follow the conditions in section 3.

You may also lend copies, under the same conditions stated above, and you may publicly display copies.

3. COPYING IN QUANTITY

If you publish printed copies (or copies in media that commonly have printed covers) of the Document, numbering more than 100, and the Document's license notice requires Cover Texts, you must enclose the copies in covers that carry, clearly and legibly, all these Cover Texts: Front-Cover Texts on the front cover, and Back-Cover Texts on the back cover. Both covers must also clearly and legibly identify you as the publisher of these copies. The front cover must present the full title with all words of the title equally prominent and visible. You may add other material on the covers in addition. Copying with changes limited to the covers, as long as they preserve the title of the Document and satisfy these conditions, can be treated as verbatim copying in other respects.

If the required texts for either cover are too voluminous to fit legibly, you should put the first ones listed (as many as fit reasonably) on the actual cover, and continue the rest onto adjacent pages.

If you publish or distribute Opaque copies of the Document numbering more than 100, you must either include a machine-readable Transparent copy along with each Opaque copy, or state in or with each Opaque copy a computer-network location from which the general network-using public has access to download using public-standard network protocols a complete Transparent copy of the Document, free of added material. If you use the latter option, you must take reasonably prudent steps, when you begin distribution of Opaque copies in quantity, to ensure that this Transparent copy will remain thus accessible at the stated location until at least one year after the last time you distribute an Opaque copy (directly or through your agents or retailers) of that edition to the public.

It is requested, but not required, that you contact the authors of the Document well before redistributing any large number of copies, to give them a chance to provide you with an updated version of the Document.

4. MODIFICATIONS

You may copy and distribute a Modified Version of the Document under the conditions of sections 2 and 3 above, provided that you release the Modified Version under precisely this License, with the Modified Version filling the role of the Document, thus licensing distribution and modification of the Modified Version to whoever possesses a copy of it. In addition, you must do these things in the Modified Version:

A. Use in the Title Page (and on the covers, if any) a title distinct from that of the Document, and from those of previous versions (which should, if there were any, be listed in the History section of the Document). You may use the same title as a previous version if the original publisher of that version gives permission.

B. List on the Title Page, as authors, one or more persons or entities responsible for authorship of the modifications in the Modified Version, together with at least five of the principal authors of the Document (all of its principal authors, if it has fewer than five), unless they release you from this requirement.

C. State on the Title page the name of the publisher of the Modified Version, as the publisher.

D. Preserve all the copyright notices of the Document.

E. Add an appropriate copyright notice for your modifications adjacent to the other copyright notices.

F. Include, immediately after the copyright notices, a license notice giving the public permission to use the Modified Version under the terms of this License, in the form shown in the Addendum below.

G. Preserve in that license notice the full lists of Invariant Sections and required Cover Texts given in the Document's license notice.

H. Include an unaltered copy of this License.

I. Preserve the section Entitled "History", Preserve its Title, and add to it an item stating at least the title, year, new authors, and publisher of the Modified Version as given on the Title Page. If there is no section Entitled "History" in the Document, create one stating the title, year, authors, and publisher of the Document as given on its Title Page, then add an item describing the Modified Version as stated in the previous sentence.

J. Preserve the network location, if any, given in the Document for public access to a Transparent copy of the Document, and likewise the network locations given in the Document for previous versions it was based on. These may be placed in the "History" section. You may omit a network location for a work that was published at least four years before the Document itself, or if the original publisher of the version it refers to gives permission.

K. For any section Entitled "Acknowledgements" or "Dedications", Preserve the Title of the section, and preserve in the section all the substance and tone of each of the contributor acknowledgements and/or dedications given therein.

L. Preserve all the Invariant Sections of the Document, unaltered in their text and in their titles. Section numbers or the equivalent are not considered part of the section titles.

M. Delete any section Entitled "Endorsements". Such a section may not be included in the Modified Version.

N. Do not retitle any existing section to be Entitled "Endorsements" or to conflict in title with any Invariant Section.

O. Preserve any Warranty Disclaimers.

If the Modified Version includes new front-matter sections or appendices that qualify as Secondary Sections and contain no material copied from the Document, you may at your option designate some or all of these sections as invariant. To do this, add their titles to the list of Invariant Sections in the Modified Version's license notice. These titles must be distinct from any other section titles.

You may add a section Entitled "Endorsements", provided it contains nothing but endorsements of your Modified Version by various parties—for example, statements of peer review or that the text has been approved by an organization as the authoritative definition of a standard.

You may add a passage of up to five words as a Front-Cover Text, and a passage of up to 25 words as a Back-Cover Text, to the end of the list of Cover Texts in the Modified Version. Only one passage of Front-Cover Text and one of Back-Cover Text may be added by (or through arrangements made by) any one entity. If the Document already includes a cover text for the same cover, previously added by you or by arrangement made by the same entity you are acting on behalf of, you may not add another; but you may replace the old one, on explicit permission from the previous publisher that added the old one.

The author(s) and publisher(s) of the Document do not by this License give permission to use their names for publicity for or to assert or imply endorsement of any Modified Version.

5. COMBINING DOCUMENTS

You may combine the Document with other documents released under this License, under the terms defined in section 4 above for modified versions, provided that you include in the combination all of the Invariant Sections of all of the original documents, unmodified, and list them all as Invariant Sections of your combined work in its license notice, and that you preserve all their Warranty Disclaimers.

The combined work need only contain one copy of this License, and multiple identical Invariant Sections may be replaced with a single copy. If there are multiple Invariant Sections with the same name but different contents, make the title of each such section unique by adding at the end of it, in parentheses, the name of the original author or publisher of that section if known, or else a unique number. Make the same adjustment to the section titles in the list of Invariant Sections in the license notice of the combined work.

In the combination, you must combine any sections Entitled "History" in the various original documents, forming one section Entitled "History"; likewise combine any sections Entitled "Acknowledgements", and any sections Entitled "Dedications". You must delete all sections Entitled "Endorsements."

6. COLLECTIONS OF DOCUMENTS

You may make a collection consisting of the Document and other documents released under this License, and replace the individual copies of this License in the various documents with a single copy that is included in the collection, provided that you follow the rules of this License for verbatim copying of each of the documents in all other respects.

You may extract a single document from such a collection, and distribute it individually under this License, provided you insert a copy of this License into the extracted document, and follow this License in all other respects regarding verbatim copying of that document.

7. AGGREGATION WITH INDEPENDENT WORKS

A compilation of the Document or its derivatives with other separate and independent documents or works, in or on a volume of a storage or distribution medium, is called an "aggregate" if the copyright resulting from the compilation is not used to limit the legal rights of the compilation's users beyond what the individual works permit. When the Document is included in an aggregate, this License does not apply to the other works in the aggregate which are not themselves derivative works of the Document.

If the Cover Text requirement of section 3 is applicable to these copies of the Document, then if the Document is less than one half of the entire aggregate, the Document's Cover Texts may be placed on covers that bracket the Document within the aggregate, or the electronic equivalent of covers if the Document is in electronic form. Otherwise they must appear on printed covers that bracket the whole aggregate.

8. TRANSLATION

Translation is considered a kind of modification, so you may distribute translations of the Document under the terms of section 4. Replacing Invariant Sections with translations requires special permission from their copyright holders, but you may include translations of some or all Invariant Sections in addition to the original versions of these Invariant Sections. You may include a translation of this License, and all the license notices in the Document, and any Warranty Disclaimers, provided that you also include the original English version of this License and the original versions of those notices and disclaimers. In case of a disagreement between the translation and the original version of this License or a notice or disclaimer, the original version will prevail.

If a section in the Document is Entitled "Acknowledgements", "Dedications", or "History", the requirement (section 4) to Preserve its Title (section 1) will typically require changing the actual title.

9. TERMINATION

You may not copy, modify, sublicense, or distribute the Document except as expressly provided under this License. Any attempt otherwise to copy, modify, sublicense, or distribute it is void, and will automatically terminate your rights under this License.

However, if you cease all violation of this License, then your license from a particular copyright holder is reinstated (a) provisionally, unless and until the copyright holder explicitly and finally terminates your license, and (b) permanently, if the copyright holder fails to notify you of the violation by some reasonable means prior to 60 days after the cessation.

Moreover, your license from a particular copyright holder is reinstated permanently if the copyright holder notifies you of the violation by some reasonable means, this is the first time you have received notice of violation of this License (for any work) from that copyright holder, and you cure the violation prior to 30 days after your receipt of the notice.

Termination of your rights under this section does not terminate the licenses of parties who have received copies or rights from you under this License. If your rights have been terminated and not permanently reinstated, receipt of a copy of some or all of the same material does not give you any rights to use it.

10. FUTURE REVISIONS OF THIS LICENSE

The Free Software Foundation may publish new, revised versions of the GNU Free Documentation License from time to time. Such new versions will be similar in spirit to the present version, but may differ in detail to address new problems or concerns. See `http://www.gnu.org/copyleft/`.

Each version of the License is given a distinguishing version number. If the Document specifies that a particular numbered version of this License "or any later version" applies to it, you have the option of following the terms and conditions either of that specified version or of any later version that has been published (not as a draft) by the Free Software Foundation. If the Document does not specify a version number of this License, you may choose any version ever published (not as a draft) by the Free Software Foundation. If the Document specifies that a proxy can decide which future versions of this License can be used, that proxy's public statement of acceptance of a version permanently authorizes you to choose that version for the Document.

11. RELICENSING

"Massive Multiauthor Collaboration Site" (or "MMC Site") means any World Wide Web server that publishes copyrightable works and also provides prominent facilities for anybody to edit those works. A public wiki that anybody can edit is an example of such a server. A "Massive Multiauthor Collaboration" (or "MMC") contained in the site means any set of copyrightable works thus published on the MMC site.

"CC-BY-SA" means the Creative Commons Attribution-Share Alike 3.0 license published by Creative Commons Corporation, a not-for-profit corporation with a principal place of business in San Francisco, California, as well as future copyleft versions of that license published by that same organization.

"Incorporate" means to publish or republish a Document, in whole or in part, as part of another Document.

An MMC is "eligible for relicensing" if it is licensed under this License, and if all works that were first published under this License somewhere other than this MMC, and subsequently incorporated in whole or in part into the MMC, (1) had no cover texts or invariant sections, and (2) were thus incorporated prior to November 1, 2008.

The operator of an MMC Site may republish an MMC contained in the site under CC-BY-SA on the same site at any time before August 1, 2009, provided the MMC is eligible for relicensing.

ADDENDUM: How to use this License for your documents

To use this License in a document you have written, include a copy of the License in the document and put the following copyright and license notices just after the title page:

```
Copyright (C)  year  your name.
Permission is granted to copy, distribute and/or modify this document
under the terms of the GNU Free Documentation License, Version 1.3
or any later version published by the Free Software Foundation;
with no Invariant Sections, no Front-Cover Texts, and no Back-Cover
Texts.  A copy of the license is included in the section entitled ''GNU
Free Documentation License''.
```

If you have Invariant Sections, Front-Cover Texts and Back-Cover Texts, replace the "with...Texts." line with this:

```
with the Invariant Sections being list their titles, with
the Front-Cover Texts being list, and with the Back-Cover Texts
being list.
```

If you have Invariant Sections without Cover Texts, or some other combination of the three, merge those two alternatives to suit the situation.

If your document contains nontrivial examples of program code, we recommend releasing these examples in parallel under your choice of free software license, such as the GNU General Public License, to permit their use in free software.

www.ingramcontent.com/pod-product-compliance
Lightning Source LLC
LaVergne TN
LVHW060132070326
832902LV00018B/2759